HISTORY OF VATICAN II

HISTORY OF VATICAN II

General Editor

GIUSEPPE ALBERIGO

Istituto per le Scienze Religiose, Bologna

Editorial Board

History of Vatican II

Vol. I

Announcing and Preparing Vatican Council II
Toward a new Era in Catholicism

edited by

Giuseppe Alberigo

English version edited by

Joseph A. Komonchak

1995

ORBIS | PEETERS
Maryknoll | Leuven

Library of Congress Cataloging-in-Publication Data

History of Vatican II / edited by Giuseppe Alberigo: English version edited by
   Joseph A. Komonchak.
     XVIII-528 p., 24 cm.
     Includes bibliographical references and index.
     Contents: v. 1. Announcing and preparing Vatican Council II.
     ISBN 1-57075-049-1 (v. 1)
     1. Vatican Council (2nd: 1962-1965) — History.
   I. Alberigo Giuseppe. II. Komonchak, Joseph A.
   BX830 1962.H55   1996
   262'.52—dc20   95-42334
                         CIP

CIP Royal Library Albert I, Brussels

History of Vatican II. — Vol. I — Announcing and Preparing Vatican Council II/
edited by G. Alberigo and J.A. Komonchak. — Leuven: Peeters, 1995

No part of this book may be used or reproduced
in any form by print, photo print, microfilm or any other means
without written permission from the publisher.

ISBN 90-6831-724-5 (PEETERS)
ISBN 1-57075-049-1 (ORBIS)
D 1995I0602I74

ORBIS BOOKS
PO Box 308
Maryknoll, NY 10545-0308

© PEETERS
Bondgenotenlaan 153
B-3000 Leuven
BELGIUM

TABLE OF CONTENTS

III. THE STRUGGLE FOR THE COUNCIL DURING THE PRE-PARATION OF VATICAN II (1960-1962) [J.A. KOMONCHAK]

IV. THE EXTERNAL CLIMATE [J.O. Beozzo]

V. ON THE EVE OF THE SECOND VATICAN COUNCIL (JULY 1 - OCTOBER 10, 1962) [K. WITTSTADT]

PREFACE
1965-1995: THIRTY YEARS AFTER VATICAN II

As we near the end of this century — and millennium — the intense
and insistent acceleration of events, at least in the northern part of the
planet, is threatening to traumatize historical memory, setting it aside as
though it were something that even though valuable is superfluous. Even
great events that have profoundly influenced the life and future of a large
part of the human race suddenly seem so distant that they can be ignored.

In the age-old course of Christian history the great conciliar assemblies constitute a spinal column. Knowledge of their unfolding offers the
church an awareness of one of its basic choral dimensions and evidence
of crucial instances of the Spirit's inteventions in history. From J. Merlin
and P. Crabbe, when printing first was beginning, to P. Labbé and G.
Cossart and down to G.D. Mansi and H. Jedin, there has been an uninterrupted historical effort to reach a correct knowledge of the Councils.

Thirty years after the close of the conciliar assembly that took place in
Rome between 1962 and 1965, it is worth asking ourselves what is the
present state of knowledge of this Council, the way it unfolded, and its
meaning.

The enthusiasm that marked the expectation and celebration of Vatican II has faded away. The generation of those who played a leading
part in it is disappearing; even the blaze of Lefebvre's rejection has died
down and left only some melancholy smoke. It is obvious that the historical context has undergone a profound change, as a result, in great
measure, of the very celebration of the Council and of the major
processes which it triggered.

Immediately after the end of the Council, attention focused on commentaries on the conciliar texts. This was the focus during the 1970s at
all levels, from the great series of books to the reading guides used in
dioceses and parishes. As a result, people acquired a somewhat overly
abstract idea of Vatican II, as though it were simply a collection of texts,
too abundant a collection!

At thirty years' distance, Vatican II appears as an event that, independently of and despite its limitations and lacunae, made the hope and
optimism of the gospel relevant once again. Satisfaction with a vision of

the Council as a collection of several hundred pages of often prolix and sometimes short-lived conclusions has until now hindered the perception of its more fruitful meaning as a stimulus to the community of believers to accept the disquieting confrontation with the word of God and with the mystery of human history.

The Council did not intend to produce a new doctrinal "Summa" (according to John XXIII, "that did not require a Council"!) nor to give answers to all problems. It is ever more pertinent to recognize the priority of the conciliar event itself, even in relation to its decisions, which are not to be read as abstract normative prescriptions but as an expression and prolongation of the event itself. The task of renewal, the anxious searching, openness to the gospel, fraternal attention to all human beings: these characteristics of Vatican II were not elements of folklore nor at all marginal and transient features. On the contrary, they sum up the spirit of the conciliar event, which any sound and correct interpretation of its decrees must take into account.

The time has come, therefore, to undertake a historical treatment of Vatican II, not in order to dismiss it by relegating it to the past, but to make it easier to move beyond the phase of controversy that marked its reception by the church. We have a duty to give generations that have not experienced the conciliar event a tool that will permit them to gain a rigorously critical understanding of its meaning for their own time.

A reconstruction not only of the facts of the Council's labors but also of the spirit and dialectic that inspired and characterized the assembly requires that the day-by-day progression of its work be interwoven with the development of the self-awareness of the assembly and its various components. Also to be reconstructed is the dialectical relationship that existed between the internal climate of the Council and the external context, both in Rome and generally.

When we look at Vatican Council II as an event and not simply as a concrete implementation of an institutional model or a sum of decrees produced, we face the problem of developing adequate hermeneutical criteria. By this I mean criteria that differ from — even if connected or complementary to — the canonical requirements for the institutional legitimacy of a Council and from the criteria for interpreting its body of decrees.

It is evident that the history of Vatican II can be reconstructed only on the basis of a rigorously critical analysis of the sources; this means all the sources that have been preserved: oral and written, official and unofficial, collective and individual, internal and external. The question that is to be answered is not simply: "How was the approval of the decrees of Vatican II reached?" but above all: "What was the actual course of Vatican II, and what was its significance?"

But, we may ask, can a reliable historical reconstruction of so recent an event be made at such an early date? Is a rigorous historical treatment already possible after thirty years? In 1988 an international team of historians asked itself precisely that question as it examined the feasibility of a history of Vatican II. After wide-ranging discussion the historians agreed that a history was indeed possible. While the closeness of the event calls for special methodological precautions, it is no less true that it is possible today to avoid the consequences of the fact that the documentation is still scattered and at the same time to profit from the valuable testimonies of those who took part in the Council. After all, after 1870, despite the fact that Vatican I was only suspended and not ended, there was no wait before the first attempts were made at a history of the event.

It was thought possible, therefore, to begin a multi-year project of research that would lead to the composition of a history of the Council. The project is sponsored by the Istituto per le Scienze Religiose in Bologna and has been coordinated by an international team of scholars who have put together an intercontinental and interconfessional group of collaborators, as indicated by the list placed at the beginning of this volume.

Most importantly, the project has encouraged many analytical studies that have patiently retraced the many paths followed in the preparation for the Council, from the ripening of John XXIII's decision to the analysis of the results of the very wide-ranging consultation conducted in 1959-1960 with a view to deciding the agenda for the Council and, finally, to the preparation, in the full and proper sense, of the material on which the assembly was to work.

It has been possible to profit from dozens of rich archival collections of documents that bring together the papers of many Council fathers or periti.[1] This has made it possible to combine in a coherent way published documents and those kept in the Vatican archive of the Council, which Paul VI established and for which he provided sound regulations so as to facilitate research into Vatican II. These various sources have been the

---

[1] See: *Concile Vatican II et Église contemporaine (Archives de Louvain-la-Neuve)*, ed. by Cl. Soetens, J. Famerée, and L. Hulsbosch (3 vols.; Louvain-la-Neuve, 1989-93); *Documents pour une histoire du Concile Vatican II. Inventaire du Fonds P. Haubtmann*, ed. by A.-M. Abel and J.-P. Ribaut (Paris, 1992); *Documents pour une histoire du Concile Vatican II. Inventaire du Fonds J. Cordier* ed. by A.-M. Abel and J.-P. Ribaut (Paris, 1993). A list of over sixty collections of documents is given on pp. 483-92 of *Verso il Concilio Vatican II* (see the next note).

basis for studies of previously quite unknown aspects of the complex preparation for the Council; the result has been highly interesting information.[2]

During these years, in addition to biannual meetings of the international coordinating team (O. Beozzo, Sao Paulo; G. Fogarty, Charlottesville; E. Fouilloux, Lyon; J. Grootaers, Leuven; A. Hastings; Leeds; J. Komonchak, Washington; M. Lamberigts, Leuven; A. Melloni, Bologna; H. Raguer, Montserrat; A. Riccardi, Rome; Cl. Soetens, Louvain-la-Neuve; E. Vilanova, Montserrat; K. Wittstadt, Würzburg), scholarly colloquia have been held in Louvain-la-Neuve/Leuven, in Houston, Texas, in La Tourette (Lyons), in Würzburg, at Louvain-la-Neuve, and at Moscow.[3] The generous and intelligent labor of A. Melloni has made these meetings and the entire project possible and fruitful. The climate of mutual complementarity that prevailed at the Council has been renewed among the collaborators in our project, so that a profound harmony has gradually been created amid the diversity of sensibilities, origin, and training.

The research, promoted by the availability, as extensive as it was unexpected, of documentary material of exceptional value and by many qualified collaborators, both historians and theologians, is producing highly interesting results.

This first volume, which deals with the preparatory phase of the Council (1959-1962), has been written by G. Alberigo of Bologna (introduction, first chapter, and conclusion), E. Fouilloux of Lyons (second chapter), J. Komonchak of Washington, D.C. (third chapter), O. Beozzo of Sao Paulo (fourth chapter), and K. Wittstadt of Würzburg

[2] A. Indelicato, *Difendere la dottrina o annunciare l'evangelo. Il dibattito nella Commissione centrale preparatoria del Vaticano II* (Genoa, 1992; pp. XIV + 346); *Per la storicizzazione del Vaticano II*, ed. by G. Alberigo and A. Melloni (Bologna, 1992; a monograph issue of *Cristanesimo nella Storia*; pp. 185); *Verso il concilio Vaticano II (1960-1962). Passaggi e problemi della preparazione conciliare*, ed. by G. Alberigo and A. Melloni (Genoa, 1993; pp. 504); and many articles in scholarly journals. Also of great value is *Le Deuxième Concile du Vatican (1959-1965)*, published by the École française de Rome; Rome, 1989).

[3] The proceedings have been published: *Sources locales de Vatican II*, ed. by J. Grootaers and Cl. Soetens (Leuven, 1990); *À la Veille du Concile Vatican II. Vota et Réactions en Europe et dans le Catholicisme oriental*, ed. by M. Lamberigts and Cl. Soetens (Leuven, 1992); *Cristianismo e iglesia de América Latina en vísperas del Vaticano II*, ed. by J. O. Beozzo (San José, Costa Rica, 1992); *Vatican II commence... Approches Francophones*, ed. by É. Fouilloux (Leuven, 1993); *A Igreia latinoamericana às vésperas do concilio. História do Concilio Ecumênico Vaticano II*, ed. by J. O. Beozzo (Sao Paulo, 1993). The proceedings of the colloquium held in Würzburg in December, 1993, will be published soon.

(fifth chapter). All chapters, except the third, have been translated by Matthew J. O'Connell.

We flatter ourselves that we are providing an understanding that is in large measure new, even for participants in the Council, of the route followed by Catholicism as it approached the Council. The authors have endeavored to respect the course which the preparation concretely took, even though this meant some repetition. We thought it absolutely necessary to allow readers not only to have as much information as possible but also to experience this "from within" by allowing them to follow closely the course of the preparatory work with all its meanderings and contradictions. We hope that the commitment to research and collaborative effort that inspired our undertaking may be evident, at least in some small degree, and help readers to enter into the fascinating event that began on January 25, 1959, and ended on December 8, 1965.

Four more volumes will follow this one, each devoted to a period of the assembly's work. Each volume will be the collaborative work of scholars from different language groups and continents and will be published in the major languages.

The implementation of the research project has been facilitated and supported by numerous forms of financial assistance and by the understanding attitude of the Peeters publishing house.

Bologna, January 25, 1995   Giuseppe Alberigo

ABBREVIATIONS

Books

ADA   *Acta et documenta Concilio oecumenico Vaticano II apparando; Series prima (antepraeparatoria).* Typis Polyglottis Vaticanis, 1960-61

ADP   *Acta et documenta Concilio oecumenico Vaticano II apparando; Series secunda (praeparatoria).* Typis Polyglottis Vaticanis, 1969

AS   *Acta Synodalia Sacrosancti Concilii Vaticani II.* Typis Polyglottis Vaticanis, 1970- .

Attese   Il Vaticano II fra attese e celebrazione, ed. G. Alberigo. Bologna 1995.

Caprile   G. Caprile, *Il Concilio Vaticano*, 4 vols. Rome, 1966-68

COD   *Conciliorum Oecumenicorum Decreta*, ed. Istituto per le Scienze Religiose. Bologna 1973

Deuxième   *Le deuxième Concile du Vatican (1959-1965).* Rome 1989

DMC   *Discorsi Messaggi Colloqui del S. Padre Giovanni XXIII*, 6 vols. Città del Vaticano, 1960-67

Schemata   *Schemata Constitutionum et Decretorum de quibus disceptabitur in Concilii sessionibus.* Series I and II. Typis Polyglottis Vaticanis, 1962. *Schemata Constitutionum et Decretorum ex quibus argumenta in Concilio disceptanda seligentur.* Series III and IV. Typis Polyglottis Vaticanis, 1963.

Storicizzazione   *Per la storicizzazione del Vaticano II*, ed. G. Alberigo and A. Melloni. Bologna 1992

Vatican II commence   Vatican II commence... Approches Francophones, ed. É. Fouilloux. Leuven 1993

Veille   *À la veille du Concile Vatican II. Vota et réactions en Europe et dans le catholicisme oriental*, ed. M. Lamberigts and C. Soetens. Leuven 1992

Vísperas   *Cristianismo e iglesias de América Latina en*
                           vísperas del Vaticano II, ed. O. Beozzo. Costa
                           Rica 1992
Verso il concilio   *Verso il concilio Vaticano II (1960-1962): Pas-*
                           saggi e problemi della preparazione conciliare,
                           ed. G. Alberigo and A. Melloni. Genoa 1993

Journals

With few exceptions, easily decipherable, abbreviations of journals
follow those given in *Theologische Realenzyklopädie: Abkurzungsver-*
zeichnis, ed. S. Schwertner (Berlin/New York 1976).

Pre-conciliar Bodies

AL	Commission for the Apostolate of the Laity
BG	Commission for Bishops and the Governance of Dioceses
CLP	Commission for the Discipline of the Clergy and the Christian People
CPC	Central Preparatory Commission
LI	Commission on the Sacred Liturgy
MI	Commission on the Missions
OR	Commission for the Oriental Churches
PrC	Preparatory Commissions
RE	Commission for Religious
SA	Commission for the Sacraments
SCM	Secretariat for Communications Media
SCU	Secretariat for Christian Unity
ST	Commission for Studies and Seminaries
TC	Theological Commission

CHAPTER I

THE ANNOUNCEMENT OF THE COUNCIL
FROM THE SECURITY OF THE FORTRESS TO
THE LURE OF THE QUEST

GIUSEPPE ALBERIGO

I. "A GESTURE OF SERENE BOLDNESS."[1]

1. *January 25, 1959.*

"Trembling a little with emotion but at the same time humbly resolute in my purpose, I announce to you a double celebration which I propose to undertake: a diocesan synod for the City and a general Council for the universal Church."[2] It was thus, on January 25, 1959, that John XXIII announced his decision to convoke a new Council, He did so less than ninety days after his election as successor to Pius XII, during the course of a short address to a small group of cardinals gathered in the Basilica of St. Paul Outside the Walls for a consistory at the close of the Week of Prayer for the Unity of the Churches. Pope John added that the synod and the Council would "happily lead to the desired and awaited modernization of the Code of Canon Law." These are "the more noteworthy aspects of apostolic activity that these three months of presence in and contact with the Roman ecclesiastical world have prompted me to undertake."

The pope says that he is motivated "solely by a concern for the 'good of souls' and in order that the new pontificate may come to grips, in a clear and well-defined way, with the spiritual needs of the present time."

---

[1] This was the title which *La Croix* (January 30, 1959) gave to P. Glorieux's commentary on the announcement of the council.

[2] For the critical text of the allocution see A. Melloni, "'Questa festiva ricorrenza.' Prodromi e preparazione del discorso di annuncio del Vaticano II (25 gennaio 1959)," *RSLR* 28 (1992) 607-43. In his preparatory drafts the pope had always written "general council," whereas in the official version the words "ecumenical council" appear, representing a qualitative jump to a higher level, and one that could not fail to perplex the non-Roman Churches. We have no information about this change from the pope's autograph; it is certain that the shift to the language of the Code of Canon Law caused many of the uncertainties and ambiguities that were to mark the first months after the announcement. [The allocution is translated in *The Pope Speaks* 5 (1958-59) 398-401; I have used this Vatican translation as a base but have altered it for the sake of closer fidelity to the Italian original. — Tr.]

This "decision was formed by the recollection of certain ancient ways of making doctrinal statements and certain wise practices of ecclesiastical discipline that in ages of renewal in the history of the Church have yielded especially effective results for the strengthening of religious unity and the kindling of a more intense Christian fervor."

No accounts of this short consistory are presently known; consequently we do not know the reactions of those present. Two years later, the pope would note that the cardinals had received the announcement in "impressive, devout silence." Not only that: although all the cardinals, present and absent, were invited to submit "a confidential and sincere statement that would let me know how each one feels and would give friendly...suggestions for carrying out" the plan, few accepted the invitation, and almost all who did did so in cold and formal language. The disturbance felt by these churchmen is easily understood. The conclave had elected Cardinal Roncalli on October 28, 1958, with the confident expectation that his would be a "transitional" pontificate, that is, one that would be short and would peacefully heal the traumas inflicted by Pius XII's long and dramatic reign.

Some of John XIII's first actions — from the revival of scheduled audiences for those in charge of the departments of the Roman Curia to the rapid appointment of a secretary of state — were interpreted as signals of a return to normality. This made the announcement of a Council all the more disconcerting to almost everyone.[3] Their confusion was intensified by the repeated assertions in the allocution of January 25 that the announced Council was not a vague project or an idea concerning which the pope intended to poll the cardinals for their views. Pope John had left no doubt that his decision was final. He had shown himself fully aware of the extraordinary character of his action, that is, that he thought of it as an exercise of an essentially primatial responsibility. It is not an accident that in his allocution the pope had spoken of a "crucial decision" and that later on, in the *Journal of a Soul*, he would note that "the ecumenical Council is entirely the initiative and, in principle, under the jurisdiction" of the pope.[4]

On January 24, 1960, in his address at the opening of the Roman Synod, the pope took the occasion to say, with regard to the idea of calling an ecumenical Council, that "someone, speaking with feeling, suggested to Us: 'Holy Father! The idea of an ecumenical Council is a

---

[3] But the plan for a Roman synod also elicited very stubborn resistance; see M. Manzo, *Papa Giovanni vescovo a Roma* (Cinisello B., 1991) 51-59.

[4] Pope John XXIII, *Journal of a Soul*, trans. D. White (rev. ed.; New York, 1980) 345.

fine one, but why not think first of all of the immediate needs of Rome by preparing for a diocesan synod for the City that is the center of Christianity....?'" If the pope did not hesitate to let it be known that the idea of a Roman synod and a revision of the Code of Canon Law had been proposed to him by others,[5] we may conclude that the decision to convoke a Council was entirely his own.

The possibility cannot indeed be excluded that during the conclave some cardinals exchanged views on this subject too. However, the hypothesis that there was agreement at that time on the convocation of a Council is less persuasive; it would hardly be compatible with the advanced age of the cardinal who was now elected pope and to whose energies the carrying out of a Council would be entrusted, nor would it be compatible with the surprise felt by the cardinals present in St. Paul Outside the Walls. As early as November 2, 1958, in one of the very first audience-lists of his pontificate, the pope wrote alongside the typewritten name of Cardinal Ruffini that something had been said (by Ruffini? by himself? by both?) about a Council. On the other hand, Cardinal Ruffini had been, along with Ottaviani, one of those promoting Pacelli's plan. According to leaks which there is no way of checking, Cardinal Ottaviani himself supposedly spoke of the matter with Roncalli during the conclave.[6]

A great many people thought the historical situation unsuitable for the calling of a great assembly of churchmen.[7] The announcement was unexpected and unforeseen and a surprise to almost all circles, dominated as they were by the climate of the "cold war" and comfortable in their acceptance of a Catholicism rendered immobile by its certainties. But in that same January allocution the pope had referred to "ages of renewal"; in his view, the Church, and this meant, first of all, Catholicism, was on the threshold of an extraordinarily important historical juncture in which it would be necessary "to define clearly and distinguish

[5] *DMC* 2:128. The role of others in regard to both the Roman synod and the revision of the *CIC* is made clear in the testimony of P. Felici, "Il primo incontro con Papa Giovanni," *OR* June 3, 1973.

[6] Fondo Roncalli, Istituto delle scienze religiose [ISR], Bologna. See E. Cavaterra, *Il prefetto del S. Offizio. Le opere e i giorni del card. Ottaviani* (Milan, 1990) 5. On his way home from the conclave, Cardinal Frings told his secretary that it was possible that a council would soon be called. See *Für die Menschen bestellt. Erinnerungen des Alterzbisschofs von Köln J. Kard. Frings* (Cologne, 1973) 247.

[7] See G. Martina, "The Historical Context in Which the Idea of a New Ecumenical Council was born," in *Vatican II: Assessment and Perspectives Twenty-Five Years After (1962-1987)*, ed. R. Latourelle (New York/Mahwah: Paulist Press, 1988) I, 3-73. This essay is of interest especially for the Roman context.

between what is sacred principle and eternal gospel and what belongs
rather to the changing times."[8] To the extent that "we are entering upon
an age that can be called one of universal mission,"[9] we must "make
ours the recommendation of Jesus that one should know how to distinguish the 'signs of the times'... and ...see now, in the midst of so much
darkness, a few indications which auger well," as the pope would later
say in the Apostolic Constitution convoking the Council.[10]

In other words, Pope John placed the decision for a Council in an
epochal context, assessed on the basis at once of historical judgments and
of intuitions of faith, the conclusions of which significantly coincided.
We should bear in mind that, due in part to his personal experience
of diplomacy over a thirty-year period, Roncalli was sensitive and
attentive to the signs of the developing world situation, which was
marked by the increasingly rapid ending of colonialism (involving the
human situation of at least three continents) and by the imminent,
although still unnoticed, passing of the cold war.

Objectively, however, the confrontation between the Soviet and
Western blocs was always on the brink of turning into a conflict: from
the Korean War (1950) to the blockade of Berlin and the building of the
wall (1961) to the Cuban crisis (1962). The world seemed locked into a
stalemate with no way out. The dynamic factors at work were confined
in their operation to the interior of the blocs: in the northern sector there
were the spread of a new stage of industrialization and a corresponding
cutback in the agricultural sphere, and the progressive domination of the
mass media; while in the continents that had largely been under colonial
rule, the agitation for independence and the rejection of economic
exploitation were growing ever more intense.

In heavily Christian areas the widespread view that the churches had
no choice but to support the anti-communist commitment of the western
bloc was being challenged by a growing unrest, fed by the conviction
that the long-standing mutual support of political institutions and
churches — which had even outlasted the age of ideologies — was
definitely on the wane. The modern version of "Christendom" was less
and less a relevant and convincing model.

In the minds of many the age of the pope (he was 77) seemed to contradict the complex and lengthy project of a Council. It was symptomatic

[8] Allocution to the Franciscan Order (April 16, 1959): *DMC* 1:250.
[9] *DMC* 2:654.
[10] *DMC* 4:868. Translation in *The Documents of Vatican II*, ed. W. M. Abbott
(New York, 1966) 704.

of this view that its proponents thought of a very short and hurried celebration, one that would take place in that same year, 1959. In fact, the
notion of a Council that would be very brief had already been proposed
at the time of the preliminary work done under Pius XII and was surely
attractive to some.

But the Catholic Church was quickly to discover that it was unprepared for a Council. Doctrinal and institutional reflection on general
Councils had stopped at least a century earlier. Canons 222-229 of the
1917 *Code of Canon Law* had produced an essentially hybrid marriage
of medieval and modern tradition with what had happened at the Vatican
Council of 1870. But was the model thus described adequate for the celebration of a new Council despite the vast cultural, social, and political
changes that had occurred in the interval? The canonists had lazily based
their teaching on past situations and neglected to make the profound
changes that were needed.[11]

Doctrinal development of the major themes of renewal (liturgy, ecumenism, the return to the biblical and patristic sources, the "rediscovery" of the Church) had likewise been slow and was lagging,[12] even as
compared with the new pastoral experiments that were going on in
important areas of Catholic life.

This was due not only to the absence of any climate of expectation of
a Council (such as had existed before the Council of Florence and during the exhausting wait for Trent). It was due also, and no less, to the
anti-Modernist repression at the beginning of the twentieth century and
the renewed atmosphere of mistrust that had spread abroad especially
during the second part of the pontificate of Pius XII in response to
efforts at renewal. According to French theologian Yves Congar,

> from the viewpoint of theology and especially of reunion it seemed that the
> Council was coming twenty years too soon. In fact, too few years had passed
> since things had begun to move. Already many ideas had changed. But in
> twenty years' time there would be an episcopate made up of men who had fed
> on ideas nourished by the Bible and tradition and on a practical awareness of
> missionary and pastoral needs. We weren't there yet. On the other hand, some
> ideas had made progress, and the very announcement of a Council with an
> ecumenical goal could speed up certain processes, given the more benevolent
> and more Christian atmosphere of the pontificate of John XXIII.[13]

[11] See the article "Concile," in the *Dictionnaire de Droit canonique*; this was written
in the early forties by N. Jung and devotes almost the same number of pages to other
kinds of council (III, 1267-80) as to ecumenical councils (III, 1280-1301).

[12] See É. Fouilloux, "'Mouvements' théologico-spirituels et concile (1959-1962),"
in *Veille*, 185-99.

[13] *Mon Journal du Concile*, copy at the ISR, Bologna, p. 1.

Only slowly would the complicated machinery involved in preparation of a Council and, above all, the gradual instruction given by John
XXIII on the subject spread an awareness of this lag. And yet we must
ask whether the euphoria created by the announcement of 1959 did not
hinder an adequate assessment of the amount of preparation required
by a Council that was intended to be pastoral rather than "doctrinal."
This euphoria compelled those who were resisting or even opposed to
the idea of a Council to adopt the guise of an assent that cloaked mini-
malizing intentions.

What, then, was intended in the announcement made on January 25,
1959? Were people to expect a conclusion to the Council that had been
adjourned in 1870? Would the Council provide a solemn, formal occasion for reasserting a Roman Catholic self-consciousness that was in
substantial continuity with the stateliness of the Pacelli era? Was there
room for anything different? If the answer was Yes, what would
the Council be able to accomplish? The enthusiasm with which public
opinion received the announcement did not provide an answer to any of
these questions, although it did show the existence of an unsuspected
area of expectation and readiness.

2. Why a Council?

But how did Pope Roncalli come to so demanding a decision?
He himself would say at the opening of the Council that the idea of a
Council came "like a flash of heavenly light," a "sudden emergence in
our heart and on our lips of the simple words 'Ecumenical Council.'"
A note in the *Journal of a Soul* for January 20, 1959, says that he "had
not thought of it before"; on April 21, 1959, he told the clergy of Venice
that it had been an inspiration; on May 7, 1960, he spoke to the superiors of the Missionary Societies of "the first idea...which emerged like a
lowly, hidden flower in the fields: it is not even visible, but you advert
to its perfume"; on May 8, 1962, addressing pilgrims from Venice, he
referred to "an unexpected illumination."[14]

---

[14] Allocution *Gaudet Mater Ecclesia*, ed. A. Melloni in *Fede Tradizione Profezia.
Studi su Giovanni XXIII e sul Vaticano II* (Brescia, 1984) 248-49, lines 198-235,
especially line 225 (translated in Abbott, *Documents*, 711-12); *DMC* 1, 897; *OR*, May 11,
1960; *DMC* 4, 258-59. Fr. Lombardi also left a testimony based on what the pope said;
see G. Zizola, *Il microfono di Dio. Pio XII, p. Lombardi e i cattolici italiani* (Milan, 1990)
444-45. G. Martina has several times raised the question of the sincerity of John XXIII's
statements, but he presents the problem in a schematic and inadequately developed way;
see G. Martina and E. Ruffini, *La Chiesa in Italia tra fede e storia* (Rome, 1975) 51-52.

These are all typically spiritual formulations that do not tell us whether he had already considered the possibility or opportuneness of a Council, still less the periods, organization, and carrying out of this enterprise. In essence, they have to do only with the pope's irrevocable decision to convoke a Council that was to be "an encounter with the face of the risen Jesus" and "a liturgical action."[15] But on October 13, 1962, addressing the noncatholic observers at the Council, he explained in more detail: "I do not like to appeal to special inspirations. I am satisfied with the orthodox teaching that everything is from God. In light of that teaching I regarded the idea of a Council as likewise an inspiration from heaven."[16]

Who was this pope who less than a hundred days after his election called the Catholic world to a Council, thereby launching the Roman Church on an adventurous undertaking, the very thought of which had made his predecessors draw back? The conclave had found itself choosing between the Armenian but Romanized Agagianian and the patriarch of Venice; it had chosen the latter: another Italian. Angelo Giuseppe Roncalli, born into a patriarchal family at Sotto il Monte (Bergamo) on November 25, 1881, had received a traditional training. The family, which was large and possessed of very slender economic resources, was marked by a solid piety of the peasant and parochial type. Roncalli always kept in touch with his origins, even when he became separated from them. His way of maintaining family relationships was the faithful application of the ideal set before priests; it was an ideal which he made personal for himself, adapting it to his own temperament and to circumstances. At the age of twelve, in 1892, he began his training for the priesthood in the seminary at Bergamo.

The notes at the beginning of his *Journal of a Soul* — a spiritual diary which he kept faithfully down to the last days of his life[17] — bear witness

[15] Radio talk of September 11, 1962 (*DMC* 4, 521), and *Gaudet Mater Ecclesia*, in Melloni (see note 14), lines 158-64 and especially lines 306-16.

[16] *DMC* 4, 609.

[17] *Il giornale dell'anima*, ed. L. Capovilla (Cinesello B., 1990[10]); ET from the original ed. of 1964: *Journal of a Soul*, trans. D. White (London, 1965; rev. ed., 1980). A critically more complex edition (of the Italian) has been published by A. Melloni (Bologna, 1989). Also published are the *Lettere ai familiari 1901-1962*, ed. L. Capovilla (2 vols.; Rome, 1968). Especially important among Roncalli's writings are the memorial of *Il cardinale Cesare Baronio* (1907) and the biography of *Mons. Giacomo Maria Tedeschi, vescovo di Bergamo* (1916); both were reprinted at Rome in 1963. For Roncalli's preaching: *La predicazione a Istanbul. Omelie, discorsi e note pastorali (1935-1944)* (Florence, 1993). Over the course of several decades Roncalli worked on an edition of *Gli atti della vista apostolica di S. Carlo Borromeo a Bergamo* (5 vols.; Florence, 1936-57).

to a normal interior outlook and spiritual enthusiasm. The first personal note occurs in September, 1896, when he experienced the sudden death of his parish priest in Sotto il Monte and was given as a memento the man's copy of *The Imitation of Christ*, a little book that was to have a profound influence on Roncalli's spirituality.

From 1901 to 1904, with a break for military service as a conscript between November, 1901, and the end of 1902, Roncalli pursued his theological studies at the Roman Seminary in Rome and was ordained a priest. In 1902, a gifted spiritual director, Francesco Pitocchi, a Redemptorist, led him to embrace an elementary but radical principle: "God is everything; I am nothing." In the years between his retreat of December, 1903, and a public celebration of Cardinal Cesare Baronio at Bergamo in 1907, Don Angelo reached some important conclusions about his future. Following a path similar to that of John Henry Newman, he refused to renounce either faith or rational inquiry; he sharpened the distinction between substance and accidents in the matter of faith: that which faith must accept without reservation is different from that which reason is able to analyze because the latter is the contingent product of historical development.

Immediately after his ordination to the priesthood (August 10, 1904), he was appointed secretary to Giacomo Radini Tedeschi, the new bishop of Bergamo. In this association with Radini in Bergamo for a decade, he experienced what it is to "think big"; he saw at work a shepherd whose commitment was unbounded; he came in contact with liturgical and ecumenical issues uncommon in Italy; and he shared the initial experiences of Catholic Action. The diocesan synod which Radini celebrated would remain Roncalli's model. After Radini's death (1914), Roncalli was in military service from May, 1915, to September, 1918, first in the medical corps, then as a military chaplain. At the end of the war, he established a house for students in Bergamo and was spiritual director of the seminary for two years. From 1921 to 1925 he lived in Rome, where as president of the Society for the Propagation of the Faith he had the task of collecting funds for the missions.

In 1925 Pius XII elevated Roncalli to the episcopate and sent him to far-off Orthodox Bulgaria, first as Apostolic Visitor, then as Apostolic Delegate (until 1934). For another decade (1935-1944) his sphere of work was the Apostolic Delegation in Istanbul, at a time when Islam was being radically laicized, and in Athens, the center of the Greek Orthodox Church. These were the decades in which he experienced both embryonic ecumenical relationships and difficult relations with the

Roman Congregations. In 1938-39 the storm of war suddenly struck; Roncalli found himself in an important but uncomfortable position. Pastoral needs had first call on his zeal; to everything else he gave only a qualitatively secondary attention. At the end of 1944, when he had completed his sixty-third year and had but a modest résumé to offer, Pius XII appointed him nuncio in Paris, where he remained from 1945 to 1953, in a Catholic environment that was full of turmoil and fraught with problems.

In November, 1952, he was asked to be ready to succeed the patriarch of Venice, who was dying. Once again, Roncalli obeyed and wrote in his *Journal* (for 1953):

> It is interesting to note that Providence has brought me back to where I began to exercise my priestly vocation, that is to pastoral work....To tell the truth, I have always believed that, for an ecclesiastic, diplomacy (so-called!) must be imbued with a pastoral spirit; otherwise it is of no use and makes a sacred mission look ridiculous. Now I am confronted with the Church's real interests, relating to her final purpose, which is to save souls....This is enough for me and I thank the Lord for it.[18]

He remained in Venice a little more than five years: the last five-year period of Pacelli's pontificate, which was marked by the Cold War between the opposing blocs.

On October 28, 1958, after a rather short conclave, Roncalli was elected to succeed Pope Pacelli. The election of an elderly pope — a man whose reign would be of short duration; a man with few distinguishing marks and therefore without prejudicial enmities; a man with a long and varied career behind him; and a man known personally to many for his geniality — seemed the most suitable and prudent solution; the electors trusted that in the meantime problems would have cleared up by themselves. The choice of the almost eighty-year-old patriarch of Venice was made in this atmosphere and with this understanding. On August 10, 1961, Roncalli would write in his *Journal*:

> When on 28 October 1958, the Cardinals of the Holy Roman Church chose me to assume the supreme responsibility of ruling the universal flock of Jesus Christ, at seventy-seven years of age, everyone was convinced that I would be a provisional and transitional Pope. Yet here I am, already on the eve of the fourth year of my pontificate, with an immense program of work in front of me to be carried out before the eyes of the whole world, which is watching and waiting.[19]

---

[18] *Journal of a Soul*, 304-5.
[19] Ibid., 325.

"Let Our work cry out to the clergy and all the people, for by it We want to 'prepare a perfect people for the Lord, to make their paths straight, so that the twisted ways may become straight and the rough ways smooth, so that every human being may see the salvation of God.'" These were the words with which Roncalli, after unexpectedly choosing the name of John, summed up the purpose of his pontificate on October 28, the day of his election. A few days later, on the occasion of his coronation, the pope stressed his commitment to being a good shepherd according to the image in the tenth chapter of John's gospel; he added that "other human qualities, such as knowledge, shrewdness, diplomatic tact, and organizational skills, can give the finishing touches to a pope's rule, but they can by no means be a substitute for his duty as pastor."

Such were the statements with which Roncalli explained the meaning he gave to the choice of himself as pope. In so doing he distanced himself from many who at that time wanted to saddle him with a variety of tasks: "There are those," he added, "who expect the pope to be a statesman, a diplomat, a man of learning, an organizer of collective life, or, in other words, a man whose mind accepts all the standards, without exception, that are used to determine progress in modern life." On November 23, when taking possession of the Lateran Basilica in his capacity as bishop of Rome, he politely pointed out that his predecessors had omitted this action or treated it lightly, whereas he intended to restore its solemn meaning as a sign of the fact that the pope is in reality, and not just symbolically, the bishop of the church that lives in Rome. Some days later, a month after his election, he noted: "I have in mind a program of work that is not exhausting but is indeed definite."[20]

---

[20] There is as yet no critically satisfactory biography of Roncalli. The following may be consulted:

For the spiritual aspect: G. Alberigo, "L'itinerario spirituale di papa Giovanni," *Servitium* 22 (1988) 35-57; A. and G. Alberigo, "La miséricorde chez Jean XXIII," *La vie spirituelle* 72 (1992) 201-15.

For the years of formation: G. Battelli, "La formazione spirituale del giovane A. G. Roncalli. Il rapporto col redentorista F. Pitocchi," in *Fede Tradizione Profezia*, 15-103; and idem, *Un pastore tra fede e ideologia. Giacomo M. Radini Tedeschi (1857-1914)* (Genoa, 1988), and *Cultura e spiritualità a Bergamo nel tempo di papa Giovanni* (Bergamo, 1983).

For the activity in Rome: S. Beltrami, *L'Opera della propagazione della fede in Italia* (Rome, 1961); S. Trinchese, *Roncalli e le missioni* (Brescia, 1989).

For the decade in Bulgaria: F. Della Salfa, *Obbedienza e pace. Il vescovo A. G. Roncalli tra Sofia e Roma (1925-1934)* (Genoa, 1988).

For the time in Istanbul: A. Melloni, *La fine del passato. A. G. Roncalli vicario e delegato apostolico fra Istanbul, Atene e la guerra (1935-1944)* (Genoa, 1993).

For the period in Paris there is still no organized study; see É. Fouilloux, "Straordinario ambasciatore? Parigi, 1944-1953," in G. Alberigo, ed., *Papa Giovanni* (Rome-Bari, 1988) 67-96.

Roncalli's long life was marked by a progression, but at a deep level; it did not find expression so much in an easily discernible itinerary, but must be grasped by attending to the symptoms or affects to which his experience gave rise. Still less was there any recognizable "plan" for the attainment of a goal or the playing of a role which Roncalli himself supposedly decided to set for his life. Just as he did not manage his own career in diplomacy, so he did not "study to be pope"; in fact, he regarded his appointment to Venice as a final harbor, "quiet after a storm."

No less important was the attitude and temperament of Roncalli himself, whom many too hastily regarded as simply "a good-natured fellow." In fact, his temperament led him to "chew the cud" of his experiences, that is, to sort out the data of experience according to unconventional standards and to store up the results at different levels. Everything that touched him was transformed within him into a lasting memory of his experiences and a sharpening of his perceptions and capacity for judgment, or, in short, into a possession that made him openminded and ready to look for the signs of the times in everyone and everything he encountered. Everything was an occasion for growth in wisdom: his close involvement in the social activism of Radini Tedeschi and his fraternal contacts with Orthodox Christianity in Bulgaria; his painful but never hopeless experience of the secularization of Turkish society and his encounter with the theological and historical optimism of a man like Suhard in post-war Paris (marked by the dechristianization of the working classes) until the Algerian tragedy began to have its impact.

None of these experiences, however, was assimilated without being sorted out. Roncalli's devotion to Radini led him to repeat in his own

---

For the period in Venice there is still no organized study: see *Angelo Giuseppe Roncalli dal patriarcato di Venezia alla catedra di S. Pietro* (Florence, 1984), and G. Alberigo, "Stili di governo episcopale: A. G. Roncalli patriarca di Venezia," in *I cattolici nel mondo contemporaneo (1922-1958)* (Milan, 1991) 237-54.

On the pontificate: G. Lercaro and G. Da Rosa, *John XXIII: Simpleton or Saint?*, trans. D. White (Chicago, 1967); F. M. Willam, *Vom jungen Angelo Roncalli (1903-1907) zum Papst Johannes XXIII (1903-1963)* (Innsbruck, 1967); J. Gritti, *Jean XXIII dans l'opinion publique. Son image à travers la presse et les sondages d'opinion publique* (Paris, 1967); L. Capovilla, *Giovanni XXIII. Quindici letture* (Rome, 1970); G. Zizola, *The Utopia of Pope John XXIII*, trans. H. Barolini (Maryknoll, 1978); *Fede Tradizione Profezia. Studi su Giovanni XXIII e sul Vaticano II* (Brescia, 1984); *Giovanni XXIII transizione del papato e della chiesa*, ed. G. Alberigo (Rome, 1988); "L'Età di Roncalli," *CrSt* 8 (1987) 1-217; *Papa Giovanni*, ed. G. Alberigo (Rome-Bari, 1988); P. Hebblethwaite, *Pope John XXIII. The Pope of the Council* (New York, 1984); M. Manzo, *Papa Giovanni vescovo a Roma* (Cinisello B., 1991); A. Riccardi, *Il potere del papa. Da Pio XII a Paolo VI* (Rome-Bari, 1988) 154-219; S. Trinchese, *Roncalli storico 1905-1958* (Chieti, 1988); G. Zizola, *Giovanni XXIII. La fede e la politica* (Rome-Bari, 1988).

life the life-journey of "his bishop," but also to share Radini's social involvement although in ways quite different from those of Radini and even with a different intensity. In like manner, his Bulgarian experience led him to a rich and open conception of Christian unity, but also to a distancing of himself both from the various forms of "uniatism" and from ecclesial uniformism. Again, his experience of a-religious secularism in the "new" Turkey quickened his attentiveness to the deeper meanings of human history that transcend the accidental aspects, but at the same time it did not affect his perception of the gospel or impoverish his rich interior life. In France, his friendly attention to the riches and turmoil of a Church so different from the Church of Italy added to the store of his experiences; his life there located him for the first time in a very important ecclesial and social situation, widened his horizons, and seemed to prepare him, in ways that go beyond rational plausibility, for the pastoral undertaking that would occupy him in Venice and Rome during the final decade of his life.

A man like Roncalli, for whom the Church was a natural habitat and for whom the study of history always had a great fascination, had reflected with interest on the important role which Councils had played in the life of the Christian communities; it was an interest outside the average education of the Italian clergy of his time. But this interest in the history of the Councils did not make him an expert in the strict sense; instead, his attention was focused chiefly on the aspects of the Councils that paved the way for union and on their pastoral role. The fascination which the period of the application of Trent had for him, a period dominated by the emblematic figure of Charles Borromeo, is explained by the leading part that pastoral practice played during it. This priority given to pastoral care was one of the clearest elements in and most intensely sought goals first of his service as bishop and then of his Petrine office.[21]

A factor that may have more directly caused Roncalli to regard a Council as timely was the proposals that surfaced in the Christian world throughout the first half of the twentieth century: from the plans of the Eastern "Orthodox" Churches (to which Roncalli seems to allude in his radio message for Christmas, 1958) to the proposals entertained first by Pius XI and then by Pius XII to resume and complete the Vatican Council that had been interrupted in 1870 (but Roncalli played no part in

---

[21] See Caprile I/1, 39-45, and G. Alberigo, "L'ispirazione di un concilio ecumenico: le esperienze del card. Roncalli," in *Deuxième*, 81-99.

these proposals).[22] We do not know whether Roncalli read the articles published in *La Palestra del clero* for May 15 and June 1, 1958, by G. A. Scaltriti, O.P., in which the author called for "a universal Council to continue the work of the Vatican Council that was broken off in 1870."[23]

In any case, the assumption of the primatial office was a turning point for Roncalli. Between the election of October 28 and the allocution on January 25 there was a constant trickle (perhaps not yet completely reconstructed) of references, often simple allusions, by John XXIII to his intention of holding a Council. We are apparently dealing here with confidential communications, except for a single consultation on January 20, when the pope "rather hesitantly and uncertainly" informed Secretary of State Tardini about the "program for his pontificate" — Roman synod, ecumenical Council, updating of the *Codex iuris canonici* — and received Tardini's complete and liberating assent.[24] It is difficult to decide whether Tardini's assent was read by the pope in even more unconditional terms than those contained in the suggestion "to cultivate, develop, and broadcast" the idea of a Council (annotation by the pope). In any case, it seems that at the moment of this conversation the pope had already begun the draft of his address on January 25.

The calling of a new Council was, then, the fruit of a personal conviction of the pope, one that slowly took form in his mind, was strengthened by others, and finally became an authoritative and irrevocable decision during the three-month period after his election to the pontificate. It was a free and independent decision such as perhaps was never made before in the history of ecumenical or general Councils. This convocation was not preceded by diplomatic negotiations or by formal consultations with churchmen, and therefore it took all by surprise: friends and opponents, inside and outside the Catholic Church, from top to bottom. It was an upsetting action; was it destined to prove barren or even to be judged the result of a rash impulse?

[22] See G. Alberigo, "Giovanni XXIII e il Vaticano II," in *Papa Roncalli* (Rome-Bari, 1987) 211-13, and Melloni, "'Questa festiva ricorrenza,'" 612-16.

[23] See Melloni, "'Questa festiva ricorrenza,'" 609-12. S. Oddi claims, however, that Roncalli gave a positive response to the inquiry conducted by Pius XII in 1948 on the opportuneness of a council; see C. Barthe, "Aux origines du Concile: la défaite du 'parti romain,'" *Catholica* 42, no. 8 (1988) 43.

[24] See L. Capovilla, "Il concilio ecumenico Vaticano II: la decisione di Giovanni XXIII. Precedenti storici e motivazioni personali," in *Come si é giunti al concilio Vaticano II*, ed. G. Galeazzi (Milan, 1988) 15-60, and C. F. Casula, "Tardini e la preparazione del concilio," ibid., 172-75.

Before turning to the responses elicited by the announcement in St. Paul Outside the Walls, it is expedient to analyze its content. The short address to the cardinals had an explicit content: it set out a program relating to the tasks for which John XXIII felt responsible as successor of Peter. Taking as his point of reference a conception of the papacy that had fallen into disuse for centuries, the pope broke his task down into "a twofold responsibility as bishop of Rome and as pastor of the universal Church: two expressions of a single suprahuman investiture; two assignments that cannot be separated and that must in fact fit together." Consistently with this vision, the address devoted a first set of reflections to the human and spiritual condition of Rome and then sketched some characteristics of the universal human situation.[25] Against this background the pope then announced the convocation of a diocesan synod for Rome and a general Council for the whole of Roman Catholicism.

Both synod and Council were undertakings that could not have been predicted. It had become unusual to give much attention to the diocesan aspects of the church of Rome and of its bishop. In more recent times the custom had gradually grown of focusing on the Holy See as an institutional and spiritual reality that absorbed and in a sense cancelled out the local Church of Rome, just as the responsibilities of the pope as "Vicar of Christ" went beyond and absorbed those of the bishop of the diocesan Roman Church, which was traditionally entrusted to the care of the anomalous figure known as the "Cardinal Vicar." The announcement of a Roman synod suddenly brought the spiritual identity of Rome to the fore by raising in their full seriousness the pastoral problems to be found at the center of the Catholic world and by reasserting the direct and inalienable responsibility of the pope.

In parallel fashion, after the authoritative approval in 1870 of the papal prerogatives of primacy and infallibility, many thought that a new Council would no longer be necessary. The widely held conception of the Church as a pyramid in which authority was communicated from the top (the pope) to the lower levels had given this view an authority almost beyond question. Admittedly, calls for a new Council had not been lacking: during the vacancy after the death of Pius XI, C. Constantini, urged by his own experience in the Far East and echoing requests from missionary circles, had drawn up a plan for a Council. But Roncalli was told of this only in June, 1959.[26] In any case, the only official initiatives had been directed to a

[25] Melloni, "'Questa festiva ricorrenza,'" lines 82-98, 102-206, 207-95.
[26] See G. Butturini, "Per un concilio di riforma: una proposta inedita (1939) di C. Costantini," *CrSt* 7 (1986) 87-139.

continuation of the Vatican Council that had been broken off in 1870. Pius XI at the beginning of his pontificate and Pius XII in the early 1950s had thought in these terms. Even so, their plans, which were kept strictly secret, had run aground well before the stage of implementation.[27]

To these two synodal undertakings, both of them disruptive, though not in the same way or degree, John XXIII added the updating of the *Codex iuris canonici*, which had been promulgated in 1917 but had been composed, in substance, during the first decade of the century and was therefore showing signs of its age. Desires for such a revision came from many sides, and this fact had also been taken into consideration during the preliminary work on a Council that had been done under Pius XII.[28] Pope John made this third program subordinate to the completion of the Roman synod and especially of the Council. On the other hand, it would soon become clear that the attention of the curial staffs and of the bishops themselves turned spontaneously to this undertaking, the outlines of which were sufficiently clear, rather than to the Council, which was foreign to the perspectives of churchmen during those years. This general outlook was echoed in a note of Msgr. Villot in April, 1962, in which he said: "Most of the commissions spent their time much more on the plan for a reform of the Code than on deliberations about a Council."[29]

The allocution on January 25 described the Council in sober terms. After invoking the intercession of Mary and the protection of the saints, the pope devoted only two phrases to the aims of the Council: on the one hand, "the enlightenment, edification, and joy of the entire Christian people" and, on the other, "a renewed cordial invitation to the faithful of the separated Churches to participate with us in this feast of grace and brotherhood, for which so many souls long in all parts of the world."[30]

[27] C. Caprile, "Pio XI e la ripresa del concilio Vaticano," *CC* 117 (1966/3) 27-39, and "Pio XI, la Curia romana e il concilio," ibid., 120 (1969/2) 563-75; idem, "Pio XII e un nuovo progetto di concilio ecumenico," *CC* 117 (1966/3) 209-27. This last article was reprinted in German with some interesting variations: "Pius XII. und das zweite Vatikanische Konzil," in *Pius XII. zum Gedächtnis*, ed. H. Schambeck (Berlin, 1977) 649-91.

[28] Caprile, "Pio XII e un nuovo progetto," 210 and 212. See F. D'Ostilio, *La storia del nuovo Codice di diritto canonico* (Vatican City, 1983).

[29] A. Wenger, "Mgr Villot et le concile Vatican II," in *Deuxième*, 244. See also A. Melloni, "Per un approccio storico-critico ai 'Consilia et vota' della fase ante-praeparatoria del Vaticano II," *RSLR* 26 (1990) 556-76.

[30] I cite, as always, from the pope's own redaction of the speech (Melloni, "'Questa festiva ricorrenza,'" lines 415-56), which has been considerably "polished" in the official edition, according to which the second purpose was "a renewed invitation to the faithful of the separated communities graciously to follow us in the search for unity and grace, for which...." No longer "Churches" but "communities"; not "participate" but "follow"; not "feast" but "search." The pope's incisive language was thus sytematically blunted.

John XXIII himself was perhaps not yet fully clear in his own mind or at least did not wish to say too much in this first announcement, which was already sufficiently disruptive, all the more so since he did not return to the by now classical formula according to which Councils were convoked in order to decide on matters of "faith and morals." He was not proposing to condemn errors or to meet threats of schism. His description was so concise that it created uncertainties in an ecclesial public opinion that was used rather to receiving "directives." In addition, it seems that the determination with which the pope announced his decision was not matched by an equally complete idea of the Council. The clarification and fuller conception of the shape and aims of the Council would be achieved by Pope John during the ensuing months and years and would also be affected by the broad debate that followed upon the announcement.

3. *The Announcement of Earlier Councils.*

The way chosen for announcing Vatican II differed from those followed for the major Councils and especially those of Paul III in the sixteenth century and Pius IX in the nineteenth for the two most recent Councils. In antiquity the action of the emperor depended on the political situation, on existing causes for concern in the Church, and, from a certain point on, on the consent of the Patriarch of the West. Later on, in the Middle Ages, the popes acted with complete independence in exercising their authority to convoke Councils, although this authority extended only to the Latin Church. After the conciliar crisis of the fifteenth century it was anticipated that Councils would be held regularly and independently of the initiative of the popes, who had shown themselves reluctant or wanting. It was only in view of a reunification with the Eastern Church that Rome and Constantinople agreed on the convocation of the Councils of Lyons and Florence.

Amid the tragic difficulties which Western Christianity was experiencing in the early decades of the sixteenth century many voices were raised asking for a Council to be held and also falling back, as Martin Luther himself did, on the canonical right of "appeal" to a Council. Finally, Pope Farnese succeeded with great effort in overcoming the tenacious resistance to the convocation of a Council for which people had been asking in vain for decades. At last, in 1536, at the height of intense diplomatic activity and exhausting ecclesiastical maneuvering, Paul III decided to announce a Council to be held in Mantua. Then, in

keeping with the practice of the time, papal nuncios were sent throughout Europe to the princes and the main ecclesiastical centers in order to
communicate the decision to convoke the Council and to obtain the real
participation of the bishops.

The result was disastrous and a Council became impossible for
another decade, despite other papal attempts to convoke one. When there
came at last a convocation that would be successful, a great part of Christendom remained uncertain about whether the pope really wished the
Council to take place. Long before papal primacy became a formal
dogma, the Latin Church had interiorized a now unconquerable dependence on the pope, to the point of being dubious about so solemn an
action as the convocation of a Council. In Rome more than elsewhere
there were those who refused to accept the possibility of a Council, and
in fact one scholar has observed that "while the nuncios were busy, as in
duty bound, making the Bull known, a hush fell upon Rome in respect to
the Council."[31] Paradoxically, the same contradiction would show up
over four centuries later: in Rome the *Osservatore Romano* never published the text of the allocution in St. Paul's, but only a skimpy bulletin,
whereas the announcement created widespread interest among the public.

Pius IX considered the possibility of holding a Council in 1849, that
is, immediately after his election (as John XXIII was to do in the same
situation), but the Italian political situation and resistance from the Curia
put off for decades the formalizing of the pope's intention (1864) and,
all the more, the beginning of preparation for the Council and its actual
opening. Only when the gathering of the members was imminent did
public debate become lively, overwhelming the preparatory work itself,[32]
to the point that the First Vatican Council took a course considerably
different from that envisaged by Pius IX himself.

As I said earlier, the "conciliar" proposals of Pius XI and Pius XII,
both of them halted before any convocation, were not made known to
the public at all.

* * *

In any case, the announcement of January 25 was an irreversible act; in
the months and years to come Catholicism and with it the other Christian

---

[31] H. Jedin, *A History of the Council at Trent* I. *The Struggle for the Council*, trans.
E. Graf (St. Louis, 1957) 508-9. See 313-54 (convocation at Mantua), 331-34 (convocation at Vicenza), 459-61 (first convocation at Trent), 504-9 (second convocation at Trent).

[32] R. Aubert, *Vatican I* (Paris, 1964) 39-53, and especially G. Martina, *Pio IX (1967-
1878)* (Rome, 1990) 111-66.

traditions and even the lay world would have to come to grips with Roncalli's project. The Catholic Church had entered a new and unforeseen
phase of its history. Having been a principle of continuity and identity
for Western societies, the Roman papacy and Catholicism were about to
become agents of movement and thus forces of renewal, even of those
same societies. The large Soviet-controlled area that for almost half a
century had drawn strength from an institutionalized controversy with post-
tridentine Christianity could not but be aware of so important a novelty;
this awareness was attested by the sudden attention which Moscow paid
to Pope John's enterprise. It had been centuries since an act so typically
ecclesial had such a complex and enormous historical impact.

II. ECHOES, HOPES, CONCERNS[33]

The sympathy which John XXIII had won for himself during the first
months of his pontificate by his pastoral attitudes created a context for
the expression of reactions to the announcement of a new Council.[34] But
the echoes awakened by his action were also much more far-reaching,
extending to very different circles, social groups, and cultural strata, far
beyond the usual confines of Roman Catholicism.[35] Geographically, too,
his action crossed the bounds of the usual Atlantic world of Europe and
North America; the response was a first sign of the intercontinental
importance that both John's pontificate and the Council were to have.[36]

[33] I am making use here of my essay "Giovanni XXIII e il Vaticano II," in *Papa
Giovanni* (Rome-Bari, 1987) 211-43, especially 211-22. In the archive of the council
there are several dozen cartons of press clippings about the council from 1959 on; they
are organized by country, but have thus far not been studied.

[34] For the approval of John by the Italian press during the first months of his pontificate see M. Marazziti, *I Papi di carta. Nascita e svolta dell'informazione religiosa da Pio
XII a Giovanni XXIII* (Genoa, 1990) 47-126. There is also worthwile information in
A. and F. Manoukian, *La Chiesa dei giornali. Ricerca sociologica sull'interessamento dei
quotidiani italiani ai fatti della Chiesa dal 1945 al 1965* (Bologna, 1968).

[35] Caprile I/1, 57-67, reprints a survey of comments that was published in *CC* for April
25, 1959; the first footnote lists various similar surveys published in the main religious
newspapers. Oddly enough, the survey in *CC* classifies as "dissents" the comments in
various publications, among them *Le Monde*, that the calling of a council by John XXIII in
fact represented the movement of his pontificate away from that of his predecessor.

[36] Private sources are especially scarce for these months in the first half of 1959. The
many diaries of the conciliar period (Siri, Döpfner, Congar, Chenu, Edelby, Bartoletti,
Musty, Perraudin, Jedin, Tromp, Felici, Léger, Tucci, Moeller, Fenton, Dupont) usually
begin only in October, 1962, or shortly before. Consequently, the rare notes concerning
this period are especially valuable: W. A. Visser't Hooft, *Memoirs* (London, 1973); *Für
die Menschen bestellt. Erinnerungen des alterzbischofs von Köln J. Kard. Frings*
(Cologne, 1973) 247-304; H. Jedin, *Lebensbericht*, ed. K. Repgen (Mainz, 1984).

It is almost impossible to make a complete survey of the reactions and early comments elicited by the announcement. The news circled the globe in a few hours, exciting attention, interest, and expectations that were so varied in their emphases, nuances, and outlooks that even the most careful account of them will succeed only in summarizing with examples.

At once there was a widespread sense that a profound change was taking place at the heart of Catholicism, with each individual imagining the substance of the change and the most desirable ways for it to develop. The most striking thing, however, was the hope and expectation that were stirred to life.

1. *Catholic Circles.*

Over and above the disconcerted or perhaps defensive silence of the cardinals present in St. Paul Outside the Walls, the responses elicited by the communication of the text of the papal allocution to all the members of the college of cardinals were characterized chiefly by bewilderment and worry. On January 25 seventeen cardinals were present. Twenty-five cardinals (seven of whom had been in St. Paul) responded by letter between January 26 and April 14; in ten instances the reply was purely formal, while only three expressed a considered opinion. Thirty-eight others did not reply at all.

Cardinals Fossati and Tappouni emphasized the ecumenical aspect of the Council; Urbani tactfully recalled the conversation he had had with Roncalli regarding "the updating of Church laws." Pizzardo, adopting the viewpoint of the Congregation for Seminaries, hoped for a renewal of the encyclical *Humani generis* and an intervention that would resolve the conflicts between the secular and the regular clergy. Spellman, from the United States, took the occasion to express a complaint that he had learned of the papal announcement only through the press; he added that the decision seemed to him "destined for certain failure." In Milan Cardinal Montini reacted "coldly" and told Father Bevilacqua of his concern that they would find themselves in a "hornet's nest." In Bologna Lercaro, according to a newspaper report, had been moved and astonished.[37]

---

[37] *ADA*, I, 114-49. *ADA* did not publish the response of Cardinal Micara, papal vicar for Rome, who in fact took note only of the calling of the Roman synod (Manzo, *Papa Giovanni vescovo*, 288-89). Pizzardo sent his reply to the Secretary of State on February 15: *AS App.* 25-28. See also Caprile, I/1, 46-54. For Montini: A. Fappani and F. Molinari, *G. B. Montini giovane* (Turin, 1979) 171; for Lercaro: V. Gorresio, *La nuova missione* (Milan, 1968) 176.

In Rome *L'Osservatore Romano* published only the communiqué from the Secretariat of State and not the text of the papal allocution in St. Paul's, since it assumed that each cardinal would receive a copy. For this reason, official information about the pope's announcement was especially scarce,[38] even though the communiqué was mistakenly sent to the press even before John XXIII delivered his address at the consistory. In its issues for the first three months of 1959 *La Civiltà Cattolica* completely ignored the announcement, except for printing the scanty communiqué in its "Chronicle." The first isolated sign of its attention came only in the issue of April 25, 1959, in the form of a survey of comments from the press.[39] During the whole of 1959 this authoritative journal did not publish a single article in the proper sense of the word on the announcement of the Council.

As an authoritative witness wrote at the beginning of August to the archbishop of Milan,

> the Rome which you knew and from which you were exiled gives no sign of changing, as it seemed it would have to do, in the end. After an initial scare the circle of elderly vultures is returning. Slowly indeed, but it is returning. And it returns with a thirst for new torments, new vendettas. Around the *carum caput* [dear head, i.e., the pope] this macabre circle presses close. It has regained its composure, that's for sure.[40]

---

[38] The complete text of the papal allocution was published in *AAS* 51 (1959) 65-69 and then in *Documentation catholique* (issue of March 29, pp. 385-88), in *Informations catholiques internationales* (issue of April 1, no. 93, pp. 27-28), and in *Herder Korrespondenz* for May (387-88), while *La Civiltà Cattolica* and *Il Regno* never published it.

[39] On February 1 *L'Osservatore Romano* published an article of commentary on the allocution of January 29: "Il triplice annuncio"; during the first three months of 1959 this daily newspaper of the Holy See returned to the subject of the council on February 11 with an article of A. Bacci who expressed his wish that Latin be the language of the council; indirectly, on March 15, with an article of R. Spiazzi on "S. Tommaso e i concili ecumenici" and on May 21 with an article of the same Dominican, "Il senso del concilio ecumenico." The issue of April 6-7 contained an article by C. Boyer, "Significati diversi della parola 'ecumenico'"; this point—a sensitive one due especially to the wide range of meanings of the adjective—was emphasized by the *Times* of London in an article of April 21. See also G. Caprile, "Primi commenti all'annunzio del futuro concilio," *CC* 110 (1959/2) 292-95. When Fr. Caprile gathered his chronicles about the preparation for the council into a volume (*Il concilio Vaticano II. Annunzio e preparazione* I/1 [Rome, 1966]), he had to add some short chapters (pp. 39-54 and 107-81) on the period between 1959 and the first half of 1960, during which the periodical had been almost completely silent. Another shrewd commentary was that of R. Rouquette, S.J., in *Études* 300 (1959) 394-401 and again in 301 (1959) 235-36 and 386-89. *Informations catholiques internationales* also devoted a great deal of space to the announcement, beginning with its issue of February 1. *Stimmen der Zeit*, on the other hand, was quite restrained and after a short notice in its March issue (462-64) published nothing more on the subject for the remainder of 1959.

[40] G. De Luca to G. B. Montini, August 6, 1959, in *Carteggio 1930-1962*, ed. P. Vian (Brescia, 1992) 232.

The announcement of the Council had perhaps hastened the mustering of powerful resistance forces after the conciliatory atmosphere of the first weeks following upon Roncalli's election.

Of the episcopal conferences that of Western Germany was especially prompt to respond and gave particular attention to the announcement; its response was based on a report which Archbishop Jaeger delivered as early as the Fulda meeting in mid-February. A month later, at a special meeting in Bühl, the Conference began to draw up German proposals for the Council. During that same period the Polish episcopate published a joint letter on the event and on April 14 established a conciliar commission within the episcopal conference.[41]

At a meeting on June 11 the board of the Italian Episcopal Conference did not approve a proposal of the archbishop of Bologna that a commission of Italian bishops be set up to study proposals from the various regions of the conference concerning subjects for the Council. Montini regarded such a move as premature and preferred to wait for signals from Rome. Urbani, Roncalli's successor in Venice, likewise confessed himself to be undecided. Instead, the board focused its attention on the decision to prepare a joint pastoral letter on laicism. At the next meeting, in October, of the presidents of the various regions of the conference, their final communiqué did not mention the announcement of the Council at all. The regional conference of Piedmont had spoken of it a month earlier, noting that each bishop had already responded individually to the antepreparatory request for opinions.[42] Meanwhile Archbishop Montini of Milan had already addressed a *Messaggio* to his faithful on January 26, having presumably been informed in advance of the papal announcement. In July, Mons. Ursi of the little southern diocese of Nardo emphasized the ecumenical significance of the coming Council.[43]

The Dutch bishops discussed the antepreparatory request for opinions in their meeting at the end of July; on the other hand, the announcement

[41] J. Kloczowski, "Les Évêques polonais et le concile Vatican II," in *Deuxième*, 167-68.

[42] On the occasion of the June meeting, John XXIII appointed Cardinal Siri, the archbishop of Genoa, to replace the elderly Cardinal Fossati as president of the Italian episcopate; see F. Sportelli, *La Conferenza Episcopale Italiana (1952-1972)* (doctoral dissertation; Sassari, 1993) 167-95. See M. Velati, "I 'consilia et vota' dei vescovi italiani," in *Veille*, 101.

[43] The text of Cardinal Montini's *Messaggio* was attached to his reply to the invitation issued in the papal allocution: *ADA*, I, 119-21, and in G. B. Montini, *Discorsi e scritti sul concilio (1959-1963)*, ed. A. Rimoldi (Brescia-Rome, 1983) 25-26. See A. Rimoldi, "La preparazione del Concilio," in *G. B. Montini, arcivescovo di Milano e il Concilio ecumenico Vaticano II. Preparazione e primo periodo* (Brescia, 1985) 202-5. For Ursi see Caprile I/1, 142-43.

of the preceding January had not been the subject of discussion by the Netherlands conference.[44]

In the United States J. J. Wright, bishop of Pittsburgh, used the feast of Sts. Peter and Paul as an occasion for bringing out the importance of the announcement.[45] In a document published in February, 1959, the Canadian Episcopal Conference emphasized the pastoral and ecumenical description given in John XXIII's announcement and asked the questions which everyone was asking to some extent: Would or would not the Council be a continuation of the Council of Pius IX? Who would be invited to the Council? Would the Orthodox Churches also take part?[46]

While the episcopate seems to have been rather slow, at least in expressing a public opinion of the papal initiative, the pope's action received an especially thoughtful and sympathetic reception in circles that for years had been committed to the desire for, development of, and experimentation in the renewal of various aspects of Catholicism. There were also some uncertain judgments, due to the fact that the initial news was limited to the communiqué from the Secretariat of State, which also spoke of coping with errors.[47] But people in these movements very quickly saw that the new pope's attitude was less intransigeant than that of his predecessor.[48] Some pastoral actions — from the importance which the pope assigned to his responsibilities as bishop of Rome, to his solemn taking possession of the Cathedral of St. John Lateran, to his visits to hospitals and prisons, and even to his removal of the adjective *perfidi* from the solemn intercession for the Jews on Good Friday — heralded a different kind of pontificate and one more attentive to the calls for renewal. Congar, for his part, wrote:

> Here was a pope threatening to abandon a number of positions. The Church was going to speak out. Some were talking of giving the bishops more independence. While the little team of co-opted Roman theologians used to

[44] J. Y. A. Jacobs, "L''aggiornamento' est mis en relief. Les 'vota' des évêques néerlandais pour Vatican II," *CrSt* 12 (1991) 323-40, and in *Veille*, 101. On the echoes of the announcement in the Netherlands see J. Y. A. Jacobs, *Met het oog op een andere Kerk. Katholiek Nederland en de voorbereiding van het Tweede Vaticaans Oecumenisch Concilie 1959-1962* (Baarn, 1986) 17-24.

[45] Caprile I/1, 158-59.

[46] But *La Semaine religieuse de Montréal* and *La Semaine religieuse de Québec* were very reserved in regard to the pope's announcement. I owe this information to the kindness of my colleague A. Naud, a former secretary of Cardinal Léger.

[47] Thus Brazilian scholar A. Amoroso Lima in a letter from New York dated January 26, 1959: *João XXIII* (Rio de Janeiro, 1966) 22-24.

[48] See É. Fouilloux, "'Mouvements' théologico-spirituels et concile (1959-1962)," in *Veille*, 185-89.

impose its views on everyone else, now the others were going to be given an independent chance. All was proceeding, it seemed to me, as if the curia of Pius XII, which had remained in place, was quite aware of the danger and would bend as much as was necessary but would not break and would try to limit the damage to the system as much as possible.[49]

While it is relatively easy to gain information about the reactions of more qualified people, it is almost impossible to give an account of the countless thoughts conveyed by quite widely differing communications media, ranging from diocesan and parish newspapers to radio and the television networks.

It is significant that only a few months after the allocution in St. Paul's and after epistolary and personal contacts with German Bishop Höfer and Jesuit Augustin Bea, Otto Karrer, a Swiss priest active in the ecumenical movement, wrote a memorandum on the prospects which the coming Council could open up for union among Christians, and sent this to bishops and theologians.[50] Looking at matters from an ecumenical viewpoint, Karrer hoped that the Council would abstain from proclaiming any new dogmatic propositions of any kind and would reinterpret the definitions of 1870, using for this purpose the declaration of the German bishops in 1875, which Pius IX had approved. In order to facilitate relations with the Eastern Orthodox, Karrer thought it necessary to harmonize the Roman primatial claims with the fraternal communion that governs interecclesial relations in the Orthodox tradition. Recognition of the right of local churches to choose their own bishops would be a very significant step. Karrer was less optimistic when it came to the Protestants, but he nonetheless suggested the fostering of contacts at many levels and especially with the World Council of Churches in Geneva. A third part of Karrer's document dealt with the internal renewal of Catholicism, a renewal based on episcopal collegiality, the central place of the Bible, the use of the vernaculars in the liturgy and the Divine Office, and, finally, the simplification of many elements of ecclesiastical practice.

[49] *Mon Journal*, 3.

[50] Karrer was one of the precursors of Vatican II; in an article entitled "Wie stellt sich der katholische Glaube in der Wirklichkeit des Lebens dar?" and published in the ecumenical journal *Una Sancta* in 1955 (pp. 24-34), he had expressed a desire that a new council be held. On this see L. Höfer, *O. Karrer 1888-1976. Kämpfen und Leiden für eine weltoffene Kirche* (Freiburg i. B., 1985); the "Memorandum" is given on pp. 394-400. See also V. Conzemius, "Otto Karrer (1888-1976)," in *Deuxième*, 340-58, and É. Fouilloux, "Des Observateurs non-catholiques," in *Vatican II commence*, 235-61.

A. Bea, too, drew up his own set of "reflections" on the Council and its ecumenical aims, and sent this to various correspondents.[51] In his view, it would be a mistake to expect too much of the Council in the matter of reunion; there are other, no less important ecclesiological problems, chiefly

> doctrine concerning the church, especially the position of bishops. In my opinion bishops must be involved to a greater extent in government both of the universal church and more specifically of their own diocese. It should not be possible for an order to be given or a decision taken on a question concerning a diocese without consulting the local ordinary. Such centralization is certainly not a blessing for the church.

Bea also maintains that "the question of the royal rule of Christ seems to me an important one for ecclesiology. Another concept that ought to be made very clear is that of the Holy Spirit as the principle that guides and enlightens the mystical body of Christ; the teaching authority of the Church will thereby receive its intrinsic justification." In his "Reflections" Bea also raises the question of "the make-up of the Roman Curia and in particular of the Congregations. It seems indispensable that each congregation be headed by a specialist, even if he is not a cardinal. In addition, the body of advisors should be international in character."[52]

In mid-June the board of the Catholic Conference for Ecumenical Affairs circulated a "Note on the restoration of Christian unity on the occasion of the coming Council." This had been composed during the preceding weeks and was sent first to many bishops and theologians and later to all the Council fathers.[53] This compact and carefully constructed note is completely faithful to its title, for it contains not so much suggestions for the Council as a working "guide" for undertakings of

[51] Stejpan Schmidt, *Augustine: The Cardinal of Unity*, trans. L. Wearne (New Rochelle, NY: New City Press, 1992) 294. Unfortunately, the text has been lost and only bits of it are known from letters of Bea.

[52] Ibid., 295.

[53] The governing board had held a well-timed meeting in Rome on February 26, 1959, as the French ambassador to the Holy See wrote in his report of March 16. The same board signed the "Note du Comité directeur de la 'Conférence catholique pour les Questions oecuméniques' sur la restauration de l'Unité chrétienne à l'occasion du prochain Concile" (14 pp. typewritten); it was composed by Ch. Boyer, F. Davis, C. J. Dumont, J. Höfer, and J. G. M. Willebrands. The note had six parts, plus an introduction (I) and conclusion. The six parts dealt with: (II) "Psychological prejudices"; (III) "Minds unprepared"; (IV) "Distinguish but do not separate"; (V) "Fundamental difficulties"; (VI) "The present situation"; (VII) "The enthusiasm expected from the good will of the Catholic Church." See also M. Velati, "La proposta ecumenica del Segretariato per l'unità dei cristiani," in *Verso il Concilio*, 273-343.

the Catholic Church with a view to the reunification of Christians. The Conference's courageous document was an important witness to the extent to which the mere announcement of the Council released and encouraged latent energies. It must be added that while this memorandum was intended chiefly for the Roman authorities of the Church, it allows us to glimpse in the background emphases and suggestions that would be heard again during the work of the Council. We may not overlook the undeniable impact which this document had on the climate of the preconciliar period by helping to strengthen the sector of opinion that was in favor of a commitment to ecumenism.

It might be said that the prevailing tone of the document is an awareness of the difficulties besetting an ecumenical activity that could successfully avoid the recurrent contradictions in the Catholic outlook. The note realistically emphasizes the difficulties and obstacles in the way of any rapprochement. The probably decisive contribution of Fr. Dumont may explain the repeated confidence that an agreement with the Orthodox is easier and closer than with the Protestants (no. 22). The fact that Fr. Boyer had a part in the work may explain the use of language — "separated brethren," "separated Churches" — that would be quickly abandoned.

With an eye on the Council, the note warns against the catastrophic effects of possible new dogmatic definitions or emphases on Mary; it also calls for a recognition of the powers proper to bishops and for the creation of intermediate ecclesiastical jurisdictions (episcopal conferences; patriarchates) that would balance Roman centralization. A surprising element in the note is the clear-sighted anticipation with which it warns against the kinds of relationship between the bishops and Rome in which haste, the spectacular, and the use of prepackaged texts are prevailing traits. The note shrewdly expresses the conviction that a union between the Churches that is based on a concern to present a united front against Communism would be ephemeral, like the reunion of Florence, which was suggested by the Muslim threat. Also mentioned in the note is the ecumenical importance of recognizing the "legitimacy of forms of theology that are purely biblical and patristic" and not Scholastic. Finally, the value of baptism, however administered, as the distinguishing mark of Christians, and communion (*koinonia*) as the basis of the idea of the Church are singled out as theological points that are crucial for any agreement.

During almost the same days, a meeting of Christian journalists, Catholic and noncatholic, was held at the Benedictine monastery of

Maria Laach, one of the centers of the liturgical renewal, on the subject
of "The Council and the Unity of Christians."[54] The introductory
talk given by the archbishop of Paderborn referred to the prevailing
uncertainty about the form the future Council would take; his talk was,
however, devoted exclusively to a summary explanation of traditional
Roman Catholic doctrine on Councils, as confirmed by the *Code of
Canon Law*.

In circles devoted to theological and historical research the prospect of
a new Council likewise spurred undertakings aimed at producing tools or
thematic studies that might facilitate the work of the Council. The most
authoritative historian of Councils, H. Jedin, immediately began work on
a summary presentation of the entire series of Councils; this appeared in
1959 and was to be very successful.[55] An institute in Bologna, encouraged by G. Dossetti and with the collaboration of an international team,
undertook a complete edition, in the original languages, of the texts of the
decrees of all the ecumenical or general Councils.[56]

The announcement did not escape the watchful eye of G. La Pira:
"An event of immense supernatural and historical significance." A few
months later, the mayor of Florence observed that "the Council is the
essential 'political' fact on which the peace of peoples and their new
political, social, cultural, and religious structures depend."[57] It would be
a difficult but possible and worthwhile task to make an inventory of the
reactions spontaneously elicited by the announcement of the Council.[58]

2. *Noncatholic Christians*.

The intensely active interchristian contacts that followed upon the
Second World War, due to the efforts of the World Council of Churches

---

[54] Caprile I/1, 89-90 and 145-46; *HK* 13 (1959) 507-9. The text of Bishop Jaeger's
report is in *DC* 56 (1959) 945-54.

[55] H. Jedin, *Kleine Konziliengeschichte* (Freiburg, 1959); ET: *Ecumenical Councils of
the Catholic Church: An Historical Outline*, trans. E. Graf (New York, 1959, 1962⁴).

[56] *Conciliorum Oecumenicorum Decreta*, ed. Istituto per le Scienze Religiose
(Bologna), curantibus J. Alberigo, P.-P. Joannou, C. Leonardi, P. Prodi, consultante H. Jedin
(Freiburg, 1962). ET: *Decrees of the Ecumenical Councils*, ed. N. P. Tanner (Washington,
1990).

[57] Notes of January 26 and April 24; see F. Mazzei, "Giovanni XXIII e La Pira," in
Giovanni XXIII transizione del papato e della chiesa, ed. G. Alberigo (Rome, 1988) 73.

[58] In the conciliar archive there are several boxes containing petitions or studies
spontaneously sent to Rome in view of the council, starting in 1959; they are organized
by subject: Marian definitions, peace, celibacy, etc. Unfortunately this material has not
yet been studied.

in Geneva and to the subsequent participation of the Eastern Orthodox Churches, did not extend to Catholicism. As Visser't Hooft noted, "during those years we had no official links with the Vatican."[59] There was nothing to make anyone think that Christian ecumenism was on the eve of a turning point. An authoritative journal had written, at the beginning of 1959, that "the desired remedy for doing away with the schism [between Latins and Orientals], namely, an ecumenical Council, seems doubtless a sheer fantasy for the time being."[60] In point of fact, John XXIII's announcement unexpectedly accelerated things and represented from the very outset a turning point in the journey toward Christian unity.

Toward the end of March, the representative of Constantinople to the World Council of Churches, Metropolitan Iakovos (Koukouzis) of Malta,[61] came to Rome, accompanied by theologian N. Nissiotis, and was received by Pope John as the special representative of the Ecumenical Patriarch Athenagoras.[62] The meeting was a result of the reference the pope had made in his Christmas message to long-standing Constantinopolitan plans for a Council. The ecumenical importance of his action did not go unnoticed, and Patriarch Athenagoras had quickly responded

---

[59] *Memoirs*, 326.

[60] G. Dejaifve in *NRT* 81 (1959) 86, cited in an editorial in *Irénikon* 32 (1959) 4; the editor remarks that the pope's announcement had stirred "extraordinary interest." Each issue of this quarterly journal contained a careful survey of the echos of the announcement in ecumenical circles (pp. 58-61, 80-90, 93-98, 221-27, 489-92); the Fall issue published an authoritative summary of ecumenical reactions: O. Rousseau, "Le prochain concile et l'Unité de l'Église" (309-33). *Una Sancta. Rundbriefe für interkonfessionelle Begegnung* (August 1959) likewise contained commentaries on the announcement by Orthodox theologian G. Florovsky and Catholic theologian J. Chrysostomus. *Vers l'Unité Chrétienne*, bulletin of the Istina Center, published a special issue entitled *Le prochain Concile et l'Unité chrétienne* (February, 1959) and containing a lengthy commentary by Fr. C. J. Dumont, who observed that people should not speak of a "council of union," that is, a council in which all the Christian Churches were included, but rather of a "council of unity," that is, a council whose purpose was to prepare for unity. The attainment of this goal should be facilitated, said Dumont, by the creation of a Catholic body for ecumenical contacts. During this same year (1959), as a result of the announcement of the council, this bulletin from Paris became a more permanent entity, while continuing to devote a great deal of space to the ecumenical significance of the prospective council; to this end it sought the collaboration of non-Roman theologians (G. Florovsky, Bishop Cassien, J. Meyendorff, A. Schmemann, N. Arsenieff, H. Alivisatos).

[61] G. Poulos, *A Breath of God. Portrait of a Prelate. A Biography of Archbishop Iakovos* (Brookline, MA, 1974) 30 ("an historic meeting"), 105. News of the audience was published in *La Croix* for April 17; see *Irénikon* 32 (1959) 218, and *Il Regno* 4 (1959/5) 28; the audience lists from the papal antechamber make no mention of the visit.

[62] Strachwitz, the German ambassador, made a brief mention of the meeting; his information was derived from a meeting of his own with the Metropolitan; see A. Melloni, "Governi e diplomazie," in *Veille*, 238-39.

in a message of his own on January 1, 1959.[63] The prospect of a Council
awakened a very lively interest in the other Orthodox Churches as well.

In April, the Papal Delegate in Turkey, Mons. Giacomo Testa, the
pope's right-hand man, paid a return visit to the patriarchate of Constantinople.[64] Metropolitan Iakovos again made Athenagoras' openness
known at the end of April, this time in the United States, where he took
part in a meeting of Christian Churches.[65] While one Greek newspaper
quickly insisted that "we are now faced with a new situation," an influential Greek theologian, H. Alivisatos, voiced reservations. In their turn,
the Coptic Church and the Patriarchate of Antioch expressed great interest in John's enterprise. It was natural to attribute to Pope John a special
sensitivity to the "Orthodox" world, since he had had direct experience
of it in the Balkans and since Roman Catholics had traditionally felt
closer to it than to other Churches. In fact, these same assumptions
would on more than one occasion trigger worries in Protestant circles
about being relegated to a secondary place. There was a first sign of this
in August when on the occasion of the meeting of the central committee
of the World Council of Churches in Rhodes Roman and Orthodox
theologians agreed on a study session to be held in Venice; this immediately set off serious Protestant reactions and the plan was cancelled.[66]

On the other hand the earliest responses to John's allocution came
from the headquarters of the World Council of Churches in Geneva, at
the instigation of W. A. Visser't Hooft, the Dutch Reformed pastor who
was General Secretary of the Council.[67] As early as January 27 Visser't
Hooft was expressing a "very special interest" in John XXIII's reference to Christian unity; two weeks later, the executive committee of the
World Council approved his statement as representing it.[68] In fact, not

[63] Irénikon 32 (1959) 91-93; Caprile, I/1, 71-72; Études 92 (1959) 251.

[64] On March 9 Mons. Testa had been given an audience by John XXIII: OR 1959,
no. 57; see Caprile, I/1, 68-81. La Croix for April 22 carried the news of the audience
with Athenagoras.

[65] New York Times, April 23, 1959. On April 21 the Times carried the news that the
Patriarchate of Moscow had denied reports that it had been in contact with the nuncio in
Vienna with a view to participation in the council.

[66] See HK for October, 1959, and the notes of Visser't Hooft in his Memoirs, 327-28.

[67] See the chapter on the Catholic Church in his Memoirs. See also Ph. Chenaux,
"Le Conseil oecuménique des Églises et la convocation du Concile," in Veille, 200-13.
Caprile I/1, 86-103, reprints two articles which Cardinal Bea wrote for La Civiltà Cat-
tolica in 1961 on Protestant reactions to the announcement of the council. Well-informed
reports on reactions in noncatholic circles and the noncatholic press appeared also in
HK 13 (1959) 354-59, 401-5, 436-38, 534-36.

[68] Time for February 23, 1959, published an article entitled "Reply to the Pope" with
interesting data on the complex development of the committee's statement.

only were the people in Geneva alert to the new accents coming from Rome; they were also concerned lest the Roman Church monopolize a new period in ecumenism.

In any case, the World Council undertook to activate channels of information about the projected Council, information not easily obtainable given the uncertainty that prevailed in Rome.[69] Members of the Council were asking what "ecumenical" meant in the designation "ecumenical Council": Did it imply a direct participation of the other Christian Churches or simply an invitation to a common search for unity?[70] In a report of March 23, Visser't Hooft expressed his conviction that the Council would not be a reunion Council, such as Florence had been; this timely conclusion should not, however, dissuade the World Council from paying very close attention to John's enterprise, and in fact he, Visser't Hooft, proposed the establishment in Rome of a "specialized and permanent agency" of the Council that could monitor the ecumenical situation at first hand. On that same occasion, he suggested immediately raising the problem of the recognition of religious freedom as a preliminary step.

On February 22-23 a first meeting was held in Geneva between the Secretary General and his Catholic fellow-countryman, Willebrands, who was organizer and secretary of the Catholic Conference for Ecumenical Affairs. In March H. H. Harms journeyed to Rome looking for information on behalf of the World Council; the result seems to have been completely negative, in part perhaps because Harms had gotten in touch with an unsuitable contact, Cardinal Tisserant, instead of with Bea, who had quickly become the pope's trusted collaborator for ecumenical matters.[71]

At the beginning of the summer the Anglicans took the step of sending a churchman, I. Rea, to John XXIII with a letter from the archbishop of Canterbury; this was a prelude to a visit of the archbishop himself to Rome.

But the interest roused by the announcement from Rome also found expression in uncertainties and reservations based on mistrust of the Catholic Church and its dogmatic and institutional positions. Those who felt thus thought it absolutely necessary to avoid any facile irenicism.

---

[69] As early as March, the office of the nuncio in Bern assigned Bishop E. Chavaz to keep the World Council informed about preparations for the council: Chenaux, "Le Conseil," 202.

[70] Visser't Hooft noted that "in the course of conversations some Catholic friends did not tell us what the council would be doing but rather asked us if we had any idea of what it would do" (*Memoirs*, 327).

[71] See Melloni, "Governi e diplomazie," in *Veille*, 239.

Some months after the initial announcement of the Council, it became clear that while the pope's desire to give the Council a strong ecumenical thrust inspired great interest and expectation in public opinion, it was meeting with notable obstacles in Rome but also in the more influential noncatholic centers.[72] Although the age-old distrust of Rome had been to some extent overcome by John's initiative, it had its lasting effects and was shown in reluctance of a not insignificant kind. Consequently, interested non-Roman Christians tended to cut the event down to size. In the West they took the attitude that a Council might be possible but that they would only gradually commit themselves; meanwhile they would focus on fostering close contacts and on the question of religious freedom. In the East, disappointment was more obvious, as would be seen when the invitation came to send "observers." As early as May 1, Patriarch Athenagoras, perhaps in order to avoid apprehensions about excessive compliance with Rome on his part, published a note that excluded any willingness to accept a separate invitation to the Council.

3. *Diplomatic Intelligence and Comments in the Press.*

An interesting confirmation of the effect of the allocution of January 25 is provided by the reports sent from Rome by diplomatic representatives accredited with the Holy See or the Republic of Italy.[73] During the days immediately following the address some more or less ignored the announcement and concentrated on the uncertain fate of the Italian government. Thus only on January 31 did the American ambassador refer to the Council; he expanded on the theme of Christian unity but also on the Chinese situation (he was echoing the reference the pope had made to this in the public homily in St. Paul's that preceded his allocution to the cardinals). The French ambassador was quicker to report the announcement; when he returned to the subject a few days later, he thought he should emphasize an interesting attitude on the part of the Roman Curia, which wanted a better division of responsibilities after the intense concentration of power during Pacelli's reign. R. de Margerie was the first to try to forecast the time needed for carrying out Roncalli's plan, and he reported that the Council could not begin until 1962.

The work of the embassy of the Federal Republic of Germany was facilitated by the presence, as ecclesiastical adviser, of a bishop,

---

[72] Bea took timely note of this (Schmidt, *Augustin Bea*, 296), as did Jedin, *Lebensbericht*, 199.

[73] See Melloni, "Governi," especially 224-40.

J. Höfer, who was involved in the ecumenical movement and therefore in a position to give an insider's judgment and have access to expert information. As a result, the ambassador was able, on January 29, to send Bonn a well structured report from Höfer that emphasized ecumenical prospects, these obviously being of special interest to a country like Germany with its mingling of confessions. The next day, a new report was sent, this one on a problem that was beginning to be discussed in Rome: the relation between the new Council and those that had preceded it.

The question was raised in several quarters of the concrete ways in which the Council might be given its desired ecumenical character. More than one person thought that the Christian confessions which had retained the episcopate might be able to send at least some observers; the participation of the confessions that had sprung from the Reformation would be more problematic. When questioned by an official of the consul general's office in Geneva (on March 10), Visser't Hooft, for his part, supposedly stressed the point that the ecumenical dimension of the Council would be determined strictly by the pope.

The problems raised by this central aspect were explicitly posed to Secretary of State Tardini by French ambassador de Margerie on February 26, in the context of a request for information which the patriarchate in Istanbul had sent to the French ambassador in Turkey. Tardini simply clarified that the Council would be "a Catholic Council, held among Catholics"; observers from the other Christian confessions would be admitted only to the public sessions.[74] There was a general conviction that there should be no repetition of the mistake made by the reunion Councils of 1274 (Lyons) and 1438 (Florence), nor of the mistake made just before the first Vatican Council, when the "separated" Churches had been publicly invited to "return" to Rome.

Toward the end of spring the diplomats, like the noncatholics, lost interest to some extent. Once competence in preparation for the Council was assigned to the Secretariat of State, the undertaking was normalized from their point of view.

It is surprising how, despite the increasing secularization (at least in the West) that rendered dubious the very idea of a "Council," John XXIII's announcement triggered a burst of attention, interest, and, above all, expectation in the public mind. This was not the result of any action of leadership groups; we have in fact seen how these were cautious and

74 Ibid., 234-35.

in some cases suspicious, having been caught by surprise.[75] The people, on the other hand, whether believers or nonbelievers, Catholics or noncatholics, saw in the elderly pope's undertaking an act of great significance; they read it as a sign of hope and of confidence in the future and in renewal. They saw in it a determination, perhaps naive but nonetheless authentic, to be involved. Almost without intermediaries, John's initiative came to the attention of millions of women and men and convinced them of its importance. Just as centuries before, in completely different cultural contexts, so now the prospect of a "Council" stirred expectation, generated trust, and won consent. The resigned and stagnant atmosphere of the fifties, when the mutual hostility of the great power blocs seemed destined to last indefinitely and paralyze any vitality in societies and in the churches, was swept away and revealed to be insubstantial.

From the very earliest days, the *New York Times* analyzed the responses to the announcement of a Council, but initially it adopted the perspective that was dominant in the West and had prevailed in the preceding pontificate, namely, resistance to communism. Even the possibility of a rapprochement with the eastern Orthodox Churches was interpreted against the background of a strategy for undoing the Soviet bloc. But as the weeks passed, the *Times* gradually added nuances to this interpretive key until finally it abandoned it completely and emphasized exclusively the ecumenical implications of the coming Council. The continual stream of articles and reports was an interesting sign of the response which the announcement was receiving in the United States of America. The *Times* of London, on the other hand, was much more sparing of articles, although it too emphasized the ecumenical aspect.

The *New York Times* for February 20 also reported a plea of Rabbi M. N. Eisendrath that the Council be expanded to include all the religions that were committed to the advancement of brotherhood. The Israeli press, on the other hand, does not seem to have paid any heed to the announcement from Rome, at least until the audience granted to J. Isaac.

The approval by public opinion, which was unexpected both in its rapidity and in its extent, raised its own problems. In fact, if it provided John XXIII with a very significant confirmation and created difficulties for those who wanted to rein in his initiative, it also made it quite clear how important it was to make some decisions on the nature and purposes

---

[75] This judgment is confirmed for Italy by the studies of R. Sani, "Gli intellettuali italiani e Giovanni XXIII," *Humanitas* 43 (1988) 204 and 212, and, more recently, of Marazziti, *I papa di carta*, 150-51 and 183.

of the Council. Would it be a Council that would resume and bring to a conclusion the Council that had been interrupted in 1870? The length of time that had passed since then and the changes that had taken place in the meanwhile made this very unlikely. On the other hand, it did not seem that any problems were surfacing (heresies, schisms) such as had quite often occasioned earlier Councils and that would call for a conciliar gathering. Nor did the widespread expectation revealed in responses to the January 25 announcement refer to any such problems.

III. DETERMINING THE CHARACTER OF THE COUNCIL

The official communiqué on the papal allocution, issued that same day, January 25, 1959, said that "as far as the celebration of an ecumenical Council is concerned, this not only has for its purpose, in the thinking of the Holy Father, the upbuilding of the Christian people; it is also meant to be an invitation to the separated communities to join in the search for the unity for which so many yearn all around the world."[76]

In the first unofficial commentary on the announcement, *L'Osservatore Romano* wrote that the Council would not be a "Council of fear but a Council of unity."[77] This did not say much, but it did advert to the change of climate: as the Church set out for the Council, it no longer felt fearful and under siege, but was breathing a new air and was free to face the supreme problem of unity.

However, not only the communiqué but even the complete text of the allocution of January 25 failed to answer the host of questions which the announcement had raised. People instinctively took as their point of reference the Councils of past centuries, although the difference in historical situation struck one immediately, nor were there any of the traditional reasons for which the great Councils had been held: doctrinal errors or disciplinary divisions. The most recent point of reference was the Vatican Council of 1869-70, especially since that had remained unfinished; on several occasions the question had been raised of the opportuneness of reconvening that Council and completing its program. Particularly in circles interested in renewal there was an especially

---

[76] *OR*, January 26-27, 1959.
[77] "Il triplice annuncio," *OR*, February 1, 1959; the article is signed "T."

earnest call for steps that would restore balance to the hard and fast conception of the Church that had become prevalent.[78] Was this what the pope had in mind?

The available sources for constructing a description of the coming Council were very sparse and left ample room for the most disparate hypotheses and fantasies. In the allocution of January 25 the pope had shown that he regarded a Council as opportune because the Church was entering upon a historical conjuncture of exceptional complexity, in which it would be necessary to distinguish among "the signs of the times" and "to see...in the midst of so much darkness, a few indications which auger well," as the Apostolic Constitution convoking the Council would later say. The exhortation *Sacrae laudes* would later emphasize the same line of thought; according to this document the Church is "crossing the line into a new age."[79]

Among the reasons for his decision the pope would also emphasize his positive assessment of the conciliar tradition: "a form which the history of the Church teaches us and which has always achieved fertile results." He had in mind in particular the Council of Trent and the benefits it brought to Catholicism; this was a view widespread among the clergy. But even in these first months Trent was not John XXIII's "model." He himself would take the occasion to explain the limitations of the analogy: "The historical circumstances are different from those of four hundred years ago when Trent was held, but the moment is no less serious for the Church and for the salvation of the world."[80]

John XXIII did not give birth to a fully formed Council, like Minerva born from the brain of Jupiter. The purposes and nature of the Council were only gradually sketched out, brought into focus, and fully understood in their substance and implications as a result of the pope's personal reflection and also in light of the responses and criticisms which the announcement of the convocation elicited in the Church and among Christians, as well as in light of the developing world situation and the start of preparations for the event.

During the two months after the announcement, it was only with difficulty that discussion of the coming Council got under way. No one

---

[78] This call found perhaps its fullest and most well considered expression in the volume entitled *L'épiscopat et l'Église universelle*, ed. Y. Congar and B.-D. Dupuy (Paris, 1962), in which were assembled authoritative studies that agreed on the urgent need of restoring the episcopate to its true place.

[79] *DMC* 4, 868 and 882.

[80] *DMC* 2, 653; *OR*, December 22, 1962; *DMC* 5, 13. In the allocution of January 25 no reference was made to particular councils, not even to Trent.

seemed to know what to say about it. Did they not dare to express viewpoints that might prove displeasing to the pope? Did they still hope that
the announcement might fall on deaf ears? Were they really bewildered
by an unexpected prospect? Those who had thought themselves immo-
bilized by an ecclesial and theological fixism now found themselves
alive and free, but they had a hard time exercising this freedom once
again.

But something was moving. Immediately after the announcement,
Dominican Y. Congar wrote an authoritative commentary on it. After a
learned disquisition on the tradition of ecumenical and general Councils,
the French theologian (who did not sign the article, because of censures
imposed under the preceding pontificate) devoted some pages to the
coming Council.[81] He was confident that it would be a new Council and
not the continuation of Vatican I; he then went on to suggest five
thematic areas for the work of the assembly. First and foremost,
the assembly would combat doctrinal errors; it would then reassert
the spiritual vocation of the human person as against the attractions of
material goods and would confirm the unity of the Church in the face of
threats of fragmentation like the one in China. Finally, pastoral activity
would be promoted, and the teaching on the Church, left incomplete by
the discontinuation of the Council of Pius IX, would be completed.

Only after offering this list, which was obviously controlled by the
ecclesiastical climate of the fifties, did Congar express his desire that the
Council also face the problem of peace and of the prohibition of atomic
weapons. He also hoped that pressures from Marian groups for new
mariological proclamations would not be successful. He touched on the
ecumenical problem, recalling the unfortunate and fruitless invitations
issued to the Orthodox and Protestant Churches in 1868 and expressing
the hope that an entity would be established in Rome for contacts with
non-Roman Christians. The concluding lines of the article made clear
the full depth of Congar's anxiety and gave a positive interpretation
to the many expectations roused by the announcement of the Council.
"Are not the events of the day the first snowdrops, as it were, of an
ecumenical springtime? Do they not foretell the coming of the time of
mercy?" Did Congar have an intuition of that season of mercy which
John XXIII was to proclaim on October 11, 1962?

---

[81] "Les conciles dans la vie de l'Église," *Informations catholiques internationales*,
no. 90 (February 15, 1959) 17-26. In his own *Journal* Congar mentions having written
this article.

Later on, Congar observed:

> I saw in the Council an opportunity for the cause not only of unity but also
> of ecclesiology. I saw it as an occasion, one that needed to be exploited as
> completely as possible, for accelerating the recovery of the true meaning of
> "episcopate" and "church" in ecclesiology and for making substantial
> progress in matters ecumenical. I committed myself to the task of stoking
> public opinion so that it would expect and demand much. I did not weary
> of saying wherever I was that perhaps only five percent of what we ask
> for will be passed. All the more reason for increasing our demands. The
> pressure of Christian public opinion must compel the Council to be a real
> Council and accomplish something.[82]

On May 23, during an audience, Maximos IV, Patriarch of the
Melkites, presented John XXIII with a note suggesting the creation
in Rome of "a new congregation or special Roman commission" for
relations with the non-Roman Christian Churches. "Everything having
to do with ecumenism will fall within the competence of this new
institution," congregation, or commission, thereby contributing in an
effective way to reconciliation with the "separated brethren."

In like manner, French Dominican C. Dumont sent two notes, in
March and June of 1959 respectively, to the Congregation for the Oriental Churches (Cardinal Tisserant), suggesting the establishment within
that Congregation and within the Congregation for the Propagation of
the Faith of two sections that would deal respectively with relations with
the Orthodox Christians and with the Protestant Christians.[83] Dumont
wrote: "The prospects which the announcement of the coming Council
has opened up in the area of Christian unity require that relationships
undertaken have increasingly a more than private character." Not only
the Congregation for the Eastern Churches but also the Congregation for
the Propagation of the Faith ought to be involved together. No less
urgent was a change of style. In fact, "the Orthodox Churches are
repeatedly offended by the fact that the Roman Church pretends not to
know them, whether by abstaining from any official contact with them
or by addressing their faithful over the heads of their Churches or by
cultivating relations with the civil authorities of the respective countries
without taking into account the ecclesiological problem posed by the

---

[82] Congar, *Journal*, first page.

[83] An extract from the memorandum is in *Le Lien* 33 (1968) 65. I take my citations of
Dumont's notes from M. Velati, *"Un indirizzo a Roma." La nascita del Segretariato per
l'unità dei cristiani (1959-1960)*, in *Attese*, 92-94; this author was able to consult unpublished documents.

separation." The signals already exchanged between John XXIII and Athenagoras marked the dawn of a turnabout that even a specialist like Dumont found it hard to think possible.

Toward the end of April Pope John formulated the fundamental purpose of the Council: to expand the commitment of Christians, "to enlarge the scope of love...with clarity of thought and magnanimity of heart."[84] Formulas of this kind have frequently been taken simply as expressions suited to an occasion, but this interpretation has obscured the hermeneutical criterion supplied by Roncalli's habitual style, for while he avoided polemics and cutting phrases, he did not on this account refrain from communicating his own points of view and making responsible and pertinent judgments. This must be kept in mind in connection with the statement about the essentially pastoral purposes of the Council,[85] a statement often thought not to have much weight. But for Pope Roncalli it was a way both to distance himself from doctrinal goals (definitions), condemnations, and ideological purposes, which immediately and spontaneously suggested themselves to the minds of many, and to emphasize the urgency of a commitment to a renewal of the Church's spirit and forms of witness and of its evangelical presence in history.

Did the pope mean to place the Council in the same perspective in which he placed his pontificate itself immediately following upon his election: that of the "good shepherd"?

As we saw earlier, in the allocution of January 25 the pope pointed out, with particular enthusiasm, that the Council was meant to be "a renewed invitation to the faithful of the separated Churches to participate with us in this feast of grace and brotherhood." A few days later (January 29), speaking to the parish priests of Rome, he confirmed that, along with its "eminently pastoral" purpose, the Council would also have an ecumenical dimension. According to one of the press agencies, the pope said that "he was not overlooking the difficulties in the way of implementing such a program, because, among other things, it will be very difficult to restore harmony and to reconcile the various Churches

---

[84] Exhortation to the bishops and clergy of the Veneto (the Three Venices), April 21 (23), 1959: *DMC* 1, 903.

[85] Even in the allocution of January 25 the council was said to be motivated by "a concern for the *bonum animarum*." "Pastoral" is a key word that expresses the central aspect of Roncalli's ecclesiology, and in fact he preferred to describe the council he had convoked as a "pastoral council." "Pastoral" and words with the same root occupied a very important place in Roncalli's vocabulary. They run through all his many writings and occur about 2000 times, according to the verbal concordance which A. Melloni has prepared at the Istituto per le scienze religiose in Bologna.

that, in addition to being too long separated, are often troubled by internal dissent." The pope wanted "to tell them to put an end to discord and come together without going through a detailed historical examination to find out who was wrong and who right; it may be that all sides shared the responsibility."[86]

The ecumenical aspect, more than any other, caught the public's attention, but it also raised very lively apprehensions. The very concern of the Vatican bureaucracy to keep hidden the papal statements now being reported is resounding proof of this fear. The official publication, at the end of February, of the allocution in St. Paul's only increased their bewilderment; for, while according to the initial communiqué the Council was also to be "an invitation to the separated communities to the search for unity," the allocution read, rather reductively: "an invitation to the faithful of the separated communities."

On April 1, addressing the Association of Catholic Universities, the pope confirmed that "while the Council will present a magnificent spectacle of the cohesion, unity, and harmony of the Church of God, the city set on a hill, it will also by its nature be an invitation to the separated brethren who glory in the name of Christian, to return to the one flock."[87]

The pope's meaning was further explained when, at the already mentioned meeting at the end of April, he outlined a sequence that was truly and properly ecumenical: "In the East, first a rapprochement, then a reconciliation, and finally a complete reunion of so many separated brethren with the ancient, common mother; and in the West a generous pastoral collaboration between the two clergies."[88] Such an approach may have been surprising to those who did not know Roncalli and the way in which he had absorbed the experiences of several decades in the East and then in Paris as well.

If we may judge by the repeated "omissions" from *L'Osservatore Romano* of reports of the pope's statements on this subject,[89] this aspect

[86] The official summary in the *OR* (= *DMC* 1, 575-78) omitted the passage in which the pope spoke of the council as a council of union; see Caprile I/1, 107, note, and G. F. Svidercoschi, *Storia del Concilio* (Milan, 1967) 39-40.

[87] *DMC* 1, 228.

[88] Exhortation to the bishops and clergy of the Veneto (the Three Venices), April, 1959: *DMC* 1, 903.

[89] A systematic study of this matter has not yet been made; a good many instances have been patiently identified by G. Zagni as part of a research program being carried out in the Istituto per le scienze religiose in Bologna. I may mention here the general audience of August 30, 1959: neither *OR* nor *DMC* report the pope's address, in which he is said to have made important statements that noncatholics would be welcome at the council. See R. Rouquette, *La fin d'une chrétienté. Chroniques* I (Paris, 1968) 33; and T. F. Stransky, "The Foundation of the Secretariat for Promoting Christian Unity," in *Vatican II By Those Who Were There*, ed. A. Stacpole (London, 1986) 62-87.

of the future Council elicited prompt and very determined resistance, even from circles very close to the pope and from men whose position in the institution made them the ones to carry out his decision.

Our reconstruction is hindered, especially for these first weeks, by institutional traits of the Roman pontificate (although these are similar to traits found in any other center of public power). It is therefore difficult, not to say impossible, to reconstruct the pressures informally brought to bear on a man who has the supreme responsibility. There are questions which we are not in a position to answer: What attitudes did John XXIII's collaborators display toward him in the matter of the Council? Was pressure brought to bear on him to re-evaluate his announcement or to water down the ecumenical aspect? What difficulties were raised in order to dissuade the pope from his plans or to slow down their implementation?

That a pope should take the initiative in promoting unity among the Christian Churches and should present this process as a matter of "cooperation" leading to a "single flock"[90] and no longer as simply a "return" — this was so unexpected and almost unlikely that it elicited diverse reactions and required a rethinking of the entire approach to ecumenism. Many asked: "What does John XXIII want?" How was it possible simply to leave behind a lengthy stage of intransigent polemics and accusations? The pope gave his answer to this bewilderment almost daily and on the most diverse occasions. A few days after his announcement of the Council he was able to emphasize his conviction that the Church "is on a journey ...and the task of the one who leads it is not to preserve it as though it were a museum." In this living Church, which is committed "to the journey of life" and is jealous of its variety, the pope is first and foremost the bishop of the Church of Rome.[91] Here were ideas that gave a glimpse of a vision of the Church different from the one that had been predominant in the preceding decades and that was summarized in *Mystici Corporis*.

Swings were also to be seen in John XXIII's references to the Council, the emphasis on each occasion being controlled by different points of view. Thus on April 6 he said he was convinced that the Council "will not immediately do away with all the divisions that exist among Christians";

---

[90] *ADA*, I, 16 and 28.

[91] *ADA*, I, 10; *Lettere*, no. 44; Caprile I/1, 108, note 2; *ADA*, I, 30. On March 15 he said to pilgrims from Venice: "Jesus established not several churches but a single Church...an apostolic and universal Church. Yes, and this Church is the Church of Rome" (*DMC* 1, 193).

twenty days later he said that the Council would have "to deal with the questions that concern mainly the good of the universal Church," and again on May 17 he seemed to insist on the goal of the Council being "internal" to the Roman Church; but on June 15 he expressed the wish that as a result of the Council "the internal structure [of the Catholic Church] would acquire a new vigor and that all the sheep would hear the voice of the shepherd, follow him, and become that one flock for which the heart of Jesus so ardently longs,"[92] thus once again connecting internal renewal with the search for unity.

The main part of the first encyclical letter of the new pontificate, *Ad Petri cathedram* (June 29, 1959), was devoted to a full explanation of the pope's thought on Church unity.[93] This vision of unity had for its points of reference both historical conditions and the eschatological dimension of the Church. It maintained that complete unity would be achieved only at the end of time, but for this reason it placed a higher value than was customary on the degree of unity already attained. Did this mean that the vision of Christian unity was being projected entirely into an uncertain and elusive future? Or did it rather imply that a unity worthy of the name was seen as already a reality, even if in an unsatisfactory degree and amid an insufficient awareness of it? A unity, then, that was sustained by a real communion in faith, a union that was indeed imperfect by comparison with the riches of the mystery of the gospel, but one that was already the gift of the Almighty and the fruit of his work.

At this point Pope John's horizon seems to have expanded still more, to the point of explicitly embracing the entire human race, in terms not only of the missionary impulse but of an increasingly urgent commitment to peace in the world, a commitment that was later intensified by events in Cuba and that would reach its high point in *Pacem in terris*.

With regard to relations with noncatholic Christians, Roncalli's preference for emphasizing what unites rather than what divides was combined in a substantive way with pastoral renewal. After saying in his encyclical of late June that "the main purpose of the Council will be to promote the growth of the Catholic faith and a salutary renewal of the morals of the Christian people and to modernize ecclesiastical discipline in order to meet the needs of our time," the pope added that "this will undoubtedly be a marvelous spectacle of truth, unity, and love that when

---

[92] *ADA*, I, 16; *DMC* 1, 288; *DMC* 1, 335; *DMC* 1, 371.
[93] *ADA*, I, 33-39.

seen by those separated from this Apostolic See will be for them a gentle invitation to seek and enter into that unity for which Jesus Christ prayed so ardently to his heavenly Father."[94]

But many problems remained unsolved. According to Bea, who would play a decisive role in the Council's ecumenical activity, "the question of unity is a centuries-old problem that cannot be solved all at once. It is not possible, humanly speaking, to expect that the Council will suddenly bring about unity, apart from a great miracle of the Holy Spirit." He even added that in his view "minds are not yet prepared for effective unity." For this reason, the Jesuit exegete preferred to stress the point that the Council would be "an internal affair of the Church" and would have to concentrate on ecclesiological problems and those concerning relations between Church and state.[95]

What kind of Council, then, did Pope John intend to have? Or could this question not be realistically asked, due to the vagueness of the aims of a pope whose alleged naivete caused him to waver between an impossible Council of unity, such as Florence had been, and a reform Council like Trent, the effectiveness and authoritativeness of which he had learned and experienced throughout his entire formation as a churchman? Or, again, was the pope's intention specific and fully worked out, even though its object eluded classification according to preexisting models and therefore created ticklish problems? Did John XXIII intend to limn, within the traditional genre of "Council," a new species suited to enabling the Church to respond to new demands in the sphere of evangelization?

Pope John did not hesitate to describe the coming Council in a manner completely traditional. It was to be, then, a Council of bishops, but with a unique participation of representatives of the noncatholic Churches[96]; it was to be free and responsible, that is, a genuinely deliberative body. Therefore the pope was always careful to distinguish between Council and Curia. But these were not the salient characteristics of the Council which he had described as a "harking back to certain ancient ways,"[97] that is, as a creative synthesis of the main Christian tradition and the

[94] *Ad Petri cathedram, ADA*, I, 34.

[95] Schmidt, *Augustin Bea*, 293-96.

[96] See G. Alberigo, *Ecclesiologia in divenire. A proposito di 'concilio pastorale' e di Osservatori a-cattolici al Vaticano II* (Bologna, 1990; 39 pp.) [= "Ekklesiologie im Werden, Bemerkungen zum 'Pastoralkonzil' und zu den Beobachtern des II. Vatikanums," *Ökumenische Rundschau* 40 (1991) 109-28]; and M. Velati "La proposta ecumenica," in *Verso il Concilio*, 273-343.

[97] *DMC* 1, 132.

demands of renewal, this being the classic attitude that has underlain all authentic movements of "re-form" or renewal of the *"forma Christi."*[98]

Here we have the reason why Roncalli leaned toward a Council that would not be a Council of all Christendom, like Lateran IV, which was justly renowned for having shaped the later medieval West, but that would also not a be a Council of union, like Florence, whose failed ambitions are even today a stumbling-block on the road to unity. Still less did John XXIII draw his inspiration from an embattled Council like Trent, nor from a Council of resistance and opposition to modern society, like Vatican I.

Pope John wanted a Council that would mark a transition between two eras, that is, that would bring the Church out of the post-tridentine period and, to a degree, out of the centuries-long Constantinian era, into a new phase of witness and proclamation, and would also recover substantial and abiding elements of the tradition considered able to nourish and ensure fidelity to the gospel during so difficult a transition. Seen in this perspective, the Council was taking on a very special importance, and this simply as an "event," even before being considered as a setting for the development and working out of norms.

This is the Council that was illumined by the "flash of heavenly light," of which Pope John spoke several times, and that, as the feast drew near, he began to describe as a "new Pentecost."[99] The image of the new Pentecost was henceforth habitually associated with the ecumenical Council, until it was sanctioned by the pope's prayer for the Council, in which he asked the Holy Spirit to "renew Thy wonders in this our day, as by a new Pentecost."[100]

Roncalli was well aware of the theological and historical significance of Pentecost, and to speak of it as being repeated was a carefully chosen and unequivocal way of underscoring, in typically Christian language, the exceptional character of the present historical juncture, the extraordinary prospects which it opened up, and the obligation of the Church to face it through a radical renewal, so that the Church would then be able to present the gospel message to the world and explain it to human beings with the same power and immediacy that

[98] See G. Alberigo, "'Réforme' en tant que critère de l'Histoire de l'Église," *RHE* 76 (1981) 72-81; idem, "Dalla riforma all'aggiornamento," in *"Con tute le tue forze." I nodi della fede cristiana oggi. Omaggio a G. Dossetti*, ed. A. and G. Alberigo (Genoa, 1993) 169-94.

[99] To the clergy of the Veneto (the Three Venices) on April 21 and then in the homily for Pentecost: *ADA*, I, 19 and 24.

[100] *DMC* 4, 875; trans. in Abbott, *Documents*, 793.

marked the first Pentecost. The reminder of Pentecost also placed in the foreground the action of the Spirit and not that of the pope or the Church, just as had been the case with the apostles and disciples who had been the objects of the Spirit's mighty and indeed overwhelming action. It was in this setting that the aim and expectation of John XXIII for the Council revealed their true scope in relation to the Church's internal life, its unity, and its place in the world of human beings.

It is from this point of view that we must interpret the tenacity and insistence with which the pope took every occasion, from January 25, 1959, on, to reassert the importance of the Council and to speak of its pastoral character. In the background was the worry about being misunderstood and the consequent risk of summoning a Council that, instead of helping the Church enter upon a new historical age, would set further obstacles and hindrances in the way, thus aggravating the suffocation from which contemporary Christianity was suffering. The entire relationship between pope and Council would be determined by, on the one side, John's deep-seated and unshakable conviction of the need for a leap forward and, on the other, the deafness or at least the initial myopia of a great many bishops, even the open-minded and enlightened among them, who were convinced that a Council could indeed overcome the lag of the Church behind the modern age, but who were distracted and almost uninterested when it came to broader perspectives. The opinions sent to Rome in connection with the antepreparatory consultation (1959-60) would bear ample witness to this attitude. To it was added the Curia's institutional antipathy to a Council, an antipathy which the Curia seemed disposed to overcome only if it meant preparing for a Council that would be an appendix to Vatican I and an occasion for a solemn approbation of Pacelli's omnipresent teaching.

> The hopes raised by the announcement of the Council were gradually covered over with a thin layer of ash. There was a lengthy silence, a kind of blackout, that was hardly broken by one or other reassuring statement from the pope. But even these statements were rather vague, and it seemed that the pope had drawn back from his original announcement. This was noted in several quarters, even though the pope himself said publicly that he had not changed.... The impression was abroad — confirmed by people coming from Rome and reporting the latest gossip from the wretched Curia — that in Rome a whole team was busy sabotaging the pope's plan. They also said that the pope was fully aware of this.

These notes of Father Congar, written later, at the beginning of his *Journal du Concile*,[101] but referring to the middle of 1959, express nicely his perception and appraisal of the Roman situation during those months. Perhaps they expressed not only the pessimism of the Dominican theologian, but also the first symptoms of "institutional isolation" that would characterize the entire pontificate of John.[102]

IV. ESTABLISHMENT OF THE ANTEPREPARATORY COMMISSION[103]

For almost four months (January 26 to May 17) of 1959 no institutional decision was made in connection with the Council. Nor did John XXIII's allocution in St. Paul Outside the Walls contain any such reference. It was not possible, however, that there should be no follow up on the announcement, especially after it had attracted so much attention.[104] Nor would the pope's advanced age allow lengthy periods of inaction without endangering the very possibility of the Council. And yet the decision, made public on Pentecost, May 17, 1959, that established an "Antepreparatory Commission," was unexpected. Councils had almost always been preceded by discussions; in particular, the medieval Councils in the West had been preceded by preparatory labors in the true and proper sense. Normally it has been the pope, the head and undisputed protagonist in a Council, who has taken the initiative in various kinds of preparation, including rather full consultations, as in the case of the "inquiries" carried out in 1213 in preparation for the Fourth Lateran Council and, later on, by Gregory X in 1273, on the eve of the Second Council of Lyons. The complicated and troubled course of the Council of Trent had deposited in the historical memory of the Roman Church the conviction that the difficulties that had accompanied that Council at every point were due in large measure to insufficient preparation.

[101] While declaring himself "disappointed," Congar did not cease keeping carefully abreast of developments in the Roman climate, and he had this further note: "Beginning at Easter, 1959" he was confirmed in his "impression that in Rome the Curia, the old guard of the Curia, had become aware of a danger and was endeavoring to exorcize it by trying to play the game of the new pontificate" (pp. 2 and 3).

[102] This hermeneutical hypothesis for explaining John's pontificate was formulated by G. Lercaro in a conference on February 23, 1965, now reprinted in *Per la forza dello Spirito. Discorsi conciliari* (Bologna, 1984) 287-310.

[103] I am making use here of my essay "Passaggi cruciali della fase antepreparatoria (1959-1960)," in *Verso il Concilio*, 15-42.

[104] For example, like many other newspapers, *La Croix* of Paris asked as early as January 27 how many council fathers there would be. On February 6 and again on February 26 it hypothesized that the council would require two years of preparation.

The idea that the problems and difficulties that surfaced at Trent were due to inadequate preparation was rather a myth; in fact, Trent had gone through a very long incubation period in which doctrinal and disciplinary problems had been discussed and dissected from every point of view. The almost twenty years that the Council took for completion were due both to the hesitations of the popes and to complicated political ups and downs, while the setbacks which the Roman See suffered were due above all to resistance to the idea that the Council should address not only doctrinal controversies but also the matter of ecclesiastical decadence.

When, three centuries later, Pius IX decided to hold a new Council, he immediately thought of holding it in Rome and of a preparation that would be institutionally defined and directed by a limited group of cardinals. Pius IX's plan came to a standstill after consultation with a limited number of prelates in 1865. The next year five preparatory commissions were established which began their work in 1868, still before the bull of convocation. In 1867 bishops who had come to Rome for canonizations answered a series of questions about the future Council.[105] Finally, the nuncios were asked to suggest the names of consultors for the Council. The preparatory commissions worked up a good sixty drafts of decrees.[106]

In 1948, when Pius XII considered the possibility of calling a Council, he decided that preparation for it should be entrusted to the supreme Congregation of the Holy Office in view of the authority it possessed and in view also of the fact that from it had come the proposal of a Council.[107]

Cardinal Tardini's collaborators developed possible scripts and outlined scenarios in view of developments since the January announcement.[108] The first draft of an antepreparatory commission goes back to February 6, 1959; it was composed on the model of what had been done in preparation for Vatican Council I. It supposed a small commission of cardinals, aided by a secretariat that would be made up of specialists in

[105] Mansi 49, 242-44.

[106] Aubert, *Vatican*, 40, 54-56. There were significant analogies with the preparation for Vatican II; see Martina, *Pio IX*, 136-66.

[107] G. Caprile, "Pio XII e un nuovo progetto di concilio ecumenico," *CC* 177 (1966/3) 210-27, and F. C. Uginet, "Les projets de concile général sous Pie XI et Pie XII," in *Deuxième*, 65-78.

[108] In the Archive of the Council there are some boxes containing documents that preceded the antepreparatory commission and came from the Secretariat of State and the Congregation for Extraordinary Ecclesiastical Affairs. These would all have been sent to the pope for his information. On this phase in general see V. Carbone, "Il cardinale Domenico Tardini e la preparazione del concilio Vaticano II," *RSCI* 45 (1991) 42-88.

doctrine, law, discipline, and the separated Churches. This group was to
have as its first task to prepare a questionnaire to be sent to the bishops
for their views and then to analyze their responses. A list of "probable
subjects" for the work of the Council foresaw the following: the priestly
apostolate (including a permanent deaconate of married men), the
lay apostolate, the family, the teaching on the Church, Church-state
relations, the adapting of the organization of the Church to meet the
needs of the day, the missions, relations between bishops and religious,
and social teaching.[109] While there is a symmetry here between the topics and the areas of competence of the various congregations, we note
the absence of subjects that would in fact become central in the work of
the Council, for example, liturgical renewal and the ecclesial importance
of the Bible. Completely missing was any synthetic overview of the
Council's activity.

The papal action on Pentecost, which was quite sober and restrained,
determined the membership on the commission and defined its tasks.[110]
The members, mostly Italian, were: G. Ferretto, P. Sigismondi, A. Samoré,
A. Coussa, C. Zerba, P. Palazzini, A. Larraona, D. Staffa, E. Dante, and
P. Philippe; the first three were bishops, the others not.

The makeup of the commission was evidently dictated by a criterion
that ensured representation of all the congregations composing the
Roman Curia. The secretary of each congregation, or his equivalent in
the hierarchy, was a member of the commission; the presidency went to
Cardinal D. Tardini, who was in charge of the Congregation for Extraordinary Ecclesiastical Affairs as well as Secretary of State; an obscure
auditor of the Rota, P. Felici, was called upon to be secretary.[111] Not
even the analogous commission appointed by Pius XII had been so
monopolized by the Curia.

The task of the commission was to gather material for beginning
the "proximate preparation" for the work of the Council. Mention was
therefore made of collecting the advice and suggestions of the Catholic
episcopate as well as the suggestions of the Roman congregations. The
commission also had the task of sketching the broad lines of the subjects
to be discussed at the Council, in keeping also with the views of the faculties of theology and canon law, and, finally, of formulating proposals

109 Carbone, "Tardini e la preparazione," 49.
110 *ADA*, I, 22-23.
111 Tardini summoned him on May 13, and on May 17 the first meeting with John
XXIII took place; see V. Carbone, "[P. Felici] Segretario generale del concilio ecumenico Vaticano II," in *Il cardinale Pericle Felici* (Rome, 1992) 159-94.

for the membership of the various groups to be put in charge of proximate preparation of the Council itself.

We have no information about the preparation of this papal document nor about the options that governed it. Two points leap to the eye, however: the decision to have the preparation preceded by a preliminary phase (for which a new term was coined) and, above all, the assignment of this phase to the Congregation for Extraordinary Ecclesiastical Affairs. From a technical viewpoint, the reason for this choice was the greater suitabilty of this part of the bureaucracy when it came to sending the request for opinions to all the bishops. The reason for having an "antepreparatory" phase was to minimize surprise and opposition to the pope's decision; at the same time, it was intended to create a flexible structure that could take the steps necessary for a full and unconditional consultation of the universal Church. Given the surprise caused by the announcement of the Council, it was an act of prudent responsibility to introduce a period of transition, and yet the pope's action provoked spirited reservations.[112]

The reason for putting an exclusively "Roman" body[113] in charge of this phase, without however placing the Council in the hands of the Curia, was to involve the Curia from the very outset and keep it from adopting a hostile position. At the same time, John XXIII assigned the direction of this phase to the Congregation for Extraordinary Ecclesiastical Affairs and not to the powerful Holy Office.[114] At the beginning of March, 1959, Msgr. Samoré had suggested a commission of nine members, chosen from among the assessors and secretaries of the Roman congregations, with Cardinal A. Ottaviani as its president. Cardinal Ciriaci then supposedly suggested to John XXIII that he entrust the presidency to Tardini and not to Ottaviani.

When the pope decided not to follow the road taken by Pius XII only ten years earlier, did he want to prevent the "supreme congregation" from monopolizing the Council? The choice was pregnant with consequences, and it showed the pope's desire that preparation for the Council be made in a different atmosphere and style from those of the Holy

---

[112] See A. Riccardi, *Il potere del papa* (Rome-Bari, 1988) 179.

[113] The non-Italians (though they had an established place in the Roman Curia) were quickly reduced to two, because when Father Larraona was made a cardinal on December 14, 1959, he was replaced by Philippe, and when the latter was made Commissary of the Holy Office, he was in turn replaced by P. Parente, an Italian.

[114] Carbone, "Tardini e la preparazione," 50. According to the testimony of Cardinal Confalonieri it was Cardinal Canali who raised doubts about the assignment of the preparation to the Holy Office; see C. Confalonieri, *Momenti romani* (Rome, 1979) 86.

Office, which was traditionally doctrinaire and intransigeant. In response to this blow the Holy Office tried to exercise leadership in the ensuing preparation through its control of the theological commission. Did the importance given to Cardinal Tardini also represent the pope's decision to give greater weight to the secretary of state?

When the pope created a special commission and specifically named the prelates to serve on it (instead of simply appointing the man occupying a certain office within each congregation), he was indeed acting "timidly," inasmuch as he refrained, for example, from putting a commission from outside the Curia in charge of the preparation for the Council. Did his action, however, at least indicate his intention to distinguish between the organs of ordinary government and the preparation for the Council?[115] And yet on June 30, when Tardini opened the meeting of the commission, with the pope presiding, he took the occasion to offset that interpretation by thanking John XXIII "for being willing to entrust the important task of concrete preparation for the Council to representatives of the sacred congregations of the Roman Curia."

The pope's decision, then, gave some definition to the Council he had announced four months earlier and confirmed his intention of following through on it. But while his action was a signal meant to remove uncertainties and fears, it also aroused deep-felt concerns. The Roman and Curial make-up of the commission set off lively reactions, especially outside of Italy. Was the Council to be put in the hands, then, of a narrow group of high bureaucrats, most of whom were not even bishops? People asked whether the Council had not already been monopolized by very small circles of men who were steeped in the intransigent spirit that had characterized the last years of the pontificate of Pius XII. There seemed to be a sharp contrast with John XXIII's repeatedly expressed intention to have the broadest possible involvement in the Council. There was now a risk of disaffection even before preparation began!

In entrusting the presidency of the antepreparatory commission to Cardinal Tardini, the pope performed an act of confidence as well as of delegation, one dictated, like others, by the attempt to win the loyalty of the Curia in regard to the Council. It is hard to believe that Pope John was not aware of the price he would have to pay to achieve this result. He refused to get involved in a dialectical confrontation with the various

---

[115] See the allocutions of May 30 and June 5: *ADA*, I, 92 and 102. For Tardini: *ADA*, I, 12. It is odd that the *Annuario Pontificio* for 1960 (pp. 1011 and 1651) lists the Antepreparatory Commission among the "Permanent Commissions of the Holy See."

antepreparatory actions, if we except the decision to consult the entire episcopate without reliance on a controlling questionnaire.

It was inevitable that if this choice were not to amount to an unconditional delegation (as perhaps not a few representatives of the Curia wanted to believe), John XXIII would be forced to find other occasions and other settings for airing his own ideas on the direction the Council was to take and especially for increasing the awareness of Catholic public opinion and especially the awareness of the bishops as to the historic occasion which this event could be. This represented an itinerary of preparation parallel to the one over which Tardini was presiding. The two itineraries were inspired by the same purpose of preparing the Council, but they were clearly different and perhaps contradictory in tendency, in their methods and in their conception of the purpose and character of the Council itself. John pursued a gradual and charismatic pedagogy; his nearly exclusive concern was to set out to everyone ideas that were clear and appropriate to the epochal moment, thus showing his trust in the instinct of faith in the body of the Church and in the creative abilities of the assembly of bishops. On the other hand, still prisoners of the Pacellian style of governing, the preparatory structure, acting with the greatest secrecy and in total isolation, amassed an improbable number of texts. It is hard to know if this situation did or did not have a negative impact on the unfolding of the Council.

The tasks of the antepreparatory commission also included the different phases of the work. A first phase was occupied with consultation of the episcopate and the Roman Curia: the principle was established that this consultation was to be universal and not limited,[116] as had been the case first under Pius IX and then under Pius XI and Pius XII. A second phase was to be devoted to drawing up a broad outline of the subjects to be discussed at the Council. This outline, however, would not be made by the antepreparatory commission; in fact, the *quaestiones* for the preparatory commissions were never discussed in the antepreparatory commission. The latter commission would, in this area, exert only an indirect influence through its classification of the suggestions received and through its own suggestions regarding the competencies of the groups involved in the preparation. Finally, in a third and last phase, suggestions were to be made regarding the membership of the preparatory groups.

---

[116] It may also be observed that the formula "the Catholic episcopate of the various countries" would seem to imply an appeal especially to the episcopal conferences that were now active in many nations. It is also of interest that the text does not mention any kind of secrecy. But the request for *vota* was later addressed only to individual bishops.

V. John XXIII Decides on the Name Vatican II

A turning point, and one all the more important in this atmosphere, was marked by John XXIII's communication of the name of the Council to Cardinal Tardini on July 14. Three days later Tardini in turn informed the heads of the ecclesiastical faculties: the Council was to be known as *Vatican II*. We do not know how this decision came to be made,[117] but we are not rash in thinking that this decision, like that of the preceding January, was reached by the pope on his own. With disconcerting simplicity he noted on July 4, 1959, after a visit to the Vatican gardens, "when I got back to the house, I found that the ecumenical Council now in preparation ought to be called 'the Second Vatican Council,' because the last one, celebrated by Pope Pius IX in 1870, bore the name of Vatican Council I — *Vatican le premier*."[118]

It was necessary, in fact, to get rid of the uncertainties that were abroad about the possible reopening of the Council that had been suspended in 1870[119]; the pope thus stepped out of the groove in which Pius XI and Pius XII had remained in their plans for a Council. By naming the future Council "Vatican II," he was putting it beyond doubt that it would be a "new" Council, and even a "new Pentecost," even though he did not reject some continuity with the Council of Pius IX. He thus avoided being encumbered by the necessity of carrying to a conclusion the ecclesiological plan left incomplete in the Constitution *Pastor Aeternus*; the new Council would have a free and open agenda and would be a new page in the many-centuried history of the Councils. At the moment when this decision was announced, its purpose was to leave a quite definite stamp, as it were, on the atmosphere in which the preparation was beginning, by implicitly denying the secondary and sometimes even slavish references being made to Vatican I and to Pacelli's project of 1948-52.

[117] According to P. Felici, in an article in *L'Avvenire d'Italia* for January 28, 1960, a suggestion had been made that the council be called "Ostiense I," in an obvious reference to the fact that the pope's announcement had been made in St. Paul Outside the Walls, the "Ostian" basilica (i.e., on the Via Ostia or road between Ostia and Rome).

[118] Handwritten note on the July 1959 agenda for this day (Fondo Roncalli, ISR, Bologna). In the present state of our knowledge it is impossible to say whether the pope's decision was suggested to him by his reading of some French text, as the concluding words in French might lead us to think. The same holds for the degree to which the pope consciously excluded any continuation of the council that had been broken off a century before.

[119] Even a theologian as thoughtful and as involved in renewal as O. Rousseau was still asking, in *Irénikon* 32 (1959) 332, whether the council was to be a continuation of the Vatican Council of Pius IX. On February 6, the French Catholic daily, *La Croix*, had asked in its turn whether the Council was to be a "Lateran" or a "Vatican" council.

John XXIII's insistence that the Council was to take a "pastoral" approach likewise acquired a more pregnant meaning. Was the pope not saying that the conciliar discussions should follow an inductive method rather than the deductive method dear to Scholasticism but now undermined by epochal changes? Would the Council not have to take as its starting point those "problems of greater importance which the Church has to face at the present time," as Pope John himself had suggested to the bishops in connection with the opinions requested of them a few weeks earlier? By the choice of name the pope was placing the Council within an open horizon; this was to be Pope Roncalli's primary and constant concern during the preparation for the Council and then during its celebration.

This did not mean that he refrained from suggesting particular goals for the conciliar assembly, but he was eager to focus, above all else, on safeguarding the freedom of the Council. If this freedom was no longer threatened, as it had been at critical moments in past conciliar history, by political powers or heretical currents, it was threatened no less seriously and even more subtly by the drag resulting from the "settled" state of Catholicism and the illusion that one could answer the challenge of the ideologies by accepting their style and methods. But the full import of John's decision was not immediately realized; the machinery of antepreparatory consultation had been set in motion, and its operators tended to measure its suitability solely by the criterion, valuable enough in itself, of efficiency.[120]

John's decision implied a further aspect of the coming Council: its venue. The choice of the city that would serve as venue had repeatedly caused troublesome problems in the past; these reached their climax during the incubation period for Trent. At that time the different and often conflicting viewpoints of the pope, the European sovereigns, and the Protestants were pitted against one another. There was an obvious divergence in the interpretations given of the principle that the Council should be celebrated in the country where the problem had arisen which the Council was called upon to resolve. The disagreement was finally settled by a compromise: the choice of Trent, a city that was imperial and Germanic in its politics but Latin in its culture and geography.

John XXIII did not explicitly name the city in which the Council would be held, but the decision that the Council would be called "Vatican II" also implied the choice of Rome. In the complex effort to achieve a balance between novelty and continuity in relation to the Council of Pius

---

[120] Only on December 7, 1959, during an allocution in the Basilica of the Twelve Apostles, did John XXIII announce in a public and solemn manner that the council was to be "Vatican II": *ADA*, I, 60-61.

IX, this choice would reassure the "Romans" that they could easily influence the Council. For the same reasons, the bishops and theologians of the Catholic world might fear that the holding of the Council in Rome would limit their impact on its work. Furthermore, would not a Roman location for the Council hinder the rapprochement with noncatholic Christians? On the other hand, in view of the uncertain international situation and the advanced age of the pope, would it have been realistic to imagine a different venue? The celebration of a Council of renewal in Rome and right in St. Peter's was a challenge but also a commitment that the center of the Catholic Church would be involved in it.

* * *

Expectation of the Council did not cause a suspension of the Church's ordinary life at any level. But while the pope was concerned to see to it that the preparation of the gathering be distinct from the daily routine of the Holy See, so as to stress the exceptional character of the conciliar event, it was inevitable that the entire Church should begin to live in a "conciliar" state of mind and that even everyday activities should be affected by it and in turn have an effect before the Council opened.

A clear norm for Roncalli, one that had been confirmed by his entire previous life, was that his pastoral commitment and service should be kept distinct from politics. He had felt the need of repeating this conviction immediately after his election, perhaps in order to distance himself from certain aspects of the preceding pontificate and from pressures, domestic and foreign, that would try to force specific political roles on the pope.[121]

Pope John was not in fact insensitive to the suffering of Christians and of the Church in eastern Europe, the USSR, and China, and he had repeated the Church's opposition to materialism and Marxism, as well as the incompatibility of these with Christianity. And yet it was easy to see something new in comparison with preceding pontificates. The struggle against Communism no longer took first place in papal teaching; John did not underrate the importance of this struggle, but he relativized it, for in his view the historical horizon of the Church's activity is much broader and more complex. At the beginning of Lent, 1959, he had warned preachers "to enlighten consciences, not to confuse them and coerce them,...to heal the brethren, not to frighten them."[122] The pope made this

---

[121] At the beginning of April, 1959, the Holy Office confirmed the excommunication of 1949 against those who voted for Communist parties. On July 3 came the definitive prohibition of the French worker-priest experiment.

[122] *DMC* 1, 142.

attitude part of a serene appraisal of the present time, unlike many who "are discouraged or give up or are tempted to give up the effort, or at least to slacken it." In his view, the Church on its pilgrimage through the centuries has not always triumphed nor, because it overcame so many enemies in the past, may it consider itself victorious over present enemies; rather it must "trust entirely in the never-failing help of its founder."[123]

John's main interest was not in political interventions, which had often been dictated by circumstances internal to Italy, but in the various aspects of the problem of peace, which was to enter a new phase during the coming years, due in part to his contribution. On several occasions he stressed the legitimate aspirations of human beings for peace.[124] From this point of view his political horizon was the world; one stimulus to this broad outlook was the imminent achievement of independence throughout the African continent. The pope was quite convinced that "the Church is not an archeological museum, but is alive, tireless, and life-giving; and it makes its way forward, often in unexpected ways."[125] The first audiences to heads of state, after the one to the president of Italy on May 6, were reserved for the rulers of Greece, who were Orthodox, and the president of Turkey, who was a Muslim.

At the end of June Msgr. F. Lardone was transferred from the nunciature in Peru to the apostolic delegation in Turkey, occupied at one time by Roncalli himself. Msgr. Lardone was to become the pope's right-hand man in initiating contacts with the Soviet Union for the purpose, at least in the beginning, of obtaining permission for bishops in countries behind the "iron curtain," that is, in the Soviet sphere, to attend the Council.[126]

As early as February 23, 1959, the pope had set up the preparatory commission for the Roman synod; this was then organized into eight subcommissions. On June 18 he received all those involved in preparation for the synod itself.

---

[123] *DMC* 1, 351.

[124] Roncalli had not in the past made any important show of militancy against war and for peace. During his long life he did indeed have direct or indirect experience of two great world conflicts and this had confirmed his instinctive human horror of war, but it had not yielded doctrinal insights or arguments for the rejection of war. Nor do we know that he gave much attention to persons and movements in the Christian world or specifically in the Catholic world that had taken positions going beyond the classical ones of the Church's magisterium, from "the useless slaughter" of Benedict XV to the "everything can be lost through war" of Pius XII. On the other hand, we must not forget that one of his inherent traits was to be a man of peace, opposed to conflict, and a peacemaker, beginning with the little family strains with which so many of his letters were concerned. Along with truth and unity, peace was at the center of his first encyclical, *Ad Petri cathedram* (June 29, 1959).

[125] *DMC* 2, 652.

[126] See A. Riccardi, *Il Vaticano e Mosca* (Rome-Bari, 1992) 232-38.

Resistance to this pontificate's renewal efforts and therefore to the prospect of a Council was shown from the very first weeks. In particular, the Holy Office pursued its habitual policy of censorship and elicited lively reactions in the process. The prohibition of the granting of a doctorate *honoris causa* to J. Maritain, the order to withdraw L. Milani's book, *Esperieze pastorali*, from the bookstores, the censure of E. Balducci's journal, *Testimonianza*, the renewal of the excommunication of the Communists and their supporters, the hostility to the worker-priest experiment in France: all these were alarming signs. People were asking whether John XXIII's desire for a relaxation of tension and a return to normality, indicated by his early creation of cardinals on December 15, 1958, after a lengthy period under Pacelli in which none were appointed,[127] was in fact only a velleity. Could not a Council held in such an atmosphere as this become an occasion for further harshness? Was the pope able to control the Curia?

* * *

The first six months of the prehistory of Vatican II seemed intended primarily to allay the surprise and confusion caused by the announcement. The pope repeatedly confirmed his decision and gradually sketched out his view of the Council. The Roman Curia accepted the prospect of a Council while entertaining the hope that they could win control of it. The Catholic episcopate was jolted by the invitation to take an active role at the level of the universal Church; for them these were perhaps months during which a nostalgic desire for the Pacellian style of governing still prevailed, while the transition to an outlook of inquiry was proving difficult. Theological circles, which had more quickly seen the novelty of the pontificate and the announcement, busied themselves in organizing their ideas, though often not believing that room was really being made for renewal. Noncatholic Christians seemed torn between an initial sympathy and a subsequent wariness: they seemed to be asking themselves, "Can Rome change?"

To the extent that the announcement of the Council had not died a premature death, the way was now open for the complex and hard-fought process of preparation.

---

[127] In a shrewd and effective balancing-act, the first cardinal "created" was G. B. Montini, who had been kept at a distance by Pius XII and was feared by curial circles, while Tardini, a man much more acceptable to the same circles, was appointed secretary of state. On this occasion the pope asked the cardinals who held two curial offices to choose only one of them; the request, desired and approved by many people, was resented by some of those concerned.

CHAPTER II

THE ANTEPREPARATORY PHASE
THE SLOW EMERGENCE FROM INERTIA
(JANUARY, 1959 — OCTOBER, 1962)

ÉTIENNE FOUILLOUX

I. VATICAN II, AN ISOLATED EVENT?

In what way was the convocation of the twenty-first general Council of the Catholic Church connected with the climate peculiar to the end of the 1950s and the beginning of the 1960s? The interpretation of the action of John XXIII already depends, at least in part, on the answer to this question: Was his action completely independent or was it determined to some extent by that climate?[1] The question is all the more relevant since the history of the Councils, ancient and modern, of which I shall speak in a moment, certainly argues for the second answer. We need think only of the many interactions between the wars of religion and the chaotic course of the Council of Trent, which for this reason stretched from 1545 to 1563; the unexpected interruption of the previous Vatican Council by the Franco-Prussian War and the entrance of the Italians into Rome in 1870.

Could it be that Pius XII himself abandoned the idea of reopening the interrupted Vatican Council because of the "Cold War"? But as far as we can tell, his reasons were primarily domestic: the cost of the operation on the morrow of a terrible worldwide conflict; differences regarding the future assembly within the team assigned with its preparation; and so on.[2] Does this mean that his retreat from the idea had nothing to do with the crisis in the East-West confrontation that would in all probability have kept episcopates under communist control from attending

---

[1] The information that follows in the text is indispensable but also sparse. I cannot here provide a complete history of the era, yet I must at least sketch the background of Vatican II. Among those who have attempted this before me is Giacomo Martina, "The Historical Context in Which the Idea of a New Ecumenical Council Was Born," in *Vatican II: Assessment and Perspectives Twenty-Five Years After (1962-1987)*, ed. René Latourelle (New York, 1988) I, 3-73.

[2] François-Charles Uginet, "Les projets de concile général sous Pie XI et Pie XII," *Deuxième*, 75-78.

his Council and thus have signaled a new breach in catholicity? I need only mention that the preparatory activities began on March 15, 1948 (shortly after the "Prague Coup") and concluded in January, 1951 (while war was raging in Korea).

Precedents of this kind bid us turn our attention to the setting in which the announcement and preparation of Vatican II took place, in order to attempt to measure the convergences or discordances between the coming assembly and its environment. But, while not claiming a clearcut picture, may we not suggest that the former were far more numerous than the latter? In many respects, the situation which John XXIII inherited was no longer the one that had chilled his predecessor's enthusiasm. The world that had emerged from the "cold war" was changing, although it was still unsure of the direction to take, but this very recovery of flexibility facilitated the holding of a Council which its initiator presented as chiefly a Council of movement.

Unsure of the direction to take? To people wearing dark glasses, the after-effects of the "cold war" still provided only too many occasions for predicting the worst: an atomic conflict which the first results of a rapid conquest of space made a dizzying possibility: the Soviet Sputnik in 1957; the American Explorer in the following year; Gagarin in space on April 12, 1961; and so on. We know now the extent to which the Soviets were bluffing, but who then doubted their superpower?

In addition, at this time the fire was still smoldering under the ashes almost everywhere. In Europe, Imre Nagy, held responsible for the Hungarian uprising in the autumn of 1956, was executed on June 16, 1958. Twice the Communist position on Berlin hardened: first in November, 1959, and then especially in August, 1961, with the building of the famous wall, intended to stop the flight of East Germans into the Federal Republic, which caused the lively reaction of Kennedy, the American President. But this was to be the last crisis.

Outside of Europe the extension of Communism tended to multiply areas of confrontation. At the beginning of January, 1959, Fidel Castro and his men entered Havana, which had been abandoned by the dictator Batista. The regime they set up quickly took a radical form; the Americans clumsily and ineffectively tried to eliminate it, for they could not bear to have a "Red base" so close to their shores. Khrushchev supported Cuba to the point of sending atomic weapons by sea, and at the very moment when Vatican II first met, the "missile-crisis" brought the world to the brink of a direct USA-USSR confrontation in October-November, 1962. This crisis, the last to involve the two great powers to such a degree, was also the most serious.

All this did nothing to encourage a pope! A widespread conflagration involving new arsenals of destruction was still a possibility. And yet it did not occur: Kennedy's firmness, but also Khrushchev's prudence, prevailed; the Soviet leader in particular was able to force caution upon his fiery Cuban ally, as their correspondence shows.[3]

From the spring of 1962 on, the official doctrine followed by McNamara, the American Secretary of Defense, allowed for graduated reprisals, blow for blow, but not a global reprisal in every situation; the balance of terror imposed its own laws. In addition, recurrent crises occurred at longer intervals by comparison with the preceding period. They were now only rents, tragic indeed at times, in the fabric of uninterrupted though sensitive negotiations between the Americans and the Soviets; neither side thought of lowering its guard, but at least they were talking. The two K's — Kennedy and Khrushchev — are too much the subject of controversy today in their respective countries to let us refrain from doing them justice for what they accomplished: they avoided the risk of a "hot war" that the "cold war" entailed, and they replaced it with a constant competition that was not yet "peaceful coexistence."

This fragile détente brought notable changes to the world checkerboard, and these in turn fostered the détente. In the area of international relations there was, first of all, if not a breakup of the blocs, at least a return to a degree of pluralism within each of them. In July, 1959, de Gaulle began to show his desire for independence from NATO. In the East, something much more serious: the break between the Soviets and the Chinese that began in 1958. In the West, on the contrary, geographical areas that had hitherto played a subordinate part strengthened their cohesion within the western world. This was true especially of the six-nation "little Europe" with a new departure for their economic development between 1957 and 1962. August 17, 1961, at Punta del Este, saw the inception in Latin America of the Alliance for Progress, which Washington had proposed. At the time, this represented a hope for a less unbalanced partnership with a continent that was still under American tutelage despite its having been formally independent since the beginning of the nineteenth century.

But the most important factor in the diversification of the world at that time was a second wave of decolonization. Conflicts did accompany the latter in some areas: in the former Belgian Congo (1960-61), in French

[3] *Le Monde* (Paris), November 24, 1990. On the entire international situation at the time see Robert Frank, "Vatican II entre guerre froide et détente (1962)," in *Vatican II commence*, 3-13.

Algeria (1954-62), and especially in Vietnam, where the situation had
badly deteriorated since the end of the 1950s. But painful though these
conflicts were, they were only the reverse side of a worldwide phenomenon of emancipation that was for the moment full of hope, for at the
beginning of the 1960s the majority of peoples who had been colonized
in the nineteenth century achieved their independence without too many
obstacles. A major source of conflicts disappeared, while after Bandung
(1955) there appeared in what was increasingly called the Third World
the beginnings of a third international power defined by the refusal of
some of the charismatic agents of decolonization (Nasser, Nehru,
Sukarno) to align themselves with the great blocs. At the same time, the
Third World became for these same blocs a kind of challenge, a kind of
"frontier," over whose development they quarreled with one another,
though in a peaceful manner at the time.

    This new "frontier," created by the ideology of development that was
triumphant at the beginning of the 1960s, was itself only one factor in
the prevailing optimism of the time. The rebuilding after the devastation
caused by the war proceeded more quickly than had been anticipated.
On both sides of the "iron curtain," thanks to new technologies, indus-
try and cities had taken definitive precedence over the changeless order
of the agricultural world. But who saw that these socio-demographic
upheavals were also affecting the Third World, but without any real
compensating factors? For the economic growth that had been pursued
after the end of the reconstruction seemed limitless both in space and in
time. Once again, a revitalized capitalism dreamed of both the end of
crises and a limitless expansion. Khrushchevian communism, meanwhile, promised more than ever that it was on the verge of making up for
lost time. Moreover, the two rivals engaged, each with its own methods,
in a keen competition to bring the Third World out of its state of underdevelopment: the Soviets committed themselves to the Aswan Dam in
September, 1958; the European Organization for Economic Cooperation, the function of which was to manage American aid, was changed,
beginning in 1960, into the Organization for Economic Cooperation and
Development. Not only was the hope of a lasting world peace springing
up again, despite annoying local conflicts, but to it there was joined the
hope of prosperity for all the inhabitants of the earth. How could people
not have confidence when they saw this break in the clouds after so
many storms?

    The only ones who refused homage to the optimism around them
were some young intellectuals who would quickly make a name for

themselves. In the realm of thought also the move from the 1950s to the 1960s seemed to be a decisive turning point. It saw the beginnings of a radical challenge to the values by which the world had been living after Auschwitz and Hiroshima, values based on a progressive humanism, on a concern for commitment to peace and human dignity. But this was a liberal humanism blind to the defects of the "free world," a Christian humanism with little sensitivity to the errors of the Churches, a Marxist humanism deaf to the cries from the gulag.

There were, however, minds that did not acknowledge kinship with any of the orthodoxies, whether Stalin's, Truman's, or even Pius XII's. The horrors of the colonial wars and the rise of indigenous nationalisms had left a profound mark on these individuals. As a result, they began very bluntly to denounce the hypocrisy of these orthodoxies, which had no qualms about destroying those who resisted their several forms of indoctrination. In Cuba, in Algeria, and then in Vietnam, they saw the armed struggles for independence as pregnant with revolutions still to come. And they based a theory on what they observed: far from mastering nature, consciousness or history, human beings are driven by obscure and implacable forces at work in those areas; thus was Marx revised by Althusser and Freud by Lacan.

The philosophical challenge to humanism was accompanied by a deconstruction of its esthetic corollaries: linear narrative (the "new novel" or, in film, the "new wave"), severance of the usual melodic line ("free jazz"; synthesizer music), disappearance or fragmentation of the human figure (plastic arts). This elitist attack on a classical culture that had claimed universality was contemporary with another and much more formidable attack, that of a mass culture based on sounds and images carried to the entire world by television — Vatican II would be the first televised Council, at least for its official ceremonies. This mass culture was hedonist and uncritical, but it met with stunning success among the children of the baby boom, as can be seen from the popularity of the Beatles among the young, beginning in ... 1962.

Such in its broad lines was the setting in which Vatican II would be prepared. Who can say that any of these factors was present in the pope's mind when he came to his decision? At least, however, such was the context of that decision, a context in which the pope himself was steeped in a greater or lesser degree, and the positive aspects of which seemed to be his primary focus. The convocation of the Council benefitted, doubtless indirectly, from the environing economic, political, and cultural optimism. We would look in vain for any closer connections and

must be content to say — but this is not negligible! — that the papal
decision, with its desire for union and openness, seemed to be in line
with one of the major tendencies of that period and one which it would
greatly help to reinforce.

But John XXIII did not underestimate the risks of the undertaking,
especially since he had a foreboding about (rather than a real understanding of) the new sources of challenge.[4] Is it not part of the drama of
Vatican II that while it prepared the Catholic Church for peaceful
renewal, it resulted in a crisis that caught it in the pincer movement of a
new hedonistic culture and a new critical culture? As early as 1964-
1965, that is, too quickly for the Council to adjust its own aim, its
remarkable adaptation to the optimism of the "golden sixties" became a
handicap in the face of a renascent pessimism.

II. A CHURCH READY FOR A COUNCIL?

But let us not end before beginning! We must shift now from a summary survey of a rapidly changing world to a less impressionistic picture
of the Catholic world to which, on January 25, 1959, John XXIII proposed an ecumenical (in the Roman sense of the term) Council.

1. Survival of a Conciliar Tradition?

The surprise which that world felt would not surprise a historian. The
surprise was, in fact, two-fold: first, that the Supreme Pontiff should
admit the need to update or modernize the Catholic Church; and, second, that this *aggiornamento* would take the form of a Council. Let me
concern myself with the second point, before handling the first.

Had the conciliar tradition disappeared from twentieth-century Christendom? Certainly not! But it was much less present within Catholicism

---

[4] See Charles de Gaulle, *Memoirs of Hope: Renewal and Endeavor*, trans. T. Kilmartin
(New York, 1971) 193: "Then, with an anxiety tempered by his natural serenity, the
sovereign pontiff spoke of the spiritual perturbation inflicted on Christendom by the gigan-
tic upheavals of the century. Among all the peoples of Europe and Asia which had been
subjected to Communism, the Catholic community was oppressed and cut off from Rome.
But everywhere else, under free regimes, a sort of diffuse rebelliousness was undermining,
if not religion then at least its practice, its rules, its hierarchy and its rites. Nevertheless,
however much anxiety this situation might cause him, the Pope saw it as no more than
another in the long series of crises which the Church had faced and surmounted ever since
the time of Christ. He believed that by putting into practice its own values of inspiration
and self-examination it would not fail once more to regain its equilibrium" (account of an
audience of the president of the French Republic with John XXIII on June 27, 1959).

than outside it. It had remained most alive in the Orthodox world and, due to the urgent situation, had even been given a new vitality there. As evidence, we may point to the reform Council of the Russian Church that took place, against all odds, in the midst of the revolutionary upheavals of 1917-1918. Not only did that Council restore the Patriarchate of Moscow that Peter the Great had suppressed, but it also based its entire work on *sobornost*, that is, conciliarity. Without this reorganization the Russian Church would perhaps not have survived the subsequent persecution.

Was the Russian example contagious? In the aftermath of the Great War and the dismantling of the Ottoman Empire, the Church of Constantinople was in no better a position than before, and yet this was the moment, in 1920, that its synod chose for launching an appeal to the Christian world to set up some sort of league of Churches on the model of the League of Nations, as a way of better responding to the challenges of the hour. Their document would feed the beginnings of the ecumenical movement, but it had hardly any effect in the East. Once again, it was at Constantinople, in the spring of 1923, that a panorthodox assembly was held that contemplated a conciliar gathering of all the Byzantino-Slavic Churches. The plan was recalled once again at the Congress of Orthodox Theology in Athens in the autumn of 1936. But numerous rivalries within the Church (conservatives vs. reformers; Moscow vs. Constantinople) and, even more, the difficulty that some of the main Churches involved had in surviving hindered implementation of the plan. Not until 1952 would another Patriarch of Constantinople, Athenagoras, revive the idea in a wise and prudent way. It was an idea that did not escape the attention of the former Apostolic Delegate in Turkey, Angelo Giuseppe Roncalli. The idea of a panorthodox Council thus persisted through the first half of the twentieth century, but without the least step being taken to make it a reality.

The ecclesiastical landscape changed more quickly in the Anglo-Protestant world, although with not inconsiderable eastern support. I am alluding here to the emergence of the ecumenical movement, the success of which Rome could not ignore. The two branches of this movement, both of them springing from the post-World War I situation, held their initial conferences: the movement for a practical Christianity, that is, Life and Work, in Stockholm in 1925, and the doctrinal branch, that is, Faith and Order, in Lausanne in 1927. In 1937, in Oxford and Edinburgh, the two organizations agreed to merge and form a World Council of Churches, although World War II delayed its formation for ten years.

The deed was done in Amsterdam in 1948: reversing an age-old centrifugal movement, Christians separated from Rome entered officially on the way of cooperation and dialogue.

The World Council, with its permanent headquarters in Geneva, was not intended to be either the Church of Jesus Christ on earth or even a super-Church; it was satisfied to be, in the language adopted in Amsterdam, "a fellowship of churches which accept our Lord Jesus Christ as God and Saviour." On this "basis," which brought together at the beginning 147 different denominations, the Genevan organization developed to the point of accepting into itself, at the third general assembly in New Delhi (1961), the International Missionary Council and the majority of the Churches in the Soviet camp. At that time it also amended its "basis" along explicitly Trinitarian lines in order to satisfy its new eastern members. Thus, at the time when the Roman Council was announced, the ecumenical movement, of which the World Council had become the expression, was, despite some reservations by fundamentalists, approaching its high point as far as representativeness was concerned, for almost all non-Catholic Christians would shortly belong to it.

Its various proceedings were not properly conciliar at all, since they were but the products of the member Churches and had no authority over these. But practice overturned juridical boundaries; the very existence of the Council and of the numerous undertakings which the Council inspired led within the non-Roman sectors of Christendom to a flood of exchanges that would have been unthinkable in the last century. And into these exchanges something of the collective life of the Church found its way.[5]

But for a long time Rome failed to take any official notice of the ecumenical movement. Not only did the Holy See refuse to join it, as had been proposed to it at the outset, but it forbade its members to participate in it. After the small opening at Lund (Faith and Order, 1952) and the closing of the way again at Evanston (second general assembly, 1954), the question of "observers" was still one of the ones that haunted the experts on the eve of Vatican II: they were to be present for the first time both in New Delhi and in Rome the following year.[6] By and large, the Vatican remained cautious, not to say mistrustful, toward the religious,

[5] Ruth Rouse and Stephen Charles Neill, eds., *A History of the Ecumenical Movement, 1517-1948* (London, 1967[2]); Harold E. Fey, ed., *The Ecumenical Advance, 1948-1968* (London, 1970).

[6] Etienne Fouilloux, *Les catholiques et l'unité chrétienne du XIXe au XXe siècle. Itinéraires européens d'expression française* (Paris, 1982) 777-817.

nongovernmental organization that the Genevan Council had become. It could not fail to take its existence into account, but it did not favor taking it as a model. It seems therefore that despite John XXIII's interest in things eastern it would be excessive to speak of an influence of noncatholic conciliarism, except in a very diluted form.

As for the Catholic conciliar tradition, it seemed to be in a rather poor state. Of course, after the suspension of the Vatican assembly in 1870, the question was whether or not under certain conditions that Council should be completed, since it had been intended to do more than define the dogma of papal primacy and infallibility. Fourteen preparatory schemas, or drafts of documents, had been distributed to the fathers, and the latter had begun discussion of three of them, two being on the tasks and duties of bishops. This point is not irrelevant, since the interruption of the proceedings led to a heavy emphasis on papal authority over against that of the episcopate. In fact, the great question left hanging after 1870 was: What position do the bishops have alongside the pope?[7]

Although we still do not have any of the original documentation, we might hypthesize that the various successors of Pius IX considered a possible reopening of the Vatican Council. If signs of this concern are very slight in Pius X and Benedict XV, they are especially clear for Pius XI and Pius XII; both popes went so far as to initiate a process of relaunching the Council. Pope Ratti's attempt began in 1922 with the establishment of a small commission of theologians who were to assess the Council of Pius IX. But the commission could not stop there. Not only had the Code of Canon Law published in 1917 settled a number of questions that were to have been discussed at Vatican I, but the development of the Church during the preceding half-century had raised other questions, beginning with the question of modernism, both doctrinal and social, which it would be difficult to avoid. But this inevitable expansion of the program multiplied the differences between those who wanted a confirmation of previous condemnations and those, like Cardinal Ehrle, who wanted too loosen the antimodernist noose. Furthermore, was it advisable to hold a Council and thereby anticipate the possible settlement of the Roman question? In proportions still difficult to measure, these two factors militated in favor of halting the preparation in 1924, despite the favorable response of a large majority of the episcopate, which had been consulted during the preceding year.[8]

---

[7] Jacques Gadille, "Vatican I, concile incomplet?" *Deuxième*, 33-45.

[8] On this episode, and the parallel one under Pius XII, see François-Charles Uginet, in *Deuxième*, 68-75; like everyone else, Uginet uses the articles of Giovanni Caprile in *CC*: "Pio XI e la ripresa del concilio Vaticano," 117 (1966/3) 27-33; "Pio XI, la Curia romana e il concilio," 129 (1969/2) 121-33, 563-75.

In the years after the burden of the Roman question had been lifted by the Lateran accords of 1929, soundings taken in favor of a continuation of Vatican I multiplied. They have been recently collected by Giuseppe Butturini, who sees them as culminating, ten years later, in a memorandum composed by Msgr. Celso Costantini, Secretary of the Congregation of Propaganda Fide, at the time of the conclave that elected Cardinal Pacelli to succeed Pius XI. But Costantini's plan was rather different: he disregarded both the idea of concluding the assembly of 1869-70 and the idea of condemning modern errors and, instead, proposed a program of prudent reform (re-evaluation of the episcopal office; return of the Protestants; the vernacular in the liturgy; and so on) for the Church of the second half of the twentieth century. In this respect, what Costantini envisaged was closer to what Vatican II would be than to the preceding Council. But who knew of his plan, even though it was updated ten years later? John XXIII himself became aware of it only in the spring of 1959, several months after announcing his own decision.[9]

In any case, the Second World War made other tasks more urgent! But shortly after it ended, the idea of a Council reappeared, although in a rather different context. Besieged as it was by hostile forces under communist direction in the world of the "cold war," the Church had to think first of all of defending itself, and this meant also defending itself against those within its own bosom who were, or were thought to be, conspiring with these hostile forces. Such was the opinion submitted to Pius XII by such prelates as Ottaviani and Ruffini. And it was in this spirit that the pope at the beginning of 1949 put the question back on the table.

Without knowing about the work done by his predecessor (which is rather strange!), Pius XII ordered a new appraisal of the Vatican assembly and an inventory of questions that had arisen since. But the method followed was no longer the same: whereas Pius XI had assigned the task to a small commission, Pius XII put the preparation in the hands of the Holy Office in the person of its assessor, Msgr. Ottaviani, and of theologians who worked for him. The preparation progressed rapidly but along limited lines that did not satisfy everyone, beginning with the secretary of the central commission, Pierre Charles, a Belgian Jesuit. These differing views on the direction to be taken by the future Council, together with material difficulties and the constraints of time, since the pope was growing old, put the lid on a plan that had excluded any consultation of

[9] Giuseppe Butturini, *Alle origini del Concilio Vaticano secondo. Una proposta di Celso Costantini* (Pordenone, 1988; 350 pp.). The plan, dated February 12-25, 1939, is given on pp. 69-116.

the bishops. It has been said, but without any real proof, that the materials developed at that time were used in the composition of later encyclicals, especially *Humani generis* (August 12, 1950).[10] If this was indeed the case, the inhibiting atmosphere of the latter text would be enough to show the direction that the planned Council would have taken!

What does this brief survey of conciliar history from 1870 on allow us to conclude as to the genesis of Vatican II? As a matter of fact, not very much, except elements of discontinuity. It is true, of course, that the unruffled passage of time was taking people further and further away from the nineteenth century and that a continuation pure and simple of Vatican I was becoming less and less conceivable. Yet the preparatory work done in the 1920s and 1940s was controlled by a determination to deal with new problems in the same essentially defensive perspective that had been at work in 1870. The two sets of preparations had no obvious connection with one another, but neither did they resemble in any way the idea of a Council which John XXIII gradually unveiled between 1959 and 1962. In fact, it is in the reversal of sides that we must look for whatever fragmentary continuity there was. Ehrle, Costantini, and Charles had not wanted the closed kind of Council that was most likely to occur at that time; Ottaviani and his followers, who had been very involved in the Pacellian program, would try, without success, to substitute it for the plan that John XXIII gradually sketched out — which accounts for the upheavals during the first session of Vatican II. But we would be engaging in dubious acrobatics were we to turn earlier efforts at a resumption of Vatican I into so many steps toward Vatican II. All in all, the spectacle of eastern synodal practice despite its imperfection influenced Pope Roncalli more than did episodes discovered only at a late date and incompletely.[11]

In any case, such a search for linear causality is somewhat illusory. It forgets the institutional and theological context in which these various efforts took place, a context important for different reasons. If Vatican I had been completed normally, of course, it would no doubt have restored the balance between pope and bishops. But given the way it ended, that Council was nonetheless very representative of the development of

---

[10] Uginet, "Les projets," 75-78, where he is using the work of Giovanni Caprile, "Pio XII e un nuovo progetto di concilio ecumenico," *CC* 117 (1966/3) 209-27 (revised as "Pius XII, und das zweite Vatikanische Konzil," in *Pius XII. zum Gedächtnis*, ed. H. Schambeck [Berlin, 1977] 649-91).

[11] Alberto Melloni, "'Questa festiva ricorrenza.' Prodromi e preparazione del discorso di annuncio del Vatican II (25 Gennaio 1959)," *RSLR* 28 (1992) 607-16.

Catholic ecclesiology since the French Revolution and even since the Catholic Reformation. Non-egalitarian and hierarchical according to Bellarmine, the Church-society developed these two characteristics to the almost exclusive benefit of the pope and the organs of the Roman Curia. The Romanization of the Church was symbolic to the extent that, after 1870 even more than before, the white-haired old man of the Vatican embodied the resistance to the forces of evil that were leagued against the Church.

But the Romanization was also very real, less perhaps because of the dogmatic definition of the pope's personal infallibility in matters of faith and morals, an infallibility of which he would make only restricted use, than because of the simultaneous appearance of the concept of the ordinary magisterium in 1863, a concept that would have far more concrete effectiveness, since for lack of clear delimitation "ordinary magisterium" often extended beyond papal acts to include decisions of the Roman congregations, especially the supreme congregation, the Holy Office.[12] This ecclesiology, confirmed by subsequent encyclicals and by the *Code* of 1917, made the Vatican more than ever the summit of Catholicism and the pope the apex of the summit: a kind of absolute sovereign in matters doctrinal, with no authority able to oppose him. The spreading practice of pilgrimages to Rome and of personal devotion to the pope were the spiritual echo of this theological development.

In this scheme of things, and despite attempts to resume the Vatican assembly, Councils had hardly any place, although the *Code* of 1917 maintained their possibility (canons 222-29). Nor was it unusual to read in popular theological literature unqualified condemnations of the Councils, for example, this statement, at the beginning of the century, in the very authoritative *Dictionnaire de théologie catholique*: "Ecumenical Councils are not necessary to the Church."[13] This was indeed not the view of informed ecclesiologists, but by the time the announcement came of what was to be Vatican II, even they had come to have little expectation of any future Council. Summing up the views of the "Catholic public" in whose name he spoke, Olivier Rousseau, a Benedictine of Chevetogne, could write in 1960: "At last, despairing of ever seeing a

---

[12] Giuseppe Ruggieri, "'Magistère ordinaire.' La lettre *Tuas libenter* de Pie IX de 21 décembre 1863," in *Le Magistère. Institutions et fonctionnements = RSR* 71 (1983) 259-67.

[13] J. Forget, "Conciles," *DTC* 3/1, 669: "In the primacy of the Roman pontiff the Church has the ordinary and essential instrument for the exercise of supreme authority, and this instrument has of itself the power and grace to decide all questions and to deal with all difficulties."

continuation of the great assemblies, people had reached the point of saying that once papal infallibility had been defined the age of the Councils was over."[14]

On the other hand, some people maintained that the consultation of the episcopate before the definition of the dogma of the Assumption (1946) had been a kind of Council by correspondence. From our point of view it was nothing of the sort, for what does an inquiry made of isolated individuals have in common with genuine collegial discussion? Collegial — that is the important word.

What could be said, at the middle of the twentieth century, of a possible practice of episcopal collegiality in the Catholic Church? For the most part, individual bishops settled the problems of their dioceses together with the Roman congregations at the time of their *ad limina* visits, a practice which greatly limited the chances of the bishops acting in concert. Canon law did indeed require that a provincial Council be convoked at least every twenty years. But reality fell short of the ideal, for this institution, which had been so vital after Trent, had badly declined since the end of the nineteenth century.

As for national or continental Councils, which required authorization from the Holy See, the position differed greatly depending on the origin and nature of the undertaking. When an episcopate of a country long Christian expressed a desire to take counsel together, whether regularly or in special circumstances, it was rare that Rome did not show its suspicion of an initiative that brought the risk of autonomous action. Since the middle of the nineteenth century the Fulda conference had been able to elude Rome in a Germany imbued with Protestantism and eager for unity. But French Catholicism was not so successful, for it was always suspect of Gallicanism. Thus Pius X regretted the three plenary assemblies of the French episcopate that were held in 1906-7 in the setting of the separation of the Churches and the state. After these meetings only the cardinals and archbishops could meet periodically between 1919 and 1951, this last being the date of a new plenary assembly that would be repeated every three years until Vatican II. The Italian episcopate, for its part, was even more fragmented despite its large numbers; the episcopal conference dated only from 1954, and it included only the presidents of the regional conferences. Unless the initiative came from Rome, any attempt at horizontal coordination within this

---

[14] In *Le Concile et les conciles* (Paris-Chevetogne, 1960) XV; see also *L'ecclésiologie au XIXe siècle* (Paris, 1960).

kind of vertical or pyramidal structure was for a long time regarded by the Vatican as a potential threat.

On the other hand, Rome never hesitated to use Councils as an instrument in structuring or consolidating young Churches in mission lands or in Protestant countries. This was true of the United States and its three national Councils of 1852, 1866, and 1884. Such too, and even more significantly, was the case in China and its Council of 1924, the driving force for which was the apostolic delegate — Celso Costantini. But the first of these examples is especially instructive, for the remarkable adaptation of Catholicism to local life in the United States quickly excited anxieties that were exorcised in 1899 under the name of "Americanism," but that reappeared in 1917 when American Catholicism equipped itself with a coordinating agency, the "National Catholic War Council." Despite difficulties, this body managed to survive the war under the name of the "National Catholic Welfare Conference" (1922).

The case of Latin America, which falls half-way between the two just mentioned (United States and China), is no less interesting. This subcontinent, of course, had undergone a hasty christianization that, with the help of population growth, turned it into one of the world's main reservoirs of Catholicism, but it was dramatically lacking in religious structures and divided by national boundaries that showed little openness. As a result, in 1899 the Holy See called a plenary meeting in Rome of the Latin American bishops to try to harmonize rules and practices and to energize the apostolate; this meeting was followed by national Councils to implement the decisions. But in the middle of the twentieth century, social and religious transformations (the stunning advance of Pentecostalism and of Afro-American cults in particular) called for new concerted efforts. The International Eucharistic Congress held in Rio de Janeiro at the end of July and the beginning of August, 1955, provided the occasion for asking for the creation of a Latin American Episcopal Council.[15] Rome agreed, and the new organization was set up in Bogotá, although not without some initial hesitations. The Vatican Commission for Latin America, founded in 1958, kept watch over the new organization.

Toward the end of the 1950s Rome began to show important signs of change on the subject of episcopal conferences. These were springing up like mushrooms, and Pius XII on several occasions expressed regret at

---

[15] Consejo Episcopal Latinoamericano or CELAM.

the isolation of dioceses and advocated a better coordination of efforts.[16] Not until 1959, however, did the episcopal conferences appear in the *Annuario Pontificio*, along with the date of the approval of their statutes and a listing of those in charge. At that time there were about forty conferences, most of which had won recognition only quite recently.[17]

Do these signs justify saying that there was no break in continuity between the preconciliar period and the conciliar period, as has been suggested?[18] Such an interpretation would surely be exaggerated. Indeed, the practice of collegiality had undoubtedly developed to some degree during the 1950s. It was, however, still limited, since in matters judged to be sensitive Rome continued to make decisions without worrying too much about the local dignitaries; Cardinals Feltin, Gerlier, and Liénart had bitter experience of this in the fall of 1953 in the matter of the worker-priests. Most importantly, theory hardly kept pace with the developing practice; the widespread feeling that a reappraisal of the individual and collective episcopal office was needed gave rise to very little theological reflection on the idea of collegiality. Such reflection as did occur was enough to inspire the votum of Archbishop Alfrink of Utrecht in 1959, but these reflections had gained only a small audience by the eve of Vatican II.[19]

From whatever angle the question was approached, then, there was little if any likelihood of a general Council of the Catholic Church at the end of the 1950s. Despite real efforts to improve its local operation, since the end of the nineteenth century this Church had increasingly

---

[16] Pius XII, Allocution on November 2, 1954, to the cardinals and bishops gathered in Rome for the proclamation of the Queenship of Mary: "Frequent and mutual communication among Bishops is very helpful for the fruitful and effective exercise of the pastoral office. Thus one perfects the other in assaying the lessons of past experience; government is made more uniform, the wonder of the faithful is avoided, for often they do not understand why in one diocese a certain policy is followed, while in another, which is perhaps adjacent, a different or even a quite contrary policy is followed. To realize these purposes general assemblies, which are now held almost everywhere, are very helpful, and also the more solemnly convened Provincial and Plenary Councils, for which the Code of Canon Law provides, and which are governed by definite laws." The pope immediately added: "In addition to this union and intercourse between brothers in the episcopacy there should be added close union and frequent communication with this Apostolic See" (*TPS* 1 [1954] 375-85 at 384).

[17] *Annuario Pontificio* (Vatican City, 1959) 858-63 (thirteen conferences approved after 1955).

[18] Giorgio Feliciani, *Le Conferenze episcopali* (Bologna, 1974).

[19] Jan Grootaers, "Une restauration de la théologie de l'épiscopat. Contribution du Cardinal Alfrink à la préparation de Vatican II," *Glaube im Prozess. Christsein nach dem II. Vatikanum. Für Karl Rahner*, ed. Elmar Klinger and Klaus Wittstadt (Freiburg — Basel — Vienna, 1984) 778-97.

become a Roman Church, in which only a pope would be able to take
the initiative in restoring the institution of Councils, which was in a poor
state.

Furthermore, what would a Council do? In the long history of the
Church general Councils had been held in four typical situations and for
four different purposes which make it possible to define four kinds of
Councils. First of all, there can be a Council for reunion with a branch
that has separated itself from the main body of Christians and now
returns to the Roman fold on the basis of an agreement made in due
form and putting an end to the schism. Such, for example, were Lyons
in 1274 and Florence in 1439, which sought union with the Byzantine
East. Was Vatican II to be a new Council of union, since John XXIII
was placing so much emphasis on his ecumenical task? So great was the
uncertainty that such a Council was rumored for several weeks, that is,
the time needed for authorized denials to be issued. No! Vatican II
would be a Catholic Council, but one that looked to the future, much-
desired reconciliation of Christians whom history had separated.

Then there is the Council that is convoked for the opposite reason:
to condemn one or more heresies, to anathematize errors, and to excom-
municate their adherents, before redefining the Catholic faith in opposition to them. The exemplar here is Trent in the sixteenth century,
after the Protestant revolt. But what errors were there for Vatican II to
condemn that had not already been recently and solemnly condemned?
The encyclical *Quanta cura* and the *Syllabus* of 1864 had given an
exhaustive list of the deviations attributed to the nineteenth century. The
encyclical *Pascendi* and the decree *Lamentabili* of 1907 had assailed,
under the name of modernism, some of these deviations that had made
their way into the very bosom of the Catholic Church. Condemnations
had indeed been rarer in the twentieth century, as well as more on target
and sometimes less resolute.

This last could not be said in regard to communism, which Pius XI
had called "intrinsically perverted" in the encyclical *Divini Redemptoris*
of 1937. Did the spread of communism after the Second World War and
the fear it aroused in the Vatican justify repetition of the condemnation?
Two disciplinary interventions of the Holy Office took care of the
matter: the one in 1949 caused a great deal of ink to flow, but the one in
1959, ten years later, went almost unnoticed. Those who wanted a
solemn proscription did not indeed lay down their arms, but where was
the urgency, now that, at the end of the 1950s, there were undeniable
signs of international détente? If the Catholic Church were once again,

belatedly, to condemn communism, would it not risk swimming against the current?

Whatever its sources may have been, the encyclical *Humani generis* of August, 1950, was meant to put a brake on the desires for openness that had survived the condemnation of modernism almost a half-century before. But while quite restrictive, it was more nuanced than *Pascendi* had been, and even sufficiently ambiguous for the main suspects to be able to issue strong denials of any interpretation that found them guilty. French Jesuit Henri de Lubac, for example, continued to issue such denials until his death.[20] In his favor, it must be said that the text made no explicit reference to any author or doctrine and that the frequently announced decree that was to accompany the encyclical never appeared. Was there a need then to dot the i's by proscribing the neomodernisms and paramodernisms of every stripe? There was undoubtedly a tendency in this direction within Catholicism, and it was strong in the Curia. But John XXIII would gradually make it clear that he was not looking for any condemnation, either of the so-called "new theology" or of communism.

A third kind of Council was one which Rome convoked, not to ban but rather solemnly to include in the structure of dogmas an element in the Church's body of beliefs. The exemplar here was Vatican I, which external events turned into what was, when all was said and done, the Council of papal infallibility. Was there an urgent need, at the end of the 1950s and beginning of the 1960s, to define new truths of faith? Nothing could be less certain. To begin with, there had quite recently been one such definition, but Pius XII had not thought it useful to convoke a Council in order to define the dogma of the Assumption on November 1, 1950. He was content with a written consultation within the Catholic body, an action that, as we have seen, cannot be likened to a conciliar process. In fact, in this matter he was making use of his infallibility for the first time.

The powerful Marian lobby did indeed hope for further definitions, close on the heels of the first. But it seems that the most advanced causes — universal mediation of all grace; coredemption — had been blocked even before the death of Pius XII. Their supporters remained numerous, but it was a long and difficult way from such support to the convocation of a Council specifically for the definition of these dogmas, especially since John XXIII was also showing that he had little taste for new dogmas. Vatican II could provide an important occasion whether

[20] Henri de Lubac, *A Theologian Speaks* (Los Angeles, 1985) 3-4.

for condemnations or for definitions, but, to say the least, the pope's gradual revelations regarding his Council hardly pointed in either of these two directions.

There remained the fourth kind of Council, one hardly seen since the resounding failure of Lateran V (1512-1517), namely, a Council of reform that could avoid Reform with a capital R, the latter now being a synonym for the rupture at the heart of western Christianity. In its own way, Trent too had been a Council of this type, since it had not been satisfied to build a wall against Protestantism but had profoundly improved the lax Catholicism of the Renaissance that had partly been to blame for the division. And contemporary historians prefer "Catholic Reform" to "Counter-Reformation" as a name for the period which Trent inaugurated.

But in the middle of the twentieth century the word "reform" was still suspect in Catholicism, as the French Dominican Yves Congar learned when his book *Vraie et fausse réforme dans l'Église* barely escaped being condemned in 1952 because he had used the word, even with many cautions.[21] But what else could the word *aggiornamento* be, in John XXIII's use of it, but the euphemistic replacement of the proscribed word with a neologism which he did not invent[22] but which he endowed with the value and power of an emblem? In his view, the Church which he was leading had less need to confront the world around it by either affirmation or condemnation than to update itself in relation to its own true self in order better to respond to the new challenges with which the world was confronting it. In short, it had to adapt itself to the world around it, while remaining faithful to its principles, instead of simply presenting the world with its own conviction or with a blunt rejection. Or, again, it had to surrender its age-old intransigence and try to cultivate opportunities for a new integration. How can we not see in this behavior a "new look" reformism?[23]

2. *The Catholic Church at the End of the 1950s*

It was suggested earlier how Pope Roncalli's "absurd itinerary" could have led him to the surprising decision to convoke a Council that must

---

[21] Etienne Fouilloux, "Recherche théologique et magistère romain en 1952. Une 'affaire' parmi d'autres," in *Le Magistère*, 269-86.

[22] The first International Congress of Religious, which was held in Rome, November-December, 1950, had for its purpose "the 'appropriate renewal,' or, in the vernacular, the 'updating' (*aggiornamento*) of the orders and congregations," according to Cardinal Piazza, in *DC*, December 31, 1950, col. 1699.

[23] Giuseppe Alberigo places a great deal of emphasis on this originality in comparison with earlier attempts at reform: see his "L'amore alla chiesa: dalla riforma all'aggiornamento," in *"Con tutte le tue forze." I nodi della fede cristiana oggi. Omaggio a Giuseppe Dossetti* (Genoa, 1993) 169-94.

be understood, in the final analysis, as a reform Council that would enable the Catholic Church to face the challenges around it under the best possible conditions. Much remains to be explained about the way in which this decision took form in the pope's mind, but that is not my purpose here. What especially needs to be explained is whether his perception of the need for *aggiornamento*, updating, that is, his perception of a certain time-lag between the Catholic Church and the modern world, one that was causing a certain uneasiness, corresponded to the facts or only to the elderly pontiff's idea of the facts. For this reason it will be worth our examining, from this point of view, the Catholicism of the preceding century and even of the preceding centuries.[24]

2a. The Roman Model

A first characteristic of the development over the course of several centuries has already been brought out: the progressive centralization of all the forms of Church authority in the hands of the pope, his entourage, and his administration. This included authority in dogma (infallibility), authority in doctrine (ordinary magisterium), and authority in discipline (canonical sanctions). But there was also a correlative centralization in the same hands of all symbolic honors, to the point of engendering a real devotion not only to Rome, which was visited by growing numbers of pilgrimages (think of the throngs in the Holy Year of 1950), but also to the pope himself. Pius IX barely missed being canonized and Pius X was actually canonized under Pius XII, devotion to whom reached summits which later criticisms of the man have caused to be largely forgotten. Here and there Pius XII is also lauded as the last pope to have maintained the integrity of the "Roman system," which at that time was close to its peak of perfection, despite its failures.

We will find this centralization surprising only if we fail to take a look outside the Catholic world. Have not the last three centuries seen the creation and then the consolidation of the modern state and of the executive power within it? In this respect, the case of Rome is not an exception to the rule. The personalization of power has brought many

[24] A summary of the contemporary history of the Church in a few pages is as risky an undertaking as a summary of the era of Vatican II in a few paragraphs. I refer the reader for further information to some recent surveys: *Guerres mondiales et totalitarismes (1954-1968)* = *Histoire du christianisme* 12 (Paris, 1990), Jean-Marie Mayeur, general editor; *Chiesa e papato nel mondo contemporaneo*, ed. Giuseppe Alberigo and Andrea Riccardi (Bari, 1990); *Storia della Chiesa*, vol. 23: *I cattolici nel mondo contemporaneo (1922-1958)*; vol. 24: *Dalle missioni alle Chiese locali (1846-1965)* (Cinisello Balsamo [Milan], 1990-91).

other excesses in the twentieth century, some of them deadly. From
Benedict XV to Pius XII, the popes used this trait of the age in order to
increase to a notable degree the papacy's moral prestige that had been so
often challenged before their time.

The logical corollary of this centripetal movement was the withering
away of the various other centers of responsibility in the Church.
General Councils were not the only ones to feel the loss. Along with
local Councils (unless willed by Rome) the areas of ecclesiastical autonomy tended to disappear. One proof: the liturgical Romanization of the
second half of the nineteenth century, with the resultant elimination of
local rites (the Rite of Lyons, for example). Another proof: the disciplinary alignment carried out by the *Code* of 1917; the only ones not
affected by this were the eastern-rite Catholic Churches, but they too
would be provided — by Rome — with their own disciplinary reform.
Nuncios, whose numbers were increased by the extension of the Vatican
network of international relations, saw their competencies expanded
according to the interests of the Holy See; in many countries, especially
in Latin America, their official diplomatic functions were coupled with
unofficial religious functions that made them the real heads of an episcopate whose members were appointed at their urging and deprived of
cohesiveness among themselves.

The majority of future bishops went to Rome to complete their clerical studies and there developed a strong Roman outlook that was ready
to be activated in all circumstances, especially during their *ad limina*
visits when they besieged the Vatican offices to obtain a good report or
an authorization or an auxiliary. Some of these bishops were very
conscious of the humiliating character of this subordination, as a number
of the preconciliar vota would show, but the passage from dissatisfaction
to an organized effort to shake off this tutelage was made only by a few
isolated bishops and some episcopates of western Europe.

And yet this undeniable centralization, which reached its high point
under Pius XII, was not an end in itself. At least in theory, it was for
the sake of a far more important goal: unity among the troops, unity of
command and operation, were needed in order better to withstand
assaults from outside. This idea bordered on an obsession during the
1950s; any linguistic departure from the Vatican norm, extensively commented on by Pius XII, was interpreted as potential support for the
enemy and for communism in particular. Moreover, sanctions rained
down to close the ranks of the front that had to be united *ad extra*; if this
phenomenon has sometimes been compared, exaggeratedly, to the

"witch hunt" that occurred in the United States in the time of Senator McCarthy, it was, in a minor mode, of a piece with that era.

It was in the sixteenth century that the Roman Church began to think of itself as a fortress of truth, besieged by successive waves of heresy and then of wickedness. But this exhausting war of defense — when it was not a rear-guard action — left its marks on the Church. Each of the threats, which were growing in severity, led to a new hardening, which in turn grew more pronounced. We may, for convenience's sake, distinguish four such threats, which many pamphleteers often showed, in a more or less strained way, as fitting one inside another, like Russian dolls.

The first threat, the Protestant Reformation, introduced the worm of free inquiry into the act of faith, which until then had been regulated by authority alone. To limit the damage done, if not to root out the worm entirely, the intense battle of the Counter-Reformation was needed, and from it issued Catholicism in the full sense which the term came to have.

Next came the Enlightenment and its child, the Revolution (first and foremost, the French Revolution). The Church struggled against it, but always in retreat, by a resolute antiliberalism, which rejected both the laicization of public life and the privatization of religion. This antiliberalism was triumphant under Pius IX, but it lasted, longer than people sometimes think, under Leo XIII.

Then came twentieth-century scientism, which attacked the faith itself in its biblical sources and their dogmatic interpretation. The harsh antimodernism of Pius X was an effort to ward off the threat that was to be found in the very bosom of the ecclesial body. At the end of the 1950s the effects of the crisis at the beginning of the century were still being felt, as can be seen from the sanctions against the thinking of Abbé Duméry in 1958 or against that of the Jesuit Teilhard de Chardin in 1962, that is, under John XXIII himself, a few weeks before the opening of the Council. At the heart of the debate, just as in 1907, was philosophy and Christianity in the case of Duméry, and science and faith in the case of Teilhard.[25]

Finally, there was the Russian Revolution of 1917, the communist regimes to which this led, and the totalitarianisms of the right, which arose by reaction. Pius XI built his reputation mainly on his firm and even-handed condemnation of both in 1937. The fall of the various fascisms, however, rendered obsolete this symmetry that was in any case

[25] For Duméry: Decree of the Holy Office, June 4, 1958, and commentary in *OR* for June 21; see *DC* for July 6, 1958, cols. 841-42. For Teilhard: Monitum of June 30, 1962, and commentary in *OR* for July 1; see *DC*, July 15, 1962, cols. 949-56.

debatable. As a result, the pontificate of Pius XII saw the high point of a Catholic anticommunism that had already begun to harden during the 1930s. In this perspective, people liked to point out that Soviet communism was a scientism, that it presented itself as a (false) response to the (real) defects of liberalism, which in turn was heir to the free inquiry of the Reformers.

But we would be going too far if we were to reduce post-tridentine Catholicism entirely to its defensive side. The Catholicism of this period was not one of simple reaction; it was also in movement, in all the senses of this word. It was not satisfied to condemn out of self-protection, but tirelessly proposed the ideal of an integral Christian countersociety that would allow no aspect of life, personal or collective, to fall outside its scope. For this Catholicism would have denied itself if it were to accept the existence of a profane realm on which it had no purchase. But this model did not therefore remain inviolable, for while its constitutive integralism persisted through the various periods, its degree of intransigence toward these ages varied appreciably. We could say that it was at its most intense until around 1920, except in one area, that of technology, which the Church rather quickly laid hold of, despite its frequent initial reservations, especially in regard to electricity. The example of the railroad, before radio and television, is an obvious one: no great mass pilgrimages, beginning with those to Lourdes, would have been possible without a judicious use of rail and locomotive, those symbols of a modernity which in other areas was rejected with horror.

But in all areas except technology the concern to maintain a distance was clear; the condemnation of liberal society and of its "collectivist" counterpart was accompanied by the often repeated call for a return to "Christendom." A great deal might be said about this call, which had a greater fondness for medieval myths than for their revival. In any case, the Thomism restored by Leo XIII provided this countersociety with an intellectual structure that was imposed, to the exclusion of any other, in the formation of Catholic elites — down to the eve of Vatican II.

From Thomism it derived its social foundations: neither liberalism nor socialism, but an organic vision that subordinated self-interest, whether individual or collective (that of a class, for example), to the common good. Each entity was to find its place therein, from the family at the base to the communities of peoples, and, in between, trades or professions and provinces or countries (rather than nations, "nation" being an inheritance from the Revolution). This plan for a largely utopian society represented what could be called "social Catholicism," provided the term is not applied solely to the "labor question." Its show-case, the "Catholic movement," a collection of associations of every kind that exerted a real power in Germany, Belgium, and Italy, could be taken as an anticipatory image of the dreamed-of society.

This third way, though it did not want to present itself as such, read-ily adapted itself to various political options, among which it refused to choose: monarchy, obviously, but also the republic, and even democ-racy, provided, of course, it were Christian. While partisans of the projected Catholic society were pleased to see it realized in Salazar's Portugal, they were careful not to absolutize a contingent regime, and they loudly condemned any attempt to subordinate it to a particular political line, whether pro-democratic or pro-monarchical. Consider the symmetry in Rome's condemnations of the Sillon in 1910 and Action Française in 1926-27.

In the properly religious sphere, the intransigence was marked by a determination consistently to stress the difference between the Catholic Church and other Christian denominations and other religions. This justified the continuation of interconfessional polemics and of reserva-tions in regard to any "ecumenical" (as it would later be called) rapprochement (failure of the two Anglo-Roman campaigns: for the re-examination of Anglican ordinations in 1896, and the Malines Con-versations thirty years later). But the intransigence could be seen even more in the deepening of attachment to Rome, both in the realm of dogma (the definitions not only of papal infallibility in 1870 but of the Immaculate Conception of Mary in 1854 and of her Assumption in 1950) and in the realm of spirituality or devotion: exaltation of the "three white things" (the Host, the Virgin, the Pope) and of the Sacred Heart and of little Thérèse of Lisieux. This religious pedagogy strength-ened the cohesiveness of the besieged fortress by setting it a little more apart from the rest of believers and by subjecting it to the sarcasm of nonbelievers.

But as a return to the Middle Ages became increasingly implausible, Catholic intransigence had to adapt itself to some developments in the world around it that were judged to be irreversible. As a result, after the First World War there appeared the idea of a "new Christendom" that would be less sacral than traditional "Christendom" to the extent that it distinguished various levels, following Maritain's distinction, which soon became canonical, between the habitual activity of believers "as Christians" in the profane world and their exceptional activity "precisely insofar as they are Christians," when religious values were threatened there. Such was the outlook of the second wave of Catholic Action, which took on a specific character in each life setting, when it asserted, as did the Young Catholic Worker movement (a movement greatly encouraged by Pius XI who committed himself fully to the "new Christendom" project): "We will make our brothers Christians once again, we swear it through Jesus Christ." Or, as another well-known slogan put it, the aim was to inject "the whole of Christianity into the whole of life" by stripping it of its now outdated medieval trappings — except for the scout movement, which won a brief triumph for the ideal of knighthood.

The ultimate goal was still an integral christianization or, better, rechristianization, but the strategy had changed: it was no longer a question simply of protecting what was left of Christendom by presenting it as a hypothetical model for a reluctant world; rather it was necessary to leave the ecclesiastical fortress and propose an open-air Christianity, a "shock" Christianity, as it was sometimes called, and offer it to a world in process of secularization as the only way by which it could achieve a properly human salvation in the face of totalitarian ideologies. In its own way this integral Christianity was all-embracing, if not totalitarian, but it could not be imposed from above by an unlimited power (whence the reservations, beginning with those of Maritain, against the Francoism that was arising in Spain).

To achieve these goals, the Catholic Church adjusted to its age in quite real ways, even though it did not admit this very openly. Its adaptation was especially remarkable in the area of the mass-media; between the two World Wars it realized the use it could make of radio, which Pius XII used very effectively during the Second World War. Then came television, which was to spread images of Rome throughout the world. The scruples of some theologians about the validity of a broadcasted Mass weighed little against the expected spiritual profit.

Another and more disputed adaptation was the division of twentieth-century society, if not into classes, at least into groups that were separated by customs and particular interests and that had to be won over by pastoral methods geared to them. Whence the sometimes quite lively debate between what was called "general" Catholic Action, Italian in origin, which took no account of special conditions of life in its parish-based mass-movements (men, women, young people, girls), and what was called "specialized" Catholic Action, which was broken down into groups (workers, farmers, students, sailors...) and was national in structure. The first of these two sometimes suspected the second of introducing (horrible to say) the class struggle into the bosom of the Church. In both types, a Catholicism focused on preservation gradually gave way to a Catholicism in movement, "proud, pure, joyful, and triumphant," according to another slogan of the time.

This Catholicism would have its successes but also its failures, which led it after 1945 to shelve the plan for a "new Christendom" in favor, on the one hand, of a humanization of the living conditions of the populations in which it was present, and, on the other, of a mission, whether of layper-sons or of priests, to the working classes that had drifted away, a mission that brought with it all sorts of problems. Initial enthusiasm would give way to realism as well as to confrontations between the different tactics used by groups, themselves different, within the Catholic movement: social Catholicism, Catholic Action, missionary trend.

This diversification should not obscure the common aim: in one or other way to win back the ground that had been lost among both the elites and the people. But the variety of choices did compromise the ini-tial intransigence; and it was excessive conformity to the world, or what was taken to be such, that led Rome first to be disturbed and then to order sanctions in the affair of the worker-priests in 1954 and then in 1959 — at the beginning of the pontificate of John XXIII.[26]

Must it therefore be claimed that the hardly deniable changes in the intransigent attitude were imposed from the periphery or even from out-side on a Roman center that was incapable of reforming itself? Nothing could be more inaccurate. In opposition to all the prejudices about Roman immobilism, the picture must be completed by including the by no means negligible attempts at reform that came from Rome during the half-century before Vatican II.

In this respect, the traditional images are often deceptive. Pius X was indeed the untiring slayer of modernism, the "crossroad of all heresies," as he called it, but he was also the architect of an important reform of the Curia that notably improved its functioning (1908). He also began the reform of canon law that would be completed under his successor in 1917. Finally, he was the pope of frequent Communion, even of children (1910). Unlike the first two actions mentioned, this last, which met with strong reservations here and there, touched the entire Christian people, encouraging them to break out of an age-old rigorism that was now Jansenist only in the sense that this term was abusively used to describe

---

[26] Letter of Cardinal Pizzardo, Prefect of the Holy Office, to Cardinal Feltin, Arch-bishop of Paris, July 3, 1959, published in *Le Monde* for September 15 and in *DC* for October 4, 1959, cols. 1222-26.

it. The restoration of frequent Communion was an important element in the improvement of eucharistic practice and not simply of eucharistic piety. It gave encouragement to a fruitful liturgical movement that came into being in Belgium on the eve of the war.

The next pope, Benedict XV, who is often insufficiently appreciated because he was absorbed mainly by the Great War and its consequences, nonetheless left his mark in at least two areas of religion. First, the area of unionism, for he extended a hand to a Christian East that was in total disarray after its Czarist and Ottoman protectors had been swept away in the fire of war and revolution. In 1917 — and the timing was not accidental — the Congregation for the Oriental Church and the Pontifical Oriental Institute were established in Rome. The second and more important area was the foreign missions: foreseeing the inevitable emancipation of the colonized peoples, Rome began to pay more attention to the indigenous cultures as stepping-stones to Christianity and to prepare a sound native clergy. The impetus begun by *Maximum illud* in 1919 lasted down to *Fidei donum* in 1957.

Pius XI, for his part, as has already been repeatedly noted, was the "pope of Catholic Action" before becoming the pope of the struggles against Stalin's and Hitler's totalitarianisms. But to this pope, who was diplomat as need required, we also owe the extension of the field of Vatican action in international relations through his signing of numerous concordats, though these differed in their effectiveness. A genuine scholar himself, he tried to improve the system of ecclesiastical formation in the context of an unqualified respect for St. Thomas Aquinas (Constitution *Deus scientiarum Dominus*, 1931).

Pius XII: a reforming pope? Impossible! Yet we need only clear our minds of clichés to be persuaded that he was indeed a reformer, at least during the first period of his pontificate, a period that ended around 1950, for after that date circumstances strengthened the naturally defensive tendency of old age. In 1943, the encyclical on biblical studies, *Divino afflante Spiritu*, was unanimously regarded as freeing scholars from the leaden cloak that had weighed on biblical study since the modernist crisis. Less open, because it attacked the two fronts of spiritualism and juridical formalism, the encyclical *Mystici Corporis Christi*, issued in that same year, replaced a purely conceptual ecclesiology with an organic one, even while asserting that the Roman Church is coextensive with the Church of Jesus Christ.

Better known are his liturgical reforms; these were begun in 1947-48 and reached their full form some time later. The masterpiece of these reforms was the restoration of the feast of Easter to its ancient splendor by assigning the central role once again to the Vigil, the nocturnal service celebrated between Holy Saturday and Easter Sunday.

The already evident decline in priestly and religious vocations prompted a comprehensive reflection on the states of life. On the one hand, this led to the creation in 1947 of secular institutes, that is, institutes that did not oblige their members to make a rigid or definitive choice between the lay state and the religious life. On the other hand, at the World Congresses for the Lay Apostolate that were convened in Rome in 1951 and 1957, it promoted dialogue between the different branches of the laity. Of course, this initiative fits well with centralization through the establishment of a permanent Roman committee (COPECIAL), but it also succeeded in making the laity an agent and partner in dialogue at the heart of the Church. It was in order to promote this role of the laity that at the second of these Congresses Pius XII launched a trial balloon that would reappear later in the vota for Vatican II: the restoration of the permanent diaconate within Catholicism.[27] If we add to all these actions the beginning of an internationalization of the Curia that was decided on in connection with the creation of cardinals, to a greater extent in 1946 than in 1953, the balance sheet was by no means negligible.

Essentially, however, the "Roman system" derived vitality from these adaptations but was not radically altered by them. Proof of this was the rapid Romanization of the non-Romans who became part of the Curia. The system, which was not without its good points, had enough internal resources to evolve slowly and smoothly, in its own way and by its own rhythm. On the whole, despite changes aimed at improving its effficiency, changes it would be idle to deny, Roman Catholicism under Pius XII resembled what it had been under Pius IX more than what it would be under Paul VI. By then, the Second Vatican Council had occurred.

2b. A Certain Discontent

I have thus far chosen to tell the recent history of Catholicism in terms of its source of cohesion, Rome. I might just as well have reconstructed it as a series of recurrent crises due to tension between this principle of

---

[27] Pius XII, Allocution at the audience of October 5, 1957: "The duties connected with Minor Orders have long been performed by laymen, and We know that thought is being given at present to the introduction of a diaconate conceived as an ecclesiastical office independent of the priesthood. Today, at least, the idea is not yet ready for implementation" (*TPS* 4 [1957-58] 122).

cohesion and the manifold efforts to transform it or even to subvert it.
Examples are plentiful, from the Lamennais crisis to that of the worker-
priests, with, in between, the modernist crisis and the crisis caused by
the Action Française movement. Although the angles of attack differed
according to period and country, all of these crises raised one and the
same question: Instead of planning to build a Christian city that was
both anachronistic and utopian, would it not be better to go out, once
and for all, to the "barbarians" of the modern world by undertaking an
evangelization that is really adapted to them?

Many of these were attempts, then, to do more than to soften the
intransigence; they struck at the postulate of integralism when, for
example, they explored paths that might lead to freedom of religion.
In these efforts the issue was one of adaptating Catholic ways of thought
and action to the modern world (though this language became unusable
after 1907) or, as people would say later on, to modernity. All these
attempts were more or less tactfully dismissed, of course; in the
nineteenth century alone, Lamennais, Möhler, and Newman could all tell
stories of this kind. But these incidents also created not only a genealogy
but a kind of "antiroman complex," as one of its opponents, the Swiss
German theologian Urs von Balthasar, has christened it.[28] While it did
not foster any real break from Rome after the Old Catholic schism that
followed on the definition of papal infallibility, this "complex" nonetheless did survive repeated blows, especially when these were spaced out
as those in high places substituted an offensive strategy for a purely
defensive one. As a result, the real birth of the "antiroman complex" can
be dated to the 1930s when the high-point of antimodernist reaction was
receding into the past.

The critical side of the complex is obviously the one that was most
visible. Prudently, because Rome was watching, a good many thinkers
expressed regrets that the methods of a bygone age were being used to
reduce protesters to silence: a plague of anonymous denunciations;
secret investigations in which the accused parties had no role; the obso-
lescence of the procedure used for the Index; appeals to authority to get
a sentence accepted without any real explanation; demands for quasi-
military obedience. The protests were directed chiefly at the methods
used by the Supreme Sacred Congregation of the Holy Office, the power
of which increased less quickly in the twentieth century than did the
dark legend that grew up around it.

[28] *Die antirömische Effekt* (Freiburg, 1974). English trans.: *The Office of Peter and
the Structure of the Church* (San Francisco, 1986).

More serious were doubts voiced about the intellectual tool imposed by Rome on Catholic philosophers and theologians: a Thomism desiccated by having been too often compressed into succinct theses; a deductive Thomism that ground up contemporary realities according to the rhythm of its impeccable conceptualizations. Had it not thereby lost sight of what is unique, that is, essential? And when it succumbed to the temptation of rationalism and sought God at the end of syllogisms, was it really adapted to a world, our world, in which personal and collective experience and the history of humanity and human beings play an ever greater role? "Subjectivism! Historicism! Relativism!" some disciples of the Angelic Doctor replied, although they too disagreed on the genesis of his work and, even more, on its posterity. Was there no access to the Christian faith except by way of St. Thomas and his school?

This appetite for rationality, which did not hesitate to accuse sceptics of anti-intellectualism, was accompanied, in an oddly logical way (since it gladly skipped over the stage of critical inquiry), by a great credulity when it came to the most varied, and even the least solidly grounded, devotions: dubious Marian apparitions, stigmatizations not officially acknowledged, sulphurous types of sanctity. The result was a widespread mysticism, but a mysticism that obscured to some extent what is specific in Christian faith, namely, Jesus Christ, true man and true God, dead and risen. The chief object of criticism was the diversification and proliferation of Mariology or the cult of Mary, for these tended to turn Catholicism into a "Mariano-Christianity," as French Dominican Yves Congar wittily put it, that is, into an appreciably different religion.[29]

Finally, reservations were repeatedly expressed about the way in which Roman Catholicism had closed in on itself, bypassing the main intellectual and social currents of the age without really understanding them or even being much interested in them. This was the attitude toward separated Christians, whom Rome hoped to win over through unionism in the case of the Easterners or through conversion pure and simple in the case of the Anglo-Protestants. The emerging ecumenical movement was deliberately ignored. While traditional Catholic anti-judaism gave signs of weakening and some feelers were put out toward Islam, these all remained embryonic velleities. As for the new missionary strategy, which won initial successes in China, it quite often ran up against the assimilative tendencies of the Congregation of Propaganda and the religious organizations that specialized in this work.

[29] Letter to Maurice Villain, a Marist, November 23, 1950.

As far as contemporary agnosticism or atheism was concerned, the lag was considerable. On the eve of Vatican II, a number of Roman documents were arguing that Kant remained the great adversary, the one held responsible for modern individualism. While "atheistic communism" in its Soviet version was known and combatted, little attention was paid to Hegel and Marx, or Freud for that matter, to say nothing of Nietzsche. While these "masters of suspicion" were influencing an ever greater number of young people in the universities, the "Roman system" continued to cross swords with Kant, Comte, or Renan. As a result, ever more numerous voices were raised, though quickly stifled, calling for a genuine reflection on these new challenges. Should we build our own world or rather participate as best we can in the world that exists? That was the real question.

But these criticisms of a triumphant Romanism, though they were both scattered and in a minority, were not purely negative. On the contrary, they suggested, cautiously in view of the way they had to operate, that there was another way to present Catholicism to the people of the twentieth century. This alternative program, though not at all systematic, did include some fundamental options that then led to a series of concrete choices.

All the minds that were closely or distantly touched by the "antiroman complex" were led by it to make use of an inductive approach that, instead of measuring reality by the yardstick of intangible truths, started from human life and experience, and even from human history, and attempted to understand these in relation to God. Whatever the depth and quality of their attempts, this preliminary effort to understand at least avoided the tragic mistakes of the past, because it kept its practitioners from excessively caricaturing their adversaries in order the more easily to slay them.

On a parallel track, an effort was made to focus on Christology in order to explain the essence of the Christian faith while clearing away the accidental undergrowth that had been proliferating around it for at least three centuries and was becoming more and more invasive. If the mystery of God become man and dying and rising for the salvation of the human race is indeed the heart of the Christian message, of its kerygma, then an appropriate intellectual approach to it ought to be able to separate it out from its devotional straitjacket and make it widely known, especially through catechesis. This was the perspective adopted by a group of German theologians from which the Jesuit, Karl Rahner, emerged, and which had its imitators on the other side of the Rhine, as can be seen in the work of French Dominican Pierre-André Liégé.

This concentration on Christology was of great ecumenical value since it echoed in Catholicism the approach of the greatest Protestant thinker of the period, Karl Barth of Basel; and it also had consequences in the realm of concrete practices of piety. A kerygmatic theology meant a purified spirituality or even, according to some of its most active supporters, a spirituality that had been "purged," with all that this term conveyed right after the Second World War. It meant a shelving of secondary devotions for the sake of the only adoration in spirit and in truth that counts: adoration of the trinitarian mystery, although, despite the links established with Russian émigré thinkers, even here the Holy Spirit was still given a subordinate place. In any case, ecumenical contacts played a large part in the clarification of the position I am trying to describe. The ecumenical influence could be seen concretely in quiet reservations toward the dogma of the Assumption of the Virgin (1950), which was regarded as inopportune and even as insufficiently founded in the Bible.

In fact, this concern for a return to essentials in the hope of being better understood by outsiders, even if not more acceptable to them, entered the twentieth century through the rise, toward the end of the 1920s, of nebulous intellectual and pastoral "movements" (as they were somewhat improperly called) in the setting provided by the birth and expansion of Catholic Action movements of the second type. Whatever the analogical value of the term, which became current after 1945, all these "movements" were inspired by the same conviction: In order to do away with "baroque" theology and the "Sulpician" piety begotten of it, it was necessary to go back beyond the superfluous elaborations of the Counter-Reformation and the Counter-Revolution to the very sources of Christianity. These could and should directly feed the faith and piety of the faithful through a scrupulous adherence to the intentions of the Founder and his first disciples.

Return to the sources: this approach played a determining role in the Catholic system, since this depends to a very large degree on tradition. If one is to be able to challenge what is being done at the moment without snapping the thread of continuity through the centuries, one must appeal from a recent tradition to one that is earlier and closer to the origins. But did either the defenders or the censors of this approach really grasp the ambiguity of this recourse to antiquity? Both saw it as an innovation, whereas by definition it focused on a distant past, while wagering that this past was closer to one's contemporaries than were the constructions of the seventeenth or nineteenth centuries. But suppose that this hitch-up did not occur? Should it be a surprise to find some "reformers" among those who were to be disappointed by *aggiornamento*?

Clearly, we have still not reached the eve of the Council. Since the end of the nineteenth century there had developed in varying forms, in France, Belgium, and Germany, a powerful movement of return to the Bible, which meant both the Old and the New Testaments; the movement had arisen despite earlier warnings that had been given teeth by the condemnation of modernism. This biblical movement had three elements. It was scholarly: it used all the resources of archeology and philology the better to understand the texts themselves in their historical, intellectual, and spiritual context. It was pastoral: it put this exegesis, which was more rigorous than some of the older imaginative interpretations, at the service of better editions of the Bible that would take the place of pious literature in the meditation of the faithful (the Bonn and Jerusalem Bibles, for example). It was theological: it was to help construct a body of thought that would bypass the hitherto obligatory tool, the medieval Scholasticism that had been impoverished by the manuals. It must be acknowledged, however, that on the eve of Vatican II biblical theology was still in its infancy. Less important but no less scholarly and perhaps more effective in the area of theology, was a patristic movement in England, France, and Germany. This provided educated Catholics with accessible editions of and commentaries on the Fathers of the western and eastern Churches, the first authoritative interpreters of the Christian message.

The period just before the First World War saw the birth, in Belgium, of a liturgical movement. Originating with the Benedictines, it experienced considerable growth first in Germany and then in France, before moving more or less easily into other areas of the Catholic world. Like its biblical counterpart, with which it cultivated close relations, this movement aimed at transcending what it called the rubricism of the preceding century with its fussiness and rigidity and its demand for uniformity. This movement, too, turned back to the early Church with a view to restoring venerable ways and putting an end to the countless later additions, a work of learned dust-removal that occupied many monasteries. The movement also attempted to derive from all this work a theology at prayer; Louis Bouyer's *The Paschal Mystery* (1945) was one of the finest products of this endeavor. Finally, this movement made an effort to change passive believers into active participants, both by emphasizing the principal rites at the expense of the others and by explaining them, and even celebrating them, in the language of the people.

At the conjuncture of these several returns to the sources and profiting by modern pedagogical research, the catechetical movement worked to change catechesis into a real initiation into the faith, an initiation that focused on essentials and used a progressive method in accordance with successive age groups.[30]

A final movement calls for special mention, because it has to do with Catholicism not so much in itself as in its relations with other confessions, religions, and ideologies. Like the other Christian confessions, although with greater difficulty, the Catholic Church of the twentieth century, through the impetus given by the Portals, the Beauduins, the Congars, and even the Couturiers and Metzgers, saw the rise within it of an ecumenical movement that aimed at a reconciliation and, if possible, a union of Christians who had been separated since the eleventh or the sixteenth century.[31] In an even more delicate area, some bold spirits extended a hand to their brothers in the other two branches descended from Abraham: Judaism and Islam. Were these people really aware of the significance of one of the major events of the twentieth century, the Muslim, Arab revival? In addition, the great religions of Asia exerted a great fascination on men like Vincent Lebbe and Jules Monchanin, who went off to bury themselves in China and India respectively.

Outside the area of the religions, flimsy foot-bridges were thrown out in all directions: to Freemasonry and even to Communism. Was not the French worker-priest experiment in many respects an attempt to make room for the Church in the Marxist world of the workers through the complete immersion therein of a handful of men whose environment still regarded them as personifications of the Church, namely, her priests?[32] At the same time, some theologians were endeavoring, with varying success and degrees of commitment, to make a place in Catholic teaching for the infinite variety of "earthly realities."

At the moment when John XXIII announced the Council, what influence was really exerted by this two-fold convergent effort to rejuvenate Catholicism through a return to its sources and to open it to the outside

---

[30] Some handy syntheses, though they deal primarily with the French scene: Gilbert Adler and Gérard Vogeleisen, *Un siècle de catéchèse en France, 1893-1980* (Paris, 1981); Mary Coke, *Le mouvement catéchétique de Jules Ferry à Vatican II* (Paris, 1988).

[31] See Fouilloux, *Les catholiques et l'unité chrétienne* (note 6, above).

[32] On this subject, which is especially well documented, see Émile Poulat, *Naissance des prêtres-ouvriers* (Tournai-Paris, 1965); François Leprieur, *Quand Rome condamne. Dominicains et prêtres-ouvriers* (Paris, 1989); Oscar L. Cole-Arnal, *Prêtres en bleu de chauffe. Histoire des prêtres-ouvriers (1943-1954)* (Paris, 1992).

world? It is not easy to decide with even a minimum of certainty, since
the subsequent endorsement of them by Vatican II has understandably
caused their importance to be magnified in retrospect. Quantitatively, the
movements did not amount to much when compared to the big Roman
battalions. Qualitatively, however, things were somewhat different.
Consider: A growing number of middle-class people in the cities of
northwest Europe were experiencing, in varying degrees, a certain discontent with Rome's chilling certainties and were calling for an expression of the faith more adapted to their intellectual or professional standing. In addition, a growing number of militants in the Catholic Action
movement among the people, both workers and countryfolk, were daily
learning through contact with their fellow workers how difficult it was to
make credible a Church whose language, ceremonies, organization, and
positions seemed to be the product of another age. Convert writers and
university laypeople were calling for an apologetics open to the real
world; teenagers in the movements and young couples were calling for
a conjugal spirituality marked less by prohibitions than by taking human
love seriously.

These various groups found no little support from the clerical chaplains whose duty it was to bear them company on their journeys. These
chaplains themselves were among the intellectual leaders of the "antiroman complex," some of them being theologians of renown who often
sacrificed their scholarly research to attend countless meetings, draw up
working plans, and write articles of sound popularization for those who
were becoming their flock. Thus between 1942 and 1954 French
Dominican Marie-Dominique Chenu devoted himself completely to the
Christians of the 13th District in Paris, to teams of teachers, groups in
the "little clubs," priests and militant workers; he gave himself to them
with exemplary constancy, because he saw in them so many ways of
introducing the gospel into his own age (to paraphrase the title of the
volume containing some of these scattered contributions[33]).

Further study of local differences as reflected in the episcopal answers
to the antepreparatory consultation would make it possible to determine
more closely the influence of the various factors I have mentioned. But
it is already possible to say that this informal, respectful challenge from
within was putting pressure on Rome, which, rightly or wrongly, saw it
as containing in germ a possible different line for Catholicism to follow
in the second half of the twentieth century: a Catholicism more sober in

[33] *La Parole de Dieu* II. *L'Évangile dans le temps* (Paris, 1964). See *L'hommage
différé au Père Chenu* (Paris, 1990).

its faith and more flexible and dynamic in dealing with the outside world. The various milieus which I have mentioned were important and would become increasingly important because of their knowledge or their responsibilities; it was not a good policy for Rome to cut itself off from them. As for the theologians who were working for these groups, their books were far more widely known than the products of their Roman confreres, which were often privately published. There was evidently a demand for theology that could be read by the non-specialist — thus the acute problem when works were translated from German or French into Italian or Spanish.

While it was not possible to speak of an organized opposition, much less of a plot, a dissatisfaction could be seen in Northern European Catholicism beginning in the 1930s. Perceptible on the spot, it was also known to Rome, which was uncertain whether to use the carrot or the stick. On the one hand, the recurrent and prevailing fear of a resurgence of modernism made indulgence unattractive; on the other, a vague perception in some curial circles of the risk of a splendid but barren isolation made compromise more appealing. The compromise took the form first of a frowning examination of these "novelties" in a Roman court, then of a careful sorting out of those that seemed acceptable and those that were not. The result was the reforms mentioned earlier. This procedure was far from satisfying those to whom it was applied, because it consistently treated the "innovators," that is, those who took the risk of not sticking to the manuals and waiting for interventions of the magisterium, as suspects, and this was a position from which they could not easily extricate themselves, since even after a negative finding the file containing the accusation remained.

Roman uneasiness became less vague and more explicit as the pontificate of Pius XII continued. During his first years, until about 1946-48, advances were in balance with setbacks; thus the warning against the so-called "new theology" in 1946 and a letter to Cardinal Suhard in 1948 allowing a free interpretation of the Pentateuch framed the ambiguous liturgical encyclical *Mediator Dei* (1947). Beginning in 1950, the ambivalence was no longer to be found; most Roman interventions were of the same kind, undeniably restrictive. To mention only the two episodes that elicited the strongest reactions both in the Church and outside it, in 1950 the great doctrinal encyclical *Humani generis* was issued, right after the Jesuit school at Fourvière, in Lyons, had been brought to heel; in 1954 came the halting of the worker-priest experiment, preceded by stern measures against the Dominican theologians who supposedly supported it.

The multiplication of sanctions, whether light or more serious, only accentuated the same division into two camps: as seen from Rome, it was always the same national Churches and the same people within them that were causing problems; as seen from France or Germany, it was always the same local informers and the same Roman censors who were blocking the way, especially since the multiplication of vacancies in the Roman Curia meant that officials often exercised several functions there. As a result, what is sometimes called, somewhat fuzzily, the "marching wing" in Catholicism got the impression that it was being blocked or even smothered; this was clear from numerous opinion polls.[34]

Nor did this group expect anything from the new pope, John XXIII. From what they knew of him as nuncio in Paris, they regarded him as at best a happy dilettante, at worst a clever conservative. It took the unshakeable optimism of Belgian Benedictine Lambert Beaudiun, who had known Roncalli not long before, to maintain that despite appearances this articulate and urbane diplomat had indeed understood something of the apostolic stirrings around him and was ready to give it a chance by reviving an institution everyone thought moribund: a general Council. If the convocation of what would become Vatican II had any logical justification, apart from the inspiration of the Spirit, which by definition eludes the historian's grasp, then it could only be the one just described.

But we have to admit that this explanation is not entirely clear. It presupposes that the new pontiff realized that an *aggiornamento* in relation to the world was needed and at the same time that it had been made possible by the existence of this minority and multiform current that had paid the price, especially under Pius X and Pius XII, for its reservations in regard to the intransigent line followed by the Vatican. But in a world of rapid decolonization, we may not limit ourselves to this Eurocentric problematic. How are we to anticipate the influence of young nations and young Churches, proud of their recent independence, on the excitement that the preparation for the Council would nourish? There was no doubt about the Romanization of these young Churches; on the other hand, they also depended largely on priests and religious who were receptive to at least some elements of the "antiroman complex."

Where, moreover, were the "movements" that could provide support for the *aggiornamento*? It has been shown that up to the very eve of the Council nothing was settled for them. The ones that had suffered least from the harsh measures of the Pacelli era and were in the best position

---

[34] For example, "Voeux pour un concile," *Études* (Paris), December, 1961.

as the 1960s began were the liturgical movement and the ecumenical movement. Despite the setback represented by Pius XII's address to the participants in the Assisi Congress in 1956 regarding both use of the vernacular and concelebration, the liturgical movement benefited extensively from earlier reforms and from the fact that it had now become world-wide, extending far beyond its places of origin. As for the ecumenical movement, it enjoyed unofficial recognition through the Catholic Conference for Ecumenical Affairs, a modest organization that since 1952 had brought experts together from around the world, each year in a different venue, and served as mediator with the other Churches and the World Council to which those Churches belonged. While the study of the Fathers of the Church and the diffusion of their works were well established, the biblical movement could not say as much, faced as it was by a new series of attacks of a fundamentalist kind in which some professors at the Lateran had become specialists. The critics admittedly seemed more and more isolated among specialists, while the Bible was becoming the bedside book of educated believers, but the raising of their academy to the rank of a pontifical university in 1959 showed that they remained influential.[35]

Was the attack of these professors on the Jesuit-run Biblical Institute a rear-guard action, or was it the harbinger of a general settling of accounts with the "innovations" of the last half-century? Shrewd indeed was anyone who could give the answer, even in 1962. But there would not have been a Council unless John XXIII himself had also sensed, in his own way, a call for change that had already been audible for years in various parts of the Catholic world.

III. ROMAN CONSULTATIONS

But it is only a retrospective vision of events that can see the future Council as facing a dilemma right from the earliest preparations for it. These began slowly, for the antepreparatory commission appointed on May 17, 1959, had first to consolidate its position, which initially was quite unsettled. It soon acquired a minimum of technical and intellectual infrastructures: a place to meet, volunteer clerics to man the secretariat, and a library of materials about the Councils.[36]

---

[35] Etienne Fouilloux, "'Mouvements' théologico-spirituels et concile (1959-1962)," *Veille*, 185-99.

[36] On June 30 Tardini announced that the secretariat of the commission would be quartered at Via Serristori 10 (*AS* App. I, p. 15).

It is to be noted, however, that the commission did not meet very often: two sessions to launch the work, on May 26 and June 30, 1959, and one on April 8, 1960, to review what had been done; to which must be added two limited meetings, on July 3 and 17, 1959, with the authorities of the Roman universities and schools of theology. Five meetings in all and for everything: not very much. On each occasion, the scenario was the same: on the one hand, Tardini, the president, presumably representing the pope, provided those present with the first news of important information about the direction to be taken by the future Council; on the other hand, he asked for their reaction to documents which he presented to them but which had been composed by others.[37]

Under the first heading of information: Latin would be the language of an assembly that was not to be a simple continuation of the Council of 1870 (May 26); it would be a Catholic Council and not a Council of union — this from John XXIII himself (30 June); it was to be more a pastoral than a dogmatic Council (meeting of July 3 with the deans of the schools of theology). On all these points, which were important for various reasons, the members of the commission and the individuals it consulted were presented with faits accomplis and were not given a real opportunity to raise objections.

Was the situation any different when it came to the tasks of the commission? On the surface, yes, but what of the reality? Before its final meeting on April 8, 1960, the commission had in fact been asked for its views on only one of the points on its original list of responsibilities, namely, the consultation of the bishops and the Catholic universities. A draft of a letter to the bishops, accompanied by a questionnaire intended to guide their responses, was submitted to the commission by its president on May 26, 1959. The first of the two documents was neutral enough, but the second was not, as both its structure and its content prove. Its five headings paid hardly any heed to the problems really facing the Catholic Church at the middle of the twentieth century and, when they did point to such problems, they did so in a rather restrictive way. Thus the first heading *De veritate sancte custodienda* ("On religiously guarding the truth") contained a list of current errors, doctrinal and moral, that the Council might discuss. The fifth heading, *De Ecclesiae unitate* ("The unity of the Church") combined missionary work and work for the "return of the dissident brothers and sisters to the Roman Church," thus using the curious terminology that was beginning to date.[38]

[37] Commission report, in Italian, in *AS* App. I, pp. 7-24.
[38] *AS* App I, pp. 11-14 ("reditum fratrum dissidentium ad Ecclesiam Romanam," p. 14).

These measures seem to have elicited hardly any objections. Msgr. Staffa, of the Congregation for Seminaries and Universities, not only approved the texts that were presented but asked that the Council concentrate chiefly on defense of the truth. In both spirit and letter he thereby confirmed the response of his patron, Cardinal Pizzardo, to the announcement of the Council.[39] In fact, the discussion focused on three other points. The question whether the new Council would be a continuation of the previous one, on which there was disagreement between Msgr. Palazzini of the Council for Public Affairs (in favor) and Father Coussa of the Oriental Churches (against), seems to have been decided in the negative by Tardini. On the other hand, Tardini agreed to send the pope the request of Paul Philippe, representative of the Holy Office, that the secrecy binding the Holy Office be lifted to allow use of conciliar materials developed earlier (meaning: under Pius XII) by the supreme congregation. Finally, Tardini announced that the offices of the Curia were immediately to set to work composing "proposals" (*proposte*), but only within the area of the competence of each, a limitation deplored by Msgr. Sigismondi of Propaganda. A letter to this effect was sent by the commission on May 29: the recipients were first to emend documents submitted to them; further down the road, they were to form study groups dealing with subjects for the future Council.[40]

But at the solemn meeting of the full commission in the presence of the pope (June 30, 1959) the procedure for consulting the bishops was completely changed. There would be no questionnaire, but only a simple letter, couched in rather general terms and dated June 18 (therefore already being sent). This was John XXIII's wish.[41] The letter had undergone a noteworthy development when compared to the draft on which the members of the commission had been asked to comment. Far from presupposing the multitude of restrictive answers that the questionnaire would have elicited, the letter left the bishops relatively free to send to Rome the problems they thought could be usefully discussed at the Council. The content of the letter is well-known today:

> Your Excellency,
> It is a great pleasure for me to inform Your Excellency that on the feast of Pentecost, May 17, 1959, John XXIII, the happily reigning Supreme Pontiff, established an antepreparatory commission for the

[39] Letter of February 15, 1959 (*AS* App. I, pp. 25-28).
[40] *ADA* III, p. x.
[41] As is proved by Tardini's note, published by Giuseppe Alberigo, "Passaggi cruciali della fase antepreparatoria (1959-1960), in *Verso il concilio*, p. 22-23.

future ecumenical Council; the undersigned has the honor of presiding
over this commission.

The Venerable Pontiff wants especially to know the opinions or views
and to obtain the suggestions and wishes of their excellencies the
bishops and prelates who are summoned by law (Canon 223) to take
part in the ecumenical Council. For His Holiness regards as highly
important the views, suggestions, and wishes of those who will be the
fathers of the coming Council. These will be most useful in preparing
the topics to be discussed at the Council.

I urge Your Excellency, therefore, kindly to communicate to this
pontifical commission the critiques, suggestions, and wishes which
your pastoral concern and your zeal for souls urges you to offer in
connection with matters and subjects of possible discussion at the
coming Council, and to do so with complete freedom and honesty.

The subjects for the Council can be points of doctrine, the discipline of
the clergy and Christian people, the manifold activities of today's
Church, matters of greater importance with which the Church must
deal nowadays, or, finally, anything else that Your Excellency thinks it
good to discuss and clarify.

In tackling this task Your Excellency may make discreet use of the
advice of expert and prudent churchmen.

This venerable pontifical commission will give full and careful consideration to whatever Your Excellency thinks will be to the advantage of
the Church and of souls.

All answers should be given in Latin. Your Excellency is asked to forward them as soon as possible to this pontifical commission (Vatican
City), but, if at all possible, not later than September 1 of this year.
Meanwhile I offer Your Excellency my heartfelt good wishes and pray
every favor for you from the Lord.

Your Excellency's servant,
Domenico Cardinal Tardini[42]

When we realize that a good many of the answers followed the
suggested list of topics (doctrine, clergy, Christian people, current problems), we can imagine what they would have been to a questionnaire
that was far more directive and slanted! But despite the omission of the
questionnaire the typology which it had contained would not be completely abandoned.

Faced with a fait accompli, the members of the commission could
only approve a change of direction that was obviously inspired from
higher up and in which they played no part. Several of them had already
composed remarks in response to the initial draft; Dante had been dissuaded from doing so by a telephone call from Felici. Only Sigismondi
had sketched a gallant last stand.

---

[42] *ADA* II/1, pp. x-xi.

The discussion turned to other matters.[43] Tardini renewed his call to the Roman congregations; he was immediately followed by Palazzini who said that his, the Congregation of the Council, had already submitted propositions. (I shall return to the question of the role of the Curial offices in this antepreparatory phase.) Paul Philippe, for his part, thanked the pope for having authorized the consultation of the Pacellian documents at the Holy Office, an authorization which must therefore have come between May 26 and June 30, although we know nothing more about it. The only debate of any importance was on the use of Latin in the replies of the consulted bishops. Understandably, Coussa (Oriental Churches) and Sigismondi (Propaganda) suggested that the Council fathers they dealt with be able to reply in French or even in English. Tardini noted that this had been considered, but the idea had not been accepted. The idea was met, moreover, on June 30 by a violent barrage in favor of Latin from Dante (Rites), Philippe (Holy Office), Zerba (Sacraments), and, of course, from Staffa (Seminaries and Universities), who stressed the close connection between the abandonment of Latin and the abandonment of doctrines, which he deplored.

Under these conditions, what value, other than to soothe feelings, was to be found in Tardini's expression of gratitude to the pope "for having chosen to entrust the important duty of concrete preparation for the Council to the representatives of the Sacred Congregations of the Roman Curia, who in virtue of their functions are in a position to have specialized knowledge of present needs, to assess accurately the obstacles to be overcome, and to make timely suggestions"?[44] Of course, the antepreparatory commission was made up entirely of acknowledged curialists; moreover, as far as we can judge from the published records of their meetings, they took rather restrictive positions. But they submitted without much complaint to the will of the president, which directly mirrored the will of the pope on essential points. If in fact the curial offices were linked from the outset to the preparation for the Council, their influence on the launching of the enterprise, on the whole, seems to have been limited. So true is this that we can even ask whether the antepreparatory commission, except for its president and secretariat, played any really effective part.

Restricted meetings on July 3 and 17 with those in charge of institutions of higher education only confirm this impression, although the limiting of the invitation to Romans was not a guileless action. What was

[43] Meeting of June 30 (*AS* App. I, p. 16).
[44] Ibid., p. 14.

asked of them was neither "proposals" (as with the curial offices) nor
"suggestions and wishes" (as with the bishops), but "a series of studies,
not lengthy but clear and precise: not on all matters or on all topics, but
on the most important and contemporary ones."[45] In the absence (confirmed by Tardini on July 3) of more precise information on the program
of the future Council, Msgr. Piolanti of the Lateran University suggested
a dogmatic constitution on the magisterium; Fathers Gillon (Angelicum)
and Mayer (San Anselmo) proposed a document on the Church that
would recapitulate all the work done since the previous Council, beginning with the encyclical *Mystici Corporis Christi*. It is impossible not to
see some discrepancy between these proposals, especially the first, and
the information which Tardini had just given the group on the nature of
the future Council: "more practical than dogmatic in character; more
pastoral than ideological; it will provide norms rather than definitions."[46]

The discrepancy became even clearer on July 17: after Tardini had
just announced, without commentary, that the Council would be called
Vatican II, Father Di Fonzo (St. Bonaventure) asked that the unfinished
labors of Vatican I be taken into account; Fathers Roschini (Marianum)
and Philippe de la Trinité (Discalced Carmelites) called for severity
against the errors of the age: it was the *French* religious who specified
"certain French ideologies which it would be opportune to attack with
great clarity."[47]

The documentation already available thus casts a rather harsh light on
Roman disagreements regarding the future Council from the very first
days of its preparation. The preparation was seemingly under the control
of the Curia; the antepreparatory commission had been chosen from its
members; the offices were approached before the bishops were,
and those in charge of the Roman universities and colleges before their
counterparts in the rest of the Catholic world (the letter asking for the
assistance of the latter was dated July 18, the day after the second
Roman meeting[48]).

But was not this entire scenario more or less an illusion? The commission was informed by its president of the most important decisions

[45] *AS* App. I, p. 18.
[46] Ibid.
[47] *AS* App. I, p. 20.
[48] "The subject matter in which you may interest yourselves can be of different kinds:
dogmatic first of all, biblical, liturgical, philosophical, moral and juridical, pastoral,
social, and so on. You also may discuss the discipline of the clergy and Christian people:
seminaries, schools, Catholic Action; and anything else you think to the advantage of the
Church and souls" (*ADA* IV, I/1, p. xi). A vast program indeed!

on the nature of the Council, but the commission played no part in reaching them. It was consulted on the procedure to be followed in the consultations that came under its list of responsibilities, but its backing was not judged necessary when it came to modifying an important aspect of this procedure, for in fact the way in which the bishops were consulted was taken out of its hands.

When, therefore, some years later,[49] Msgr. Carbone expressed his pleasure at the good work done between May, 1959, and June, 1960, he came close to expressing satisfaction merely with himself, since what he said applied to the president and secretariat of the commission rather than to the commission as a whole. For the role of the latter was remarkably reduced after the summer of 1959: consultation of the curial offices (May 29), of the bishops (June 18), and the universities (July 18), without forgetting the nuncios, who on July 13 were told of the consultation of the bishops and asked to reply to it themselves.

IV. The Responses

As early as July 1959 for the promptest and as late as the summer of 1960 for the slowest, the replies came to Tardini, who passed them on to the secretariat of the antepreparatory commission. This impressive mass of over two thousand documents would later supply the material for eight volumes of *Acta et documenta Concilio Vaticano II apparando* (Records and Documents of the Preparation for Vatican Council II).[50]

This enormous material, still poorly known despite numerous surveys by nations, has been the subject of divergent judgments by historians. Some have compared the attitudes of the bishops during the Council with their vota and denied the latter any value: prisoners of a preconciliar mentality, they in no way presaged the coming event. Some other historians have taken a different approach and been tempted to look to these documents for a kind of self-portrait of the Catholic Church on the eve of the Council.

But the material to which the consultation gave rise deserves neither excessive disparagement nor exorbitant esteem. In response to the negative

---

[49] Special issue of *Osservatore della Domenica*, March 6, 1996, p. 21; see his further contributions: "Il cardinale Domenico Tardini e la preparazione del concilio Vaticano II," *RSCI* 45 (1991) 42-88; "(Pericle Felici) Segretario generale del Vaticano II," in *Il cardinale Pericle Felici* (Rome, 1992) 159-94. For a critical perspective see Giuseppe Alberigo, "Passaggi cruciali" (note 41, above) 7-34.

[50] Vincenzo Carbone, "Genesi e criteri della pubblicazione degli atti del Concilio Vaticano II," *Lateranum* (Rome) 44 (1978) 579-94.

appraisal, there is the richness of the material, which means that it cannot be simply ignored, even though there would be hardly any reference to it in the subsequent debates. The second group of historians, on the other hand, needs to be more cautious in its assessment, lest the material be taken for something it could not be, for it certainly does not give a picture of the Catholic Church in the middle of the twentieth century but rather a picture of those elements that the bishops chose to record in the context of a consultation by Rome. But even this much is not negligible! Who, after all, could complain about having available such a wide-ranging poll of the opinions of the leaders of the Catholic world?

We must not forget, however, that the votum was not the only means the bishops had of preparing the Council. At the time when they were replying to Cardinal Tardini, a number of prelates were engaged in the process that would lead to the creation of the Secretariat for Christian Unity, a process much more important than their replies to the antepreparatory consultation, however interesting these replies may have been.[51]

1. *How to Use the Vota*[52]

A few hermeneutical precautions can save us from either a naive or a reductive reading of these documents. The first task is to grasp the sheer volume of the material thus assembled. Those who were asked to write down their desires for the future Council included not only the Catholic universities and the congregations of the Roman Curia, which were specifically approached, but all those who had a right to attend a general Council according to a broad interpretation of Canon 223 of the 1917 Code; this included titular bishops and prelates in the missions among others, although there was some ambiguity regarding the former. The request was sent to each individual, even though the initial list of the antepreparatory commission's tasks spoke simply of consulting the episcopate. The result was a mountain of replies that soon submerged the secretariat.

Out of a possible total of 2812 individuals and groups, 2150 replied (76.4%). We may quickly set the groups aside, at least for statistical purposes, for while the ten Roman congregations submitted their "proposals," only 51 of 62 institutions of higher education (82.2%) complied

---

[51] See below, pp. 263-271.

[52] I owe a good deal to the pioneering article of Alberto Melloni, "Per un approccio storico-critico ai consilia et vota della fase antepreparatoria del Vaticano II," *RSLR* 26 (1990) 556-76.

— one might have expected more from institutions the Church devotes to intellectual work. But these raw figures are deceptive. Besides Chicago and Sherbrooke (Canada), six Latin American institutions failed to reply. To this we need only add the three short, conventional replies from Bogotá, Ecuador, and Chile to see how very slight was the contribution made by the universities of the subcontinent to the antepreparatory consultation.[53] This geographical oddity has no obvious explanation.

Let me turn now to the figures for the answers from future fathers of the Council. Of the 2594 who were sounded out 1998 replied (77%).[54] An astonishing proportion for any poll of a specific population! The first lesson taught by the consultation is, therefore, the interest it aroused. But dealing with large numbers has the drawback that full or reasoned replies are indiscriminately lumped with those that are terse or have little to say. Thomas McCabe, Bishop of Wollongong in Australia took six months to reply in six lines that he had almost nothing to suggest.[55] On the other hand, the Cardinal Archbishop of Guadalajara, who was president of the episcopal conference, sent 27 pages, which amounted to 18% of the individual Mexican contributions, 17 of which were no more than a page in length.[56] Two extremes of size!

But a breakdown of the results according to a classification of the future conciliar fathers and according to pastoral source is not completely without its interest. The most assiduous in replying were the diplomats — nuncios or other representatives — whose role made them accustomed to submitting reports (91.8% replied). Next came the residential bishops with 87.2% replying, which was a remarkable figure.

After these, however, the figures drop quickly: the groups that felt least involved were apostolic vicars (68.4%), religious superiors (64.7%), and titular bishops (56.5%), while apostolic prefects brought up the rear with fewer than one out of two replying (46.9%). It is clear that auxiliary bishops and those in charge of missionary areas felt less zeal in replying than did those in full charge of dioceses, that is, ordinaries or residential bishops.

The great variety in the reaction of auxiliaries is especially revealing of the way in which they conceived of their position in the hierarchy. Of

[53] *ADA* IV/2, pp. 46-50, 533-38, 555-60.
[54] *ADA* Indices, Indici statistici, pp. 207-433.
[55] *ADA* II, December 15, 1959, p. 608: "Therefore I have nothing to suggest except that some thought be given to the power and authority of the bishops."
[56] Jesús García, "México," *Vísperas*, 200.

the seven Mexican bishops in this category, two did not reply, two signed the reply of the ordinaries, and only three sent personal replies, although at least two of these were among the most original and relevant of all the responses.[57] The Mexican example can be taken as typical: the low percentage of personal responses from auxiliaries reflected a low degree of involvement and even an uncertainty on their part about their right to take part in the process: the lack of response, the signing of the ordinary's response, or the addition to his of an identical response were so many unmistakable signs of this. A sharing of responsibilities, such as was to be seen in New York between Cardinal Spellman and his assistant, Maguire,[58] was itself evidence of a better integration of the auxiliary into the diocese. Those personal responses that had no connection with that of the "boss" call for careful reading, because they often expressed the outlook of a younger generation of bishops; I may mention here such European examples as the replies of Bishop Pignedoli, auxiliary of Milan, and Bishop Elchinger, coadjutor of Strasbourg.

A breakdown of responses according to geographical origin is no less instructive, provided we move away from the usual continental setting and look at nations. There was little difference, after all, between Central America, which led the class in responses (88.1%) and Oceania, which brought up the rear 68.5%). I note only the excellent African response, which was better than that of Europe (83.3% to 79.9%) and the relatively weak Asian response (70.2%). These differences, which were in any case minimal, were explainable not only by the lesser influence of auxiliaries or missionaries in the hierarchy but also by the politico-religious effect of local situations. Thus Asia was handicapped by the enforced silence of many Chinese and Vietnamese bishops; Europe by that of many bishops under communist control, except for Poland and Yugoslavia (there was no reply from Czechoslovakia, or from the Uniate Ukrainians except for those in exile; only one reply from Hungary).

Although less noticeable, other seemingly more surprising silences were in fact to be explained similarly. Thus Cardinal Coppello, Archbishop of Buenos Aires, who was considered to have been overly involved in the Peron regime, had to retire under pressure from the Argentine dictator's successors; his replacement died, and Cardinal Caggiano, who succeeded, had just arrived from Rosario; the Church of Buenos Aires was in turmoil because of these events and did not reply to Tardini.[59]

[57] Ibid., 199.
[58] Melloni, "Per un approccio," 568.
[59] Fortunato Mallimaci, "Argentina," *Visperas*, 102-3.

There is another piece of evidence that deserves closer attention: the rapidity with which the responses were sent. In his letter the Cardinal Secretary of State had asked that they be received by September 1, 1959. In October, a month after that deadline, many responses had come in but several hundred were still lacking.[60] A reminder was therefore sent on March 21, 1960,[61] which pushed the close of the consultation period back to the end of April of that year; even so, a number of vota did not come in until mid-summer. There is no check-list that would allow us to identify the late responders or the reason for their slowness. Difficulties of communication, the excuse of some bishops far distant from Rome, may have played a part, as in the case of the Apostolic Vicar of Bui-Chu in North Vietnam.[62] But this was surely not the only explanation. These belated responses would not carry the same weight as the others, since they could not be included in the summaries by country that were drawn up at the beginning of 1960, much less in the final synthesis.

For various reasons, then, a little less than 600 Council fathers did not respond. Like all silences, this one is difficult to interpret. One might be tempted to conclude that it was the result of either unfavorable political conditions or a relative indifference. It is indeed likely that these explanations held for the majority of cases, but they did not hold for all. Thus Bishop Mendez Arceo of Cuernavaca in Mexico would be one of the most active Latin American prelates at the Council, but he did not respond. His colleagues, Larrain of Talca (Chile) and Blomjous of Mwanza (Tanganyika), sent terse and innocuous replies that gave no hint of the energy they would show at the Council.[63] On the other hand, account must also be taken of multiple replies, for second thoughts or supplementary replies undoubtedly revealed great interest in the consultation. Thus Cardinal Gracias, Archbishop of Bombay sent two rather lengthy replies, dated August 17 and August 28, 1959; he was imitated by his colleague, Archbishop Cooray of Colombo (August 29, 1959 and July 20, 1960).[64]

There is the same difficulty in assessing the delays in responding. How many prompt replies were of no importance or stereotyped? Three lines of text and four of polite phrases were all that the Bishop of

---

[60] 1988 responses out of a possible 2600, according to Melloni, "Per un approccio," 562.

[61] *ADA* II/1, p. xiii.

[62] His reply, which had very little substance, was dated September 9, 1960 (*ADA* II/4, pp. 639-41).

[63] Their replies were dated September 5, 1959 (*ADA* II/7, p. 377) and April 18, 1960 (*ADA* II/5, pp. 479-80), respectively.

[64] *ADA* II/4. pp. 109-16 and 37-47.

Maurienne (France) sent, whereas it took a year for the Bishop of Palo (Philippines) to say that he had not prepared any proposal.[65] On the other hand, a late reply might indicate, in addition to a cautious approach, a lively interest in the coming Council that was fed either by encouraging remarks from the pope (to which few vota make reference) or by information about other replies, since the instructions about secrecy were not always very strictly obeyed. Can we think that Cardinal Montini of Milan had no interest in the Council, even though his votum was dated as late as May 8, 1960?[66] Some delays were even explained as proof of that kind of heightened interest; thus on May 20, 1960 Bishop Van Bekkum, Apostolic Vicar of Ruteng in Indonesia, referred to the joint text which he had helped to compose in his role as secretary of the episcopal conference.[67] While a number of late vota were obviously sent only to set the sender's mind at rest, this does not seem to account for the majority of cases: six months or more after Tardini's letter the changed ecclesial situation was having its first effects on the minds of some prelates.

This last remark allows me to pass from the number, length, and dates of the responses to their form. In keeping with the wishes of the antepreparatory commission, a large majority of the replies were in Latin. There was one well-known and deliberate exception to this rule: a number of Uniate hierarchies, and not unimportant ones, replied either in French or in Italian, in order to show that they would not tolerate a Latinization that would only discredit them still further in the East.[68]

In addition, the language-rule suffered a number of other infringements that, though involving only individuals, were no less significant. Thus some bishops did not hesitate to reply in their native language, most often French (Tahiti; Wallis and Futuna Islands) but also English (four Americans), Spanish (two Argentinians), and Italian. The Bishop of Krishnagar in India was not afraid to say, in Italian, that "the Latin language is no longer a means of unifying the Church."[69] Even some nuncios (Austria, France, Philippines) and one superior general of a religious order (the Salesians) replied in the language of Dante. But the proportion of nonconformists was small, doubtless no more than 5% of the whole.

---

[65] Yves-Marie Hilaire, "Les voeux des évêques français après l'annonce du concile de Vatican II (1959)," *Deuxième*, 102; *ADA* II/4, p. 299 (May 5, 1960).

[66] *ADA* II/3, pp. 374-81.

[67] *ADA* II/4, p. 252. Bishop Hurley of Durban (Union of South Africa) also used a meeting of bishops as an excuse (*ADA* II/5, p. 538, April 15, 1960).

[68] Roberto Morozzo della Rocca, "I 'voti' degli orientali nella preparazione del Vaticano II," *Veille*, 120-21.

[69] *ADA* II/4, p. 156.

Still and all, the matter needs to be looked at a little more closely. There were a good many prelates who accompanied their Latin votum with a letter in their native tongue. Very few, on the other hand, were those who began in Latin and ended in the vernacular, as did the University of Montreal, which used Latin for theological questions but French when dealing with the spirituality of business people or with an assessment of "non-theological factors" in ecclesial problems.[70] Finally, how many imitated Pignedoli, auxiliary of Milan, who sent two texts, the first in Italian and the second in Latin, although only the second was published in the *Acta*?[71] If other cases could be discovered, a comparison of the two versions would obviously be of interest.

It becomes clear, then, that in addition to the case of the Uniate Orientals, who paraded their disagreement, there was a creeping rebellion against the language of the Church; it was indeed limited but not on that account negligible. In the Catholic world of the mid-twentieth century, some prelates, especially in the missions, no longer had enough mastery of Latin to be willing or able to use it in their responses.[72]

Like the consultation itself, the overwhelming majority of vota came from individuals. But even this rule had a number of exceptions. (I shall not say anything more of the auxiliary bishops who signed the votum of their ordinaries.) It is necessary, however, to mention some deliberate doublets. Thus the ordinaries of Roermond and Rotterdam, who were dissatisfied with the collective response of the Netherlands episcopate, sent two identical responses, one in French, the other in Latin.[73] The responses of the bishops of Palai and Trichur (India) were dated the same day, August 25, 1959, and resembled each other too closely not to have been composed in concert, as were the replies of their colleagues in Copenhagen (Denmark) and Helsinki (Finland).[74] Some archbishops and their suffragans also spoke with a single voice: the Province of Vienna (Austria), the Indian Province of Verapoly, in Kerala, and the Italian Province of Emilia.

Attempts at national responses also ran into internal disagreements or Roman prejudices. The former scuttled the joint response of the Swiss

[70] *ADA* IV/2, pp. 461-65.

[71] Melloni, "Per un approccio," 461-62; *ADA* II/3, pp. 847-51.

[72] The (Italian) Dominican bishop of Multan (Pakistan) admitted: "I have lost the ability to write in Latin" (*ADA* II/4, p. 431).

[73] *ADA* II/2, pp. 492-504.

[74] *ADA* II/4, pp. 185-89 and 208-12; *ADA* II/1, pp. 159 (no date) and 163 (August 29). Bishop Smith of Pembroke (Canada) obviously drew his inspiration from the votum of his colleague, Bishop Cody of London (*ADA* II/6, pp. 68-69 and 34-36; dated August 26 and 1).

episcopal conference that had been suggested by nuncio Gustave Testa, who was close to the pope.[75] Both reasons combined to frustrate a joint response of the Dutch conference.[76] Nevertheless, three such undertakings did succeed in the Latin Catholic world, despite the fact that the latter was less steeped in the synodal tradition than its sister Church in the East: these successes came in Germany, Mexico, and Indonesia. Fifteen prelates also took advantage of a meeting of the Episcopal Conference of Central America (CEDAC) to compose the only international votum in the entire collection.[77]

These signs of collegiality at work in the preparation of the Council are not insignificant, but neither do they necessarily indicate openness. Everything depended on those involved and on the subject of their joint effort; thus the Province of Emilia sent a bare list of detailed suggestions; the Province of Luluabourg in Congo-Leopoldville came out strongly against native nationalism; on May 5, 1960, the standing committee of the ordinaries of the Congo and Rwanda-Burundi composed a list of eleven requests that added nothing to the vota of the individual bishops; and the Mexican conference was content to submit a single votum: for the definition of the spiritual motherhood of Mary.[78] On the other hand, if the universal interest of the German response is well-known,[79] too little attention has been paid to that of its Indonesian counterpart, which also came in late and to which I must return below.

These collective responses did not take away the right of individuals to respond, but they did, logically enough, anticipate the content of individual responses; thus the votum of retired missionary Bishop Van Valenberg was very close to that of the Indonesian conference to which he belonged.[80]

Only an especially careful reading of the vota might provide some information on the way in which they were composed. Thus it seems possible to eliminate, at least to some extent, the hypothesis that the nuncios and other delegates exerted influence. For at least two reasons this influence does not seem to have been extensive. The first is chronological: a number of bishops did not wait for the nuncios to express their wishes before preparing and sending their own answers. Above all, however, it has been noted that the vota of the diplomats were impersonal and sterotyped, so much so as to suggest the need for a comparative

[75] Philippe Chenaux, "Les 'vota' des évêques suisses," *Veille*, 111-13.
[76] J. Y. H. A. Jacobs, "Les 'vota' des évêques néerlandais pour le concile," ibid., 101-2.
[77] *ADA* II/6, pp. 521-23 (August 27, 1959).
[78] Ibid., pp. 260-63 (October 16, 1959).
[79] *ADA* II/1, pp. 734-71 (May 15, 1960).
[80] *ADA* II/4, pp. 260-64 and 271-78 (May 15, 1960).

study.[81] There were exceptions, of course. Thus the responses of the internuncio in Pakistan and the apostolic delegate in Great Britain were more open than most of the episcopal responses from those countries. That of the apostolic delegate to Mexico was one of the very few to mention the Indian populations.

But despite these exceptions it is impossible to miss the almost complete absence of concrete reference in the vota of the diplomats. Such prudence was understandable in the difficult case of Cuba but was less justifiable in Europe or North America. Everything suggests that many of these officials, coming from other places and having few roots in the country in which they were temporarily representing the Holy See, responded less in terms of a specific situation than according to their formation and the Roman outlook they had acquired. That is why I have been hesitant to treat of them here rather than as part of the Vatican reception of the results of the consultation.

Tardini's request had encouraged the bishops to consult a few prudent and enlightened advisers before responding. The need of seeking advice could, of course, provide an excuse for delaying any reply. It is rather difficult to determine from the episcopal vota themselves whether or not the bishops took extensive advantage of the permission to seek advice. The responses of religious superiors, on the other hand, are often more explicit, to the extent that, despite the differences in the constitutions of their institute, they each had at their disposal a consultative group for the government of their subjects.

The range of actual situations seems to have been quite broad. Two French replies from two branches working in the same area exemplify two extremes. Father Houdiard, superior general of the religious (Fathers and Brothers) of St. Vincent de Paul, said in the letter accompanying his reply: "I have written these few notes in the presence of God," leaving us to infer with certainty that he consulted no one[82]; the same can be said of his colleague in the Society of St. Sulpice, Pierre Girard, who replied in longhand from his vacation in the Auvergne.[83] On the other hand, Father Goison, of the Sons of Charity, explicitly relied on the experience of his subordinates, who were parish priests among the suburban have-nots or chaplains of popular-level Catholic Action.[84]

---

[81] Joseph A. Komonchak, "U.S. Bishops' Suggestions for Vatican II," *CrSt* 15 (1994) 313-71, at 324.

[82] *ADA* II/8, pp. 207-16 at p. 207 (August 21, 1959).

[83] Ibid., pp. 318-19 (August 25, 1959).

[84] Ibid., pp. 270-82 (September 4, 1959).

There was also a middle position: a votum that was a collection of "wishes and suggestions from the General Curia and the professors of our houses of study"; the words are those of Albain Collette, Vicar General of the Assumptionists,[85] but the thought applies to many of those in comparable positions outside of Rome.

It is far more difficult to discern any typology in the maze of episcopal vota. Many of them repeated Tardini's language word for word,[86] suggesting that their consultation hardly amounted to much: at most, members of the diocesan curia, directors of the seminary, some preferred theologian, even some influential parish priests; only about ten individuals in the more fortunate cases of Cardinal Cushing of Boston or the archbishop of Asunción (Paraguay).[87] Examples of more extensive samplings, especially outside the clergy, were extremely rare. Apart from the official votum, thirty-seven professors of Louvain University, among them eighteen laypersons, belatedly composed a very interesting "Note on the Conditions for the Intellectual Apostolate," which would make the rounds, although unofficially.[88] But the most surprising case, and one that shows how mysterious the Lord's ways are, was undoubtedly that of Bahia Blanca in Argentina, where the reputedly conservative Bishop Esorto, without turning a hair, sent a Latin translation of reflections from one of the most active parishes in Buenos Aires, reflections which one of the men close to him had asked for.[89]

As a matter of fact, the majority of the prelates either composed their own votum or assigned the task to one of their right-hand men. Only occasional evidence enables us to know a little more about the real authors of some of the vota. Thus the Bishop of Foggia (Italy) immediately signaled his reservations regarding any challenge to the Pacellian heritage by asking the help of Jesuit Riccardo Lombardi, who had been close to Pius XII but had little liking for his successor and favored a reform from on high; it would be of interest to discover what influence Lombardi may have had on others.[90] The talents of the American

---

[85] Ibid., pp. 186-95 at 186 (December 26, 1959).

[86] "In tackling this task Your Excellency may make discreet use of the advice of expert and prudent churchmen" (*ADA* II/1, p. x).

[87] Komonchak, "U.S. Bishops' Suggestions," 317; Margarita Duran Estrago, "Paraguay," *Vísperas*, 147.

[88] Mathijs Lamberigts, "The 'vota antepraeparatoria' of the Faculties of Theology of Louvain and Lovanium (Zaïre)," in *Veille*, 169-75.

[89] Mallimaci, "Argentina," 105 (note 59, above).

[90] Roberto Morozzo della Rocca, "I 'vota' degli vescovi italiani per il concilio," *Deuxième*, 134.

Redemptorist theologian Francis Connell were exercised along even more conservative lines; while his offer of service to Bishops Leech (Harrisburg) and Floersh (Louisville) produced no results, the same was not true of Cardinal O'Boyle of Washington and his auxiliaries nor of Bishop McManus of Ponce (Puerto Rico).[91]

The influence of the ecumenical monastery of Chevetogne in Belgium would have been in a quite different direction. Some have thought to detect — but without decisive proof — the mark of Dom Olivier Rousseau on some of the Oriental vota.[92] More certain is the influence that a memorandum composed in May, 1959, by Swiss theologian Otto Karrer had on some German-language responses.[93] Nor is there is any doubt in one last case: Four of the seven Dutch responses readily admit their debt to the "Note on the Restoration of Christian Unity on the Occasion of the Coming Council," which came from the Catholic Conference for Ecumenical Affairs and was dated June 15, 1959.[94]

From a strictly formal point of view the vota wavered between the two extremes of conformism and originality; in this respect it made no difference who the authors were. Conformism could be seen in the arid lists of unrelated items or in extreme examples of polite phrases that emphasized the dependence of the ordinaries on Rome.[95] Originality, though of opposing kinds, was to be seen in the obsessions of the archbishop of Delhi and the inventiveness of the vicar apostolic of Purkowerto in Indonesia. The former was interested only in the glorification of Mary and Joseph.[96] The latter suggested an organization of the Council according to cultural areas and a further calendar of meetings that must have left his Roman addressees wondering: seven geographical sections; a plenary Council every fifty years and a worldwide conference every twenty-five years.[97]

We must not, therefore, underestimate the variety, sometimes the rich profuseness, of the collection of vota. Why then has the collection often had a bad press among specialists dealing with the Council? The reason is that, quantitatively, it displayed considerably more conformism than

---

[91] Komonchak, "U.S. Bishops's Suggestions," 318-19.
[92] Melloni, "Per un approccio," 566.
[93] Victor Conzemius, "Otto Karrer (1888-1976)," *Deuxième*, 354-58.
[94] Jacobs, "Les 'vota' des évêques néerlandais," 102-4 (note 76, above).
[95] For example, Archbishop Lacchio of Changsa (China) wrote on August 18, 1959: "With deep respect and reverence I kiss the sacred purple and beg a holy blessing" (*ADA* II/4, p. 481).
[96] Ibid., p. 125 (March 22, 1960).
[97] Ibid., pp. 242-51 (August 20, 1959).

originality. If we adopt Fortunato Mallimaci's sound distinction between
"canonical vota" and "pastoral vota," which are better adapted to the
variety of situations,[98] the former clearly predominate. How are they to
be recognized? by their juridical vocabulary, inherited from the Code of
1917 or from the theological manuals; their often tedious lists of many
pointed suggestions; their chiefly ternary structure in which doctrine is
quickly dispatched, before dwelling at length on discipline, while not
showing much interest in concrete situations or in the keenly debated
questions of the moment, which were often written off. Thus over 2000
of the 9438 suggestions inventoried in the *Analyticus Conspectus* have
to do with the clergy.[99]

Before finding fault with the vota for their silences or their omissions,
we ought to ask what the reasons were for this conformism on the part
of the majority. Although the request made to them was not very precise,
most of the bishops thought of this as a typical situation with which they
were well acquainted and whose exceptional character in this instance
few of them perceived: they had to answer an inquiry from Rome. They
responded therefore in accord with a mentality long since instilled into
them and then reinforced by experience of their relations with the
nuncios or the Vatican offices.

This mind-set predetermined the excessively respectful tone, the
canonical form, and, above all, the notorious cautiousness of many of
the responses, which therefore have to be decoded, with the help of a
familiarity with the rules of the game, in order to detect nuances. Thus
many vota were satisfied with suggesting questions, sometimes hotly
debated ones, while avoiding giving any answers.[100] Or else the anti-
quated vocabulary that they used in connection with problems whose
recent developments eluded them, such as the unity of Christians,
showed their desire to satisfy the pope's expectations without really
subscribing to them.[101] Accustomed to conform to what Rome desired,
they went on groping, because this time they lacked the help of a firm
directive. This makes the strongly personal vota, whether defensive or
"pastoral," that violated these rules all the more interesting. In all cases,
however, we must not forget that the votum belonged to a well defined

[98] Mallimaci, "Argentina," *Vísperas*, 106.

[99] Caprile, I/1, 174.

[100] There were no less than forty such questions in the votum of Father Milwaukee on
behalf of the Capuchins; *ADA* II/8, pp. 77-82 (August 28, 1959).

[101] The American Franciscans of the Atonement were pursuing their unionist aim of
"reconciling the dissidents"; ibid., 307-9.

literary genre, that of a reply to Rome, and this fact must be very carefully kept in mind for a correct interpretation of the considerable amount of material produced by the antepreparatory consultation. On the whole, the responses were a rather conformist echo of an appeal, the new tone of which it was not easy to perceive.

2. *Three Sets of Attitudes*

When we move from form to content we quickly face the difficult problem of a grill for classification that can take us beyond the obvious minimal consensus that can be discerned in most of the vota. In essence it includes three desires: better definition of the role of the bishop, speeding up liturgical reform, and restoration of the permanent diaconate, which had been proposed by Pius XII to compensate for the growing dearth of priestly vocations. This third measure raised hardly any questions, but the same was not true of the first two, the ambiguity of which needs to brought out more clearly.

Vatican II was obviously going to be the Council that would speak about bishops, but in what sense? A sizable gap appears between a minority of vota, which offered a theological substructure, individual or collective, for such a re-evaluation, and the great mass of vota, which were content to make disciplinary demands that would turn each bishop into a pope in his own diocese: an often virulent denunciation of the exemption of religious, something that many superiors general, however, were endeavoring to preserve[102]; elimination of parish priests' right not to be moved; a better distribution of the clergy as a whole. This second and clearly dominant tendency held fast to what had been done at Vatican I, while the former, minority group made more or less open calls for more collegiality. But there is no small danger here of a confusion that would interpret every desire to strengthen episcopal authority into a sign of openness, when it was far from being this in all cases.

A comparable ambiguity becomes apparent in connection with two quite different conceptions of liturgical reform; we might call them the "pastoral" and the "canonical." Both sought to improve the conduct of worship along the lines begun by the preceding pontificate. The second, however, which was clearly that of the majority, went no further than a dusting off of the rubrics and was timid when it came to the use of the vernacular, whereas the former, which took a bolder tack on this point as

---

[102] For example, the superiors of the Franciscan Third Order Regular, the Redemptorists, and the Holy Ghost Fathers.

on others, sought to restore rites to their ecclesial context. In this perspective, the liturgy was to be taken from the hands of the specialists and become once again a vital apostolic tool, since what was at issue was a closer bond between the mass of the faithful and the Church. Almost all the responses suggested improvements, sometimes going into great detail. But could anyone believe that the signers were all resolute supporters of *aggiornamento*? There were very few explicitly conservative warnings against the decline of Latin, praised as the language for universal communication.[103]

In the light of all this, we need a more functional method for sorting out the vota according to their content. I have deliberately set aside as unsatisfactory the classification in the *Acta et documenta*, which is according to categories of respondents and according to continent. My reason is simple: such a classification makes it impossible to pinpoint the main trends expressed in the consultation, since it juxtaposes merely on the basis of geography or of logic vota that follow very different lines. I have therefore chosen another kind of classification, set out in two distinct stages. The "Roman" vota — replies from prelates in the Curia and from religious superiors with an ultramontane outlook, as well as texts from the Roman universities and proposals from the curial offices — will not be studied here but later on, after we have studied the work of the secretariat of the antepreparatory commission on the results of the consultation. As far as the curial offices are concerned, no doubt is possible: they were asked to participate in the work by reason of their position. The other three categories of Roman respondents, on the other hand, made up the common cultural reservoir from which the authorities who interpreted and condensed the replies drew men and ideas. Their suggestions undoubtedly make it possible to understand better the spirit in which the secretariat's work was done.

In dealing with the material that reached Rome from the entire Catholic world (dioceses, universities, non-Roman religious congregations) I have decided to divide it roughly into three large bodies. The first brings together responses which basically paid hardly any heed to the pope's objectives and were even more or less openly opposed to them. The second, on the contrary, brings together responses that, with varying degrees of decisiveness, followed the path broken by John XXIII. The third is not a mere "morass" nor, still worse, a residue of unclassifiable vota, but brings together vota coming most often from the

---

[103] But the warnings came in proportionally greater numbers from religious superiors than from bishops.

young Churches in process of emancipation; the characteristic of these
vota is that they show such contrasts to the two preceding trends, sometimes within one and the same votum, as to render any bipartite breakdown impossible.

The reader should, of course, consider this typology a provisional one,
for it has had to take into account the difficulties already seen in using
the sources, as well as the unequal treatment so far given to them by
scholars: the European and American responses have been thoroughly
studied, whereas the African and even more the Asian are still poorly
known, as are the responses of the religious and of the universities.

2a. Capping Four Centuries of Intransigence

The first category of responses is not the most difficult to delimit
because it is marked by a homogeneity hardly disturbed by the
inevitable nuances. The thrust of these responses was that the coming
Council should be the climactic moment in the centuries-old movement
that opposed the Roman Catholic model to its competitors and enemies
who claimed the modern world for themselves. In this perspective, the
need was to complete the work begun at Trent in the sixteenth
century and pursued, though incompletely, by Vatican I in the nineteenth. To use Jeffrey Klaiber's accurate summation in speaking of Peru,
"The proposals of the bishops give the impression, on the whole, that
they are preparing for the Council of Trent...and not for an ecumenical
Council of the entire Church in the twentieth century."[104]

This twofold desire to preserve and to affirm can be read not only in the
content of the vota but also in their form, although here it is more subtle.
The intransigence finds expression most often in individual responses
behind which there does not seem to have been any common effort or
which had been entrusted to a safe theologian. Thus many episcopates were
like dust-specks, isolated individuals with no visible concern for collegiality. For example, efforts at coordination between dioceses can be counted
on one hand for the whole of Italy.[105] "Canonical" replies were clearly in
the majority here: discipline was more important than doctrine and reduced
the "signs of the times" to next to nothing. Few Latin American bishops
dwelt on the already critical problem of the impoverishment of an increasingly large part of the population, while the same problem claimed the
attention of only a single Spanish prelate, the Archbishop of Grenada.[106]

[104] Vísperas, 162.

[105] Mauro Velati, "I 'consilia et vota' dei vescovi italiani," Veille, 85.

[106] Evangelista Vilanova, "Los 'vota' de los obispos españoles después del anuncio
del concilio Vaticano II," ibid., 82.

Yet the literary genre of the consultation is not enough to explain such silences, which have forcibly struck many observers. The overwhelming majority of them were written in good Church Latin, and they copied the organization and formulas of canon law for what was very often a mere catalogue of scattered or unimportant suggestions. As a result, they leave an impression of triviality and repetitiveness on anyone who goes through them one after another: as Roberto Morozzo della Rocca sums it up a propos of the Italian vota, they are marked by conventionalism, uniformity, conformism, and lack of originality.[107]

Two main characteristics mark the responses in this category: they show little restraint in advocating a Council that would define and that would condemn, so as better to distinguish Roman Catholicism from its environment. First, definitions: While some vota suggested exalting St. Joseph or turning Pius XII's doctrine of the Church as the Mystical Body into a dogma, most of the suggestions in this area were concerned with Mary. The Mexican episcopate was alone in its defense of her spiritual motherhood, although this suggestion would be retained by Paul VI. There were a good many defenders of coredemption, but far fewer than the partisans of Mary's universal mediation of all graces, which was the object of four-fifths of the petitions on behalf of the Virgin.[108]

This undeniable Marian thrust revealed a twofold time-lag when related to a context that was rapidly evolving, and in this area too. On the one hand, it showed absolutely no concern for possible ecumenical troubles caused by new definitions; many Latin American prelates not only paid no heed to the cause of unity but wanted a condemnation, if not of Protestantism itself, of the Protestant proselytism they were experiencing.[109] On the other hand, the Marian thrust took almost no account of the shift toward moderation that had begun as early as the end of the pontificate of Pius XII, a shift that in the opinion even of specialists caused the shelving of both the universal mediation and the coredemptive role of Mary. But would not the Council provide an opportunity to increase the momentum once again?

These calls for definitions were often accompanied by corresponding calls for condemnations. The errors to be proscribed were chiefly those of the contemporary world that was moving further and further away

[107] Morozzo della Rocca,'vota' dei vescovi italiani," 122 (note 90, above).

[108] There were 280 of these according to the *Sintesi finale sui consigli e suggerimenti* (March 12, 1960), p. 4.

[109] This defensive anxiety was present especially in the Argentinian and Mexican vota.

from the bosom of the Church. Although the old nineteenth-century ene-mies were not forgotten, they now came far behind the new dangers of the present age: communism first of all, or even existentialism and situ-ation morality, which had recently been denounced by Pius XII. But the calls for condemnation were also aimed at the infiltration of these errors into the bosom of the Church under the form of modernism or neomod-ernism or dogmatic relativism. The argument for condemnation followed the defensive line that had begun with the *Syllabus* of 1864, had been continued by the encyclical *Pascendi* and the decree that applied it in 1907, and had ended, in muted form, in the encyclical *Humani generis* of 1950. References to this last document, sometimes with the addition of sybilline allusions to the theses of living theologians, are enough to place a votum in our first category.

The vota in this category were not, however, lacking in weak desires for reform, although "reform" was not the word willingly used of them. But these desires were marked by an exceptional cautiousness: improve-ment in the functioning of the Vatican machine, for example, but few explicit criticisms of its methods, especially those used in censuring. The often proposed assertion of the authority of the bishop over his dioceses could be obtained only at the expense of religious and laity and even of priests. The restoration of the permanent diaconate should not be allowed to cause a lowering of esteem for priestly celibacy, nor were needed liturgical improvements to detract from the preeminence of Latin as the language of the universal Church — no concern was shown for the East that was in union with the Roman Catholic Church.

It is not very difficult to link this profile with ecclesiastical geogra-phy. Two sets of responses correspond to it rather exactly. On the one hand, there were the responses from Latin Churches that were dominant in their territories and knew how to remain in this position by protecting themselves against all harmful influences. The clearest and also the most fully studied case was none other than the plethora of Italian bishops, so closely dependent on the Roman Curia. Almost half of their vota called for at least one condemnation, and a third of them asked for at least one new Marian definition: all doubts had to be dissipated and all certainties strengthened.[110] Apart from an emphatic distrust of modern society, there was no sign of any awareness of the radical transformations going on in the peninsula: urbanization, industrialization, and the heightened standard of living, even though the pastoral implications of these

---

[110] Velati, "I 'consilia et vota' dei vescovi italiani," 92 and 94.

changes were obvious. Only one current question occupied the attention
of these Italian pastors at any length: in a country in which the voca-
tional crisis was acute, the energetic defense of the traditional priesthood, which had been the subject of a recent discussion in the Catholic
press.[111] Apart from this one exception, the great problems of the Church
were not handled any better than were the problems of the world; only
one fifth of the vota paid any attention to the disunity of Christians.[112]
This explains the repeated criticisms observers have made of the cultural
lag or provincialism of Italian Catholicism.

The same remarks apply to the Spanish vota, with which the
Portuguese may be combined. The bishop of Leiria, guardian of Fatima,
distinguished himself by his obsession with Mary (three requests for
definitions), and the archbishops of Braga and Coimbra by their stric-
tures against modern errors. In a hierarchy overly identified with its
national Catholicism, the surprise announcement of a Council triggered
a movement of withdrawal that could be felt at all levels: lack of
thought about the situation of the country and of the Church within it;
the timidity of the weak desires for reform, except when it came to the
powers of bishops; biblical and liturgical conservatism. This withdrawal was especially clear in the area of doctrine; more than the
requests for definitions, which were numerous enough, the striking
thing here was the vigor and precision of the calls for condemnation.
Condemnations of outsiders, of which Evangelista Vilanova gives a
lengthy list that includes philosophers Ortega y Gasset and Una-
muno,[113] but condemnations also of insiders: whereas only one votum
suggested doing away with the antimodernist oath, ten (out of 81)
denounced the French "new theology,"[114] against which the experts of
the Spanish episcopate had, since the end of the 1940s, been conducting
a campaign which they now had a chance to revitalize. The condemnation of "the so-called 'new theology'" occupied a prominent place
among the vota of the University of Comillas, in a lengthy response that
was over 80% "canonical." The University of Salamanca, in its turn,
called for a new syllabus of the biblical, dogmatic, and moral errors that
were proliferating.[115]

[111] Morozzo della Rocca, "I 'vota' dei vescovi italiani," 123-24 (note 90, above), and
Velati (note 105), 86-91.
[112] Velati, 86.
[113] Vilanova, "Los 'vota' de los obispos españoles," 67 and 69.
[114] Ibid., 64.
[115] ADA IV/2, pp. 539-54 and 50-159 (especially 544 and 56).

The responses from Spanish-speaking America, which have likewise been carefully studied, suggest comparable findings, except for the set from Brazil, which was quite different. The most striking aspect of these responses was undoubtedly their often glaring lack of connection with the sad realities of the subcontinent. It is true, of course, that popular devotion to Mary was intense in those lands, that liberal or Masonic anticlericalism was formidable, and that Evangelical proselytism was making progress among populations that were now subproletarian. But communism? This had never been a real threat either in the streets or at the ballot box.[116] The stern denunciation was due to the fright caused by the Cuban revolution, which was quite recent when the bishops were sending their vota.

On the other hand, few criticized the dictatorships, even though these were not always fond of the Church; almost the only one to risk such a criticism was the American Redemptorist Reilly, who had been physically threatened in Trujillo's Dominican Republic.[117] Meanwhile the bishops of Paraguay would receive financial aid from the Stroessner government to pay for their trip to Rome in 1962.[118] If it might be anachronistic to fault the vota of 1959-60 for their almost complete silence about the poverty of a subcontinent that was at that time enchanted by hopes of development, still the frequent laments about the poor distribution of the clergy would have made it possible to raise the problem caused by galloping urbanization amid the worst possible material conditions. The evidence cannot be denied: the concrete situation of Spanish-speaking America did not figure among the concerns which its bishops wanted to bring to Vatican II.

Within these sets of vota few voices stood out: two in Argentina, a single but important one in Paraguay. The diocese of Misiones, which had been created in 1957, had been entrusted to Bishop Bogarin in order to remove him from Catholic Action where his influence had been judged to be politically and religious harmful.[119] Often, in fact, "black sheep" had gained their openness from contacts with lay movements and attendance at international meetings of these movements.

Unlike in Spain, for which no future leader of the majority can be cited, Italy provided some weighty exceptions to the conformism of the

---

[116] According to Mallimaci (*Vísperas*, 112), the communists had no more than three percent of the votes in Argentina.

[117] Ibid., 208-9 (Armando Lampe).

[118] Ibid., 146 (Margarita Duran Estrago).

[119] Ibid., 148-51.

majority. The first concern of Bishop Sentin of Trieste was the preservation of international peace.[120] Cardinal Lercaro of Bologna, for his
part, thought that communism had already been condemned enough and
that more room should be made for the vernacular in the liturgy.[121]
As for the delayed votum of Cardinal Montini of Milan, it deserves
attention both for the breadth of its thinking on the Church and for its
prudence.[122] For the moment, however, these exceptions were drowned
in a flood of almost interchangeable responses.

A second distinct group, which is less well known, brings together the
responses from Churches that were threatened by a more or less hostile
environment. Catholic Churches that were weak or whose members
were a minority had traditionally been all the more Roman because
their connection with the Chair of Peter served them both as a point of
reference and as a protection against their enemies. A first group in this
category consists of almost all the responses from countries under communist control.

I mentioned earlier the small number of such responses, which were
reduced to great simplicity by the hostility of the authorities. Still and
all, we must look at the ones that in spite of everything did reach Rome.
Quite understandably, the harshest attacks on communism were not to
be found in the vota of those belonging to nations under its yoke; neither
the Polish bishops nor even their Yugoslav confreres could frankly state
their position on this subject. If they had done so, they would probably
have been censored and deprived of any chance to take part in the future
assembly. Thus a condemnation of materialism came from Belgrade and
from Székesfehérvár (Hungary); but Poland, following the lead of Cardinal Primate Wyszynski, showed very great prudence.[123] On the other
hand, their attitude in matters religious was completely unambiguous:
the majority of the vota from the East pleaded, in a very "canonical"
manner, for a Council that would stand firm on the Catholic positions
that served them as their "business card" — against the Marxist threat,
we might be tempted to add, although this was nowhere said. Is this not

---

[120] Morozzo della Rocca, 134; Velati, 97.

[121] Original Italian of the votum, with a commentary by Giuseppe Alberigo, in
Giacomo Lercaro, *Per la forza dello spirito* (Bologna, 1984) 10-13 and 65-70.

[122] Antonio Rimoldi, "La preparazione del Concilio," in *Giovanni Battista Montini
arcivescovo di Milano e il Concilio ecumenico Vaticano II* (Brescia, 1985) 205-9.

[123] "There should be an exposition of Catholic social teaching on economics, labor,
property and the social obligations attaching to property. Also of social life in common
and of the account that society must render for the gifts of nature and grace" (*AD* I/II, 2,
p. 679).

the explanation for their attachment to Latin or their legendary Marian piety? When it came to theology, the only two vota sent by the University of Lublin asked that the privileges of the Virgin be explicated.[124]

Missionaries expelled from territories behind the "Bamboo Curtain" were not subject to the same restraints. From Hong Kong, Formosa, and the Philippines, but also from Spain, France, and the United States, where such missionaries were living in forced retirement, they sent Rome vota in which their call for a renewal of the solemn condemnation of communism was based on their experience of Chinese prisons before their expulsion.[125] Having been cut off from their people for years, they did not think they could offer constructive proposals and they often fell back on clearly conservative positions that were closer to those of their few Vietnamese colleagues than to those of missionary prelates who had been able to remain at their post in the rest of Indochina.[126]

The case of Catholic minorities in Protestant countries was much less indicative. Strengthened by support from Rome, they had with varying success finally won acceptance in countries in which, with the advance of secularization, confessional discrimination was playing an increasingly smaller role. But they retained a very strong ultramontane outlook that caused them to emphasize what characterized their Catholic identity in order to distinguish themselves more clearly from the Protestant world that surrounded them. The Irish responses, and the British to a lesser degree, were impregnated by this outlook. Their environment did indeed make them fear any new Marian definitions, which were likely to be poorly received there, but this fear coincided also with undeniable reservations regarding the union of Christians as well as the surrounding society. Similarly, criticisms of Roman bureaucratization did not imply a resolutely reformist outlook; on the contrary, a legalist mentality and a concern to stick firmly to classical positions begot a scrupulous or timid conformism, as, for example, in liturgical matters. This was the tone of most of the Irish responses, which were often short and skimpy. The archbishop of Dublin was more articulate but he called for condemnations of modern errors and the proclamation of Mary's mediating role.[127]

In Great Britain, on the other hand, Solange Dayras notes some signs of progress. Although Archbishop Godfrey of Westminster and a former

[124] *ADA* IV/2, p. 243.
[125] For example, Archbishop Melendro of Anking, writing from Palencia (Spain), *ADA* II/4, pp. 472-81 (August 7, 1959).
[126] See especially the votum of the Apostolic Vicar of Saigon, ibid., pp. 646-48 (August 28, 1959).
[127] *ADA* II/2, pp. 77-80 (August 24, 1959).

Apostolic Delegate, still thought himself authorized to answer for
prelates whom he had recently met in Rome, he no longer had the great
influence he had had in the past. A minority of responses showed
concerns that reflected a little more openness: four out of twenty, which
is not a negligible figure.[128] These few indicators, though still tenuous,
presaged a further development, which the Council would accelerate,
along the lines of what may be called the Dutch model: full national
integration and a cutting of the umbilical cord with Rome. But the
prevailing tone of the episcopal responses showed that this point had not
yet been reached in 1959-60.

It is not surprising to see the Catholic universities of these geographical areas adopting similar positions, since these institutions had formed
or were inspiring a good many members of the local hierarchies. To the
Spanish and Polish examples already given may be added some others,
notably the Italians. Thus the University of the Sacred Heart in Milan,
with its eye on Henri Duméry, who had recently been condemned,
emphasized the need for a rational presentation of the faith.[129] This
alignment, which might have been anticipated, allowed for some exceptions: no one will be surprised by the relative openness with regard to
the theology of the Church that was shown in the votum of the Lombard
school of Venegono, which was closely allied in every way with its
archbishop, Giovanni Battista Montini.[130]

2b. Toward Vatican II

Despite the small number of explicit references to the wishes of John
XXIII, even in the most belated vota, a second category of responses
came out, though with countless nuances, in favor of a substantial adaptation of the Catholic Church to its times in very diverse areas.

The majority of these vota, which were written in Latin, were of
course strictly individual and classic in their construction; only some
Uniate Oriental hierarchies deliberately used French. But the division
into "pastoral" responses and "canonical" responses was here less unfavorable to the former, a fact which suggests the exercise of a greater
freedom in regard to the literary genre. Thus lists of secondary points are

[128] Solange Dayras, "Les voeux de l'épiscopat britannique: reflets d'une Eglise
minoritaire," *Deuxième*, 139-53.
[129] *ADA* IV/2, p. 453.
[130] Ibid., 678-93 (dated May 11, 1960, only three days after that of the future Paul VI).
Although the votum was unsigned, the hand of Carlo Colombo could be discerned. Antonio
Rimoldi shows that there was definitely a division of labor: pastoral matters for the archbishop, doctrinal for the university (Rimoldi, "La preparazione del Concilio," 220-22).

less numerous; the tripartite division into doctrine, discipline, and context is sometimes dropped and gives way to truly thematic vota that give extensive development only to some points regarded as major (for example, the vota of Bishops Schoenmaeckers and Suenens, auxiliaries of Malines, on Catholic Action and the permanent diaconate[131]). But even when the tripartite division suggested in Tardini's letter was not drastically changed, the importance assigned to the several headings shifted away from discipline to doctrine, or else to consideration of the environing world.

One of the distinctive marks of vota of this second kind was the quality of their theological reflection; if this was not true of them all, it was far more frequent than in vota of the preceding category. This also accounted for vota that were fuller and less arid. If signs of prior consultation are not found only in this category, they are more numerous here, as I had occasion to point out earlier. Efforts, fruitless or successful, to produce a joint text were not infrequent, and the most interesting of the successful efforts come from this category: the Fulda Conference, the Indonesian episcopate, and three Oriental synods. Even before the Council, concern for effective collegiality seems undeniably to have been rather widespread in these areas.

But the main difference by comparison with the preceding trend was in the content of the vota. As the way in which the material was divided would already suggest, the difference was not that they paid more attention to the world around them, although the Indonesian conference did place the growth in world population at the head of the list of its concerns.[132] This accounts for the disappointment of some commentators who stress how little attention these vota paid to the world as context of the Church.[133] But this judgment seems to me rather severe when the entire body of vota is taken into account.

It is true that the vota in this second category are much more concerned with solving problems within the Church than with meeting the expectations of people of the twentieth century. But within the limits of this narrow framework, it has to be said that these vota show a reversal of tendency by comparison with the conformism of which I spoke earlier, for here the reform current clearly prevails over the conservative

---

[131] Claude Soetens, "Les 'vota' des évêques belges en vue du concile," in *Veille*, 41, and 43-44.

[132] *ADA* II/4, p. 271.

[133] See the nuanced judgments of Claude Soetens on Belgium and Philippe Chenaux on Switzerland in *Veille*, 38-52 and 111-18.

current. Admittedly, we still find in these responses calls for dogmatic definitions, especially concerning Mary, as Yves-Marie Hilaire notes for France,[134] but they are now balanced by very explicit refusals of anything that would intensify interconfessional disputes. In this second type of response a concern for ecumenism occupies a central place and is translated into calls for the creation of a Roman organization for dialogue among Christians. True enough, this body of vota also includes calls for condemnation, especially of communism, but there are fewer of them and they have to do more with movements outside of Catholicism than with deviations within it. Here again, France stood out somewhat because it already had doubts about the temporal involvement of priests and militants. On the other hand, a good many voices were raised to preserve scholarly study, especially of the Bible, from repressive measures now regarded as outdated. Reform of the Index, elimination of the antimodernist oath, and a change in the methods of the Holy Office: these three demands are among the surest signs of a reforming spirit.

But the vota in this second category were not content to criticize the operation of the ecclesiastical machine. They often proposed that it be radically transformed, and the basis for the proposals was not juridical considerations so much as theological reflection. The issue was the Church, looked at chiefly from the viewpoint of its nature as the body of Christ, a body whose various members, often atrophied to the profit of the head, would have to regain their full role. Rather than simply strengthening the position of the bishops, these responses offered a real theology of the episcopate; in some responses, for example, that of Archbishop Alfrink of Utrecht,[135] this led to a plea for collegiality. This theology of the episcopate was frequently accompanied by a theology of the laity, in terms of Catholic Action or otherwise. Already caught in the pincer movement of these two forces, clerics were an item of interest less for their own sake than in terms of the disciplinary questions that they raised.

Although the theological basis was less often brought out, the desire for liturgical reform extended to more than a mere adjustment of the rubrics; the issue was rather the participation of the laity, and the concern was therefore pastoral and apostolic. Consequently, the two decisive areas were the right to concelebrate and the extension of the use of the vernacular, despite Pius XII's recent restrictions in these two sensitive areas. From time to time, vota even contained explicit references

134 Hilaire, "Les voeux des evêques français," 106 (note 65, above).
135 *ADA* II/2, pp. 509-16 (December 22, 1959).

to the liturgical movement to support such requests; this was true, in particular, of the calls for the *Deutsche Singmesse* in Austria and Germany.[136] But it was one of the most active centers of the liturgical movement, the faculty of theology in Trier, that set forth the program in a well-argued way.[137]

The examples already given suggest a geography that I must now clarify. The responses most favorable to *aggiornamento* came essentially from two well-defined areas of the Catholic world: the northwestern part of continental Europe and the Churches of the Eastern rite. But the motivations of the two were not quite the same. In the former, a desire for adaptation brought together the more or less reformist aspirations of the "movements" (biblical, liturgical, ecumenical) that had arisen and grown in various places, movements for which John XXIII's Council came as a divine surprise.

In German Catholicism the pope's undertaking aroused early and sustained interest. Out of the many dialogues to which that interest gave rise and which extended far beyond the hierarchy, there came a document that can still be regarded as a model of a response that was collegial before this term became common: the collective response of the Fulda Conference, April 27, 1960. If the text did indeed suggest the condemnation of the surrounding materialism, whatever that was, this was not the backbone of the document, which instead was wholly permeated by a concern for ecumenism in a country in which Catholics and Protestants had been living side by side for years. In this perspective it proposed a substantial rewriting of the treatise *De Ecclesia* with a reassessment of the role of bishops, a definition of the place of the laity, and, of course, liturgical reform, which was already well advanced in German-speaking countries.[138] By comparison, the individual vota in German seem colorless,[139] and even frankly disappointing in the case of some renowned faculties of theology such as Bonn or Innsbruck in Austria.[140]

The collective response from Indonesia (May 15, 1960), though less well known, was no less representative of the same reformist current,

[136] Vicar Apostolic (a Capuchin) of Medan (Indonesia), *ADA* II/4, p. 238 (August 22, 1959).

[137] *ADA* II/2, pp. 754-70.

[138] See the analysis by Klaus Wittstadt, "L'episcopato tedesco e il Vatican II: preparazione e prima sessione," *Giovanni XXIII. Transizione del papato e della chiesa* (Rome, 1988) 111-13.

[139] Klaus Wittstadt, "Die bayerischen Bischöfe vor dem Zweiten Vatikanischen Konzil," *Veille*, 24-37.

[140] *ADA* IV/2, pp. 773-74 and 793-94.

both in its structure and in its content. Disdaining the usual tripartite division suggested in the Roman letter of inquiry, this response began with some "General Points." After bringing up the demographic question, it went on to raise in an emphatic way the question of the universality of the Church: adaptation of Church law and worship to the variety of situations in which Churches found themselves; collaboration between local Churches; and the participation of the entire Catholic world in its central government. A second doctrinal chapter called for a constitution on the Church and another on the status of the laity. Only then came some headings on moral and pastoral theology, the liturgy, law, and catechesis. In passing, there was a call for the establishment of a curial office that would carry on a dialogue with the World Council of Churches, which was explicitly named.[141] No discordant notes were sounded in the individual responses of the members of the conference, whether these preceded or were contemporaneous with the collective response. It is this homogeneity that persuaded me to place this missionary Church of the Third World here rather than in the third category.

But we must immediately note that the Indonesian response was indebted to Dutch Catholicism, since it was from this that the bishops came who were posted to the Indian Ocean. And when we turn to the Church of the Netherlands we are in contact with a Church that was in the process of freeing itself completely from its minority and ultramontane complex; the same could be said of its younger sisters in Scandinavia.[142] Nonetheless, Roman reservations and the conservatism of Bishop Huibers of Haarlem made any collective response impossible. The situation was the same in Belgium, where Bishop Callewaert of Ghent was cautious about the diaconate and the decline of Latin, and in Switzerland, where Bishop Charrière of Fribourg made it clear that he would not sign a document that he thought was too open on several points, although he himself unhesitatingly issued a firm condemnation of atomic weapons.

With the exception of these individuals, these three European episcopates of modest size came out in behalf of the adaptation that was being asked for, although not without introducing many qualifications. The Dutch, led by Archbishop Alfrink, who was the only one to describe the Church as "community of believers" and "people of God,"[143] were

---

[141] *ADA* II/4, p. 277.

[142] The bishop of Stockholm was still talking of regions "infected by the heresy of the Reformers," but his colleagues in Copenhagen, Helsinki, and Oslo were clearly much more open in matters ecumenical.

[143] Jacobs, "Les 'vota' des évêques néerlandais," 104 (note 76, above).

bolder than the Belgians, except for Bishop Charue of Namur, and bolder especially than the Swiss, who had no real leader.[144] The split was not along language lines: it was the German speakers who showed a greater openness in Switzerland and the French speakers in Belgium. In the three cases, the universities adopted comparable positions despite quite different styles: bolder in Louvain and Nijmegen than in Fribourg, which sent a text that was heavily Thomistic but that also contained a strong plea against Christian antisemitism.[145]

Some observers have been misled by the part played by some French bishops in the reversal of trend during the first session of the Council and have given too early a date for the fine conciliar attitudes of the bishops of France. Yves-Marie Hilaire has clarified the time-sequence by showing the existence of a strong minority of vota that represent our first model, although they called for condemnations of surrounding errors rather than for definitions.[146] This minority also found voice, sometimes an aggressive one, in some responses from universities and religious institutes. For example, the faculty of Angers sent two texts: one from its dean, Msgr. Lusseau, for whom the modernist crisis was not yet past, and another, from "many professors," that can only be read as a return of fire to the first.[147]

More pugnacious still were the proposals sent from two religious institutes that were bastions of integrist Catholicism in France. Dom Jean Prou, abbot of Solesmes, speaking in the name of the Benedictines of France, did not conceal his views: in ten two-columned pages he listed erroneous doctrines (Hegelian dialectic, for example, and the theodicy of Teilhard) and, opposite them, the remedies to be applied.[148] The superior of the fathers and brothers of St. Vincent de Paul not only deplored the relative ineffectiveness of *Humani generis*, but also denounced the numerous accusations of integrism that were being made against defenders of the true faith; he then energetically attacked every form of specialized Catholic Action in pastoral practice.[149] The votum sent by Pierre Girard for the Society of Saint-Sulpice was less violent and, above all, less fully argued, but it followed the same line.[150]

[144] Soetens on Belgium and Chenaux on Switzerland, in *Veille*.

[145] *ADA* IV/2, pp. 784-86 (Fribourg); on the votum from Louvain see Mathijs Lamberigts in *Veille*, 169-75 (note 88, above).

[146] See the table drawn up by Hilaire in *Deuxième*, 105.

[147] *ADA* IV/2, pp. 11-23 and 23-28 (no declaration of new heresies; unity of Christians; episcopal collegiality, etc.).

[148] *ADA* II/8, pp. 20-29.

[149] Ibid., 207-26.

[150] Ibid., 318-19.

The French hierarchy thus displayed a greater variety of attitudes than commentators have thought as they looked back. Dom Sortais, Abbot General of the Trappists, deplored the public differences of opinion within his institute on the education question (the future Debré law concerning aid to private schools was exciting passions when the first prelates were drafting their replies).[151] In the concerns that come to light in many vóta with regard to the definition of Catholic Action or to priestly activism Yves-Marie Hilaire detects signs pointing ahead to the crisis in the French Church. He does not, however, fall into the trap of anachronism and notes that the majority of the episcopal responses to the antepreparatory consultation bear witness to a calm and moderate spirit of reform that was supported by the five other Catholic faculties, especially Lyons,[152] and by a number of congregations that were French in origin and spirit, above all, the Sons of Charity, but also the Assumptionists, Marists, and White Fathers.

As for the bishops, their proposals dealt with standard issues: role of the bishop, place of the laity, reform of worship and of the central government of the Church, and ecumenism (37 vota out of 84). Bishop Weber of Strasbourg, who had for his adviser Dominican Yves Congar, whom he had taken into his diocese, was the only one, or almost the only one, to show greater boldness and breadth of vision in the statement on the situation of the Church, with which he introduced his votum.[153] But the award for anti-curial vigor went to Msgr. Bruno de Solages, rector of the Catholic Institute of Toulouse.[154] More French responses than one would have expected were in half-tones: if this is the main lesson which an investigation of the vota teaches, it is not enough to challenge the placing of the body of French vota in the "conciliar" category.

The borderline between this category and the preceding is clear enough to cut through a religious Order as decentralized as the Benedictines. Thus the Italian Congregation of Vallombrosa joined Solesmes in its opposition to any slackening of intransigence, while the Austrian and Bavarian congregations came out clearly on the side of the Swiss Abbot Primate against any new condemnations or definitions and for ecumenical dialogue and important internal reforms. They were followed, although in a minor key, by their Belgian, Brazilian, and British counterparts.[155]

151 Ibid., 53-54 (August 30, 1959).
152 Lyons submitted a very clear theological *Declaratio*: *ADA* IV/2, pp. 199-201.
153 Hilaire, op. cit., 102.
154 "De ecclesiasticae administrationis reformatione," *ADA* IV/2, pp. 577-80.
155 *ADA* II/8, pp. 13-46.

Generally speaking, among these monks the responses from German speakers went further and cut more deeply than those of the French speakers, with the paradoxical result that out of a concern for ecumenism the abbot of the Swiss Marian sanctuary of Einsiedeln rejected any new dogmatic definition![156]

The responses from the Uniate Orient, the variety of which does not hide their family resemblance, constitute the second main group in our second category. Even the Ukrainian emigrants in Canada and the United States, who most often wrote in Latin and launched strong attacks on communism, openly claimed their national uniqueness and their role in reunion with the Orthodox.[157] The Maronites of Lebanon, though traditionally closely tied to Rome, were not on that account any less Oriental. The synodal responses of the Armenians, the Syrians, and above all the Melkites were indeed more incisive. But a simple comparison with the Latin vota from the Near East, that of the archbishop of Smyrna, for example,[158] makes the difference obvious.

At the risk of uttering a truism, I must repeat that these vota came from Orientals living in a Church in which the overwhelming majority were Latins. Their primary aim was to maintain their distinctness in order not to cut themselves off still more from their separated brethren. As Roberto Morozzo della Rocca very soundly observes, in this situation the Orientals did not ask for "a new *Syllabus* or a new *Pascendi* or new Codes (liturgical, social, missionary, lay), such as the most Latin of the western fathers did in order to restore order amid the 'confusion' caused by the contemporary world. What the Orientals feared especially was the proclamation of new dogmatic definitions and further development of the Roman Catholic tradition, because this would separate them still further from Orthodoxy."[159] This is why the Oriental vota were obsessed with the question of the reabsorption of schism into unity and showed little apparent concern for the world around them, especially the Arab-Muslim world. This is also why these vota often took the typical form of real "lists of grievances" against Latin encroachments that too often were discrediting them in their own regions.

In both of the typical cases I have singled out, concern for union — with the Protestants in northwestern Europe, and with the Byzantino-Slavs or nonchalcedonians in the Orient — played a determining role in

---

[156] *ADA* II/2, p. 47.
[157] Roberto Morozzo della Rocca, "I 'voti' degli Orientali," *Veille*, 123-24.
[158] *ADA* IV/2, pp. 623-25.
[159] *Veille*, 125.

the openness which these responses showed to the conciliar perspectives sketched by John XXIII.

2c. Contrasts and Uncertainties

The third category of responses to the antepreparatory consultation is not the easiest to define. In fact, does it really exist? Could we not, in fact, do what we just did for Indonesia: divide the vota from the peripheral areas of the Catholic world according to the two, essentially European, criteria of withdrawal from and receptiveness to the pope's proposed *aggiornamento*? Such a division into two groups would have the merit of simplicity: hierarchies of Iberian or British origin, on the one side; hierarchies of French-speaking or Dutch origin, on the other. But it is only a short step from simplicity to simplism. A division into two camps would anticipate the fact that the majority of the fathers concerned would rally to the future majority at the Council while a minority joined the conciliar minority. But this was by no means obvious in 1959-60, a period at which no clear tendency emerged from the combined vota of this third group.

What was it, in fact, that distinguished the vota of Portuguese-speaking Brazil from those of the remainder of Spanish-speaking Latin America? It is the heterogeneity of their suggestions that constitutes, in my view, the chief characteristic of the Brazilians. Third largest in the world, after the Italian and the American, the Brazilian episcopate sent Rome responses that covered the entire spectrum of possible positions. At one extreme, Bishop Proença Sigaud, at that time bishop of Jacarézinho, described the Church as a fortress being attacked from without by a mob of enemies and threatened from within by advocates of a "Trojan Horse strategy"; his inflexible integralism looked to the Council for the condemnation of both groups, beginning with a condemnation of Maritain, who in his view had done a great deal of harm to Catholicism in Latin America.[160]

At the other extreme, Bishop Helder Câmara, secretary of the episcopal conference and vice-president of CELAM, in a short but quite nonconformist response, suggested that Latin not be the language of the Council and that the Church commit itself there to the formation of a better world first of all in economic and social areas, but also in esthetic, scientific, and political areas.[161] Between these two extremes were all the nuances separating candid reserve from confident openness.[162]

[160] *ADA* II/7, pp. 180-95 (August 22, 1959), especially p. 190.

[161] Ibid., pp. 325-27 (August 15, 1959).

[162] On the situation of the Church in Brazil see José Oscar Beozzo's essay in *Vísperas*, 49-81.

The dissimilarity in these vota is found at the various levels of the Catholic world; it was neither a morass nor a third party. First of all, within the same continent: in the case of Africa or Oceania we need only compare the responses from French speakers with those from English speakers. Neither nuances nor exceptions, such as the bold statements of Archbishop Roberts, former Archbishop of Bombay,[163] suffice to do away with the contrasts between two religious sensibilities that were quite removed each from the other. The missions or young Churches of British origin were more timid about accepting the possibility of an adaptation of the apostolate to local conditions.

The same contrasts were to be seen in the smaller setting of two geographically proximate nations. The gulf separating the Philippine bishops, mostly of Spanish origin, from the Indonesian bishops of Dutch origin is striking: the latter, spokesmen for a minority community in a Muslim country, were much more open than the former, who were leaders in a predominantly Latin Catholic world from which they gladly drew their inspiration. Thus the auxiliary of Manila called for a reorganization of Catholic Action along the lines of the centralized Italian model and under Roman supervision.[164] Under these conditions, the local religious environment easily prevailed over a bishop's origin; thus Bishop Van den Ouwelant of Surigao wanted the exaltation of Mary and Joseph as well as the continuation of Latin in the Mass.[165]

The same contrasts were also to be seen within a single country or a single linguistic area; for example, between the English speaking and French speaking responses in Canada. Joseph Komonchak has shown the great variety in the American vota, from the resolute conservatism of a Mc Intyre of Los Angeles to the ecumenical openness of many of his confreres. The Catholic University of America was not spared such divisions; the faculties of theology and of law were clearly not on the same wavelength, and yet it was the faculty of law, once this is distinguished from custom, that showed itself less uneasy about novelty.[166] In French-speaking Africa, too, differences of view about the future Council were considerable; indeed, this adjective is too weak to describe the gulf between a Marcel Lefebvre, Archbishop of Dakar, and a Louis Durrieu, Bishop of Ouagadougou (Upper Volta).[167]

---

[163] Solange Dayras, "Les voeux de l'épiscopat britannique," *Deuxième*, 151-52.

[164] *ADA* II/4, pp. 327-30 (September 1, 1959).

[165] Ibid., pp. 301-4 (March 31 and June 15, 1960).

[166] Komonchak, "U.S. Bishops' Suggestions," p. 369-70; *ADA* IV/2, pp. 615-31.

[167] *ADA* II/5, pp. 47-54 (February 26, 1960((attacks on Fathers Rétif and Congar, p. 48); pp. 61-83 (February 12, 1959; *sic*: 1960?) (theology of the episcopate, pp. 65-68). The only thing the two texts have is common is that they are in French.

Finally, the same contrasts show up even within some individual responses. Cardinal Gracias of Bombay obviously wanted a fairly radical reform of the Roman system, but he did not think this incompatible with the definition of new Marian dogmas.[168] Cardinal Doi of Tokyo, who was close to Gracias on more than one point, was reserved when it came to new definitions but did want an investigation and condemnation of such intellectual trends as existentialism and relativism.[169] But the award for inconsistency undoubtedly went to their colleague, the Archbishop of Taipei (Formosa) who asked for the eradication of every trace of colonialism in evangelization and for the internationalization of the Church's central curia, but at the same called for definitions (Mystical Body, Mary as mediatrix and coredemptrix) and condemnations (of communism, atheistic humanism, existentialism) in accordance with *Humani generis*.[170] Such contradictions are not adequately explained by appealing to human inconsistency. Should we not see in them rather a reflection of the conflict, henceforth difficult to resolve, between the Roman cast of mind and the pressures of the environment?

As this first overview shows, there was in this third category of vota an overlapping of religious cultures so different that one would have been venturesome indeed to anticipate how they would behave toward one another at the Council. Unlike the first two categories, whose sympathies were hardly in doubt from 1959-60 on, the responses of this third kind came from episcopates too divided for any clear tendency to emerge. That is why the fall of 1962 brought so many surprises.

Let me go back to the responses from Brazil. Both Helder Câmara and Proença Sigaud were worried about the state of Catholicism in their country, although for opposite reasons. This seems to me to be the second element that distinguishes this third group of vota. Unlike responses from Europe, these most often started from intraecclesial problems and then evoked local situations. The American situation, for example, included theological questions: a quarter of the bishops suggested tackling the problem of religious freedom that had become acute since the controversy of the 1950s caused by the work of Jesuit John Courtney Murray. Moreover, seventeen of the American bishops questioned the formula "No salvation outside the Church," which since the end of the 1940s had been given a rigorist interpretation by another, now dissenting, Jesuit, Leonard Feeney.[171]

---

[168] *ADA* II/4, pp. 109-16.
[169] Ibid., pp. 84-88 (no date).
[170] Ibid., pp. 341-43 (August 23, 1960).
[171] Komonchak, "U.S. Bishops' Suggestions," p. 343-49.

This theme was, moreover, a characteristic mark of English-speaking Catholicism, whereas little attention was paid to it elsewhere; thus it appeared again in the vota of the British, Australian, and Indian bishops.

In Southeast Asia, the desire for a dialogue with Buddhism cropped up here and there. In an especially well informed votum, Archbishop Bazin of Rangoon (Burma) expressed a desire that in regard to Buddhism the Council should decide between the view that it is atheistic and the view of Daniélou, de Lubac, Guardini, and Karrer, that it is an incomplete religion; the archbishop clearly favored this second view.[172]

But the role of the Church in the surrounding world also had the attention of the bishops. In a happy surprise, more than a third of the American responses paid some heed to it. While the prelates chiefly concerned fell short of the position they had taken earlier on the integration of chicanos, racial segregation was a challenge to those from the south, and they rejected it, sometimes vigorously, as did Bishop Rummel of New Orleans.[173] On the other hand, Archbishop Hurley of Durban in the Union of South Africa, did not say a word about apartheid, although he had often criticized it publicly; did he think that this was not a question for a Council to take up?[174]

In Africa, the burning problems connected with decolonization were rarely brought up as such but did crop up rather frequently in the vota, but in more or less roundabout ways. The bishops of the province of Luluabourg (in Congo-Léopoldville), a province shaken by demands for independence, came out clearly for the missions and against nationalism.[175] How else are we to interpret the sharp condemnation of communism by their colleagues in Angola and Mozambique if not as a reaction to the movements of emancipation, behind which they saw the hand of Moscow and even, at this early date, of Cuba? Was not the obvious difference in assessment of Islam by Archbishop Duval of Algiers and Bishop Lacaste, his suffragan in Oran, an echo of their other, well-known disagreement on the Algerian conflict? Lacaste, who was closely associated with the view that Algeria belonged to France, was certainly less disposed to dialogue than Duval, who was rather critical of that view.[176]

---

[172] *ADA* II/4, pp. 24-26 (August 25, 1959).

[173] *ADA* II/6, pp. 382-91 (August 27, 1959).

[174] *ADA* II/5, pp. 537-59 (April 15, 1960) (votum cited).

[175] Claude Soetens, "L'apport du Congo-Léopoldville (Zaïre), du Rwanda et du Burundi au concile Vatican II," in *Vatican II commence....*, pp. 189-208.

[176] *ADA* II/5, pp. 99-103 (August 22, 1959); pp. 110-15 (August 29, 1959). On the disagreements between the two men see André Nozière, *Algérie: les chrétiens dans la guerre* (Paris, 1979).

On the strictly religious level, a number of missionary bishops of Belgian and French origin pleaded for an Africanization of Catholicism, a view that supposed colonization to be now in the past.

Do the responses of this third kind allow us, then, to define a kind of Catholic Third World that was a distant echo of Bandung or of its consequences? Not really, because properly Third World concerns were infrequent and allusive in a set of vota which includes those of North America and Australasia but not those of Spanish-speaking America. Less worried about using Latin (a fourth of the vota from Africa were in the vernaculars), less often respectful also of canonical forms, very diverse in their content, and more sensitive to the variety of local situations, these sometimes unpredictable responses often stand out against the grayness of the rest of the vota.

A negative criterion (the divergence in the responses) and a positive criterion (their closer attention to the surrounding world) thus define this group of vota sent by bishops whose future behavior at the Council no one could have predicted. An accurate inventory of these responses is often hindered by the lack of first-hand studies. Those of Avery Dulles on American theology and of Joseph Komonchak on the American vota show that the North American episcopate was better prepared for Vatican II than is generally thought. There were indeed sharp differences within this episcopate, but the common distinction between the openness of the Midwest and the conservatism of the two coasts is not a compelling one. "If none of the bishops was a revolutionary, a good number could be considered reformists," is Komonchak's conclusion at the end of a work that does not, however, gloss over the less open-minded reactions.[177] At first sight, tensions seemed more acute in Brazil; it would be of interest here to clarify further the influence of Father Lombardi, who preached a retreat to the bishops May 5-8, 1960.[178] On the other hand, such tensions seemed less acute in southern and eastern Asia.

The African continent, for its part, also provided well known examples of sharp contrasting and bold views that in fact surprised John XXIII.[179] It is interesting, however, to see that these views came less

[177] Komonchak, "U.S. Bishops' Suggestions," p. 366; Avery Dulles, "Theological Orientations. American Catholic Theology," *CrSt* 13/2 (1992) 361-82.

[178] José Oscar Beozzo, in *Vísperas*, 71.

[179] On the report of March 7, 1960, that consolidated the African vota, the pope wrote: "Copious and detailed remarks, sometimes rather bizarre and debatable, but an expression of apostolic zeal and worthy of attention"; see Carbone, "Il cardinale Domenico Tardini," 69. Is it not likely that the pope's surprise was caused by the eight requests for the relaxing of priestly celibacy?

from native prelates than from their missionary colleagues who carried European quarrels over to Africa. The former were faithful to Latin and to proven canonical forms, and their vota were marked by a great caution that was hardly visible later at the Council.[180] It must be said, however, that in 1959-60 there were still few native bishops in countries in which de colonization was imminent; by 1962 several of them would be the leaders of young Churches in new states, and that changed everything.[181]

I have already noted the linguistic division: the Italians, Iberians, and British were less inclined to challenge the Roman system than were the Belgians and the French — from this point of view, Archbishop Lefebvre of Dakar was rather an exception. On the other hand, continuity with the various European positions was often striking. Like his English colleagues, Bishop McCann of Cape Town advocated condemnations but no new definitions that might alarm noncatholics; and Archbishop McCarthy of Nairobi meant to keep Latin as the predominant language of the Mass.[182] On the other side, the votum of the faculty of theology of the Lovanium in Leopoldville, recently established by Louvain and staffed by graduates of Louvain, revealed an inspiration very like that of the mother university.[183]

The difference between the responses of missionary priests of the Spiritan congregation and those of their colleagues, the White Fathers, has not gone unnoticed. The former (in addition to Archbishop Lefebvre, we may think, for example, of Archbishop Bernard of Brazzaville) were not outstanding for their boldness. The second group, on the other hand, sketched an unworried Africanization of Catholicism, and this without regard to linguistic barriers. To the example, already mentioned, of Bishop Durrieu must be added that of Bishop Blomjous of Mwanza in Tanganyika, although he was quite discreet in his response, and, above all, that of Bishop Matthijsen, Vicar Apostolic of Lake Albert, who came out in favor of establishing within the universal Church cultural regions that would have far-reaching liturgical autonomy.[184] We recall that the votum submitted by the superior of the White Fathers was pretty much along the same lines.

---

[180] See, e.g., the votum of Bishop Rugambwa of Rutabo (Tanganyika), *ADA* II/5, pp. 480-81 (August 6, 1959).

[181] Claude Prudhomme, "Les évêques d'Afrique noire anciennement française et le Concile," in *Vatican II commence*, 163-88.

[182] *ADA* II/5, pp. 535-37 (August 22, 1960); pp. 256-58 (August 25, 1959).

[183] Lamberigts, in *Veille*, 175-82.

[184] Claude Soetens, "L'apport du Congo-Léopoldville (Zaïre)," in *Vatican II commence*, 189-208.

The body of vota that have been studied does not allow us to go further in determining patterns to be seen in the responses of the religious congregations, although such a study would be worthwhile, since it would provide another key for interpreting the third type of response to the antepreparatory consultation.

When seen from the observation point provided by the non-Roman vota, the antepreparatory consultation brought out less the unity of the Catholic world than its diversity. Innovative views were not lacking in this enormous body of material, but their impact was diluted by a mass of responses that were timid and in a good number of cases frankly narrow-minded. Many bishops were surprised by the pope's decision and toward it adopted an attitude of cautious waiting. It was on these bishops that curial circles relied in order to impose on this kaleidoscopic material a coherence deriving from their own vision of the Council, a vision that was rather far removed from the enigmatic *aggiornamento* from which they might have everything to fear.

V. FROM CONTEMPT TO COOPTATION

When we turn now to the Roman viewpoint, the antepreparatory consultation should enable us to answer two major questions that remain. On the one hand, how did the secretariat of the Tardini commission handle the raw material of the responses from throughout the Catholic world so as to derive from them, if not a program, at least a synthesis that would point a clear way for future activity? This labor, however, was not unaffected by Roman thinking at this time about the future Council. On the other hand, then, what was the reaction of Vatican circles to the appeals of the cardinal Secretary of State? A study of the Roman vota can provide useful details of their feelings about the event that had been announced.

These Roman vota were of two quite different kinds. The initial consultation also involved future Council fathers who were then residing in Rome, both prelates and religious. The request made of them was followed, as we know, by invitations to the institutions of higher learning and the curial offices that they submit collective observations and proposals. An accurate assessment of the Roman position during the antepreparatory phase must therefore take into account these three sets of data. In light of the documentation presently available, I suggest that there was a seemingly paradoxical but nonetheless real connection between the lack of interest shown in the individual consultation and the great effort made to channel its results in a resolute manner. The more ludicrous such a consultation seemed, the more important it was to forestall its possible harmful effects.

1. *Between Indifference and Distrust: The Roman Vota*

Andrea Riccardi's study of the Roman vota leaves no doubt on this point:[185] Curial officials, those in charge of the vicariate of Rome and of the suburbican dioceses, the Romans who would participate in the Council, did not pay much attention to Tardini's consultation. A first typical instance: the surprising lack of any response from such cardinals as Tisserant, who, as we know, had no great love for John XXIII. A second typical case, and, it seems, the most common: responses whose brevity or poverty make their conventional character all the clearer. A third and final typical case, though this is in fact only a variant of the second: some responses openly displayed a firm conservatism that closely links them to our first category of vota. These are all the more noteworthy in that some of them came from princes of the Church who exerted great influence in the curia. Thus Cardinal Micara, Vicar of Rome, did not hesitate to attack openly the "theories" of Maritain and of the journal *Esprit*, which in his view were guilty of inciting the laity to an excessive independence of the hierarchy.[186]

The only two exceptions to a casualness that bordered on contempt were nonetheless significant. More articulate, if not more open, vota came both from foreign prelates resident in Rome (Gawlina of Poland, for example, and Hudal of Germany) and from Italian prelates loyal to Pacelli and more or less influenced by the theses of Jesuit Riccardo Lombardi: these called for reform, but one controlled by Rome, and designed to improve the functioning of the Vatican machinery.[187]

These rare evidences of attention were not enough, however, to reverse the general trend. How, then, are we to interpret a lack of interest too obvious for it not to have been deliberate? One factor was undoubtedly reservations about the whole idea of a general Council, since the preparation for it and the celebration itself would uselessly disrupt the ordinary government of the Church. In this respect, the poverty of the Roman vota confirm the lukewarmness (to put it mildly)

---

[185] "I 'vota' romani," in *Veille*, 148-56.
[186] Ibid., 150-51.
[187] Ibid., 152-56.

of the approvals from the cardinals after the announcement of January 25, 1959.

To a lesser degree, there were reservations with regard to the procedure being followed: Vatican circles were not very enthusiastic about a universal consultation without any limitations imposed to keep the sparks from flying; but they also doubted that the whole matter concerned them directly, destined as they were to have a deliberative and not simply consultative role. How could their views be simply set alongside those of far-distant prelates who for them were often only names in the *Annuario Pontificio*? Many of them were also convinced that the serious work would begin only when the shapeless mass of vota were processed...in Rome. Why, then, should they prematurely waste their energies on useless skirmishes that might give the unfortunate impression of a last-ditch struggle against the pope's decision? Only those members of the curia who more clearly foresaw the danger immediately began taking countermeasures. Furthermore, it was this mixture of disbelief in the coming event and of deep-rooted conservatism that caused the failure, early in 1960, of the Roman synod, which John XXIII had announced at the same time as the Council.

Almost all the general superiors of the religious congregations that had been founded under Roman influence or that had long since set up their headquarters there showed a greater interest in the antepreparatory consultation. This was not true, however, of Michael Browne, Master General of the Dominicans. His votum, sent on May 16, 1960, was content to suggest, in addition to the restoration of the permanent diaconate, the elevation of the Oriental patriarchs to the rank of cardinal and the establishment of a new curial office for studies.[188] Both form and content make it clear that in the eyes of this de jure member of the Holy Office the consultation meant only an unnecessary chore.

Browne's votum was in striking contrast to a response that undoubtedly stood out from the pack: that of Augustin Sepinski, Minister General of the Franciscans. It was submitted rather quickly (September 30, 1959) and was more detailed. The author took a stand against the unbridled theological passion (*rabies theologica*) that was so fond of definitions and condemnations, and, more clearly still, against atomic weaponry. On the positive side, he came out not only for continued

[188] *ADA* II/8, pp. 65-68.

liturgical reform and the restoration of the diaconate but also for the establishment in Rome of an ecumenical commission (*coetus oecumenicus*) for dialogue with the separated brethren.[189]

As usual, the votum of John Baptist Janssens, General of the Jesuits, took a position halfway between these two extremes. He signaled the danger of a godless humanism and a relativistic philosophy that had freed itself from Scholasticism, but he also came out for more extensive use of the vernaculars in the liturgy. In fact, on a series of issues ranging from the authority of the ordinary magisterium to ecumenism to the place of the laity in the Church, he raised a number of important questions, but refrained from giving his own answer to them.[190]

Most of his counterparts were not so cautious. Although they were not alone in this respect, their collective volleys nonetheless helped to turn the Roman and quasi-Roman vota in a consciously defensive direction. The only element of openness, if it can be called that, in the vota of these religious superiors was often their determination to maintain their exemption in face of episcopal hunger. But they also rivalled one another in their inflexibility in matters doctrinal and liturgical as well as in their inventiveness in matters dogmatic as they strove to give Joseph a place at Mary's side. Especially indicative in this respect were the responses from the Hermits of St. Augustine, the Discalced Carmelites, and the Servites.[191] But the same tendency was to be seen in other religious families marked by the Roman spirit; for example, the Conventual Franciscans, the Capuchins, and the Trinitarians.

All in all, two distinct points emerge from the vota of the future Council fathers then residing in Rome: on the one hand, their undeniably conservative, rather than wait-and-see, attitude, despite some exceptions that were all the less commonplace for being isolated; on the other, their authors' lack of respect for the consultation, which they regarded as merely a concession to the democratic spirit of the age and which for that very reason could not, in their view, play a decisive role in the preparation of the program for the Council. But that this preparation did in fact concern them very greatly is proved both by the theological reflection on the future Council that went on in Rome at this same period and by the effort at normalization to which the vota from the four quarters of the Catholic world were subjected.

[189] Ibid., pp. 69-72.
[190] Ibid., pp. 124-27.

2. Roman Theology Confronts the Council

We need only page through the journals published by the Roman universities and analyze the responses to Tardini's call in which their thinking is summarized, and we will see something far from indifference: a watchful and unremitting attention to the process by which Vatican II was being brought to birth. These collective developments make it quite clear that the Roman centers of study meant to play at the Council their traditional role as the Vatican's official intellectuals, even before they provided the Council with its chief experts. But in what direction were they moving? That is the main question.

A cursory reading of Roman theological production during the antepreparatory phase leaves hardly any doubt on this point.[192] Admittedly, this whole body of material contained too many nuances for any deceptive homogeneity to be claimed for it. There is also a remarkably close similarity between the vota of the general superiors and those of the Roman institutes belonging to their congregations. There was but one exception to this rule: the gulf between the closed mind of the Antonianum and the openness of Father Sepinski.[193] On the other hand, there can be no better example of consistency than that provided by the Dominicans: like the response of Master General Browne, that of the Angelicum, which is exactly contemporaneous, is distinguished by its skimpiness; it thus confirms the lack of interest of the higher echelons of the Order in the preliminary stages of preparation for the Council.[194]

The same correspondence can be seen in the openness to reform of the Salesian vota, apart from doctrinal questions, and in the skilful balance shown in the Jesuit vota, although the Gregorian University would later, under pressure from John XXIII, have to revise its material on relations

[191] Ibid., pp. 84-96, 104-6, 112-14.

[192] Etienne Fouilloux, "Théologiens romains et Vatican II (1959-1962)," *CrSt* 15 (1994) 373-94.

[193] *ADA* IV/I/2, pp. 51-109. The use of the vota of the Roman colleges and universities raises a problem of chronology. These vota, which were requested for Easter, 1960, and were sent between March 7 (the Angelicum) and May 25 (the Anselmianum), completed the consultation cycle and should therefore be discussed *after* the summarizing reports of the secretariat of Tardini's commission and the proposals of the curial agencies, since these reports and proposals preceded the vota of the colleges and universities. I have chosen to bring the latter in at this point because they seem to me to be the result of a process of reflection that had been going on for over a year and because this very process explains to some extent the spirit of the reports and proposals of the curial agencies.

[194] Ibid., pp. 7-27, of which four deal with theological questions and three come from Father Garrigou-Langrange.

between pope and bishops.[195] In contrast, the appendices to the text of this renowned university do not all show the same caution. The lengthy classical votum on marriage by Franz Hürth, Pius XII's moral theologian,[196] has rightly been contrasted with the positive proposals submitted by the Institute of Social Sciences regarding the struggle against poverty and, even more, the response of the Biblical Institute, which stands out clearly from the entire body of vota. Although they were suspected of serious errors, the exegetes of the Society of Jesus had the courage forcefully to recall three pressing needs: freedom for biblical scholarship, the reform of disciplinary procedures, and, above all, a radical change in the way Catholics spoke of Judaism.[197] But this boldness, which suggests that even in Rome the Society of Jesus was less homogeneous than it had been ten years earlier, was an isolated phenomenon.

Small or large, secular or belonging to religious congregations, the other Roman institutions of higher learning were at one in their frankly conservative views, although the emphases differed slightly in each case. Since the Gregorianum could not conceal certain disagreements between the older men in charge and a new generation of more flexible professors, its hitherto undisputed leadership was henceforth challenged by a rapidly rising Lateranum. Once John XXIII turned the Roman college where he had done his ecclesiastical studies into a full-fledged university (May 17, 1959), the Lateranum appointed itself the watchdog of Catholicism, as was shown by its attack on the Biblical Institute. Moreover, it provided itself with the weapons for this attack: its journal *Divinitas* was also the vehicle for the Pontifical Academy of Theology, an organization that served as a rallying point for *zelanti* (zealots) of every kind. The vota of the Lateran professors are impressive both for their volume and for the impression they give of already being conciliar drafts.[198] A number of these men, who were already consultors to the Curia, evidently wanted to imprint the mark of their thinking on the future Council.

What these men had in mind seemed, to say the least, far removed from the *aggiornamento* of which John XXIII was speaking. In a very explicit and much more structured way than in the vota of those bishops whose intuitions these professors were reducing to systematic form, they in effect sketched a plan as it were to bring four centuries of intransigent

---

[195] Incident reported in Carbone, "Il cardinale Domenico Tardini," 70. Compare the two versions: *ADA* IV/I/1, p. 14, and the one in Carbone.

[196] *ADA* IV, pp. 90-118.

[197] Ibid., 125-36 ("On avoiding antisemitism" [*De antisemitismo vitando*], 131-32).

[198] Ibid., pp. 169-442!

Catholicism to a climax, in regard both to the claims of the Roman Church and to protection against the countless dangers, domestic and foreign, that were threatening it.

There was no ambiguity about the first of these two goals. At the solemn start of the new school year for the Lateran University (October 28, 1959), one of its patrons and former professors, Cardinal Ruffini of Palermo, declared: "The coming Council will be able, if it thinks it appropriate, to give their principal teachings a definitive value that would set them above and beyond any discussion."[199] The teachings to which he was referring were those of Leo XIII, Pius X, Benedict XV, Pius XI, and Pius XII.

This yearning for dogmas found expression under four major headings. First of all, to see to it that Vatican II gave solemn consecration to new privileges for Joseph and, of course, for Mary. The most fervent here were the Servites of the Marianum, the Franciscans of the Antonianum, and the Conventuals of the St. Bonaventure school of theology. They were better informed about the situation in the Vatican than many bishops were and they insisted as much on the spiritual maternity of the Blessed Virgin as on her role as mediatrix and corredemptrix.

A second objective: to lock the doors in the area of exegesis in order to check the laxity that had reappeared in the wake of the encyclical *Divino afflante Spiritu*. This time it was clearly the Lateran itself that was spearheading the drive, under the leadership of its specialist, Msgr. Francesco Spadafora. To obtain this objective he proposed a definition of "the unqualified inerrancy of the Bible," since only this could drastically reduce the range of possible interpretations.[200] In the background, a number of his colleagues were hoping that monogenism would be upgraded to the status of a truth of faith.

A third urgent need: an irrevocable certification of the exclusive authority of Thomism in the teaching of philosophy and theology; on this point, the Angelicum and even the Benedictine Anselmianum agreed with the Lateran. A fourth and final concern and the one most emphasized: strengthening the hierarchical structure of the Church by making obedience to the ordinary magisterium incumbent on all, in keeping with the example given by Pius X and Pius XII, to whom our authors constantly appealed.[201] "If anyone says that the Roman Pontiff is

---

[199] *Divinitas*, 4 (1960) 15.

[200] *ADA* IV/I/1, pp. 263-70.

[201] Special issue of *Divinitas* 3 (1959, no. 4) on "Pope Pius XII and Sacred Theology."

not the immediate source of all jurisdiction in the external forum, let him be anathema": such was the new canon proposed by Msgr. Lattanzi of the Lateran.[202] Thus, almost a century after the definition of papal primacy and infallibility, many Roman theologians continued to think that an increase in papal prerogatives, which meant, secondarily, an increase in their own, was the best way to stress the distinctiveness of Catholicism and to preserve it against all attacks. We can understand why they resented the open consultation of the episcopate as a costly rebuff and why they were rather contemptuous of it.

It was a matter, after all, not simply of self-promotion but also of self-protection. As a result, the prevailing tone of the responses from the Roman universities was less positive than negative. This can be felt in the form adopted in their responses, which was that of a deductive theology that often rests upon earlier documents of the magisterium as collected by Denzinger and his successors.[203] It was also a theology-"against," the principal function of which was to identify errors and then to pillory them; thus the votum of the Carmelite faculty of theology attacked Henri Duméry, who had just been disciplined, and Pierre Teilhard de Chardin, who would be disciplined shortly before the beginning of the Council.[204] Such calls for condemnation proliferated: there were no fewer than 61 of them in the virtual draft of a *syllabus errorum* that was offered by the Conventual faculty of theology of St. Bonaventure.[205] From eugenics to communism by way of feminism and nudism,[206] few were the twentieth-century deviations, or what were thought to be such, that escaped the watchful eyes of these guardians of the temple.

But amid the universal perversion of thought and morals nothing angered these men more than its infiltration into the bosom of the Church itself. Thus Msgr. Romeo, in his attack on the Biblicum, vigorously denounced the termites that were insidiously eating away at Catholic doctrine and the Catholic faith.[207] Whatever the name given to this undermining process — irrationalism, relativism, or subjectivism, or all three combined — it had to be combatted without truce or mercy in its many forms: exegetical, liturgical, moral, philosophical, and, finally,

---

[202] *ADA* IV/I/1, p. 209.

[203] 36 of the 55 footnotes in the response of the Servites (at the Marianum) contained at least one reference to Denzinger; *ADA* IV/I/2, pp. 426-59.

[204] Ibid., pp. 321-32.

[205] Ibid., pp. 235-59.

[206] The section on "The 'new morality'" (*De "morali nova"*) in the response from the Franciscan Antonianum, ibid., pp. 86-88.

[207] *Divinitas*, 4 (1960) 454.

theological. In addition, these attackers still had their sights set on the French "new theology": and especially on Henri de Lubac, even now, ten years after hierarchial lightning had struck him down. In other words, and contrary to what an overly French-centered history of contemporary theology might believe, that thick file had not been closed.

All this accounts for the omnipresence, among the *zelanti*, of references to the encyclical *Humani generis* of August 12, 1950, in which the earlier crisis had culminated.[208] Far from being outdated, this restrictive document remained utterly relevant. To the extent that its warnings had not been heeded, they had to be renewed and brought up to date, that is, expanded and systematized. Thus Msgr. Garafalo, rector of the College of the Propaganda, expected the Council to compose a new formula of faith that would include the recent warnings, as well as a new universal catechism that would spell out the meaning of the new formula.[209] Bluntly and effectively the Salesianum neatly summed up the deep feelings of Roman theological circles: "As for modern errors, the Council could refute those listed in the encyclical *Humani generis* of Pius XII."[210] My conclusions thus match those of Antonino Indelicato in his study of the theological preparation made in Rome for Vatican II: a supreme effort to bar the approaches to Catholic truth, in the spirit that marked the end of the preceding pontificate.[211]

This intellectual environment with its oscillation between coolness and pugnacity surely played a larger part in the Roman reaction to the antepreparatory consultation than did the individual incomplete or skimpy vota. It also sheds light on the spirit in which the episcopal responses would be dealt with.

3. *The Work on the Vota*

The close examination of the vota, which historians are undertaking today, was done by the secretariat of the Tardini Commission throughout the fall and winter of 1959-60, but for an entirely different purpose: to provide the future preparatory commissions with key ideas so that they would not get lost amid so many divergent paths. Msgr. Carbone,

---

[208] There are six mentions of this document in the votum of Dom Vagaggini of the Anselmianum; *ADA* IV/I/2, pp. 33-43.

[209] "De symbolo et professione fidei noviter proponendis in concilio," *ADA* IV/I/1, pp. 447-52.

[210] Ibid., IV/I/2, p. 124.

[211] "Lo schema 'De deposito fidei pure custodiendo' e la preparazione del Vaticano II," *CrSt* 11 (1990) 345-51.

who took part in that labor, has carefully complemented the published documents with a description of the method and time-table that were followed. He says nothing, however, of the mental frameworks that were applied, doubtless because they are still too deeply impressed on him for him to be able to look at them critically.[212]

As early as the end of August, 1959, Tardini, it seems, set two phases for the work: a thematic analysis of the vota, and then syntheses by areas prior to a final synthesis. For the analysis, the plan was to use large-size cards, with meticulous regulations for their use: only one subject on a card; all the cards in Latin; a summary of the subject matter or a copy of it if it proved to be too complex; identification of the prelate submitting the votum. The example given for advice about subject matter: the rejection of "situation morality."[213]

The examination started, then, at the beginning of September, 1959, and with the Italian responses. This, too, was by no means accidental, for it gave the workers in the secretariat time to get the operation running smoothly. A first batch of cards, with doctrinal material, was sent to the members of the antepreparatory commission on November 3. Four more followed during the period until December 15, all still dealing with the Italian vota. The division of the material was significant: first, proposals concerning the clergy and religious, then the laity, the liturgy, and social and charitable activities, and finally the missions, and, right at the end because quite novel, ecumenism.[214]

As the introduction to the *Analyticus Conspectus* would later confirm, the order followed was not an insignificant one: "Cards were filled out, beginning with doctrinal subjects in the order established by theologians and moving on to the various areas in the ecclesiastical disciplines, arranged for the most part in accordance with the Code."[215] Thus the two tools used in classifying the wishes of the bishops were the division into treatises followed by textbook theology and the Code of Canon Law. We have already seen, of course, that these tools were suitable for dealing with that part of the responses that had spontaneously followed the same plan. But did this procedure not risk neglecting other responses, those, for example, whose purpose was to analyze a situation rather provide a list of suggestions? Did it not risk pruning others that used other interpretive grids, by forcing them into a mould that by its nature had no place for what was original in the responses?

[212] Carbone, "Il cardinale Domenico Tardini," 67-70.
[213] "Normae praecipuae," *ADA* II, App. 1, p. vii.
[214] *ADA* III, p. xii.
[215] *ADA* II, App. 1, p. v.

There is no doubt that the method followed made it easier to combine differing positions, but it also meant that it would not draw attention to those that seemed — in the Roman view of things — the most unexpected. The metaphor of the gospel comes quickly to mind: the new wine would in all likelihood be lost in these old wineskins.[216] It is not surprising that the secretariat of the Tardini Commission took a body of material the richness of which we have seen and imposed on it the only conceptual framework familiar to them, but it was a framework that would both impoverish the material and predetermine the result of the operation.

The work continued its unruffled way to the end of January, 1960; the last cards, extracted from the vota of the religious superiors, were sent on February 8. The examination had begun with Italy and moved on to France and the rest of Europe except for the German-speaking countries, then to Latin America, Germany and Austria; only then did it turn to Asia, Oceania, North America, and Africa.[217] It is difficult not to see in this progression a reflection of the Vatican's symbolic geography, which was Eurocentric — even Italocentric. The approximately 2000 thematic cards, carrying over 9000 proposals, were not, however, exhaustive, since several hundred responses were still outstanding. Only on March 21, 1960, was a reminder sent to those still delaying.

The work done was nevertheless enormous. To be usable, it required some kind of index that would facilitate consultation of it. This tool would be the *Analyticus Conspectus consiliorum et votorum quae ab episcopis et praelatis data sunt* (An analytic survey of the suggestions and vota submitted by the bishops and prelates). This was itself imposing: over 1500 printed pages in two volumes.[218] Its origin and function, however, remain obscure. The date it bears, February 1, 1961, is obviously the date of the printing that climaxed the compilation. But when was it conceived and for what purpose? All the available evidence points to a desire to help the preparatory commissions in their work; faced with this overwhelming mass of responses, the commissions would need a guide to keep them from getting lost in it. Rather than add the entire set of thematic cards to their burden, why not provide the commissions with a substantial digest of them? The result: the *Conspectus*, which must therefore have been composed at the beginning of the

[216] Giuseppe Alberigo, "Passaggi cruciali della fase antepreparatoria," *Verso il concilio*, 15-42.

[217] *ADA* III, p. xii.

[218] *AD* II, App. 1 and 2, 806 and 733 pages respectively.

preparatory phase, probably during the second half of 1960. If this hypothesis regarding chronology is accurate, it suggests that the *Conspectus* played no part in the development of the program for the Council, unlike the synthesizing reports of which I shall speak later. It would simply have served, as Caprile has written, as a "repertory of ideas" for the use of the preparatory commissions.[219]

This determination of the purpose in no way detracts from the real value of the *Conspectus*, provided we do not misjudge its character. Far from being "a panoramic photograph of the desires and problems of the Catholic world,"[220] the *Conspectus* displays the results of the screening of the vota by Felici's secretariat with the two sieves provided by the theology of the manuals and by canon law. It would therefore be a mistake to look to the *Conspectus* for a faithful echo of the antepreparatory consultation. On the other hand, it is indeed a valuable source for a better understanding of the spirit in which this consultation was handled in Rome.[221]

The *Conspectus* divides the material under eighteen headings of very unequal extent but very close to those used from the beginning for sorting out the Italian vota. The proportion between doctrinal suggestions and canonical suggestions is one to eight in volume. More than 3000 proposals, or one third of the total, have to do with the clergy, secular or religious, and 250 with the laity. With only 300 references ecumenism nonetheless makes a spectacular breakthrough.[222]

Unable to go through the two volumes with a fine comb, I shall single out only the subject of catechesis and the 200 pages of the doctrinal section. With regard to the former, Maurice Simon's detailed study is definitive: random choices, erroneous classifications, and dubious combinations make it necessary to do the entire job all over again.[223] After a clearly restrictive chapter on sacred scripture, the doctrinal section deals at great length with the Church, following a descending order: from the pope to the members of the mystical Body, with, of course, the bishops in between; only one entry deals with the relationship of the bishops to their priests. Next come the divine Persons and those classified with

[219] Caprile, I/1, 173-74, and Carbone, "Il cardinale Domenico Tardini," 67-68. Both writers rely on the introduction, "Propositum et mens," of the *Conspectus* (*ADA* II, App. 1, pp. V-VI).

[220] Caprile I/1, 174.

[221] Melloni saw this clearly from the outset: "Per un approccio," 573-75.

[222] The estimates are from Caprile, I/1, 174.

[223] Maurice Simon, *Un catéchisme universel pour l'Église catholique du concile de Trente à nos jours* (Leuven, 1992) 145-92.

them: God the Father gets seven pages, the incarnate Word five, and the Virgin Mary as many as the first two together, that is, twelve pages (there is no point in looking for the Holy Spirit...). This doctrinal section ends with a fourteenth chapter on "Errors to be Condemned" (*De erroribus damnandis*) of about thirty pages that contains no fewer than 69 items in alphabetical order, from Adventism to Utilitarianism. How can we keep from smiling as we see, one after the other, National- ism, Naturalism, Neopaganism, and Pantheism? The *Syllabus* model is certainly in firm possession here! Communism is well in the lead with 200 mentions (to which must be added many of the entries under mate- rialism); it is followed by existentialism (100), laicism, the chief sur- vivor of the adversaries of a former day (97), and situation ethics (85).[224]

Admittedly, none of this was simply made up. But the systematic abridgement of the proposals scattered throughout the vota according to a predetermined grid of a Scholastico-canonical type has the effect of magnifying by accumulation. This clearly distorts the antepreparatory consultation by reducing it to its skeletal structure. An examination of the earlier syntheses, which had more importance as the operation was still going on, shows that such was indeed the goal implicitly sought.

From the outset Tardini had planned on this second phase of the work — syntheses by area —, but it was delayed somewhat, as his assistant, Felici, admitted when the first set of cards was sent out on November 3. This phase was reactivated by the cardinal secretary of state on January 27, 1960, at the urging of the pope himself, if we may believe Carbone. This produced the intermediate stages, consisting of synthetic reports of the responses according to nation, region, or continent, as the case might be. A month and a half of work, from February 13 to April 1, 1960, was needed before John XXIII was acquainted with these twelve documents, all dated February 11. The time-lapse suggests, however, that further work was done on the reports, and this supposition is confirmed by the dates on which they were sent to the members of the antepreparatory commission: from February 20 to March 7.

The two lists are only partially the same; it is difficult to derive any information from them regarding the geographical areas that were handled first. Apart from some crossovers, the geographical order seems to have been the same as that followed in the examination of the vota: Europe in general and Italy in particular came first. As for the thematic

---

[224] The figures derived from the *Conspectus* (*ADA* II, App. 1, pp. 197-231) by Maurice Simon, *Un catéchisme universel*, 183, are more accurate than those in the *Sintesi finale* (pp. 5-6), which were compiled before the final vota were in.

organization, it repeats essentially the grid applied to the Italian vota, a grid which the *Analyticus Conspectus* would later be content simply to refine.[225] We may challenge the criteria, but we may not challenge the seriousness or consistency with which they were applied from the beginning of the process to its end.

It would be a most valuable help to have access to the approximately 300 typewritten pages of these reports, since it was through them that John XXIII and doubtless many Curial officials as well came to know the expectations of the bishops. But they have not been published. Two examples, however, make possible an evaluation of this first piece of work when compared to the conclusions drawn from the studies still being made of the vota themselves.

In less than thirty pages the report on Italy sums up rather accurately what Morozzo della Rocca and Velati have told us about the responses from the peninsula. Whereas the activity of the Church in the world and the role of the laity are dealt with succinctly, canonical questions occupy a far more important place. There are four pages on the discipline of the sacraments and thirteen lines on ecumenism; this last low figure seems to correspond to the reality in the vota. Internal disagreements are not eliminated but they are relativized by the figures: a strong majority for the extension of the use of the vernaculars in the liturgy, a strong majority also in favor of dogmatic definitions and of condemnations; almost complete unanimity, finally, in calling for a "full restoration of the authority and power of the bishops in their own dioceses."[226] The concluding summary simply schematizes the material a bit more but does not distort it: "Universal mediation of our Lady: a few discordant views."[227]

The case is rather different with the report on the United States and Canada, which is the shortest of all the reports (thirteen typewritten pages). It does take account of local characteristics: the practical bent of the responses; the references to racism and nuclear war; import of the adage "Outside the Church no salvation." Nor does the report hide disagreements, especially between Latins and Orientals on changes of rite, but also on the opportuneness of definitions and condemnations in countries that are confessionally heterogeneous.

But Joseph Komonchak, who has carefully studied the responses from the United States, thinks that the decision to apply an a priori

[225] *ADA* III, p. xv, and Carbone, "Il cardinale Domenico Tardini," 68-69.
[226] Copy in the archives of the Istituto per le scienze religiose, Bologna, p. 8.
[227] Ibid., p. 26.

interpretive grid instead of an inductive method prevented a grasp of the whole substance of the responses. I may add that even without any intention of doing so, the application of such a grid erased to some extent some sharp differences between the United States and Canada and, in particular, the debate, keen though it was, on the problem of religious freedom. But Komonchak is especially critical of the conclusion, which he regards as more unfaithful to the report than the report was to the vota, for it claims the existence of an unnuanced desire for a definition of Mary's mediatorial role, reduces liturgical reform to a reform of the breviary, and suppresses any reference to ecumenism. The hurried reader who would be satisfied to read this conclusion would take away a greatly distorted view of the wishes of the American bishops.[228]

Is this an isolated example due to the brevity of the document or does it reflect a general tendency? Lack of other data makes it difficult to judge. At most one may risk the hypothesis that the reliability of the national syntheses is in proportion to the homogeneity of the responses and their closeness to Roman ideas. The secretariat of the antepreparatory commission was fully at home with the Italian vota; they had no need to curtail the range of the responses or to alter their meaning. The North American vota, on the other hand, created problems for the secretariat by reason of their diversity; as a result, there was the temptation to reduce them to their lowest common denominator or even to present only the views of the majority. The degree of distortion would be all the more important because many Vatican dignitaries, including John XXIII himself, whose handwritten remarks Carbone cites,[229] knew nothing about the vota except what the summarizing reports told them.

This reduction of the complex to the simple, the heterogeneous to the homogeneous, and pluriformity to majority, was an inseparable element of the deductive method adopted, a method which itself was part of the Roman cast of mind. The reduction reached its peak in the final outcome of the process: the "Final Synthesis of the Resolutions and Suggestions for the Coming Ecumenical Council from Their Excellencies the Bishops and Prelates of the Entire World,"[230] which was dated March 12, 1960, and was read by John XXIII on April 7, the eve of the final meeting of the antepreparatory commission. Like the national reports, this important text, which sought to summarize the input of over 2000

---

[228] Copy of the report in the archives of the Istituto per le scienze religiose, Bologna; commentary in Komonchak, "U.S. Bishops' Suggestions," pp. 367-68.

[229] "Il cardinale Domenico Tardini," 68-69.

[230] Copy in the archives of the Istituto per le scienze religiose, Bologna.

responses, has not been published or even properly analyzed by historians of the Council.[231]

Consider, first of all, how concise the document is: everything is contained in eighteen not too tightly packed typewritten pages. Above all, consider its presuppositions, which are clearly set down in the introduction. In such a general document there can be no question of taking account of particular proposals, whether from individuals or from groups, whatever their importance.[232] For proposals that did not concern the entire Catholic world, the secretariat of the commission refers the reader to the regional summaries. Within this already limited framework two criteria are applied in choosing the points to be mentioned: the criterion of number[233] and the criterion of moderation, evoked with regard to the power of a bishop over his diocese.[234] Once again, the rule of the least common denominator was being followed.

The text, which is identical in structure with the national syntheses, has another striking characteristic: its kinship with the report on Italy, even down to the detail of the formulas used. Here are at least two examples of this kinship: the call for a definition of episcopal consecration as a sacrament distinct from priestly ordination; the almost complete repetition of the statement about the restoration of episcopal authority and, in particular, of the statement about disorder in seminaries: "The spread of the methods, so called, of 'self-education, self-control, and personal autonomy,' is (however) deplored, and the restoration of discipline is requested (desired)."[235] The coincidence is surely not accidental. What seems to have happened is that throughout the work on the vota, the Italian model, which permeated the members of the commission's secretariat, played a determining role far greater than the interest of the responses from Italy warranted: it served as a kind of yardstick.

Given this hypothesis, it is hardly surprising that the synthetic report should emphasize the conservative tendency to be seen in the majority of the vota entered on the cards.[236] And yet the tenor of the document is

[231] There are only brief mentions in Caprile, I/1, 173, and Carbone, "Il cardinale Domenico Tardini," 69.

[232] "Therefore no reference is made here to topics that have a national character, even ones of some importance," p. 1.

[233] The text says: "winning the greatest number of votes," ibid., 1.

[234] "We note that, on this subject as on the preceding, moderate voices far outnumbered the extremists," ibid., 10 (the reference is to the exemption of religious and the immovability of pastors).

[235] Page 11 in both cases; the words in parentheses are those in the final summary that differ from those in the report on Italy.

[236] I remind the reader that neither the collective German text nor its Indonesian counterpart, to give two examples, were taken into account.

quite different depending on whether it is dealing with doctrine or with internal organization. In the area of doctrine, which occupies the first third of the text, the controlling idea is that Vatican II was to be the Council that deals with the Church: a Church presented (following Pius XII) as the mystical body of Christ and endowed with a theology of the laity but, most importantly, with a theology of the bishop (rather than of the episcopate).

In addition to this major theme, four other major dogmatic concerns are extracted from the body of vota: clarification of the Church's socio-political teaching; extension of Marian privileges; condemnation of errors abroad in the world, beginning with communism; condemnation also of deviations in the interpretation of scripture "which encourage rationalism and naturalism," no less.[237] It is doubtless in this last point that the fingerprints of the maximalists are to be seen most clearly: no view opposed to this rigorism is mentioned, although in the matter of def-initions and condemnations the opposed minority is allowed to speak.[238]

A single theme also dominates in the other two thirds of the document, which are devoted to intra-ecclesial problems: "the full re-establishment of the authority and power of the bishops in the government of dioce-ses."[239] This restoration was, of course, to be at the expense chiefly of pastors and religious (the latter were defended only by some of their superiors). But the summary once again does not overlook the griev-ances, formulated "at times in a lively manner,"[240] against the Vatican Curia, which was regarded as too centralized, too large, too Italian, and not always competent.[241] The tone was thus set for a second part that was not frightened by "reforms," provided these respect the Roman primacy and are applied in a level-headed way to limited objectives. There were only eleven voices opposed to the restoration of the perma-nen diaconate; about sixty to cutting back on Latin; sixty-six to the modification of ecclesiastical garb. Thus the summary unflinchingly records a clear reversal of trend in favor of prudent majorities that wanted movement, concerned to improve the Church's image and func-tioning.

The "Final Synthesis" is therefore unambiguous to the extent that it clearly follows the main lines of the consultation and even reflects some

---

[237] "Sintesi finale," 2.
[238] Over 300 requests for Marian definitions and 61 against; ibid., 4.
[239] Ibid., 9 (the report on Italy had said: "in their own dioceses").
[240] Ibid., 8.
[241] 130 prelates called for a reform of the Index; ibid., 17.

of its nuances. Despite everything, however, I cannot help thinking that it also positions all this material along three main lines that run through the document. First, there is an ecclesiocentrism that reduces any openness to the outside world to a minimum: five rather off-hand lines, at the end of the text, on the missions and on ecumenism, though these had been brought up in 160 and 300 vota respectively.[242] Next, there is an obsessive defensiveness that leads to endless references to "dangerous modern theories" (in exegesis), "erroneous opinions" (in ecclesiology), "dangers" threatening the clergy, or "modern errors" (in morality). Final, there is the document's preoccupation with protecting the faithful by erecting a wall of words and paper: a dogmatic constitution on the Church," a "summa of social teaching" and a "collection of the principal modern errors."[243]

All this is to be found, of course, in the vota, but the latter also contain much else that such a process of classification and then reduction dessicates and hardens, without, however, completing erasing the diversity.

4. The Reaction of the Curial Congregations

Despite what might have been expected, the "Final Synthesis" did not mean the end of work on the antepreparatory consultation. In fact, it was the "proposals" of the curial offices that provided the logical completion of the cycle. Having been present at the beginning of the process, the offices naturally had a place in it at the end, after having meanwhile been closely associated with its different stages. At the first meeting of the antepreparatory commission on May 26, 1959, Tardini spoke of his desire that each office establish "study commissions and organizational committees in which consultors and research assistants would take part, in order to be ready to supply the preparatory commissions of the future Council with proposals most in keeping with the interests of the Church and of souls."[244] This wish was confirmed in a letter of May 29, although with another important detail: these internal commissions were to become active only during a second period. Thus it quickly became clear that the proposals from the Curia were not simply to be added to those of the bishops but were rather to respond to the latter.

That is why, on November 3, 1959, Bishop Felici sent several copies of the first cards extracted from the vota to the members of the

---

[242] "For their specific suggestions we refer the reader to the cards and the summary reports on the individual countries," ibid., 18.

[243] Ibid., 4 and 6.

[244] AS, App. I, p. 7.

antepreparatory commission, who were also the seconds-in-command in the curial offices, so that they could begin to familiarize themselves with this material. The dispatches continued until February 8, 1960.[245] Then, on February 16, judging the transmitted documentation to have been sufficient, Tardini reactivated the process: the congregations were to provide their own proposals by mid-March, so that the antepreparatory commission could meet during the last two weeks of the same month, in accordance with the wishes of the pope.[246] There was only a slight delay in meeting this schedule. Beginning on February 20, the national summaries were also sent to the Curia by the same channels: first, Italy and Canada-United States, with Africa and Germany-Austria bringing up the rear on March 7.[247] In all likelihood, although there is no documentary confirmation, the curial offices also received the "Final Synthesis" of March 12. Thus, while they were drawing up their proposals, they had at their disposal all the work that had been done on the responses to the consultation, work which everything suggests was done with them in view, although John XXIII had been the primary recipient of the documentation and was making clear his desire to be kept au courant with the preparation for the conciliar assembly.[248]

The curial proposals, sent to Tardini between March 6 (Congregation for the Oriental Churches) and April 5 (Congregation for Religious), were not very homogeneous. They differed in every or almost every way. First, their size: four and eight pages containing curt lists of 28 and 23 points to be discussed, from the Congregation for the Oriental Churches and from Propaganda respectively; about 100 pages of closely-written text containing little treatises of theology from the Council for Extraordinary Ecclesiastical Affairs (apostolate of the laity) and from the Congregation for Seminaries and Universities ("On keeping to the teaching of St. Thomas").[249]

They differed also in their language: Consistory, Oriental Churches, and Extraordinary Ecclesiastical Affairs answered in Italian. They differed in their working methods: While most of the offices waited to receive the cards or reports from Felici's secretariat and then very carefully took note of the bishops' suggestions, which the Congregation of the Consistory in particular tackled point by point, this was not true of

---

[245] *ADA* III, pp. xi-xii.

[246] Ibid., xiii.

[247] Ibid., xiv-xv.

[248] Letters, already cited, of February 16 and 20, 1960.

[249] *ADA* III, pp. 157-214 and 333-57. On these proposals see Andrea Riccardi, "I 'vota' romani," *Veille*, 163-68.

the Congregation of the Council: according to the premature announcement of its secretary, Bishop Palazzini, on June 30, seven area commissions had been at work in that Congregation between October 27, 1959, and March 8, 1960, with much less concern for the consultation that was then being analyzed.[250]

Finally, they differed in the areas of reflection: in the main, the specialized offices (Sacraments, Rites, Seminaries) respected the compartmentalization of the curial system; other reactions, however, displayed an overlapping of competencies that gave validity to some of the episcopal criticisms. The scattering of the several foci of concern and their possible overlapping were to be seen especially in the Congregation of the Consistory, the Congregation of the Council, and the Congregation for Extraordinary Ecclesiastical Affairs. As a result, all three conjured up a possible reform of the Curia. The commissions of the second of these three dealt with the cultural heritage of the Church, attention to Protestants and communists, the role of the media, the administration of ecclesiastical property, catechetics and Catholic schools, and finally the laity. In contrast, the very compact and summary document of the Holy Office was explicitly offered as a future doctrinal draft.

To a large extent, however, the homogeneity of the content serves as a corrective to the heterogeneity of the manner. It is true that the several offices of the Curia did not show themselves opposed to every kind of *aggiornamento* (a word which the Congregation of Rites used unenthusiastically in connection with the liturgy[251]). The reforms contemplated in the preceding pontificate were, of course, accepted: restoration of the permanent diaconate, even for married men (Holy Office) and the giving of official status to the episcopal conferences (Consistory). Propaganda and Religious tried, understandably, to check the episcopal attack on exemption. The Congregation of the Oriental Churches, though not very articulate in other areas, did suggest a fuller role for the bishops in the coming Council and a consultation of the "dissidents" in connection with it. Propaganda, once again, showed itself less timid in taking a stand, for obvious reasons, in favor not only of the diaconate but also of a lay apostolate and the use of the vernaculars in the liturgy in mission lands.

But the modest boldness of the Curia stopped there. If the real dissatisfaction with Roman centralization that existed in other parts of the world was clearly perceived (Consistory; Extraordinary Ecclesiastical

[250] *ADA* III, p. 151.
[251] Ibid., 281.

Affairs), few of the offices were ready to do anything about it. On the contrary, the Congregation of the Consistory defended its prerogatives with tooth and claw against possible encroachments; thus it rejected any discussion of the role of nuncios as well as of the procedure for nominating bishops, and it proposed the creation of the post of permanent visitor for each country in order better to control the local hierarchies. The Congregation of the Council, for its part, suggested the creation, in Rome, of a commission to coordinate the anticommunist struggle and a center for coordinating the apostolate of the laity. Thus, contrary to the wish expressed by numerous bishops, this Congregation was not afraid of greater centralization in order to meet new needs.

As for the basic directions taken by the different offices, these proved to be more restrictive and, above all, more one-sided than those seen in the synthesis of the vota. The Holy Office set its tone from the very outset, for its introduction contained a lengthy list of errors, ancient and modern, to be rooted out, before it went on to advocate clearly conservative solutions in the areas of dogma, the Church, and morality. With regard to ecumenism, which was shunted off to the end among the "special questions," the Holy Office left no doubt about its determination to supervise it: interconfessional dialogue, which was a praiseworthy but "dangerous" undertaking, gave rise to too many abuses for it not to be strictly regulated; thus the word "Church" could not be used except of Catholicism.[252]

The Congregation of the Council, for its part, devoted a great deal of attention to the progress of communism. The Congregation of Rites, though ready to discuss with Propaganda possible concessions for the missions, was otherwise opposed not only to any general liturgical reform but also to the spread of concelebration and to an extension of the use of the vernaculars that would endanger the liturgical supremacy of Latin. The Congregation for Seminaries and Universities agreed with it on this point, while also proposing, once again, that in the name of St. Thomas the teaching of the twenty-four theses of 1914 be made obligatory in all the seminaries and scholasticates of the Catholic world.[253] Not surprisingly, these four offices formed the hard nucleus of curial resistance, together with the Congregation of the Consistory, which would have nothing to do with any relaxation in relations between center and periphery. Especially on Latin and centralization, they were not afraid to show their colors by contradicting the trend among a potential majority

---

[252] Ibid., 17.
[253] Ibid., 341.

of the bishops — something which the "Final Synthesis" had not done. In these circumstances, the laudatory judgments of John XXIII on such proposals were puzzling.[254]

Shall we say, then, that the mountain of the antepreparatory consultation brought forth a mouse? Eighteen pages of impoverished summary for thousands of pages of responses from around the world were certainly not much in comparison with the solid collection of opinions from the Roman universities that was passed on unchanged, and with the no less solid collection of proposals from the curial congregations, especially since many of these proposals unabashedly contradicted the wishes of hundreds of bishops, as though the important thing were less to do justice to a forced consultation than to ward off in advance the unforeseeable repercussions of such a consultation. At this point in the demonstration, then, an affirmative answer seems possible.

5. Toward the Preparation Proper

But before giving a definitive answer, we must look closely at the final weeks of the antepreparatory phase, for they were to prove decisive. Now that the results of the consultation had been gathered in, two of the three duties of the Tardini commission had still to be carried out: the structure and composition of the preparatory agencies and suggestions for the program they would undertake. If the commission or its secretariat were to echo, in both cases, what they had derived from the episcopal responses, then a provisional pessimistic judgment would have to be revised.

First of all, what about the program for the Council's work? In fact, although this was one of the things that Tardini's commission was supposed to discuss, it was never really asked to do so. At its last meeting, on April 8, 1960, its president informed the members that the pope had reserved to himself the right to choose the themes or subjects for discussion from among the various proposals assembled, although the commission would be informed of his choice.[255] Without giving any more details, but with a great deal of optimism, the Motu Proprio *Superno Dei nutu* of June 5, 1960, which marked the beginning of the preparatory phase, stated that these themes emerged clearly from the episcopal consultation, the curial proposals, and the responses of the universities, all of which were placed on the same level.[256]

---

[254] Thus the comment, "read with lively satisfaction," on the proposals of the Congregation of the Consistory, May 10, 1960, in Carbone, "Il cardinale Domenico Tardini," 69.

[255] *AS* App. I, p. 21.

[256] *ADA* I, pp. 93-99 (Latin and Italian texts).

On July 9, however, the secretariat of the antepreparatory commission sent to the appointed presidents the *Quaestiones commissionibus praeparatoriis Concilii Oecumenici Vaticani II positae* ("Questions for the commissions preparing for the Second Vatican Ecumenical Council"). These the pope had approved on July 2, while allowing some freedom of movement: other subjects could be studied and joint subcommissions could discuss matters involving more than one commission.[257] An exhaustive analysis of the *Quaestiones* shows their direct connection with the "Final Synthesis" of the episcopal consultation, which evidently served as the basis for the composition of the questions.[258]

We do, of course, see differences between the two documents at various points, and these differences are not accidental. In the case of the missions, it was necessary to go back to the area reports in order to make up for the deficiencies of the Synthesis. All mentions of possible reforms in the Curia have disappeared from the *Quaestiones*. In addition, the latter seem to entrust the entire ecumenical problem solely to the Congregation for the Oriental Churches, while the Secretariat for Christian Unity is ignored. Nor is the problem that this organization is simply a secretariat, since four questions are sent to the Secretariat for the Mass Media. This omission therefore represents a deliberate decision to consider the new office as nothing more than a conveyor belt for dealing with noncatholics and certainly not as an organ of preparation for Vatican II. Bea's secretariat was thus given, willy-nilly, a complete freedom of action, but it would still have to overcome a severe initial handicap.

But these noteworthy differences, as well as numerous adjustments in detail due to the division into commissions, cannot hide the essential fact of the close connection between the *Quaestiones* and the "Final Synthesis" of the episcopal consultation: the same themes appear subdivided in the same way and expressed in similar if not identical ways. In both letter and spirit, then, the *Quaestiones* faithfully reflect the prevailing tendency of the antepreparatory work. They suggest a Council bent on preserving the integrity of Catholicism from the doctrinal errors threatening it,[259] errors the disciplinary consequences of which imply the definition of new norms as well as reforms in details.

---

[257] Carbone, "Il cardinale Domenico Tardini," 81-82. The *Quaestiones* are published in *ADP* II/1, pp. 408-15.

[258] This work of analysis was done at the Istituto per le scienze religiose, Bologna, and is summarized by Giuseppe Alberigo and Alberto Melloni in *Verso il concilio*, pp. 34-37, 465-69.

[259] But the aim is defensive rather than positive, since the proposals for Marian definitions are no longer included.

The fragmentary character of the *Quaestiones*, which often verges on a kind of pointillism, underscores the absence of any comprehensive reflection on what Vatican II should mean for the Church in the middle of the twentieth century. Lacking any overall direction, each preparatory commission would develop its own drafts covering the limited set of *Quaestiones* that reached it; the danger was a scattering of energies and, at the same time, overlappings that would hardly be avoided by the permission to establish joint subcommissions. As the link connecting the two preliminary phases, the *Quaestiones* leave one skeptical about how coherent the preparation of the Council would be; but in them, as in the *Conspectus*, we do find a digest, as it were, of the method which the Tardini commission applied to the antepreparatory consultation. Do we not also see in them a distant echo of the questionnaire that was planned at the beginning but then ruled out by John XXIII?

And yet, did the *Quaestiones* really have to be used? In this regard, the best known case, that of the theological commission, is perhaps not the most significant because this commission went to work so early. Officially, every step was taken there to claim that the preparatory work was connected with the antepreparatory by way of the *Quaestiones*, as was shown by a letter of July 13 which Jesuit Sebastian Tromp of the Gregorian University addressed to the members of a working group that had been recruited as early as mid-June from people connected to the Holy Office. But this letter was accompanied by three draft constitutions (on the Church, the deposit of faith, and morality), which Tromp himself had composed in the second half of June, that is, well before the reception of the *Quaestiones*, recorded by the secretariat of the theological commission on July 22, the day after a first, unofficial meeting. The *Quaestiones* did, however, lead to the composition of a fourth draft, on the sources of the faith.[260]

The other preparatory commissions, which were set up during the following weeks, proved more conformist, in that they would essentially follow the order of the *Quaestiones*, although with changes in details and with their own interpretation of the importance of the various questions. The commissions that showed themselves most independent of the grid provided seem to have been the commission on the lay apostolate, the commission on the missions, and especially the commission on the liturgy, which added the mystery of worship, respect for local traditions, and the participation of the faithful, or, in other words, the essential

---

[260] Riccardo Burigana, "Progetto dogmatico del Vaticano II: la commissione teologica preparatoria (1960-1962)," in *Verso il concilio*, 150-54.

demands of the liturgical movement; this commission thus went well beyond the rubricism of the *Quaestiones*.[261] With these qualifications, which were not negligible, we can say that, both for better and for worse, the *Quaestiones* played their part as an intellectual transition between the antepreparatory and preparatory phases.

But what about the structures that were set up and the persons who were going to fill them? In both of these areas Msgr. Carbone has provided us with a chronology that is quite detailed but also difficult to interpret because it is not explained in any depth. According to him, at a very early date Tardini had the idea of opening the future preparatory commissions to pastors from the entire Catholic world.[262] But the real beginning of the process goes back only to March 12, 1960, the day on which the cardinal asked the secretariat of his commission for a first plan, which was given to him on March 17 and which Felici submitted to John XXIII on March 24. This *Proposta per la costituzione delle commissioni preparatorie del concilio Vaticano II* ("Proposal for the Establishment of Preparatory Commissions for the Second Vatican Council") was sent to the members of the antepreparatory commission on April 1, for discussion at their final meeting on April 8.[263]

But by April 2, the pope had approved of the Tardini proposals which Felici had transmitted, and so it was already possible to send a request for names to the nuncios, the secretaries of the curial offices, the rectors of the universities, and "other ecclesiastical personnages" such as Cardinal Wyszynski, Primate of Poland.[264] What were the suggested criteria for the selection of members? "Priestly virtues," therefore no laypersons; competence, of course, in philosophy, theology, and canon law; but also, and no less, "sound doctrine."[265] With regard to the recipients of this request, the reader will note the absence of religious superiors and the presidents of the episcopal conferences, although they had been included in the list which Felici had given to the pope on March 24, while the secretaries of the curial offices are included although they had not figured in that list. Although there is no proof of it, these omissions and inclusions were not accidental; rather they brought the consultation into compliance with the usual norms governing Vatican administration.[266]

[261] Comparative analysis in the archives of the Istituto per le scienze religiose, Bologna.

[262] Remarks to Felici, August 29, 1950; see Carbone, "Il cardinale Domenico Tardini," 75.

[263] Analysis in the archives of the Istituto per le scienze religiose, Bologna.

[264] Carbone, "Il cardinale Domenico Tardini," 73-74.

[265] Ibid., 74 ("sicurezza di dottrina").

[266] I am still following Carbone here.

On April 8, then, Tardini presented the antepreparatory commission not only with a report on the work that had been done but also with the plan approved by John XXIII; this last, in Tardini's view, could be turned into a solemn Motu Proprio. Following Vatican I as a model, the plan provided for a central commission of sixteen members whom the Cardinal Secretary of State wanted chosen from among cardinals not overly involved in the Curia. This commission would have the pope or his representative as president and would be assisted by a Council made up of the secretaries of the congregations or comparable individuals. The central commission would have extensive powers, since it would have to establish the specialized commissions and appoint their members, draw up the general guidelines for the work of these commissions, and coordinate their activity. For this purpose, the secretary general (of the central commission) would be assisted by the secretaries of the various commissions.

Sixteen such commissions were then listed, all of them structured in the same way: with a president and a secretary in charge, they would consist of members, consultors, and advisers and experts, all of whom either lived in Rome or could easily travel to Rome. Three of these commissions could be regarded as technical; four were doctrinal (biblical, dogmatic, moral, socio-juridical); seven were disciplinary, each corresponding to a curial congregation. Only two were newcomers to this classic arrangement: a puzzling "pastoral commission," about the nature of which Ferretto, secretary of the Congregation of the Consistory, inquired on April 8, probably not without an ulterior motive;[267] and a commission for Christian unity, which thus had the same rank as the others.

After emphasizing the extent and quality of the work done on the consultation in so short a time, Tardini gave great credit for it to the Roman Curia, while at the same time rejecting the view that the Curia had coopted the antepreparatory phase for its own ends. But before yielding the floor to the members of the commission, Tardini added that such a view did exist and would have to be taken into account in the next phase.

In a muffled but still perceptible way, two struggles then ensued that occupied the final moments of the antepreparatory period: on the number of commissions and on the place of the curialists in them. Regarding

[267] Tardini's answer was that this commission was to deal with modern forms of the apostolate. My description is based on the minutes of the meeting of April 8, in AS App. 1, pp. 21-24.

the former, two opposed kinds of criticism were voiced. Sigismondi (Propaganda), Palazzini (Council), Philippe (Religious) Staffa (Seminaries and Universities), and Parente (Holy Office) all wanted a greater concentration of commissions. Parente, the new assessor of the Holy Office even called for a radical concentration: he wanted only a central commission that would be subdivided into two sections, a doctrinal and a disciplinary, the first of these being, of course, closely connected with the Holy Office. Without going that far, the first three of the men named tried indirectly to channel water to their own mills by suggesting the creation of a major doctrinal commission; this for reasons which Palazzini did not conceal: in order, for example, to avoid the erring ways (scantonamenti) of the biblical scholars.

On the other hand, the representatives of offices that had no equivalent in the list of commissions expressed their dissatisfaction. Such was the case of Father Coussa (Oriental Churches) who asked at least that the ecumenical commission be divided into two sections, a western and an eastern, in order not to hurt the feelings of the Orthodox; like Parente, he based his complaint on the precedent set by Vatican I. Such especially was the case of Msgr. Ferretto (Consistory), who suggested no less than three further commissions: for bishops, the government of dioceses, and pastoral care of migrants (a more original suggestion).

Following the example of Paul Philippe, who was the most candid, Parente and Sigismondo also expressed a desire that "the complaint" of the episcopate about the composition of the antepreparatory commission should be heeded. Besides, no one was opposed to drawing recruits from a wider pool. But these same men demanded nonetheless that the Curia exert "a broad influence" on the preparation for the Council,[268] an influence which Parente conceived in terms of providing a framework for these labors. Was the initial concession, then, a pure formality? Divergent viewpoints were expressed regarding the role of the seconds-in-command of the congregations. Tardini gave little encouragement to Staffa, who asked that these men be part of the commissions in their area of competence, and hardly any more to Zerba (Sacraments) who would have liked to have the prefects of the congregations be members of the central commission, while making them at the same time presidents of the particular commissions and, for good measure, turning their assistants into the secretariats of these commissions. And yet, except for the

---

[268] "After recalling the complaint of the episcopate regarding the composition of the antepreparatory commission, Father Philippe said he was in favor of the Roman Curia exerting a broad influence on the work of preparation for the Council": ibid., 24.

last proposal, the final outcome would be fairly close to what was thus desired.

After this meeting, Tardini gave the secretariat of the antepreparatory commission his directions for composing a draft of a Motu Proprio: in addition to the central commission, a blunt reduction to five particular commissions, plus the Secretariat for Christian Unity, so described because of its novelty, says Carbone.[269] The text was given to the pope for a first reading on April 30. John XXIII accepted it in principle but made a few changes, especially the introduction of a commission for the Oriental Churches. Was this due to his own attachment to these Churches or to pressure from the corresponding congregation? Probably a bit of each. Publication of the document was set for May 8.

Four days before that date, the pope told Tardini, who had come to receive his views on the second version, that he wanted to delay any publicity on the document until all the Roman cardinals had been personally consulted. The Secretary of State objected that this would be a time-consuming procedure, and he got the pope to agree instead to an oral communication to those cardinals who could attend a meeting scheduled for May 30. After having approved the final revision of the Motu Proprio on May 10, John XXIII authorized the addition of three commissions prior to the meeting (bishops and government of dioceses; religious; liturgy) and one more after the meeting: the Commission for the Lay Apostolate, which he spoke of on June 2 as a real innovation.[270]

Superno Dei nutu was presented to the cardinals on May 30, dated June 5, and commented on by its signer on that same day, after Vespers for Pentecost. According to custom, it was published in the issue of *Osservatore romano* that had appeared the evening before. It had three parts. The first described the coming Council: Vatican II would assemble "around" the pope to work for the renewal of the Church and the union of Christians. The second part gave a broad outline of the antepreparatory phase that was then ending. The third, finally, introduced the next phase. The plan was for ten commissions in addition to a central commission; nine of these corresponded to the congregations of the Curia, while the tenth could readily be compared to the standing committee of the Congresses of the Lay Apostolate. Apart from the secretariat for the mass media, which was introduced at Tardini's suggestion to take its place alongside its technico-administrative counterparts, the only real novelty was the "Council" or secretariat for unity. The role of this last was, however, confined to one of liaison with separated Christians.

[269] Carbone, "Il cardinale Domenico Tardini," 75.
[270] "This to be the final suggestion": said to Felici on June 1, ibid., 78.

All members of the commissions were to be appointed by the pope, but their identity was left vague, except for the central commission, the arrangement of which required several revisions because Tardini refused to accept the burden of heading it. Its membership was to include, in addition to prelates from around the world, the presidents and secretaries of the specific commissions; the pope or his representative was to preside over it. But the central commission's powers had melted away: not only would it no longer appoint the members of the other commissions, it would have to be content with keeping an eye on their work and coordinating it; to this end it would have a secretary general. The central commission did, however, retain the power to propose the rules for the functioning of the Council. The particular commissions, whose members were likewise to be recruited from around the Catholic world, were to have a cardinal as president and a secretary whose rank was not specified.[271]

Although certain episodes are still obscure, the direction which the development of the structure took from the initial outlines of it is clear enough. The reduction of the authority and prerogatives of the central commission gave greater autonomy to the specific commissions; as a result it made still more difficult any harmonious unfolding of the Council; this would in the final analysis depend on the pope alone. The number of commissions, which ended up half-way between the initial proliferation and the later severe limitation, was simply the empirical result of interacting pressures: in response to the wishes of its representatives at the April 8 meeting, the Holy Office won the establishment of a powerful Theological Commission, while the congregations that had been overlooked won the establishment of commissions corresponding to each.[272] The modelling of the commissions on the organization of the Curia was almost total. The introduction of a commission for the Oriental Churches deprived the Secretariat for Unity, which was no long a full-ranking commission, of part of its scope. In fact, only the confirmation of a degree of internationalization in the preparation maintained the different course set by John XXIII in the preceding year.

The victory of the Curia was completed on June 6 by the appointment of the presidents of the commissions, who turned out to be...the prefects of the corresponding congregations, except for Cento (Lay Apostolate) and Bea (Secretariat for Unity). This selection, which reduced still further the room to manoeuvre of the central commission, of which all these cardinals were de jure members, was hardly a surprise to insiders,

---

[271] *ADA* I, pp. 93-99.

[272] These pressures are mentioned by Carbone, "Il cardinale Domenico Tardini," 81.

since it simply made official a decision taken on April 30 at the recommendation of Tardini.[273] But people were all the more surprised at the selection, because the pope had just insisted on two occasions, to the cardinals on May 30 and publicly on June 5, that he wanted to avoid any confusion between Council and Curia. How could anyone believe in such a distinction after these appointments, which looked like a takeover? On June 7, at an audience for the editor of *La Civiltà Cattolica*, John XXIII defended the appointments on the ground that he wanted to gain the support of his closest collaborators.[274]

At the same time, the pope had to check the zeal of some of the cardinals who on their own initiative had already approached one of their assistants for the job of secretary. Thus on the evening of June 6 Tardini told Felici, on behalf of the pope, that being a member of the secretariat of a curial congregation was incompatible with participation in the preparatory commissions. The secretaries of the latter were to be looked for outside the curial personnel and, as far as possible, outside Italy.[275] The appointments made during the second half of June formally respected these two wishes in that only four were Italian, but the overwhelming majority were Romans by adoption: professors in the colleges and universities and consultors of the congregations. Only Jan Willebrands, who was promoted from the unofficial Catholic Conference for Ecumenical Affairs to the Roman Secretariat, was truly a new man, whereas Bugnini, a Lazarist, had been one of the architects of Pacelli's liturgical reforms. It would also be made clear, on July 19, that these ecclesiastics were indeed members of the commissions whose operation they were to ensure.

The fate of the suggestions collected by the secretariat of the antepreparatory commission regarding the selection of members is still unclear. The only reliable information we have has to do, once again, with the Theological Commission, which was atypical. Riccardo Burigana has shown the decisive role played in its composition by the informal working group set up by the Holy Office as early as June 13.[276] For the overall membership of the commissions, which was in place by mid-June, beginning with the central commission, we have only the quantitative analysis made by Antonino Indelicato, but this is just as revealing.

[273] Ibid., 75.
[274] Caprile, I/1, 181; for reactions see Antonino Indelicato, "La 'Formula nova professionis fidei' nella preparazione del Vaticano II," *CrSt* 7, no. 2 (1986) 305-6.
[275] Carbone, "Il cardinale Domenico Tardini," 80.
[276] Burigana, "Progetto dogmatico del Vaticano II," 145-48 and 151-52 (note 260, above).

With regard to the only point that concerns us here, we can derive from this analysis two contradictory sets of data. A little less than two-thirds of the 842 individuals finally chosen did not live in Rome and were recruited from the entire Catholic world, especially from Europe. More than a third (37.71%), however, lived in Rome, and more than a quarter (26.36%) belonged to the Curia, which placed about two-thirds of its own consultors (61.2%) in this group.[277] If we add to this top-heavy numerical representation some qualitative advantages, such as lengthy experience of joint work on dossiers, the outcome of the problems raised earlier was hardly in question.

The topics submitted to the preparatory commission could, of course, be regarded as distant echoes of the vota of many bishops, but only after these had been carefully screened by the secretariat of the Tardini Commission. Admittedly, too, many of those bishops and their advisers would be sitting on the commission, and this was an important bit of progress; but they would be surrounded by a far more experienced Roman personnel and would be under the direction of the chief dignitaries of the Vatican or of their right-hand men. In other words, while the antepreparatory commission had not as such participated in the consultation process, its secretariat had from beginning to end controlled how it was used; in addition, it worked closely with the curial offices through the secretaries or comparable personnel of the latter. Thus what the Curia had initially been forced to let slip from its grasp on orders from the pope, it won back to a great extent at the end, without serious opposition from John XXIII, who accepted a tacit compromise in which, however, his desire for *aggiornamento* seemed to be losing out.

In these circumstances, how could the antepreparatory phase have brought forth new leaders, men ready to give the pope effective support in the carrying out of his plan? Augustin Bea's name has sometimes been mentioned. But is that a correct evaluation? This Jesuit, who was unknown to John XXIII in the spring of 1959, was made a cardinal at the consistory of December 14 of that same year. "A German, a biblical scholar, was confessor to Pius XII," was the temperate observation of Tardini, who thus emphasized continuity rather than innovation.[278] It is true that some of Bea's German friends immediately suggested to him the creation of what would become the Secretariat for Christian Unity, but his influence in the Curia remained limited and his views uncertain; thus he was not appointed to the Holy Office, and he preached caution

[277] "Formazione e composizione delle commissioni preparatorie," ibid., 35-60.
[278] Stejpan Schmidt, *Augustin Bea: The Cardinal of Unity*, trans. Leslie Wearne (New Rochelle, N.Y., 1992) 308.

in his address at the closing of the Sixteenth Italian Biblical Week in September, 1960.[279] His star would rise only a little later, as the secretariat that had been put in his charge in June became increasingly important.

As a matter of fact, the two supervisors of the antepreparatory phase were not unknowns. This is obvious in the case of Tardini. He had become a close collaborator of Pius XII after the death of Cardinal Maglione in 1944 and even more once his alter ego, Montini, had been sent into pleasant exile in Milan in 1954. He became the first secretary of state of John XXIII, who bestowed the cardinal's hat on him at the consistory of December 15, 1958. His biographers, who have been eager to show not only his full agreement with the pope but even his anticipation of some of the pope's wishes, have done little to shed light on his real role during the period with which we are dealing here.[280]

Tardini was in fact a complex individual. On the one hand, this top-ranking servant of the Church, a man renowned for his administrative severity, his political realism, and his lack of enthusiasm for bold ventures, had undoubtedly been surprised by the pontifical initiative, all the more so since, after being one of the first to be told of it, he was called upon to get it launched. On the other hand, this loyal servant, who because of his age and his health had no personal ambitions, could not have shown any possible disagreement except by offering his resignation, which he in fact attempted to do. He would later vigorously refuse the presidency of the central commission and, with it, any important role in the subsequent phase. But the pope nonetheless created a buffer for himself by entrusting responsibility for the burgeoning idea of a Council to a man known for his independence of the curial clans; thus the idea would escape the control of the "Roman party," or what was left of it, and especially that element of it that was in the Holy Office's sphere of influence.

Tardini thus found himself precisely at the meeting point of two different pressures, which he sought to bring into harmony: to the Roman Congregations he made the will of John XXIII known via the members of the antepreparatory commission (universal consultation without a questionnaire; participation of non-Roman prelates in the preparatory commissions); he convinced John XXIII that there could be no Council

---

[279] "Les méthodes des études bibliques selon l'enseignement de l'Église," *DC*, November 6, 1960, cols. 1315-19.

[280] In addition to Carlo Felice Casula, "Il cardinale Domenico Tardini," *Deuxième*, 208-27, see especially Carbone, "Il cardinale Domenico Tardini."

without the Curia (therefore the prefects of the congregations were made
presidents of the preparatory commissions). The Secretary of State
proved, then, to be a dedicated worker for the Council, but for a low-
profile Council: at the grand opening act that was his press conference
of October 30, 1959, he used the word *aggiornamento*, but applied it to
"ecclesiastical discipline."[281]

Tardini was supported in his task by the man who seems to have been
the only real "newcomer" of the antepreparatory phase and who during
this phase made himself the indispensable work-horse, as it were, of the
coming Council. Msgr. Pericle Felici thus began a Vatican career that
was as brilliant as it had been unforeseen. This prelate of the second
rank was indeed hardly known when he was chosen to head the
secretariat of the antepreparatory commission. But was he really a
"newcomer"? We must look beyond the limited circumstantial reasons
for his selection and pay heed to the later judgment of his colleague,
Fagiolo, who compared him to Tardini's successor, Cicognani: "The
two men shared the same Roman formation, the same classical and
juridical education, and a healthy realism that helped them avoid being
overly elated by successes and discouraged by difficulties."[282] There
could be no better description of a good curial servant of the Church:
Felici was a worthy product of the Vatican administrative tradition.

He rose irresistibly and precociously, despite the fact that John XXIII
had not previously been acquainted with him.[283] At the press conference
on October 30, 1959, he made a first public appearance at Tardini's
side; he accompanied the latter again on French television on the following January 24. When the Cardinal Secretary of State replaced his
deceased colleague Tedeschini as dean of the chapter of St. Peter's in
November, 1959, he immediately called upon Felici to be his assistant.
For what purpose, if not to see to the material preparation of the basilica
for the coming assembly? Tardini's illness at the end of January, 1960,
hastened Felici's advancement; thus on February 3, he became the regular go-between with the pope's personal secretary, Don Loris
Capovilla, in conciliar matters; as such, he was thenceforth given a
special audience each week. On March 24, John XXIII asked Felici to
prepare to head the secretariat of the future central commission; the

---

[281] *ADA* I p. 154.

[282] Vincenzo Fagiolo, "Il cardinale Amleto Cicognani e Mons. Pericle Felici," *Deuxième*, 230.

[283] According to a note of Bartolomeo Migone on an audience with the pope; see
Alberto Melloni, "Governi e diplomazie davanti all'annuncio del Vaticano II," *Veille*, 250.

promise was confirmed on April 30 and honored by an appointment in due form on June 7.[284]

Felici thus found himself, like Tardini, at the point of contact between the desires of the pope and those of the Curia. In addition, he had shown his ability to handle the vast number of vota. Between Pentecost, 1959, and Pentecost, 1960, that is, during the period planned by Tardini, Felici's secretariat was occupied in providing an organizational structure for the next phase and a *status quaestionis* for the commissions who would comprise it. From a Roman point of view, the contract was fulfilled and fulfilled well.

But what about the point of view of the outside world, of other believers or Christians, of the faithful in the ranks, or even of the bishops who had sent in their vota? The seal of secrecy had been placed on almost the entire antepreparatory work; and this, of course, gave rise to numerous hypotheses. The most eloquent example of the misunderstandings that that kind of blackout could produce was undoubtedly the way in which the World Council of Churches responded to the announcement of a Council. The news did, of course, elicit varied reactions from Christians separated from Rome. These ranged from the confirmed skepticism of Protestants who were convinced that a reform of Roman Catholicism was impossible, to the foreseeable enthusiasm of Patriarch Athenagoras after his response to the pope's Christmas message of 1958. But at the end of the 1950s and beginning of the 1960s Geneva occupied a key place in the ecumenical order; consequently its opinion of the announced event was most important.

Philippe Chenaux has shown that because they lacked first-hand information the World Council's officials, and first and foremost its secretary general, Visser't Hooft, quickly experienced two quite different reactions.[285] First, for a few months they were baffled by a Council which, as they gradually learned, was to concern itself with the union of Christians but was not to be a Council of union; even the Catholic ecumenists who had for a dozen years or so been engaged in regular dialogue with Geneva could not say anything more, and for good reason.

Then came a period of distrust as a result of what was remembered as "the Rhodes incident." It was on this island, at the end of August, 1959, that the central committee of the Genevan Council held its first meeting

---

[284] Vincenzo Carbone, "(Pericle Felici) Segretario generale del concilio ecumenico Vaticano II," in *Il cardinal Pericle Felici* (Rome, 1992) 159-96.

[285] Philippe Chenaux, "Le Conseil oecuménique des Églises et la convocation du Concile," *Veille*, 200-9.

in an Orthodox country. The Catholic observers present took advantage
of the occasion to meet in private with a number of the Oriental dignitaries. But the awkward publicity given to these informal conversations
over dinner left the impression that Rome, preparing for a Council, had
not abandoned its ancient unionist dream of a special reconciliation with
the East. And this happened during a meeting of the World Council
which itself was at an advanced stage in negotiations to win the adherence of the Byzantino-Slavic Churches of the Soviet world. Visser't
Hooft was angry; the participants in the conversations offered embarrassed explanations; there were reciprocal efforts to restore peace; but
the discontent took some time to quiet down.

Misfortune can, however, be good for something: "the Rhodes
incident" shed a harsh light on the lack of a Roman office to handle
ecumenical information and dialogue; it thus helped in a major way to
the accomplishment of a plan already under consideration. But it took a
long time to restore trust, including trust about the real goals of the
Council as far as unity was concerned.

This well-known episode emphasized the gap that had been created
between the exclusively Roman origin of the Council and the still confused expectations found in public opinion, whether Catholic, Christian,
or neutral. The wide-ranging consultation handled by Felici's secretariat
had remained a one-way street; apart from the official texts, John
XXIII's comments on them, and Tardini's two public appearances, there
had been no real communication in the other direction. The first non-
Romans to become acquainted with the results of the work that had been
done would be the members of the preparatory commissions, and they
would learn of it only through the *Quaestiones*.

This gap between consultation and *Quaestiones* was not simply material
but intellectual and spiritual as well. The reductive treatment of the
antepreparatory consultation left aside a good many of the urgent problems
the world was facing, especially decolonization. While the disquiet felt by
part of the Catholic world at this time-lag was clearly seen, there seemed to
be no willingness, in the document that resulted from the consultation, to
do justice to that disquiet, except on some scattered points of detail. Quite
the contrary: the spirit in which the antepreparatory work was done was
one of strengthening the Church's defenses against dangers from outside.
The individuals selected for the work, their conceptual frameworks, and
their working methods led, after considerable effort, to a result that could
have been foreseen: an evident Romanization of the plan for the Council,
both in the organization of the preparation and in the subjects it would treat.

CHAPTER III

THE STRUGGLE FOR THE COUNCIL DURING THE PREPARATION OF VATICAN II (1960-1962)

JOSEPH A. KOMONCHAK

INTRODUCTION: THE PAPAL VISION OF THE COUNCIL

During the two years of the preparation of the Council, Pope John XXIII continued to set forth his grand vision of the opportunity the Council represented for the Church at a particularly propitious moment of history.[1] The Pope made a great number of statements about the Council,[2] many of them primarily homiletic and hortatory. Those that were more precise presented variations on themes which he set out with greatest clarity and force on two major occasions: the speech on 14 November 1960 in which he inaugurated the work of the preparatory commissions and the *Bulla indictionis, Humanae salutis*, of 25 December 1961.[3] There is a remarkable continuity of theme and emphasis in these statements, which, if it had been more carefully studied, might have made his opening address at the Council seem less startling and bold.[4]

In these texts Pope John set out the significance of the Council in its historical moment. Here he was following the instincts of an historian, who cannot make sense of previous Councils unless he studies not only the circumstances in which they met but also the difficulties, often greater than those today, they confronted.[5] Such a study prompted the effort to describe the difficulties and opportunities the Church faced in

---

[1] See G. Alberigo, "Giovanni XXIII e il Vaticano II," in *Papa Giovanni*, ed. G. Alberigo (Bari 1987) 211-43; *idem*, "Passaggi cruciali della fase antepreparatoria (1959-1960)," in *Verso il Concilio*, 15-42.

[2] The first volume of the *ADP* provides a fairly comprehensive set of the Pope's remarks, both major and minor, about the Council; for an index by topic and concern, see Caprile, I/2, 742-45.

[3] *DMC* III 15-26, IV 867-76; *ADP* I 32-41, 132-43.

[4] See G. Alberigo, "Formazione, contenuto e fortuna dell'allocuzione," in *Fede Tradizione Profezia: Studi su Giovanni XXIII e sul Vaticano II* (Brescia 1984) 187-222.

[5] *DMC* III 16; *ADA* I 32-33. Another aspect of the Pope's historical judgement of earlier Councils, which cannot be developed here, is his frequent reference to the political entanglements which often affected them, from which the present Council would be blessedly free; see *ADP* I, 240, 260-61, 332, 363, 370.

the world in which the Second Vatican Council would meet. The Pope considered the modern world to have undergone and to be undergoing such great changes that it could be said to be on the threshhold of a new era.[6] These transformations brought with them great technological advantages and great dangers, particularly the threat of the loss of all sense of the spiritual, since man's moral progress had not kept pace with his material progress, often pursued in deliberate independence from God.[7]

The Pope reveals himself to have been very aware of the mixed blessings of modernity. There are even some passages in his speeches that recall the sometimes apocalyptic catastrophism that had marked a great part of the papal and episcopal Catholic response to modernity ever since the French Revolution. But where he differed remarkably from many of his predecessors was in the spirit of faith and confidence with which he faced this prospect.[8] He repeatedly warned against exaggerating the evils, as if Christ and his Spirit had abandoned the world. This confidence is still often trivialized by people who reduce it to an alleged native (and naive!) optimism. But it is clear that the roots of the Pope's attitude lay in his faith in Christ and his Spirit and that this faith grounded the need for a Church, "which feels the rhythm of time" and can discern the "signs of the times." All of this is particularly clear in his remarks in *Humanae salutis*:

> These painful considerations are a reminder of the duty to be vigilant and to keep a sense of responsibility awake. Distrustful souls see only darkness burdening the face of the earth. Instead we like to reaffirm all our confidence in our Savior who has not left the world which he redeemed. Indeed, we make our own the recommendation of Jesus that we know how to distinguish "the signs of the times" (Mt 16:4); and we seem to see now, in the midst of so much darkness, more than a few indications that augur well for the fate of the Church and of humanity.[9]

The Pope found such reasons for hope in the world's experience of immense evil in this century and in its awareness of contemporary threats, which had led people to become more thoughtful, more open to spiritual values, more eager to work for the integration of individuals, classes and nations. All this had made the world more open to the Church's teachings.

[6] "The Church today is witnessing a crisis underway in society. While humanity is at the turning-point of a new age, tasks of immense seriousness and size await the Church, as before in the most tragic ages of its history;" *ADP* I 139, 132; *DMC* IV 867-68.

[7] *DMC* III 18, *ADP* I 34; *DMC* IV 867-69, ADP I 139-40, 132-33.

[8] See G. Ruggieri, "Appunti per una teologia in Papa Roncalli," in *Papa Giovanni* 259-64.

[9] *DMC* IV 868, *ADP* I 140, 133. See the remarkably similar development in his earlier speech to the PrC, *DMC* III 18-19; *ADP* I 34. See also the Pentecost address, 5 June 1960: *ADA* I 105-106, *DMC* 397-99.

The Church in turn was showing itself ready to meet the challenges it faced: vast energies were being expended by both clergy and laity in the apostolate, in prayer, in action in all areas; and the persecuted communities were revealing a faith and a heroism equal to that of the greatest periods in the Church's history. Only the presence of the Holy Spirit could account for such vitality in the midst of difficulty.[10] These were the reasons that led the Pope to convoke the Council:

> In the face of this twofold spectacle — a world which reveals a grave state of spiritual need and the Church of Christ, still so vibrant with vitality — we, from the time we ascended to the supreme pontificate,... felt at once the urgent duty to call our sons together in order to enable the Church to contribute more effectively to the solution of the problems of the modern age.[11]

It was precisely because the Council was placed before such general challenges that, in the Pope's mind, its attention would not focus, as had many previous Councils, on particular points of doctrine or discipline;[12] instead, it would "revalidate and illumine the substance of the human and Christian thought and life of which the Church throughout the centuries is the depository and teacher."[13] He set out a grand vision of the Council's work:

[10] *DMC* II 399; *ADA* I 106.

[11] *DMC* IV 870; *ADP* I 140-41, 134.

[12] There is only one place in which the Pope seems to contract his vision of the Council's work, his Pentecost address, 10 June 1962: "The coming Council will not cast light one by one on all the points of Catholic doctrine; it will give special attention to the ones that concern the fundamental truths that have come under discussion or stand in contrast to the contradictions of modern thought, derived from errors that are eternal but vary in their influence." But this observation, which may reflect the orientation of the doctrinal texts prepared by the TC, is almost immediately contradicted by the familiar contrast between Vatican II and earlier Councils: "Twenty Ecumenical Councils, countless national and provincial councils, and diocesan synods have made a priceless contribution to the knowledge of one or more theological or moral truths. The Second Vatican Council presents itself to the Catholic world, to humanity, in the strength of the apostolic Creed, proclaimed by the immense assembly, and with the experience of a nearly universal illumination of doctrine, in an integral vision that better corresponds to the soul of the modern era;" *ADP* I 256-57.

[13] *DMC* III 18, *ADP* I 34. A month later, on 3 Dec 1960, the Pope repeated this distinction between a concentration on "one or more points of Catholic doctrine," as had been necessary at Trent and at Vatican I, and the more general scope he wished the Council to have: "Today's situation is different. Our soul is as it were pervaded by supernatural joy before a true Epiphany, a revelation that is not limited to this or that topic, but touches upon everything, every benefit brought by Christianity.... It is a burning, felt renewal of souls, beginning with one's own personal sanctification, for the sake of representing the Church in all its permanent, immaculate and unchanged splendor to today's world;" *ADP* I 44.

> We expect great things indeed — we wish to repeat it — from this Council,
> which wishes to reinvigorate faith, doctrine, Church discipline, religious and
> spiritual life; we also expect it to make a great contribution to the reaffir-
> mation of those principles of the Christian order which also inspire and gov-
> ern developments in civic, economic, political and social life.[14]

The success of the Council, then, would consist in what he called a
"restoration and renewal of the universal Church."[15] If the Council were
to carry it through, then the Church too would stand at the beginning of
a new era in its history.[16]

In the mind of the Pope, the renewal of the Church was to serve its
ability to be of redemptive significance in the modern world. There are
already present here in these earlier texts the two dimensions that were
set out in the Pope's speech a month before the Council opened, when
he spoke of the Church's vitality *ad intra* and *ad extra*.[17] This language
has often been given too schematic a sense by later authors, suggesting
that one can easily divide off questions internal to the Church from those
that affect its relations with the world. But in the Pope's mind these were
closely linked: it was for the sake of its redemptive effectiveness
precisely in the modern world that he urged the Church's renewal. This
is what gives all its force and breadth to Pope John's appeal to the
primarily "pastoral" character of the Council. The Council was to be the
Church's engagement with a particular moment of history, and the
Council's review of its doctrine and practice thus had to be an exercise
in what has nicely been called "pastoral theology as the historical
hermeneutics of Christian truth."[18]

---

[14] *DMC* III 24; *ADP* I 39. Compare the statement in *Humanae salutis*: "The coming
Council will fortunately be meeting at a moment in which the Church is feeling a very
strong desire to fortify its faith and to look at itself again in its own awe-inspiring unity.
It also is feeling the urgent duty to give greater effectiveness to its activity and to promote
the sanctification of its members, the spread of revealed truth, and the consolidation of its
structures. It will be a demonstration of the Church, always living and always young, that
senses the rhythm of time, that in every century adorns itself with new splendor, radiates
new light, achieves new conquests, while remaining ever the same, faithful to the divine
image impressed on its countenance by its Spouse, who loves it and protects it, Jesus
Christ;" *DMC* IV 870-71; *ADP* I 141, 135.

[15] *ADP* I 169-70; *DMC* IV 163.

[16] See the apostolic exhortation, *Sacrae laudis*, 23 January 1962: "It can rightly be
said that we all feel ourselves to be near the goal of a new age, based upon fidelity to the
ancient patrimony and open to the wonders of a genuine spiritual progress;" Caprile, I/2
310; *ADP* I 152, *DMC* IV 882. Earlier in the same month, he had spoken of "the tasks of
the new age that will open with the Ecumenical Council;" *ADP* I 147.

[17] *DMC* IV 522; *ADP* I 350.

[18] G. Ruggieri, "Appunti per una teologia in papa Roncalli," in *Papa Giovanni* 256.

This broad and challenging vision of the Council had to be set out here first as a reminder that it was not first articulated in the Pope's opening speech to the Council and therefore can serve as a criterion by which to assess the results of the preparatory work that the Pope set in motion. The two papal statements on which we have focused were made at the beginning and in the middle of the preparatory period. The more solemn assertion and expansion of their themes at the opening of the Council was, then, in the nature of a reminder of the reasons and motives that had inspired the idea of the Council and also of a not so subtle criticism of the results of the work of the previous two years.

This chapter will describe how the preparatory work was organized, the pastoral and doctrinal texts it produced, and the struggle for the definition of the Council that was always the at least implicit drama being played out in its course. At the end of the chapter, we will return to the question of the correspondence between the papal vision and the preparatory process and work.

I. THE ORGANIZATION OF THE PREPARATORY WORK

A. GENERAL ORGANIZATION

The previous chapter has set out the schematic provisions for the organization of the preparatory work established by Pope John's *motu proprio*, *Superno Dei nutu*. The task of studying the topics that might be treated at the Council was entrusted to ten commissions, corresponding, except for the AL, to the congregations of the Roman Curia.[19] Three secretariats were also set up, one for the media of communication, one for economic and technical aspects, and one to help the separated brethren follow the work of the Council.

The Pope also established a central commission (CPC), which he himself would head, to follow and to coordinate the work of the preparatory commissions, to review their work and evaluate it for submission to the pope, and to draw up the rules of procedure for the Council itself. The secretary of the CPC, P. Felici, served as the General Secretary of the whole preparatory effort. The CPC did not meet until mid-June 1961, however, a year after it had been established and when the preparatory work was already well advanced. It was only at its second plenary session, 7-12 Nov 1961, that three sub-commissions were established

---

[19] Another commission, for ceremonies, was announced on 17 Nov 1960.

within the CPC to draw up the conciliar regulations, to deal with mixed matters, and to amend the schemas according to the proposals of the CPC.

The CPC's role in the organization and coordination of the preparatory work appears to have been very modest. At its first meeting in June 1961, it heard reports on the progress of the work, but neither then nor at any other time, it seems, were its members asked their views about the structure, methods, or themes of the conciliar preparation itself, which remained almost exclusively the competence of Felici's secretariat, at least for the greater part of the preparatory period.

Little documentary evidence of the general directions given to the PrC is now available, but some information can be gleaned from the diary of Sebastien Tromp, which records four occasions when Felici met with all the secretaries of the PrC between September 1960 and May 1961.[20] At these meetings, Felici explained the more minute details of the secretaries' roles as well as more important guidelines. They were to make monthly reports to him, who would in turn regularly report to the Pope. Felici urged the PrC to hold plenary sessions monthly in order to keep things moving. Secretaries were not to communicate with the media,[21] a task reserved to the CPC, which would also issue a monthly bulletin reporting nominations and the progress of the work.

Little information is available on more precise activities of the General Secretariat, particularly with regard to the coordination of efforts. The letter that accompanied the transmission of the official *Quaestiones* envisaged the constitution of mixed commissions on matters of joint interest, and on 19 December 1960 Felici sent out norms for the study of such matters.[22] Eleven months later, however, at the second meeting of the CPC, the secretary general had to admit that, despite the efforts of his office to promote them, few mixed commissions had been established among the PrC.[23]

[20] Tromp Diary, 22 September 1960, 10 November 1960, 18 February 1961, 25 May 1961. (I have had access to this invaluable source only through July 1961.) No other documentation on the transmission of these reports to the Pope is now available.

[21] He repeated this requirement at the meeting on 10 November 1960, noting that the Pope had not been happy at the publicity given in *OssRom* to the first plenary session of the TC. On this prohibition of contact with the press, Cicognani told the LI: "His Holiness, Pope John XXIII, gave a special warning on this matter." (A-McManus).

[22] *ADP* I/1 416.

[23] *ADP* II/1 609.

In fact, the PrC set about their their work in relative independence of one another.[24] Several of them did collaborate on certain particular matters either through mixed subcommissions or through exchanges of information, but the great mass of the materials was considered by the PrC separately.[25] If in some cases, this insured that distinct and sometimes new perspectives would be properly represented in the conciliar preparation, it also resulted in much duplication of effort and an absence of coherence.

The problem was aggravated by the separation of practical or pastoral questions from doctrinal questions, a division that was encouraged by the fact that in the official *Quaestiones* only the TC received doctrinal topics. This monopoly was jealously guarded by the TC which worsened matters by resolutely refusing any formal collaboration with the other PrC. In the first two months of 1961, the TC received requests from several PrC asking either for assistance or for the establishment of mixed commissions. At the February 1961 plenary session of the TC, Tromp explained the principle that had guided its negative reply: the TC had exclusive competence in doctrinal matters, and as it refrained from entering into merely disciplinary questions unless they raised doctrinal issues, so it expected other PrC to refrain from doctrinal matters. Mixed commissions were appropriate when the same disciplinary question affected several commissions, but not when the issue was purely dogmatic.[26] Tromp did not publicly report to the TC that Ottaviani had refused a request for a mixed commission with the SCU on another ground: the latter was not a commission. "We are going to remain," the Cardinal had added, "masters in our own house." Dogmatic issues being the sole competence of the TC, the SCU would have to be content with submitting proposals and with friendly conversations.[27] Ottaviani would maintain this principle until the end, giving a particularly forceful

[24] The question of relationships with other PrC was raised at an organizational meeting of the AL on 15 Oct 1960, at which Msgr. Glorieux reported that Felici had told him: "Each commission is autonomous in its own work, since unification and harmonization will be done by the Central Commission itself;" "Acta primae sessionis Pont. Comm. 'De apostolatu laicorum' ad Conc. Oecum. Vaticanum II apparandum," 3 (A-Ligutti).

[25] For details, see V. Carbone, "Gli schemi preparatori del Concilio Ecumenico Vaticano Secondo," *ME* 96 (1971) 76-86.

[26] "Relatio Secretarii," 13 Feb 1961. At the same time, Ottaviani told Tromp that the Pope had agreed that the TC should review the texts prepared by other PrC for their theological content; Tromp Diary, 16 and 23 Feb 1961.

[27] Tromp Diary, 28 Jan and 23 Feb 1961. This reply reflects some of the anger felt in the TC over the "propaganda," as Tromp called it, that Bea was making on behalf of his views on membership in the Church.

defence of it at the last meeting of the CPC after Bea had justified his
secretariat's having prepared a text on religious freedom on the grounds
that the TC had refused all cooperation.[28]

Concern about a lack of coordination in the preparatory work was
expressed at a fairly early stage of the work. It may have lain behind a
proposal that Frings and Döpfner, backed by the French bishops,
brought to the Pope in May 1961. As reported by Felici to the secretaries
of the PrC and summarized in Tromp's Diary, their idea was that to
insure that the conciliar decrees had a pastoral character, they should all
be gathered into a single pastoral decree.[29] Tromp also records a possible solution: that after the work of the individual PrC was completed,
there would be an "'intercommission' to redact everything in a pastoral
form."[30]

A month later, at the first meeting of the CPC, Larraona proposed that
it establish subcommissions to facilitate its work, among them one
that would put into an order appropriate for conciliar consideration
documents on matters which fell under the competency of two or more
curial congregations and preparatory commissions.[31] Felici seemed to be
echoing this idea when twice in September 1961 he anticipated the
establishment of an organism within the CPC to assure that all the texts
on "the principal problems of pastoral technique" would have an organic
unity.[32] This response is doubly significant: it reduced the problem to a

[28] "First I have to make it clear that I do not agree that the Theological Commission
has to work with other commissions on matters of doctrine. The Theological Commission
is fully independent on these matters; they are matters of doctrine, and it is not as in other
commissions, where mixed matters are discussed.... There can be matters that concern the
doctrinal Commission in other commissions, but these must be sent to the doctrinal
Commission; and the Secretariat for Christian Unity should have sent its schema (since it
addresses a doctrinal and not merely a sociological matter...) to the doctrinal Commission
to see whether it agrees with the doctrinal Commission;" *ADP* II/4, 688, 691.

[29] According to K. Wittstadt, Frings, writing to the Pope in the name of the Bishops
of Germany, had already on 20 June 1960 proposed the establishment of a "Commission
on Pastoral Matters": "A special group should be appointed to work actively and closely
with the other commissions on pastoral problems;" "L'episcopato tedesco e il Vaticano
II: preparazione e prima sessione," in *Giovanni XXIII: transizione del Papato e della
Chiesa*, ed. G. Alberigo (Rome 1988) 114-15. I have no information on the Pope's reply.

[30] Tromp Diary, 25 May 1961.

[31] *ADP* II/1 291-93.

[32] Caprile, I/2 191; see also 175. There seems to be an echo of this proposal in a
discussion within the SCU in November 1961: After Willebrands had noted that "it
seems that the Holy Father was asked to create a pastoral commission, but the idea was
not accepted," Bea explained that "The Holy Father replied that pastoral questions were
to be considered by all the commissions;" SCU, "De Verbo Dei, 29 Nov - 1 Dec 1961"
(A-Stransky).

simple matter of "*la tecnica pastorale*" and it postponed a solution until after all the texts were prepared, as if it need not affect the deliberations that would produce them. It was not until the second meeting of the CPC in November 1961 that the establishment of the Subcommission on Mixed Matters was announced, whose role would be to give unity to schemata of the PrC on the same or similar material.[33]

This November meeting saw the problem again raised by the CPC members as they began to discuss the first prepared texts. Felici felt obliged to defend the preparatory process from the accusation of a lack of coordination. After noting that the efforts of his secretariat to promote cooperation among the PrC had not succeeded, he minimized the difficulty on the grounds that the subcommission on mixed matters could easily make a single text out of the many prepared by the several PrC.[34]

The criticism continued to recur, however, in subsequent meetings of the CPC. Many members expressed impatience (a) that they had to address particular disciplinary questions before they had seen the relevant theological texts (e.g., discussing structural relations affecting bishops before they considered the TC's text *De Ecclesia*), (b) that they had to discuss similar if not identical questions two or three times as they appeared in texts submitted by different PrC, and (c) that materials were being brought to them that were so specific and so minor that they were unworthy of a Council and should be left to the revision of the Code.

While Felici agreed with at least the last of these criticisms and urged that the Council limit itself to programmatic statements of principle,[35] he maintained until the end that the two subcommissions on mixed matters and on amendments could meet the concerns expressed at the CPC. In fact, as we shall see later, this assurance did not satisfy many important members of the CPC, who as the Council approached multiplied appeals to the Pope that a coherent pastoral plan give greater unity to the conciliar agenda than had guided its preparation.

---

[33] *ADP* II/1 434: Tisserant was its president, L. Governatori its secretary, with Ferretto, Liénart, Tappouni, and Muench its members. Montini and Suenens were added as members later, and Coussa replaced Muench upon the latter's death.

[34] *ADP* II/1 608-609. In observations written for the Pope on 4 December 1961, Card. Testa urged that future sessions of the CPC should be conducted with greater logic and illustrated its lack in the November meeting: "Don't present the text of the profession of faith before the possible condemnation of theological, biblical, moral errors. Don't put in the same session ecclesiastical dress (which ought to be left to regional councils) and the profession of faith;" copy found in Roncalli papers, ISR, Bologna.

[35] See *ADP* II/3 207, 438.

B. Internal Organization and Methods

1. *Distribution of Roles*

The personnel of each of the PrC were divided into two groups: members and consultors. The norm Felici recommended was the one followed by the TC: members had a vote and could speak freely, whereas consultors had no vote and could only speak when invited to do so.[36] Practices, however, seem to have differed greatly. In several PrC, the difference between members and consultors was purely formal. Even in the TC, both in subcommissions and in plenary meetings, consultors were often called on for comments. In most of the PrC, including the TC, consultors were asked not only to submit *vota* on various themes but even to prepare texts. All but one of the PrC divided their work among subcommissions composed both of members and consultors; the exception was the RE, which kept a sharper distinction between members, most of them resident in Rome, who wrote the texts, and consultors, whose views were solicited and then considered at meetings of the members.

The more important distinction was between members and consultors who lived in Rome and those who lived elsewhere; Felici once even spoke of distant members as "honorary members."[37] In most of the PrC the subcommissions worked in Rome, preparing texts that were then reviewed in plenary sessions of both members and consultors. In the TC, for example, the five subcommissions were composed of a few members and a few consultors living in Rome. Consultors living outside of Rome, while not participating in the actual writing, received and were invited to comment on the drafts before each of the plenary sessions, but they could only participate in the work of the subcommissions when these met during the plenary sessions and they had little role in the decisions made between such sessions. The great exceptions to this rule were the LI and the SCU, which, as we will see, entrusted more responsibility to their subcommissions, which seldom met in Rome and often communicated by mail.

All of the PrC had begun preliminary work before the formal inauguration of the preparatory period on 14 November 1960. The TC and the RE began as early as July and were able to bring to their first plenary session well-elaborated agendas, which were not greatly altered then or

[36] Tromp Diary, 18 Feb 1961.
[37] Tromp Diary, 10 Nov 1960.

later. Greater elasticity in establishing the agenda seems to have marked the other PrC.

2. *Secrecy*

All of the PrC were bound to keep their proceedings secret, although they seem to have interpreted this obligation rather differently. The TC was the strictest: members and consultors were told that they could not communicate even with members of other PrC because of the close links between the TC and the Holy Office.[38] The LI was told by its president, G. Cicognani, that the secret affected the purposes it set itself and everything said and done at its meetings.[39] The SCU, on the other hand, explicitly distinguished its secret from that of the Holy Office,[40] and many of its members did not scruple to converse and correspond with members of other commissions.

The political implications of the oath of secrecy were well perceived by Congar as he deliberated whether to accept his appointment to the TC. While there was a need for discretion with regard to the press and public opinion, the secret would also serve to atomize and neutralize opposition, inhibiting horizontal relationships in favor of vertical ones with Rome.

> In contrast, the members of the Commission who work at Rome, at least at times, could speak to one another. The result will be a non-Roman world that is scattered, atomized and vowed to secrecy and a compact Roman organ that is free to express itself.[41]

Frustration at the secrecy was just as great in the press, both secular and religious, which chafed over the lack of information. Inaugurating the preparatory work, the Pope invoked the *amor silentii* that appropriately characterizes a Council devoted primarily to the Catholic Church and its internal organization.[42] When the complaints became stronger he returned to the issue at the conclusion of the first meeting of the CPC. While grateful for journalists' interest, he reminded them that the Council was not an academy or legislature, but a solemn meeting of the

[38] Tromp Diary, 13 Dec 1960; Tromp to Philips, 13 Jan 1961 (A-Philips).

[39] "Allocutio Em.mi Cardinalis Caietani Cicognani initio sessionis diei 15 novembris 1960," 2 (A-Stransky).

[40] Bea, "Sermo introductorius Em.mi Cardinalis Praesidis," 14 Nov 1960, with an appeal to the Code, c. 243:2.

[41] Y. Congar, *Mon journal du Concile*, "Fin de juillet 1960," ts 8, ms 12.

[42] *DMC* III 21; see also Felici's remarks to journalists two weeks later, *DC* 58 (1961) 669-71.

hierarchy that requires respect, reserve and prudence. He promised more information, when the work had proceeded further; meanwhile he asked them to avoid "idle curiosity" and "bitter quarrels."[43] These comments did not greatly reassure people, and the press and Catholic people continued to complain about the "Wall of China" that hid the preparatory work from their view.

3. *The Absence of the Laity*

Similar complaints were also registered about the lack of lay participation in the preparation of the Council. Seven laymen served on the administrative secretariat, but in all of the PrC that prepared texts for the Council there was only one layman, F. Vito, who served on the ST. In fact, despite the efforts of its president and secretary, no lay people were appointed even to the AL, the commission set up to discuss their apostolate.[44] Needless to say, no women, lay or religious, served on any preparatory commissions.

On 25 May 1961 Felici informed the secretaries of the PrC that Frings and Döpfner had raised the question of the role of the laity with the Pope and that it was being raised also in Austria and Holland.[45] Felici reported that the Pope's answer was that, because the Council was an act of the teaching and not the learning Church, lay people were not to be members or consultors of the PrC, but should express their desires to their bishops and might also be asked to submit proposals, particularly to the AL and the SCM.[46] A month later, the Pope told the CPC that the proposals submitted by those consulted during the antepreparatory period should be considered to represent also the desires of the lower clergy and of the laity.[47] Lay people, then, remained excluded from direct participation in the preparation of the Council.

---

[43] *DMC*, III, 330-31; for examples of the kinds of complaints the Pope was addressing see *DC* 58 (1961) 853-58.

[44] Many of the national and international associations of lay people, however, did submit *vota* and were represented on the AL by priests long associated with their work. See G. Turbanti, "I laici nella chiesa e nel mondo," in *Verso il Concilio*, 212-18.

[45] In a widely quoted speech on 30 Jan 1960, König had declared his desire that the laity, especially the large international Catholic organizations, might officially participate in the preparation (*DC* 58 [1961] 445-46); and at Pentecost Alfrink expressed a similar hope for the Council itself (Caprile, II/2, 129-30). For Döpfner's regret that lay people were not involved in the preparatory commissions, see *ADP* II/1 264-65. For other voices, see *DC* 58 (1961) 895-902.

[46] Tromp Diary, 25 May 1961.

[47] *DMC* III 329.

II. PREPARING FOR A "PASTORAL" COUNCIL

From a very early date, it was understood that the Pope wished the Second Vatican Council to be primarily "pastoral" in nature. While this word was regularly echoed by many of the participants in the preparation, it was not always used in the same sense. A genuine exploration of the meaning of the term was, however, inhibited by the disjunction that the official *"Quaestiones"* promoted when they assigned all the doctrinal questions to the TC and left all the practical "pastoral" questions to the other PrC. This structural distribution of competencies reinforced the view that prevailed in the TC that doctrinal clarification, over which it had a monopoly, was the primary role of the Council, with "pastoral" considerations something that bishops could see to when they returned to their sees. On the other hand, it also encouraged the other PrC to think of their role as primarily one of addressing individual and often rather minor problems of what Felici called "pastoral technique." Only the LI consistently refused this fatal disjunction and undertook an effective *ressourcement* to provide a basis for its specific proposals for liturgical reform.

As theologically questionable as is this disjunction of competencies, in fact it is the one that marked the preparation of the Council and may usefully be employed in a review of the work. This section, then, will study the work of the more pragmatically oriented commissions, contrast to it the work of the LI, and end with a study of a particular matter of pastoral reform, the question of languages in the Church, over which the two visions of the Church came into rather dramatic conflict. The next section will then review the struggle over the determination of the Council's doctrinal purpose.

A. THE REFORM OF PASTORAL PRACTICE

1. *Commission on Bishops and the Governance of Dioceses (BG)*

Chaired, after the death of Card. Mimmi, by Card. Marella, with G. Gawlina as secretary, it had a majority of bishops (36 of the 51) and, to deal with the question of exemption, of high officials of religious orders. Only fifteen per cent of its personnel were associated with the Roman Curia.[48] The BG formed seven subcommissions and three mixed

---

[48] For fuller information on the membership of this and other PrC, see A. Indelicato, "Formazione e composizione delle commissioni preparatorie," in *Verso il Concilio*, 43-66.

commissions: with the commission for religious, for the discipline of the clergy, and with both of these commissions. There is no evidence of cooperation with the TC, which was preparing two chapters on bishops.[49]

The *Quaestiones* assigned to the BG concerned the partition of dioceses; three problems connected with the power of bishops: their relations with the Roman Curia,[50] with pastors, and with exempt religious; the principal pastoral problems in today's conditions (including the question of establishing personal parishes in large cities), and the care of emigrants.[51] Only these last two questions suggested the need to relate pastoral care to contemporary problems.

The BG understood its task to be that of preparing statements of principle and general proposals for an eventual reform of canon law to accommodate Church discipline to contemporary needs.[52] It brought seven texts to the CPC. The first, on the division of dioceses,[53] after rather banal observations that dioceses should be neither too large nor too small, was content to propose some particular changes in church law.

The second schema, on episcopal conferences,[54] addressed an issue not included among the *Quaestiones* assigned to the BG but one too important to neglect. Two drafts were prepared, a long text that dealt with the conferences at some length and in some detail, and a shorter one, eventually selected, that had only four sections: on the nature and establishment of episcopal conferences, on their governance, on the

---

[49] This separation of the doctrinal and disciplinary aspects ignored the acute comment made in the "Final Synthesis," 8: "The logical connection between this disciplinary problem and the doctrinal problem of the divine origin and the power of bishops is evident. Catholic doctrine on the episcopate needs to be clarified in order then to arrive in the disciplinary field at concrete determinations of the powers of bishops."

[50] This reference reflects a paragraph in the "Final Synthesis," 9, but neither here nor anywhere else do the *Quaestiones* reflect another paragraph (p. 8) in that text which summarized the many proposals, "sometimes expressed quite animatedly," for reform of the Roman Curia by decentralization, bureaucratic simplification, internationalization, and improvements in the choice of personnel.

[51] *ADP* II/1 409.

[52] Card. Marella's comment to the CPC; *ADP* II/2 500. For a discussion of the texts of the BG, CLP, and ST concerning the Church's pastoral practice, see M. Guasco, "Verso un aggiornamento della pastorale," in *Verso il Concilio*, 351-95; A. Indelicato, *Difendere la dottrina o annunicare l'Evangelo: Il dibattito nella Commission centrale preparatoria del Vaticano II* (Genoa 1992) 147-57, 217-29, 277-79.

[53] *ADP* II/2 496-518. The BG worked with a purely juridical notion of a diocese: "Dioceses are particular Churches which under the authority of the Roman Pontiff are entrusted for governance to bishops who are by divine institution successors of the Apostles" (496).

[54] *ADP* II/2 518-41.

force of their decisions, and on relations among bishops of various nations. Marella's report to the CPC indicates that there were often significant differences within the BG over certain issues, in particular over the juridical authority of decisions made by conferences.[55]

The third schema concerned relations between bishops and the congregations of the Roman Curia.[56] As Marella reported to the CPC, this material, even in its juridical aspects, involved the theological question of the relation between the power of bishops in their dioceses and the jurisdictional primacy of the pope. The BG offered as its statement of theological principle that while the office of bishops derived directly from Christ's institution, the particular jurisdiction a bishop enjoys in his diocese derives from the pope as its "proximate cause."[57] Although this means that the pope can extend or restrict the powers of a bishop, both theological principle — lest bishops be thought to be "decapitated" — and practical necessity suggested that changes be made in church law. The BG therefore proposed expanding the rights and faculties, privileges and indults of bishops, altering some canons in the code, and improving relations with the Roman Curia.

The fourth schema, on relations between bishops and pastors,[58] after a rather hortatory exposition, addressed the problem of the irremovability of pastors. Insisting that the governing principle should be the good of souls, the BG proposed that the distinction between movable and irremovable pastors be abolished in church law, and it outlined a procedure by which a bishop for just cause could remove any pastor, with the right of the latter to appeal to the Holy See also eliminated.

The BG's fifth schema, on coadjutor and auxiliary bishops and the resignation of bishops,[59] addressed two issues that were not mentioned in the *Quaestiones* and on which the Code was lacking: the problems caused by ill or aged bishops and by dioceses that are too large or too populous for one bishop. To meet the first problem, the schema urged permanently ill and aged bishops to submit their resignations; aged bishops would be considered to have offered their resignation upon reaching

[55] For the compromise text, see *ADP* II/2 525: "Decisions reached by the episcopal conference do not bind juridically but morally; for the sake of unity, then, they are to be received with the greatest respect and religiously observed."

[56] *ADP* II/2 541-76.

[57] At the discussion in the CPC, Frings, echoing the views of Maximos IV, suggested that this serious question be reserved for the chapter on bishops that would be offered by the TC; Döpfner later agreed with this proposal; *ADP* II/2 553, 557.

[58] *ADP* IV/2 577-97. This schema was drawn up in collaboration with the CLP.

[59] *ADP* II/3 643-75.

the age of seventy-five.[60] To meet the second problem, the schema set out several norms for the appointment of coadjutor or auxiliary bishops.

The sixth schema of the BG addressed the chief problems concerning the care of souls.[61] The first part dealt with general doctrinal and practical principles, the second with more particular questions. The doctrinal principles set out the Church as the effect and instrument of Christ's redemption, in which bishops exercise the three tasks of preaching and teaching, sanctifying, and governing.[62] The general practical principles, after a section on ecclesiastical vocations, follow this threefold scheme and offer what Marella called a "Pastoral Directory" for bishops in the areas of education, worship and government. A last section considers the bishop as a *sponsor Ecclesiae universalis*.[63]

The first five chapters of the section on more particular problems addressed in considerable detail the pastoral needs of emigrants, sailors, air-travellers, nomads, and tourists. Marella explained that originally there had also been a discussion of the pastoral care of workers ("Question du monde ouvrier"), but that it had disappeared in the course of the redaction of the texts. "But," he noted, "it will be easy to prepare a new schema on the subject."[64]

On the other hand, the BG did feel obliged to offer a chapter "on the care of souls for Christians infected with communism." The threat of atheistic communism, both as doctrine and as practice, was one of those evils that the Church has a right and duty to oppose, not for economic or political but for religious reasons. For areas not oppressed by communism,

---

[60] Marella told the CPC that there was much disagreement on the question of resignation, particularly because of age. To those who invoked the Church's tradition and the dignity of the episcopal office, it was replied that no theological difficulty stood in the way, since "the episcopal power is by divine law capable of being limited by the Supreme Pontiff not only with regard to territorial extent but also with regard to time;" *ADP* II/3 650.

[61] *ADP* II/3 676-790.

[62] Marella told the CPC that there had been some debate over whether the VG should address these questions "since it was the task of the Theological Commmission to deal with the doctrine on the institution, nature, and power of bishops;" but canonical precedent was invoked to authorize this section; see *ADP* II/3 696-97. There is no indication of consultation with the TC on this material.

[63] In his report, Marella made clear that: "Obviously, we are not dealing here with a participation in the jurisdiction that is proper to the Supreme Pontiff, but with co-responsibility in sollicitude for the whole Church of Christ;" *ADP* II/3 698.

[64] *ADP* II/3 741. This appears to be the only reference in all the preparatory work to the nest of problems to which a host of pastoral and even missionary initiatives had been addressed in the previous twenty years.

the schema proposed an extensive campaign of instruction and of action; it recommended a program of re-education for young people trained under communism; and it asked for support of the "Church of silence."[65]

The last schema proposed by the BG concerned relations between bishops and religious.[66] Drawn up by a mixed commission of select members of the BG and the RE,[67] the text first established four general principles to govern the question: the authority of the local bishop and the respect due to him; the need to respect the distinct character of religious; the principle of exemption, founded in the supreme authority of the pope, yet not absolute or unlimited; the need for cooperation between religious and the secular clergy. Fairly detailed recommendations then followed to implement each principle.

The texts prepared by the BG, as is clear from this summary, were primarily practical in character. For the most part, this commission avoided doctrinal matters, assuming that these could either be safely taken for granted or left for the TC to consider. Its approach was primarily juridical, aimed at reform of the Code, whose ecclesiology and ideas about the distribution of authority in the Church the BG tended to assume. While the bishop's office was said to be of divine right in the Church, his jurisdiction was considered to derive from papal delegation and to be limitable by papal decision. Some sense of collective responsibility is visible in its texts on episcopal conferences and in the idea of the bishop as *sponsor Ecclesiae universalis*, but this is not very well developed; and the primarily juridical orientation prevented the elaboration of a theology of the local Church.

These texts were presented and discussed at the CPC before the chapters on bishops in the TC's schema *De Ecclesia* had been seen. But the debate there,[68] particularly on episcopal conferences and on relations with the Roman Curia, raised important doctrinal questions on the relationship between pope and bishops and on the nature of collegiality and its relation both to the pope and to the individual bishop.

[65] Marella explained to the CPC that his commission was aware that the CLP was also drafting a text on this subject which agreed on many points with his schema but addressed different aspects of the problem; *ADP* II/3 768. There does not seem to have been any real coordination of the two efforts.

[66] *ADP* II/4 220-83.

[67] See *ADP* II/4 233, where Marella speaks of the "sometimes very lively discussions" which took place in the course of the redaction of the text. Valeri also made a report on the text to the CPC; *ADP* II/4 234-37.

[68] For the CPC discussions, see Indelicato, *Difendere la dottrina*, 147-57, 220-29, 277-79.

After the discussion in the CPC, these seven schemata were grouped into two texts, *De episcopis ac dioceseon regimine* and *De cura animarum*, to each of which were also joined material from the texts prepared by the commission on the discipline of the clergy.[69]

2. *Commission for the Discipline of the Clergy and the Christian People (CLP)*

Chaired by Card. Ciriaci, with C. Berutti as secretary, it began in October 1960 by establishing general norms for its work. Its first plenary session established nineteen subcommissions, the heads of which prepared texts on the basis of proposals submitted by members and consultors; these texts were then sent out before plenary meetings. Plenary sessions were held every two months, from January 1961 to April 1962. Three mixed commissions were formed: with the BG, RE, and SCM.

The official *Quaestiones* had assigned the CLP seven topics to consider in the light of contemporary needs: the distribution of the clergy, the irremovability of pastors, clerical dress, ecclesiastical precepts, catechetical instruction, ecclesiastical benefices, and confraternities.[70] To these the commission added ten other topics, so that it was able to present the CPC no fewer than seventeen texts.[71] All of these texts kept very close to the ground, offering very practical advice as to how the Council might, as Ciriaci put it to the CPC, "adapt the Church to changed and quite fluid conditions."[72]

The texts prepared came before the CPC in several groups, seven of them in November 1961, two others in February 1962, five more in May 1962, and the final three in June 1962.[73] Of these, as a result of discussions in the CPC, nine were removed from the conciliar agenda by

---

[69] See Carbone, "Gli schemi preparatori," 56-57.

[70] *ADP* II/1 410.

[71] In addition to texts on the seven topics listed above, the CP presented these others: De clericorum vitae sanctitate; De paroeciarum provisione, unione, divisione; De obligationibus parochorum; De patrimonio historico et artistico ecclesiastico; De parochorum obligationibus quoad curam animarum; De cura animarum et communismo; De praevia librorum censura eorumque prohibitione; De censuris earumque reservatione; De modo procedendi in poenis in via administrativa infligendis; De Missarum stipendiis, de Missarum onerum reductione, de piis ultimis voluntatibus; De promovendis ad Ordines sacros iis qui fuerunt pastores seu ministri acatholici.

[72] *ADP* II/1 566.

[73] *ADP* I/2, 563-733; II/2, 597-653; II/3 790-893; II/4, 220-336. Ciriaci's comments on these various texts, most of them apparently spoken extemporaneously and primarily anecdotal and hortatory, are singularly uninformative about the process by which they were constructed.

suppression (on the historical and artistic patrimony) or by reservation either to the Holy See (the ordination of convert pastors), to episcopal conferences (clerical dress and tonsure), or to the revision of the Code of Canon Law (ecclesiastical precepts, censorship and prohibition of books, censures, administrative penalties, associations of the faithful, Mass stipends). Of the other eight texts, three (distribution of the clergy, holiness, benefices) formed the single conciliar schema attributed to this Commission, the *De clericis*, while the other five (parishes, obligations of pastors, pastors and the cure of souls, catechesis, communism) formed parts either of the schema *De episcopis et dioeceseon regime* or of the schema *De cura animarum*.[74]

As these decisions themselves indicate, the texts prepared by the CLP were less appropriate for an ecumenical Council than for a commission for the reform of the Code. Practical and pastoral in intention, often descending into details, they showed little serious effort either to examine and describe the social and cultural developments that might make the changes proposed advisable or to provide a theological and particularly an ecclesiological basis for the proposals made. The reigning notion and structures of the Church were largely taken for granted, as is the assumption that the parish is the primary locus for the ministry of priests. There is no evidence that the commission spent any time considering the serious sociological and ecclesiological discussions of the Church's pastoral activity in the modern world that had been going on for three decades.

3. *Commission for Religious (RE)*[75]

Chaired by Card. Valeri with J. Rousseau as secretary, it was composed mostly of religious, thirty-five of them resident in Rome. Half of its membership were affiliated with the Roman Curia, most of them from the Congregation for Religious. In July 1960 it began to gather and arrange material for its work. In late October and early November twenty topics were identified and accepted at the first plenary session. Studies were sought from members and consultors, which were then synthesized by a *ponens*, who drafted a text to prepare for general discussions particularly of the practical consequences. This was distributed

---

[74] See Carbone, "Gli schemi preparatori," 57-58; Indelicato, *Difendere la dottrina*, 91-103, 157-60, 224-29, 234-35, 279-80.

[75] See L.C. Marques, "Per il rinnovamento della vita religiosa," in *Verso il Concilio*, 425-44.

before meetings and the observations of members and consultors were
again synthesized. Since most of the members resided in Rome, frequent
meetings were held, usually twice a week.

The official *Quaestiones* proposed five general questions for the RE
to consider: the renewal of religious life, the union or federation of religious institutes, the exemption of religious, and the religious habit.[76]
The commission expanded this program and produced a single schema
De statibus perfectionis acquirendae with thirty-two chapters.[77] This
was presented to the CPC in two unequal parts, the first presenting the
doctrine about the nature and character of the religious life, the second
offering practical suggestions for its renewal.

By "doctrine" the RE's text meant not the theological but the juridical nature of religious institutes. The theological aspects were left to the
TC to present, a task the latter undertook at the express invitation of the
RE.[78] The schema assumed the classic interpretation of the words of
Christ to the rich young man, distinguishing between the ordinary Christian life of obedience to the commandments and the state of perfection
pursued by following the evangelical counsels. The text was presented
as in continuity with a similar effort at Vatican I to discuss and to defend
the religious life. Opposition and scorn for this vocation were being
expressed, and the development of new forms in which it can be lived
required the Council to speak clearly in order to avoid confusion and
error. The two particular errors the RE thought it necessary to combat
were those already condemned by Pius XII: an activism that neglects the
interior life of prayer and a naturalism that neglects properly supernatural motivations. In addition, the RE proposed a condemnation of the
views that honor marriage more than virginity or celibacy, that see the
religious life as simply a refuge for the timid, and that describe it as too
difficult because involving a surrender of freedom.

The renewal of the religious life proposed by the RE was to go in two
directions: a restoration where needed of those elements that belong to
the nature of religious life or are proper to the original intention of the

[76] *ADP* II/1 410-11.

[77] Valeri informed the CPC that this "single organic schema" had been constructed
"on the model of what was done at the Council of Trent *pro Regularibus et Monialibus*,
Session XXV;" *ADP* II/2 659.

[78] See the comments of Valeri, *ADP* II/4 354-55, and of Ottaviani, *ADP* II/3 1095.
The TC's chapter *De statibus evangelicae perfectionis adquirendae* was prepared by
U. Betti, who showed a first draft to Rousseau, secretary of the RE, and took his remarks
into account in revising it; see R. Burigana, "Progetto dogmatico del Vaticano II: la commissione teologica preparatoria (1960-1962)," in *Verso il Concilio*, 175n.

institute or were legitimately introduced since; and an adaptation to meet developing exigencies of time and place. The criterion offered for the latter, however, closely resembled those proposed for the former, fidelity to the intentions and spirit of the founders and respect for the historic patrimony; any changes in purpose, however, would only be possible with the approval of the Holy See.

The chapters of the RE's schema came to the CPC in no logical order; in fact the basic doctrinal sections on the juridical nature and character of the religious life were brought to the CPC *after* it had already discussed the practical sections.[79] The schema remained substantially the same in structure and content after the discussion in the CPC.[80]

4. *Commission for the Discipline of the Sacraments (SA)*[81]

This was chaired by Card. Masella with R. Bidagor as its secretary. Sixteen of its forty-one members and consultors resided in Rome. Curial figures constituted 40% of its membership, fifteen of them from the Congregation for Sacraments. It formed six subcommissions and one mixed commission, with the Secretariat for Christian Unity, on mixed marriages. It does not seem to have had any relations with the Commission on the Liturgy.

The official *Quaestiones* assigned five topics to the SA: extension of the faculty to administer confirmation; extension of jurisdiction to hear confessions and the question of reserved sins; whether to restore the minor orders and the diaconate and the age and interstices for minor orders; reducing the number of marriage impediments and making marriage procedures more expeditious; the problem of priests who have left the ministry.[82] The primarily practical character of these topics was reflected also in those the SA added, as when it considered also the question of the age for confirmation and sponsors for the sacrament, when it briefly discussed the power of particular Councils to grant faculties to hear confessions, and when it prepared schemata on preparation for marriage, on the sacramental form of marriage, and on mixed marriages. The horizon of interest remained very narrow, confined to proposing technical and canonical reforms, governing theological notions being assumed without apparent question.

---

[79] See *ADP* II,2 653-737; II/3 1116-1180; II/4 337-83; Indelicato, *Difendere la dottrina*, 161-65, 256-58.

[80] See Carbone, "Gli schemi preparatori," 58-60.

[81] See M. Paiano, "La commissione preparatoria *De disciplina sacramentorum*," in *Verso il Concilio*, 138-40.

[82] *ADP* II/1 411-12.

The only truly innovative text was the schema *De sacramento ordinis*,[83] which proposed the restoration of the diaconate and of the minor orders. Two motives were invoked for this proposal: a growing dedication of the faithful to the work of the apostolate and the lack of priests. The text proposed that the diaconate be restored especially in those areas where the latter problem is acute. The diaconal functions would include various liturgical roles, catechesis and preaching, work in diocesan curias and tribunals, and administrative roles. Married men could be ordained to the diaconate by general statute of the Holy See for specific areas or by particular dispensation.[84] As for the minor orders, these would be reduced from four to two, lectors and acolytes, with real functions assigned.

In another important schema, *De matrimoniis mixtis*,[85] the SA began by deploring the great increase of such marriages, which posed great dangers for the Catholic party. To meet the problem, the text urged that bishops and pastors warn the faithful against entering into such marriages, and where they could not be prevented, that they diminish the likelihood of harm by devising norms to meet particular situations. For this purpose and to avoid giving ecumenical offense, the SA proposed some reforms of canon law on the subject, "leaving the substance intact." These changes in the Code reflected the influence of the *votum* which the SA had received from the SCU. In his report to the CPC, Masella claimed that his commission's proposals were in agreement, "for the most part," with the *vota* of the SCU, a judgement with which, however, Bea immediately disagreed on several minor points and on one very important one.[86]

Bea's serious criticism was that the SA's text did not address the problem which ecumenical conversations had indicated was the "test" of the Church's good will: the reform of the canon that declared invalid a mixed marriage performed without proper canonical form. The SCU had discussed, with much disagreement, whether the Code should return to the more lenient policy which Pius X had permitted in some regions, which was to consider such marriages illicit, but not invalid. Unable to agree upon this, the SCU's *votum* proposed that this primarily pastoral

[83] *ADP* II/2 138-79.

[84] Five members of the SA disagreed with this proposal, and Masella went out of his way to assure the CPC that his commission was unanimous in agreeing that celibacy was never to be dissociated from the priesthood; *ADP* II/2 152.

[85] For the text and discussion at the CPC, see *ADP* II/3 1186-1221.

[86] *ADP* II/3 1191-94.

question be left to the several episcopal conferences to decide for their own areas.[87] The SA had considered the question but decided, without giving reasons, not to accept the SCU's recommendation.

Of the ten texts which the SA brought to the CPC, only the six schemata on marriage were retained for presentation to the Council in the form of a schema *De matrimonii sacramento*. The CPC judged that the question of lapsed priests should be reserved to the Holy See, and the other three texts were left for the reform of the Code.[88]

5. *Commission for Studies and Seminaries (ST)*

Chaired by Card. Pizzardo, with A. Mayer its secretary, it began its work in November 1960 and concluded it in February 1962. It was divided into twelve sub-commissions which met regularly; there were six plenary sessions. It had mixed commissions with the LI and with the SCU. It also made use of the chapter on the magisterium prepared by the TC for its own text on the subject.

The ST was assigned six topics. Four of these (on the nature of the ecclesiastical vocation and how to promote them, on spiritual formation, on pastoral formation, and on Catholic schools) were stated very generally in the *Quaestiones*, which were, however, more precise on the other two. The reform of the *ratio studiorum* was to give special attention to the integrity of doctrine in submission to the magisterium and to the teaching of Scripture. Similarly, the question of clerical discipline should include a rejection of recent errors that promote a certain specious "autonomy."[89] The latter remark echoes concerns found in the "Final Synthesis", which lamented "the spread of so-called methods of 'self-education, self-control, personal autonomy;'"[90] but the remark about the course of studies introduces concerns that were not found in the CAP's summary of episcopal *vota* but had been strongly emphasized in the *votum* prepared by the Congregation for Seminaries and Universities.[91]

---

[87] *ADP* II/3 1192-94.

[88] See Carbone, "Gli schemi preparatori," 60-61; Indelicato, *Difendere la dottrina*, 133-37, 258-59, 282-84.

[89] *ADP* II/1 412-13.

[90] "Sintesi finale," 11. A letter from the Congregation for Seminaries and Universities to the world's bishops, 27 September 1960, had raised these same issues; see *Seminarium* (1961) 1-18.

[91] See *ADA* III 315-406. The Congregation's first three proposals asked for conciliar statements on soundness and integrity of doctrine, on the relation between theology and the magisterium, and on the teaching of Scripture, particularly in seminaries.

The ST completed six texts for consideration by the CPC.[92] The first, *De vocationibus ecclesiasticis fovendis*,[93] deliberately abstained from addressing disputed theological questions about the nature of a vocation and the duty to follow it. Instead it contained a set of exhortations to all members of the Church that they do all they can to meet the crisis of what in a note is called the "lamentable lack of vocations."

The ST's second text, *De sacrorum alumnis formandis*, came before the CPC in an odd order, the fourth chapter, "De studiorum ratione in Seminariis" being discussed on 26 February 1961 and the other five chapters only on 12 June 1962.[94] The text provided sets of general laws, principles and criteria which would have to be accommodated to various times and places. The chapter on discipline in seminaries was intended to meet widespread concern about the spread of disobedience in the Church in the name of freedom and autonomy.[95] The chapter on the course of studies required that seminarians be given as good a general education as the laity receive, that they be trained well in Latin, that in a two-year course they be taught scholastic philosophy according to the principles and methods of St. Thomas Aquinas and learn how to analyze and reply to contemporary philosophies, that their four-year theology curriculum also follow Aquinas' principles, that they study Scripture according to norms to be given by the Council, that they become acquainted with separated Christian communities, and that they learn enough about modern religious errors to be able to show the erring the way to truth.

In the text, *De studiis academicis ab universitatibus tum catholicis tum ecclesiasticis provehendis*,[96] the ST speaks very briefly about Catholic universities in general, descending, however, into much greater detail when it comes to ecclesiastical universities. The special place of the study of St. Thomas in both philosophy and theology is again noted. The ST's text *De scholis catholicis*[97] sets out general principles applicable not only to all Catholic educational institutions but also to such modern inventions as the cinema, radio and television.[98] The rather scholastic

[92] The last of these, on the use of Latin in clerical studies, was not submitted for discussion by the CPC because of the promulgation in the meantime of *Veterum sapientia*. The ST's text on the subject is discussed below in the section on languages.

[93] *ADP* II/2 738-56.

[94] *ADP* II/2 756-99, II/4 24-110.

[95] *ADP* II/4 45.

[96] *ADP* II/2 800-862.

[97] *ADP* II/4 110-57.

[98] *ADP* II/4 118: "for it is quite unjust that there should be a monopoly on this kind of inventions and helps."

presentation is aimed at a host of various errors identified in the notes.[99] The rights of the family and of the Church are set out, and standards set for various aspects of the schools.

The final text presented to the CPC by the ST was the schema *De obsequio erga ecclesiae magisterium in tradendis disciplinis sacris*,[100] which addresses three topics not found in the official *Quaestiones* assigned to the ST but proposed in the *votum* of the Congregation for Seminaries and Universities. The first chapter, relying almost wholly on the documents of Pius XII but also drawing on a draft of the chapter on the magisterium prepared by the TC, sets out the unique authority and rights of the official magisterium of pope and bishops. This is described as the "proximate norm of truth in matters of faith and morals" to which teachers must submit. Teachers have the duty to defend official teaching and the right to explore it more thoroughly, but any view that denies or deforms the obvious sense of a truth proposed by the magisterium by that very fact is to be considered mistaken. Even the non-infallible magisterium demands an inner religious assent.

The second chapter is devoted to the teaching of Scripture, which should begin with the divine origin of the sacred books, their inspiration, inerrancy, and historical and objective truth.[101] Teachers of the Bible should focus on the literal sense, which is to be interpreted in the light of magisterial statements, the Fathers and the analogy of faith.[102]

The final chapter of the schema solemnly make its own the last five pope's repeated exaltation of St. Thomas.[103] From the Code the text then borrows the obligation that Catholic philosophers and theologians follow his "teaching, method, and distinctive principles," words which are

---

[99] See *ADP* II/4 119-20, where the following are mentioned: atheistic communism, socialism, naturalism, materialism, laicism, liberalism, statism, evolutionism, exaggerated humanism, rationalism, racism, intellectualism, voluntarism, agnosticism, and pragmatism..

[100] *ADP* II/4 157-220.

[101] The text refers at this point to the Holy Office monitum of 20 June 1961; *ADP* II/4 164.

[102] This chapter, all things considered, is much less aggressive against current dangers than the *votum* of the Congregation; see *ADA* III 328-34.

[103] *ADP* II/4, 165; on the next page this endorsement is extended even further: "it should be extended to the faithful themselves and especially to those who are exercising some apostolic function, so that all of them, faithfully imbued with this teaching in proportion to their state and ability, may be able to grasp the universal character of the truth itself and, led by the Angelic Doctor, may more surely and more strongly come to a better knowledge of Christ's revelation."

given a very strict meaning in the notes. To the text of this chapter the ST appended some "Additamenta" which set out Aquinas' first principles in philosophy and theology.[104]

The five texts of the ST that were discussed at the CPC were in the end combined to form two schemata: *De sacrorum alumnis formandis* and *De scholis catholicis et de studiis academicis*.[105]

6. *Commission on Missions (MI)*[106]

The Commission was chaired by Card. Agagianian, with D. Matthew as secretary, but in fact this latter role was played by S. Paventi, a consultor to the Congregation for Religious and *minutante* in the Congregation for the Propagation of the Faith.[107] Although all continents were represented, forty-one of the fifty-four members and consultors of the MI were from Europe. Over half of them resided in Rome, where many worked at the headquarters of missionary orders or taught at Roman academies. Twenty-nine per cent of the commission were from the Curia, most of them from the Congregation for the Propagation of the Faith.

The official *Quaestiones* asked for a study of the promotion of missionary work, missionary vocations, the formation of missionaries and the coordination of their work, the indigenous clergy, and relations between dioceses and the missions.[108] Paventi developed a program of work that appears to be heavily dependent on the proposals of his

---

[104] At the end the ST declared its opinion with regard to the famous 24 Theses or "Pronuntiata maiora" prepared by the Congregation in 1914: "With the aid of further historical and theoretical investigations by a group of experts, these theses should be rewritten in briefer form and extended to cover other parts of philosophy (e.g., ethics, natural law, economics, philosophy of history and of religion, esthetics, etc.);" *ADP* II/4 172. This nearly exclusive exaltation of Aquinas was strongly criticized when the text was brought to the CPC; see Indelicato, *Difendere la dottrina*, 270-71.

[105] See Carbone, "Gli schemi preparatori," 61-62; Indelicato, *Difendere la dottrina*, 165-70, 266-76.

[106] See S. Paventi, "'Iter' dello schema 'De activitate missionali Ecclesiae,'" *Euntes Docete* 19 (1966) 98-126; J. B. Anderson, *A Vatican II Pneumatology of the Paschal Mystery: The Historical-Doctrinal Genesis of Ad Gentes I, 2-5* (Anal. Greg. 250; Rome, 1988) 7-21; G. Butturini, "Missioni e concilio: La storia, i testi e i criteri della commissione preparatoria," *Verso il Concilio*, 397-423.

[107] Paventi had been secretary of a subcommission established within the latter Congregation to review the episcopal *vota* on the missions and to prepare a set of proposals for the CAP. Of the twenty-three proposals submitted by the Congregation, all but one (which urged that no new dogmas be proclaimed by the Council) concerned particular questions of the canon law of missions; see *ADA* III 243-50.

[108] *ADP* II/1 413-14.

Congregation and which he divided among five subcommissions, three of which were chaired by men who had been on the Congregation's earlier subcommission.

The subcommissions, composed of members and consultors resident in Rome, met about twice a month from October 1960 until April 1961. In January and February 1961, joint meetings were held with representatives of the LI; material on the laity was communicated to the AL, but lack of time prevented discussions with it.[109] It does not appear that any conversations took place with the TC, which was itself to prepare a chapter on the Church's missionary rights.[110]

The MI sent the CPC seven brief texts, which were intended to form a single schema. A preface, written after some controversy by Paventi, provided a very brief history of the Church's missionary efforts, described it as a wholly spiritual and not political or temporal work, rapidly pointed out hopeful and difficult aspects facing it, and urged all Catholics to commit themselves to the work. The preface does not even allude to the recent theological controversy about the nature and place of the missions in the Church. Although constrained by the monopoly the TC claimed on doctrinal matters, the MI seems also to have thought the theological issues to be settled. At the CPC Agaganian made the remarkable claim that the work of evangelization posed no special doctrinal problems since recent Popes had clarified the basis and purposes of missionary work.[111]

This statement ignored the lively and interesting debate about the definition of the Church's mission that had marked the previous half-century. In brief, this debate had seen an original emphasis on the salvation of souls as the purpose of the missions replaced by an emphasis on the *plantatio Ecclesiae*, understood at first in a largely institutional sense. At the point when it was becoming generally agreed that it was a mistake to counterpose these approaches, a more radical challenge arose, particularly from France, with the proposal that the term "mission" be

[109] See Agagianian's comment, *ADP*, II/3 402. On the other hand, Seumois, in a letter to Agagianian, 19 December 1962, speaks of a successful intervention of Msgr. Glorieux on behalf of a statement on the lay apostolate in the missions; see Anderson, *A Vatican II Pneumatology*, 297.

[110] Agaganian felt obliged to explain to the CPC why his commission had not consulted other PrC. From the conversations with the LI and the AL, it had become apparent, he said, "that it was first necessary to establish definite and precise norms for evangelization, better adapted to the apostolate, and then to examine problems concerning the missions in their light;" *ADP* II/3 166.

[111] *ADP* II/3 164.

given a more basic and comprehensive meaning to include both the
evangelization of dechristianized zones in historically Christian lands
and the Church's general engagement in all aspects of human history.[112]

The Preface does not offer a precise definition of the missions, but from
its indirect comments emerges the dominant idea of the *plantatio Ecclesiae*, the generation of new particular Churches, diversified by their social
and cultural locations.[113] The proposal that the missions be understood in
the context of the Church's single and general mission nowhere appears.

After this preface the MI offered the seven schemata that set out more
precise questions.[114] Taking for granted that missionary work was the
proper responsibility of the pope, of the Roman Curia, and of the
missionary institutes,[115] these chapters were chiefly concerned with introducing various practical adaptations into the Church's pastoral activity
in missionary lands: in other words, the reform of the Church's *ius
missionale*.[116] The guiding principle was that the Roman Congregation

[112] For reviews of these developments, see E. Loffeld, *Le problème cardinal de la
missiologie et des missions catholiques* (Rhenen 1956); A. Seumois, "The Evolution of
Mission Theology among Roman Catholics," in *The Theology of the Christian Mission*,
ed. G.H. Anderson (New York 1961) 123-34; R. Hoffman, "The Development of
Mission Theology in the Twentieth Century," *TS* 23 (1962) 419-41; E. Loffeld,
"Convergences actuelles en théologie missionnaire," *Eglise vivante* 15 (1963) 44-58,
131-46; M.-J. Le Guillou, "Mission as an Ecclesiological Theme," in *Re-thinking the
Church's Mission* (Concilium 13; New York 1966) 81-130; S. Dianich, *Chiesa in
missione: Per una ecclesiologia dinamica* (Milan 1985) 15-133. Interesting comments
and bibliographies can also be found in Y. Congar, "Principes doctrinaux (nᵒˢ 2 à 9),"
in *L'activité missionnaire de l'Eglise* (Unam Sanctam 67; Paris 1967) 198-208.
[113] "The Church, like any true human mother, also desires that her children be similar
to her and yet also different and individual, all of whom, though born from different
races, she embraces with a single love;" *ADP* II/3 145.
[114] I. De regimine missionum; II. De disciplina cleri; III. De religiosis; IV. De Sacramentis et de S. Liturgia; V. De disciplina populi christiani; VI. De studiis clericorum;
VII. De cooperatione missionali.
[115] The first section of the schema regularly stresses the unique role of the pope,
immediately said to be carried out through the Congregation, and quotes the Code
of Canon Law: "universal responsibility for the missions to non-Catholics is reserved
exclusively to the Apostolic See" (*ADP*, II/3 152), a position that not only falls short of
the view of Pius XII but also differs from the one adopted by the TC in its schema
De Ecclesia: "The right and duty to proclaim the Gospel of Christ everywhere on earth
belongs to the body of Pastors along with the Vicar of Christ, and to all of them in
solidarity Christ gave the mandate, imposing on them a common duty" (*ADP* II/4 673).
At the CPC Maximos IV Saigh sharply criticized the MI's emphasis on the role of the
pope as "a tendency to flattery of the Supreme Pontiffs" (*ADP* II/3 610).
[116] See Agaganian's comment: "The reason lies in the fact that the current law for the
most part does not correspond to the present state of the missions. Because of this lacuna,
there is an urgent need to give some flexibility to the general laws in accord with what
recent Supreme Pontiffs have stated in their documents on missionary adaptation;" *ADP*
II/3 165; see also 166-67.

should not have to direct this activity by way of dispensations and particular faculties. Present norms were delaying the adaptation that is needed "so that the spread of the Gospel may keep up with those peoples who are seeing their aspirations and rights acknowledged even in international politics."[117] The proposals, which often descended into some detail and replicated materials already considered by other preparatory commissions, were often quite open, seeking various ways in which missionary activity could be adapted to local situations so that it would not be encumbered by the Church's "western dress."

After the discussions in the CPC,[118] it was decided that five of the texts prepared by the MI (on the discipline of the clergy, on religious, on sacraments and liturgy, on the discipline of the people, and on clerical studies) should not be brought to the Council. The other two schemata (on the direction of the missions and on missionary cooperation) were united to form the *Schema decreti de missionibus*.[119]

It is difficult now to know in any detail what sort of discussions may have arisen within the MI during the preparatory period, but there are some indications of disagreements. Paventi's report mentions only conflicts over the nature of the "Prooemium" that would introduce its text. At the end of the first session of the Council, A. Seumois would attribute the weaknesses of the text to the "triumvirate" of canonists (Paventi, Buijs and Kowalski) who dominated the MI and despotically refused to introduce the proposals of theologians of the missions.[120] This view is confirmed but also nuanced in a journal entry written by Yves Congar, during the Council, when he was involved in furious debates over the theological orientation of *Ad gentes*. Congar blamed the canonists Buijs and Paventi for their inability to conceive of anything but a juridical approach, but he also associated A. Seumois with them,

---

[117] *ADP*, II/3 165. This brief comment is one of the few places in which the text makes any reference to the larger context in which missionary activity is carried out. Otherwise the schema ignores the new problems created by the process of de-colonialization.

[118] *ADP*, II/3 144-275, 369-460.

[119] See Carbone, "Gli schemi preparatori," 65-66; Indelicato, *Difendere la dottrina*, 198-208..

[120] A. Seumois to Cardinal Agagianian, 19 December 1962, published in Anderson, *A Vatican II Pneumatology*, 297. Later in the same letter Seumois, commenting on efforts to revise the schema at the end of the first session of the Council, says that these canonists were not "able to fulfill this task well, stuck as they were in the old canonical schema that the Council could not accept and unable to conceive a new authentically missionary schema that would really and frankly address the major missionary problems that face the Church today and would be in accord with the basic orientations, now well known, of the majority of the Fathers of the Council." See also the interview with Seumois, 320-21.

perhaps because the latter was a determined foe of efforts to extend the
notion of mission as far as Congar wished.[121]

These two remarks, which remain to be verified in detail, would seem
to indicate that within the MI the chief discussions concerned the dominance of the juridical over the theological and not the question of the
adequacy of the *plantatio Ecclesiae* orientation. When this also was
challenged during the Council, the Roman missiologists reunited in an
effort to defend the traditional territorial approach to the missions and
the latter's dependence on the pope and the Congregation for the Propagation of the Faith. It would take four years of the Council's deliberations to resolve this issue.

7. Commission on the Apostolate of the Laity (AL)[122]

This Commission was a last-minute addition to the PrC, expressly
desired by Pope John as the "newest mark" of the Council and entrusted
with the study of "the apostolate of the laity, religious and social
Catholic action."[123] The official *Quaestiones* set out three general areas
of work: (a) the apostolate of the laity: its scope and purposes, its
subordination to the hierarchy, and how it may be adapted to meet
contemporary needs; (b) Catholic Action: the notion, scope and subjec-
tion to the hierarchy, adapting its constitution to present needs, the relation between it and other associations; (c) associations: how they can
better accomplish their charitable and social activity.[124] The clearest
point in these brief topics was the subordination of the lay apostolate to
the hierarchy; "today's needs" were left quite unspecified. No mention
was made of the theological foundations of the question, which were

---

[121] Y. Congar, *Mon Journal du Concile*, 30 March 1965, quoted in Anderson, *A Vatican II Pneumatology*, 131. According to Congar, A. Seumois himself was a fierce
defender of the idea that the goal of the missions was the *plantatio Ecclesiae* and feared
that Congar's approach would lead to a depreciation of the distinctive tasks of classical
missionary activity in favor of a single, undifferentiated "mission" of the Church. Shortly
before the Council Seumois referred to such phrases as "*l'Eglise en état de mission*" as a
"misuse of terms," rejected by missiologists and repudiated by Propaganda, which "has
shown no inclination to extend its missionary jurisdiction to those dechristianized
'espaces', which are left in the care of the apostolic activity, not of the properly missionary action;" "Mission Theology among Roman Catholics," 131.

[122] See G. Turbanti, "I laici nella chiesa e nel mondo," *Verso il Concilio Vaticano II*,
207-71. For the immediate context, see R. Goldie, "L'avant-concile des 'Christifideles
laici' (1945-1959)," *RHE* 88 (1993) 131-71.

[123] See the Pope's autograph note, 1 June 1960, quoted in V. Carbone, "Il Cardinale
Domenico Tardini e la preparazione del Concilio Vaticano II," *RSChIt* 45 (1991) 78n.

[124] *ADP* II/I 414.

presumably to be studied by the TC, whose mandate on the Church included a discussion of the place of the laity.[125]

The AL was chaired by Card. Cento, with A. Glorieux as secretary. Probably because it did not correspond to any existing curial congregation, only ten percent of its personnel were from the Curia. No lay people served on this commission, but various lay organizations were represented by clerics, these constituting about a third of the commission's personnel. Regular contacts were maintained with these associations, some of which also submitted texts for consideration. Conspicuously absent were the theologians who in the previous decade had done the most to advance the theology of the laity: Congar, Philips, Rahner, Schillebeeckx, von Balthasar, Chenu.[126]

Three subcommissions were established within the AL: on the general notion and on Catholic Action; on social action; on charitable activity. Seven plenary sessions of the whole AL were held between November 1960 and April 1962. Most of the work of elaborating a text, however, was accomplished by small groups, largely Italian in membership, within the subcommissions. On the basis of reports solicited from the members, these groups worked up a text, sent it out for review by the other members, and then proposed revisions in the light of the comments received. The result of this work was a single, 172-page text, *Schema constitutionis de apostolatu laicorum*, which was approved at the AL's plenary session in April 1962 and sent to the CPC.[127]

The first parts of this text dealt with the general notion of the apostolate of the laity and with Catholic Action. Within the subcommission that prepared these sections, serious disagreements on the definition of the lay apostolate emerged very quickly, particularly over the question of the basis and the status of lay activity in the world and the significance to be assigned to a public "mandate" officially accrediting certain forms of the lay apostolate. Closely related was the question of the definition of "Catholic Action," with opinions divided between those

[125] Writing to Henri Caffarel, a consultor to the AL, on 19 Dec 1960, Congar commented: "An unfortunate impression that I had in Rome is the fatal partitioning between the different bodies and, worse still, between the different topics of specific doctrines. It is clear that a real work '*De laicis*' can only be presented in an ecclesiological synthesis: it's all of one piece. What is said about the laity will be worth as much as the presentation that is made of the Church" (A-Congar).

[126] Congar and Philips served on the TC, where the latter wrote the chapter on laity; Rahner had been exiled to the SA; the other three were not appointed to any preparatory body.

[127] *ADP* II/IV 468-520, 565-97.

who wished to expand the reference of the term to include many different types of lay activity and those who wished it to be restricted to a particular type, the one developed particularly in Italy and marked by direct dependence on the hierarchy. Involved in these two questions were fundamental questions on the relation between the temporal order and the spiritual or supernatural order, on the scope of the Church's redemptive mission, on the roles of the hierarchy and the laity in accomplishing it, and on the freedom and autonomy of the laity.

The final text first offered a rather diffuse presentation of fundamental notions. It insisted that all the members of the Church, in virtue of their baptism and confirmation, have a right and duty to be actively involved in the life of the Church. A rather juridical definition of lay people was offered: "By 'the laity' is here meant Christian believers to whom the common rights and duties of persons in the Church belong and who, while not belonging to the clerical state or to the state of perfection, are called to attain their Christian perfection amid the affairs of the world."[128] The text then simply enumerated the various ways in which various activities undertaken by lay people are related to the hierarchy: by canonical mission, by hierarchical mandate, by simple approval, or by free initiatives subject to the vigilance of the hierarchy.

The second part of the final text discussed *De apostolatu laicorum in actione ad regnum Christi directe provehendum*. Among the various forms of this direct apostolate, "Catholic Action" was treated first and given the narrower meaning of those forms of lay activity which are undertaken under the direction of the hierarchy; other activities were simply referred to as "other forms" of the direct apostolate.[129] This part ended with discussions of the various areas in which the lay apostolate is to be exercised.

The third part of the AL's schema was devoted to the laity's charitable activities. Within the subcommission that elaborated this section, the chief problem lay in defining the relation between the Church's charitable work and state-sponsored programs of social welfare. One group of members wished to approach the issue in a priori fashion, on the basis of an abstract insistence on the superiority of the supernatural virtue of charity, which disparagingly regarded works of justice and social welfare as at best merely "naturalistic." Others found this approach unrealistic and paternalistic. There was also a sharp disagreement on the

---

[128] *ADP* II/IV 473-74.

[129] Perhaps a little defensively, the Declaration that introduced this schema said that questions of terminology were not yet ripe for solution; *ADP* II/IV 469.

degree to which the Church's charitable activities ought to be centralized and placed under greater Roman control. On the central point, while indicating that the works of charity surpass forms of assistance that proceed "from merely human or social impulses," the final text praised modern societies for developing such institutions and encouraged the faithful to promote them.

The last section of the schema, *De apostolatu laicorum in actione sociali*, was the most organically constructed. It offered a strong defence of the right and duty of the Church to participate in what it called the "Christian restoration of the natural order," an effort it considered an implication of Christ's redemption of the world. This was developed in what became a little summa of the Church's social teaching. In the course of elaborating this text, the principal subject of dispute was the participation of the laity in mixed or neutral associations for social justice. The final text came down on the side of the defenders of this practice, at least in certain places and circumstances.[130]

The work of the AL and the text it produced illustrate once again the lack of coordination in the preparatory period. The commission was supposed to deal primarily with practical questions affecting the lay apostolate, leaving the theological bases for the TC.[131] That this was an impossible division of responsibilities became quickly apparent in the subcommissions. The determination of the laity's role in both Church and society and of its relationship with the hierarchy rested upon ecclesiological bases. When Msgr. Glorieux consulted Tromp about some particular questions, he was told that the TC would deal with the foundations in accord with the brochure he and Philips had prepared for the Second World Congress on the Lay Apostolate.[132] It does not seem that there were any other formal discussions with the TC, and when Cento presented his commission's text to the CPC, he expressed his relief that those doctrinal notions the AL had had to develop agreed in substance with the views of the TC in its chapter on the laity.[133]

---

[130] The AL's text was revised after the CPC discussion for presentation to the Council; see Carbone, "Gli schemi preparatori," 66-67.

[131] In the Declaration which preceded the text presented to the CPC, it is remarked: "...doctrinal questions exceded the competency of our commission; our documents do not touch upon doctrine except to the degree that this is needed to understand the questions. In these cases we invoke the traditional doctrine;" *ADP* II/IV 469.

[132] Tromp Diary, 17 Jan 1961. On 2 Feb 1961 Tromp also met with Henri Caffarel, whose views on marriage he does not appear to have agreed with. The work to which Tromp referred was *De laicorum apostolatus fundamento, indole, formis*, prepared in 1956.

[133] *ADP*, II/IV 524. On the other hand, the AL did receive the SCU's text *De sacerdotio fidelium et de officiis laicorum* in May 1961, but it is hard to see any influence on the brief paragraph devoted to that theme in the AL's text.

In two other areas of its concern, the AL apparently also worked alone. The section "De laicorum apostolatu in ambitibus materialismo, praesertim marxistico, imbutis" appears to have been drawn up without any consultation with the CLP, which had produced a text of its own, *De cura animarum et communismo*.[134] Similarly, the section on the laity's social activity covers much of the same material that was entrusted to the TC's subcommission *De ordine sociali*. The presence on both subcommissions of Pavan, Jarlot and Ferrari Toniolo (who were also involved in the preparation of *Mater et magistra*) does not suffice to prevent the impression of another example of needless duplication of effort.

8. *Commission for the Oriental Churches (OR)*[135]

Chaired by Card. G. Cicognani, with A.G. Wilykyj as secretary, this commission was composed of prelates representing nearly all of the eastern Churches in communion with Rome and of experts in oriental affairs, among whom professors at the Pontifical Oriental Institute dominated.

The CAP sent this commission four topics: transfers of rite, shared worship with eastern Christians, how to reconcile the eastern dissidents, and the chief disciplinary problems assigned to other PrC, but from the standpoint of the eastern Churches.[136] This was not a very ambitious list, and the way in which the third of these topics was stated ("de modo reconciliandi Orientales dissidentes") was a weak response to the extraordinary interest in the Council that had already been expressed by many of the Orthodox, most notably by Patriarch Athenagoras.

To promote the ecumenical purpose of the Council, Pope John had divided responsibilities between the SCU, which would deal with the Protestant communities, and the OR, which would deal with the Orthodox. Although the OR established a special subcommission to promote relations with the Orthodox, it proved itself remarkably unresponsive to the challenges of the moment. There was only one unfruitful meeting between the OR and the SCU. Despite urging from the SCU, the OR did not initiate any contacts with the Orthodox until June 1961 when a delegation went to Constantinople to inform Athenagoras of the progress

[134] For the two texts see *ADP* II/IV 510-13 and II/III 798-803.
[135] See *Les églises orientales catholiques: Décret 'Orientalium Ecclesiarum'*, ed. N. Edelby and I. Dick (Paris 1970); M. Velati, "La proposta ecumenica," *Verso il Concilio*, 344-50.
[136] *ADP* II/1 413.

of the preparation of the Council. As the Council neared, in part because of the desire of the Orthodox, Pope John removed the task of engaging in conversations with the Orthodox from the OR and assigned it to the SCU.

At its first plenary session in November 1960, the OR divided itself into six study sections according to competencies (theological, juridical, pastoral, liturgical, ecumenical, historical). Three outlines had already been prepared and were presented at this meeting: on rites in the Church, on the oriental Patriarchs, and on *communicatio in sacris*. Edelby, representing the Melkites, came to the meeting with counter-proposals which succeeded in expanding the agenda and deepening its theological problematic.

The OR met in five more plenary sessions, largely completing its work in October 1961 (a sixth plenary session was held in May 1962 to make suggestions for the reform of the code of oriental canon law). The OR prepared twelve schemata, one of which, *De habitu clericorum*, never came before the CPC.[137] Except for the schema *De Ecclesiae unitate*, the texts were intended to form chapters in a single text *De Ecclesiis Orientalibus*.

The first of the OR texts, *De ritibus in Ecclesia*,[138] went far beyond the precise question assigned to the commission: transfers from rite to rite. An initial project had presented only three themes: the superiority of the pope over all rites; the equality of rites; and freedom to change rites. Edelby's counter-proposal, presented at the November meeting, expanded the question to include a theological justification of the variety of rites in the Church. This formed the basis of further discussion which in April 1961 produced the final text in twelve paragraphs that was presented to the CPC.

Whereas the initial draft had so stressed the supremacy of the pope as almost to suggest that he belonged to none,[139] the final text recalled that

---

[137] De Ecclesiae sacramentis; De ritibus in Ecclesia; De Patriarchis orientalibus; De communicatione in sacris cum christianis orientalibus non catholicis; De usu linguarum vernacularum in liturgiis; De Ecclesiae praeceptis; De facultatibus Episcoporum; De catechismo et catechetica institutione; De kalendario perpetuo et celebratione Paschatis; De officio divino Ecclesiarum orientalium; De habitu clericorum; De Ecclesiae unitate: "ut omnes unum sint." Carbone, "Gli schemi preparatori," 62-63, does not include the text *De habitu clericorum*, apparently because it was never even printed for presentation to the CCP; see Edelby, *Le décret sur les églises orientales*, 71, who counts fifteen texts because he considers the four chapters *De Ecclesiae sacramentis* as separate schemata.

[138] *ADP* II/2 179-97.

[139] "The Roman Pontiff, successor of Blessed Peter in his primacy, is not bound, as such, to any rite (liturgical or canonical); he can freely choose the rite that he wants and practice it according to circumstances;" see Edelby, *Les églises orientales*, 130.

as bishop of Rome, the pope has his own rite, which does not limit his universal primacy over all rites. It also stressed that all the particular Churches or rites are equal in holiness and dignity, enjoy the same rights and privileges, and are bound by the same obligations, so that none of them is superior to the others. The text also saw the variety of rites as an expression of catholicity, which both requires the preservation of legitimate traditions and the Church's adaptation to various needs of time and place. The OR's schema even envisaged the formation of new rites to provide for the good of souls and to display even more the Church's universality.[140] This text, then, expanded the original topic to offer the first outline of a theology of the local Church.[141]

Another set of important ecclesiological questions was raised in the preparation of a second text, *De patriarchis orientalibus*.[142] An initial plan would have exhausted this topic in a consideration of whether patriarchs should be made Cardinals and what order of precedence they should have. At Edelby's suggestion, this narrow focus was broadened to include several other questions: whether patriarchs should have a role in the election of the pope, whether new patriarchates should be created, whether the Latin patriarchates and titular patriarchates should be retained, whether there should be a single patriarchate in any one territory, and whether the juridical authority of a patriarch should be clarified.

The result was a schema that set out thirteen proposals. The "very broad authority" of oriental patriarchs, "given or admitted by the Roman Pontiff or by an Ecumenical Council," was acknowledged and detailed, along with a desire that the patriarchal dignity be revived and flourish. The possibility of establishing new patriarchates in the East was stated, and the suppression of titular Latin patriarchates was recommended, but with the Latin patriarchate of Jerusalem to be preserved. Another proposal was that some oriental patriarchs be made Cardinals and that they take part in the election of the pope. Patriarchs would also be given precedence over all other prelates, including Cardinals, except for legates *a latere* of the pope.

When this text was presented to the CPC, however, it was prefaced by several paragraphs that reflected a rather different theological assessment of the authority and role of patriarchs. This preface, which Edelby says was prepared by a small group of Roman experts and was never

---

[140] *ADP* II/2 180-81.

[141] The CPC received this text with general favor, although some thought it exaggerated the significance of variety and several objected to the paragraph on possible new rites.

[142] *ADP* II/2 197-229.

approved by the OR,[143] began with the assertion that by divine right there are only two levels of jurisdictional authority in the Church, the "supreme pontificate" and the "subordinated episcopate" (the text also says that bishops receive their authority "at the mediation of the Roman Pontiff"). All other degrees of authority exist only "by ecclesiastical institution."[144] Among these was the authority of patriarchs, a supra-episcopal power that is a participation in the Roman Pontiff's primatial authority and thus subject to his power to change, increase or diminish it.[145] The assumption here is that any jurisdictional authority in the Church superior to that of the local bishop must be a participation in the primatial power of the pope, a view that Maximos IV would challenge when this text came before the CPC.[146]

It remains unclear whether there were any conversations between the OR and either the TC or the SCU over the place of patriarchs. The doctrine set out in the preface is the same as that which Tromp held,[147] while the call for the restoration of patriarchal rights and privileges coincided with the *votum* on the subject prepared by the SCU and sent to the OR.[148]

In its text *De communicatione in sacris*,[149] the OR proposed a mitigation of the Church's practice by means, first, of the distinction between formal and merely material communion and, second, of the difference between the situations of those who initiate a schism and those who in good faith find themselves separated from the Church.

The most ambitious of the texts prepared by the OR was the schema "De Ecclesiae unitate: 'Ut omnes unum sint'",[150] in which it addressed

[143] *Les églises orientales*, 284.

[144] *ADP* II/2 197. A certain animus against the Melkites may be visible in the fact that in support of this claim the preface cites not only the motu proprio *Cleri Sanctitati*, which in their minds had denigrated the office of the patriarch, but also a statement made by Melkite bishops in 1900: "We consider it most certain that the patriarchal dignity was not established by divine law but only by ecclesiastical law, in this differing from the authority of the Roman Pontiff which we acknowledge to be of divine law and to stand above all others."

[145] *ADP* II/2 197-98. The non-historical character of these claims is also reflected in Cicognani's remarks to the CPC (201): "Already the Fathers of Nicaea thought that some participation in the authority of the Apostolic See was linked to the patriarchal sees."

[146] *ADP* II/2 210; Indelicato, *Difendere la dottrina*, 137-43.

[147] When Philips sent Tromp a paper on the patriarchs written by C. Moeller, Tromp replied that it was useful as history but not as theology, since the main point was that patriarchal authority was only a participation in papal power.

[148] "In the rite and discipline of the Orientals all those things should be retained or restored which can be retained without damage to the divine laws, especially with regard to the ancient rights of patriarchs and metropolitans and with regard to the election and confirmation of bishops, as Leo XIII solemnly promised;" SCU, "De structura hierarchica Ecclesiae votorum conspectus," 7 (A-Stransky).

[149] *ADP* II/2 229-48.

[150] *ADP* II/4 436-67.

the challenge of promoting the reconciliation of the eastern Orthodox churches. In a first section deliberately written in biblical language more familiar to the Orthodox,[151] the schema set out a short treatise on the Church, its hierarchical structure and visible unity under Peter (which has not been destroyed by the unfortunate divisions that have occurred), the variety in which this unity is realized, the harm the divisions have caused, especially outside the Church, the *vestigia unitatis* that can still be found among the dissidents, and the Church's work to restore unity. The text then sets out various means, supernatural, theological, liturgical, disciplinary, psychological, and practical, by which unity can be sought. This schema appears to have been drawn up without any consultation with the TC or even with the SCU.

The other texts prepared by the OR were on a series of mainly disciplinary questions.[152] The schema *De Ecclesiae sacramentis*[153] addresses the question of the minister of confirmation and of penance, recommends the restoration of the permanent diaconate, and proposes an alteration in the discipline with regard to mixed marriages. The schema *De Ecclesiae praeceptis*[154] made specific proposals with regard to feast days, fast and abstinence, Easter communion, financial contributions, and the celebration of marriages. The text *De facultatibus episcoporum*[155] asked that the principle be established that the authority of bishops in their own sees not be limited except by what is necessary or suitable for the common good of the whole Church. The text *De catechismo et catechetica institutione*[156] proposed that a single catechism of Christian doctrine be issued for the whole Church, western and eastern, and that its preparation give full respect to the variety and distinctiveness of the oriental rites. In two other short texts, *De kalendario perpetuo et celebratione Paschatis* and *De officio divino*,[157] the OR supported a common civil calendar, urged all Christians to agree upon a common date for Easter, and asked that the divine office take greater account of oriental traditions.

[151] Pope John, however, did not like it: "The mosaic of biblical texts which it begins does not seem to be in good taste;" Giovanni XXIII, *Lettere 1958-1963*, ed. L.F. Capovilla (Roma 1978) 546.

[152] I do not discuss here the text *De habitu clericorum*, which was not presented to the CPC, or the text *De usu linguarum vernacularum*, which is discussed later in this paper.

[153] *ADP* II/2 258-79.

[154] *ADP* II/2 862-77.

[155] *ADP* II/3 1280-91.

[156] *ADP* II/3 1291-1304.

[157] *ADP* II/3 1304-22.

After the discussion of all the texts of the OR by the CPC, the one on ecclesiastical precepts was remanded to the revision of the Code, the one on *communicatio in sacris* was reserved to the Holy See, and the other minor texts, with various changes, were grouped into a single schema *De Ecclesiis Orientalibus*. The CPC also recommended that the schema *De Ecclesiae unitate* be fused with the other texts on ecumenism drawn up by the TC and the SCU; but the Secretariate of State, for reasons still unclear, decided that it should remain a distinct text, and it was therefore printed in the first volume of the texts presented for discussion at the first Session of the Council.[158]

9. *Secretariat for Communications Media (SCM)*

Chaired by Archbishop M.J. O'Connor, with A. Deskur as secretary, this secretariat received very general topics from the CAP: to present the Church's teaching, to promote means by which Catholics will learn how to use the media according to Catholic principles, to discuss how they can be made to conform to faith and morals and to promote the works of the apostolate.[159] All forty-six of the members and consultors of the SCM were either bishops or priests, fourteen resident in Rome. Almost all had some competence or experience in the area. The SCM formed three subcommissions, on the press, radio and television, and the cinema. It established a mixed commission with the CLP. Four small subcommissions prepared proposals sent to the MI, ST, OR, and AL.

At its plenary session, 19 October 1961, it approved the draft of a schema, which was further modified through correspondence and definitively approved in January 1962. The CPC discussed the text in March-April 1962.[160] A first part of the schema set out the Church's right, an implication of its religious freedom, to make use of all the modern instruments of communication. The second part presented authoritative solutions to the chief moral questions about the use of such media. The last part discussed the responsibilities of those who work in such media, a sort of code of professional ethics. Alone among all the PrC, the SCM added to each of these sections canons censuring those who disagree with the teachings set out: "Si quis dixerit... a doctrina catholica est alienus."[161]

---

[158] See Carbone, "Gli schemi preparatori," 62-64; Indelicato, *Difendere la dottrina*, 290-94.

[159] *ADP* II/1 415.

[160] *ADP* II/3 493-590.

[161] At the CPC discussion, there was a general consensus that these canons should either be dropped or turned into positively stated norms; see Carbone, "Gli schemi preparatori," 67-68; Indelicato, *Difendere la dottrina*, 208-13.

B. The Liturgical Commission (LI)[162]

The LI was chaired by the prefect of the Congregation for Rites, G. Cicognani, with A. Bugnini serving as its secretary. Many of the most important figures in the liturgical movement were represented on the commission: C. Vagaggini, B. Capelle, B. Botte, A. Chavasse, P. Jounel, G. Martimort, J. Jungmann, P.-M. Gy. Eleven of the sixty-one members had some association with the Curia, but only three of them resided in Rome. Within the LI the distinction between members and consultors was purely formal.

The official *Quaestiones* had proposed in very dry language seven areas in which the LI should consider appropriate reforms: the calendar, the texts and rubrics of the Mass, certain other rites, baptism, confirmation, extreme unction, and marriage, the Breviary, the use of the vernacular, and liturgical vestments.[163] The secretary of the LI did not feel obliged to confine its work to these topics, however, and in late October 1960 he sent out a program of twelve questions for as many subcommissions. To the seven proposed in the *Quaestiones* were added concelebration, liturgical formation, the participation of the faithful, liturgical adaptation, sacred music and sacred art. The additional topics proposed by Bugnini expanded the horizon of the LI's work to include theological and pastoral questions of the first order.

The LI began its work at a plenary meeting of members on 12 November 1960, which approved the twelve questions but decided also to add an important topic: a doctrinal prologue "On the mystery of the sacred liturgy and its relation to the life of the Church."[164] Norms for the subcommissions' work were also agreed upon.[165] The suggested themes

---

[162] See C. Braga, "La 'Sacrosanctum Concilium' nei lavori della Commissione preparatoria," *Notitiae* 20 (1984) 87-134; P. Jounel, "Genèse et théologie de la Constitution Sacrosanctum Concilium," *M-D*, 155 (1983) 6-20; A. Bugnini, *The Reform of the Liturgy, 1948-1975*, trans. by Matthew J. O'Connell (Collegeville 1990) 26-39; A.-G. Martimort, "La Constitution sur la Liturgie de Vatican II," *BLE* 85 (1984) 60-74; idem, "L'histoire de la réforme liturgique à travers le témoignage de Mgr Annibale Bugnini," *M-D* 162 (1985) 125-55; M. Paiano, "Il rinnovamento della liturgia: dai movimenti alla chiesa universale," in *Verso il Concilio*, 67-140.

[163] *ADP* I/1 412.

[164] For the thirteen topics assigned to the subcommissions, see Braga, "La 'Sacrosanctum Concilium,'" 114-17.

[165] See Braga, "La 'Sacrosanctum Concilium,'" 111-14. Not included in these norms was the advice given by Cicognani in his opening address: that the members of the LI refrain from any actions outside the commission "which might be intended to arouse disagreement either for or against any question proposed or to be proposed or which might seek by some passion to influence superior authority. The greatest sincerity and probity are, therefore, required;" "Allocutio Em.mi Cardinalis Caietani Cicognanii initio sessionis diei 15 novembris 1960," 2 (A-McManus).

listed under each question were recommendations and the subcommissions were free to modify them or to add others. They were to concentrate on the "more general principles" rather than on precise determinations or applications, which could be left to the experts in the Congregation for Rites.[166] Their work was to provide a complete exploration of all aspects of a question, theological, historical, pastoral, practical, legislative, with every assertion given scholarly documentation, and then to propose the conclusions drawn from it. The subcommissions would work on their own for four months, preparing texts that would be studied at a second plenary session in April when they would be examined and revised for submission to the Central Commission, it was hoped, in June. Since the members of the subcommissions did not live near one another, they would have to collaborate by correspondence or at occasional meetings. The secretariat of the LI would serve a coordinating role.

Organizationally, then, especially during the crucial initial period of work, the LI was the least centralized of all the PrC. Substantively, by comparison with the other PrC, what is most noticeable about the LI's work was the close connection always drawn between doctrine and practice: pastoral reform was always related to theological principle. Methodologically, it differed from other PrC by its commitment to comprehensive scholarly work on which to base its proposals for reform.

In general the subcommissions appear to have been able to work well both individually and in communication with one another. Some important theological differences arose, as, for example, within the subcommission *De mysterio*, between emphasis on the incarnation and focus on the paschal mystery, or in the subcommission *De participatione fidelium* over the question whether this should be based on the common priesthood of the faithful or on the ecclesial nature of the liturgy; but these differences were minor compared to a common commitment to serious and well grounded pastoral reform. Perhaps the only major exception to this harmony occurred in the subcommission *De musica sacra* which was dominated by I. Anglés, whose fierce defence of the primacy of Gregorian chant included very critical judgements about movements for liturgical reform.[167]

---

[166] This distinction had already been used by Pope John when he approved the new rubrics for the Breviary and Missal, 25 July 1960: "...we decided that the more general principles affecting the general reform of the liturgy are to be proposed to the Fathers in the coming Ecumenical Council, but that the afore-mentioned reform of the rubrics of the Breviary and Missal is not to be postponed any longer;" *ADP* I 13.

[167] Anglés' Pontifical Institute of Sacred Music submitted a *votum* to the CAP in which the defence of Gregorian chant and of Latin took the form of an attack upon the liturgical movement; *ADA* IV/II/1 225, 227.

The subcommissions worked separately from November 1960 to March 1961, when reports of their work were gathered in preparation for the plenary session of the LI in April 1961. The inner dynamics of the LI's functioning were affected in the weeks before the plenary session by tensions between the commission and certain Roman circles that were concerned about the question of Latin in the liturgy. (This problem is discussed separately below.) The secretariat of the LI now found it necessary not only to coordinate the work of the subcommissions but to defend the whole LI from curial interference. This led to the only serious tensions between the secretariat and the subcommissions, which were less inclined to tactical prudence.

At the April plenary session, besides the question of Latin, the principal debates concerned the introduction of eschatology into the discussion of the mystery of the liturgy, the relation between liturgy and devotions, the theological ground of the participation of the faithful and its relation to the hierarchical nature of the Church, and the principle that the criterion of participation should determine what was said about sacred music.

After the April session, the secretariat began to compose an organic schema on the basis of the subcommissions' work and the comments received. This schema, largely the work of Bugnini and Vagaggini, continued to express the reforming thrust of the subcommissions, but also reflected an effort to make sure that the general principles of reform would not be imperilled by relatively minor but controversial issues. Bugnini stated the problem quite frankly in the letter with which he sent out the completed draft on 10 August 1961. The "climate and inspiration" of the Council had been in their minds in preparing it: "And for that reason we have sometimes preferred to attenuate or even to neglect some things than to endanger everything."[168]

The abundant comments that were received from the members included criticisms both of the interference of the Congregation for Rites and of certain theological orientations, particularly in the first chapter into which most of the general and doctrinal questions had been gathered. Martimort and Jenny thought that the text of the subcommission *De mysterio* had been "disfigured" by the introduction of several scholastic terms.[169] Martimort wrote an alternate text, which centered the

---

[168] "Constitutio de sacra Liturgia fovenda atque instauranda, Schema transmissum Sodalibus Commissionis die 10 augusti 1961," iii (A-McManus).

[169] See Martimort, "La Constitution," 65. He appears to be referring to Vagaggini's use of the categories of instrumental causality to explain the schema's underlying christology and ecclesiology.

liturgy on the paschal mystery, whereas Vagaggini's text focused on the incarnation. To deal with these criticisms, a special meeting was held in mid-October. Although two orientations were visible, not only theological (incarnation vs. eschatology) but also strategic (how much prudence to show with regard to Roman disquiet), the meeting was generally harmonious and resulted in a revision of the text that tried to take both orientations into account.[170]

The newly revised text was sent out on 15 November 1961. Minor criticisms of its language and style were registered, but at another meeting of the subcommission *De mysterio* held just before the plenary session in January, further changes strengthened the text's references to the paschal mystery and to the eschatological dimensions of the liturgy.[171] On questions known to be causing alarm in certain Roman circles, the history of the text — from the August draft, through the November draft, to the text revised at the January plenary session and submitted to the CPC — shows a mixed picture. For example, the August draft contained a cautious paragraph entitled "Preserving the tradition while admitting legitimate progress," which ended with the statement: "Innovations are not to be made except where true necessity requires it and then only with caution so that the new forms will in a way grow organically out of the forms already existing." In the November draft "true necessity" was weakened to "what would truly be useful to the Church." The paragraph on the relation between the worshipping and didactic purposes of the liturgy was altered to remove the false dichotomy the first draft had expressed, probably in order to address a theological criticism often brought against the liturgical reforms. In discussing the limitations to be placed on liturgical adaptation to different cultures, the words "with the approval of the Holy See" were dropped in the statement on the authority of episcopal conferences. A paragraph that called for the establishment in the Congregation for Rites of a "Central Office on Liturgy, Music and Sacred Art" to coordinate and promote the work of diocesan and national liturgical offices was dropped entirely.

After revisions and unanimous approval of the text at the plenary session in January, all that remained was for it to receive the signature of

---

[170] Braga reports that this special meeting became the object of criticisms that the secretariat of the LI was secretly manipulating the work of the commission in progressive directions; "La 'Sacrosanctum Concilium," 101.

[171] Particular examples of the textual history are given in "Les étapes préparatoires du schéma de la Constitution sur la Liturgie," *M-D* 155 (1983) 31-53, and in Braga, "La 'Sacrosanctum Concilium,'" 117-34.

the president of the LI, Cardinal Cicognani. Martimort says that strong
external pressure was brought to bear on the Cardinal.[172] After much
hesitation Cicognani signed the schema on 1 February, four days before
his death.

The schema of the LI contained a preface and eight chapters.[173]
The first chapter, on the general principles, is notable for its theological
content, grounding liturgical renewal in a strong christological confession, which combines nicely the incarnational and paschal emphases,
and in an ecclesiology in which the "wondrous sacrament of the whole
Church" is realized in its liturgical actions, themselves anticipations of
the Church's eschatological fulfilment. The liturgy is then related to the
Church's total mission and to the spiritual life of the faithful. The greater
participation of the faithful serves as the supreme criterion of liturgical
renewal and reform, for which general norms are then outlined, followed
by particular norms derived from the need to adapt the liturgy to local
circumstances and cultures, to express the liturgy's didactic and pastoral
functions, and to respect the Church's communal and hierarchical
nature. The section on the liturgical life of dioceses and parishes briefly
offers a liturgical basis for a theology of the local Church: the episcopal
liturgy is described as the "chief manifestation of the Church" and a theological notion of the parish as a visible representation of the whole
Church replaces an earlier sterile definition of it as simply a "portion of
a diocese." Finally, the local Church is also validated in the sections on
national and diocesan structures to promote the liturgical renewal, with
episcopal conferences having authority to make decisions, subject to
recognitio by the Holy See, with regard to certain liturgical adaptations,
including greater use of the vernacular.

The subsequent chapters offer briefer theological statements on which
to base specific recommendations for the reform of the liturgy. Among
the most important practical reforms proposed were the reform of the
lectionary, more use of the vernacular in the Mass, wider use of
communion under both species, and more frequent opportunities for
concelebration.

---

[172] "Cardinals Pizzardo and Bacci, along with the musicians, sounded the alarm
for the defense of endangered Latin; others objected to the decentralization envisaged,
while others rejected the reform of the breviary;" Martimort, "La Constitution sur la
Liturgie," 66.

[173] Prooemium; I. De principiis generalibus ad S. Liturgiam instaurandam atque
fovendam; II. De sacrosancto Eucharistiae mysterio; III. De sacramentis et sacramental-
ibus; IV. De officio divino; V. De anno liturgico; VI. De sacra supellectile; VII.
De musica sacra; VIII. De arte sacra. See *ADP* II/3 26-144, 275-368, 460-93.

For each theological statement and practical reform, the schema also offered a "Declaratio," technically not part of the text for the Council but added to provide the members of the CPC fuller explanations and justifications of the points made.[174] These statements would become an object of some controversy, particularly when they were omitted from the text as revised after the CPC discussion and submitted to the Council.

Among all the schemas prepared for the Council, the schema *De Liturgia* stands out for the successful effort its redactors made to link the doctrinal and pastoral dimensions of the questions they were assigned. The principles were derived from a serious effort at *ressourcement*, obvious both in the effort to relate the Church's liturgical life to its christological center and in the biblical and patristic language the schema favored. The pastoral reforms were grounded in the doctrine, but also in the fundamental principle, also theologically grounded, of the right and duty of the faithful to participate in the liturgy. It was this intrinsic synthesis of the doctrinal and the pastoral that chiefly accounts for the fact that the LI's text was the only text that was generally well received when the Council Fathers began their review of the preparatory material.

C. THE QUESTION OF LANGUAGES

Special attention is usefully given to this question for a number of reasons. First, it illustrates well the tensions that often arose between the preparatory bodies and some circles within the Roman Curia. Second, in its various aspects, at least as it was argued, it raised the issue of the relationship between the doctrinal and the pastoral. Third, it represented a more than symbolic issue over which to discuss what is involved in a genuinely pastoral renewal of the Church and in an apostolic engagement with the modern world: at stake in the question, in other words, were basic notions of the Church and its role in the world.

1. *The Language of the Council*

The question was first raised with regard to the language that would be used at the Council. That this must be Latin had been urged by

---

[174] The fascicle in which the schema was presented to the CPC stated this clearly on the Table of Contents page: "The Declarations do not belong to the conciliar text but are presented only in order to explain the canons;" see also Larraona's report to the CPC, *ADP* II/3 54.

A. Bacci in *OssRom* only two weeks after the announcement of the Council.[175] This was also the view of Tardini, who in his first press conference called Latin "the Church's language, especially adapted to express doctrinal concepts and disciplinary norms." No thought was being given to simultaneous translations, he added, because of the danger of confusion if they are done poorly or inaccurately.[176]

Assistance in the use of Latin was the only subject on which the counsellors and members of the CPC were asked to comment as the conciliar rules began to be elaborated: "It being established that the Council's language must be Latin, should some helps be provided to facilitate its use and understanding?"[177] Among the responses prepared for the June 1961 meeting of the CPC there was some support for exceptional use of vernacular languages, at least in commission meetings; there was, on the other hand, considerable support for a system of simultaneous translation.[178] The strongest case against the use of the vernacular came from Pizzardo and Staffa, the prefect and the secretary of the Congregation for Seminaries and Universities, whose arguments in favor of Latin anticipate *Veterum sapientia* by invoking the primacy of Rome and the Pope's universal and immediate authority.[179] The ecclesiological assumptions of this argument were challenged by Bea and by Maximos IV.[180]

At the conclusion of this CPC discussion, Pope John said that Latin would be the official language of the Council, but that occasionally,

[175] A. Bacci, "In quale lingua si parlerà nel futuro Concilio ecumenico?" *OssRom*, 11 Feb 1959; he returned to the argument in *OssRom*, 3 July 1960; see *DC* 57 (1960) 1001-1008.

[176] *ADA* I 157; discussions were continuing, he said, about the use of other languages at the Council and about means for assisting the conciliar participants in the use of Latin. Tardini had already made a similar announcement to the CAP on 26 May 1959; see *AS App*, 8.

[177] *ADP* II/1 22.

[178] See Indelicato, *Difendere la dottrina*, 48-52.

[179] See *ADP* II/1 47-48 (Staffa) and 219-20 (Pizzardo). Pizzardo's remark anticipates, at times verbatim, the argument of *Veterum sapientia* (see *AAS* 54 [1962] 131) and probably explains the appearance in that text, for the only time in Roncalli's writings, of the Latin text of canon 218 § 2; see A. Melloni, "Tensioni e timori nella preparazione del Vaticano II: La *Veterum sapientia* di Giovanni XXIII (22 febbraio 1962)," *CrSt* 11 (1990) 291. In a speech given on 28 October 1961, Staffa also invoked the universal primacy of the pope and cited the same canon; see "L'unità della fede e l'unificazione dei popoli nel magistero del Sommo Pontefice Giovanni XXIII," *Divinitas* 6 (1962) 30.

[180] *ADP* II/1 306 (Bea): "On this question we should not proceed on the basis of a principle, quite debatable, that Latin is the language of the Church 'because of its superior authority'. For the superior Church of Rome spoke Greek until the second century, and the definitive Latinizing of liturgical language was not accomplished until the second half of the fourth century. In the seventh century, when Greeks were numerous in Rome, the liturgy again became bilingual;" for Maximos IV see 379-80.

when necessary, other languages could be used.[181] Discussions and experiments about the use of simultaneous translation went on well into 1962, but the *Ordo Concilii* in the end imposed Latin for all public sessions and general congregations, offered only the help of translators, and left room for the vernacular only in the commissions.

This decision in favor of Latin as the official language of the Council was significant on several counts. The arguments for retaining it were often based on its value as an instrument of unity and of doctrinal exactitude. Ecclesiologically, this was a problematic argument, since Churches that used other languages were within the catholic unity and retained the orthodox faith. On a practical level, the choice of Latin also served to limit the degree to which many of the bishops would be able to participate in or even to understand the conciliar debates.

2. *Languages in Clerical Studies*

Another element in the debate was the place of Latin in the education of the clergy. Concern about the decline in the clergy's ability to understand and use Latin had been expressed most recently in a letter of the Congregation for Seminaries and Universities, 27 October 1957.[182] The antepreparatory *votum* of the same Congregation contained a section *De cognitione et usu linguae latinae in studiis ecclesiasticis.*[183]

Although this topic had not been included in the official *Quaestiones* assigned to it, the ST designated a subcommission to prepare a text *De lingua Latina in studiis ecclesiasticis rite excolenda*; this text was approved at the plenary session of the ST in October 1961.[184] After describing Latin as the "language eminently proper to ministers of the Catholic Church" and a clear sign and instrument of unity, the text deplored the neglect of and opposition to Latin. Its own *vota* required that clerical students learn Latin before beginning their study of philosophy and theology and that it be used in teaching and learning those

[181] *ADP* II/1 128; cp. Staffa's *votum*, 52. On 7 Oct 1961, the Pope spoke briefly about the usefulness of Latin as an instrument of unity and added that the Council "would offer another occasion for the Fathers, that is, the Bishops, to understand one another by using the old and venerable Latin;" *ADP* I, 114.

[182] *AAS* 50 (1958) 292-96. On this letter, which, Romita says, "contains *in nuce* the material in *Veterum Sapientia*" (*ME* 87 [1962] 251), see the commentaries of I. Parisella, *ME* 83 (1958) 248-61, and M. Noirot, "Le Latin, langue vivante de l'Eglise," *Ami du Clergé* 68 (1958) 537-46.

[183] *ADA* III 358-63.

[184] See *ADP* IV,2 181-85; A. Stickler, "A 25 anni della costituzione apostolica 'Veterum Sapientia' di Giovanni XXIII: Rievocazione storica e prospettive," *Salesianum* 2 (1988) 372 (but note that it was the ST that approved this text on that date, not the CPC).

higher studies. H. Jedin interprets the introduction of the adverb "suitably" in the norm on using Latin in teaching and learning philosophy and theology as an effort to mitigate the prescription,[185] an attempt perhaps also visible in the following norm, which acknowledged the need for local situations to be taken into account and allowed episcopal conferences to draw up appropriate norms, subject to Roman approval.

The question also arose in the MI, one of whose texts proposed that clerical studies, including the textbooks and languages used in teaching, be prudently adapted by bishops to local cultures. But by the time this text came before the CPC, the general principle had been settled by *Veterum sapientia*.[186] Before discussing this document, it will be helpful to consider the last of the issues involved in the question of languages.

3. *Languages in the Liturgy*

The most controversial aspect of the question was the use of the vernacular in the liturgy, a matter of hot debate in the previous decade.[187] As proponents of the introduction of the vernacular multiplied their efforts, there began what an opponent called "a veritable barrage which the Church intends to oppose to any desire for solemn liturgy in the vernacular."[188] On 29 April 1955, the Holy Office issued a decree restricting appeals to exceptions of the general law about Latin in the liturgy.[189] At the end of that same year the Encyclical *Musicae sacrae* confirmed the principle of Latin as the liturgical language with exhortations to obtain greater participation of the faithful by means of better catechesis. This was thought to have settled the issue.[190]

[185] See H. Jedin, *Lebensbericht* (Mainz 1984) 202.

[186] Agagianian thus felt it necessary to assure the CPC: "Allow me to note that the study of Latin has always been and still is respected and used in all our seminaries in the missions. It will now be even more inculcated by our bishops and missionaries in accord with the recent Encyclical *Veterum sapientia*;" *ADP* II/3 424. In the discussion that followed, only Godfrey (427) and Micara (433) referred to *Veterum sapientia*, the latter proposing that "perhaps it is useful that it be stated in the program of clerical studies everywhere that the exclusion or disparagement of Latin is not permitted."

[187] See A.-G. Martimort, "Le problème des langues liturgiques de 1946 à 1957," *M-D* 53 (1958) 23-55.

[188] J. Claire, "La Messe basse solennisée," *RevGrég* 35 (1956) 82.

[189] J. Claire, "Un Décret du Saint-Office à propos des concessions faites aux diocèses allemands concernant l'usage de la langue vulgaire dans la liturgie," *RevGrég* 34 (1955) 231-37.

[190] *AAS* 48 (1956) 5-25. For rather different commentaries, see A. Stohr, "The Encyclical 'On Sacred Music' and its Significance for the Care of Souls," in *The Assisi Papers: Proceedings of the First International Congress of Pastoral Liturgy, Assisi-Rome, September 18-22, 1956* (Collegeville 1957) 186-200; F. Romita, "Langue et catéchèse liturgique d'après l'Encyclique *Musicae sacrae disciplina*," *RevGrég* 35 (1957) 95-107, 168-76.

In fact it did not end discussion, and the First International Congress of Pastoral Liturgy held in Assisi in September 1956 saw the two sides of the issue confront one another again. The announced theme of the Congress was pastoral liturgy, but the undercurrent that directed its preparation and the content of many of its reports was the introduction of the vernacular. Aware that such movements were abroad, Cardinal Cicognani, in the opening address of the Congress, tried to limit the concerns to the implementation of already given papal directives with regard to liturgy. In a section apparently added at the last minute, he reminded the participants that in *Mediator Dei* Pius XII had spoken of the use of Latin as "at once an imposing sign of unity and an effective safeguard against the corruption of true doctrine."[191]

Cicognani's words, however, did not inhibit other speakers from addressing the question of liturgical languages either directly or by implication. But when the participants were received by Pope Pius XII at the end of the Congress, they received an admonition that was not encouraging for defenders of the vernacular:

> On the part of the Church, the liturgy today entails a concern for progress but also for conservation and defence. She returns to the past without slavishly copying it and creates anew in the ceremonies themselves, in the use of the vernacular, in popular song and in the building of churches. It would be superfluous, nevertheless, to recall once again that the Church has serious reasons for steadfastly retaining in the Latin rite the unconditional obligation of the celebrating priest to use the Latin language and, likewise, for insisting that the Gregorian chant in the holy sacrifice be in the language of the Church.[192]

Once again, defenders of Latin thought they now had another papal text that definitively settled the issue.[193]

Despite these Roman interventions, the issue did not die. It was raised often in the antepreparatory *vota* submitted by the world's bishops.[194]

[191] See *The Assisi Papers*, 13-16; for the circumstances of Cicognani's speech, see Bugnini, *The Reform of the Liturgy*, 11-13.

[192] *AAS* 48 (1956) 725.

[193] See J. Claire, "Le Ier Congrès International de Pastorale Liturgique," *RevGrég Supp* 35 (1956) 33-43; F. Romita, "Commentaire," *ME* 82 (1957) 21-5; M. Noirot, "Le Saint-Siège et le mouvement liturgique contemporain," *RevGrég* 35 (1957) 45: "If on certain points of Church legislation, one might admit that a rejection is not quite definitive, here the adjectives and adverbs used by the Holy Father, which a canonist owes it to himself to underline, show clearly that the Holy See, in full consciousness of the matter and for the good of the Church, can make no concessions on this point."

[194] See the summary in the "Sintesi finale" 16: "Only about sixty bishops and prelates ask that Latin be preserved in the liturgy. A much larger number, however, hope for greater use of the vernacular in the Mass, at least for the catechetical parts (354 bishops and

Although in the official *Quaestiones*, the question of the vernacular appeared only among the topics assigned to the LI — "It should be diligently considered whether it is expedient to allow the vernacular in some parts of the Mass and in administering the sacraments,"[195] — two other commissions also took it up.

In April 1961 the OR approved a text *De usu linguarum vernacularum in liturgiis*, which was brought before the CPC in January 1962.[196] It seems likely that the subject was placed on the agenda of the OR because of N. Edelby, representative of the Melkite rite, which for the last three years had been engaged in a struggle with the Holy Office over the use of the vernacular in its liturgies in the United States.[197] In December 1959 bishops there were informed by the Apostolic Delegate, acting on instructions from the Holy See, that Eastern-rite priests in their dioceses were to cease any use of English in the liturgy. The Delegate made clear the reason: "But they must avoid causing confusion by introducing the vernacular language into the mass, for, in so doing, they offer to promoters of the abandonment of the Latin language in the Sacred Liturgy an opportunity to cite as an example and a precedent what the Oriental priests are doing in their midst." Inquiry by the Melkite discovered that the instructions came, not from the Congregation for the Oriental Church, but from the Holy Office, which had reserved to itself all questions on the liturgical use of the vernacular. Maximos IV appealed the issue directly to the Pope on 5 February 1960,[198] and on 31 March the Holy Office issued a formal decree permitting the use of the vernacular except for the Anaphora. Despite the rather profound ignorance of the Byzantine liturgy that this

---

prelates), in the administration of the sacraments, except for the formula (305 bishops and prelates), and in other rites." The antepreparaatory *votum* of the Congregation for Rites had included a section "De lingua liturgica latina et de linguis vernaculis in celebranda liturgia admittendis" (*ADA* III 266-75), in which there was an extensive and not unsympathetic review of all the arguments against the use of Latin. But this was followed by rather cautious recommendations: 1) "Every effort should be made that the use of Latin in the liturgy of the 'Latin' Church be kept in its present state;" 2) that the clergy be well trained in the understanding and use of Latin, "so that every complaint on this basis against liturgical Latin can be removed;" 3) that in a revised Roman Ritual in Latin there also be indicated "those texts which can be translated into the vernacular where this may be needed or opportune."

[195] *ADP* II/1 412.

[196] *ADP* II/2 248-58.

[197] See *Les églises orientales catholiques*, 443-44; N. Edelby, "Comments on a Recent Decision of the Holy Office," typescript, dated "Cairo, May 1960" (A-McManus).

[198] An English translation of the "Declaratio Beatitudinis Suae Maximos IV, Patriarchae Antiochen. Melchitarum," can be found in the A-McManus.

[199] See the editorial remarks in *Irénikon* 33 (1960) 232-33 and in *Proche Orient Chrétien* 10 (1960) 134-35.

decree revealed,[199] it was received with satisfaction by Maximos IV, who urged obedience to it "while we await an amendment." It is understandable, then, that the Melkites would wish to see their immemorial privileges in the matter of languages safeguarded by the Council.

The OR's schema asked the Council to confirm the ancient customary law that permitted the Oriental churches to use whatever languages they considered best for the good of souls. The four *vota* in which this position was articulated were preceded by a brief preface which vindicated the practice biblically and traditionally and argued that it did no damage to the Church's unity but rather displayed it more splendidly. In his presentation of the text to the CPC, A. Cicognani at several points reviewed the differences between western and eastern practice in the question of popular languages and noted that the western practice had, especially since Trent, affected the legitimate practice of the eastern churches. Three of the four formal responses (Ruffini, Jullien, Browne) urged caution because of the probable impact of this provision for the eastern churches upon the question of Latin in the western church: "Lest the Latins say," remarked Jullien, "if these and those, why not we also?"[200]

The issue was addressed also by the MI, in its schema *De sacramentis ac de s. liturgia*, discussed by the CPC at the end of March 1962.[201] The MI's text also proposed a general principle: "From Scripture we know that all languages are ordered towards the praise of Christ. Such praise is expressed especially in the liturgy, where the law of intelligibility of liturgical language for all gathered was stated by the Apostle. A diversity of customs and of rites has always existed in the Church, showing most clearly the riches of the Church's unity." The text was very cautious, however, in drawing conclusions from this apostolic "law of intelligibility;" it sought only "some use of the vernacular and some adaptation of rites to the genius of peoples and to local conditions."[202] Here too caution was urged at the CPC discussion, particularly by Ruffini, Lefebvre, and D'Alton, who offered the principle that "the visible unity of the Catholic Church is chiefly manifested by the visible uniformity of its worship."[203]

---

[200] *ADP*, II/II 251; Jullien had defended Latin as an instrument of culture in *Cultura cristiana alla luce di Roma* (Rome 1956), 34-43, and in *Etudes ecclésiastiques dans la lumière de Rome* (Paris 1958). For the discussion in the CPC, see Indelicato, *Difendere la dottrina*, 143.

[201] *ADP* II/3 369-94.

[202] *ADP* II/3 370.

[203] *ADP* II/3 388.

For its part, the LI, at its first plenary session in November 1960, established a subcommission *De lingua latina* for which the topic was articulated in three questions: whether the use of Latin was to be fully retained; whether some use of the vernacular was to be allowed, and if so, in what parts and to what degree; how clerics could be trained in Latin in order to be able to understand and use it in the liturgy.[204]

At the first meeting of the subcommission, 15 November 1960, its relator, D. Borella, expressed the view that the matter could be handled rather easily on the basis of the comments presented by several Roman Congregations, which revealed the mind of the Holy See.[205] Other members disagreed very strongly, however, and argued that it was necessary to approach the issue from the point of view of principles that would be valid for the whole Church, both eastern and western.[206] Botte then prepared a report on liturgical languages in which he briefly reviewed the history and the present situation before addressing the reasons for and against the use of the vernacular.[207] According to Botte, this was used as the basis for the report that Borella prepared for the April 1961 plenary session of the LI.[208] This text documented the variety of liturgical languages in the Church's tradition and how conflicts had regularly ended with the Church legitimizing local liturgical languages.[209]

Within the subcommission the strongest opposition to the greater use of the vernacular came from Anglés, a zealous defender of Gregorian Chant whose fortunes he knew to depend on the retention of Latin.[210] He seems to have been responsible for arousing the fear in several Roman circles that the LI was hostile to Latin and intended to propose radical innovations in the use of the vernacular.

---

[204] See Braga, "La 'Sacrosanctum Concilium,'" 115-116.

[205] Borella was concerned that to ask for too much with respect to the vernacular might compromise the whole cause; he sought a gradual change "so as to provoke not a revolution but an evolution, which will gradually prepare the ground;" cited in Paiano, "Il rinnovamento della liturgia," 106-107.

[206] "Relatio de sessione Subcommissionis 'De lingua latina' Romae", die 15a novembris, ... habitae (A-McManus). B. Botte argued that the very title of the subcommission should be changed, since it restricted its attention to the Latin church.

[207] "Relatio de linguis liturgicis", undated, but probably late 1960 (A-McManus).

[208] B. Botte, *From Silence to Participation: An Insider's View of Liturgical Renewal* (Washington 1988) 120-21. Borella's report, which was removed from the agenda of the April plenary session, was later published by him in *Ambrosius* 44 (1968) 71-94, 137-68, 237-66.

[209] Paiano, "Il rinnovamento della liturgia," 109.

[210] See H. Anglés, "Il prossimo Concilio Ecumenico e la Musica Sacra," *Bollettino degli Amici del Pont. Istituto di Musica Sacra* 11 (1959) 6; and the *votum* submitted to the CAP by Anglés' Institute, *ADA* IV/II/1 226.

Apparently because of Anglés' opposition, on 4 March 1961 Bugnini submitted a pro-memoria defending his commission against these charges.[211] While noting that the LI had not yet reached any definitive conclusions, he said that it was likely that two guidelines would be followed: that Latin must be preserved "without qualification" for the clergy, and that the vernacular in the liturgy for the faithful would follow the principles set out by Pius XII and the Holy Office. Bugnini noted that a mixed commission with the ST had reached an agreement on the necessity of retaining Latin in the education of the clergy; on the other hand, a similar commission with the MI had asked for a "more functional form" when it came to mission territories. As for the LI, its subcommissions would be asked to include minority positions on controverted topics, with the decision to be made by the plenary commission. If the whole LI could not reach agreement, the issue would be left to the Council. In any case, Bugnini concluded, the CPC would be in a position to coordinate material which several commissions had addressed, to choose "the position it thinks most opportune and present it to the Fathers of the Council for their consideration," a subtle reminder that questions raised in the preparatory process belonged to the CPC and not to the Curia to resolve.

Bugnini's pro-memoria had little effect, however, and on 25 March 1961 *OssRom* published a three-starred anonymous article, "Latin, the Language of the Church," which was a vigorous defence of the Church's need of a language which is "universal, immutable, and not vulgar."[212] The article became particularly vigorous when it turned to "the campaign underway against liturgical Latin," of which it used words like speciousness, disloyalty, iconoclastic fanaticism, and intemperance. It ended by calling upon priests to give submission and obedience to the "admonitions" of Pius XII at the Assisi Congress.[213]

---

[211] See Bugnini, *The Reform of the Liturgy*, 22-24; on p. 22 he names Anglés as the source of the complaint that the LI was "the number one enemy of Latin." He does not identify to whom he addressed his pro-memoria.

[212] The article was also published in French in *DC* 58 (1961) 593-610 and in *RevGrég* 40 (1962) 32-41, which borrowed its translation from *Nouvelles de Chrétienté*. There is reason to think that the article was aimed not only at the LI but also at the recently published book by Paul Winninger, *Langues vivantes et liturgie* (Paris 1961), perhaps particularly because it had received a lengthy and favorable notice in *Etudes*.

[213] As a result, it seems, of the *OssRom* article, rumors began to circulate that the TC was trying to appropriate the question of liturgical languages. "Which is false," wrote Tromp, drily adding: "Perhaps they are confusing the Theological Commission and the Holy Office;" Tromp Diary, 12 April 1961.

In response to such pressure, at its second plenary session in April, the secretariat of the LI thought it more prudent to withdraw from the agenda the report prepared by the subcommission *De lingua latina* and instead to consider the question as it arose in the reports of the other subcommissions.[214] Bugnini had Vagaggini prepare a text on liturgical languages, which proposed a compromise solution: the vernacular would be permitted in the didactic parts of the liturgy but Latin retained in others. At the session a very vigorous debate on the issue took place among the members, during which Cicognani cautioned against altering the tradition. An appeal seems to have been made to the Pope,[215] and remarks of Felici a few days later about the freedom of discussion in the commissions were interpreted as a sign that the LI could continue to discuss the matter.[216]

While all this was going on in the LI, the SCU was preparing to lend its support. The Secretariat had taken up the question of Latin particularly in connection with the relation between unity and uniformity.[217] In February 1961, the SCU's subcommission on liturgical questions had prepared a *votum* that asked for "the widest possible use of the vernacular" in the Mass and sacraments. Even before the plenary session of April, perhaps because of the Roman controversy, the text had been weakened to read "a wider use."

By the time the SCU met for its April session, Bea had already participated in the CPC discussion of the schema prepared by the OR and heard the arguments on behalf of Latin as a sign of unity. He might also have seen the ecumenical implications of the universalistic and uniformist ecclesiology presupposed in the *OssRom* article on Latin. This may account for the vigor of his statement at the beginning of the meeting: "We must strongly oppose the idea that Latin is a sign of unity. It is more a sign of uniformity than a sign of unity." While the members heard from defenders of the universal value of Latin, Bea's position, defended theologically by Thils,[218] was reflected in the SCU's clear and

---

[214] In a note written at the time about the withdrawal of the report on Latin, A.-G. Martimort commented: "This report was not read, and the subcommission was buried in silence, because Cardinal Pizzardo and others had criticized Cardinal Cicognani for having allowed a debate about so burning an issue;" La Constitution sur la Liturgie," 64.

[215] See Jounel, "Genèse et théologie," 15; K. Hughes, *The Monk's Tale: A Biography of Godfrey Diekmann, O.S.B.* (Collegeville 1991) 189.

[216] See C. Braga, "La 'Sacrosanctum Concilium,'" 97-99, 106; P. Jounel, "Genèse et théologie," 15, 48-51; Paiano, "Il rinnovamento della liturgia," 109-13.

[217] For what follows, see Velati, "La proposta ecumenica," 296-300.

[218] "It is of the essence of unity that it reveals itself in diversity; the unity of the world appears more clearly at the moment that its multiformity becomes more manifest. The

strong *votum*, which it forwarded to the LI: "That the Council, when it presents the principles of liturgical renewal, carefully refrain from any expressions which might suggest that the Catholic liturgy is identified with the Latin Roman liturgy and that the Latin language is a necessary bond of Catholic unity."

The first draft of the schema on the liturgy (August 1961), prepared by the LI's secretariat after the April meeting, continued to call for the introduction of the vernacular, especially in the didactic parts, a principle later applied to the Mass and the divine office.[219] In its "Declaratio" on the Breviary the LI put out its most forceful statement on the matter. It acknowledged that Latin should be retained since it was a "bond of unity." But it went on immediately to point out that the study of Latin was diminishing rapidly everywhere and that the Church is powerless to halt this decline. It also made a pointed remark that "the question of language in the liturgy was in itself a cultural question and not a religious question in the strict sense." It was not spiritually useful to force priests who do not understand Latin to continue to use it in their daily prayer. Lastly, the LI said, the use of the vernacular would promote the reunion of Christians. The general principle and its particular applications remained the same in the revised schema that was sent out to members of the LI in November.[220]

It was at this point, however, that the first of two interventions of Pope John took place. On 7 December 1961 his apostolic letter to Anglés for the fiftieth anniversary of the Pontifical Institute for Sacred Music appeared to vindicate its director's position. The Pope praised the Institute for its cultivation and defense of Latin in solemn liturgies, for

plurality of languages does not threaten unity; on the contrary, it is of the essence of unity that it expresses itself in a pluriform richness." Pope John, in a speech on 19 August 1961, recorded only indirectly in *OssRom*, addressed the question of unity in variety. He noted that while Latin is used in the Roman and Ambrosian rites, Greek and Slavic languages are in use in other rites. The Church's unity was to be found elsewhere: "Now, if there are many different rites — and this confirms beauty and enchantment — the foundation is one and the faith is identical;" *ADP* I, 103.

[219] "In the liturgy, more room should be allowed for the vernacular, especially in the directly didactic parts and at least in songs and prayers more proper to the people. The episcopal conferences in the individual regions should have the authority, with the approval of the Holy See, to set the limits and the manner for the introduction of the vernacular into the liturgy." A similar proposal was made explicitly about the Mass in #48. Jungmann protested to Bugnini that he had changed the language approved in April ("modum et mensuram") to "modum et limites;" see Paiano, "Il rinnovamento della liturgia" 118.

[220] The "Declaratio" that accompanied the paragraph on the use of the vernacular in the Divine Office was somewhat abbreviated and made slightly less aggressive.

which he borrowed a phrase from *Mediator Dei*: "a clear and beautiful sign of unity."[221] For many reasons Latin should continue to occupy that chief place; difficulties of comprehension could be met by greater liturgical catechesis and by the use of missals by the faithful. While greater adaptation was possible in non-solemn liturgies, the Pope concluded, "in solemn liturgies, whether in magnificent temples or in small churches in towns, Latin must always hold its royal sceptre and exercise its noble rule."[222]

Both sides immediately tried to use the Pope's letter as a weapon in their battle. Anglés saw it as a vindication of his long and painful campaign in defence of Gregorian chant and of Latin.[223] Bugnini, however, warned against exaggerating the juridical force of the letter and saw in the close link the Pope drew between Latin and chant a reason for arguing that the latter could not be adapted to modern musical languages![224]

Despite Bugnini's effort to minimize the import of Pope John's letter, the LI thought it prudent to make certain adjustments in its schema. The November draft had described the solemn liturgy as "celebrated with song" but at the January plenary session of the LI, this was changed to "celebrated in Latin."[225] More serious was the change that Bugnini insisted had to be inserted into the article on liturgical languages: "The use of Latin in the western liturgy must absolutely be preserved."[226] The insertion of this strong statement appears to have been the price of gaining Cicognani's support for the schema.[227] On the other hand, all the

---

[221] See *AAS* 39 (1947) 544-45: "The use of Latin is a clear and beautiful sign of unity and an effective remedy against any corruptions of true doctrine." These remarks of the Encyclical were constantly invoked by supporters of Latin, and it is perhaps significant that Pope John makes use only of the first of Pius XII's two arguments.

[222] *AAS* 53 (1961) 812. For the opponents of Latin, the preservation of the supreme place of the solemn liturgy was fundamental.

[223] See H. Anglés' commentary, written after *Veterum sapientia* had been promulgated, "La Lettera Apostolica 'Iucunda laudatio,'" *Bollettino degli Amici del P. Istituto di Musica Sacra* 14 (March-December 1962) 57.

[224] A. Bugnini, "Adnotationes," *Ephemerides Liturgicae* 76 (1962) 63-68. In his "Adnotationes," *ME* 87 (1962) 96-103, F. Romita replied in detail to many of Bugnini's points. For a similarly grateful reception of the papal letter, see J. Gajard, "Lettre 'Jucunda laudatio' de S.S. Jean XXIII à Mgr H. Anglés," *Etudes Grégoriennes* 5 (1962) 7-8.

[225] *ADP* II/3 462; see Paiano, "Il rinnovamento della liturgia," 128, 130.

[226] This severe principle was then followed, however, by two paragraphs that came close to contradicting it, by legitimizing greater use of the vernacular where this is useful to the people and by allowing the episcopal conferences to establish the "limits and manner for introducing the vernacular into the liturgy."

[227] "Bugnini had been overtaken by all sorts of doubts or fears; he stated quite frankly that the text had to be palatable to Eminenza who must present it to the central commission. Eminenza in turn is alarmed over 2 things only — vernacular and an apparent attempt to shorten the Divine Office unduly.... On language, there was no substantive change but a sentence had to be inserted (to please Pizzardo I guess!): Lingua Latina

particular calls for greater use of the vernacular remained in the text. This last plenary session of the LI was held only ten days before Pope John announced the proximate publication of a document on the use of Latin in clerical studies;[228] and it is possible that the new caution in the LI reflects knowledge of what was in the works.

On 22 February 1962, amidst much pomp and ceremony, the Pope signed the Apostolic Constitution, *Veterum sapientia*.[229] Much about this action remains to be clarified: its textual history, the relationship between the document and the question of Latin as it had appeared in several texts being prepared for the Council, and the Pope's motives.

With regard to its origins, it is known that the *votum* of the Congregation for Seminaries and Universities had proposed the preparation of a "Constitutio de linguae latinae disciplina" whose structure closely anticipated that of *Veterum sapientia*.[230] The Congregation appears to have continued to work on this project even while the ST was working on its schema on Latin in clerical studies,[231] perhaps in part because it considered the latter's document too lenient.[232] Stickler thinks that both texts were brought to the Pope and that he assigned the task of redacting the apostolic constitution to Msgr. Tondini.[233] Brief instructions from the

omnino retinenda est. This is of course interpreted à la Rome: the exceptions are far more numerous than the rule;" McManus to Diekmann, undated, but probably January 1962 (A-McManus).

[228] See *DMC* IV 147; Caprile, I/2, 276.

[229] *AAS* 54 (1962) 129-35, with the "Ordinationes" published by the Congregation for Studies and Seminaries on 22 April 1962, 339-68. See Stickler, "A 25 anni dalla constituzione apostolica;" and A. Melloni, "Tensioni e timori," 275-307. For contemporary comments, see A. Bacci, *OssRom* 26-27 Feb 1962 (=*DC* 59 [1962] 399-406; F. Romita, "Adnotationes," *ME* 87 (1962) 199-275; O. Rousseau, "Veterum Sapientia," *Revue Nouvelle*, 35 (1962) 361-67; M. Noirot, "Etude et usage de la langue latine: La Constitution apostolique *Veterum Sapientia*," *RevGrég* 40 (1962) 75-101; K. Rahner, "Über das Latein als Kirchensprache," *ZKTh* 84 (1962) 275-99; D. Staffa, "De Constitutione Apostolica 'Veterum sapientia' rite exsequenda," *Seminarium* 14 (1962) 428-38.

[230] *ADA* III 363.

[231] But, apparently, without the knowledge of the subcommission within the ST that was preparing a text for the Council! See Stickler, "A 25 anni dalla costituzione apostolica 'Veterum Sapientia'", 372-74, where he speaks about the issuance of *Veterum sapientia* as "a dramatic surprise."

[232] This is the view of Jedin, who in the ST had opposed the use of Latin in clerical education and reports that a compromise formula had been reached: "The action was without doubt aimed at the Commission; the neo-Latinists in the Curia wanted to anticipate it and the Council, and they succeeded in getting the pope to approve a decree whose impracticability was obvious;" H. Jedin, *Lebensbericht* 202-203. Caprile, I/2 386n, records a similar view in Rome that *Veterum sapientia* was designed "to offset the text of a schema already prepared for the Council, although not with the unanimous agreement of the commission for studies and seminaries."

[233] Stickler, "A 25 anni," 372.

Pope have been made available: the text should avoid all harshness, affirm the dignity also of Greek and other ancient languages, and make a serious effort to explain to Asians and Africans why the Church treasures Latin.[234]

In content, the first and expository part of *Veterum sapientia* closely follows the main arguments of the *OssRom* article, of which at some points it is a simple translation.[235] The papal text differs most notably by the brief statement of respect for other ancient sacred languages and above all by the absence from it of the more exuberant expressions of the Church as a "super-culture."

Towards the end of this exposition, the Pope presents *Veterum sapientia* as an authoritative response to recent controversies over Latin and to requests received from many bishops for the Holy See to declare its opinion. The response took the form of eight norms, the first two of which urge bishops not only to implement the prescriptions but to see to it that none of their subjects, "eager for novelties," write against the use of Latin "either in teaching the higher sacred disciplines or in the liturgy" or try to extenuate the will of Rome. The other norms require that clerical students achieve a good knowledge of Latin before beginning their higher studies, that the length of their studies be extended if necessary to achieve this purpose, that Latin be used in lectures and textbooks, that the Congregation for Studies establish an institute to promote the study of Latin and of Greek, that bishops also take care that their clerical students gain a good knowledge of Greek, and that the Congregation elaborate norms for the implementation of the apostolic constitution.

These prescriptions, particularly the prohibition of questioning the use of Latin in the liturgy, were widely interpreted as settling the issues before the Council could even discuss them, a view that was accepted with a certain satisfaction in some circles,[236] but with dismay in others.

---

[234] See Melloni, "Tensioni e timori," 289.

[235] Similarly in the address he gave on the occasion of his promulgation of *Veterum sapientia*, the Pope's arguments closely follow those of the *OssRom* article; see *DMC* IV, 169-71.

[236] See Romita, "Adnotationes," 257-58; Noirot, "Etude et usage de la langue latine," 88-89, was untroubled that the Pope should have taken this measure just before the Council: "Is not the Pope the head of the Church? And if he wished precisely to promulgate his resolute will to see the revival of the Latin education of clerics on the very eve of the Council — the preparation for which has no doubt shown clearly the urgency of such a measure — does he not have at once the authority and the grace to do so? When one reads that some people are waging a campaign to have the Council return to the question (that is, in order to modify the papal decision), one wonders if the authors of such requests have not forgotten that no conciliar decision (even if one were proposed!) has any value against the papal will." Noirot went on to remind them that anyone who appeals from a pope to a general Council is suspect of heresy and automatically excommunicated (c. 2332)!

A group of Dutch Catholics issued an open letter to their bishops protesting the foreclosing of the question of liturgical languages. In response to this and other criticisms, assurances came that the question of liturgical language would remain on the conciliar agenda.[237] (On the other hand, *Veterum sapientia* required the ST's decree on that subject to be withdrawn from the agenda of the CPC.[238])

In the end, the schema *De sacra liturgia* sent to the CPC presented in #24 a general principle — "The use of Latin in the western liturgy is absolutely to be preserved" — which was much qualified, however, by the continued calls for the vernacular in the Mass, in the rituals, and in the Breviary.

By the time this text came before the CPC, Cardinal Larraona had succeeded Cicognani as president of the LI. Larraona's lack of enthusiasm for the introduction of the vernacular became clear in his remarks to the CPC on the general principles set out in #24. Larraona said that the principle applied only for those strictly liturgical actions for which it had already been expressly conceded in certain regions. As for introducing other cases, he appealed to *Veterum sapientia* and its prohibition of further discussion of greater use of the vernacular in the liturgy.[239] This not very subtle reference, echoed at the CPC meeting only by Spellman,[240] did not inhibit a discussion which revealed a clear division of opinion on the matter. The strongest support for the introduction of the vernacular came from Léger, who urged therefore that the text about Latin be changed from "must absolutely be preserved" to "should be preserved," and from Montini, who presented a long argument which even appealed to the statement in *Veterum sapientia* about the Church's use of the ancient liturgical languages.[241]

---

[237] See Caprile, I/2, 386, 538; R. Rouquette, *Etudes* 313 (April 1962) 104-107 (=*La fin d'une chrétienté*, I, 172-75). It is interesting to note that Staffa, in a speech given at The Catholic University of America on 9 July 1962 reached the same conclusion: "In no way does the Constitution settle the question of the use of the vernacular in the liturgy. For example, the use of the vernacular in the Mass of Catechumens, if it is proposed for their judgement, will be determined by the Fathers of the Council;" "De Constitutione Apostolica 'Veterum sapientia' rite exsequenda," 435.

[238] By whom this decision was made is not known. It is worth remarking that when the Pope, less than a week after promulgating *Veterum sapientia*, addressed the CPC and reflected on the text on seminaries it had just been studying, he made no reference to this document, even though he referred to the "solemn encounter" at which he had signed it; see *ADP* I 177-79.

[239] *ADP* II/3 63.

[240] *ADP* II/3 67.

[241] *ADP* II/3 70-71, 84-87.

The issue returned when the CPC considered the LI's proposal to allow the use of the vernacular in the Divine Office. While support for this seems to have been great, there was also some sharp opposition, particularly to the statement that the Church should accommodate itself to the nearly universal decline in the knowledge of Latin. *Veterum sapientia* was explicitly appealed to by four cardinals, among them Ottaviani.[242] There is also an oblique reference to it in the remarks of Alfrink who, after noting that about a third of his priests desire to say the Breviary in the vernacular, defended them against the charge that this made them "eager for novelties."[243]

The many-sided controversy over Latin is of interest for several reasons. On an organizational level, it illustrates the complex relations that existed not only among the various PrC and between them and various Curial congregations but also between the Pope and the preparation of the Council and between the Curia and the Council itself. Substantively, a review of the controversies that preceded *Veterum sapientia* and of the commentaries on it, both favorable and critical, reveals how many important issues were considered to be at stake in the question of the Church's language. Space does not permit me here to do more than mention some of them: in ecclesiology, the contest between a universalistic notion of the Church, for which the universal primacy of the pope is the starting point, and a theology of the local Church, for which the relation between Church and culture is primary — for the first unity is so linked to universality that it threatens to be reduced to uniformity, while for the second the Church's unity is conceived within variety; in liturgy, besides the question of the relation between Latin and Gregorian chant, there are the questions of the relations between the roles of the clergy and the laity in liturgical activities and between the "latreutic" and salvific purposes of the liturgy; finally, on a larger cultural level, there is the question of the abiding normative character both of classical Latin culture and of the medieval Christendom of the West, the question that was perhaps most relevant to the desire of the Pope that the Council engage the Church in a new encounter with history and culture.

---

[242] "What most horifies me is the new wound being inflicted on Latin in the liturgy. The possibility is being insinuated of priests saying the Breviary in the vernacular. The reason would be that many do not understand Latin. I am astonished that anyone could be ordained a priest without knowing Latin well. And I especially regret that a remedy should be suggested that is not in accord with the latest pontifical document, *Veterum sapientia*, and that consecrates by its concessions ignorance of the liturgical, scholastic, theological language of the Church itself;" *ADP* I/3 350-51.

[243] *ADP* II/3 349. The phrase "rerum novarum studiosi" had occurred in the warning of *Veterum sapientia* against speaking against the use of Latin in the liturgy.

III. Preparing a "Doctrinal" Council

Pope John's call for a renewal of the whole substance of Christian thought and life in the circumstances of the last third of the twentieth century required also a re-appropriation of the doctrinal heritage of Catholic Christianity. In the division of labor suggested by the official "*Quaestiones*," this task fell in particular to the TC. But the larger finalities of the Council required that this re-appropriation be undertaken in and for a world undergoing rapid change and in particular with an eye on the work of overcoming the divisions of Christianity, which remained one of the major obstacles to effective Christian action in the world. The ecumenical finality of the Gospel was the special responsibility of the SCU, which with papal encouragement quickly became something more than an information-center and undertook the task of ensuring that concern for the "separated brethren" would enter the horizons of the other PrC.

In this section, we will review how the TC understood its task with regard to the doctrinal work of the Gospel, how the SCU sought to bring ecumenical concerns to bear, and how the two preparatory bodies eventually entered into open contest with one another.

A. The Preparatory Theological Commission

1. *Agenda and Orientation*

In *Superno Dei nutu*, Pope John assigned the TC the task of investigating "questions concerning Sacred Scripture, Sacred Tradition, faith and morals."[244] Cardinal Alfredo Ottaviani was named its president and Sebastien Tromp its secretary.[245]

The two men set to work very quickly, establishing a "prior subcommission," composed of several men, all associated in various ways with the Holy Office, to prepare the work of the TC.[246] A week after the announcement of the preparatory commissions, this group had already begun to review the names of possible members on a list provided, it

---

[244] *ADA* I 95. See R. Burigana, "Progetto dogmatico del Vaticano II: la commissione teologica preparatoria (1960-1962)," in *Verso il Concilio*, 141-206.

[245] There is some evidence that Tromp was not Ottaviani's first choice, which fell rather on the rector of a Roman pontifical university or academy (probably Piolanti); see Burigana, "Progetto dogmatico," 198-99.

[246] The following took part at one or another of the several meetings of this subcommission: P. Parente, D. Staffa, P. Philippe, C. Balic, L. Ciappi, A. Piolanti, R. Gagnebet, F. Hürth, S. Garofalo, R. Verardo.

seems, by the general secretariat. On 24 June a shorter and considerably altered list was reviewed and the members of the subcommission were asked to send in their opinions.[247] Three weeks later the Vatican announced the names of the first 27 members and 29 consultors of the TC, later names being announced in the course of the preparatory period.[248] The initial numerical predominance of men linked either to the Holy Office or to the Roman academies was not notably altered by the later nominations.[249]

In July the same prior subcommission took up the question of the matters on which the TC would work. On this question it could be guided by several documents. There was, first, the *votum* submitted to the CAP by the Holy Office on 10 March 1960.[250] This text, which, unlike many of the other curial proposals, made no references to the *vota* of the bishops, began with a warning that errors condemned at Vatican I and in the modernist era were being revived, among them naturalism, atheistic humanism, evolutionism, relativism, indifferentism, Marxism, laicism, and immanentism. It then proposed that the Council, after restating Catholic doctrine on man's ability to know the truth, on God, and on revelation, defend and confirm the chief doctrines under attack, particularly by a coherent exposition about the Church. Its last recommendation was that a new formula for the profession of faith be elaborated.

---

[247] See Burigana, "Progetto dogmatico," 251-54, where the views of F.X. Hürth on A. Janssen, Philippe de la Trinité, H. de Lubac, and Y. Congar are particularly revealing. Of the last two men, Hürth commented that their "appointment would silence many opponents."

[248] The appearance of the names of Y. Congar and H. de Lubac among the consultors aroused much comment. The two men met to discuss their nomination, and although they feared that it might prove to be mere window-dressing and an effort to curtail their freedom, making them in effect hostages to the TC, they did not believe they could turn down the appointment. In presenting the TC's text *De deposito fidei* to the CPC, Ottaviani would refer to de Lubac's participation as proof "that the Doctrinal Commission had included men who certainly cannot be considered benighted, the common description of the Holy Office;" *ADP* II/2 310.

[249] See Burigana, "Progetto dogmatico," 151-54, which discusses the exclusion of P. Benoit and K. Rahner from the TC.

[250] *ADA* III, 3-17. According to internal criteria and to Parente's own testimony to A. Riccardi, this text was written by Parente and lightly revised by Ottaviani. Parente had served on the commission within the Holy Office to which Pius XII assigned the task of preparing a possible ecumenical Council. An enthusiastic defender of *Humani generis*, he had submitted as Archbishop of Perugia a brief *votum*, all but one of whose dogmatic issues is introduced into the Holy Office's proposal; see *ADA* II/III, 529-31. Even after the Council, Parente continued to see it in continuity with *Humani generis* and with Pius XII's conciliar project; see *La crisi della verità e il Concilio Vaticano II* (Rovigo, 1983) 19-32, and *A venti anni dal Concilio Vaticano II: Esperienze e prospettive* (Rome, 1985) 14: "This disorder prepared the atmosphere of the Council which Pius XII had already initiated with a commission within the Holy Office, which John XXIII then brought to reality, and which Paul VI brought to a happy end."

Closely related to this *votum* was a text also drawn up within the Holy Office by M. Leclercq: "Synopsis of the Things in the Bishops' Vota That Concern Faith and Morals." This divided the material into five large sections: A) Fundamental Questions; B) the Church as the Mystical Body; C) the Hierarchy in the Church; D) the Apostolate of the Church; E) Moral Matters — a structure fairly close to that of the Holy Office's *votum*. It too noted requests of bishops for a new formula of the profession of faith.[251]

Meanwhile the CAP was completing its own "Final Synthesis" of the proposals submitted by the worldwide episcopate. This document identified the following doctrinal problems: (1) the interpretation of Scripture, particularly in the light of dangerous modern theories, (2) ecclesiology (which it said was the dominant theme in the bishops' letters and included the nature of the Church), the Mystical Body, and the episcopate, (3) new dogmatic definitions, particularly in Mariology, on which, however, it noted that the bishops were divided, (4) social questions, particularly the relationship between Church and State, and (5) a set of errors to be condemned at the Council: communism, laicism, atheistic existentialism, moral relativism, materialism, naturalism, liberalism, exaggerated nationalism, modernism, and Masonry.[252]

This synthesis seems to have been the chief source of the official *Quaestiones* which assigned the TC five topics: the sources of revelation, the Church, the supernatural order, particularly in moral matters, marriage, and social teaching.[253]

Tromp seems to have begun to outline possible dogmatic constitutions even before receiving the official questions. By 13 July, at Ottaviani's request, he had already composed outlines of three schemata: "*De Ecclesia*," "*De deposito*," "*De rebus moralibus et socialibus*." The Pope's wishes, expressed in the "*Quaestiones*," however, required Tromp, aided by S. Garofalo, hastily to prepare a fourth outline, "*De fontibus revelationis*."[254] Tromp's four outlines omit a good deal of what was proposed in the Holy Office's *votum* and arrange the material in a different manner.

At the meeting of the prior subcommission on 21 July, the four outlines were explained and discussed; Garofalo ("*De fontibus*"), Tromp

---

[251] The structure and content of this text and the absence from of it of the question of Scripture suggest that it was drawn up before the official "*Quaestiones*" were known.

[252] "Sintesi finale" 1-6.

[253] *ADP* II/1 408-409.

[254] The inspiration and inerrancy of Scripture were among the particular questions contained in Tromp's original outline *De deposito fidei custodiendo*. These draft texts can be found in the Gagnebet papers.

("*De Ecclesia*" and "*De ordine morali et sociali*"), and Ciappi ("*De depo-sito*"), spent the last days of the month revising the schemata. Before sending the texts to the members, Ottaviani and Tromp sought a *nihil obstat* from the Pope, lest they be embarrassed by his subsequent disap-proval. Tardini replied on 22 September approving the schemata, but cautioning that the final texts of the constitutions should not be too long and should speak briefly about undisputed points in order to be able to expand upon new elements or responses to current errors.[255] On 24 Sep-tember Ottaviani sent the members the four "*Schemata compendiosa*," on which he invited their comments. With the letter he also enclosed a copy of the *votum* of the Holy Office and of its "Synopsis" of episcopal comments on matters of faith and morals.[256]

The first plenary session of the TC was held on 27 October 1960.[257] Tromp introduced the four summary schemata, explaining that the prior subcommission had simply followed the suggestions of the Pope, the bishops, and the Curia and had not sought to construct an inevitably "artificial and scholastic" synthesis without relevance to contemporary questions. He then raised an at first sight minor question — the number and order of schemata — that would in fact prove illustrative of tensions within the TC and in its relations with the Holy Office.

The initial idea, Tromp said, had been to prepare only two constitu-tions, on the Church and on defending the deposit of faith, but this idea had been set aside because of the pope's insistence that the question of the sources of revelation be considered. It had also been decided to divide the material on the deposit into doctrinal and moral sections. But Tromp then went on to defend the original idea of two constitutions, offering his vision of how they would fit into the work of the whole Council. The text on the Church would reflect on its nature, mission and witness to the world, while that on the deposit would present those salvific truths that were being neglected or distorted today. Tromp's effort to justify his program seems to have been aimed, at least in part, to offset the view of Parente, who continued to press upon Ottaviani the program outlined in the Holy Office's *votum*.

[255] V. Carbone, "Il cardinale Domenico Tardini," 85-86.
[256] In his diary, 17 Sept. 1960, next to this information Tromp noted "The Assessor, Msgr. Parente, is joyful." Ironic references to the Holy Office and to Parente in particu-lar recur in Tromp's Diary.
[257] Tromp's Diary confirms the statement of Caprile, I/1 272-73, that the TC's antici-pation of the Pope's solemn inauguration of the preparatory period was not viewed favor-ably by many in Rome, including the Pope himself.

After Tromp's opening report, the TC began to debate the question of the number and the order of the doctrinal texts. No consensus was reached, opinions being divided in favor of the order as presented, the one proposed by Tromp, and the one reflected in the Holy Office's *votum*, with a few others suggesting inversions of the order of the texts. To resolve this conflict, Ottaviani appointed a small subcommission, from which he excluded Tromp, who interpreted its establishment as a maneuver inspired by Parente.

Four reports were then given on the *schemata compendiosa*, explaining their topics, emphases, and purposes. Only Ciappi's report on the *De deposito* text made any effort to relate its content to the proposals gathered in the antepreparatory consultation.[258] The full TC then decided to constitute five subcommissions to prepare five texts, the material on morality being divided now into two schemata, on individual and on social morality. After each report Ottaviani announced the members of the respective subcommissions except for that on the social order, it being considered prudent to wait for this until the names of those who were preparing the Pope's encyclical on social questions were known.[259]

The special subcommission on the order of the schemata met on 28 and 29 October.[260] According to the report of its work, received by Tromp on 7 November, the subcommission began by noting that most of the TC's members wished to begin with a statement of the truths, denied by many today, that underlie the whole natural and supernatural order; they also wished the dominant unifying idea to be the idea of the Church, as had been proposed both by Tromp and in the Holy Office's *votum*. The subcommission recommended that the TC begin with a first constitution which, in the face of such errors as immanentism, atheistic humanism, materialistic Marxism, and integral evolutionism, should present the truth about God as author of nature and grace, revelation, and Christ's redemption. This would be followed by the constitutions on the Church as the instrument of salvation, on the sources in which the Church finds the revelation of salvation, and on the Christian moral order which embodies the subjective way to salvation.

---

[258] For Ciappi's view of the doctrinal work of the Council, see "Che cosa la Teologia si attende dal Concilio," *Sacra Doctrina* 6 (1961) 89-107; "Le attese della teologia di fronte al Concilio Vaticano II," *Divinitas* 2 (1961) 494-502.

[259] Tromp noted in his Diary, 27 Oct 1960, that he had also not been consulted on the constitution of the subcommission *De Ecclesia*.

[260] The subcommission was chaired by Msgr. F. Carpino; its other members were J. Schröffer, L. Gillon, E. Dhanis, J. Ramirez, A. Trapè, with M. Leclercq taking notes.

Not content with determining the order of the texts, however, the subcommission also offered an outline of how these texts might be structured. Here at several points the subcommission referred to the proposals made in the *votum* of the Holy Office from which it also borrowed a quite new outline of the text on the Church. Tromp's diary reveals that the day after he received this report, he complained to Ottaviani that the subcommission had exceeded its competency by proposing a total change in the schema on the Church, warning him also that the TC might be regarded as a commission of the Holy Office and he himself as "a clerk of the Holy Office."[261]

Ottaviani decided that the question of the order of the schemata should be submitted also to the consultors of the TC before the members made a final decision. According to Tromp's notes, the majority of responses from consultors favored his view. On 21 December Tromp met with the chairs of the four subcommissions; they decided that a profession of faith in God and Christ should precede the five schemata: *De Ecclesia, De fontibus, De deposito, De ordine morali individuali, De ordine morali sociali*. Whether these should be reduced to two schemata could be left for a later decision, after they had been written.

This debate reveals the existence of tensions within even the Roman contingent. Tromp's schemata departed from the order of the Holy Office's *votum* and omitted some of its content, and Tromp saw in the objections to his plan and in the appointment of a subcommission to settle the issue an effort on Parente's part to control the agenda and work of the TC. Tromp's Diary shows frequent concern to preserve the independence of the TC.

A minor incident revealed another source of tensions. Tromp wanted the subcommissions *De ecclesia* and *De ordine morali* to meet at the

---

[261] On 11 November Tromp made the same complaint to Felici; he then repeated it in nearly the same language in a report to the Pope, 3 December 1960: "Finally, allow me to say that the work of the secretary is not easy. On the one hand, he was told to take great care that the Theological Commission not be considered a part of the S.S. Congregation of the Holy Office; on the other hand, many things are being done and perhaps have to be done that very strongly suggest that idea" (A-Florit).

Ottaviani's reply to this complaint is not recorded; perhaps it might be inferred from his remarks at the January 1962 CCP meeting, where he addressed a possible objection to the TC's use of the *votum* of the Holy Office, "as if we were slaves of the demands of that Congregation": "But the Holy Office is especially competent because of the constant reports it has from consultations, indications, and communications that it receives from all over the world. It seems to me, then, that from its experience it can give some idea of the things that are most necessary, in today's time and circumstances, with regard to the doctrine of faith and morals;" *ADP* II/2 310.

Gregorian University. When this was objected to by Garofalo or Piolanti,[262] Ottaviani directed that all subcommissions should meet at the Holy Office. When Tromp nevertheless called the members to meet at the Gregorian, Piolanti and Fenton went to the Holy Office where Ottaviani telephoned Tromp and ordered the subcommission to come from the Gregorian to the Holy Office. Behind this little dispute lay tensions between the Gregorian and the Lateran and perhaps other Roman academies as well.[263] Piolanti soon asked to be moved from the *De Ecclesia* to the *De deposito* subcommission; but the Lateran would continue to be represented on the former by U. Lattanzi, appointed by Ottaviani over Tromp's objections.

On the other hand, the differences between Parente, Piolanti, and Tromp were minor compared to the differences between them and some of the non-Roman members and consultors. G. Philips and L. Cerfaux, for example, favored a constitution on Catholic faith which would be a simple presentation, offering an objective exposition rather than a condemnation of errors and expressed in scriptural, conciliar and patristic language. Cerfaux even prepared a "Schema Constitutionis praeviae de fide catholica," which presented the order of creation, the order of Christian revelation, the apostolic preaching and tradition, and the Scriptures.[264] At the first plenary session, several other members, including Tromp, declared themselves in favor of an initial profession of faith, but events were to show that there was little agreement as to what this should be like.

A second example of alternate visions, communicated to the TC, is the paper in which in late September Congar gave his views on the tasks of the Council and commented on the TC's *schemata*.[265] He urged that the Council undertake its work with a clear view of the world in which the Church was living: where one of every four people was Chinese and one of every

---

[262] Tromp's Diary, 27 Oct 1960, mentions Garofalo, while Fenton's Diary, 27 Oct 1960, names Piolanti; Leclercq also told Tromp that the Dominicans objected to two of the subcommissions meeting at the Gregorian.

[263] These tensions were high throughout the preparatory period, pitting not only individual theologians against one another, but Roman academic institutions as well. Besides the public attack of the Lateran upon the Biblical Institute (discussed below), there was also talk of an effort to unite all the Roman institutions into a single great body, under the leadership of the Congregation for Seminaries and Studies, whose prefect would be its Chancellor; see A. Stickler, "'Pontificia Universitas Romana,'" *Seminarium* 14 (1962) 651-70, and X. Rynne, *Letters from Vatican City* (New York 1963) 51-52.

[264] This text can be found in the A-Philips.

[265] This seventeen-page, untitled paper begins "Conformement à l'invitation..." and is dated 24 September 1960. Congar sent this text not only to Tromp but to the other members and consultors of the TC.

234 234

three was under communist domination, where divided Christians were
nurturing hope for reunion, where practical atheism and technocracy were
prevalent, where colonialism and paternalism were rejected, where women
were seeking to advance themselves. The *schemata compendiosa*, on the
other hand, appeared to Congar to have been written for the world in which
the First Vatican Council met. He criticized their emphasis upon formal
questions of authority, neglect of the substantive content of the Gospel, primarily negative view of the contemporary world, abstract and scholastic
style, omission of crucial current issues, and lack of ecumenical interest.

This perspective was also reflected in Congar's reply on the question
of the number and order of the schemata.[266] If he preferred Tromp's idea
of two large texts because it would permit a unified and dynamic
presentation, he wished this to be developed kerygmatically rather than
analytically or scholastically. Congar also agreed with the proposal of
several members that the schemata be preceded by a profession of faith
in God and in Christ, which would avoid accusations of ecclesiological
positivism, would provide an organic unity to the developed schemata,
and would ground and reveal the dynamic and missionary aspect of the
Church, providing a proclamation of Christian hope as well as of faith.[267]

The texts of Cerfaux and Congar represented a quite different orientation for the TC, one with which Philips was also sympathetic, but they had
little effect on its program. While there was some agreement at the plenary
session that the schemata should be preceded by a positive declaration of
the Church's faith in God and Christ, it is doubtful that members intended
the same thing by this suggestion and in the end it was never acted upon.
The *schemata compendiosa* continued to define the TC's program.

2. *Norms and Methods*.

By the end of November, Tromp had prepared and Ottaviani had
approved twelve norms to guide the work of the subcommissions.[268]
They should be chiefly concerned with the needs of the Church today

[266] Congar, "Animadversiones de Systemate quo ordinanda sunt ea quae fuerunt
Commissioni Theologicae subjecta seu De ordine servando," 13 Dec 1960 (A-Congar).

[267] While in Rome on 16 November 1960, Congar found Tromp disinclined to his
views: "Fr. Tromp dismissed my idea that we ought right away to adopt an order of
exposition, which I would hope would be a dynamic order, a proclamation of salvation.
For him precise technical *theses* have to be drawn up; later we can consider in what order
to present them. But for me, the unity of Church, Scripture, Tradition, laity, etc... are
conceived differently in accord with the total order in which they are considered;"
Y. Congar, *Mon Journal du Concile*, 16 Nov 1960.

[268] "Normae generales pro subcommissionibus," 20 Nov 1960.

and should not prepare scientific treatises. They should not address obsolete or generally accepted matters, individual errors that pose no threat to the Church's faith, or disputed questions not yet ripe for judgment. If matters already defined needed to be stressed, this should be done briefly. In condemning errors, they should usually condemn the falsehood without naming it, which might only cause disputes later. The subcommissions were to confine themselves to doctrinal matters, leaving disciplinary questions to the other commissions.

These norms, which reflected Tardini's views as well as Ottaviani's, meant that the texts prepared by the TC would not be organic or synthetic presentations of the Church's doctrines, but would focus on contemporary needs, defined almost exclusively in terms of defending the deposit against errors. Even though Tromp noted that the presentation should be devoted more to elucidating the truth than to condemning errors, he reminded the subcommissions of the advice given to the members of the Theological Commission at Vatican I: "Before anything else, carefully gather the errors of this time."

As for their method, the subcommissions were to develop the outlines given them, dropping or adding things only after consulting the TC. They were to take into account the proposals made in the antepreparatory consultation and the observations already made by members and consultors of the TC. For more difficult questions, they were to give special attention to recent decisions of the Holy See, being familiar in particular with the acts of Vatican I. No reference was made to the need for new studies of the Scriptures or earlier Tradition. They could seek the advice of experts outside the TC only after consulting Ottaviani.

From the beginning the subcommissions were both to undertake particular studies of the more difficult and disputed matters and to begin composing the whole schema with provisional texts that would then be discussed and improved. This significant procedural decision meant that first drafts of texts would be undertaken *before* the studies of particular questions were received. Although a good number of *vota* were in fact solicited from both members and consultors, they were seldom able to alter either the orientation or the substance of the early drafts, which closely followed the lines of the *schemata compendiosa*.

By and large the texts composed by the subcommissions were written by members and by consultors living in Rome; draft-texts submitted by such non-Romans as Salaverri, Häring, Delhaye, and Congar had little success. Of non-Romans only Philips and C. Colombo prepared drafts that found their way into the definitive schemata. *Vota* were solicited

from many of the non-Roman members and consultors, all of them were
sent regular reports on the work, and their comments on successive
drafts were requested, faithfully reported, and considered seriously. But
most of the real redactional work of the TC was done in the subcommissions whose meetings were attended by the non-Romans only during
the four plenary sessions. While only members had a right to vote and to
speak at meetings, the evidence is that both at subcommission and at
plenary sessions, consultors were often called upon for their opinions.

Special skills were required, of course, for writing texts that would
meet the requirements of the TC's stated purposes; and it was quickly
clear that not all the authors of early drafts possessed them. Tromp spent
a great deal of time revising texts in a more "conciliar style." This task
perhaps compensated for Ottaviani's decision that Tromp was not to be
a member of any particular subcommission, although he could attend
their meetings and express his opinions; in particular Tromp was not to
be the *relator* for the subcommission *De Ecclesia*, where, Ottaviani told
him, several people had said that he would urge his own views too
strongly.[269] Tromp certainly was the strongest figure in the TC, directing
its work very closely and defending his own opinions very forcefully.
While the many reports of the TC's work show him to have been very
faithful in reporting the different views, they do not reveal a man much
inclined to self-doubt or to conciliation; and this and the caustic wit he
employed even in official reports and comments help explain why both
Roman and non-Roman participants in the work of the TC could
describe his manner as "dictatorial" and "tyrannical."

B. The Texts Produced by the Theological Commission

In the twenty months of its work, the TC produced eight texts: a new
formula for the profession of the faith and drafts of seven constitutions:
on the sources of revelation, on the moral order, on the defence of the
deposit of faith, on chastity, virginity, marriage and the family, on the
Church, on the Blessed Virgin Mary, on the community of nations, and
on the social order. Of these we will leave the schemas on the sources of
revelation and on the Church for separate treatment below in relation to
the rival approaches of the SCU. Here we will briefly describe the other
texts produced by the TC.

[269] Tromp Diary, 31 Oct 1960. From what must have been a painful meeting Tromp
says that he departed "with mixed joy and tears."

1. *A New Formula for the Profession of Faith*

While the proposals made by Congar, Cerfaux, and several others that the Council begin with a positive statement of the Church's faith in God and Christ never bore fruit, the TC did undertake a project similar in title but quite different in character: a new formula for the profession of faith.[270] In presenting this text to the CPC, Ottaviani said that the Holy Office had received requests for a new formula even before the announcement of the Council; he did not mention that it also appeared in the Holy Office's *votum*. Although the "Synopsis" of episcopal proposals drawn up within the Holy Office claimed that around eighty bishops had requested it, the "Final Synthesis" of the episcopal consultation made no mention of it and it was not found among the questions officially proposed to the TC.[271]

At the first plenary session of the TC the topic of a new formula was briefly discussed but no decision reached. At the end of December Ottaviani brought the proposal to Pope John who approved it early in January but ordered that it be prepared within the TC and not by the Holy Office.[272] On 7 Jan 1961 Ottaviani assigned the task to the subcommission *De deposito* with Tromp to be the final redactor.[273]

This project was announced to the TC at its plenary session on 13 February 1961. At the end of the meeting, Tromp clarified the instructions he had been given: the new text would precede the Council and not be approved by it; instead it would be submitted to the Cardinals of the Holy Office where it would proceed through the usual channels.[274] If the preparation of the new formula was assigned to the TC by the Pope, then, it was still thought that its approval would be in the hands of the Holy Office.

A meeting of the subcommission *De deposito* on 17 March approved a set of guidelines and gave Tromp the task of writing a text. Tromp spent the next week preparing a draft and a report, which Ottaviani approved on 11 April. Tromp gave his text to the subcommission on 19 April and on the 22nd its chairman, Ciappi, sent Tromp some written comments. By the end of July Tromp had finished a slight revision of his text.

[270] See A. Indelicato, "La 'Formula nova professionis fidei' nella preparazione del Vaticano II," *CrSt* 7 (1986) 305-40; Burigana, "Progetto dogmatico," 186-88.

[271] In the published schematic summary of the antepreparatory consultation, under the title "De symbolis fidei," nine proposals are listed, only four of which, supported by fifteen bishops, call for anything like a new profession of faith; see *ADA App*, II/1 9-10.

[272] See *ADP* II/1 499-500.

[273] Tromp Diary, 7 Jan 1961.

[274] "Epilogus Secretarii," 16 Feb 1961. This procedure was repeated by Ottaviani in a conversation with Tromp on 11 April 1961; Tromp Diary.

Whether the new formula was ever sent to the Holy Office is not known; but in early August it was sent out as part of the agenda for discussion at the September plenary session of the TC. On the basis of comments received from the members and consultors the new formula was revised at two meetings of the subcommission *De deposito* just prior to the meeting. At the plenary sessions further slight revisions were made, and the whole text was approved on 18 September. The final revised text was sent to the CPC on 4 October.[275]

After the Nicene-Constantinopolitan Creed, the new formula proposed thirteen paragraphs that were framed by two paragraphs on the magisterium. No. 2 called for reception of everything taught either solemnly or through the ordinary universal magisterium, especially doctrines opposed to contemporary errors. No. 16 expected profession of the things defined by ecumenical Councils, particularly by Trent and Vatican I and called for rejection of whatever is condemned not only in those Councils but also in Encyclicals, particularly in *Pascendi* and *Humani generis*.

The thirteen central paragraphs called for adherence to statements on natural reason's ability to demonstrate the existence of God and on the duty also of civil society to acknowledge God, on christology and the atonement, on the Blessed Virgin and the devotion to her, on the Church as the ark of salvation, on papal government and magisterium, on bishops as successors of the Apostles, on the seven sacraments and the necessity of baptism for salvation, on the ordained priest as the only valid offerer of the Mass, on the real presence in the Eucharist, on sacramentals, indulgences, and relics, on original sin, on miracles, prophecies, and the Church itself as manifest signs of divine revelation, on the development of doctrine, on the close of revelation with the death of the last apostle, on the inerrancy and the interpretation of Scripture, and on faith as intellectual assent to revealed truths because of the authority of God.

Footnotes supplied the sources from which each paragraph was drawn and often explained the contemporary errors the statements excluded. The Scriptures are never cited; no magisterial source earlier than Trent is cited, and only two Eucharistic hymns break the monopoly of references to recent magisterial texts. *Pascendi*, *Lamentabili*, and the anti-modernist oath are cited eight times and *Humani generis* seven times. Among the errors opposed are: laicism, mistaken notions of Christ's satisfaction, minimalism in Mariology and errors on her virginity, denials that the Catholic Church is the one true Church, new theories about the salvation of infants who die without baptism, denials of the difference

[275] See *ADP* II/1, 495-99.

between the universal and hierarchical priesthood, emphases on the Church's sins, and neglect of the doctrine of Hell.

When he brought the new formula to the CPC on 8 November 1961, Ottaviani explained it as an effort to combine the Tridentine profession with the anti-modernist oath, eliminating repetitions, removing no longer relevant material, and making some changes to address new and current errors. Anticipating two objections, he said that the new formula contained no doctrines that were not already beyond debate, so that there should be no problem in approving it even before the Council, and that the frequent references to *Pascendi* and *Humani generis* should cause no difficulty because everything stated was already in the antimodernist oath: what really counts, in any case, is less the source of a truth than the truth itself.[276]

Despite these clarifications, many members of the CPC severely criticized the new formula for its negative character, inflation of the authority of encyclicals, neglect of the varying doctrinal authority of its statements, and attempt to close many legitimately disputed questions. A majority voted that an approval of the text be deferred until it could be revised in the light of the comments made and at least until after the CPC had reviewed all the other constitutions.[277]

The new formula was remanded to the subcommission on amendments, where it was discussed on 22 January 1962. A report for the subcommission expressed sharp annoyance that the TC now was describing the text as a *presynodal* document to be approved by the Pope and imposed upon the Council, a view of it that the report claimed differed from the understanding common at the November meeting of the CPC, that the text would be submitted to the Council Fathers for definitive approval.[278] It recommended that the text not be approved by the Pope prior to the Council without the Fathers having an opportunity to express their views, especially since another formula would have to be drawn up after the Council to include whatever truths the Council defined. This recommendation was accepted and the new formula was not in fact used to begin the Council.[279]

[276] *ADP* II/1 499-502.

[277] *ADP* II/1 502-23; see Indelicato, *Difendere la dottrina*, 67-77.

[278] The report appears to be mistaken here; certainly Ottaviani said at the November meeting that he wished the text to be used at the beginning of the Council.

[279] See *De emendatione schematum decretorum quae discussa fuerunt in sessione generali Pontificiae Commissionis Centralis mense novembri 1961 habita* (TPV 1962), 3-5. It is curious to note, however, that in an article published in a special number of *OssRom*, 11 October 1962, the very eve of the Council, L. Ciappi was still expecting the Council to open "with a solemn profession of faith according to a new formula inspired by the most recent documents of the Church's magisteri." Does this indicate that the use of the new formula was still a matter of debate and struggle?

Although it became a dead letter, the new formula has some significance for an understanding of the TC's program for the Council. First, its content provides a useful summary of the vision of the faith that the leaders of the TC believed it necessary to present in response to the doctrinal crisis they saw all around them and which they would unfold at greater length in their several schemata.[280] Tactically, the proposal that it be approved before the Council and then used at its beginning would have been a decisive action, settling in advance some of the most important of the questions the doctrinal schemata would address. There could be no clearer illustration that the leaders of the TC expected these schemata to be approved without serious challenge; and if one did arise, they would have been able to appeal to the new profession of faith, solemnly adopted by pope and the body of bishops at the beginning of their work, to settle the issue. Finally, although much remains obscure here, the history of the text seems to reveal another point at which the Holy Office obscured the lines between itself and the TC, thus blurring the distinction between Curia and Council the Pope had called for.

2. *De deposito fidei pure custodiendo*[281]

Tromp's initial *schema compendiosum* proposed nine general topics: the notion of objective truth, the existence of a personal God and the force of apologetical demonstrations, cosmic evolution, monogenism, the true concept of revelation, certitude of the fact of revelation, the notion of faith, distinction and harmony between the natural and supernatural orders, no new revelations after the close of the deposit. To these were added five particular questions: biblical inspiration and inerrancy,[282] original sin, the real presence of Christ in the Eucharist, the sacrificial character of the Mass, the Blessed Virgin Mary. This list had been largely drawn, Tromp told the prior subcommission, from the experience of the Holy Office and reflected the doctrinal questions most in need of defence today.

---

[280] This connection between the new formula of faith and the doctrinal schemata was made explicit by Ottaviani himself when he accepted a deferral of approval until after the CPC had discussed the other texts: "It may be that some things in the other constitutions will not be accepted, and the formula for the profession of faith was drawn up in harmony with the other constitutions;" *ADP* II/1 514.

[281] See A. Indelicato, "Lo schema 'De deposito fidei pure custodiendo' e la preparazione del Vaticano II," *CrSt* 11 (1990) 309-55; Burigana, "Progetto dogmatico," 182-86.

[282] This, Tromp explained to the prior subcommission, had already been taken from this schema to form part of the new schema *De fontibus*.

Tromp's outline, accepted by the prior subcommission, was then revised by Ciappi who provided for each question a set of more precise topics along with indications of magisterial sources (Vatican I, Pius X, Pius XII) for many of them. When he presented this *schema compendiosum* at the first plenary session in October, Ciappi also provided excerpts from the antepreparatory consultation, giving in particular references to the *votum* of the Holy Office.[283] The October plenary session accepted this outline, but moved the question of the Blessed Virgin to the subcommission on the Church. Although several people had asked that the schema *De deposito* be given a more positive orientation and synthetic character, no such effort was undertaken, and from beginning to end the subcommission *De deposito* followed the outline first offered by Tromp.

Most of the redactional work was done by the Roman subcommission, closely followed and assisted by Tromp.[284] A large number of studies were requested not only from other members and consultors of the TC, but also, something rare among the subcommissions of the TC, from outside experts.[285] But, like the other subcommissions, this one also did not wait for the commissioned studies to arrive before it began drafting its texts.

By mid-December the subcommission was already discussing the first drafts of four chapters, three of which were typed and distributed for discussion at the plenary session in February where they were generally approved and it was decided to accept Tromp's proposal that the subcommission also address the question of the salvation of unbaptized infants. After the February meeting the subcommission met regularly for the next two months. At the end of April, Ciappi's progress-report noted that the first four chapters were closest to completion, while studies were underway on the other subjects. While Tromp would write the chapter on unbaptized children, two other topics remained to be assigned: the

[283] At the end Ciappi mentioned other possible topics raised in the consultation: on the nature of man, on the necessity of baptism for infants, on christology, the causality of the sacraments, the last things. Of these only the question of unbaptized infants was added to the original list.

[284] The members of the subcommission: F. Carpino, A. Stohr, L. Audet, A. Piolanti, A. Ciappi, J. Ramirez, E. Dhanis, A. Trapè.

[285] Cerfaux and Kerrigan studied monogenism in the Bible, de Lubac the argument from causality for the existence of God, Labourdette recent views on original sin, and Dander the salvation of unbaptized childen and the satisfaction of Christ. Of the outside experts, V. Marcozzi submitted three *vota* on evolution and paleo-anthropology, E. Boné two on evolution and monogenism, Z. Alszeghy and M. Flick one on recent errors on original sin, C. Fabro one on existentialistic atheism, and A. Rossi one on the demonstrability of revelation.

real presence of Christ in the Eucharist and the sacrificial character of the Mass.[286] From then on the work progressed so rapidly that the whole text, consisting of eleven chapters, was completed by 13 July and could be printed for discussion by the whole TC in September.[287]

The members and consultors sent in forty-seven pages of comments on the schema,[288] all but three of whose chapters most of them had not seen before, which may explain why many of their comments were quite critical. Several respondents complained about the overly philosophical character of the first two chapters and also questioned whether the schema should begin with such *praeambula* rather than with the chapter on revelation and faith. The formalism and extrinsicism of the latter chapter were criticized by Congar and de Lubac. But the sharpest criticisms fell on the chapters on original sin, on monogenism, and on unbaptized infants, whose severity was criticized by all those who submitted written comments.

At subcommission meetings during the September plenary session, many revisions were made in the text. The plenary assembly discussed the text on 25-28 September. A few significant changes were introduced into the earlier chapters, including one by de Lubac that introduced the only reference to the Trinity in the chapter on God. In his journal Congar noted a certain lassitude among the participants, not least of all because the Roman theologians seemed to be controlling everything;[289] even the lively debate on original sin and monogenism ended with only minor changes in the tone and content of the chapters. No agreement, despite several efforts to compose compromise-texts, could be reached on the question of the salvation of unbaptized infants. In October Tromp and Ciappi revised the text in the light of the amendments accepted by the subcommission and approved by the plenary. This text was then sent to the CPC.[290]

After a preface that declared that the right and duty of defending the deposit fell also upon the universal episcopate, a first chapter vindicated the power of the human mind to reach the truth, that is, a knowledge of an objective order of things, and warned against calling into question the

[286] No chapters on these two subjects were ever prepared by the subcommission *De deposito*.

[287] "Constitutio de deposito fidei pure custodiendo" (CT 7/61:56; TPV 1961).

[288] "Animadversiones in constitutionem de deposito fidei pure custodiendo" (CT 7/61:62).

[289] Encountering Janssen, Delhaye, and de Lubac, Congar found them "rather discouraged and bitter. Their views have not been and are not being taken into account. The Romans are doing everything;" Y. Congar, *Mon Journal du Concile*, 22 Sept 1961.

[290] For the text and discussions at the CPC, see *ADP* II/2 279-443; see Indelicato, *Difendere la dottrina*, 115-31.

first principles of metaphysics and epistemology. The second chapter built on this a statement of the ability of natural reason to demonstrate the existence of God, offered arguments drawn from the perfections and imperfections of creatures, and warned against efforts to weaken their probative force. Throughout the redactional process, members and consultors questioned whether it was the role of an ecumenical Council to address these issues philosophically and to enter into questions that were freely debated even among Christian philosophers. De Lubac's argument that the Council should not attempt even in general to outline proofs for the existence of God was disregarded, as were proposals that a properly theological discussion of these questions follow the chapter on revelation and faith. The approach remained one of abstract logic, following the classical course of clerical education and moving from the truths that reason can discover to those that revelation adds.

Chapter three defended the creation of the world at the beginning of time and condemned evolutionism; after statements thought to represent the opinions of Teilhard de Chardin were condemned,[291] the chapter briefly discussed the relation between faith and science, particularly with regard to human evolution.

Revelation and faith were the subject of chapter four. The classic modern definition of revelation as *locutio Dei attestantis* was presented and then related to the history of salvation. The accent fell on revelation as doctrine, carefully distinguished from mere experience. One paragraph warned against a recent form of relativism that questions the adequacy and permanence of traditional doctrinal concepts. This de Lubac recognized to be aimed at himself, but his and Congar's energetic protests were unable to remove it from the text.[292] The last several

---

[291] In his comments on the section, de Lubac vigorously defended Teilhard from the accusations here brought against him; but he was successful only in having Teilhard's name removed from the notes. On June 30, 1962, the Holy Office would publish a monitum about the theological and philosophical ambiguities and errors in Teilhard's works. The next day, *OssRom* published an anonymous article commenting on Teilhard's thought, finding grave errors in it, and criticizing de Lubac's recent book on Teilhard, particularly his assertion that Teilhard is for our century "an authentic witness to Jesus Christ." See *DC* 59 (1962) 949-56.

[292] In #22 of Dhanis' chapter, de Lubac recognized the same criticism that had been directed at him by his Father General in 1951. When De Lubac asked Dhanis who were the targets of this criticism, Dhanis refused to reply. De Lubac told Congar he intended to write Tromp demanding an explanation of the targets of this criticism, and if he found that he was among them, he would submit his resignation to the Pope. What de Lubac did is not known, but the paragraph remained in the text that was submitted to the CPC. Congar himself wrote to Dhanis hoping to change his mind but received no satisfaction; Y. Congar, *Mon Journal du Concile*, 28 Sept 1961.

paragraphs stressed the importance of the external signs of revelation and assigned a much slighter role to the inner witness of grace.

The chapter, in other words, continued the classical modern approach, echoing a first-year course in a seminary. Revelation was presented as the communication of a body of truths, extrinsically guaranteed by external signs which legitimate the trustworthiness of the "divine legates," of whom Christ was simply the most important one. The uniqueness of Christ as the embodiment of God's wisdom and knowledge was even eliminated and there was no reference to the content of the revelation he brought.[293] Faith was an assent to the doctrines revealed based upon the authority of the revealing God. Chapter five developed this notion of revelation with a brief discussion of dogmatic development and a warning against exaggerated interest in private revelations.

Chapter six discussed the natural and supernatural orders and rejected errors that question the gratuity of the supernatural order or deny its necessity. After a seventh chapter condemned various forms of spiritualism and reincarnation, the eighth and ninth took up the related questions of original sin and monogenism. On the latter question the subcommission had commissioned no fewer than seven special studies, two on the Bible and five on contemporary scientific opinions. The modesty and careful distinctions of these studies[294] were not reflected in the text prepared by Trapè and vigorously defended by Tromp, which by expressly declaring that any form of polygenism was contrary to Catholic faith closed the slight opening in *Humani generis* to a possible revision of the doctrine of monogenism. The proposal of several participants at the September plenary session that the conciliar text simply repeat the language of *Humani generis* was rejected.

A similar fate befell criticisms of the chapter on original sin. Here too careful studies of recent opinions on this doctrine by Labourdette and by Flick and Alszeghy had little effect on the text, which gave a rapid and

---

[293] See P. Levillain, *La mécanique politique de Vatican II: La majorité et l'unanimité dans un Concile* (Paris 1975) 82, where he quotes from de Lubac's journal: "Fr. X, who plays an important role, seems to want to minimize the person of Jesus Christ, who is no more than one of the *legatores divini* (this is how he is designated, anonymously, in the chapter on revelation). The teaching Christ does not possess "the treasures of wisdom and knowledge" (he had this Pauline text suppressed in this very chapter)."

[294] While Cerfaux argued that the New Testament left the question open, Kerrigan found monogenism an implication of the whole biblical revelation. Marcozzi and Boné reported that contemporary scientists assume evolution in general and the evolution of man as the starting-point of their investigations and that methodologically they can only work under the hypothesis of an original group of human beings and not a single person or couple.

bald statement of the classical doctrine with no effort to make it more intelligible to contemporaries or to respond to serious questions. The text even wished to enter into the warmly debated question of the interpretation of the fifth chapter of the Epistle to the Romans,[295] although the flat assertion that it could be found in Rm 5:12 was nuanced when the chapter was revised at the September meeting.

Chapter ten addressed the question of the salvation of children who die without baptism. The text brought to the CPC reflected the dispute within the TC itself. In April 1961, after the Innsbruck theologian Dander had submitted a study which concluded that the question was still under discussion and should be left open, Tromp himself wrote a lengthy *votum* on the subject whose conclusion was the opposite. He then wrote a very brief chapter that asserted that supernatural beatitude was closed to such infants and rebuked recent theories as rash and dangerous. On this point, however, Tromp was not able to carry the day either within the subcommission or at the plenary session, and the text that was sent to the CPC contained three possible ways of addressing the issue.

The last chapter defended the classical doctrine of sin as an offense against God for which Christ's satisfaction was necessary. Little is known about the author or the history of this text.

Even this brief outline shows that the schema *De deposito* was not intended as a full and systematic presentation of Catholic doctrine. The first five chapters might be said to follow a certain order, but the last six do not: in fact, the only criterion for treatment of the latter doctrines was the perceived need to defend them from contemporary threats. In nearly every case the primary purpose was either to echo and to develop the teaching of Vatican I or to confirm by supreme conciliar authority the teachings of *Pascendi* and *Humani generis*, particularly the latter whose effort to squelch "*la nouvelle théologie*" was not considered to have succeeded.

The spirit that guided the group that prepared the text was described well by de Lubac:

> They know their craft, but little else. You sense in them a certain indifference to Scripture, the Fathers, the Eastern Church; a lack of interest in and

[295] S. Lyonnet, a professor at the Biblical Institute, had for some years been arguing that the text of Rom 5:12 did not refer to original sin but to personal sins; see "Le sens d'*eph'hô* en Rom. 5,12 et l'exégèse des Pères grecs," *Biblica* 36 (1955) 436-56; "Le Péché originel et l'exégèse de Rom 5,12-14," *RSR* 44 (1956) 63-84. Several Roman theologians believed this to contradict the infallible interpretation of this verse given at the Council of Trent; see F. Spadafora, "Rom. 5,12: Esegesi e riflessi dogmatici," *Divinitas* 4 (1960) 289-98. Lyonnet's position was one of the reasons for the effort to remove him from the faculty of the Pontifical Biblical Institute.

uneasiness with regard to contemporary doctrines and intellectual currents contrary to Christian faith. They are, it seems, too certain of their own superiority; their practice of judging does not incline them to work. It is the milieu of the Holy Office. Observations, studies, suggestions from theologians, or even bishops, from elsewhere (except those of some friends or spokesmen) scarcely retain their attention. The result is a little academic system, ultra-intellectualistic but without much intellectual quality. The Gospel is folded into this system, which is the constant *a priori*.[296]

It is no wonder that de Lubac felt like a hostage, even a defendant, in the midst of this subcommission.[297]

3. *De ordine morali*[298]

Three of the five "*Quaestiones*" proposed to the TC by the Pope concerned moral questions. Its presentation of the supernatural order should condemn the chief contemporary errors: naturalism, materialism, communism, and laicism. On the basis of recent papal teachings, it should explain Catholic doctrine on marriage and condemn "the widespread errors of naturalism." Finally, it should provide a concise presentation of Catholic doctrine on social issues.[299]

Tromp's initial outline of a constitution on moral and social matters first made a general point: there is a natural law that the Church has the right to explain and use as a criterion for moral and social matters. Under moral questions, it then listed the absolute value of the moral order, situation ethics, and freedom of conscience; love as a criterion of morality; the notion of sin and its deformation; sex and marriage.[300] F. Hürth reviewed Tromp's schema, made some changes, and added some observations;[301] and it was his text that was presented to the first plenary session of the TC, where it was adopted as the basic program for

---

[296] Quoted in Levillain, *La mécanique politique*, 82; see also 84-85.

[297] H. de Lubac, *At the Service of the Church*, trans. A.E. Englund (San Francisco 1993) 116-17.

[298] Burigana, "Progetto dogmatico," 188-91.

[299] *ADP* II/1 408-409. The vagueness of these questions reflects the "Sintesi finale," which did not even include a section on moral issues, although among the errors to be condemned it did include "moral relativism (situation ethics)" (5) and urged a new presentation of Catholic doctrine on the nature and purposes of marriage in order to counteract the spread of divorce, contraception, and other errors (15). On the other hand, both the Holy Office's *votum*, ADA III 14-16, and its "Synopsis" of episcopal views were more precise and provided most of the topics the subcommission on morality took up.

[300] S. Tromp, "Constitutio de rebus moralibus et socialibus", undated but sent out on 13 July 1960.

[301] F. Hürth, "Schema de ordine morali et sociali," (CT 4/60; 20.7.1960).

the subcommision, with the work divided, however, between two sub-commissions, one for a text *De ordine morali individuali* and the other a text *De ordine sociali*.

The work of the small group that prepared the first of these texts[302] fell chiefly to three Roman theologians, F.X. Hürth, L. Gillon, and E. Lio, who worked largely on their own, without a regular chairman and with little help from commissioned studies.[303] Two papers were eventually requested of B. Häring,[304] but only after he had been excluded from direct participation in the work because his approach was thought incompatible with that of the group.[305]

The three Romans set to work immediately and by mid-January a draft was ready for discussion at the February plenary meeting. Hürth presented a lengthy explanation that the text was a necessary response to a host of contemporary errors in moral matters. The text took as its guiding notion the idea of an objectively existing, absolute and immutable moral order as the sum of norms by which human life was to be governed and led to its final end.[306]

During the February session, a number of changes were agreed upon, most of them clarifying or nuancing statements but without substantively

---

[302] Members: J. Wright, F. Franic, P. Philippe, L. Gillon, F. Hürth; Consultors: Anastasius a SS. Rosario, E. Lio; P. Delhaye B. Häring, L. Janssens.

[303] In April Tromp reported that besides the texts of Häring (see next note), this subcommission had drawn only upon a *votum* on the moral order by Lio and that of F. Hürth, both prepared for the CAP; see *ADA* IV/I/2 95-109, IV/I/1 90-119.

[304] In the note with which he accepted his appointment to the CT, Häring had offered his expertise on fundamental questions, on situation ethics and juridical positivism, on true and false humanism, on venial sin, on marriage and family, and on social questions (A-Häring). On 7 Jan 1961 Tromp asked him to prepare two *"disputationes"*: "Against naturalism and laicism" and "The true and religious responsibility of spouses with regard to the procreation and educatin of children." Häring submitted these two studies and added a draft of a constitution on the second.

[305] See minutes of the meeting, 2 Nov 1960, where Hürth said Häring would be an "disturbing *element*" and Gillon that he represents a "tendency foreign to our work" (A-VC II). These comments reflect the suspicions Häring had aroused in Rome, particularly through his book, *Das Gesetz Christi* (Freiburg i. Br. 1954), which had been examined by the Holy Office but in which Hürth told Häring he had found much to disagree with but nothing heretical; see Häring, *Fede Storia Morale, intervista di Gianni Licheri* (Rome 1989) 48-49. But the remarks might also be a response to Häring's critique of the *schema compendiosum* for emphasizing obligations and for neglecting the law of grace written on Christian hearts, which ought to be the starting-point. Another moral theologian who had difficulty in contributing to the work of the subcommission was P. Delhaye of Louvain, who had written an article calling for a renewal of moral theology, "La théologie morale d'hier et d'aujourd'hui," *RevSR* 27 (1953) 112-30.

[306] These qualities were to be defended against agnosticism, relativism, subjectivism, materialism, liberalism, moral "autonomism," libertinism, personalism, totalitarianism, laicism, humanism, immanentism, and evolutionism.

modifying the text and, despite a number of observations in this direction, without enlarging its vision or deepening its analysis. It was
decided, however, to expand and to clarify the single paragraph devoted
to conscience and to include a discussion of venial sins. The subcommission returned to work, Lio's chapters on chastity and marriage were
completed and added,[307] and the whole text was finished at the end of
May. It was then printed and sent out to the TC in July in preparation for
the September plenary session.[308]

By September 12th, fifty-two pages of observations had been gathered
and typed.[309] Besides a host of particular suggestions, the two most general criticisms received were that the text was too negative, neglected the
elements of truth in mistaken positions, and should be more positive and
biblical in tone and content; in particular, it neglected or even down-
played the central and formal role of charity in the Christian life.

During the September plenary session, the subcommission met at
three afternoon meetings and proposed minor changes in the text,[310]
which was then brought for discussion to the whole TC. Both in the subcommission and in the plenary sessions, a principal topic of debate was
the role of charity in the Christian moral life. Delhaye complained that
his written proposal about the section on charity was not even read at the
subcommission's meeting.[311] Laurentin circulated a proposal that a reference to Rom 8:10 about love as the fulfillment of the law be added to
the text; although he received a number of signatures on his petition, his
attempt failed.[312]

---

[307] Because these chapters were eventually to form part of a separate schema, they
will be treated in the next section.

[308] "Constitutio de ordine morali" (CT 8/61:28): I. De fundamento ordinis moralis;
II. De conscientia christiana; III. De subiectivismo et relativismo morali; IV. De naturali
et supernaturali dignitate personae humanae; V. De peccato; VI. De castitate et pudicitia
christiana; VII. De matrimonio christiano.

[309] "Animadversiones membrorum et consultorum in Constit. de ordine morali (C.T.
8/61:28)" (C.T. 8/61:30; 12 sept. 1961)

[310] When Janssen, Delhaye and Häring showed up at one of the subcommission meetings, Tromp told them that they had not been invited. They remained, however, and
Tromp would later regard their presence as providential because he could inform the plenary session that all present at the meeting had approved the text and accepted the proposed amendments.

[311] Y. Congar, *Mon Journal du Concile*, 21 and 25 Sept 1961. This appears to refer to
Delhaye's alternate text, which would have expanded the paragraph on charity into a
whole chapter entitled, "Praestantia caritatis in ordine morali christiano;" it is reproduced
in the "Observationes membrorum...," 18-21. For Delhaye's judgment on the preparatory
text see "Les points forts de la morale à Vatican II," *StMor* 24 (1986) 5-40, at 9-12.

[312] The text can be found in the papers of Congar, Griffith, and Häring.

At the plenary sessions, the general criticisms of the text do not seem to have been discussed, and the text was approved with mostly minor changes which did not alter its general structure or content. Over the objections of Fr. Hürth,[313] the Subcommission did agree, however, to insert a sentence into no. 5 that states that Christ recapitulated his moral teaching in the two great commandments of love of God and of neighbor.[314] It was also decided, while keeping the chapter on chastity in this text, to make the one on marriage part of a separate constitution. After the plenary meeting, Tromp and a small group made the final revisions which enabled them to send the text on October 7th to Felici for transmission to the CPC.[315]

The text *De ordine morali* essentially continued to present the themes and to use the arguments advanced in the first text written by Hürth and Gillon in January, 1961. The final text differs principally by the expansion of a single paragraph on conscience into five paragraphs and by the addition of treatments of venial sin, growth in holiness, frequent confession, and voluntary mortifications.

The chief emphasis of the text is the objectivity and absolute character of the moral order, the essence of which is the observation of the positive and negative laws laid down by God. A certain voluntarism pervades the whole, efforts to ground Christian imperatives in basic Christian indicatives having been resisted. Moral decisions are usually presented as simply matters of deducing particular applications of general laws or principles. There is hardly any reference to the liberation by grace of the person for the good, and only a brief reference to the virtue of prudence suggests the necessity of concrete moral discernment. Even in the final version, the role of love in the Christian life is scarcely acknowledged before warnings are issued about misunderstanding and exaggerating its significance. In short, from the beginning of the TC's elaboration of the text on morality to its conclusion, the presentation was dominated by the need to defend certain aspects of the Christian life against contemporary errors. This, and not an effort to make a positive and coherent statement of the basis and defining characteristics of Christian morality, was the controlling interest and purpose.

[313] Delhaye told Congar that Hürth had defended his position that morality consists primarily of commands and prohibitions by remarking that Christ "had only spoken of charity 'per transennam', in reply to a question a Pharisee happened to ask him;" Y. Congar, *Mon Journal du Concile*, 25 Sept 1961.

[314] A reference to the divine sonship of the Christian was also added to no. 16, and footnote references to Teilhard and to M. Oraison were removed.

[315] *ADP* I/2 28-96.

But the guiding theme and the responses to current problems also reflected clear choices with regard to the recent history of Catholic moral theology. In the votum that he submitted to the CAP, Lio had maintained that the concept of the moral order was more traditional and appropriate than the new central ideas for presenting Catholic moral teaching that had been proposed by Tillman, Mersch, Gilleman, etc.[316] The three men cited had sought to renew moral theology by focusing it on discipleship (Tillmann), on participation in the life of the Mystical Body (Mersch), or on the role of charity (Gilleman).[317] Common to these authors was a criticism of modern moral theology for its legalism, casuistry, minimalism, and lack of biblical inspiration.[318] The common response of defenders of traditional approaches and methods was that these more positive orientations often confused moral theology with Christian asceticism, would not be helpful to confessors in dealing with concrete cases, and verged on the errors of situation ethics.[319]

Closely related was the Roman concern about the rise of a "new morality," a term used by Pius XII in two addresses in 1952 and surely designed to echo the "new theology" that he had repudiated in *Humani generis*.[320] The central vice of this new morality, the Pope said, was the effort to subordinate ethical criteria to the individual conscience. The repudiation of objective norms was also the primary criticism of situation ethics in a 1956 instruction of the Holy Office.[321] These

---

[316] *ADA* IV/I/2 95-109.

[317] See F. Tillmann, *Handbuch der katholischen Sittenlehre*. vol. III: *Die Idee der Nachfolge Christi* (Düsseldorf 1934), vol. IV: *Die Verwirklichung der Nachfolge Christi* (Düsseldorf 1935-36); E. Mersch, *Morale et corps mystique* (Bruxelles 1949³); G. Gilleman, *Le primat de la charité en théologie morale: Essai méthodoloqique* (Bruxelles 1954²). For the modern history of moral theology, see J.A. Gallagher, *Time Past and Time Future: An Historical Study of Catholic Moral Theology* (New York 1990).

[318] Many of these criticisms were repeated by J. Leclercq, *L'enseignement de la morale chrétienne* (Paris 1950); but in 1956 this book was the object of a severe critique in *OssRom*, 2 Feb 1956, which announced that the work had been ordered withdrawn from circulation and all translations forbidden.

[319] See, for example, L. Gillon, "La théologie morale et l'éthique de l'exemplarité personnelle," *Ang* 34 (1957) 241-59, 361-78; "L'imitation du Christ et la morale de saint Thomas," *Ang* 36 (1959) 263-86.

[320] F. Hürth provided the texts and a long commentary on these speeches in *PRMCL* 41 (1952) 183-249.

[321] *AAS* 48 (1956) 144-45; once again Hürth provided the text and commentary in *PRMCL* 45 (1956) 137-204. For a useful survey and bibliography, see A. Poppi, "La 'morale di situazione': Presentazione e analisi delle fonti," *MF* 57 (Gennaio-Marzo 1957) 3-63; "Elementi di una critica alla 'morale di situazione,'" *Ibid.*, 168-222.

criticisms were presented synthetically by Hürth in an essay on conscience which anticipates the themes and emphases of the chapter on the subject he wrote for the TC.[322]

These recent controversies help to explain the orientation and the content of the schema *De ordine morali*. Its governing theme was a rejection of the efforts to build moral theology on evangelical and spiritual grounds and to give it a more positive and specifically Christian orientation. The overriding preoccupation with the objective and universal character of the moral order not only excluded situation ethics but displayed a fear and suspicion of any effort to validate subjective dimensions of Christian life, even the effort to promote charity into a central role. The stress on magisterial sources, particularly those of Pius XII, represented an implicit rejection of the idea that Catholic moral theology much needed a renewed contact with the Scriptures or with the great theological tradition. The Council would be asked to confirm not only this magisterial teaching but the orientation, methods and emphases of classical modern moral theology.

4. *De castitate, matrimonio, familia, virginitate*[323]

The official *Quaestiones* asked the TC to present the Catholic doctrine on marriage in the light of the recent papal magisterium and to oppose the spreading errors of naturalism.[324] This vague proposal was clarified in the Holy Office's votum which called for a presentation of the origin, ends, properties, and use of marriage, identifying a number of particular questions, and asking for a confirmation of traditional doctrine on chastity, continence, and modesty, along with bans against divorce and the emancipation of women and children and a defence of parental rights over the education of their children.[325]

This full agenda was divided by Tromp and Hürth between the two sections of the outline on moral matters presented to the small prior subcommission in July 1960. The section on individual moral order included the objective sexual order, chastity and modesty, and opposed "libertinism, nudism, and hedonism," while the section on social moral order listed the natural and divine order of the family, the essentials of marriage, birth control and artificial fertilization, and the problem of

---

[322] Hürth, "Metaphysica, psychologica, theologica hodierna conscientiae christianae problemata," in *Problemi scelti di teologia contemporanea* (Rome 1954) 393-414.
[323] Burigana, "Progetto dogmatico," 194-95.
[324] *ADP*, II/I, 408-409.
[325] *ADA* III 15.

overpopulation. At the October 1960 plenary session, it was decided to establish a separate subcommission to deal with social morality, with the material on marriage divided between it and the subcommission on individual morality.

E. Lio was entrusted the task of writing the schema in the subcommission *De ordine morali individuali*. By 21 February 1961 he had finished a first draft of nine chapters *De ordine morali sexuali*, directed against the spread of errors even among Catholics, a recent issue of the journal *Esprit* being cited as an example.[326] The text vindicated the goodness of sexuality and the duty to subordinate it to the divine order; it opposed attempts to reduce all of human life to matters of sexuality, defended the equality of men and women while insisting on their distinct natural qualities and roles; it argued that sexuality can only be morally exercised within legitimate marriages and that God's dominion over man's body limits man's control over it and forbids such actions as sterilization, sex-changes, and artificial fertilization; it condemned various practices that violate the natural and Christian order; it defended the possibility of sexual continence in unmarried people and the superiority of virginity to the married state; finally it listed a host of contemporary assaults on chastity and urged civil authorities to be vigilant in the area.[327] In support of his arguments Lio adduced primarily the papal magisterium, especially that of Pius XII.

Lio then developed this draft into distinct chapters on chastity and on marriage. These were completed in late May and printed as the last two chapters of the schema *De ordine morali*. The chapter "De castitate et de pudicitia christiana," was almost completely rewritten but retained much of the argument of the first draft. The three and a half pages of text were supplemented by ten pages of notes, once again drawn mainly from Pius XII and now naming as examples of contemporary errors works by Oraison and Hesnard[328] and the special issue of *Esprit*. The chapter

---

[326] Among the errors named by Lio were: a denigration of sex or its mystical exaltation, pansexualism and sexuolatry, false feminism, the separation of sex from marriage, racism and eugenicism, psychologism, sexual libertinism, biological determinism, false personalism in sexual matters, sensualism, hedonism and public immorality. A whole issue of *Esprit* 28 (Nov 1960) 1665-1964, had just been devoted to "La Sexualité," containing the results of a survey of intellectuals and many articles of reflection.

[327] Lio's initial description of these assaults would be found too specific and detailed for the subcommission's taste: nudity, indiscriminate sex-education, modern dress and dances, shows and images, beauty-contests, songs, etc.; and he was persuaded to tone it down, "lest the Constitution itself be judged to be crude and 'realistic;'" *ADP* II/3 904.

[328] The notes refer to Hesnard, *Morale sans péché*, placed on the Index in January 1956 and to M. Oraison, *Vie chrétienne et le problème de la sexualité* (Paris 1951), also condemned by the Holy Office.

"De matrimonio christiano," had fifteen paragraphs set out in seven pages and supplemented by seventeen pages of notes. Marriage was presented as God's institution for the procreation of the human race, whose essential properties are unity and indissolubility, and whose "natural, objective, specific, principal, primary, single and indivisible end" is the procreation and education of children. The respective rights and duties of Church and State and of individuals are set out. The three traditional goods of marriage are expounded, the *bonum prolis* forbidding artificial contraception and abortion; the number of children is left to the judgment of the couple who should prefer moral and religious values over eugenic, economic or social values. The *bonum fidei* forbids all adultery and requires couples to obey the natural law. Married love is exalted but there is a warning that it not be thought so necessary that its absence is considered to invalidate a marriage. The *bonum sacramenti* forbids civil marriages and divorce and grounds the Church's concern about mixed marriages. The final paragraph sets out a long list of opposed errors.

Meanwhile, within the subcommission *De ordine sociali* R. Sigmund had been preparing his two chapters on marriage and the family.[329] The first, "De matrimonio ut fonte familiae," argued that marriage was the only legitimate source of a family and defended the rights of parents over the education of their children. Three paragraphs were devoted to the number of children, who should be received as a gift from God. A difference in tone from Lio's text is noticed, however, when this text argues that parents may reasonably take into account the health of the wife and their economic situation in deciding how many children to have. Artificial birth control, of course, remains forbidden. The text then goes on to treat the problem of overpopulation, denying that absolute and definitive overpopulation is a possibility, urging parents not to surrender to merely materialistic criteria, and urging that the growth of populations be influenced rather by social transformations.

The chapter "De familiae seu societatis domesticae origine naturali et divina" defended the priority of the family to civil society and its right to receive help from the state. The final paragraph described the structure of authority within the family, confirming the natural priority of the father, confirmed and elevated by the Christian sacrament.

Both subcommissions' texts were distributed to the members and consultors of the TC in the summer of 1961 in preparation for the September plenary session. Lio's text received over twenty pages of

---

[329] "Constitutionis *De ordine sociali* Capita Varia" (CT 9/61:24).

comments, of which those of Laurentin and Häring were particularly critical: the text was too juridical and negative, focused too much on procreation, ignored the importance of married love, and was too harsh in dealing with difficult questions and cases. The subcommission *De ordine morali*, which witnessed some sharp disagreements, accepted mostly minor changes. On 23 September a public dispute broke out in the plenary session over the ends of marriage, with Häring locked in debate with Tromp and Hürth, who insisted on the unique primacy of procreation.

Sigmund's text in the schema *De ordine sociali* was not debated at the September meeting, but ten pages of comments were received from the members and consultors. Because of duplications in the two texts, the subcommission *De ordine morali* voted on 22 September to integrate the two texts into a single schema *De matrimonio et familia*. Lio's chapter on chastity and modesty, on the other hand, remained in the text *De ordine morali* that was sent on to the CPC.

After the September meeting of the TC the discussion of the ends of marriage continued. Janssen sent in suggestions that were supported by his Louvain colleagues Philips and Delhaye, but only the proposal to reduce the number of adjectives exalting the procreation of children as the sole primary end was accepted. Häring was more closely involved, invited by Tromp to take part in a small subcommission to revise the text. The new text continued to assert that procreation was the only primary end, but it also identified the other purposes of marriage as "objective" and said that although secondary, they were not for that reason to be spurned or depreciated. The result of this labor was the schema *De matrimonio et familia christiana* that was ready by the end of January 1962 and was discussed at the last plenary session of the TC in March.[330] The comments submitted and the discussions at the plenary session revealed that differences still remained, particularly on the ends of marriage, on authority within the family, and on overpopulation.[331]

[330] "Constitutio de matrimonio et familia christiana" (CT 20/61:14; 29 Jan 1962): I. De ordine divino obiectivo quoad matrimonium christianum; II. De iuribus, obligationibus et virtutibus in matrimonio christiano; III. De ordine divino quoad familiam christianam; IV. De peculiaribus iuribus et obligationibus.

[331] On the last question a debate took place on whether absolute overpopulation was a real possibility, Tromp and others arguing that it was not because this would invalidate the divine command to "increase and multiply." Bishop Peruzzo, recently appointed to the CT, was scandalized by some of the comments and, siding with Tromp, argued that if ever there were too many people, some would die, and so there could never be too many; Y. Congar, *Mon Journal du Concile*, 8 Mar 1962.

By the time of this plenary session, it was already known that the CPC had recommended that the text on chastity be taken from the text *De ordine morali* and included with the material in the text *De matrimonio et familia*, which should now also include an expanded section on virginity. The text that resulted, completed on 24 March, was the schema *De castitate, virginitate, matrimonio, familia*, which was printed and sent to the CPC.[332]

As with the schema *De ordine morali christiano*, this schema is best understood by reviewing the errors it was intended to oppose, for this preoccupation so dominated the discussion as to intrude upon almost every effort at a positive statement. In general it may be said to be opposed, first, to an over-exaltation of sexuality, not only by Freudian theory but also by some Catholics. A single brief paragraph is devoted to the origin and nature of sex. While declaring that the distinction of sexes comes from God and is "very good," the schema warns against thinking that it is a dimension of the image of God in man. The general orientation of spirit is well illustrated in a single sentence: "Here on earth, although human sex also has other qualities, it is primarily ordered towards marriage, as Scripture teaches..., until the time is fulfilled when 'at the resurrection they will neither marry nor be given in marriage.'"[333] The "other qualities" of sexuality are nowhere elaborated, and the primary orientation towards marriage is asserted, only to have even that relativized by the reference to the next age, when marriage will be no more. The next paragraph goes on to issue a set of prohibitions of actions that violate the lordship of God, and not of man, over the human body.

The chapter on chastity and virginity begins with a vigorous defence of their possibility, even in the young. Two long paragraphs urge the defense and care of chastity, condemn the general moral laxity in this area, and reject seven errors in the matter. The notes are overwhelmingly to texts of Pius XII, whose teaching appears as the only wall of defence against a horde of enemies, particularly the modern social and psychological sciences.

The primary concern of the chapter on marriage is the defence of its divinely established and objective finality, "independently, that is, of the intentions of the parties." This primary end is exclusively the procreation and education of children, which does not depend on other ends and should not be confused with them nor considered merely equal to them. A late change in the text admitted that other ends, like mutual aid and the relief of concupiscence, are also objective, but secondary.

[332] *ADP* II/3 893-986; see Indelicato, *Difendere la dottrina*, 235-41.
[333] *ADP* II/3 894.

The TC's text addressed attempts over the previous three decades to broaden and deepen the theology of marriage. Initiated by a layman, D. von Hildebrand,[334] and an object of controversy when adopted by priest-theologians,[335] this effort sought to give greater role to the personalist and interpersonal meanings of marriage in order to counter-balance the nearly exclusive insistence on procreation as the primary end of marriage. The distinction between the meaning of marriage as a communion of life and its purposes, both personal and procreational, was defended both on philosophical and theological grounds and by an appeal to a passage in Pius XI's *Casti connubii*, which stated that if marriage is not taken in its stricter sense as an institution for the procreation of children but in a broader sense as a total communion of life, then "this mutual inner moulding of husband and wife, this determined effort to perfect each other, can in a very real sense, as the Roman Catechism teaches, be said to be the chief reason and purpose of marriage."[336] The spread of these theories led the Holy Office to intervene with a decree, 1 April 1944, rejecting the views of those "who either deny that the primary purpose of marriage is the generation and education of children or teach that the secondary purposes are not essentially subordinate to the primary purpose but are equally primary and independent."[337] This same teaching was reiterated several times by Pius XII in 1951.

The authors of the TC's text on marriage were determined to defend this position not only against earlier authors,[338] but also against members of the TC itself. Häring and others did not deny that procreation was a primary purpose of marriage, but they did not wish marital love and communion to be described as a secondary and subordinate end. Häring records that at a meeting of the subcommission in which he made this case, Hürth replied that it contradicted Church teaching.[339] Hürth's

[334] D. von Hildebrand, *Die Ehe* (München 1929).

[335] H. Doms, *The Meaning of Marriage*, trans. G. Sayer (New York 1939); B. Krempel, *Die Zweckfrage der Ehe in neuer Beleuchtung* (Zürich/Köln 1941); for bibliography, see J.C. Ford and G. Kelly, "Catholic Personalists and the Ends of Marriage," in *Contemporary Moral Theology, II: Marriage Questions* (Westminster, MD, 1964) 16-35.

[336] *AAS* 22 (1930) 548.

[337] *AAS* 36 (1944) 103.

[338] Notes referred to Doms' book and to a more recent work by E. Michel, *Ehe: Eine Anthropologie der Geschlechts-gemeinschaft* (Stuttgart 1950), which had been placed on the Index in 1952.

[339] As the two men were leaving the Holy Office later, Hürth told Häring: "I hope you can understand my sharp remarks. I once had to spend a whole day trying to talk Pius XI, who wanted a similar description, out of the idea that you proposed again today." Häring, "25 Jahre katholische Sexualethik," *Studia Moralia* 20 (1982) 54-55. The same story is recounted in B. Häring, *Fede storia morale* (Rome 1989) 56-57. It may be that on this issue it was Vermeersch and not Hürth who had the greater influence on *Casti connubii*; see Ford and Kelly, *Contemporary Moral Theology*, II, 140.

concern is visible in a footnote that appears in the TC's text on the ends of marriage. After citing two texts of Pius XII in favor of the position taken in the schema, the note adds a reference to the disputed passage in *Casti connubii*, to which, in surely the only case of its kind in all the texts of the TC, a warning is appended: "although some people, on the basis of the statement in the Roman Catechism that is cited there, are unduly exalting conjugal love as the primary purpose of marriage."[340]

This dispute manifests once again that the primary concern of the TC's subcommissions on moral issues was the defence of an objective moral order against what they saw as the relativizing and debilitating effects of subjectivism. At every point where an effort was made to introduce the legitimate dimensions of subjectivity — in the discussion of conscience, of charity, of freedom, of sexuality, of married love — warning signs had to be posted. Morality had to remain a matter of objectively grounded prohibitions and commandments.

5. *De Beata Virgine Maria*[341]

The official *Quaestiones* did not include a treatment of the Blessed Virgin Mary among the topics assigned to the TC.[342] The Holy Office's *votum*, however, had mentioned several topics under the heading "De Maria, Matre Christi Capitis et Ecclesiae": her central role in the work of redemption, her subjective and objective cooperation, the defence of the "*cultus hyperduliae*" shown her (this against minimalists and people who think it an impediment to Christian unity), her *virginitas in partu*, and the question of her bodily death.[343] Tromp's original outline of the schema *De deposito*, ended with the simple phrase "Beata Maria Virgine."[344] But

[340] *ADP* II/3 918.

[341] See C. Balic, "La doctrine sur la bienheureuse Vierge Marie Mère de l'Eglise, et la Constitution 'Lumen gentium' du Concile Vatican II," *Divinitas* 9 (1965) 464-82; G.M. Besutti, "Lo schema mariano al Concilio Vaticano II: Documentazione e note di cronaca," *Marianum* 28 (1966) 1-203.

[342] The "Sintesi finale," 4, had noted that 280 bishops had asked for a definition of the universal mediation of Mary and 45 a definition of her spiritual maternity, while 61 bishops questioned the opportunity of such definitions on the grounds that they are not needed for the good of the Church and would cause problems for the return of the separated brethren. The Holy Office's own summary of the episcopal vota, said that 350 bishops had mentioned the Virgin's privileges, especially her mediation, while 60 had thought a definition inopportune "because of the separated."

[343] *ADA* III 6-7.

[344] At the meeting of the *praevia subcommissio*, 21 July 1960, Tromp said that "against recent errors it must above all be established that the Blessed Virgin Mary belongs to the center and not to the periphery of the Church." There is some evidence that Tromp was not in favor of a major statement on the Virgin.

in Ciappi's elaboration of this outline into the *Schema compendiosum De deposito*, the topic had been greatly filled out: "The Blessed Virgin Mary. Not at the periphery but at the heart of Christianity: as the Mother of the Word Incarnate. Partner of Christ the Savior, Most holy Mother of all the members of Christ, Universal Mediatrix. Virgin before giving birth, while givng birth, after giving birth." At the first plenary session of the TC, 27 October 1960, the choice of these themes was amply illustrated by statistical references to the antepreparatory *vota*.[345] A meeting between Tromp and the secretaries of the TC's subcommissions, 21 December, moved the section on the Blessed Virgin to the schema *De Ecclesia*.

The work of preparing the text was assigned to C. Balic. By the end of April 1961, he had prepared a first draft. A second draft was ready by early July 1961, which, slightly revised, was then included as the fifth chapter, "De Maria Matre Iesu et Matre Ecclesiae," of the "Capita varia" *De Ecclesia* sent out to the TC members for discussion at their November meeting. In an introductory note, Balic explained that there were no statements in his text that could not be found in papal documents,[346] that it was aimed at certain errors with regard to *virginitas in partu*, Mary's knowledge of the divinity of her Son at the time of the Annunciation, and mistakes made by both maximalists and minimalists,[347] that it had consciously avoided language that would cause difficulties to dissidents, restricted itself to the actual economy of salvation, explained how Mary's mediation did not compromise Christ's unique role, and urged everyone to pray to Mary as the "Promoter of Christian union."[348]

Sixteen pages of comments had been received and recorded by the September plenary session. Several people wondered why the text was in the schema *De Ecclesia*, since it seemed more like an independent text, without reference to the rest of the document. Particular comments were very varied, with some finding the text excessive in its claims, others wishing to strengthen it. The text does not seem to have been discussed at the plenary session, however, and Balic had to prepare another draft on the basis of the written comments.[349] If anything, this

[345] Ciappi, "Relatio de schemate tertio: De deposito fidei custodiendo," 13-15.

[346] In fact, to a three and a half-page text, Balic appended fourteen and a half pages of notes, most of them drawn from papal sources.

[347] In a footnote Balic spoke "of a minimizing tendency widespread among some Catholic men, especially those who maintain the so-called 'ecclesiological' method," that is, an approach to Mary that relates her to the Church.

[348] "De Ecclesia capita varia" (CT 5/61:86), 26-27.

[349] "De Maria, Matre Corporis Christi Mystici" (CT 19/61:20; 20 nov 1961). The title appears to have been changed because of opposition, particularly from Laurentin, against the title "Mater Ecclesiae."

text magnified the privileges of Mary even more and certainly maintained Balic's methodological and substantive options.[350]

Slightly revised, this text was sent out to the members for discussion at the final plenary meeting in March.[351] Balic's prefatory notes now raised another issue, however, whether the discussion of Our Lady should be part of the schema De Ecclesia or a separate text. "The latter would be better," Balic added, "and in that case perhaps the schema could be expanded." At a meeting of the subcommission De Ecclesia, Balic's proposal was accepted, and it was then approved at the plenary session. But at the plenary meeting, Tromp raised objections with regard to the statements about the mediation of Mary. A special subcommission was appointed to resolve the issue. The discussion continued after the meeting, and a definitive text, which met Tromp's concerns, was completed in April; after a mysterious last-minute problem, which required the intervention of the Pope,[352] it was approved for consideration by the CPC.

The discussion at the CPC was generally favorable,[353] the chief question raised by some of the members being the assertion of the mediation of Mary.[354] The subcommission on amendments sent the TC the proposed changes, most of which the TC's committee accepted. But on the major issue of the mediation of the Blessed Virgin, it refused to budge, giving as two of its reasons that to be silent on the issue would cause scandal to many of the faithful who would see it "as coming from an inferiority complex towards Protestants" and that "to reserve the title of Mediator to Christ alone would be an implicit admission that the Church has erred for centuries in matters of faith."[355]

[350] One of Balic's main concerns was to ensure that the text spoke of Mary's part in the *objective* redemption wrought by Christ; if this was not secured, he said, "there will always be those very subtle people who will find their own views in the statements offered and will reduce them to a minimum;" Balic to Hürth, November 1961.

[351] "De Maria, Matre Capitis et Matre Corporis Mystici Christi Membrorum" (CT 19/61:50; 20 ian 1962).

[352] Tromp speaks vaguely of "some difficulties about how to proceed," settled by the Pope on 27 April; "Ultima acta Pontificiae Commissionis Theologicae: Post clausum Consessum Plenarium (10 Mart. 1962) usque ad diem 20 Julii 1962," 3. Balic, "La doctrine..." 467, suggests that the problem lay in the state of the text, which was rather repetitive. "At the last minute someone suggested that the schema not be printed. At the direct intervention of John XXIII, however, it was printed." One is tempted to identify this "someone" with Tromp, who criticized the excessive length and notes of Balic's texts.

[353] ADP II/4 746-84.

[354] The chief opponents were Liénart, Montini, Godfrey, Ritter, Jullien, and Alter, several of whom mentioned the ecumenical difficulties the declaration could cause. Bea was not among them: "We should not be afraid of offending the Protestants; today many of them sincerely venerate the Blessed Virgin;" ADP II/4 781.

[355] De emendatione schematis Constitutionis De Ecclesia (Pars II) et de emendatione schematis Constitutionis De Beata Maria Virgine (TPV 1962) 27.

There is no doubt that the schema *De Beata Maria Virgine*, even in its section on her mediatorial role, met the expectations and desires of a very large number of the bishops, as expressed in their antepreparatory *vota*. A substantial minority, however, had expressed the desire that the Council not promulgate any new Marian doctrines, particularly because of the ecumenical implications. The efforts made to present Mary as the "Promoter of Christian union" were not likely to lessen these difficulties, particularly if, as Congar noted, the text was placed in the context of recent developments in Catholic Marian theology:

> One has to consider also the general situation of Mariology in important parts of the Catholic Church, if not everywhere. It is a situation of over-bidding. Very powerful groups are expressed interested in "raising" it still higher and in such a way that tomorrow's bid will only be a step toward higher bids the day after tomorrow. I am afraid that a conciliar text, with its high authority, even if it is not "*de fide*," will serve as a trampoline for the acrobats of an exaggerating and maximizing Mariology, even if the text itself is not maximizing (and it isn't, as a whole), and that these acrobats will use various expressions in the text to exaggerate it and push it further.[356]

6. *De ordine sociali and De communitate gentium*[357]

The last of the topics assigned to the TC in the official "*Quaestiones*" was stated very simply: "A concise exposition of Catholic social doctrine should be issued."[358] The early drafts of Tromp and Hürth sketched some topics that might be studied in order to meet this demand. At the first plenary session in October, it was decided to assign the work to a separate subcommission *De ordine sociali*. No members were assigned to this body, however, apparently on the assumption that its work would have to await the completion of the encyclical known to be in preparation. But on 17 December the Pope let it be known that he wished the TC's subcommission to begin working.[359]

The subcommission met for the first time at the end of February 1961, when it distributed its material: Gundlach and Pavan would deal with the foundations, Sigmond with marriage and the family, Jarlot and

---

[356] "Remarques sur le Schéma 'De B. Maria Virgine,'" prepared by Congar for Msgr. Weber (A-Congar).

[357] See Burigana, "Progetto dogmatico," 191-94.

[358] *ADP* II/1 409. This appears to reflect the "Sintesi finale" 4, which reports the desire of bishops for a systematic and organic presentation of the Church's social teaching: "People are hoping for the elaboration of a 'Summa Socialis.'"

[359] The Pope himself appointed P. Pavan and A. Ferrari Toniolo, and these were soon joined by G. Gundlach, R. Sigmond and G. Jarlot.

Ferrari Toniolo with economic matters, and Pavan and Gundlach with questions of politics, it being understood, however, that the question of Church and State would be dealt with in the subcommission *De Ecclesia.*[360]

Pavan and Jarlot, who had asssisted in the preparation of Pope John's encyclical, *Mater et magistra*, found themselves opposed both by Tromp and by Gundlach, who had been the chief writer of Pius XII's social documents but who had been excluded from an effective role in the preparation of the recent Encyclical.[361] Jarlot appears to have been urged by Tromp to stress the right to private property over the communal origin and source of created goods.

By the summer of 1961, a first draft of a text was ready to be sent out for discussion by the whole TC.[362] Besides Sigmond's two chapters on marriage and family, which were soon to be removed from the subcommission's competency, there were only two brief chapters by Pavan, on the basis of the social order and the principles of social life, and by Jarlot, on private property. This text was never discussed at the September meeting, however, although eleven pages of comments had been assembled. The most common complaint was that the text was more philosophical than theological in character; but Laurentin submitted a sharp critique of its defense of private property, which he thought neglected major elements of the tradition.

The first drafts of the material on other economic questions began to be circulated only late in 1961. But no texts *De ordine sociali* were discussed at the final plenary session of the TC in March 1962. Once again, however, the Pope made it known that he wished the work to be completed, apparently surprising Tromp by the mandate that a text be prepared also on the international social order to meet the requests of bishops who had asked that the Council address such issues as peace and the atomic bomb.

[360] Tromp Diary, 28 Feb 1961.
[361] In a comment on the first draft of a text *De ordine sociali*, Gundlach made a revealing remark: "Because of its mainly pastoral character, the Encyclical *Mater et magistra* does not preclude a dogmatic constitution presenting the Church's social doctrine as established by the Roman Pontiffs from Leo XIII on. Indeed in some matters it seems to need to be complemented by a doctrinal presentation, based upon immutable principles;" "Animadversiones membrorum et consultorum in Constitutionem De ordine sociali" (CT 9/61:25; 9 sept 1961), "Addendum."
[362] "Constitutionis De ordine sociali Capita Varia" (CT 9/61:24).

The subcommission completed its first text, *De ordine sociali*, at a special meeting in June. It had seven chapters: on foundations and principles, on private property, on work, on just salaries, on agriculture, on social peace, and on government and economy. The work of preparing a text on the international order fell to Sigmond and Cereceda, who met with Ottaviani and Tromp on 19 May to outline a text and who less than three weeks later had produced a text that was approved on 8 June by Ottaviani. The text *De communitate gentium* had five chapters: on the moral basis of international community, on its structure and authority, on the rights and duties of states in the international community, on impediments to its establishment and functioning, and on the defense of the international order and peace. These texts were sent to Felici in June.[363]

By this time, however, the CPC had completed its work, so that the texts on social questions were never discussed there. Felici appears to have sent them out to the members of the CPC, however, and in late September Tromp found himself having to work with a small committee in response to observations on the texts received from thirteen Cardinals. The TC committee sent its responses to Felici on 10 October, the day before the Council opened.[364] The revisions of the texts that resulted were mostly minor ones, so that they retained their primary methodological and substantive reference to the natural law and classic Catholic social teaching.[365]

It is clear from this brief history that the leaders of the TC were not as convinced of the importance of these texts as was the Pope himself. The appointment of members to the subcommission was delayed; it began its work much later than the other subcommissions; its drafts were never publicly discussed at any of the plenary sessions; and its final texts had to be rushed through at the very end of the preparatory period without being referred to or approved by the whole TC. This history might be taken to be emblematic of the indifference of the TC to the larger issues that were so much a part of the horizon within which the Pope wished the Council to meet.

---

[363] For all this information, see Tromp "Ultima acta Pont. Comm. Theologicae," 6-7.

[364] See Tromp, "Relatio Secretarii Commissionis Conciliaris 'de doctrina fidei et morum'" (15/62:19; 26 dec 1962), 1-2.

[365] The two texts were eventually printed in *Schemata Constitutionum et Decretorum ex quibus argumenta in Concilio disceptanda seligentur*, Series tertia (TPV 1962) 5-66.

C. The Secretariat for Promoting Christian Unity[366]

1. Membership

The personnel of the SCU were drawn from a wide variety of geographical areas, including in particular regions where ecumenical relations were especially important (North America, England, Holland, Germany, and Switzerland), and they represented all the major Catholic ecumenical organizations. The Catholic Conference for Ecumenical Questions supplied not only J. Willebrands, appointed to serve as the secretary of the SCU, but several others: J. Höfer, C.-J. Dumont, J. Hamer, F. Thijssen, F. Davis, and C. Boyer, the last of these being also the head of the closest thing to a Vatican ecumenical office, "Unitas". L. Jaeger, founder of the J.A. Möhler Institute of Paderborn, H. Volk, E. Stakemeier, F. Charrière, and J. Feiner represented the German and Swiss areas. North America was represented by five men: G. Weigel, G. Tavard, G. Baum, J. Cunningham, and E. Hanahoe. P. Dumont represented the ecumenical monastery of Chevetogne.

Of curial representation, the most important figures were C. Boyer and M. Maccarrone, both associated with the Congregation for Seminaries and Universities. Conspicuously absent from the SCU was any representative of the Holy Office, although Maccarone, Boyer and Hanahoe, a close friend of Fenton, tended to defend the Roman idea that the purpose of ecumenical conversations was the return of the erring brethren to the one true Church.

2. Competency and Topics

Willebrands claims that it was Pope John's original intention to include relations with the Orthodox Churches in the program of the SCU; but when Bea demurred because of his lack of familiarity with those questions, the Pope acceded, assigning relations with the Orthodox to the OR, in this way also assuring that the corresponding congregation would have its interests represented in the preparation of the Council.[367]

---

[366] See H. Bacht, "Kardinal Bea, Wegbereiter der Einheit," Cath(M) 35 (1981) 173-88; T. F. Stransky, "The Foundation of the Secretariat for Promoting Christian Unity," in Vatican II Revisited by Those Who Were There, ed. A. Stacpoole (Minneapolis 1986) 62-87; S. Schmidt, "Giovanni XXIII e il Segretariato per l'unione dei cristiani," CrSt 8 (1987) 95-117, M. Velati, "La proposta ecumenica del segretariato per l'unità dei cristiani," in Verso il Concilio, 273-350.

[367] J. Willebrands, "Il cardinale Agostino Bea: il suo contributo al movimento ecumenico, alla libertà religiosa e all'instaurazione di nuove relazioni con il popolo ebraico," in Atti del Simposio Card. Agostino Bea (Roma, 16-19 dicembre 1981) (Roma 1983) 6; see S. Schmidt, Augustin Bea: The Cardinal of Unity (New Rochelle, NY 1992) 344.

As events would show, however, this in itself understandable differentiation of ecumenical tasks was not accompanied by sufficient guarantees
of an equally necessary coordination and collaboration between the two
bodies. The distribution of members did not help matters. Only two
members of the SCU, Ch. Dumont and P. Dumont, had much experience
of conversations with the Orthodox, but their assignment to the SCU
deprived the OR of an expertise and an enthusiasm from which that
commission would have greatly benefitted.

In *Superno Dei nutu*, the SCU's purpose was described as that of
helping other Christians to follow the work of the Council and so to find
more easily the path to the unity for which Christ prayed.[368] This vague
description was not clarified in the *"Quaestiones,"* which did not
include any proposals for the new organism. This imprecision enabled
some Roman figures, among them Tromp, to maintain that the Secretariat was only "an information-office."[369]

Bea and the members of the SCU had grander ideas, however. In the
Cardinal's proposal for the establishment of the SCU, he had already
included among its conciliar roles the study of the hopes and fears others
were expressing about the Council and the preparation of appropriate
responses.[370] The Catholic Conference for Ecumenical Questions had
also presented a lengthy *tour d'horizon* of the ecumenical situation, its
prospects and its difficulties, and had identified areas of particular
concern and appropriate ways in which the Council might respond to
them. From the men who would soon be appointed members and
consultors of the SCU, Bea also received recommendations that its
activities not be limited to providing information to non-Catholics but
include also bringing their views to the attention of the PrC.[371]

It is not known whether the statutes of the SCU, prepared by Bea himself and still unpublished today, contained a broader agenda than that
outlined publicly by the Pope. But by July the SCU had prepared a first
draft of a program of work that included the study of doctrinal, liturgical, and spiritual questions as well as concrete actions to be taken to
promote Christian unity.[372] In mid-September Bea and Willebrands took

---

[368] *ADA* I 95.

[369] Schmidt, *Augustin Bea*, 343n.

[370] See Schmidt, *Augustin Bea*, 325-26.

[371] See, for example, C.-J. Dumont, "Le 'motu proprio' du 5 juin 1960," *Vers l'unité
chrétienne* (mai-juin 1960) 25, and Dumont's "Note sur le 'Conseil' ou 'Secrétariat' pour
les rapports avec les non-catholiques institué par le Motu Proprio du 5 juin 1960," sent to
Bea on 8 July 1960; Dumont Papers.

[372] Schmidt, *Augustin Bea*, 344-45, who suggests that the program relied heavily on
the report submitted by the Catholic Conference for Ecumenical Questions.

advantage of the meeting of the Catholic Conference for Ecumenical Questions at Gazzada to discuss problems and procedures with several of the members and consultors. At the beginning of October a program of work was sent out to the members and consultors for comments. Many of the responses listed theological and practical questions the SCU should address as it prepared, if not schemata, then *vota* that would keep the PrC informed about the ecumenical dimensions of their work.

At the first plenary session of the SCU, November 1960, a program of work was distributed and discussed. It outlined six major topics: 1) the purpose and role of the Secretariat; 2) the principles and contemporary tasks of Catholic ecumenism; 3) questions of ecclesiology; 4) theological questions: the Word of God, liturgical applications, religious freedom, mixed marriages; 5) practical questions: observers at the Council, prayers for unity, the formula of abjuration, Protestant missions in Catholic countries; 6) the Jewish question: relation between the two Testaments, liturgical texts, etc.[373]

Bea's opening address began with the purposes of the SCU. If the first of these was that of keeping the separated brethren informed about the Council, another purpose followed from the letter in which the Pope had appointed Bea president of the SCU and which, Bea argued, equated the new body to the PrC and thus authorized it also to study and investigate materials for the Council. "The Secretariat, then, is not merely an 'information-office,' but can also prepare materials regarding Christian unity and which therefore might be proposed to the Council."[374]

As for areas of competence, Bea told the SCU that, in response to many requests, Pope John had also assigned questions concerning the Jews to the SCU.[375] He also noted that many of the questions the SCU would discuss were concerns also of other PrC, particularly the TC, the BG, and the LI. The SCU would discuss the issues and then transmit its proposals to these bodies for them to consider, perhaps also by means of mixed commissions.[376]

---

[373] A copy of the program is found in the A-Stransky.

[374] Bea, "Sermo introductorius Em.mi Cardinalis Praesidis" (14 November 1960) 2 (A-Stransky). Schmidt, Willebrands, and Carbone all agree that this judgment of Bea must have been authorized by Pope John; see Schmidt, *Augustin Bea*, 345-46; Willebrands, "Il Cardinal Agostino Bea," 7; Carbone, "Gli schemi preparatori," 84.

[375] For the background of this decision, see Schmidt, *Augustin Bea*, 332-38; J.M. Oesterreicher, "Declaration on the Relationship of the Church to Non-Christian Religions: Introduction and Commentary," in *Commentary on the Documents of Vatican II* (New York 1969) III 1-17.

[376] Bea, "Sermo introductorius," 3. In the course of the discussion that followed his speech, Bea said that he had already been in contact with Ottaviani and Tromp about cooperation with the TC and that other mixed commissions would have to be considered.

At this early point, then, it does not seem that the SCU intended to prepare schemata of its own to be proposed to the Council, but rather to prepare texts that would ensure that ecumenical concerns were taken into consideration by the other PrC. It was only when it became apparent that ecumenical sensitivity would not mark the work of the other PrC, particularly the TC, that the Secretariat, with the apparent encouragement of the Pope, began to prepare texts for presentation to the CPC and, eventually, to the Council itself.[377]

As a result of the ensuing discussion it was decided to distribute the work among ten subcommissions which would study: 1. The relation of baptized non-Catholics to the Church (membership); 2. The Church's hierarchical structure; 3. The conversion of individuals and of communities; the restoration of the diaconate; 4. The priesthood of all believers and the condition of lay people in the Church; religious liberty and toleration. 5. The "Word of God" in the Church; 6. Liturgical questions: the vernacular; communion under both kinds; 7. Mixed marriages; 8. Octave of Prayers for Christian Unity: a new formula; 9. The central ecumenical problem according to today's orientation of the World Council at Geneva and especially according to that Council's concept of unity; 10. Questions concerning the Jews.[378]

3. *Method*

Within the SCU fifteen subcommissions were eventually established,[379] composed of four or five men and headed by a bishop who served as *relator*. Within each subcommission a text was prepared by the bishop or by a theologian and then sent to the other members for comments. These subcommissions do not seem to have met often, instead communicating mostly by letter. Their texts were then discussed, revised and approved at plenary sessions.

The method the subcommissions generally followed was the one the SCU recommended to the Council itself in an epilogue to its document,

---

[377] The first indication of this possibility appears to be the remarks that Bea made in an interview, 10 March 1961, when he spoke of the *vota* being prepared by the UC, "which then will be discussed, *either directly by the Central Commission* or by the other commissions interested in the same questions;" see *DC* 58 (2 April 1961) 448 (my emphasis).

[378] Stransky, "The Foundation of the SPCU," 82.

[379] This number was reached by the differentiation of subcommissions for the consideration of the questions of religious freedom and of Scripture and Tradition and by the addition of subcommissions to discuss the permanence of the Secretariat, the preparation of an ecumenical directory, and the invitation of non-Catholics to the Council.

De structura hierarchica Ecclesiae. Evoking a Pauline phrase frequently on the lips of Pope John, it inquired "How at the Council can the truth be done in charity?" It found its model in the procedures of the Council of Trent, at which Catholic scholars first gathered accurate information about the views of the Reformers, examined these in the light of Scripture and tradition to discern what was true and false in them, and finally offered a presentation of Catholic doctrine that would respond to the questions raised by the separated brethren. This method the SCU recommended to the Fathers of Vatican II:

> In this way they did not present the truth in the abstract or apart from the questions of the day, but from the beginning of their discussions they first studied the questions and views of the Reformers so that they could respond to them from the fullness of the deposit of Catholic faith by stating the true Catholic and apostolic faith. Thus from the beginning they joined the presentation of the truth with that charity which wishes to secure the salvation of the separated brethren. In the same way the Fathers of the Second Vatican Council ought to "do the truth with charity," so that our separated brethren may experience a strong and gentle invitation to seek that unity which our Lord Jesus Christ prayed for from his heavenly Father.[380]

The SCU set out to prepare the Council for this kind of ecumenical conversation. Its subcommissions studied their particular topics in the light of Protestant questions and criticisms and outlined proposals intended to help the other PrC to address the topics in a way that not only would not further alienate Protestants but would help them to understand the Catholic position. These *vota* of the SCU, then, represented an introduction to ecumenical conversation necessary for the majority of the members of the PrC, and not just the Romans, who had had very little experience of such encounters before.

4. *The Texts of the SCU*

The principal means by which the SCU sought to have an effect upon the preparatory work was the communication to other PrC of various texts that outlined the ecumenical implications of themes being considered.[381] In this section we will review several of these texts, leaving to the next section a consideration of the major points at which it found itself in direct confrontation with the orientations of the TC.

---

[380] SCU, "De structura hierarchica Ecclesiae" (May 1961) 47 (A-Stransky).

[381] The special question of the role of the SCU in preparing for the invitation to non-Catholic observers is also handled separately later.

4.1. The subcommission on the laity produced a text *De sacerdotio fidelium*, a first draft of which was ready in February 1961 and the final text of which was approved in April of that year.[382] It was intended to respond to the Protestant criticism that the Catholic Church regarded the laity simply as passive subjects and neglected the doctrine of the common priesthood. The text studied the NT doctrine of the priesthood of the faithful and then offered eighteen *vota* about how this doctrine should be taught, particularly by showing that it is an authentic and not merely metaphorical priesthood, one that is complementary to the ordained priesthood, and to be exercised by every Christian in the everyday course of his life. In May 1961 this text was sent to the TC and to the AL, upon whose texts, however, it does not appear to have had great influence. The AL's brief discussion of the universal priesthood of the faithful gives priority to their participation in worship, which was not the first emphasis of the SCU's text.[383] The TC's chapter *De laicis* agreed with the SCU in not calling the common priesthood metaphorical, but it made use of Pius XII's distinction between the two priesthoods in order to stress the superiority of the ministerial priesthood.[384]

4.2. The subcommission on liturgical questions offered a response to Protestant criticisms of the reduced role of Scripture in Catholic worship and of the passive role of the laity. This text included the statement that Latin should not be considered a sign of unity; it also asked the bishops to recognize the centrality of the eucharist over private devotions, to approve the restoration of communion under both kinds, concelebration, and *communicatio in sacris*, and to halt the practice of rebaptizing Christian converts to Catholicism. In May this text was sent to the LI, with which this subcommission had already been collaborating.[385]

4.3. The subcommission *De matrimoniis mixtis* at first proposed a text that would have asked for major changes in the Church's legislation with regard to marriages of Catholics to non-Catholic Christians: the restoration of the more lenient pre-Code attitude so that mixed marriages

---

[382] See Velati, "La proposta ecumenica," 293-96.

[383] See *ADP* II/4 473; Turbanti, "I laici nella chiesa e nel mondo," 236-37.

[384] *ADP* II/3 1087-88, 1091-92. On 1 Dec 1962, Stransky sent a copy of the SCU's text to Bishop Primeau, pointing out that the SCU had hoped the TC might consider adopting its outline and begin with the common duties of all the faithful: "the suggestion was ignored, and we have a schema that stresses 'the community of the faithful' less than did Mystici Corporis" (A-Primeau).

[385] See Velati, "La proposta ecumenica," 296-300.

without proper form would not be considered invalid, the removal of the requirement that the Catholic party seek the conversion of the non-Catholic party, and the permission of some kind of religious ceremony. Opposition to these proposals was strong, however, both in the subcommission and in the plenary sessions, with Heenan and De Smedt raising the strongest objections, so that the text was softened before it was approved in November 1961 and sent on to the SA.[386] The latter's text on the subject recommended certain changes in the Code for the sake of ecumenical sensitivity, but not enough for Bea, who at the CPC urged the SCU's position.[387]

4.4. Another subcommission in which major disagreements appeared was the one appointed to reconsider a new orientation and formula for the Octave of Prayers for Christian Unity. E. Hanahoe, an American member of the community of Paul Wattson, the founder of the Octave, resisted efforts to alter its orientation away from prayers for the return of other Christians to the Catholic Church.[388] When the effort stalled, the subcommission was reoriented so that it would prepare a text simply on the general question of prayer for Christian unity. Here too objections were posed, particularly by Hanahoe and Boyer, whose model remained that of the "return" of the separated brethren and who found the proposed text in conflict with the chapter *De oecumenismo* that was being prepared in the TC's schema *De Ecclesia*. A text was eventually completed and approved in April 1962. This was sent directly to the CPC, where it was discussed in June.[389]

4.5. In the subcommission *De conversionibus individualibus et de conversione communitatum*, similar disagreements appeared. The main problem was the relationship between ecumenism and conversion, with Hanahoe tending to reduce the first to a search for the second. An effort was undertaken to elaborate a theology of ecumenism that would be sent to the TC, but this was abandoned and work began instead on a more pastoral text that could be submitted directly to the CPC at its last meeting. This text, *De oecumenismo catholico*, was subtitled a "pastoral decree" in order to appear as a complement to the dogmatic approach

[386] See Velati, "La proposta ecumenica," 309-14.

[387] *ADP* II/3 1191-94; see above.

[388] See *One Fold: Essays and documents to commemorate the Golden Jubilee of the Chair of Unity Octave 1908-1958*, ed. E.F. Hanahoe and T.F. Cranny (Garrison, NY 1959).

[389] *ADP* II/4 813-16, 822-34.

followed in the TC's chapter on the subject in its schema *De Ecclesia* and perhaps also to avoid appearing to infringe upon the TC's competency. But besides giving practical guidance on how to engage in ecumenical activity, the SCU's text also contained important doctrinal sections on the unity and uniqueness of the Church, on the salvific value of elements of the Church found outside the Catholic Church, and on ecumenism as an exercise of the Church's catholicity.

These views contrasted rather markedly with the positions adopted in the TC's *De Ecclesia*, whose chapter on ecumenism, while acknowledging the existence of links between the Catholic Church and other Christian individuals and communities, emphasized their return as the goal of ecumenical activity, stressed the legitimacy of working for individual conversions, and devoted its longest section to a set of restrictive norms on *communicatio in sacris*. The two texts were brought together to the CPC in June 1962, where the majority of members urged that they be joined together, along with the text *De unitate Ecclesiae* of the OR, into a single schema.[390] This was not attempted before the Council opened, however, and the SCU's text was the only one of the three that was not printed for submission to the Council.[391]

4.6. Finally, a subcommission of the SCU took up the question of the Church's relationship with the Jewish people.[392] In the elaboration of the text the chief roles were played by G. Baum and J. Oesterreicher, both converts from Judaism. The latter prepared a rather lengthy draft which repeated themes contained in an earlier text by Baum but placed them in a biblical and theological context and ended with several concrete proposals urging the Council to acknowledge the Church's roots in Judaism, to oppose the idea that the Jewish people are the object of a divine curse, to proclaim that the reconciliation of Jews and Christians is part of the Church's eschatological hope, and to condemn anti-semitism. To this first draft, prepared and discussed at the April 1961 meeting, it was later proposed to add a *votum* that Catholics show a more friendly and humble attitude towards the new state of Israel.

But the discussion of the text at the August meeting already revealed the difficulties that would await a text on the Jews. Besides the objections that could be foreseen from Arab countries, there was also, as Oesterreicher

---

[390] *ADP* II/4 785-812.

[391] See Velati, "La proposta ecumenica," 320-26; Carbone, "Gli schemi preparatori," 70-71.

[392] See Velati, "La proposta ecumenica," 331-38; Oesterreicher, "The Declaration on the Relationship of the Church to Non-Christian Religions", 17-46.

notes, the fact that many Catholic bishops and theologians were simply not prepared for it, the question of the mystery of Israel in the economy of salvation being still "the Cinderella of theology."[393] By the November 1961 meeting, fears began to be expressed that the text might represent an intervention in the complex political problems of the Middle East and that it rested on disputable interpretations of the Scriptures. It was decided to prepare a much briefer statement for presentation to the Council, perhaps in the schema *De libertate religiosa*, with another text on the links between Israel and Church to be prepared for the TC's text *De Ecclesia*. A single-page text was then prepared and approved. On 2 February 1962 Pope John told Bea that the text on the Jews could be submitted directly to the CPC, "without any other commission intervening."[394]

This brief *Decretum de Judaeis* was scheduled to be discussed at the last meeting of the CPC in June 1962. But on the last day of that session, Cicognani announced that after consultation with Bea, the Secretariat of State had decided to withdraw the text from the CPC's agenda and not to submit it to the Council. After implying that the decree did not fit the purposes of the Council and asking why this particular decree was being offered — "If we speak about the Jews, why not also about the Muslims?" — Cicognani alluded to the real reasons for the decision:

> Today's bitter disputes between Jews and Arabs are well known; the suspicion of politics could easily arise, that we are favoring one or another of the parties — rumors about this are already spreading. Jews and all others who are outside the Church know that the Church will receive them with great love if they desire to embrace the Catholic faith.[395]

The rumors to which Cicognani referred were aroused by the announcement that Dr. Chaim Wardi, an official in the state of Israel's Ministry of Religious Affairs, would attend the Council as a representative of the World Jewish Congress. This announcement, which appears to have surprised the Vatican, led Arab governments to protest at the apparent special treatment being accorded to Jews and, it seemed, to Israel. In these circumstances, Cicognani decided to follow the ways of political prudence and ordered the text withdrawn.[396]

---

[393] Oesterreicher, "The Declaration," 39, and, for illustrations, see 32-36.

[394] "Prolusio Em.mi Card. Bea," Sessio generalis VI (6-10 martii 1962), 1 (A-Stransky).

[395] *ADP* II/4 22-23.

[396] See Oesterreicher, "The Declaration," 41-42; Schmidt, *Augustin Bea*, 378-79; J. Willebrands, "Cardinal Bea's Attitude to Relations with the Jews: Unpublished Details," *Simposio Card. Agostino Bea*, 79-83, who reports that the same circumstances led the Secretariat of State to ask Bea to suppress an article about to appear in *CC*, "Are the Jews a deicide people and 'cursed by God?'" Bea agreed but then allowed the article to appear, over the name of L. Hertling, in *Stimmen der Zeit* 88 (1961-62) 16-25.

D. DOCTRINE AND DIALOGUE

In the summaries given above of the texts produced by the TC and the SCU are already apparent different ideas about the Council and, more particularly, about how it should rearticulate the faith to meet contemporary challenges and questions. Relations between the two preparatory bodies remained rather distant on the matters reviewed in the previous sections. This corresponded to the TC's own notion of its own exclusive competency in doctrinal matters, but this attitude was even firmer towards the SCU than towards other PrC because the TC did not think that Bea's secretariat had any right to compose documents.

This generally frosty relationship was even colder, however, with regard to two areas of concern which were central to the determination of the Council's purpose and on which the two bodies entered into open confrontation in a struggle that foreshadowed the drama of the Council's first session. The first of these concerned the appropriation and communication of the Word of God, the second the nature and mission of the Church. On these great questions the two bodies prepared quite different texts by quite different processes; and underlying both the processes and the tasks were quite different assumptions about the nature and purpose of the Council. Nowhere else was it as clear that the history of the preparatory period was not simply an institutional tug-of-war but also a struggle over the definition of the nature and mission of the Church in the modern world. This section, then, will discuss these conflicts on the two major doctrinal questions that would confront the Council.

1. *The Word of God*

The first of the *Quaestiones* the TC received from the CAP was the following:

> ON THE SOURCES OF REVELATION: In accord with recent statements of the Supreme Pontiffs, there should be a presentation of Catholic doctrine on Sacred Scripture (i.e., on the historicity of the biblical books; on the respect which exegetes are required to show to the sacred Tradition and the Church's magisterium); recent errors in this area should be condemned; at the same time norms should be issued by which exegetes may be guided in interpreting the Scriptures according to the sense of the Church.[397]

---

[397] *ADP* II/I, 408. This text is very close to the description of the issue given in the "Sintesi finale" 1. For the TC's discussion on the sources of revelation, see Burigana, "Progetto dogmatico," 177-82.

The inclusion of this set of topics seems to have surprised Tromp who turned to S. Garofalo for help in adding a schema *De fontibus* to the three he had already written for the first meeting of the prior subcommission.[398] This *schema compendiosum* was then revised by Garofalo in July and was sent to the members of the TC on 24 September for discussion at the first plenary meeting in October.

The thirteen brief paragraphs of this early text addressed two main problems. The first concerned various aspects of the interpretation of Scripture and was developed in twelve of the paragraphs: the definition of inspiration, particularly its personal and not communal character (1), the absolute inerrancy of Scripture and the question of authorship (3), literary genres and how to identify them (4-5), the historicity of the Bible (6), particularly of the Gospels (7-9), the Church's authority over the Scriptures (10), restrictions on the reading of the Bible (11), the duty of scholars to conform to Tradition and Magisterium (11-12), and the authority of the Vulgate (13). The other distinct theme, stated in paragraph 2, had not been included in the *Quaestiones*: the necessity of Tradition as a second source, needed to know truths not found in Scripture.[399]

In his report to the first plenary session of the TC, Garofalo explained that this list had been drawn from three sources: the "Final Synthesis" of episcopal *vota*, the Holy Office's *votum*, and the *votum* of the Congregation for Seminaries and Universities. All three of these had mentioned the problem of the interpretation of the Bible,[400] but only the Holy Office had raised the question of the sufficiency of Scripture.[401] Garofalo also noted that the schema had been drawn up without access to the proposals submitted by Catholic universities and faculties (including, therefore, the *votum* of the Pontifical Biblical Institute), which had not yet been published.[402]

---

[398] "Schema de fontibus revelationis," (CT 4/60; 20 July 1960).

[399] "Schema compendiosum Constitutionis De fontibus revelationis," (CT 4/60). The only topic listed in the July schema but not included in this revised version was the last: "14. *The problem of adaptation should be treated.*" Perhaps this was thought to be one of those "pastoral" problems beyond the TC's competency.

[400] The *votum* of the Congregation for Seminaries and Universities described the abuse of the idea of literary genres by Catholics, unduly influenced by Protestant scholars and by *Formgeschichte*, who were questioning the historicity of the Gospels to the point that one feared a return to Modernism; *ADA* III 330.

[401] *ADA* III 8-9. The "Synopsis" of episcopal *vota* drawn up within the Holy Office does not mention any questions about revelation, which suggests that it was drawn up before Felici had sent out the "*Quaestiones*".

[402] Garofalo, "Relatio de schemate secundo: De Fontibus Revelationis," 1-2.

The subcommission *De fontibus* began its work soon after the October plenary session,[403] commissioning studies from several members and consultors. Advised by Tromp that they need not await these studies before beginning to draft a text, three members submitted drafts of chapters: on inspiration and inerrancy (Di Fonzo), on the Old Testament (Kerrigan), and on literary genres (Castellino). These were typed and sent out to to to the TC in preparation for the second plenary session in February.[404] The subcommission seems to have done little work for the next two months, resuming its meetings only in late April. It worked very rapidly for the next weeks, however, and finished its work on 23 June. Its schema was then printed and mailed out as part of the agenda for the September plenary session, where it was approved. In October the schema *De fontibus* was sent to the CPC, the first of the doctrinal texts completed by the TC.

The two questions to which the subcommission *De fontibus* addressed itself were the objects of wide-ranging controversy at the time. They differ from one another significantly enough to require us to treat them separately.

1.1. Scripture and Tradition in the TC

In the last half of the 1950s a dispute had broken out among Catholic theologians on the ecumenically sensitive question of what was called the "material sufficiency" of Scripture, that is, whether all of revelation is in some way contained in Scripture or whether there are some revealed truths not found there but only in tradition. This issue turned in part on the interpretation of the decree on the matter issued by the Council of Trent, which some theologians maintained had settled the issue

[403] The members of the subcommission were: Scherer, Hermaniuk, Schröffer, Cerfaux, Garofalo, Schmaus, Michel, and Van den Eynde; Kerrigan, Di Fonzo, and Castellino served as consultors. Garofalo, Cerfaux, and Kerrigan were consultors to the Pontifical Biblical Commission. The two principal centers of Catholic biblical scholarship at the time, the PBI and the Ecole biblique of Jerusalem, were not represented on the TC, nor were there any biblical scholars from Germany.

As the subcommission was about to begin its work, Garofalo asked that E. Vogt and P. Benoit be added to the TC as consultors, but Ottaviani told Tromp that the decision would have to be brought to the Cardinals of the Holy Office; see Tromp Diary, 23 Nov 1960. Vogt's appointment came only on 1 March, as a sign of the Pope's confidence in the Biblicum. Benoit was never appointed; for the hostility to him within the Holy Office, see the documents in F.M. Stabile, "Il Cardinal Ruffini e il Vaticano II: Le lettere di un 'intransigente,'" CrSt 11 (1990) 118-21.

[404] "Constitutio de fontibus Revelationis," (CT 20/60; 21 Jan 1960). At the same time Cerfaux submitted a "Constitutio de Scriptura," along with "Adnotationes" (CT 23/60, 10-11 Jan 1960), which also were reproduced but were not discussed at the February meeting and do not seem to have had any effect on the history of the schema.

once and for all, while others argued that Trent had left the question open.[405] Beneath the two particular questions often lay different views of the nature both of revelation and of tradition. The literature on the two subjects was growing rapidly, and the debate tended to be very warm.

The paragraph of the original *schema compendiosum* devoted to the question left no doubt on which side Tromp and Garofalo expected the TC to come down: "Sacred Scripture is not the only source of the revelation which is found in the Deposit of Faith. For besides the divine Tradition which is set out in Sacred Scripture, there is also the divine Tradition of truths which *are not contained* in Sacred Scripture." The task of elaborating a text to make this case was assigned to D. van den Eynde, while several members of the subcommission were also asked for their views.[406] While Cerfaux and Schmaus argued the necessity of tradition for the full and accurate interpretation of the Bible, Unger and Bertetto concluded that tradition was necessary also to supply for the material insuffiency of Scripture.[407] It was the latter opinion that was espoused in van den Eynde's May draft, which maintained that Scripture alone was the way in which such revealed truths as the integrity, inspiration and canonicity of the Scriptures are known to the Church.[408]

When this text was discussed at the plenary session in September, several members asked in vain for a return to the language of Trent, which had spoken of the Gospel as the one source that comes to us through the Scriptures and tradition. While a fuller description of tradition was added to the text, the sections on the relation between Scripture and tradition underwent only minor changes. Thus revised, the schema

[405] That Trent left the question open was argued by J.R. Geiselmann, "Das Missverständnis über das Verhältnis von Schrift und Tradition und seine Überwindung in der katholischen Theologie," *Una Sancta* 11 (1956) 132-39; "Das Konzil von Trient über das Verhältnis der Heiligen Schrift und der nicht geschriebenen Tradition," in *Die mündliche Überlieferung: Beiträge zum Begriff der Tradition*, ed. M. Schmaus (Munich 1957) 133-67, by J. Beumer, "Katholisches und protestantisches Schriftprinzip im Urteil des Trienter Konzils," *Scholastik* 34 (1959) 249-58, and by Y. Congar, *La tradition et les traditions: Essai historique* (Paris 1960), 207-32. The chief opponent of this new interpretation was the Gregorian University professor, H. Lennerz, "Scriptura sola?" *Greg* 40 (1959) 38-53; "Sine scripto traditiones," *Greg* 40 (1959) 624-35. See also Y. Congar, "Le débat sur la question du rapport entre Écriture et Tradition, au point de vue de leur contenu matériel," *RSPT* 48 (1964) 645-57.

[406] Notably not asked to write on it was Congar, the first volume of whose *Tradition et traditions* had just appeared.

[407] Cerfaux and Schmaus submitted their comments in January 1961; the dates on which Unger and Bertetto submitted theirs are not known, but the typed versions of their *vota* prepared for the TC are dated, respectively, 23 June 1961 and 3 August 1961.

[408] D. Van den Eynde, "De duplici fonte revelationis" (CT 6/61:20; 12 May 1961).

was approved by the whole TC and sent in October to the CPC, where it was discussed on 9 November 1961.[409]

Surprisingly, the relationship between Scripture and Tradition was not directly raised at the CPC discussion, not even by Bea, who might have been expected to be particularly concerned by the TC's position not only because of its general ecumenical implications, but also because a subcommission of his own Secretariat was also engaged in a study of the question.

1.2. Scripture and Tradition in the SCU

From the beginning the SCU's program had included a treatment of the Word of God,[410] but an early proposal that the subcommission assigned this task consider the relation between Scripture and Tradition had at first been refused, apparently out of fear that the issue might be prematurely closed. But at the Bühl meeting in August 1961, that is, *after* the TC's subcommission *De fontibus* had completed its work, the SCU decided to appoint a new subcommission to deal with the issue from an ecumenical standpoint.[411]

By the end of October Feiner was able to send out a first draft of a text on the question, which was then discussed at a plenary meeting on 30 November and 1 December. After a brief description of the state of the question, the text offered lengthy doctrinal and historical comments buttressed by extensive notes. A section on how to apply the principles of Catholic ecumenism to the question was followed by concrete suggestions to be offered to the TC and to the CPC. The main argument in both the text and the *vota* was that the question of the material sufficiency of the Scriptures was still a subject of legitimate debate among Catholic theologians and that the Council should not say anything that would prematurely settle the issue.

At the November meeting, Bea explained the text on Scripture and Tradition that the TC had presented to the CPC and pointed out that the question was still controverted, the Holy Office not yet having censured any Catholic work dealing with the question. The SCU's discussion showed that everyone was in general agreement with Feiner's text

---

[409] *ADP* II/1, 523-63; see Indelicato, *Difendere la dottrina*, 77-90.

[410] On the SCU's texts on Scripture, see J. Feiner, "La contribution du Secrétariat pour l'Unité ds Chrétiens à la Constitution dogmatique sur la Révélation divine," in *La Révélation divine* (US 70a; Paris 1968) 119-33; Velati, "La proposta ecumenica," 300-309.

[411] The members were: J. Feiner (reporter), C. Boyer, G. Tavard, E. Stakemeier, and M. Bévenot.

except for C. Boyer, who presented a paper arguing that Trent had settled the issue.

Approved in general at the plenary session of Nov-Dec 1961, the SCU's text was slightly revised and presented again at the next plenary session in March 1962. There Bea told the members that the TC's text *De fontibus* had been found inadequate at the CPC meeting, that he had himself sent "extensive comments" to Confalonieri, president of the CPC's subcommission on amendments, who said they had been very helpful, and that after the SCU had a definitive text on Scripture and Tradition, it too would be sent both to the TC and to Confalonieri's subcommission "so that the final redaction would take them into account."[412]

After the March discussions, a final text was prepared and distributed to the members of the SCU in April.[413] Eight *vota* were offered should the Council wish to address the question. These urged that Scripture and Tradition not be presented as two independent and parallel means of transmitting revelation, but as intimately inter-related, that the Council abstain from expressions that would exclude the view that all revealed truths are in some way contained or hinted at in the Scriptures, that tradition be presented as the living process by which the Spirit guides the Church to a full knowledge of revealed truths, so that tradition does not appear as a merely mechanical transmission of doctrines clearly known and expressed from the beginning.[414]

These proposals represent a formal repudiation of the spirit and of the positions of the TC's schema *De fontibus*. By the time the SCU's text was completed, however, not only had the CPC discussed the *De fontibus* text, but its subcommission on amendments had already revised it in the light of the criticisms made by members of the CPC and the responses of the TC. If the SCU's text arrived too late to affect the preparatory text *De fontibus*, it was available to influence initial episcopal responses to that text and the discussion of it at the first session of the Council.

1.3. Biblical Interpretation in the TC

Three chapters of the TC's text *De fontibus* (on inspiration and inerrancy, on the Old Testament, and on literary genres) were ready in very provisional form for the February 1961 plenary session, where

---

[412] Bea, "Prolusio," 4 (A-Stransky).

[413] SCU, "De Traditione et Sacra Scriptura (Relatio reformata et emendata)" (A-Stransky).

[414] Feiner explains these eight *vota* in "La contribution," 121-24.

Garofalo reported that the work was so advanced that the text should soon be finished.[415] At this point, however, the work of the subcommission seems to have been temporarily suspended, not to begin again until 21-22 April. In a progress-report a week later, Garofalo said that the chapter on the Old Testament needed only further polishing but that further study was needed of the question of the authorship of the Gospels. Discussion was also continuing, he said, on the historicity of the Gospels, with special attention being given to erroneous or incautious views that were being spread around.[416]

This comment leads one to suspect that the subcommission's work was now being affected by the controversy on biblical studies that had been raging in Rome for four months. Concerns about the direction of Catholic biblical studies had been growing for some time, especially within the Holy Office and the Congregation for Seminaries and Universities. These were given dramatic expression early in January in a long and violent attack published in *Divinitas* in a special issue in honor of Cardinal Ruffini.[417] Its author, A. Romeo, professor of Scripture at the Lateran and *aiutante di studio* at the Congregation for Seminaries and Universities, not content with sharp criticisms of several Catholic scholars, also criticized the Pontifical Biblical Institute (PBI) itself for abandoning the magisterium's positions and having become in effect a participant in what Romeo's intransigence saw as a vast campaign to substitute for the Church's faith a new Christianity inspired by Teilhard de Chardin and reminiscent of Masonry.

The PBI's response was immediate and strong. After failing to obtain a retraction and space in *Divinitas* to respond, it published a reply in one of its own journals in which it refuted Romeo's charges in great detail and expressed its grief that such a defamation should have been published in the journal of the Roman Theological Academy.[418] It was only

[415] Garofalo, "Relatio de laboribus factis et peragendis in subcommissione De fontibus revelationis," 13 Feb 1961; Tromp, "Relatio de Consessu secundo plenario Commissionis Theologicae habito diebus 13-16 Febr. 1961, in aedibus Vaticanis," June 1961 (CT 4/61); Tromp, "Epilogus Secretarii," 16 Feb 1961.

[416] Garofalo, "Relatio de laboribus factis et faciendis in subcommissione De fontibus," 27 April 1961.

[417] A. Romeo, "L'Enciclica 'Divino Afflante Spiritu' e le 'opiniones novae,'" *Divinitas* 4 (1960) 385-456. It was also published in extract-form, Fenton receiving a copy from F. Spadafora on 10 Jan 1961.

[418] "Pontificium Institutum Biblicum et recens libellus R.mi D.ni A. Romeo," *VD* 39 (1961) 3-17; also published in abstract-form.

after this reply was published that abstracts of both articles were ordered withdrawn from sale[419] and the question was reserved, it seems, to the Holy Office.[420]

The controversy echoed throughout official Rome. On 19 Jan 1961 Tromp learned about Romeo's article from Garofalo who found it "defamatory and unjust." Two days later Tromp told Ottaviani of his concern that the TC might be considered to be involved, since four of the moderators of *Divinitas* were among its members; in his journal Tromp noted that the editor had not consulted him and that he had not yet read the article. Bea wrote Piolanti an energetic letter of protest, to which Pizzardo replied that Romeo's article had been published without his knowledge and represented the views only of the author.[421] Three days later Tromp reported in his journal that the Pope had telephoned the rector of *Civiltà Cattolica* to inform him and the rector of the PBI that he had read Romeo's article "with displeasure and disgust." On 2 March, *OssRom* announced that E. Vogt, rector of the PBI, had been appointed to the TC.[422] Finally, on 5 March the consultors to the Pontifical Biblical Commission (including Cerfaux) composed a statement, sent to Vogt three days later, in which they deprecated Romeo's article and declared their solidarity with the PBI.

Three months later the Holy Office issued a text widely interpreted as its reply to the controversy. A monitum published on 20 June 1961 criticized those who questioned the historicity of the Scriptures and called upon Catholics to follow the magisterium in interpreting the Bible. Five

---

[419] Vogt, rector of the Biblicum, diplomatically expressed his view on this matter: "Msgr. Romeo's article, from the time of its publication, has been widely and quite freely circulated for seven months. But as soon as our simple correction was published, the sale of the two abstracts was forbidden (for both parties, it is true). But then other violent articles against us were published, without any impediment. We have not replied lest we descend to the same level and to avoid a formal controversy and so as not to expose ourselves to a new prohibition;" "Pro-memoria sugli attachi contro il Pontificio Istituto Biblico" (s.d.).

[420] This at least is the claim of F. Spadafora, *La tradizione contro il Concilio* (Rome 1989) 48, who says that Romeo and he were asked to submit their documentation to the Holy Office for review. It is interesting to note that Caprile's *Cronaca* for the period makes no reference to the controversy at all, not even to mention that Vogt had been made a member of the CT.

[421] Schmidt, *Augustin Bea*, 318n; Fogarty, *American Catholic Biblical Scholarship: A History from the Early Republic to Vatican II* (San Francisco 1989) 293.

[422] Vogt himself interpreted the Pope's action as "showing that His confidence in the Biblical was unshaken;" Vogt to Roland Murphy, 25 March 1961; A-CBA. Tromp noted in his Diary, 1-2 Feb 1961, that neither Ottaviani nor he knew anything about this nomination and that Felici had explained that Vogt had been appointed at the express wish of the Pope.

days later it was announced that Jean Steinmann's book, *La vie de Jésus* had been placed on the Index.[423]

The campaign continued in the following months. Ruffini entered the fray publicly with an article in *OssRom*, criticizing, in a manner that appeared to repudiate *Divino afflante Spiritu*, the appeal to literary genres in the interpretation of the Bible.[424] On the very day this article appeared, Pizzardo sent a copy of it to all rectors of diocesan seminaries in Italy, asking them to draw it to the attention of their professors because of the authority of its author and the circumstances in which it was written.[425] In September Ruffini wrote to the new Secretary of State, Cicognani, to inform him that Tardini, shortly before his death, had indicated that two or three professors would be removed from the Biblicum.[426] This appears to refer to S. Lyonnet and M. Zerwick, two of the scholars most vigorously attacked by Romeo; their suspension from teaching, however, although it had long been sought, did not occur until the end of the academic year, 1961-62.[427] Ottaviani made a similar effort, this time unsuccessful, to remove Myles M. Bourke, professor of the New Testament and another of Romeo's targets, from the faculty of the archdiocesan seminary in New York.[428]

[423] *AAS* 53 (1961) 507-508; two days later, *OssRom* published an article explaining and justifying the decree; *DC* 58 (1961) 890-94; for a sympathetic commentary, see F. Spadafora, "Adnotationes," *ME* 86 (1961) 360-73. On 9 May 1961 Ruffini had denounced Steinmann's book to Ottaviani; see Stabile, "Il Cardinal Ruffini," 115-16.

[424] E. Ruffini, "Generi Letterari e ipotesi di lavoro nei recenti studi biblici," *OssRom* (24 Aug 1961); an English translation was published in *AER* 145 (Dec. 1961) 362-65; six months later the American journal published another article by Ruffini, "The Bible and its Genuine Historical and Objective Truth," *AER* 146 (June 1962) 361-68, which Stabile, "Il Cardinal Ruffini," 118, thinks may have been written for *OssRom* but which never appeared there.

[425] Pizzardo to the rectors of diocesan seminaries in Italy, 24 Aug 1961 (A-Fenton).

[426] See Stabile, "Il Cardinal Ruffini," 116.

[427] Writing, it seems, early in 1962, Vogt commented: "First of all, I have to note that the removal of the two professors was requested or imposed without their ever having been warned not to teach this or that thing. Indeed, I myself expressly asked, in a letter to Cardinal Pizzardo on 10 April 1960 and then orally to Cardinal Ottavani in February 1961, that they warn us and give us concrete and specific indications of what might be lacking in our teaching. But I have never received any notice of this;" "Pro-memoria," 13.

[428] Bourke had written an article, cited by Romeo, "The Literary Genus of Mt. 1-2," *CBQ* 22 (Oct 1960) 160-75. Spellman not only refused Ottaviani's request, but a year later, over the objections of the Apostolic Delegate, the Congregation for Seminaries, and the Holy Office, had Bourke named a papal chamberlain. At the November meeting of the CCP, Ottaviani illustrated the dangerous trends in Catholic bibilical scholarship by referring to problems at the same seminary; see *ADP*, II/I, 549. By this time, Richard J. Dillon, a New York seminarian and author of an article which Ottaviani also criticized ("St. Luke's Infancy Account: A Study in the Interrelation of Literary Form and Theological Teaching," *Dunwoodie Review* 1 [Jan 1961] 5-37), now ordained, had been assigned by Spellman to studies at the Biblicum!

The views of Pope John XXIII in all of this are not clear. Tromp repeatedly said that it was the Pope who had placed the question of biblical interpretation on the agenda of the TC. Although at least one of his advisers thought that the criticisms of the PBI were not entirely unjustified,[429] the Pope criticized Romeo's article and honored the PBI by appointing Vogt to the TC. A year later, however, he expressed irritation at the Pontifical Biblical Commission's silence during the ongoing debate and threatened to dissolve it if it did not meet its duties.[430] On the other hand, on the very eve of the Council, in an address to a meeting of the Associazione Biblica Italiana, which had also been indicted by Romeo, Pope John contented himself with very general statements, speaking of biblical scholars as collaborators of the Church in the defence, study and transmission of revealed doctrine, but also recalling the Church's right to supervise their work.[431]

It is not now possible to say with much certainty and in any clear detail what effect this controversy had on the work of the TC's subcommission *De fontibus*. To the degree that one can reconstruct the history of its text, however, one observes a certain hardening of positions on several matters that were at the heart of the controversy.

On the hotly disputed question of *the historicity of the Gospels*, Cerfaux's January papers had detailed the differences between ancient and modern notions of history, set out the history of the oral transmission of the words and deeds of Jesus, noted the varying literary character of the four Gospels, and used this to explain variations among the Gospels in reporting the words and deeds of Jesus. But the text approved by the subcommission on 4 May and not substantially altered later, after a general statement asserting the different historical criteria used in antiquity, flatly condemns errors that "in any way and for any reason" deny or weaken the objective truth of events in the life of Christ, particularly those that touch on the foundations of faith: the infancy of Christ,

---

[429] On 7 Jan 1962, in the midst of the Lombardi controversy, A. Dell'Acqua wrote: "It is well known that the Jesuits have a lot of trouble at the Biblical Institute. Many people think they are 'half-heretical'or almost. The Biblical Institute is suspected of 'deviationism' (and in some respects not wrongly);" see G. Zizola, *Il microfono di Dio: Pio XII, padre Lombardi e i cattolici italiani* (Milan 1990) 460.

[430] *Lettere 1958-1963*, 536-37. Capovilla may reflect the Pope's mind when he speaks of the persistence of "various insidious tendencies with regard to the concept of inspiration, inerrancy, historicity, etc." For other comments on the Pope's attitude and on the silence of the Biblical Commission, see P. Grelot, "La Constitution sur la Révélation: I. La Préparation d'un schéma conciliaire," *Etudes* 324 (Jan 1966) 102, and F. Spadafora, *Leone XIII e gli studi biblici* (Rovigo 1976).

[431] *DMC* IV 540-45.

his signs and miracles, his resurrection and ascension. With regard to
Christ's teaching, the text condemns views that deny that the words
attributed to him in the Gospels, "even if not always literally at least
always substantially," were actually spoken by Christ or that they reflect
the consciousness of the early Church more than the mind and words of
Christ himself. Efforts to nuance both statements were also unavailing,
and the text that was sent out to the whole TC in June was able to add
an explicit reference to the new Holy Office monitum on the question.

Another question concerned *literary genres in the Bible*. Explicit
reference to the need to identify and study them had appeared in all three
of the texts presented in January, with Castellino offering an historical
survey and justification of their use in modern biblical interpretation
along with some cautions. Lengthy treatments of their importance continued to appear in drafts written by Di Fonzo and Castellino in April.
But a combined text written by them in May warned against concocted
theories, analyses based only on internal evidence, and efforts to reduce
supernatural events to the common course of nature. They illustrated this
problem by referring to an article on the infancy narratives that had been
at the center of the controversy sparked by Romeo's article.[432] In the
final revision of the text made in June, however, the two lengthy paragraphs on literary genres were eliminated in favor of a single sentence:
"For the truth and historical trustworthiness of Sacred Scripture is
rightly weighed only if proper attention is given to the customary and
native ways of thinking, speaking and narrating that prevailed at the time
of the sacred authors and were in common use in social relationships at
the time." A footnote at this point refers to *Divino afflante Spiritu*, but
the very term "literary genre" has disappeared from the text.[433]

On these questions, then, one notes that the positions espoused in the
schema *De fontibus* became stricter in the course of the elaboration of
the text. On each point more open views were expressed within the
subcommission, including by at least two of the Roman members,
Di Fonzo and Castellino, while Cerfaux, van den Eynde, Kerrigan and
Vogt made unsuccessful efforts to nuance the text. Although these
six constituted a majority of the subcommission, they were unable to

---

[432] Di Fonzo-Castellino, "De S. Scripturae inspiratione, inerrantia et compositione lit-
teraria" (CT 6/61:24; 22 May 1961), with a reference to the article by M.M. Bourke on
the Matthean infancy narrative.

[433] Tromp offered a not entirely convincing argument when he presented the text to
the CCP: "No. 13 in effect is speaking about 'literary genres;' the reality is clearly
described but that phrase is not used lest the doctrine be so adapted to our time that it may
perhaps later become obscure;" *ADP* I/1 535.

prevail. Even the presence of Vogt made no difference; in fact, things became stricter after he joined the subcommission. The text of the *De fontibus* that was presented to the CPC had clearly come down on one side of the public controversy. The dominant tone of the text was suspicious and condemnatory of the methods and results of contemporary biblical scholarship.

1.4. Biblical Interpretation in the SCU

Meanwhile, a subcommission within the SCU was also engaged in work on the place of the Scriptures in the doctrine and life of the Church, in preaching, in the liturgy, and in catechesis.[434] H. Volk served as the reporter for the subcommission, which was able to bring to the April 1961 plenary session an exposition of a theology of the Word of God, followed by several *vota*. The original intention was that this text, or at least the *vota* at the end, would be brought to the attention of the ST and of the TC.

Volk's text was an attempt to begin the work of elaborating a theology of the Word of God, not simply as a set of doctrines found in Scripture and Tradition but as a living source of life for the Church through the reading of the Bible, in the liturgy, in preaching and catechesis. On this basis, the Council might usefully state the Church's dependence on the Word of God and urge an expansion of the lectionary used at Mass and the use of the vernacular in worship and in the breviary.

Even after the plenary meeting held in Bühl in August 1961, the expectation was still that this text would be a *votum* for the guidance of other CPC. But in November, only days after the TC's text *De fontibus* had been discussed in the CPC, Volk was informed by the secretariat of the SCU that his subcommission should instead prepare an independent votum that would be submitted directly to the CPC. At the November plenary session, Bea explained that the decree would supply for the neglect of the spiritual and theological value of the Word of God in the TC's text *De fontibus*. The plenary session of the SCU approved the suggestion that Volk prepare such a decree. At the plenary session in March 1962, the text *De Verbo Dei: Schema decreti pastoralis* was unanimously approved for submission to the CPC where it was discussed on 20 June 1962.[435]

---

[434] The members of the subcommission were: H. Volk, J. Feiner, F. Thijssen, C. Boyer, G. Tavard.

[435] *ADP* II/4 816-34; see Indelicato, *Difendere la dottrina*, 311-13.

The schema began with a statement that was not unlike the perspective of the TC: the necessity to defend the divine gift of the Word of God against threats. But it did not see the problem as an atomized set of errors but as a general threat to the whole deposit of revelation; and the response suggested by the SCU was not a set of anathemas but the living and life-giving power of the Word of God itself. The schema then defined this Word as including "all those things which God has said to us in his revelation ..., the Word written and passed down, which echoes in the Church's worship and life." It offered a positive exposition of the Word of God as a source of life for the Church and for individual Christians. Revelation was presented as God's ongoing conversation with man through his Word. The text attributed a quasi-sacramental power to God's Word, stressed its importance in the celebration of the sacraments and in preaching, and urged that it be placed at the center of clerical education.

The counterpositions between the TC and the SCU on the Word of God are significant on several counts. There is first of all the great difference in the fundamental problematic. For the TC revelation was the communication of a set of doctrines, guaranteed in their origins by divine authority, interpreted by the magisterium, and now to be defended from various errors. For the SCU revelation was a salvific encounter by which God brings light and life to men and which has an intrinsic power of its own because of the truth it enshrines.

Secondly, for the SCU the Word of God in its primary expression in the Scriptures and Tradition stands over the Church for which it is a source of life. In the text of the TC the role of the magisterium is so stressed that the primary expressions of the Word of God recede into the background, giving way in particular to the most recent statements of the magisterium.

Third, in terms of method, the SCU constructed its texts as an engagement with a contemporary audience, particularly the partners of the ecumenical dialogue whose questions it took seriously and from whom it thought it had something also to learn. This respectful conversation led it back to new works of scholarship, biblical and historical. For the TC, on the other hand, the defence of the deposit of faith largely ignored contemporary questions except as various errors needing to be condemned. The deposit of faith was assumed to have such an objectivity and consistency, particularly as articulated in traditional concepts and as defended by the recent magisterium, that the circumstances in which it had been stated in the past were of little account, and the defence of it was a matter of confidently and deductively pursuing paths already indicated, especially by scholastic theology. Contemporary hermeneutics were so absent from its preoccupations that it could expect the Council to settle "doctrinal" issues on their own terms, leaving the engagement with contemporary concerns and questions to the "pastoral" efforts of bishops and priests.

Finally, the differences between the two bodies over revelation illustrate once again the institutional atomization of problems that marked the preparatory period. There was no cooperation between the TC and the SCU in this area, and the SCU eventually felt obliged, once it became aware of the utter lack of ecumenical sensitivity in the TC, to construct texts that represented a clear and explicit challenge to the TC's claim to exclusive competency in doctrinal matters. If this challenge was ineffective during the preparatory process, it anticipated the struggle that would define the drama of the first session of the Council.

2. *The Church*

From the time Pope John announced the Council, nearly everyone recognized that one of its chief tasks would be to articulate the nature and mission of the Church. This was in fact the mandate given to the TC in the official *Quaestiones* which called for the completion of Vatican I's Constitution *De Ecclesia* particularly by a treatment of the Mystical Body, the episcopate, and the laity.[436]

The original outline Tromp prepared contained twelve themes,[437] to which the meeting of the prior subcommission added another on the missionary rights of the Church. This outline was then presented in a slightly expanded form as the *schema compendiosum De Ecclesia* that was proposed and accepted at the October plenary meeting of the TC.

The preparation of a text *De Ecclesia* might have been expected to be particularly suited to Tromp himself, who had prepared the *schema*

---

[436] The "*Sintesi finale*" (2-4) had identified also a desire among the bishops for "an organic and complete dogmatic Constitution on the Church," in order to complete Vatican I. For the CT's text on the Church, see A. Acerbi, *Due ecclesiologie: ecclesiologia giuridica ed ecclesiologia di comunione nella "Lumen gentium"* (Bologna 1975); U. Betti, *La dottrina sull'episcopato del Concilio Vaticano II: Il capitolo III della Costituzione dommatica Lumen gentium* (Roma 1984) 17-51; Burigana, "Progetto dogmatico," 167-77.

[437] 1) Indoles et missio Ecclesiae; 2) Ecclesia et communio sanctorum; 3) Membra Ecclesiae; 4) Necessitas Ecclesiae ad salutem; 5) Auctoritas Ecclesiae magisterialis; 6) Auctoritas Ecclesiae disciplinaris; 7) Relatio Episcoporum ad S. Pontificem; 8) Episcopi et sacerdotes; 9) Positio laicorum in Ecclesia; 10) Ecclesia et reditus separatorum; 11) Ecclesia et respublica; 12) Tolerantia christiana.

compendiosum and whose role in the writing of *Mystici Corporis* was well known. That Tromp would not receive this task was hinted at when he was not even consulted by Ottaviani about the membership of the subcommission *De Ecclesia*; and it was confirmed later when Ottaviani informed Tromp of several complaints that he would try to impose his own views.[438] After Balic refused the post, Ottaviani appointed Gagnebet to head the subcommission. Tromp's weak position was also apparent when his objections did not prevent Ottaviani from appointing Lattanzi to the subcommission, perhaps in order to assure a Lateran presence after Piolanti left the subcommission.[439] The tensions reflected in all this impeded the work of the subcommission, which was one of the last among those of the TC to complete its work.

Methodologically, the subcommission *De Ecclesia* worked in roughly the same way as the other subcommissions in the TC. Many particular studies were commissioned from the members and consultors, but work on redacting the chapters often was initiated before they had all been received. Philips and Colombo were the only non-Romans asked to write chapters. Most of the work was done by the subcommission of members and Roman consultors. Gagnebet did, however, often consult the non-Roman consultors and invited them to many meetings where he also called upon them to intervene.

By the second plenary session in February 1961, only a very provisional form of Lattanzi's first chapter, on the nature of the Church, was ready for discussion, and even that encountered many serious criticisms. The work accelerated a bit after that and at a special meeting in Ariccia in June several chapters were discussed. In July five chapters were considered ready to be typed and sent out for discussion at the September plenary session. After the March 1962 plenary sessions six chapters were considered sufficiently complete to prepare them for submission to the CPC on 20 March. The subcommission then worked on revising the other chapters, completing them on 19 May. The CPC reviewed the schema *De Ecclesia* in its May and June meetings.[440] But so much work was needed to revise the text again that it was only ready to be distributed to

---

[438] Tromp Diary, 27-30 Oct 1960; see also Fenton Diary, 27-29 Oct 1960.

[439] Tromp Diary, 8 Nov 1960: "I was quite opposed; I know he is a good man, but he never stops talking. There are already enough people on the Commission de Ecclesia." The full membership of the subcommission as listed on 25 Jan 1961: M. Dubois, J. Griffiths, P. Kornyljak, J. Fenton, G. Philips, C. Colombo, C. Journet, R. Gagnebet, C. Balic, U. Lattanzi, H. Schauf, J. Witte, J. Lécuyer.

[440] Chapters I-VI were discussed in May, *ADP* II/3 986-1156, and chapters VII-XI in June, *ADP* II/4 621-812; see Indelicato, *Difendere la dottrina*, 242-54, 296-307.

the bishops in November, 1962, after the Council's work had already begun.

The slowness of the work of this subcommission had certain unfortunate effects on the preparation of the whole Council. First, it meant that the CPC itself had to deal with a host of practical questions whose resolution depended on central ecclesiological themes it had not yet considered. For example, the disciplinary material on bishops — their authority in their dioceses, their relations with the Pope, their relations with priests — was considered in the CPC long before the chapters on bishops in the *De Ecclesia* were available to them. This was the most dramatic illustration of the lack of coordination in the conciliar preparation and of the fatal separation of doctrinal and disciplinary questions — the assumption being, apparently, that there would be no major changes or developments in the doctrinal material. Secondly, the chapters on the Church were reviewed only in the rush of things in the last meetings of the CPC, when the approaching date for the opening of the Council forced the CPC to run rapidly through the very material that from the beginning had been considered to be at the heart of the conciliar program.

As with the schema *De fontibus*, the text on the Church addressed problems of great ecumenical interest, but here also the TC conducted itself in sovereign independence of the SCU. All requests from the Secretariate for the formation of a mixed commission were turned down by Ottaviani and Tromp on the grounds that the Secretariat was not a commission and that this would compromise the independence of the TC. The Secretariat was told it would have to be content with submitting texts that set out the ecumenical dimensions of several issues.

Since it would be impossible here to summarize all the chapters of the TC's schema *De Ecclesia*,[441] I will focus on four themes, important in themselves, that were also the object of the SCU's interest.

2.1. The Nature of the Church

This was the title of the first chapter of the TC's schema *De Ecclesia*, assigned to Lattanzi in November 1960. The three successive texts that the latter prepared in the next months were criticized at the February

---

[441] I. De Ecclesiae militantis natura; II. De membris Ecclesiae eiusdemque necessitate ad salutem; III. De Episcopatu ut supremo gradu sacramenti Ordinis et de Sacerdotio; IV. De Episcopis residentialibus; V. De statibus evangelicae perfectionis; VI. De laicis; VII. De Ecclesiae Magisterio; VIII. De auctoritate et oboedientia in Ecclesia; IX. De relationibus inter Ecclesiam et Statum necnon de tolerantia religiosa; X. De necessitate Eccclesiae annuntiandi Evangelium omnibus gentibus et ubique terrarum. XI. De oecumenismo. See Acerbi, *Due ecclesiologie*, 107-49.

plenary session for being very diffuse, complicated, and unclear. Although there was general agreement that Lattanzi was incapable of redacting a text in an appropriate conciliar style, Gagnebet, in an effort to avoid offending the Lateran theologian, persuaded Ottaviani to allow Tromp to become the final redactor of the whole text, thus providing for a diplomatic means to revise Lattanzi's schema. This maneuvre, however, left Lattanzi with the impression that his text had been substantially approved and required only minor improvements.

For the next several months the attention of the subcommission focused on other chapters. When it became necessary to return to the introductory text and after an effort to collaborate with Lattanzi failed, Tromp himself prepared a substitute text.[442] Lattanzi reacted bitterly and in a letter to Gagnebet complained that this "illegal" action was a serious affront to his honor and to that of his University. Insisting that his text had been substantially approved at the February plenary meeting, Lattanzi threatened to take the matter to higher authority.[443] The protest reached at least as high as Ottaviani, to whom Gagnebet had to provide an account of this history.[444] Some sort of compromise seems to have been reached, because in January a new text was composed which drew on the texts of both Lattanzi and Tromp. This was approved at the March plenary meeting of the TC and after minor revisions sent on to the CPC.

The chapter, "De Ecclesiae militantis natura,"[445] began with the Father's plan of salvation for men not as individuals but within a community. The Son's execution of the Father's plan was then briefly described, with emphasis upon Christ's providing leaders for his Church. The third paragraph rapidly evoked some of the biblical images of the Church, but then the concept of the Mystical Body was developed in two paragraphs, with emphasis upon its visibility and on the distribution of roles. The chapter ended with two paragraphs which assert the identity between the visible society and the mystical Body and conclude that only the Roman Catholic Church is rightly called the Church.

---

[442] Tromp, "De indole Ecclesiae: Nova redactio, a P. Secretario confecta" (CT 19/61:33; 14 Dec 1961).

[443] For the documentation, see F. Lattanzi, *Un uomo libero: Ugo Emilio Lattanzi* (Roma 1971²) 159-66.

[444] Two drafts of this letter from Gagnebet to Ottaviani, both dated 20 Dec 1961, can be found in Gagnebet's papers (FGn I.6.53 and I.6.55). Congar learned, perhaps from Gagnebet, that Lattanzi had taken his complaint to the Pope himself: "He insisted that the honor of the Lateran was at stake. It was all a matter of competition: the Lateran had to make a dogmatic text; (Congar Journal, 8 March 1962).

[445] *ADP* II/3 986-90.

The emphasis of the chapter, then, is on the visible and societal character of the Church, which is the one theme found in all the paragraphs and to which the few evocations of the spiritual and supernatural character of the Church are always subordinated. The dominant concept is that of the Mystical Body, the efforts within the TC to promote other images, such as the People of God, having been largely unsuccessful. Everything in the earlier paragraphs is aimed at preparing the conclusion of the chapter: the identification of the Catholic Church with the Mystical Body that had been taught by Pius XII in *Mystici Corporis* and in *Humani generis*.

While the subcommission *De Ecclesia* was developing its chapter on the Church's nature, a subcommission within the SCU, chaired by Jaeger, that originally planned to prepare *vota* on the hierarchical structure of the Church, was expanding its vision into a sketch of an integral ecclesiology. The result of its labors, approved by the whole SCU in April, 1961, was a set of twelve *vota* supplemented by forty-seven pages of justificatory comments.[446]

Before the text addressed the specific questions of the Church's hierarchical structure, it set out four *vota* on the inner reality of the Church. The first of these established the christological structure of the Church as both visible and invisible: "Thus the Church is a mystery, known only by faith, in which the sacramental worship of Christ is forever carried out." This paragraph was a response to a problem also of concern to the TC: the tendency to separate the visible Church from the invisible Church; and the appeal to the christological structure of the Church resembled the analogy employed by the subcommission *De Ecclesia*. Lattanzi's early drafts had also said that the Church is itself a mystery, but this statement vanishes in the later drafts. The primarily apologetical purposes of the TC's text did not permit it to say that the mystery of the Church is known only to faith; indeed in the schema *De deposito fidei* the statement of Vatican I that the Church itself is an irrefutable sign of its divine origin had been forcefully restated.

The christological focus of the SCU's text appeared again in the fourth of its *vota* which spoke of Christ as the sole head of the Church, enjoying full authority as chief Shepherd of souls and as always faithfully joined to his Bride the Church. This paragraph responded to Protestant objections that ecclesiastical authority often obscured or even

---

[446] "Votum subcommissionis II De structura hierarchica Ecclesiae" (May 1961) (A-Stransky).

usurped the proper authority of Christ. Its stress on the absolutely unique authority which Christ continues to exercise over the Church offered a different emphasis from that of the TC's text, which stressed instead Christ's appointment of hierarchical leaders for his Church.

The SCU's text also presented a richer view of the horizontal reality of the Church: "The Church is the group of believers, united by the bonds of faith and charity in the Holy Spirit, constituting a sacramentally structured community and supported by social bonds and authorty." This led to a discussion of the Church as the People of God, the contin-uation and consummation of Israel's history, whose life and activity is exercised by the power of the Holy Spirit and which in its earthly pilgrimage is nourished by the eucharist, is purified by the blood of Christ, and awaits fulfilment in the risen Christ. The *votum* thus stressed the invisible dimensions of the Church which Protestants accuse Catholics of neglecting. These themes are not entirely absent from the TC's text, but there they are subordinated to the emphasis upon the social and hierarchical aspects of the Church. There is a noticeable difference also in the language of the two texts, the TC's being more scholastic and heavily dependent on *Mystici Corporis*, while the SCU's is biblical and patristic in inspiration.

Another basic principle of the SCU's text is expressed in its *votum* on the Church's unity, which is presented as the gift of God and not some-thing still needing to be realized. Its principle is the Spirit of Christ received in baptism but also articulated in charisms and offices. This paragraph is the one that comes closest to the concerns of the TC's first chapter; indeed in its notes it appeals not only to J.A. Möhler but to Tromp's commentary on *Mystici Corporis*.

This text of the SCU was communicated to Tromp on 24 May, before, that is, the first chapter of the TC's schema *De Ecclesia* had been com-pleted. But, as the comparison above indicates, even where there were some common themes, there is little sign that the SCU's text had any effect on either the general orientation or the specific arguments of the TC's schema.[447]

---

[447] This was in fact the criticism that Bea made when the first two chapters of the schema *De Ecclesia* came before the CPC. He noted that after the TC had refused to join in a mixed commission with the SCU, the latter had sent its texts, whose fate in the TC he summed up: "I am grateful to see that at least some vestiges are found in the schemata of the Commission, even though, unfortunately a good number of others were not con-sidered." His judgement on the first chapter: "It lacks a section on the Christian people themselves, as if only the hierarchy has a role in the Church;" *ADP* II/3 1012.

2.2. *Membership in the Church*

This topic was the subject of great concern in both preparatory bodies. Tromp included it in his *schema compendiosum* because of false interpretations of *Mystici Corporis*, "especially in northern areas." At the same time the SCU set up a subcommission to discuss to discuss the question of the relation of baptized non-Catholics to the Church: "Members of the Church: in what sense?"

The issue became a matter of public discussion when, soon after the establishment of the SCU, Bea began to state that in virtue of their baptism non-Catholics were members of the mystical body.[448] In his Diary Tromp noted a number of the speeches in which Bea had espoused this thesis[449] and discussed the problem with Ottaviani and Parente, both of whom advised prudence, not least of all because of rumors that Bea's remarks were close to the views of Pope John.

The question was hotly debated by both preparatory bodies at plenary sessions in February 1961. Within the TC positions were divided, Schmaus and Lécuyer defending a position similar to Bea's, Fenton denying that anyone but a Roman Catholic could be considered a member of the Church, and others looking for a middle position that would acknowledge the spiritual realities present in non-Catholic Christians. The result of the February discussions in the TC was the decision to follow the teaching of *Mystici Corporis*, while looking for a more charitable way to express the doctrine.[450]

On the other hand, the first draft from the SCU's subcommission on the subject was criticized for dealing with the question in terms of "members," which could not provide the needed nuance. The key issue was to find a way to distinguish in their relation to the Church between baptized non-Catholics and pagans; to speak of an unconscious *votum* for both these cases ignored the spiritual validity and effects of baptism even outside the Church. Bea remarked that *Mystici Corporis* was too general in its position and that biblical and patristic language would be more useful.

When, after the February meetings, Willebrands repeated to Tromp the request of the SCU for a mixed commission with the TC to discuss the issue, Tromp expressed his displeasure that Bea was making "propaganda"

---

[448] See the several communications in *Simposio Card. Agostino Bea*, 159-230.

[449] Tromp's attention to this thesis is noted as early as 1 Oct 1960, as his Diary notes.

[450] In the course of the discussion *vota* were received from Brinktrine, Salaverri, Journet, Schmaus, Lécuyer, Congar, Philips, Tromp, and Balic.

for his "highly debatable theory" while knowing that neither Ottaviani
nor Tromp could publicly take issue with him.[451]

Tromp himself then assumed responsibility for the chapter on the
subject in the TC's schema *De Ecclesia*. In April he proposed a text
which spoke both of "real" members and of "members *in voto*." But
this departure from the language of *Mystici Corporis* was criticized by
others and so was dropped in subsequent drafts, which returned to the
position of the Encyclical: only Catholics were "really" members of the
mystical body, others were only "related" to it by desire. In an explana-
tory *votum* written in May, Tromp took direct issue with Bea's position
and explained that to admit that heretics and schismatics, forty-five per
cent of all Christians, are really members of the Church would make it
difficult to defend the ecumenical character of Trent and Vatican I,
would require that heretical and schismatical bishops be invited to Vatican II, would deny the unity of the Church, and would ruin its claims to
infallibility.[452] For Tromp, then, the key issue at stake in the question of
membership was the identification of the Mystical Body with the Roman
Catholic Church.

By this time the SCU had reached its own conclusions on the subject.[453]
This consisted of nine fundamental propositions the SCU believed
should guide the TC's discussion. It argued that when the Church is seen
as a "structure of means for acquiring grace," one could observe that
many of these means of grace were shared in varying but incomplete
measures in non-Catholic communities. These elements placed members
of those communities in a real relationship with the Catholic Church,
represented a partial and visible way of belonging to the Church. If they
were not in full canonical communion with the Church, neither could
they be considered in the same position as pagans, something that is
obscured if they are said to be related to the Church only by desire. Such
language also did not allow for the different forms and degrees of such
desire. A consideration of the means of grace retained in the various
non-Christian bodies provided a means to judge to what degree non-
Catholic Christians belong to the Church. The final proposition pointed
out the various biblical metaphors for the Church, one of which, body
and members, permitted one to speak of non-Catholic Christians as
members of Christ's body.

---

[451] Tromp Diary, 23 Feb 1961.
[452] Tromp, "De membris Ecclesiae" (CT 5/61:48; 15 May 1961).
[453] SCU, "De Christianorum acatholicorum ordine ad Ecclesiam. Relatio" (A-Stransky).

The SCU's proposals were communicated to the TC in mid-May. When Tromp later reworked his chapter, he introduced several of the real relations, juridical, sacramental, and mystical, by which non-Catholic Christians are linked to the Church, but he continued to deny that they could be considered "real" members of the mystical body. Noticeably lacking was any effort to explore the way outlined by the SCU: beginning with the means of grace, elements of the Church, retained in non-Christian communities. Tromp's chapter spoke only of individual non-Catholics; the word Church had to be kept exclusively for the Catholic Church.[454]

Bea made one last attempt to keep the question open when the TC's text came before the CPC, where he offered a lengthy criticism inspired by the SCU's position.[455] Ottaviani's response was vigorous, an only slightly veiled criticism of Bea's many speeches on the matter and a restatement of the main issue at stake:

> Not all of the things said by Cardinal Bea can be accepted, because some of them are quite dangerous. I understand his zeal, the very great zeal that he has shown since the Secretariat for non-Catholics was entrusted to him, and he will certainly work to keep the door open to them at the Council. But we must not exaggerate; we must not say, as was said, surprisingly, in a conference, that as soon as someone is baptized he is a member of the Mystical Body even if he is not yet a member of the Church. This is dangerous to say. There should have been a discussion, as there was later, on how to understand this. But to say to a crowd of people: "Whoever is baptized is a member of the Mystical Body even if he is not a member of the Church" is very dangerous. The Catholic Church and the Mystical Body are identical.[456]

2.3. *Episcopacy and Primacy*

It was a common view that one of the chief doctrinal aims of the Second Vatican Council would be to complete the ecclesiology of Vatican I by a treatment of the nature and role of the episcopate in the Church. Tromp's *schema compendiosum* included this topic, specifying it as a presentation of the episcopacy as a sacrament, the relationship between bishops and the pope, and the role of bishops in governing the Church. Similarly, the SCU from the beginning established a subcommission to deal with the hierarchical structure of the Church and in particular with the source of the Church's ministerial authority and the relationships between patriarchs, bishops and the pope.

---

[454] See *ADP* II/3 990-91.
[455] *ADP* II/3 1014-16.
[456] *ADP* II/3 1024.

Within the TC Lécuyer was given the task of writing the chapter on the episcopate as a sacrament. The great majority of the members and consultors were of the view that the Council should mark a doctrinal advance by confirming this doctrine, thus overcoming the medieval view which had reduced the episcopate to a merely juridical differentiation. Lécuyer's text, therefore, did not have a dramatic history, and on this point there was also no disagreement with the SCU.

Problems did arise, both within the TC and between the TC and the SCU, over the question of the role of bishops in the Church. The TC's chapter on this topic was entrusted to H. Schauf. A first question regarded the derivation of episcopal powers. Lécuyer's chapter had stated that Christ closely linked the power to teach and to govern to the power to sanctify that is given in ordination. If everyone agreed with this, the question remained whether the power of jurisdiction was also rooted in ordination or derived instead from papal delegation. Studies defending both positions were received from the members and consultors of the TC.

While Congar and others proposed that the Council not attempt to settle the issue, which they thought still the object of legitimate theological debate, Schauf's chapter defended the doctrine, emphatically asserted by Pius XII,[457] that bishops received their jurisdictional authority from the pope. In the draft submitted to the CPC, the point was thus stated:

> Bishops receive their actual jurisdiction, not by sacred ordination but, directly or indirectly, from a juridical mission, received not from the Church insofar as it is the assembly of believers, or from the faithful, gathered in whatever numbers, nor from the civil authority, but from the government of the Church and indeed from the successor of Peter himself, by whom therefore they are installed in office and also can be deposed, transferred, and restored.[458]

Meanwhile in the SCU Maccarrone defended the thesis that the bishop's authority derived from that of the pope,[459] but from a paper of Ch. Moeller the SCU's *votum* borrowed historical arguments to the contrary and concluded that the issue was not yet ready for dogmatic solution.[460]

---

[457] In his votum "De Episcopis" (CT 22/60; 4 Feb 1961), Tromp noted two points about the writing of Pius XII "*Mystici Corporis*": that he had refused to admit that bishops could be called "vicars of Christ," reserving this title to himself, and, on the derivation of episcopal jurisdiction from the pope, that "Pope Pius XII personally wanted this view introduced into the Encyclical Mystici Corporis."

[458] *ADP* II/3 1040.

[459] Maccarrone also supplied his documentation to the CT: "De S. Petro exordio episcopatus" (CT 5/61:87; 17 Aug 1961).

[460] Ch. Moeller, "De notione patriarchatus Occidentis" (April 1961). This and another paper by Moeller, "Nota de notione 'Ecclesiae particularis'", were sent by Phillips both to the SCU and to the TC in April 1961 (A-Philips).

That neither Moeller's paper nor the SCU's *votum*, both of them received by the TC in April and May 1961, had any effect on Schauf's chapter may in part be due to the difference in method between the two preparatory bodies. Moeller had offered an historical argument borrowed in part from Batiffol's threefold distinction of the areas of competence of the Bishop of Rome: his authority as bishop of a local Church, as Patriarch of the West, and as pope. The confusion of the last two of these had led to the assigning to papal prerogatives of an authority that more properly belongs to the patriarchate. The SCU's *votum* briefly echoed these considerations.

From the beginning of the TC's work, however, Tromp had argued that the issue should be decided by reference not to historical sources but to the Church's present life and practice. As for Moeller's study, Tromp told Philips that it was better history than theology, since it was clear that the authority of other patriarchs could only be a participation in the power of the pope. The patriarchate of the West and the patriarchate of Constantinople, he added, were analogous concepts, related as *ens absolutum* and *ens participatum*.[461] Tromp's reply illustrates why arguments drawn from history, even within his TC, were so ineffective.

Tromp's views were also reflected in the position taken by the TC's schema on the authority of bishops with respect to the whole Church.[462] Whether singly or collectively, bishops had no authority outside their own churches except by conferral of the pope, although they were bound in many ways to demonstrate their concern for the universal Church. Although the body of bishops, with the pope and never without him, is the subject of full and supreme authority over the whole Church, it can only exercise this authority in an extraordinary way and by the permission of the pope. Schauf's text was thus a vigorous affirmation of papal authority, and this within the chapter that was supposed to counterbalance the ecclesiology of Vatican I.

At the last plenary session of the TC, Msgr. Hermaniuk tried to introduce a stronger statement about the collegial character of the Church's magisterium and Betti urged that the chapter on the magisterium include a discussion of the authority of ecumenical Councils, but these efforts achieved only minor success, for fear that the independence of the papal magisterium might be compromised. The strict dependence of episcopal authority — whether individual or collective, in its origin and in its exercise — on the pope remained the dominant theme of the TC's text.

[461] Tromp to Philips, 24 May 1961 (A-Philips).
[462] *ADP* II/3 1040-41.

2.4. *Church and State*

The last question in Tromp's *schema compendiosum* concerned
Church and State and Christian toleration, on which, he reported to the
October 1960 plenary session, controversies continued to pit bishop
against bishop so that a "a decisive word from on high" is necessary.[463]
For rather different reasons the SCU was also concerned about the issue,
which it framed in terms of religious freedom and tolerance. The need to
address the issue had been urged by the World Council of Churches
which saw in the official teaching of the Church a serious impediment to
ecumenical conversation and cooperation. Bea also justified the SCU's
addressing the issue on the ground that the official *Quaestiones* assigned
to the TC had not included the theme.

The task of drawing up the TC's text on the questions was assigned to
R. Gagnebet. This choice was probably motivated by the fact that only
two years earlier Gagnebet had been the chief author of a document
being prepared in the Holy Office that would have condemned as
erroneous a series of propositions intended to summarize the views of
several Catholic authors — among them Jacques Maritain and John
Courtney Murray — who were calling for a revision of the classic
modern doctrine on Church and State. It appears that it was only the
death of Pius XII that prevented the publication of this text.

Gagnebet's first draft for the TC reproduced with only minimal
changes the text he had prepared for the Holy Office in 1958; even the
title was the same: "The duties of the Catholic state with regard to religion."[464] In the course of four successive drafts, the title would be
changed to "Relations between Church and State and Religious Toleration," but, despite persistent criticism within the TC, the general orientation and positions would remain generally faithful to those of the Holy
Office's 1958 text.

The text approved at the TC's March 1962 plenary meeting and sent
on to the CPC[465] distinguished between the Church and civil society and

---

[463] The themes also appeared in the section on the social order in the *schema
compendiosum De ordine morali*: "Political society, its nature, origin and functions,
according to the teaching of Pius IX, Leo XIII, Pius XI, Pius XII, against the errors of
materialism, socialism, communism, liberalism, and capitaliism. The teaching of Maritain
and laicism." The reference to Maritain was criticized by the members at the October
1960 plenary meeting.

[464] Gagnebet, "De officiis status Catholici erga religionem" (CT 5/61; 7 April 1961).
This was also the title of the published version of the notorious speech of Card. Ottaviani,
2 March 1953: *Doveri dello stato cattolico verso la religione* (Roma 1953).

[465] *ADP* II/4 657-72.

argued the subordination of the end of the latter to the end of the Church. Describing the duties of the Church towards civil society, it maintained that the Church had a right and duty to intervene in the temporal order only when its supernatural goal was at stake. It then proceeded to state that the civil power could not remain indifferent to religion but must support it; indeed the duty to perform religious obligations fell not only on individual citizens but on the civil authority itself, which was, therefore, bound to acknowledge the one way in which God wishes to be served and worshipped: within the Catholic Church. Civil authority could assume this role because such manifest signs attested to the unique divine origin of the Church. The civil authority was thus required to grant the Church complete freedom and independence in the accomplishment of its mission and also to exclude from its legislation and public actions anything that the Church considers to inhibit its purpose.

Gagnebet's text acknowledged that relations between Church and State would vary with circumstances and that the full doctrine can be applied only in a Catholic state. While even there the state could not legitimately coerce consciences, it could act in order to help its citizens persevere in the true faith, by restricting public displays of other religions and the spread of false doctrines. Even in a Catholic country, moreover, the common good both of the nation and of the Church could require that the civil authorities exercise a just tolerance of other religions. Complete religious freedom, of course, could and should be granted in non-Catholic countries. Finally, the text insisted that the principles outlined were not to be obscured by a "false laicism" and by appeal to the common good. They rested on the firm rights of God, on the immutable constitution and mission of the Church, and on the social nature of man, which is always the same and defines the essential purpose of civil society under whatever political or historical circumstances.

The TC's chapter on Church and State, then, was a restatement of the classic doctrine which many Catholics had been criticizing since the end of the Second World War. It rejected arguments common to several of them: that the classical "thesis" reflected a stage of political development that had been surpassed by the rise of modern pluralistic democracies, which require another articulation of the fundamental principles of the Church's independence and freedom. This chapter of the schema *De Ecclesia* would now accomplish the repudiation of such views that had been frustrated in 1958.

For its part the SCU's subcommission was adopting a quite different *impostazione*. At a meeting in Fribourg, 27 December 1960, a text

prepared by L. Janssen and presented by Bishop de Smedt was accepted as
a basic orientation. In a world undergoing rapid unification but also dis-
playing a great pluralism of religions, the Church had to face three great
questions: tolerance, cooperation, and Church-State relations. Tolerance
today was a necessary expression of a charity that acknowledges the fundamental significance of personal freedom both for human dignity and for
faith itself. Urgent human needs require also that Catholics cooperate with
people of other or of no faith. Relations between Church and State must be
governed by the distinction between the spiritual and the temporal established by Christ himself, by the transcendence of the spiritual over the
temporal, and by the freedom of the Church. In the course of developing
these themes, de Smedt's paper distanced itself from some of the com-
monplaces used in statements of the classic thesis: the idea that truth has
rights, the notion of "dogmatic intolerance," the distinction between "thesis" and "hypothesis," and the idea that the state itself must worship God.

Accepted in principle at the February plenary meeting, this text was
further elaborated in the course of the next months, encountering
disagreement only from C. Boyer and E. Hanahoe, who defended the
classical position.[466] An intermediate text, discussed in April, still took
the form of a series of *vota* intended for transmission to another commission. But at the April meeting Bea authorized de Smedt to elaborate
his text in the form of a constitution on religious freedom. In August
1961, the definitive text of the *"Schema Constitutionis de libertate religiosa"* was discussed and approved. It was then sent, with the Pope's
express permission,[467] directly to the CPC.[468]

The SCU text abandoned the term "toleration" in order to discuss
"De bonis fidei in caritate promovendis." This charity requires both that
unworthy types of proselytism be avoided and that full respect be
granted to those to whom the faith is to be preached. Every person had a
right to religious freedom which governs both private and public acts
and which the state must acknowledge and defend. The greatly short-
ened second section urged Catholics to become involved in the direction
of their social life and to cooperate with all men of good will in this
project. The third section stated the distinction between religious and
temporal society and the transcendent freedom of the Church. It then
went on to make a clear and forceful statement:

---

[466] See C. Boyer, "Vérité et tolérance," *Doctor Communis* 14 (1961) 111-27.
[467] On 1 February 1962, Pope John told Bea that this schema and that on the Jews could
be sent by the SCU to the CPC directly, *"without any other commission intervening."*
[468] *ADP* II/4 676-84.

The Catholic Church has never admitted and cannot admit the State positively to propose the doctrine of religious indifferentism which states that all religions are of the same value. But it quite approves modern civil societies when in the practical ordering of civic life they establish by law that religious freedom and political equality should be granted to the adherents of every religion.

Civil society has a duty to grant religious freedom to all religious communities within the bonds of public order and the common good. If civil society has a duty to serve God, it does this best by following divine laws in its legislation and by faithfully fulfilling its own distinctive mission.

The texts of the TC and of the SCU came before the CPC together and provoked the most dramatic confrontation witnessed by that body.[469] After a very brief presentation of his commission's text, Ottaviani attacked the SCU's schema "as very strongly revealing the influence of contacts with non-Catholics." After illustrating this unfortunate tendency, Ottaviani urged that only his text be considered by the TC, adding a final remark: that he did not see how the SCU had any competence to propose a text on Church and State.

Bea, for his part, vigorously denied that his secretariat had exceeded the competence assigned it by the Pope, and he deplored the refusal of the TC to collaborate with other PrC and with the SCU. The SCU text was a reply to serious criticisms of the Catholic Church's position on religious freedom and took into account that "Catholic states" no longer exist. The sociological facts had changed, and these had to lead to a new view of the competence of the state in religious matters.[470]

After Ottaviani defended the sovereign independence of the TC, which did not require it to collaborate with other bodies, the members of the CPC commented. Unusually lengthy interventions, which came closer to a genuine debate than many another discussion in the CPC, soon revealed that its members were as divided in their views as the two preparatory bodies. At the end of the discussion, Ottaviani asked the members to choose between the two texts and not leave it, as some had proposed, to a third commission to resolve. But the result of the vote was no clearer than the discussion had been, and the issue was deferred,

---

[469] *ADP* II/ 4 684-746; see Indelicato, *Difendere la dottrina*, 298-307.

[470] Bea invoked here the authority of Pius XII's speech, *Ci riesce*, 6 December 1953, which was widely interpreted as that Pope's authoritative rejection of Ottaviani's intransigent thesis.

as Confalonieri suggested,[471] to the Pope, who in July created a special commission, chaired by Ciriaci and including Ottaviani, Bea, Tromp and Willebrands, to look for an agreement.

At the end of July a new text, taking into account some of the views stated in the TC's text, was prepared by De Smedt and Hamer and sent by the SCU to Ciriaci and to Tromp. The SCU never received a response to this text from the TC, and the special papal commission never met.[472] It appears to have been the TC alone that decided on the not insubstantial changes that were introduced into its own chapter. The now much shorter text dropped the discussion of tolerance and the section on the "Catholic state," but left intact the general principles, continuing to warn against a "false laicism" that would call them into question.[473]

The texts of the TC and of the SCU on these matters represent one of the most dramatic contrasts encountered in the course of the preparation of the Council. They clearly differed in their statement of the question and in the theological methods and concepts they employed. But behind these differences lay even more fundamental differences with regard to the interpretation of the political, social and cultural developments that had produced the world in which the Council would meet. The TC's text called for a continuation of the attitude and strategy that had determined the strongly anti-modern stance of Roman Catholicism since the French Revolution. The SCU's text echoed the many efforts that had been made, especially since the 1930s, to find other ways in which the Church might meet its redemptive task in a world irremediably changed. The issue at stake between the two texts was the very one that the Pope's vision of the Council posed: how the Church was to be the Church on the threshhold of a new era.

IV. THE REVIEW AND AMENDMENT OF THE PREPARATORY TEXTS

Of the three functions assigned to the CPC, the critical review of the texts prepared by the PrC was the one that it was able to carry through

---

[471] Confalonieri's remarks, *ADP* II/4 731, are particularly important, since he was the president of the CPC's subcommission on amendments. He spoke of the "original sin" that the competencies of the PrC had not been clearly articulated; he denied that any single commission was superior to the others: ("Only the Central Commission has the task of passing judgement on the schemata proposed by the individual commissions"), and he proposed that the question be deferred to the Pope who might either refer it to the subcommission on mixed matters or appoint a committee of experts to review the question and prepare a single text.

[472] See "Note sur le Schema 'De libertate religiosa" présenté par le Secrétariat pour l'unité des chrétiens" (26 Sept 1963), 1 (A-Stransky).

[473] See *AS* I/4 65-74.

most thoroughly.[474] Its task was to determine whether the texts prepared were suitable for submission to the Pope, whose judgment it would be whether to present them to the Council.

A. THE CPC DISCUSSION OF THE TEXTS

Discussion of the preparatory texts began at the second session of the CPC in November 1961 and concluded at its seventh session in June 1962. In anticipation of the November meeting, Felici prepared norms to govern the CPC's work.[475] As the individual PrC completed work on individual schemata, they sent them to Felici's secretariat which had them printed at the Vatican press in separate fascicles. These were then sent out to the members of the CPC so that they could prepare for the open discussions at the meetings. At each meeting the president of the commission gave a brief report on the text. This was followed by an oral discussion which concluded with a vote in which members could express their opinion as *placet, placet iuxta modum*, and *non placet*. A text that received a favorable vote of two-thirds of the members would be considered approved. Votes *placet iuxta modum* would be considered favorable, but if such votes came from a quarter of the members and the matter could not be resolved by further explanation, the results of the votes would be communicated to the Pope. Schemata that were not approved would be sent back to the commission for revision in the light of the CPC comments and resubmission to the CPC.

This last provision was in fact never to be carried out. At the November session, it was announced that a subcommission on amendments was established within the CPC itself, but nothing was said about a resubmission of amended texts to the whole CPC.[476] In fact, no text was ever resubmitted to the CPC, most of whose members did not learn what amendments had been made before they, along with all the other conciliar Fathers, received the first of the texts, in the summer of 1962. As things worked out, in other words, the role of the CPC was to comment on the texts submitted by the CPC; the crucial work of revision was carried out by its subcommission on amendments and was never reviewed by the whole CPC.

[474] A faithful summary of the CPC's work may be found in Indelicato, *Difendere la dottrina*, whose concluding chapter, 315-39, offers many acute comments.

[475] *ADP* II/1 424-25. The CPC itself does not seem to have been consulted on these norms and there is no evidence that they were seriously discussed at any of its meetings.

[476] *ADP* II/1 434.

In the year and a half of its work, the CPC received 124 fascicles, containing seventy-five schemata (reducible to sixty). By the time the Council opened, as a result of the decisions of the CPC and of the work of its subcommissions, some of these schemata were suppressed, reserved to the Holy See, referred to the reform of Canon Law, or combined with other texts. The number of schemata produced during the preparatory period was thereby reduced to twenty-two.[477] This effect of the deliberations of the CPC was not known until much later, however, so that the enduring impression was of a great mass of poorly organized material, of greatly varying quality.

This impression was strengthened by the fact that the texts came before the CPC, not in any logical or coherent order, but simply in the order in which they were completed by the PrC. This could mean that a disciplinary question, addressed by a commission, would come up for discussion before the underlying doctrinal issue, addressed in a text of the TC, had been considered. It could even mean, as in the case of the RE and ST, that individual chapters of a text would not be seen in logical order but in the order of their completion.

The same impression is left by a simple review of the numbers and sequence of texts considered by the CPC in its successive meetings, which gives an idea also of the rhythm of its work. At the November 1961 meeting, it reviewed two texts of the TC, the new formula for the profession of faith and the schema on the sources of revelation, and six brief disciplinary texts from the CLP. At the January 1962 meeting the review of two doctrinal texts, on the moral order and the defence of the deposit of faith, framed the discussion of three disciplinary texts submitted by the SA and five largely disciplinary texts of the OR. A month later the CPC's agenda was devoted to questions of discipline addressed in four texts from the BG, two from the CLP, four from the RE, four from the ST, and one from the OR. Discussion at the March-April meeting of the text from the LI was interrupted by consideration of six texts from the MI and followed by review of the text from the SCM. The May meeting saw the CPC consider four texts of the BG and three from the CLP before returning to doctrinal issues with the TC's texts on chastity, virginity, marriage and the family and on the first six chapters on the Church. The discussion then turned again to disciplinary questions with the review of the remaining chapters of the text of the RE, three more

---

[477] For an outline of the work and a discussion of the number, see Carbone, "Gli schemi preparatori."

from the SA, and three more from the OR. Discussion of three texts from the ST began the final meeting in June, followed by one from the mixed commission of the BG and RE, one each from the DP and RE, two from the SA, one from the OR, two from the AL, three from the TC (the last chapters on the Church), and three from the SCU.

The acceleration of the work of the CPC, prompted by the announcement on 2 February 1962 that the Council would open on 11 October is clearly visible even in this simple review. Not only did the PrC now have to hurry the completion of their texts, but the CPC was forced also to review hastily and more superficially the series of texts that came before it pell-mell in its final meetings.[478] This was particularly unfortunate in the case of the TC's schema *De Ecclesia*, which all sides recognized to be the centerpiece of the Council's work but which came before the TC only in its last two sessions, after nearly all the other texts had been considered and so late that the revision of it was not completed until after the Council had already begun.

The *acta* of the meetings of the CPC reveal that its discussions were characterized by a great deal of freedom and that its members did not feel at all hesitant to criticize the texts prepared by the PrC either openly at the actual meetings or more indirectly in occasional comments outside.[479] Open disputes were not uncommon, some of them quite spirited, which revealed that the Council might not be as peaceful (or automatic) an event as some were anticipating and either hoping or fearing. Many of the lines of disagreement that became visible to the world at the first session of the Council were already being traced in the largely hidden debates in the CPC. Some participants spoke of it as a

---

[478] For the oral and written comments and the account of the votes, 1174 pages sufficed in the *ADP* volumes for the first three of these sessions, while nearly twice as many pages (2231) were required for the last three.

[479] An example of the latter is the remarks of König, in January 1961, after he had seen the first texts of the CPr. He warned about the possibility that there might be forces or influences "which will try to bend the course of things according to all too human desires. Perhaps certain commissions, by their methods and organization might narrow and influence the orientation and methods of the Council. It would only be much later that one would be able to see that this had been so. Many people are concerned to avoid such influences." Later, in remarks that seem to refer to the TC, he added: "One hopes that the preparatory work will be at the level of contemporary theological thought in the Roman Church. The preparatory work must prudently and discreetly reflect the multiformity and the dynamism of this thought, as well as the spiritual experiences, even those which exist outside the Roman Church;" *DC* 58 (1 April 1961) 445-47. On these remarks, see Cardinal Franz Koenig, *Where is the Church Heading?* (Middlegreen, Eng. 1986) 21.

"Council-in-miniature," and König appealed to the freedom and frankness of its debates as an assurance that the Council itself would not be a rubber-stamp assembly.[480]

The doctrinal texts of the TC often met severe criticisms in the CPC, although the sharpness of these was often blunted by the fact that most of the members chose to register their votes in the form of a *Placet iuxta modum*, which technically counted as a positive vote. The texts *De fontibus*, *De deposito fidei*, and *De ordine morali* were much criticized for their negative and defensive character, for their neglect of specifically Christian and theological arguments and motives, and for attempting to settle legitimately disputed questions. In these comments and in the rather hurried remarks on the *De Ecclesia* text were anticipated many of the criticisms that would be heard in the Council hall. Ottaviani was much more aggressive in his responses to criticism than were the presidents of the other PrC, and he strongly insisted throughout that his commission had prepared precisely for what Councils are supposed to do: to defend the Church's deposit of faith from the threat of error. Councils are supposed to be defensive and dogmatic; pastoral work is for bishops and priests, whose job it is to adapt and implement a Council's doctrines and decisions.

The deliberations in the CPC also saw the emergence of the individuals and the groups that would appear in clearly drawn formation during the Council. Among those most critical of the prepared texts were Alfrink, Döpfner, Frings, Hurley, König, Léger, Liénart, Maximos IV, Montini and Suenens. Among the defenders of the texts Browne, Lefebvre, Ottaviani, Ruffini and Siri were the most vocal. Between these two fairly well defined blocs stood the great majority of the members of the CPC, whose positions, less often reflected in formal statements than in brief comments attached to their votes, are more difficult to characterize. If one may speak of alliances at all, they often shifted depending on the topic under consideration. It would be difficult also to describe the tensions often revealed in terms of a *Curia contra mundum* opposition, since there were not lacking defenders of Roman authority among non-Romans and some acute critics of centralization among curialists, most notably Confalonieri.

[480] See Caprile, I/2 250-51; *DC* 59 (7 Oct 1962) 1275, where König also expressed the hope that communiqués on the Council itself would reveal "something of these honest controversies and frank exchanges."

B. THE SUBCOMMISSION ON AMENDMENTS

Between the CPC and the Council itself stood the very important work of the subcommission on amendments. Chaired by Confalonieri, with V. Fagiolo serving as secretary, it was composed of six Cardinals on the CPC: Micara, Copello, Siri, Léger, Frings, and Browne. It began its work on 27 January 1962 and concluded it on 20 July 1962, having met a total of fourteen times. According to its secretary, the subcommission reviewed twenty-nine texts in forty-nine hours of work, a schedule which could hardly permit serious study or debate. The rhythm of its work varied greatly. Its first four meetings were held in its first three months, its last ten in two and a half months. It had the leisure to devote two whole sessions in April and May to revising the schema *De deposito fidei*, but in July the urgency of being ready for the Council's opening forced it to consider four schemata on the 16th, to rush through the schema *De Ecclesia* on the 17th, to review twenty-one chapters of the schema *De religiosis* on the 18th, and to conclude with four schemata on the 20th.

Its method was first to catalogue as systematically as possible the remarks made at the meetings of the CPC[481] and then to send them to the appropriate commission, where a three-man committee was to prepare a reply. It then prepared a text which recorded both the CPC comments and the response of the commission. This text was then distributed to the members of the subcommission who at their meetings decided, in the light of the two sets of comments, which amendments to make in the texts.[482]

Much about the work of this subcommission remains obscure, the minutes of its meetings and the essential documentation being still unpublished. For most of the preparatory texts the only way to judge the concrete effects of CPC comments is by a laborious comparison of the texts submitted to that body with the revised texts printed for conciliar consideration, a task that it is impossible to undertake here. In the review

---

[481] This was not always an easy task, since the formal votes at the end of CPC discussions were made in terms of *Placet, Placet iuxta modum,* and *Non placet,* and because many of the members often referred to earlier speakers, even at times to two or more speakers whose views seemed contradictory! The subcommission on amendments seemed most attentive to written comments by the CPC members, which it faithfully reproduced.

[482] For the dates, method and work, see V. Fagiolo in *Le Concile Vatican II: Synthèse historico-théologique des travaux et des documents* (Paris 1966) 89-92; see also Confalonieri's defence of his subcommission's work in *AS* I/2 106-108.

above of the work of the PrC, brief indications have been given of the general remarks many of the texts received during the CPC discussion and of their subsequent fate at the hands of the subcommission.

On a few of the more important texts, however, further if still partial documentation is available, and a few examples of these may usefully be reviewed here in order to illustrate what kind of impact the CPC criticisms had in the last and crucial process of revision.

1. *The TC's Schema De fontibus revelationis*

At the November meeting of the CPC,[483] five members in particular offered rather serious criticisms of this text: König, Döpfner, Bea, Hurley, and Alfrink. Bea in particular criticized the defensive character of the schema and its restrictive attitude towards the work of Catholic exegetes; he asked that the text be revised with the help of the Pontifical Biblical Commission and of exegetes from the regions where controversy was reigning. Bea's intervention was interrupted three times by Ottaviani's defence of the schema as a needed response to Catholic scholars who were endangering the faith.

At the end of the discussion only five members voted *Placet*; only Frings and Döpfner voted *Non placet*, asking for a revision, while seventy members voted *Placet iuxta modum*, indicating often which observations of speakers they wished taken into account in a revision. (Bea's name was invoked by fifty-three of the members.) Many of them asked that the text be revised and then resubmitted for another vote. Ciriaci proposed that a revised text be sent to the members of the Commission who could respond by mail, a suggestion which Ottaviani immediately seconded and which several members also endorsed.[484] Several members asked that an attempt be made in the revised text to reconcile the positions of Bea and Ottaviani.[485]

The subcommission gathered the comments made at the CPC and sent them to the TC in a twenty-three page typed text.[486] In early January Tromp wrote a ten-page reply which was revised and approved in the

---

[483] *ADP* I/2 523-62; Indelicato, *Difendere la dottrina* 77-90.

[484] *ADP* II/I 556.

[485] Silva Santiago made the prophetical comment, "And it seems to me that this must be done before the Council, since otherwise there will be difficult discussions and controversies in the Council itself;" *ADP* II/I 560.

[486] "Observationes factae ab Em.mis, Exc.mis et Rev.mis Patribus Pont. Commissionis Centralis in Sessione habita die 10 novembris circa Constitutionem De Fontibus Revelationis" (A-Florit).

course of a conversation with Ottaviani on 9 January.[487] Tromp was willing to accept about half of the specific amendments proposed at the CPC, including some not insignificant changes in the treatment of inspiration, inerrancy, and the historicity of the Gospels. But at several points, Tromp did not hide his annoyance at some of the criticisms or his convictions about the issues at stake. To Bea he replied that the constructive and positive character of the text was obvious to anyone who read it without prejudice. It was dangerous to speak of the freedom of Catholic exegetes, since they are limited by the magisterium, the tradition and the analogy of faith, and they should not be given an opportunity to use a conciliar text to oppose a Roman decision, as had happened when some exegetes abusively cited *Divino afflante Spiritu* against other decisions of the Holy See.

Tromp could not accept Döpfner's proposal that the text speak of the Scriptures as the chief source. "For many reasons Sacred Scrripture is not the principal source. For tradition is prior in nature; it is the source from which alone the inspiration of all of Scripture can be definitively proved; it is the source from which we know the Canon with certainty; it explains Scripture; finally, the Church existed without the New Testament Scriptures, but not without the New Testament tradition." Döpfner's comment that the magisterium needs the help of theologians, Tromp said, was dangerous because it could be taken to mean a *conditio sine qua non*. To criticisms of the draft's treatment of the historicity of the Gospels, he replied that the TC did not think there could be any debate about the matter: "It is quite convinced that because of the ever cruder errors being taught in middle schools, in preaching, in catechesis, the text must speak about the infancy of Christ, his miracles, and his resurrection and ascension."

A comparison with the final text reveals that the subcommission on amendments in general accepted Tromp's guidance on almost all the significant issues. There are some changes that cannot be explained by reference either to the summary of the CPC comments or to Tromp's reply. It is possible that Bea exercised some influence on the subcommission,[488] but it was not enough substantially to alter the content or the

---

[487] "Responsio ad observationes factas in Commissione Centrali ad Constitutionem De Fontibus Revelationis;" Florit Papers. Both of these texts were then printed in *De emendatione schematum decretorum quae discussa fuerunt in sessione generali Pontificiae Commissionis Centralis mense novembri 1961 habita* (TPV 1962) 33-44.

[488] At the plenary session of the SCU in March 1962, Bea said that he had sent "extensive comments" on the *De fontibus* text to Confalonieri, who had found them helpful. It is not clear whether Bea is referring to the remarks he had made at the CPC meeting or to another document unknown to me.

tone of the TC's text. The *votum* of the SCU on the relationship between Scripture and Tradition was completed only after the subcommission had finished its revision of the text, whose position on the subject remained the same as that of the text submitted to the CPC.[489]

2. The TC's Schema De deposito fidei

This text was discussed at the January meeting of the CPC,[490] after which the many general and particular comments were communicated in an 83-page document to the TC. A small TC committee worked on a revision of the text in late February, late March and early April. Its first responses were sent to the subcommission on 22 March, with the second part sent in early April. The TC's responses totalled forty pages.[491]

The subcommission on amendments reviewed the first six chapters of the schema *De deposito fidei* on 2 April and the last five on 7 May 1962. Space does not permit us here to review all the criticisms this text had received at the CPC discussion nor all of the TC's responses to them. But some more important general discussions may be summarized on the basis of the subcommission's report.[492]

Liénart and Alfrink had criticized the heavily philosophical approach of the early chapters of the schema. The TC responded with a strong defence of the perennial Christian philosophy, no mere human invention, but "human reason itself, by which man is made in the image of God and which is common to all men, even Indians and Africans, as it reflects on itself in the light of faith and finds there the most basic principles, both speculative and practical, by which human life is governed." Certainly there are disputes among Christians about the more remote conclusions of this philosophy, into which the Council should not enter. But the TC had reservations about Alfrink's claim that the Church's preaching had to be adapted to various cultures. This is true only insofar as these cultures do not contradict natural law and natural religion,

---

[489] Tromp received permission from the Pope to show the text as revised by the subcommission on amendments to B. Wambacq, subsecretary of the Pontifical Biblical Commission on 24 April 1962: "That scholar, who because of rumors expected some sort of document of the Sacred Inquisition, was astonished at the moderation of the teaching, which he gladly approved;" "Ultima acta Pont. Comm. Theologicae," 3.

[490] *ADP* II/2 279-415; Indelicato, *Difendere la dottrina*, 115-31.

[491] For this information, see Tromp, "Ultima acta Pontificiae Commissionis Theologicae."

[492] *De emendatione schematum decretorum quae discussa fuerunt in sessione generali Pontificiae Commissionis Centralis mense ianuario 1962 habita*. Pars III and Pars IV (TPV 1962).

"which cannot be established a priori and indeed, as a result of original sin, happens rather rarely." As for the biblical authors, while the TC could grant that St. Paul, St. John, and Christ himself had not preached philosophy, it was unwilling to deny that they were imbued with the principles of Christian philosophy especially in matters of theodicy, ethics and psychology. The Commission had taken *Humani generis* as its guide in its chapters on the foundations of faith and did not wish in any way to indulge in that inferiority complex towards non-Catholic philosophy which regards Christian philosophy "as a Cinderella" and opens the way to a dangerous laicism in philosophy.

To the criticisms that the schema was too negative, too philosophical, and too condemnatory, Döpfner had added its lack of internal unity, which lack he suggested might be met by the rather Rahnerian synthesis he outlined.[493] The TC replied that it could not accept this proposal at all; the matters its texts considered were chosen only because either wholly or in part they were being corrupted by recent errors. To make a synthesis of them would be very artificial. The synthetic unity of its own text was psychological and pastoral: "the desire to defend the faithful from errors of various sorts, which are not at all in harmony with one another." The TC then proceeded to give Döpfner a lesson: a constitution in defence of the Church was fulfilling a grave duty, which bishops ought to be undertaking in their own dioceses instead of worrying so much about exemptions and decentralization.[494]

As for the objection made at the TC that issues still being disputed among theologians should not be settled by the Council, Tromp pointed out that this excellent principle was not an absolute. The consensus of theologians was not a necessary condition of a magisterial decision, and

---

[493] *ADP* II/2 287-91.

[494] Léger, who was a member of the subcommission on amendments, sent Döpfner a copy of this reply, adding: "In all honesty, I am sending you this text because I do not think that theologians have a right so impertinently to pass judgement on a Father of the Church who is, moreover, a member of the Central Commission;" Léger to Döpfner, 27 Aug 1962. Döpfner replied: "The comments of the Theological Commission on my remarks about the schema 'De Deposito pure custodiendo' I read with sorrow and surprise, not only because of the tone, inappropriate when addressing bishops, but also because the attitude is unsatisfactory and truly fruitless in terms of the tasks of the Council. I am of the view that this Constitution has to be dropped entirely; even without it there is enough material left for the Council even on theological questions. And the various errors condemned there have already been pointed out, in their dangerousness, by the Holy See;" (A-Léger).

opinions could be rejected because they conflict with other already defined truths. Vatican II should take care not to weaken what earlier Councils had declared: "For any doubt about an earlier Council necessarily lessens the authority of this one."[495]

On more particular matters, the TC was willing to separate the section *De novissimis* into a separate chapter because so many errors about this doctrine were spreading: "which is not surprising when the notion of sin is being corrupted and a final absolution is being promised even to the devil." On the condemnation of polygenism, the TC continued to think it necessary to close the door *Humani generis* had left slightly ajar, since Councils are for settling matters encyclicals leave open. As for the chapter on the salvation of unbaptized children, the TC made a frank admission: the question was addressed not because the matter in itself was so serious, but to defend the Church's ordinary and universal magisterium. The text proposed the solid and continuous doctrine of the Church. "But if with so many important documents we still do not have absolute certainty, then truly we must confess, along with the bishops of Holland when they wrote about 'the meaning of the Council,' that 'in practice the final and absolute certainty we have about a truth of faith is an extraordinary definition of the Church.' Which cannot be true." Few things in the Church's universal preaching are as certain as this doctrine. "We would have to agree with all those modern people who say that at least in matters not clearly defined by the extraordinary magisterium a '*ressourcement*' is necessary. This is why all this activity in recent years to create a new public opinion in the Church on the fate of infants who die without baptism is by no means an innocent matter. *Videant consules.*" In the end the TC could not accept any of the alternate proposals to the text it had presented on the matter: "It is clear that the Theological Commission can never agree with the majority of the Central Commission and leaves the grave responsibility on this matter to that Commission and to the Fathers gathered in Council."

Of all the texts of the TC, this schema was the one that underwent most changes as it passed through the subcommission on amendments.[496] There were now ten chapters instead of eleven, Chapter IX of the original, "The Unity of Common Origin of the Human Race," having

---

[495] The TC repeated this concern later, warning that the Council should do nothing to weaken Trent's teaching on original sin: "For if this is allowed, it also allows people to disregard its own decrees."

[496] See Tromp, "Ultima acta Pontificiae Commissionis Theologicae," 1-2, for brief indications of the exchanges between the TC and the subcommission.

been joined with Chapter VIII to form a single Chapter, "Original Sin in the Children of Adam." Chapter VII of the original, "Spiritism and the Last Things," has been divided up, with the material on the last things expanded and now forming a chapter of its own, #IX, "The Last Things," while the other material has been expanded to form Chapter VI, "Private Revelations." The titles of certain chapters have also been changed: Chapter III is now "The Creation and Evolution of the World;" Chapter IV, "Public Revelation and Catholic Faith;" Chapter VII, "The Natural and Supernatural Orders." The chapter on infants dying without baptism is dropped because only a minority in the CPC approved it.

On more particular matters, the revised text does nuance the philosophical assertions in the first chapters and the discussion of revelation and faith. The text on polygenism is altered to accord with *Humani generis*. Without going into all the details, it can be said that in general, the subcommission on amendments showed a greater independence of the TC in its judgements on the schema *De deposito fidei*.

3. *The TC's Schema De Ecclesia*

This text was considered by the CPC at its May and June meetings.[497] Many criticisms, both general and particular, were expressed, enough to fill 197 pages in the text sent to the TC for reaction. A small TC committee again set about the work of revision, in circumstances of such varied and urgent business that they may help to explain the even more aggressive character of the TC's responses, which reveal also the heights of its claims to authority.[498]

It began with a defence of the unique authority of the TC: "It alone is competent in dogmatic matters," which is the reason it felt no obligation to form mixed commissions with the other commissions, "much less with Secretariats whose purpose is not study." The TC would gladly receive suggestions, but it had no duty to agree with them all. It had had among its members both conservatives and progressives, expert in all areas, which made it highly unlikely that in the CPC anything would be said that had not been more fully discussed in the TC.

[497] *ADP* II/3 986-1115; II/4 621-746, 785-812; Indelicato, *Difendere la dottrina*, 242-54, 272-76, 290-307.

[498] *De emendatione schematis Constitutionis De Ecclesia* (TPV 1962). This committee was composed of Tromp, Gagnebet and Schauf. Drafts of the responses of the last two make it clear that the aggressive and sarcastic tone of many of the comments in the final text sent to the subcommission on amendments is due to Tromp.

The TC committee then reviewed the areas of greatest dispute that had appeared in the CPC discussion. On the relation between the Roman Catholic Church and the Mystical Body of Christ, the TC could not accept those who deny they are identical or who think that the Body of Christ is broader in extent than the Catholic Church. On membership in the Church, to accept Bea's idea would lead to the most serious consequences, among them the ruin of the unity and indivisibility, the indefectibility and infallibility, and the holiness of the Church and the loss of the ecumenical authority of any Council that did not include non-Catholic Christians.

On the question whether the mystical or juridical aspect should be dominant, the TC replied that it was the latter: while Christ might have chosen to give his grace without the Church, in fact he willed that union with him would be realized "in a social, juridical, heterogeneous organism. We are united to Christ because we are united at least by desire with the Church, and not vice-versa." On the question which should prevail, the authority of Peter or that of the college of apostles, the answer had to be that of Peter: since Christ's ascension, Peter stood towards the Church as Christ had stood towards the Apostles. As a bishop the Pope is a member of the episcopal body, but as Vicar of Christ, he stands above it. "Nor is the body of bishops with and under Peter for the sake of the ordinary governance of the Church; only Peter has this role. Otherwise the Church would cease to be monarchical."

The TC concluded its remarks on the basic and general questions with its most aggressive claim yet:

> Rightly does the Secretary General fear that disagreements on the above points may become known outside. They could not be settled in the Central Commission because it lacks both juridical and practical competence. For it has no doctrinal authority, and in it while there is very great freedom to criticize, serious replies to objections are impossible. As for the questions listed in this paragraph...., the Theological Commission, after lengthy debates, came to conclusions from which it can in no way depart.

In the more particular responses of the TC simply to the comments on the first six chapters *De Ecclesia*, which fill no fewer than forty-three pages, the same sarcastic impatience is often displayed, particularly with regard to proposals to strengthen references to episcopal authority at the expense, the TC thought, of papal prerogatives. Nevertheless, the TC did agree to many changes in the text, most of which the subcommission on amendments in turn accepted.

For example, in the first four chapters of the schema *De Ecclesia*, there is only one significant point on which the judgement of the subcommission differed from that of the TC's committee. It concerned the crucial question of the relationship between episcopal ordination and the three powers of the bishop. The text submitted to the CPC had said that bishops derive their actual jurisdiction, not from ordination, but from a juridical mission.[499] This position had been vigorously criticized at the CPC by Döpfner, Alfrink, Confalonieri and Maximos IV. The TC's committee rejected most of these criticisms and was only willing to accept a minor change, so that the prior text would be preceded by a statement that ordination by its nature is ordered towards the exercise of episcopal jurisdiction.[500] But the subcommission on amendments was dissatisfied with this response and altered the text to read: "Although sacred ordination to the supreme level of the priesthood confers, along with the office of sanctification, the offices also of teaching and governance which comprise jurisdiction, nevertheless bishops do not receive the exercise of jurisdiction by sacred ordination itself but by a mission ... from the supreme governance of the Church." It did not escape the notice of the members of the TC's committee that this change, which ran quite counter to its views, reflected the position of Confalonieri, the president of the subcommission on amendments.[501] But this change remained the only significant disagreement between the TC's committee and the CPC's subcommission in the crucial first four chapters of the schema on the Church.

4. The LI's Schema De sacra Liturgia

Considerable controversy surrounds the work of this subcommission with regard to the schema *De sacra liturgia*. At the first session of the Council, for example, Ottaviani publicly wondered why the text on communion under both kinds had not been altered by the subcommission in accordance with the unanimous wishes of the members of the CPC.[502]

---

[499] "Bishops receive their actual jurisdiction not by sacred ordination itself but, directly or indirectly, by a juridical mission from the governance of the Church and, indeed, from the successor Peter himself...."

[500] "Although sacred ordination to the supreme level of the priesthood is of its nature ordered towards the exercise of episcopal jurisdiction, nevertheless bishops do not receive their actual ordination from sacred ordination itself but by a juridical mission and indeed...from the supreme governance of the Church."

[501] See H. Schauf, "Zur Textgeschichte grundlegender Aussagen aus 'Lumen gentium' über das Bischofskollegium," *AKKR* 141 (1972) 37-40.

[502] *AS* I/2 18.

On the other hand, several men who had participated in the work of the
LI were surprised at many of the changes that had been introduced by
the subcommission.[503] Bugnini listed the changes: the omission of the
"Declarationes," the watering-down of the effort at decentralization, the
omission of communion under both kinds for the laity, limitations of the
occasions for concelebration, the omission of the possibility of using the
vernacular for the divine office.[504] Both defenders and opponents of the
liturgical reform, therefore, were unhappy with the work of the subcommission on amendments.

But there is another complicating factor, at least if Bugnini is to be
believed. He claims that besides the official three-man committee he
chaired in order to reply to the comments made at the CPC, there was
also a small, unofficial committee appointed by Larraona in order to
correct the text in a direction more pleasing to the Cardinal. Bugnini's
committee did not at first know of the existence of this second secret
committee, and, Bugnini says, the Cardinal "juggled the two, anxious
that the game not be discovered."[505]

It is not now possible to verify the existence of this other, "secret"
committee, much less to follow its work. There is available, however, a
document which contains both the remarks of the members of the CPC
and the official responses prepared, it seems, by Bugnini's official
committee.[506] This text enables one to compare the response of this
committee to the text that was presented to the Council. We may concentrate on the points at which Bugnini and others saw a weakening of the
LI's text's positions.

First, then, with regard to the omission of the *"Declarationes"* in the
conciliar text, there does not seem to have been any call at the CPC to
remove these from the text. The LI's committee explained that while not
part of the conciliar text, they were helpful for explaining the proposals
made in the text. The LI would therefore gratefully receive comments

[503] Martimort, for example, speaks of "the changes, damaging in my view, which
various influences had introduced into the text;" "La Constitution sur la Liturgie," 69.
[504] Bugnini, *The Reform of the Liturgy*, 26.
[505] Bugnini, *The Reform of the Liturgy*, 27, where he identifies F. Antonelli and
G. Löw as members of the "secret" committee. Caprile, II, 114n, gives some support to
Bugnini's claims: "It became known that besides the reply of the Liturgical Commission
to the observations of the Central Commission, the Subcommission on Amendments also
received other observations, private in nature and quite opposite in orientation, from Cardinal Larraona; these, although announced beforehand, were received when the revision
had already been completed;" see also Paiano, "Il rinnovamento della liturgia," 132-34.
[506] *De emendatione schematum decretorum quae discussa fuerunt in sessione generali
Pontificiae Commissionis Centralis mensis martii-aprilis 1962*, Pars I (TPV 1962).

and keep them for the post-conciliar commission so that the intent of the text would be clear.[507] The comment is not entirely clear and could be interpreted to mean that it was not necessary for the text presented to the Council to contain the Declarationes. On the other hand, Bugnini's committee often made proposals to revise and clarify the Declarations, which suggests that it expected them to be included in the conciliar text.

Secondly, with regard to the *authority of episcopal conferences*, in #20 of the text presented to the Council, the wording about the authority of episcopal conferences is identical to the text presented to the CPC with the exception of the addition at the end of the words: "after its acts have been recognized by the Holy See (cf. can. 291)." Except for the reference to the canon of the Code, this addition had been recommended by the LI's committee itself.[508] The same issue recurred in #24, on the language of the liturgy. Here Bugnini's committee's proposal to change the first statement of principle was accepted, so that instead of reading that the use of Latin "must absolutely be preserved," it now said, more weakly: "should be preserved." But where the LI's text had proposed that episcopal conferences would have the right "to *establish* the limits and manner of introducing the vernacular into the liturgy," the text presented to the Council changed the verb to "*propose*."[509] This change ran counter to the recommendation of the LI's committee: "The faculties that would be granted to the episcopal conferences would not be greater than they are now; the principle of authority also remains since the acts must be recognized by the Holy See."[510]

[507] *De emendatione*, 3.

[508] *De emendatione*, 16. In its general introductory responses, the LI's committee cited Ruffini's comment: "Is too much freedom being given to the episcopal conferences?" to which it replied (p. 7): "Not in the view of the Liturgical Commission. Decisions on liturgical matters are not being handed over to the episcopal conferences and remain entirely in the hands of the Holy See; what is being handed over is the role of determining or judging the limits and degree of liturgical adaptation that is to be submitted to the Holy See. In the preparatory acts for the Council there were so great many petitions from bishops that the Liturgical Conclusion thought that something had to be conceded to the episcopal conferences. This is, after all, what commonly happens when the episcopal conferences send the acts of their annual or semi-annual sessions to the Holy See."

[509] A similar change was made in the canon on the possibility of introducing vernacular hymns into the solemn liturgy.

[510] *De emendatione*, 27. In its general remarks (p. 7-8), the LI's committee replied to Montini's request for greater use of the vernacular: "For practical reasons which should not be scorned, the Commission asked for the essentials with regard to the vernacular, essentials for pastoral action. But no. 24 says 'especially,' which leaves the door open for the Holy See so that it can see to the needs of different places in the future. What is proposed can be accepted by everyone since it rests on solid arguments: the readings, some songs, prayers. A balance must be kept between tradition and pastoral needs. Thus it is the Commission's view that the question of the vernacular must be kept within the proposed limits."

With regard to *communion under both species*, #42 remained the
same, extending it not only to clerics and religious but also to lay
people,[511] except that the words "for certain well defined cases, in the
judgment of the bishops," were changed to "to certain cases well
defined by the Holy See, as, for example, in the Mass of sacred Ordination." Here the reference to the Holy See was suggested by the LI's own
committee, which had commented: "Certainly it has to be kept to
certain defined cases. But it maintains that the door should not be closed
and that the matter should be examined leniently."[512]

As for *concelebration* (#44), the LI's text proposed extending opportunities for this to the chrism Mass on Holy Thursday, to conventual
Masses and the chief Masses where there are more priests present than
are needed, to meetings of priests where it would be difficult for all of
them to celebrate singly, and to extraordinary celebrations. Although
Bugnini's committee proposed retaining all of these cases with only
some minor changes in wording,[513] the text presented to the Council
reduced them to two: the chrism Mass and meetings of priests, "if individual celebrations cannot otherwise be provided and in the judgment of
the Ordinary."

With regard to *the language of the divine office*, the permission
granted in the LI's text that the vernacular be used in certain circumstances was dropped from the text presented to the Council. This ran
counter to the response of the LI's committee, which took note of the
sharp divisions in the CPC on the matter but argued that the moderate
proposal should be retained: "But since it is a serious and important
question, the Liturgical Commission asks that the decision be left to the
Council."[514]

When one reviews these and other changes,[515] one sees in them a
regular effort, resisted by the LI's committee, to reassert Roman authority
over liturgical reform and adaptation, particularly on the matters of

[511] Bugnini, therefore, was incorrect in saying that the text presented to the Council
withdrew this practice from the laity.
[512] *De emendatione*, 37.
[513] *De emendatione*, 37-38.
[514] *De emendatione*, 52.
[515] Two paragraphs were dropped from the LI's text. The first, on stipends in concel-
ebrated Masses (#47), disappears without comment by the LI's committee; the second, on
baptisms in hospitals (#56), was opposed at the CCP, and the committee agreed that it
should be dropped. At three places also phrases were introduced to assert that the
eucharistic sacrifice is at the center of the liturgy; the source of this suggestion is not
known, and it is not mentioned in the committee's responses. Other minor changes were
made, some at the committee's suggestion, others on unknown bases.

language and of communion under both kinds. Some movement in this direction was approved by the LI's committee, but not the reduction of the role of the episcopal conferences to the mere "proposing" of use of the vernacular. It is, of course, impossible now to know whether this and other changes were made because of the intervention of the alleged "secret" committee or because the subcommission on amendments found enough ground in the remarks made at the CPC to refuse the recommendations of the LI's official committee. Further light will have to await the publication of the *acta* of that subcommission or the availability of other sources.

Space does not allow one to extend this study to other preparatory texts, but the review of the amendments to these four schemata permits certain observations. First, the CPC's subcommission usually accepted the responses the commissions gave to the CPC proposals. Second, where the CPC criticisms included an alternate text, they had a much better chance of being accepted both by the revising committees of the PrC and by the subcommission on amendments. Third, both those committees and the subcommission itself were often in the position of having to address conflicting opinions in the CPC. Fourth, the work of the subcommission was surely inhibited by the press of time. This was most obvious in the case of the schema *De Ecclesia*, on which a very large number of comments was registered, but to which it devoted only one meeting of three and a half hours.

The general conclusion, tentative until the publication of the *acta* of its meetings, is that the subcommission on amendments, while it did effect major reductions and amalgamations in many of the more practically oriented texts, did not in most cases notably alter the problematic or the content of the major doctrinal texts submitted to the CPC. The one task of the three assigned to the CPC which it was able to take up with some seriousness — the review and criticism of the texts of the PrC — was fatally flawed perhaps chiefly because its subcommission had to begin its work so late in the process and when the urgency of time prevented it from undertaking it with proper care and from submitting its own work of revision to a further judgement of the whole CPC. This delay, as we shall see, also made it impossible for the CPC to have much effect on the determination of the agenda of the first session of the Council, particularly by introducing a greater coherence than had marked the preparations. When the

Council opened, this lack of coordination, which Hurley would later call the Council's "original sin," remained unredeemed.[516]

V. The Ecumenical Presence at the Council

A. Establishing the Principle

The wave of ecumenical enthusiasm provoked by the announcement of the Council grew even stronger with the announcement of the establishment of the Secretariat for Christian Unity. Now that the Vatican had an office for ecumenical affairs, it was possible to consider new opportunities for formal conversation. These included not only path-breaking meetings between the Pope and the heads of several western Protestant churches, but also the possibility of participation, at least through observers, in one another's meetings, which would mean the presence of non-Catholic representatives at the Council itself.[517] Pope John is reported to have mentioned this possibility on 30 August 1959: if representatives of the separated brethren wished to be present at the Council, they would be welcome.[518] In his press conference, 30 October 1959, Tardini said that the question of non-Catholic observers was under study, but that he thought it probable that they would be welcome if they wished to come, in which case it would be appropriate to send them the more important documents.[519] Although both support and opposition to

---

[516] At the first session of the Council, Hurley recalled the frequency of complaints at the CPC at the insufficiently pastoral nature of many of the texts. He went on: "In the Central Commission, as I now see, when complaints were made about the non-pastoral character of the schemata, we were voices crying in the wilderness. There was no one who listened to our cry, who could or should have addressed this failure in the preparatory work. Central direction was lacking. There was no person or commission for clearly interpreting the pastoral goal of the Council, for directing and coordinating the work of the individual commissions towards the established purpose, for establishing limits to what was to be proposed to the Council. Here is the basic defect in the whole preparatory effort. Here is, as it were, the original sin of this Council;" AS I/3 199.

[517] These possibilities were raised at the first meeting between Bea and Visser't Hooft in October 1960; see Schmidt, *Augustin Bea*, 342-43; P. Chenaux, "Le Conseil oecuménique des Eglises et la convocation du Concile," in *Veille*, 200-213. The ecumenical implications of the convocation of the Council were a major interest of many diplomats; see A. Melloni, "Governi e diplomazie davanti all'annuncio del Vaticano II," *Ibid.*, 225-237.

[518] See A. Wenger, *Vatican II: Volume I: The First Session* (Westminster MD 1966) 141-42; *HerKorr* 14 (1959/60) 8.

[519] See *ICI* 108 (15 November 1959) 5; the report of Tardini's remarks published in *OssRom* and then in *ADA*, I, 154, omits the comment about sending the observers the documentation.

the idea were registered during the antepreparatory period, on 26 June 1960 the Pope seemed to settle the issue when he said that representatives of the separated brethren "will be called to assist at the great meeting of the Church."[520]

One difficulty in the way of non-Catholic presence at the Council, however, was the Holy Office's long-standing policy that no Catholics could attend meetings of the World Council of Churches in the status of official observers. Unless this difficulty could be overcome, the principle of ecumenical reciprocity would make it very difficult for Protestants to consider attending the Council. When the WCC invited the Secretariat to send observers to its third General Assembly to be held in New Delhi, 18 November-15 December 1961, the SCU was prepared to respond positively. Assuming that it had the authority to decide the issue, at its February 1961 meeting it began to identify the five representatives it would send, who included three of its own members: Willebrands, Hamer, and Weigel.

But when these names were sent to the Holy Office for a *nihil obstat* in June, Ottaviani replied that it was up to the Holy Office to decide the principle at stake and that it had decided to preserve the principle that no official Catholic observers could attend assemblies of the WCC; any Catholics who went would have to go as "journalists". Bea protested this decision, on which he had not been consulted, pointing out that it would make it impossible to invite non-Catholic observers to the Council. Although Bea sent a copy of this reply to the Pope, it does not appear that the Pope himself had to intervene. Bea and Ottaviani worked out a compromise: five Catholic observers, chosen by the SCU, could attend the New Delhi meeting, but they could not be selected from among any of the preparatory bodies of the Council. Willebrands, Weigel and Hamer were then replaced by E. Duff of the U.S., M.-J. Le Guillou of "Istina", and J.C. Groot of the Catholic Conference for Ecumenical Questions, joining J. Edamaron and I. Extross, both of India.[521]

Meanwhile, the SCU had already begun to discuss the question of non-Catholic observers at the Council, accepted in principle at a small meeting in Rome on 15 December 1960. What remained was to decide in what ways the observers could be present, the subject raised at the

---

[520] *ADP* I 8.

[521] For this episode see Stransky, "The Foundation of the SPCU," 75-76; Schmidt, *Augustin Bea*, 350-51. Willebrands wrote to Weigel, 26 July 1961: "What should make us rejoice is the *fact* that five RCC observers will be going; the granting of this principle overshadows the refusal of our personally attending;" Woodstock College Archives.

SCU's second plenary session in February 1961. Willebrands gave a report in which he summarized the many expressions of interest the Secretariat had received. After insisting on the difference between journalists and ecumenical observers, he proposed that the latter be admitted to general sessions of the Council, but without a right to speak or to vote and that the Secretariat organize special meetings in which to explain developments and learn reactions. As for whom to invite, Willebrands thought it more appropriate to invite experts in ecumenism rather than bishops or heads of communions, which could cause a number of difficulties. Willebrands' proposals were generally approved by the SCU.[522]

At the April plenary session a definitive text was approved for transmission to the CPC. The SCU's *votum* followed Willebrands' initial report rather closely.[523] It urged the necessity of providing the separated brethren more than merely external information on the deliberations of the Council, which they were sure to follow very closely; and the best way of providing this would be to invite them to send observers. It reviewed expressions of interest in the Council on the part of non-Catholics, including a desire to send observers. It then proposed a possible statute for such invitations and provided a list of ten separated communities that might be invited, in addition, of course, to representatives of the Orthodox Churches. The quality of the persons invited (bishops or experts) was left to the good judgement of the communities.

The question had also been addressed by some of the curial officials who served as counsellors to the CPC, when they responded in early March 1961 to an inquiry which included the question of whom to invite to the Council. Four of them proposed that representatives of non-Catholic communities be invited.[524] At the first session of the CPC, 12 June 1961, Bea reported on the deliberations of the SCU that had led to its *votum*;[525] and in the course of the following discussion some 21 members of the CPC declared their approval of the presence of non-Catholic observers.[526] On 13 July Felici sought a judgement on the SCU's proposal from three important figures in the Curia, F. Carpino, A. Coussa, and A. Samoré, assessors respectively of the Consistorial Congregation, the Congregation for Oriental Churches, and the Congregation for

[522] See Willebrands, "Observateurs non-catholiques;" Minutes of the discussion, 9 February 1961 (A-Stransky).

[523] The text may be found in *ADP* II/1 449-57.

[524] See *ADP* I/1 21-22, 55-57 (Palazzini), 66-71 (Brennan), 73-76 (Rossi), 98-100 (Cavagna).

[525] See Bea's report to the first session of the CPC, 12 June 1961, *ADP* II/1 165-66.

[526] *ADP* II/1 169-75, 234-401; see also *ADP* IV/1 40-41 for a summary.

Extraordinary Ecclesiastical Affairs.[527] With minor differences, their responses were favorable to the SCU's proposal.[528]

The question arose as a distinct topic at the November meeting of the CPC, where the SCU's proposal was considered.[529] By this time the SCU had specified its proposal in the form of four conclusions that were distributed at the meeting.[530] The first established the principle that "Non-Catholic Christians, who desire to be present at the Council through delegates, can be admitted in ways and under conditions to be determined in time." The second proposed that after a general announcement of the possibility of such a presence, the Secretariat would undertake contacts with various communities to find out if they wished to send observers; when the response was positive, a formal invitation would be sent to them. The third conclusion was that on the matter of who would be invited, conversations would be undertaken with the prelates of the major Oriental Churches and with the moderators of the major Protestant confederations, who would be able to choose two or three observers; but the Secretariat reserved the right also to invite a few others who were expert in ecumenical conversations. Finally, it was proposed that the observers would be present not only in the most solemn sessions, but also in sessions where discussions and votes would take place, it being understood that they would have no right to intervene in the discussions. On sessions they did not intend they would be supplied information by the Secretariat, and the observers would have an opportunity at such meetings to express their own views, which the Secretariat would transmit to the proper conciliar commission.

After Bea had briefly introduced the SCU's text and specific proposals, Cicognani, speaking on behalf of the OR, declared his general agreement with the proposals of the SCU. His remarks differed somewhat in spirit from that of Bea, however, since he cited as a precedent the quite differently inspired invitations sent out before Vatican I, described the ecumenical aim of the Council in terms of a return of the separated brethren, and questioned whether the representatives should not be called "honored guests" rather than "observers."[531]

[527] *ADP* II/1 418. Conspicuously absent from this consultation was the Holy Office which at this very time was attempting to exclude the presence of Catholic observers at the New Delhi meeting of the WCC.

[528] *ADP* I/1 427-32.

[529] See *ADP* I/1 449-58 (text), 458-66 (reports of Bea and Cicognani), 466-95 (discussion); see Indelicato, *Difendere la dottrina*, 57-67.

[530] *ADP* I/1 457-58.

[531] *ADA* I/1 465.

The members of the CPC declared themselves favorable to the SCU's proposal both in general and in its particular suggestions.[532] Only Ottaviani was reserved and even he asked only that the question be deferred because it was not yet mature and many difficulties had still to be addressed.[533] The official minutes of the discussion, however, gave special attention to this abstention, attributing it to a different motive: "because the issues were not clearly presented and there were disagreements between the report of Cardinal Bea and the remarks of Cardinal Amleto Cicognani."[534] When news began to spread of the generally positive response of the CPC, Felici's Press Office made a point of emphasizing that the vote of the CPC was purely consultative and that the definitive decision remained in the hands of the Pope alone.[535]

The papal decision became known in the *Bulla indictionis*, 25 December 1961. As Bea had recommended in his remarks to the CPC,[536] the possibility was announced by indirection as the Pope reported on the response the announcement of the Council had received among non-Catholics:

> And we know also not only that the announcement of the Council was accepted by them with joy but also that many have already promised to offer their prayers for its success and that they hope to send representatives of their communities to follow its work at close quarters. All this is for us a reason of great comfort and of hope and precisely for the purpose of facilitating these contacts we some time ago established the Secretariat for this specific purpose.[537]

With this approval, the SCU could now cooperate with the CPC's subcommission in the elaboration of the section of the conciliar rules

---

[532] S. Schmidt, *Agostino Bea*, 359, gives the result as: 56 placet, 8 placet iuxta modum, 2 non placet, and 1 abstention. I cannot find any non placets in the official report. It is worth noting also that four members of the CPC proposed that invitations be extended more widely: to Jews, Muslims, Buddhists, and representatives of other religions.

[533] *ADP* II/1 480; only Landazuri Ricketts and Bernard (490-91) made favorable references to Ottaviani's remarks.

[534] *ADP* II/1 433-36.

[535] Caprile, I/2, 228-29; see Stransky, "The Foundation of the SPCU," 77, who reports the SCU's fear that it was now facing "a New Delhi in reverse."

[536] *ADP* I/1 459: "As was already said, only those should be admitted who desire it. There should not, then, be a general invitation, but only an announcement of the possibility to be given to those who wish to be present. This could be done in the *Bulla indictionis Concilii*, at the end of which the Supreme Pontiff could say something like that he is very happy that the 'separated brethren' received the announcement of the Council with such great good will and even often indicated that they were also praying for its success."

[537] *DMC* IV 875.

that would define the presence and role of the observers. On 22 January 1962 it sent a pro-memoria indicating the number of positive responses it had already received from various bodies. Urging that its own work would be helped if precise norms could be decided as soon as possible, it also sent a draft containing five proposals drawn up in the light of the CPC discussion.[538] On 17 March a slightly revised version was discussed by the subcommission, which gave its final approval to the section on observers on 23 June 1962.[539] In three paragraphs it established that observers, except in special cases, could attend public sessions and general congregations but not meetings of the conciliar commissions, and that they could not speak or vote. They were free to communicate with their sponsoring bodies but were to keep the conciliar secret with all others. The Secretariat was made responsible for supervising relations between the observers and the Council.[540]

B. EXTENDING THE INVITATIONS

Meanwhile, the Secretariat was engaged in the task of sounding out the communities and, upon receiving favorable responses, of inviting them to send observers. Between February and July 1962 Willebrands undertook several journeys in order to carry out these negotiations.[541] They were generally successful: of the Protestant federations listed in Bea's proposal to the CPC, only the Baptist World Alliance declined to be represented. Conversations with the "non-Chalcedonian" churches were also successful, resulting in invitations to the Coptic Church of Egypt, the Syrian Orthodox Church, the Ethiopian Orthodox Church, and the Armenian Church.

Things were more complex and difficult with the other Orthodox Churches.[542] A first difficulty was already implicit in the differences in tone between the reports which Bea and Cicognani gave at the November 1961 meeting of the CPC. In fact, there had been very little cooperation between the SCU and the OR on the issue of observers or on any other question. A mixed commission of the two bodies met only once,

---

[538] *ADP* IV/1 79-81.

[539] *ADP* IV/1 86, 157, 220.

[540] *ADP* IV/1 261-62.

[541] For a rapid summary, see Stransky, "The Foundation of the SPCU," 77-78.

[542] See Wenger, *Vatican II,* 147-49, 156-94; idem, *Les trois Rome: L'Eglise des années soixante* (Paris 1991) 79-89, 95-100; Stransky, "The Foundation of the SPCU," 77-80.

discussing the question of observers on 23 March 1961.[543] But the meeting had no practical effect, and efforts to engage the OR commission
in serious collaboration on this and on many other questions proved
fruitless.[544] The result was a serious imbalance in ecumenical activities
during the preparatory period: while the Secretariat pursued multiple
contacts with representatives of Protestant communities, it was not until
June 1961 that a delegation from the OR paid a visit to Patriarch
Athenagoras, who had often expressed his appreciation of Pope John
and his hopes for the Council and whose chagrin at the lack of Vatican
attention to the Orthodox had been expressed to the Secretariat.

The visit to the ecumenical Patriarch was not followed up by the
subcommission in the OR devoted to such conversations. With Bea's
encouragement, Ch. Dumont wrote a long letter to Msgr. Testa, head
of this subcommission, urging him to develop the contacts now at last
initiated, to consider establishing a mixed commission with the SCU in
order to coordinate the two ecumenical endeavors, and to start considering the peculiar nature of a possible invitation to the Orthodox Churches,
one that to be effective and not offensive to the Orthodox would have to
be based on a principle of reciprocity.[545] Dumont received no response
to this letter.

The inaction of the OR led the Orthodox to make it clear that they
wished their conversations with Rome to be mediated by the Secretariat.
Late in 1961, Bea brought this to the attention of Pope John, who
granted the request. From then on the Secretariat was in charge of all
ecumenical concerns and conversations.

If the Secretariat now had exclusive responsibility for the conversation with the Orthodox community, it faced some major difficulties. For
one thing, the first Pan-Orthodox Conference in Rhodes in the fall
of 1961 had decided to adopt common responses on matters affecting
eastern Orthodoxy in general. Second, in May 1961 the *Journal of
the Patriarchate of Moscow* had published an article entitled "Non possumus", which on ecclesiological and political grounds fiercely rejected
the idea of participation in the Council.[546] This and other statements by
representatives of Moscow introduced Cold War tensions into the question, suggesting that the Council was part of an effort on the part of the

[543] Willebrands to Ch. Dumont, 10 March 1961 (A-Dumont).
[544] See Ch. Dumont's memoirs, ch. 5; A-Dumont.
[545] Ch. Dumont to Testa, 26 July 1961; A-Dumont.
[546] See *Journal of the Patriarchate of Moscow* 5 (1961) 73-75; excerpts are given in
A. Wenger, *Vatican II* 157-58.

Catholic Church to unify the Churches against the Communist world. Third, there were the tensions within Orthodoxy between Constantinople and Moscow, particularly Moscow's claim to be "the third Rome." Fourth, from the Vatican's side, there was the desire of the Pope that the Catholic bishops in communist-dominated countries be permitted to attend the Council, a consideration which suggested the need to deal with Moscow independently or at least with other issues in mind than those that affected its conversations with Constantinople.[547] A final complicating factor was that these negotiations had to be undertaken in the very limited time that remained before the opening of the Council on 11 October.

Willebrands made at least two visits to the ecumenical Patriarch Athenagoras, who sent accounts of the conversations to the heads of the autocephalous Orthodox churches, including Moscow. After the first of these visits, in February 1962, an ostensibly private communication from the secretary of the Synod for External Relations of the Synod of Moscow gave the first indication that his patriarchate's attitude towards the Council was not as negative as the notorious article had made it appear.[548]

On 24 July the official invitation to send observers was sent to Athenagoras. No response came from Constantinople, which, despite the Patriarch's desire to send representatives, felt constrained by the presumably still negative attitude of Moscow. Independent contacts with Moscow were initiated in August at the meeting of the central committee meeting of the WCC,[549] where Willebrands had a lengthy conversation with Archbishop Nikodim of the patriarchate's Department of External Affairs, the result of which was the possibility that Moscow might indeed send observers. Willebrands was then authorized to undertake a secret journey to Moscow, 27 September – October 2. Upon his return, Bea sent Moscow an official invitation on 4 October.

Athenagoras seems to have been kept at least partially informed of these negotiations whose result he eagerly awaited in order to be able to provide his own response. Having no reason to think that Moscow had altered its stance, he finally informed the Secretariat that the

---

[547] For the larger context of Pope John's policy towards the Soviet Union, see A. Riccardi, *Il Vaticano e Mosca: 1940-1990* (Bari 1992) 217-64.

[548] A.S. Bouevsky to Ch. Dumont, 28 February 1962 (A-Dumont).

[549] Besides this contact, a meeting also took place at Metz between Cardinal Tisserant and Archbishop Nikodim at the end of the summer; see V. Carbone, "Schema e discussioni sull'ateismo e sul marxismo nel concilio Vaticano II. Documentazione," *Rivista di Storia della Chiesa in Italia* 44 (1990) 10-68, at 67.

autocephalous churches in communion with Constantinople had unanimously agreed not to send observers. But almost simultaneously with
this disappointing news came word from Moscow that its Synod had
indeed decided to send representatives.

This conclusion, on the one hand, represented an important element in
the thawing of relations between Rome and Moscow;[550] but on the other
hand, it revealed once again the tensions within Orthodoxy itself and
raised questions as to whether Rome had not been used by Moscow in
order to press its own claims or, even worse, that Rome was continuing its
divide ut imperes policy now within the Orthodox churches themselves.

Despite the rather sour note on which these negotiations with
the Orthodox ended on the very eve of the Council, the principle was
established and generally well implemented that Vatican II would take
place in a quite different ecumenical climate than had characterized either
Trent or Vatican I. Pope John, who had from the beginning urged the
ecumenical significance of the Council, regularly contrasted the sympathetic interest his announcement had provoked among non-Catholics to
the suspicions and even hostility that had surrounded earlier Councils,
particularly Vatican I. As things turned out, the decision to invite non-
Catholics as observers was one of the most important decisions made
during the preparatory period, with consequences for the character the
Council would assume and the work it would carry out that far surpassed
the expectations of even the most optimistic. In more ways than one, their
presence at the Council marked "the end of the Counter-Reformation."[551]

VI. DETERMING THE RULES FOR THE COUNCIL

Both prior history and the great numbers of bishops expected to attend
Vatican II provided reasons for wanting rules to be established that
could provide at once for the freedom of the participants and for the

---

[550] It also gave rise to the unsubstantiated claim, still repeated today, particularly by the
intransigent press, that the sending of observers by Moscow was made dependent upon a
formal promise given by Tisserant and/or Willebrands that the Council would refrain from
condemning communism; see R. Amerio, *Iota Unum: Studio delle variazioni della Chiesa
cattolica nel secolo XX* (Milan-Naples 1986²) 66-67; V. Carbone, "Schemi e discussioni
sull'ateismo e sul marxismo"; Riccardi, *Il Vaticano e Mosca*, 277-85.

[551] See Y. Congar, "Le rôle des 'Observateurs' dans l'avancée oecuménique," in
Le Concile Vatican II: Son Eglise, Peuple de Dieu et Corps du Christ (Paris 1984) 90-98;
G. Alberigo, *Ecclesiologia in divinire: A proposito di 'concilio pastorale' e di Osservatori a-cattolici al Vaticano II* (Bologna 1990); E. Fouilloux, "Des observateurs non-
catholiques," in *Vatican II commence*, 235-61.

effective functioning of the conciliar process. Concern for efficiency was prominent in the mind of Tardini when at his first press-conference he offered his views on how the Council might proceed. The fears of some bishops that the Council might keep them away from their dioceses for long periods of time could be met if a great deal of the work were to take place by correspondence. A text would be prepared at Rome by one of the commissions and sent to the bishops. Their reactions would then be recorded and the text revised or replaced. When the bishops gathered in Council, they could then vote on an already revised text on which their general views would already be known.[552]

But besides organizational efficiency, there are also important ecclesiological questions implicit in the procedures that guide a Council, in the process by which they are elaborated, and the means by which they are made authoritative. The implications of the procedures themselves may be illustrated by the theological justification of a view like Tardini's that was offered by S. Tromp when he was consulted on the matter by Dell'Acqua in March 1961. Tromp prepared a memorandum after this discussion,[553] in which he argued that it was not even necessary for the bishops to gather in one place. It could be enough for the Pope to inform the bishops that he wished to pass definitive judgement on an issue, ask for their judgements on the matter, and if there were moral unanimity among them, solemnly define it "with the sacred Council's approval."[554] If the bishops did assemble in one place, however, a problem would arise simply because it would not be possible for 3000 of them to have the full freedom to speak to which they have a right.[555] Tromp's solution

[552] The report of Tardini's press conference in *OssRom*, reproduced in *ADA* I 153-58, does not include these remarks, which are drawn from a letter of J. Hamer to Y. Congar, 7 Nov 1959, which is confirmed by the reports in the London *Tablet*, 213 (7 Nov 1959) 972, and in *HerdKorr* 14 (1959-60) 106: "It is the pope's desire that the written preparation will be so expedited that the actual sessions of the Council will not demand too much time and the bishops will not be absent from their dioceses too long." In the margin of Hamer's letter, Congar wrote: "It's a prefabricated Council! It's the procedure followed for the Immaculate Conception and the Assumption. It wouldn't be a real Council!"

[553] Tromp Diary, 21 March 1961. It is not clear whether Dell'Acqua, who was one of the counsellors to the CPC, had been asked for his opinions or whether the request was otherwise motivated. While Dell'Acqua's own response on the matter, *ADP* II/1 50-52, shows no trace of Tromp's views, a copy of Tromp's "Memorandum: De methodo procedendi in Conc. Vat. II (ad audientiam 21-III-1961)," dated 24 March 1961, can be found in the Roncalli papers, ISR.

[554] Tromp had already made the same argument in a text written for the TC, "De Episcopis" (CT 22/60; 4 Feb 1961) 5. On his copy of this text, Congar wrote: "This is quite a different thing than a Council!"

[555] Tromp also added: "There is also a danger that it will be extremists who do most of the talking and that the voice of moderates will not be heard."

was that the proper information be sent to the bishops beforehand, so that they could approve, reject or amend it. The texts would then be revised and sent to the bishops again "so that a decision will in effect be reached before they come together in one place." For this procedure to work, the Pope would have to make it clear that he alone had a right to decide the topics the Council would consider, "all others being quite excluded," and that the bishops were being asked *only* whether the provisional texts were good and worthy of an ecumenical Council: they would not be asked to comment "whether something else could be done or even whether something could be done better." If these two rules were not observed, Tromp concluded his memorandum, "a conclusion will never be reached."

A view like Tromp's must have lain behind the remarkable proposal of P. Philippe that it would not be necessary for bishops to speak at the Council. He proposed that the texts be sent to the bishops and their responses sent to the CPC, which would decide which of them to accept and remand the text to a special commission for revision. The revised text would then be brought back to the CPC, which would send the definitive text to a general session of the Council for its deliberative vote. At this session, Philippe argued, "It is much better that each of the bishops communicate his proposals in writing. Only the Pope, President of the Council, should speak."[556]

The views of Tromp and Philippe, which should not be considered typical of curial officials,[557] represent a *reductio ad absurdum* of the very idea of an ecumenical Council.[558] They are a manifestation, how-ever, of the extreme degrees to which the papal dominance of conciliar practice could be taken. But on two other questions — who should draw up the conciliar rules and by whose authority they should be adopted — a strongly papalistic stance did prevail.

---

[556] *ADP* II/1 58-59.

[557] In fact it was probably views such as these that led other curial figures to defend the right of the bishops to speak at the Council. Parente, *ADP* II/1 33, insisted that a Council is an exercise of the teaching Church, which requires freedom to speak, since his-tory shows that the Holy Spirit often works through the comments of the least important bishops. Parente's comments were echoed by Marella (269), Pizzardo (218), and Micara (214-15), who warned "about the danger of reducing the conciliar sessions to formal, choreographed meetings." Even Ottaviani left room for bishops to intervene in speeches of two or three minutes, "either to ask for explanations or to propose difficulties," after which a vote would be taken either to accept a text or to remand it to a commission for revision (277-78).

[558] For the ecclesiological issues at stake, see Y. Congar, "Konzil als Versammlung und grundsätzliche Konziliarität der Kirche," in *Gott in Welt: Festgabe für Karl Rahner* (Freiburg 1964) II 135-65.

The elaboration of the conciliar rules was undertaken on the assumption that the norms established by Pius IX for Vatican I provided a model, later codified in the assertion of the Code of Canon Law: "It belongs to the Roman Pontiff by himself or through others to preside over an ecumenical Council, to establish and designate the matters to be discussed at it and the order to be followed, to transfer, suspend or dissolve it, and to confirm its decrees."[559] This canon both reflected the definition of papal primacy of Vatican I and turned into normative law what at that Council had been a novelty: that the rules of conciliar procedure are established *motu proprio* by the pope and without the conciliar assembly having an opportunity to vote on the rules by which it is to be governed.

A. The Preparation of the Rules

Under these assumptions the work of elaborating rules for Vatican II began in March 1961 when Felici asked the counsellors of the CPC to give their opinions on seven questions: whom to call to the Council, criteria for selecting theological and canonical periti, the composition of the conciliar commissions, how to organize the conciliar debates, the majority required for conciliar decisions, how to make the use of Latin more easy, and how to record the conciliar proceedings.[560] In May these same questions were sent out to the members of the CPC, which took them up at its first session in June.[561] As the synthesis of the comments of both counsellors and CPC members shows,[562] opinions on the questions proposed often varied greatly and seldom reflected a consensus. No formal votes on the questions seem to have been taken.

At this June meeting of the CPC, Larraona proposed the establishment of a subcommission to draw up the conciliar regulations.[563] Larraona's proposal envisaged the subcommission's draft text being brought to the full CPC and even to the episcopal conferences for review and criticism, after which it would again come before the CPC for definitive approval.

---

[559] *CIC* c. 222 § 2.

[560] *ADP* II/1 21-22; for the responses of the counsellors, see 31-103, with a summary 104-13. These replies vary considerably and might serve as a useful starting-point for a study of the varieties of expectations in the Roman Curia, particularly if the officials were not responding simply *in proprio nomine*.

[561] *ADP* II/1 169-403; see Indelicato, *Difendere la dottrina*, 17-54.

[562] *ADP*, IV/1, 21-75.

[563] *ADP* II/1 293-94.

On 7 November 1961, Felici announced the establishment of such a sub-commission,[564] but without any indication that the subcommission's product would come before the CPC for approval. In fact the members of the CPC were never to have another opportunity to declare their minds on the subject of the conciliar regulations.

The CPC's subcommission carried out its task in twenty-eight plenary sessions held between 11 November 1961 and 27 June 1962. The first three sessions were devoted to the question of whom to invite to the Council. The remainder of the subcommission's sessions were devoted to elaborating a text, of which four successive drafts were prepared. At the end of June a definitive text was unanimously approved and two days later, 29 June 1961, it was sent to Felici for submission to the Pope.[565] After further changes, some of them from Pope John, and after the elaboration of the text of the accompanying *motu proprio*, the rules were promulgated by Pope John on 6 August 1962 as the *Ordo Concilii Oecumenici Vaticani II Celebrandi*.[566]

B. Major Features of the Conciliar Rules

The *Ordo Concilii*[567] presented seventy juridical norms set out in three sections: I. Personnel; II. Norms; III. Procedures. Early in its delibera-tions the subcommission decided to include titular bishops as conciliar participants with a deliberative vote, while superiors of non-exempt reli-gious congregations with more than 3000 members would participate with only a deliberative vote. The text distinguished public sessions, when texts would be formally promulgated, from the ordinary general congregations, where discussions would take place. These working sessions would be chaired by one of the ten Cardinals, appointed by the Pope, who consti-tuted the presidency of the Council responsible for its general supervision.

Ten conciliar commissions were provided for, reproducing the preparatory commissions with the exception of the excision of the

---

[564] *ADP* II/1 434. It was to be chaired by Roberti, with V. Carbone serving as secre-tary and de Barros Câmara, Jullien, Larraona, and Heard as members. In fact, de Barros Câmara never took part in the meetings.

[565] The final text of the subcommission is in *ADP* IV/1 230-50.

[566] See *ADP* I 306-25. The text was not made public until 5 September.

[567] See H. Jedin, "Die Geschäftsordnung des Konzils," *LTHK. Das zweite Vatikani-sche Konzil*, III (Freiburg 1968) 610-23; P. Levillain, *La mécanique politique de Vatican II*, esp. pp. 107-70; G. Alberigo, "La preparazione del regolamento del Concilio Vaticano II," in *Vatican II commence*, 54-72.

ceremonial commission and the inclusion in the tasks of the commission on the apostolate of the laity of the topics attributed earlier to the Secretariate for Communications Media. The rules established that each commission would have 24 members, two-thirds of them elected by the Council,[568] the other third appointed by the Pope, and with its president appointed by the Pope. Here the subcommission departed from the example of Vatican I, where all the members of conciliar commissions were elected by the assembly. In the very last stages of the preparation of the rules, the Pope introduced, in addition to the ten commissions, a Secretariat for Extraordinary Affairs, whose members would be appointed by the Pope, and whose role was "to examine individual new questions presented by the Fathers and, if called for, to refer the matter to the Supreme Pontiff." It is unclear why this body was added at the last minute and, in particular, whether it was intended to provide a counter-weight to the Council of presidents and to the general secretariat of the Council.[569]

Theologians, canonists and other experts would be designated by the Pope; they could be present at general congregations, could speak if so invited, and could participate in writing and amending schemata.[570] Individual conciliar Fathers could also make use of their own experts, but these had no right to be present for the general congregations. Non-Catholic observers were generally permitted to attend public sessions and general congregations, but not meetings of commissions. They had no right to speak or to vote, but the requirement of secrecy would not forbid them to communicate with their own communities. The SCU had the task of helping them to follow the conciliar activities, a vague description of that body's role, which would permit it great liberty.

The general norms required all involved to keep the secret "on discussions in the Council and on the views of individuals." Latin was to be used in public sessions and general congregations, with the assistance of interpreters promised,[571] while vernacular languages could be used in

---

[568] Art. 55 provided that these elections were to take place before discussions began, but nothing was said about the procedures for this election, on which the CPC discussion had revealed a good deal of support for nominations from episcopal conferences. The issue had been discussed in the meetings of the subcommission, but no decision was reached; see *ADP* IV/1 143, 159, and G. Caprile, "La seconda giornata del Vaticano II 25 anni dopo," *CivCatt* 138/3 (1987) 382-90.

[569] Certainly this was the way in which it was seen at the first session of the Council, both by some of those appointed to it (e.g., Suenens) and by the General Secretary, Felici.

[570] Nothing was said about the criteria for their selection, a matter warmly debated at the CPC consultation.

[571] Despite considerable support for this expressed in the CPC consultation, the rules made no provision for simultaneous translation. The rule on language was stricter than the

commission meetings. All discussions and votes were to take place in the order of ecclesiastical precedence: Cardinals, patriarchs, archbishops, bishops, etc.

The provisions for the examination of schemata set out a five-step procedure. After a *relator* proposed and briefly explained a schema, any Father could speak, proposing that it be accepted, rejected or amended.[572] Such interventions had to be announced three days earlier,[573] were to address first general and only then particular issues, were not to last longer than ten minutes, and, when they included recommended amendments, were to be submitted also in writing. The third step was a vote on whether to accept or reject proposed amendments, the fourth was a revision of the schema in the light of this vote, and the fifth and final step was a vote on the whole schema.

In the commissions votes were to be taken in terms of *placet, non placet* and *placet iuxta modum*, this threefold possibility also applying in votes within general congregations on parts or the whole of a schema. Votes on particular amendments, however, and those taken in public sessions, at the end of the process, could only be either *placet* or *non placet*. In all three occasions, a two-thirds majority was required for approval, no distinction being made, as had been suggested earlier, for different majorities depending on the nature of the document under consideration. The two-thirds majority required was a last-minute change, made by the Pope; the subcommission's final draft had been content with a 60% majority.[574]

The rules provided for the proposal of new questions but only if they concerned issues of general Christian interest, were necessary or opportune for conciliar deliberation, and contained nothing contrary to the constant *sensus Ecclesiae* or to its traditions. This is the only norm that acknowledges the bishops to possess anything like a *ius proponendi*. There is a certain ambiguity in the norms over the body to which such

one the Pope had himself envisaged at the time the CPC was debating the issue: "As for Latin, it must indeed be the official language; but on occasions, when necessary, views might also be expressed in the vernacular;" *ADP* II/1 128.

[572] This provision for a possible rejection was not specified further, no rules being set out for a vote to reject a whole schema; the expectation apparently was that the prepared schemata would need only emendation.

[573] This provision, along with the requirement that speakers follow the order of ecclesiastical precedence, would prevent the conciliar discussions from being genuine debates, with argument met by argument.

[574] The Pope's reasons for this change remain obscure. On the one hand, it enhanced the search for consensus among the bishops; on the other, it could paralyze efforts to resolve highly disputed matters.

new questions were to be brought. Art. 40 § 2 says that they are to be brought to the president, but art. 7 § 2 says that it is the Secretariat for Extraordinary Affairs that is to review new questions proposed by the Fathers.[575]

As the two earlier sections, the third discussed more particular procedures in an order inverse to the one the Council would have to follow, discussing first the final public sessions, second the general congregations where the debates would take place, and third the commission in which the work of amending and elaborating the texts would be carried out. The first section is the only one in which a role for the pope is set out, consisting only in the solemn promulgation, "with the approval of the sacred Council," of the final decrees. In general, the whole *Ordo celebrandi* has little to say about the role of the pope, perhaps on the assumption that he is free to determine what it will be.

General congregations would proceed at the times and with the agenda their president sets; nothing was said about opportunities for the Council to affect the determination of the agenda. Fairly detailed provisions for the conciliar debate were then set out; perhaps because it was foreseen that this debate would proceed in orderly and expeditious manner, nothing is said about ending a debate or about making a general judgement on the suitability of a text for discussion.

The rules for the work of commissions are rather general, but give considerable authority to their presidents to decide their agenda, the languages they use, and the way in which they would vote.

C. OBSERVATIONS

From a general ecclesiological standpoint, the *Ordo Concilii* continues and legally formalizes the development, already visible at Trent, dominant at Vatican I, and enshrined in the Code of Canon Law, which magnified the authority of the pope over an ecumenical Council.[576] The very promulgation of the *Ordo Concilii* by papal act before the Council embodied this view: all the major decisions about participation, agenda, and procedure were already decided. Papally appointed preparatory

---

[575] At the first session of the Council, Suenens brought to the Secretariat for Extraordinary Affairs an unsuccessful request that an alternate text *De Ecclesia* be distributed to the Council.

[576] "For the writer of the conciliar rules the greatest maxim was the protection of the rights of papal primacy;" Jedin, "Die Geschäftsordnung des Konzils," 622.

commissions would provide the texts for conciliar discussion. Papally appointed presidents would direct its course, and a papally appointed secretary would expedite its administration. Papal appointees would chair the conciliar commissions, one-third of whose members would also be appointed by the pope.

The rules did provide for the rights of bishops to comment on the prepared texts (even to propose the rejection of a schema) and to offer, under certain conditions, new questions for the Council to consider. But no clear rules were given for the rejection of a schema or for the introduction of new topics. Clearly, the *Ordo Concilii* anticipated an unproblematic Council, whose agenda would consist in the discussion of already prepared schemata, in the apparent expectation that they might need only to be amended.[577] The great majority of specific procedural norms concerned the process of amendment either in commissions or in general congregations.

Some indication that an unproblematic Council was indeed the expectation of at least some Roman officials was given at a meeting of the Technical-Organizational Commission, of which Testa was president and Felici the secretary, on 7 June 1962,[578] as the CPC's subcommission on the rules was nearing the end of its work. Testa outlined how a typical conciliar session might unfold. Each of the Fathers would have received at his residence a printed fascicle, containing the brief schema to be discussed, the report on it that would be read by a Cardinal, and the various written interventions in both Latin and the original language. The Cardinal reporter would then speak, followed by those who had prepared written interventions. Then would begin the discussion, which would be brief, concise, and clear, avoiding "useless lessons in theology, etc." After the discussion, a vote would take place and be counted and reported.

At this point Testa made what was called a "secondary suggestion" that noted some advantages, far from merely technical, with regard to written interventions. If these were submitted a week before, the Secretariat would be able to examine them to see not only if they were relevant and brief but also if they contained any aberrant doctrine. "This

---

[577] "Its authors started out with the expectation that the schemata elaborated by the preparatory commissions and approved by the Central Commission would be accepted at least as the basis for the debates, that is, in their substance. This expectation was not fulfilled.... The author of the regulations had not counted on — in fact it would have been quite difficult for him to do so — this strong independent streak in the Council;" Jedin, "Die Geschäftsordnung des Konzils," 622.

[578] "Seduta della Commissione technico-organizzativa, 7 Giugno 1962" (A-Spellman).

will guarantee a control to keep order in the conciliar process." If any problems were found, a diplomatic visit could be made to the Council Father to ask him to improve his intervention. The reasons for these previsions were then given:

> The Council must give a good example to the observers by its order, precision, seriousness in the treatment of topics, a harmonious process to avoid useless and harmful polemics, to avoid getting bogged down and, worse still, boredom. Everything must proceed with diligence and an effort to correct little by little whatever problems may arise despite the good will of all.

The minutes of this meeting do not indicate whether there was any discussion of these suggestions. Nor is it now possible to know whether Testa's expectations were shared by others and particularly by the secretary of his commission, Felici. But a view like Testa's would help to explain why so many people thought that the Council would be able to finish its work quite expeditiously.

VII. THE DATE, DURATION AND AGENDA OF THE COUNCIL

A. THE DATE OF THE COUNCIL'S OPENING

In his press conference in October 1959, Tardini had said that three years would probably be necessary before the Council could be held.[579] When rumors began to spread in the following spring that Tardini was then thinking that the Council could not open until 1963, Pope John spoke of the matter with Felici, who assured him that Tardini had made no such statement; Felici himself thought that if the preparatory work began soon and was conducted expeditiously, it might be possible to begin as early as 1961. At the last meeting of the CAP on 8 April 1960, Tardini informed the members that the Pope desired the Council to begin no later than in 1962,[580] a date that the Pope himself mentioned in September.[581]

The preparations did not proceed as expeditiously as had been hoped, few of the PrC being able to conclude their work according to their initial schedules. Throughout 1961, the Pope expressed his hope several times that the Council could begin soon, at least within a year.[582] In May

[579] ADA I 158.

[580] ASApp 21; Tardini added: "This can be done if we work hard." See Carbone, "Il Cardinale Domenico Tardini," 74.

[581] DMC II, 689.

[582] See Caprile, I/2, 45, 111, 208, 209, 249.

1961, he had to calm the fears of Frings and Döpfner that the Council was being prepared too hastily — they asked that it not open before 1963. The Pope replied that he had not decided on any date and that the Council would open when the preparatory work was completed.[583] At a meeting of the Technical Organizational Commission, 8 November 1961, Felici said it was the Pope's desire that the Council begin in October 1962.[584]

In the *Bulla indictionis*, 25 December 1961, the Pope announced that he was convoking the Council to meet at an unspecified time in the following year. On 2 February 1962, he announced that the Council would open on 11 October. Little is known about what motivated the Pope to determine the date. It is difficult to believe that it was the quality of the work already completed, since most of the preparatory texts, including some of the most important of them, had not yet been reviewed by the CPC. It may be that the Pope believed that if a firm date were not established, the preparatory work would never be finished, or at least would not be completed in time for him to preside over at least the beginning of the Council. In any case, the Pope was not persuaded even by widely shared criticisms of the preparations to postpone the beginning of the work.[585]

B. THE ANTICIPATED DURATION OF THE COUNCIL

From the beginning, the question of the duration of the Council was a matter of considerable discussion. In his press conference, 30 October 1959, Tardini said that the Council would be so well prepared that it

---

[583] See Carbone, "Il Cardinale Domenico Tardini," 84, who reports that the mistaken fear of the German Cardinals may have been prompted by the initial consultation undertaken by Felici with regard to the convocation, opening and rules of the Council.

[584] "Verbale della prima riunione della Commissione tecnico-organizzativa" (A-Spellman).

[585] In his conciliar recollections, Frings reports that in May, Döpfner and he unsuccessfully urged the Pope to postpone the date of the opening of the Council because of the state of the preparations; see *Für die Menschen Bestellt: Erinnerungen des Alterzbischofs von Köln Josef Kardinal Frings* (Köln 1973) 251. The brief text, "De praeparatione Concilii Oecumenici Vaticani II," which Hurley composed in April and sent to Frings, Döpfner, and other Cardinals in May, had also asked that the Council's opening be put off until the preparatory texts could be carefully revised. A. Melloni, relying, it seems, on the testimony of Capovilla, maintains that Frings, Döpfner and Bengsch made another effort in this direction around August; see "Giovanni XXIII e l'avvio del Vaticano II," in *Vatican II commence*, 76.

would not need to last very long.[586] When Felici told the Technical Organizational Commission, 8 November 1961, that the Pope wished the Council to begin in October 1962 and end, if possible, before the end of the year, all the Cardinals expressed surprise at this news, given the number of questions to be treated and the freedom the bishops must have to discuss them.[587] As late as March 1962, the Administrative Secretariat was still facing the difficulties of making arrangements without knowing how long the Council would last.[588]

Remarks of the Pope on 3 April 1962, at the end of the fifth session of the CPC, led to some fears that the Council would be a rapid affair. He said that several conversations had led him to think that, because of the progress made in the discussions at the CPC, when the Council began, "the consensus of bishops will not be difficult and will be accepted by everyone."[589] In his remarks at the close of the next session of the CPC, 12 May 1962, the Pope made a point of calming apprehensions by noting that free discussion was required for the very good of the Council.[590]

What seems to be the first indication that the Council might require more than one session was given in a papal address on 8 April.[591] A clearer reference is found in a letter from the Secretariat of State to nuntios, 19 June 1962, which said that the Council, "as now anticipated, will take place in two periods of time."[592] In his retreat notes, 8 September 1962, Pope John spoke of the *first* session of the Council as running from 11 October to 8 December,[593] and in an address to an audience on 19 September he said that the Council would begin on 11 October and "and may be prolonged, after a brief interval, also into next

---

[586] *Tablet* 213 (7 Nov 1959) 972. See *HK* 14 (1959-60) 106.

[587] "Verbale della prima riunione della Commissione tecnico-organizzativa," A-Spellman.

[588] Caprile, I/2, 607.

[589] *DMC*, IV, 200. This view, according to Rouquette, *La fin d'une chrétienté*, I, 114, was then echoed by Felici in a press conference.

[590] *DMC* IV 267.

[591] See Rouquette, *La fin d'une chrétienté*, I, 114-15, who cites an article in *La Croix*. The report of this address given in *OssRom* and reprinted in *DMC* IV 685-89, does not mention this comment. On 23 May 1962, Gagnebet informed Congar of the rumors that were circulating in the TC: "It seems certain that the first session will end around the 8th of December, or the 20th, others say. The second will take place after Easter, and the third in the fall;" Congar Papers.

[592] Caprile, I/2 535.

[593] *Journal of a Soul*, 322. Elsewhere Capovilla reports a conversation with the Pope on 6 September 1962, in which he spoke of "the work of the first session," which he hoped would deal with at least four schemata: on liturgy, communications media, missions and clergy.

year."[594] This was the same view he maintained still on the very day the Council opened, when he told the crowd gathered in St. Peter's Square: "The Council has begun and we do not know when it will end. If it must not be concluded before Christmas because, perhaps, we have not succeeded saying everything, treating the various topics, then another meeting will be necessary."[595]

It is understandable that the Pope, given his age and state of health, hoped that the Council might be able to complete its work in one or at most two sessions, but it is difficult to see how the mass of material prepared for the conciliar agenda could have been dealt with in so short a time by anything other than a rubber-stamp Council. This is just another one of the pieces in the Roncalli-mystery, all the more puzzling because he had already received from important figures enough indications of dissatisfaction at the quantity and quality of the preparatory schemata to suggest that the Council would not proceed as rapidly as this time-table would seem to anticipate. Suenens' criticisms of the preparatory work had already raised in March 1962 the relationship between the agenda and the duration of the Council: "The choice of these questions must inevitably be limited according to how long it is envisaged that the Council should last. At all costs, we must avoid the bishops having the impression that they did not have time to deal seriously with the matters put before them because the Council had got bogged down in details."[596] In the letter of 4 July 1962 with which he sent his plan for the Council, Suenens said that it was the desire of the Cardinals whom he had consulted that "the Council should start with a doctrinal section that would form the matter of the first session, with the pastoral section occupying the further session or sessions."[597]

Similarly, a few days later, König felt it necessary to address fears that the Council would be all external pomp, but that nothing would be changed and the curial bureaucracy would successfully resist movements for reform. Citing the example of the frank and lengthy discussions in the CPC and the changes they had effected in many schemata, he hoped that a similar frankness would mark the conciliar discussions, something that would require time: "One can already say that if the first session of the Council ends before Christmas, in all probability next year (or the following years) many months will pass before we see the end."[598]

---

[594] Caprile, I/2, 635.
[595] Caprile, II, 8.
[596] Léon-Joseph Suenens, "A Plan for the Whole Council," in *Vatican II Revisited*, 93.
[597] Suenens, "A Plan for the Whole Council," 95.
[598] *DC* 59 (7 Oct 1962) 1275-76.

Such interventions were made in part in order to encourage Pope John not to allow the Council to proceed on the assumption that only minor adjustments might be made to the disappointing preparatory texts. There were, of course, people whose idea of conciliar procedure would suggest such a rapid course of events. The norms established in the *Ordo Concilii* seemed to presuppose and to encourage such a project. Testa's sketch of a typical conciliar work-day, perhaps reflecting the views of Felici, certainly fit this idea. In the summer of 1962 Tromp is said to have expressed his conviction that the theological schemata were so well prepared that they would require only two weeks of the Council's time.[599]

Nothing was clearly established, then, in the summer of 1962, about how long the Council's work would last. It was already clear, however, that this question would depend on a judgement on the quality of the preparatory work and that this question in turn would depend on judgements about the fundamental purposes and character of the Council itself. Like many other things about the Council, all this was in a state of dramatic tension as its opening neared.

C. Determining a Plan and Agenda for the Council

Soon after Pope John announced that the Council would begin in October 1962, the widespread complaints about the disorganized character of the preparations, confirmed by the haphazard sequence in which texts were being brought before the CPC, became fears about the Council itself and particularly that it would not correspond to the intentions of the Pope. Suenens says that he raised the issue with Pope John as early in March 1962, when he complained about the number and disorganized and often trivial character of the texts that were coming before the CPC. In response to encouragement by the Pope, Suenens drafted a text that criticized the preparatory texts, 80% of which he said were not proper matter for a Council, and proposed the establishment of a special commission — "a sort of brain trust" — to prepare a conciliar agenda that would be limited to major and vital questions that concern the whole Church and that embody the desired pastoral renewal. Other topics would be left to the reform of Canon Law or to post-conciliar commissions. According to

---

[599] P. Smulders, "Zum Werdegang des Konzilskapitels 'Die Offenbarung Selbst," in *Glaube im Prozess: Christsein nach dem II. Vatikanum*, E. Klinger and K. Wittstadt (ed., Freiburg/Basel/Wien 1984) 100.

Suenens, the Pope approved his note and asked him to develop it further and to solicit the opinions of other important Cardinals.[600]

While Suenens worked privately on a fuller statement of a coherent program for the Council, other members brought the issue out into the open at the May meeting of the CPC. During a discussion of the BG's schema *De animarum cura*, Frings twice objected to the number and relatively minor character of many of the texts being brought to the CPC. He thought it unlikely that bishops would be able to form a judgment on all these things in the few weeks or months they would have to study them.[601] Felici echoed Frings' remarks, warning that the Council should not become "an encyclopedia of sacred matters rather than, as it shoud be, the source and origin of basic constitutions and decrees."[602]

Frings' remarks were welcomed by Archbishop Hurley, who had long been frustrated both by the methods employed in the CPC discussions and by the scattered quality of the materials it had to review.[603] On 18 April he had written to Suenens, asking him to intervene with the Pope or to encourage a group of Cardinals to do so and enclosing a copy of a draft he had himself written: "De praeparatione Concilii Oecumenici Vaticani II". Hurley feared that if the Council were to lose itself in the many and very particular questions found in the prepared texts, it would never speak about the basic principles of the renewal and adaptation of Church life that the Pope desired. But he then made a proposal that would have altered the structure of the preparation: the immediate appointment of a sub-commission to reduce the mass of materials, retaining only what was worthy of a Council, with the material retained being ordered in such a way as to move from basic principles to general applications, leaving specific questions to post-conciliar commissions or to the episcopal conferences. This might require that the date of the Council be postponed; but if this were not possible, at least only the

---

[600] See Suenens, "A Plan for the Whole Council," 88-105; idem, *Souvenirs et espérances* (Paris 1991) 65-80. Suenens expressed similar ideas at the 28 March CPC discussion of the schema *De regimine missionum*, where he also made use of the distinction between the *Ecclesia ad intra* and the *Ecclesia ad extra*; *ADP* II/3 183.

[601] "Either they will deliver themselves over to the bishops or consultors who have studied the materials or they will refrain from judgment or they will cover their eyes and approve everything. Such behavior is not to be hoped for and will greatly detract from the honor and dignity of the ecumenical Council;" *ADP* II/3 745-46; see also 713, where he feared that Vatican II's documents would prove longer than those of all previous Councils.

[602] *ADP* II/3 719; see also 758.

[603] The following paragraphs are based upon materials Archbishop Hurley kindly gave to me.

basic principles of Church renewal should be taken up in the first session, with other questions deferred until later sessions. On 3 May Suenens told Hurley that while he did not think he should make such a proposal in the CPC itself, he would be willing to speak to the Pope privately.[604]

After Frings' remarks on 4 May, Hurley brought the German Cardinal a copy of the draft he had prepared. That evening Frings telephoned Hurley to say that he intended at the next morning's session to offer Hurley's proposal of a special subcommission to take charge of the preparation. Hurley also left a copy of his text with König, who promised to support Frings' proposal.

On 5 May Frings proposed at the CPC meeting that the Pope appoint a new subcommission which would have greater authority over the schemata being prepared and also enjoy a "a power of initiative in the name and by the mandate of this Commission." The role of this subcommission would be (1) to prepare an introductory constitution in which the purpose of the Council would be clearly stated: the renewal of religious life and the adaptation of the Church's apostolic activity to the modern world; (2) to combine and simplify the texts that deal with the same material; (3) to eliminate from the conciliar agenda anything that has to do with the reform of the Code, is merely a matter of organization, or does not fit the purpose of the Council.[605]

In the discussion that followed, Frings' proposal, was seconded by a large number of the most important Cardinals, of varied theological tendencies.[606] Léger flatly stated, "We are not ready to begin the Council next October," and urged that the June meeting of the CPC be devoted to a study of the amended texts to be sent out to the bishops.[607] Card.

---

[604] Suenens' response may have been prompted by a concern to keep his earlier intervention with the Pope confidential. By the end of April he had already completed a larger draft of his plan for the Council, and in a letter to the Pope on 16 May 1962, he spoke of having discussed it with "various members [presumably of the CPC] consulted on the spot in Rome;" copy in Roncalli papers, ISR.

[605] Frings concluded: "Unless we proceed in this or a similarly energetic way, I am afraid that the Council may be suffocated by the mass of material to be treated, that the discussions in the Council will be infinite or will be suppressed in an undesirable way, that in the end the whole Council will be frustrated after having been begun with such great hope and with such great expectations of Christians or the whole world;" *ADP*, II/3, 814-15.

[606] Liénart, Valeri, Siri, Quiroga y Palacios, Léger, Giobbe, Godfrey, Confalonieri, Döpfner, Marella, Santos, Rugambwa, Ritter, Di Jorio, Jullien, Larraona, Heard, Browne, Albareda, and many of the other participants supported Frings' proposal. König and Suenens did not comment on it.

[607] *ADP* II/3 828.

Roberti said that the subcommission on the conciliar rules, which he chaired, had also considered the question and concluded that it should prepare a new edition of texts, unifying them and removing what is not pertinent material for the Council. This new edition would be sent to the Fathers who would prepare their responses.[608]

Felici felt obliged to reply to the hardly disguised critique of the work he had been directing. He said that Frings' proposal would be brought to the Pope, but also pointed out that the Pope had already assigned many of the tasks envisaged to the subcommissions on amendments and on mixed matters. The former had begun the desired winnowing of texts and six important texts had already been selected and would be sent to the bishops in July. He ended by remarking that the purpose of the Council had already been determined by the Pope; any further specification of it should be the work of the Council. He did not comment on Léger's proposal that the amended texts be brought back to the CPC.[609]

At the beginning of May 1962, then, a majority of the members of the CPC not only were critical of the texts prepared for the Council and fearful that the latter would lose its way in a morass of detail, but also supported the appointment of a special commission to take the matter in hand and to select significant questions on the basis of a coherent and significant plan. This was a last effort on the part of the CPC to assume responsibility for the coordination of the preparatory work. Although Felici shared the concern about the minor character of many of the prepared texts and agreed that the Council's agenda should be limited to statements of principle, he resisted the idea of a new commission and gave the first indication that decisions about the agenda, on which he apparently did not think it necessary to consult the CPC, were already being made. The General Secretary's position remained what it had been: that the coordination could be accomplished at the end of the whole process and by the structures already in place.

At this point, the struggle over the character and agenda of the Council moved behind the scenes. On 16 May, shortly after the meeting of the CPC, Suenens sent Pope John a fuller and more positive plan for the Council. It would bring coherence to the Council by beginning with a

---

[608] *ADP* II/3 831. Hurley took up Roberti's invitation for comments on the rules of the Council and sent him a proposal on 10 May; see *ADP* IV/1, 87-89.

[609] *ADP* II/3, 833-34. Hurley said that, while Felici's remarks had partially quieted his concern, still "the work of the Council will lack unity unless there is a clear, enlightening, soul-stirring introductory schema about the Church and its apostolic activity in today's circumstances, which will also illumine all the other schemata;" 836.

text "*De Ecclesiae Christi mysterio*," followed by a grouping of schemas having to do with the *Ecclesia ad intra*, considered as evangelizing, teaching, sanctifying, and worshipping, with a final section on the *Ecclesia ad extra* that would meet the world's expectations of conciliar responses to social questions.[610] Suenens related his project to the official texts already prepared;

> These themes allow maximum possible use of the schemata drawn up: a massive and important amount of work has been done which we must take advantage of, while removing its fragmentary and mosaic character, breathing a soul into it. Most of these schemata are lifeless skeletons, due to their juridical, canonical and sometimes repressive approach. We will try in our plan to give them some life and breadth of approach and make them contribute to an overall whole.[611]

In the letter to the Pope accompanying his plan, Suenens' remarks suggest that the Pope was considering accepting the proposal, widely supported in the CPC, of a special commission to draw up the conciliar agenda:

> It would also be the role of the working group that your Holiness is thinking of establishing to examine how to insert the correct schemata into the plan proposed — or some other better plan. This same group could, moreover, propose the list of schemata which would be reserved not to the Council itself but to the Commission for the reform of the Code or to some postconciliar commissions, a desire that has been expressed many times in the course of the meetings of the Central Commission.[612]

The Pope told Suenens to meet with some Cardinals, whom he named, to get their views of the proposal.

On 19 May, Cicognani sent a select group of Cardinals a copy of Suenens' plan, which he described as "a draft of the 'pastoral plan' on which Cardinal Suenens, in agreement with other Cardinals, proposes that the forthcoming ecumenical Council proceed, with the use of the schemata already written but to be revised and with a broader vision of the pastoral ministry."[613]

---

[610] See Suenens, "A Plan for the Whole Council," 96-102; on p. 4, he calls this "the final version" of his plan, that is, after discussions with other Cardinals.

[611] Suenens, "A Plan for the Whole Council," 96.

[612] Suenens to Pope John, 16 May 1962; Suenens urged that this group not be more than four or five in number and proposed the names of Larrain, Hurley, Morcillo, and Seper.

[613] Cicognani's note is found in the Roncalli papers, ISR. To which Cardinals he sent Suenens' plan is not now known, but Liénart seems to have been among them; see his enthusiastic letter to Suenens, 14 June 1962, in Suenens, "A Plan for the Whole Council," 94-95.

The first documented response of Pope John to these efforts was his direction, 20 May, that Cicognani ensure the bishops that they would have sufficient time to review the texts before the Council opened, since the texts to be discussed at the Council would be sent to them in July and August, and not in September.[614] Perhaps in accord with this papal desire, on 27 May Felici wrote a memorandum in which he responded to the recommendations of the CPC that the many schemata be reduced in number and that only the more important and pressing topics be submitted to the Council. Felici told the Pope that the material could be reduced to twenty basic texts, seven of them theological and thirteen pastoral. Of these twenty texts, six had already been completely amended and were now being printed so that, with the Pope's approval, they could be sent to the bishops in July: *De fontibus Revelationis, De deposito Fidei pure custodiendo, De ordine morali, De castitate, virginitate, matrimonio, familia, De sacra Liturgia, De instrumentis communicationis socialis*. The subcommissions on mixed matters and on amendments were diligently at work,[615] Felici added, and it was hoped that the other schemata could be printed and sent out in the following months.[616]

It seems likely that these were the six texts to which Felici referred in his remarks to the CPC on 5 May; and these would in fact be approved by the Pope in July for transmission to the bishops.[617] But a few things remain puzzling. When Felici made his remarks to the CPC, of the six texts eventually selected only the schemas *De fontibus* and *De ordine morali* had been both discussed at the CPC and reviewed by the subcommission on amendments; the schema *De deposito fidei* had been

---

[614] See *Lettere*, 535-36; Capovilla supplies only the information that the Pope wrote this note on the back of a page that summarized a conversation between Dell'Acqua and Msgr. Gouet, secretary of the French episcopal conference.

[615] While the latter subcommission was already at work, the subcommission on mixed matters did not hold its first meeting until 15 June; see L. Governatori in *Le Concile Vatican II*. 88. In fact, the subcommission would meet only twice before the Council opened and twice more during its first session. The meagre result of its work, not completed until December 1962, was the gathering of related materials into two schemata: *De Episcopis ac de dioceseon regimine* and *De pastorali Episcoporum munere deque cura animarum*; see Caprile, I/2, 533-35, and Governatori, *Le Concile Vatican II*, 87-89.

[616] This memorandum can be found in the Roncalli papers at the ISR, Bologna.

[617] *Schemata Constitutionum et Decretorum de quibus disceptabitur in Concilii sessionibus, Series prima* (TPV 1962). Included with these texts was the schema *De unitate Ecclesiae*, which was only discussed by the CPC in mid-June, when the consensus was that it should be integrated with the two other texts on ecumenism in the TC's *De Ecclesia* and the SCU's *De oecumenismo catholico*. No such effort was undertaken, and the reason why the OR's text was chosen is unclear.

discussed at the CPC but the subcommission had only reviewed half of it; the schemas *De sacra Liturgia* and *De instrumentis communicationis socialis* had been discussed at the CPC but not yet reviewed by the subcommission; and the schema *De castitate...* had not yet even been discussed by the CPC. Even by the time Felici wrote his memorandum, 27 May, the schema *De castitate* had not yet been discussed by the subcommission on amendments.[618]

It was not true, even on 27 May, then, that all of the six schemata which Felici mentioned in his memorandum of that day, had in fact been "aleady entirely amended." When the initial choice was made, before 5 May, things were in an even more incomplete state. The basic decision about the selection of texts for the Council was made, then, before either the CPC or its subcommission had completed their work. The criteria of this selection, of course, remain quite unclear.

It is tempting to think that all this discussion about the purpose and agenda of the Council lay behind the invitation Pope John extended to the members of the CPC in his final address to them on 20 June:

> No more welcome contribution to the success of ecumenical Council that is to begin on October 11 could be given than that each Father send in good time to the new General Secretariat or to the Cardinal Secretary of State, along with a personal letter, whatever he believes, given the circumstances, is appropriate to the project. All this will be of help in examining the problems with prudence and in proper light, in avoiding difficulties, and in bringing everything to completion in utter peace.[619]

Was this invitation a response to indications of dissatisfaction and an effort to find out how widespread it was?[620] How much should be read into the specification that these private letters were to be sent either to

---

[618] See the summaries of the work of the CCP and of the subcommission on amendments by Fagiolo, *Le Concile Vatican II*, 79-85, 89-92. Note also that the schema *De unitate Ecclesiae* came before the CPC only in mid-June; if and when this text was reviewed by the subcommission is not clear, but if it was so reviewed, it could not have been before 16 July, that is, *after* it had been submitted to the Pope for his approval.

[619] *DMC* IV 386; *ADP* I 262.

[620] A week after the Pope made these remarks, Msgr. Jean Villot, auxiliary of Lyons, recorded his impressions in a letter to Henri Denis, 20 June 1962: "On the other hand, I have the impression that a certain number of bishops who were associated with the preparatory work are dissatisfied with the general orientation of that work, which as a whole seems like a mosaic of disconnected questions. At the instigation of the Cardinals of Malines and of Munich, who spoke about it recently to the pope, there may be in the months that will precede the Council a rather strong current calling this rather narrow 'problematic' into question. Here too the beginning of the Council risks being rather charged;" Villot to Denis, 20 June 1962; Denis papers, Bibliothèque des Facultés Catholiques, Lyon.

the Secretariat of State or to a *new* general secretariat? What were the "difficulties" that would need to be avoided if the Council were to proceed effectively?

Meanwhile, Suenens was pursuing his consultation with select Cardinals. In early July he met at the Belgian College with Döpfner, Montini, Siri, and Liénart, all of whom, he reported to the Pope on 4 July, warmly supported the idea that the Council have a broad and coherent plan, that the Council begin with doctrinal material in its first session, leaving pastoral topics to subsequent sessions, that the doctrinal section begin with a study "*De Ecclesiae Christi mysterio*," that the prepared texts not be sent out to the bishops pell-mell, and that Suenens should elaborate his plan to show how the prepared texts could be inserted within its general framework. With this letter Suenens enclosed a copy of this longer plan.[621]

Only days afterward, however, on 10 July, Felici sent Pope John the seven schemata that he proposed should form the first volume of documents for conciliar consideration. In the letter to Cicognani with which he sent these texts to the Pope, Felici explained that they had been discussed at the CPC, revised by the subcommission on amendments, and polished by Vatican Latinists. Felici's letter asked only for the Pope's permission to send these texts to the bishops.[622] No explanation appears to have been made as to why, out of all the texts so far discussed and revised, precisely these seven were chosen. If the selection of the first four of the eventual seven schemas could be motivated by a desire to put the chief doctrinal texts (except for the *De Ecclesia*, which was not yet complete) before the Council first, and if the choice of the text *De sacra Liturgia* would meet common expectations, what led Felici to choose, among all the texts on pastoral matters, the insignificant text on the communications media and, among the three texts on ecumenism, the OR's text *De unitate Ecclesiae*?

In an audience with Cicognani on 13 July, Pope John gave his approval that these seven texts be sent out to the conciliar Fathers. Since the permission was granted only three days after the Pope received the texts, one may wonder how carefully he was able to review them. Select marginal notations by the Pope have been cited as indications that he was generally pleased with the texts,[623] but it is not clear when he made

---

[621] Suenens, "A Plan for the Whole Council," 96-105.

[622] See V. Fagiolo, "Il cardinale Amleto Cicognani e Mons. Pericle Felici," in *Deuxième*, 233-35.

[623] See V. Carbone, "Genesi e criteri della pubblicazione degli atti del Concilio Vaticano II," *Lat* 44 (1978) 587-88; Fagiolo, "Il cardinale A. Cicognani," 234.

these notes, which, it should also be observed, had no effect.[624] It appears that the Pope was presented with something like a *fait accompli*: could he have rejected these texts at so late a date and still be able to send other texts to the bishops in time for them to review them before the Council opened?

The obscurity that surrounds this crucial decision is only increased by a note made by the Pope's secretary, Capovilla, after a conversation on 6 September 1962. Speaking of the work of the first session, the Pope commented: "At least four schemata: Liturgy, Social Communications, Missions, Clergy."[625] Only the first two of these schemata were included in the volume sent out in July; and it is striking that the four doctrinal schemata in that volume are absent from the Pope's list. By this time, of course, the Pope had received many criticisms of the preparatory schemata, particularly those on doctrine, and at least one proposal, from German bishops, that the opening of the Council be postponed because of the contrast between the schemata and the Pope's conciliar vision. Was the Pope's comment a last-minute hypothesis or a way to meet these criticisms?

A last effort to affect the Council's agenda can now be documented from the papers of Cardinal Léger, who had spoken often and critically during the sessions of the CPC and who was a member also of the sub-commission on amendments.[626] Inspired in part by an apparently similar effort of Frings,[627] in August 1962 he prepared a twelve-page letter

[624] In an audience on 27 July 1962, the Pope told the director of *La Civiltà Cattolica* of his dissatisfaction with some of the texts, which he was then reviewing and annotating; see Caprile, I/2, 279n. This date is noteworthy, coming two weeks after he had approved the sending of the texts to the bishops.

[625] See Capovilla's comments in *Giovanni Battista Montini Arcivescovo di Milano e il Concilio Ecumenico Vaticano II: Preparazione e primo periodo* (Brescia 1985) 341.

[626] See Gilles Routhier, "Les réactions du cardinal Léger à la préparation de Vatican II," *Revue d'Histoire de l'Eglise de France* 80 (1994) 281-302.

[627] In a letter to Frings, 17 Aug 1962, Léger speaks of having received from the German Cardinal some days earlier "a very suggestive text designed to illumine the Holy Father and the members of the Central Commission on the aims of the Council and on the matters that ought to be treated there." This would seem to refer to a text Frings had brought to the last meeting of the CCP. Among Léger's papers is found a six-page typed Latin text on which Léger has written "Ordo du Concile - Frings." It bears the date, added later: 11 October. The first three pages set out an introduction to the entire work of the Council as the response of faith to contemporary conditions: the renewal of the Church's inner life and the adaptation of the apostolate to modern needs. The last pages supply a list of specific topics grouped under six major headings: I. Veritates fundamentales; II. De formatione laboratorum et collaboratorum apostolicorum; III. De ipso apostolatu Ecclesiae; IV. De Ecclesia orante; V. De Ecclesia sanctificante; VI. De caritate et adjutorio sociali. Whether this is the text to which Léger was referring remains to be verified.

expressing both hopes and fears about the Council and which he hoped
to send to the Pope over the signatures of several Cardinals. Léger
declared his agreement with the Pope on the necessity of renewal in the
Church, which must follow two basic norms: that it be faithful to Christ
and the Gospel and that it meet contemporary needs of men. If Church
renewal could not mean revolution or rejection of essential elements,
neither could it be limited to "some rare and timid accommodations," to
a restoration of the past, or to simple suppression of abuses and defence
against danger. "The renewal that will make the Church fully faithful to
its mission, is, in total fidelity to the Gospel and to the needs of men, 'an
ardent and deep renewal of soul,' an adaptation of the Church's magisterium to contemporary needs, a transformation of institutions that will
put it in perfect correspondence with the complex realities of life." More
particularly, it would be important for the Council to distinguish
between the absolute and the relative, the universal and timeless and the
particular and time-bound; total fidelity to Christ would have to be
accompanied by "a total, comprehensive openness, a deeply generous
attitude toward all authentic human values;" and, finally, genuine
renewal of the Church must subordinate what is juridical to the demands
of charity and to pastoral exigencies.

Léger then used these criteria to evaluate the preparatory work as it
had passed before the CPC. Among them he had words of praise for the
schemas on the liturgy, on the apostolate of the laity, on religious freedom (the text of the SCU), on relations between bishops and the Roman
Curia. But he was apprehensive about several other texts which he found
lacking in "the deep orientation which Your Holiness himself has
wanted to give to the coming Council: the renewal of doctrine and institutions by a return to the most authentic sources and in a welcoming
attention to the realities of our times."

> Several schemata consider the Church too much as an institution under
> siege which the Council must defend; they do not see in it enough the radi-
> ant depositary of the salvation to be shared. In them the Church has the
> aspect of an institution more juridical than missionary. They don't show
> the courage to turn frankly to the present world, toward its needs, toward
> its new and legitimate demands. They seem to believe, instead, that it will
> be enough to repeat, with more insistence but without deepening the doc-
> trine, formulas which already the world no longer can understand. They
> seem to believe that the losses of faith, the deterioration of morality, the
> failures of the apostolate have no other causes than the inattention of men
> or the malice of the times; they do not ask if the obsolete character of cer-
> tain forms of the Church's thought and action also play some role in it.

Léger then exemplified these comments by criticisms of the schemas on the religious life, on the Church (except for the chapters on the laity and on authority and obedience in the Church), on the deposit of faith, on the doctrine of St. Thomas, on Church and State, on the social order, on Catholic schools, and on the communications-media.

Léger ended this letter to the Pope with two requests. The first was that only texts which make a real contribution and address the needs of the day be presented to the Council. While some schemata met these criteria, others did not, and Léger thought it unlikely that the Council itself could make the necessary changes. The second request was that the Pope repeat once again to all those involved in the Council "the urgent, overriding need for the Council to undertake really and with the courage of fidelity to Christ and to the eager expectation of all men the work of renewal in which the Church will rediscover the purest traits of its youth."

In mid-August Léger sent this text to seven other Cardinals, solliciting their signatures: Frings, Liénart, Döpfner, Montini, Suenens, Alfrink, and König. He received the agreement of all except Montini and Alfrink.[628] Léger sent his paper, co-signed by Frings, Döpfner and König, to the Pope on 11 September 1962; a week later he sent another copy with Liénart's signature. In the accompanying letters Léger repeated his anxiety and fear of great disappointment if the Council were to proceed as prepared.

On 17 September Cicognani wrote to Léger to inform him that the Pope had received the texts and that he "appreciated your gesture and thanks you greatly for this filial communication." This rather non-committal reply may reflect the fact that it was by now too late to change the agenda set by the transmission of the seven texts to the bishops. By then the Pope had already given his 11 September radio-address in which he adopted some of the language and orientation of Suenens' project in restating his vision of the Council against the larger backdrop of contemporary developments in the world. Léger's initiative may have helped, however, to sustain the Pope's confidence as he prepared his

[628] Frings said that he agreed with the general tenor of the paper, if not with every detail. Liénart and Döpfner said they were in full agreement, but the latter was worried that it would have little effect, "given the form of the schemata proposed for the first period of the conciliar sessions." Montini was unable to reply until 19 September, by which time he thought the effort might be "untimely, after the Holy Father's message of September 11." Still he thought Léger's letter contained "so many good things, which could be recalled during the Council." Suenens sent his own signed response directly to the Pope. Alfrink's response is not known.

speech for the opening of the Council which would have the character of the appeal Léger desired and would in fact liberate the conciliar Fathers to assume responsibility for their own work, to be critical, now publicly, of much of the preparatory work, and to orient the Council in a direction much closer to the Pope's own vision.

VIII. POPE JOHN AND THE PREPARATION OF THE COUNCIL

Perhaps the most important question that remains for the historian to address, one that only the availability of much more documentation will make it possible to answer, is Pope John XXIII's relationship with the preparatory process we have just reviewed. The elements of the problem are easy enough to state. On the one hand, there is the broad vision of the Council as an opportunity to promote a thorough and deep spiritual renewal of the Church and to undertake the pastoral adaptations, *aggiornamento*, that would enable it to be a more effective redemptive presence in a changed and changing world. This vision, articulated in important texts during the preparatory period, would be restated in even more authoritative form in the Pope's opening speech at the Council. By once again declaring his disagreement with "the prophets of doom," he authorized in advance the severe critique of the preparatory texts that was to be undertaken so dramatically by the conciliar Fathers at the first session. Any doubts about the Pope's own views were erased when he intervened, against the conciliar regulations, to withdraw from the conciliar agenda the schema *De fontibus revelationis*, one of the touchstones of the TC's vision of the Council. At the beginning and the end of the preparatory process, then, there are relatively clear statements of the Pope's view of the Council.

On the other hand, it does not appear that anything like this grand vision inspired most of the documents produced during the preparatory period. The doctrinal texts were all conceived as responses to contemporary threats to the purity and integrity of the deposit of revelation. For that reason, they deliberately did not present a comprehensive or synthetic restatement of the Gospel, but emphasized only those doctrines being questioned either outside or inside the Church. The stance was suspicious and negative, and it was defended to the end and quite unapologetically even when it was called into question at the CPC.

As for the pastoral texts, these most often took the form of tinkering with the reigning system, proposing relatively minor adjustments in what Felici, in a revealing comment, called "pastoral technique." Very few of the PrC responsible for addressing the pastoral questions undertook anything like a serious consideration of the challenges and opportunities posed by the contemporary world. It would be unjust to say that most of them were as negative and defensive as the TC, but certainly the texts they produced do not show much pastoral imagination and the reforms they envisaged fall rather short of what would be necessary to produce that "new age" in the Church of which the Pope spoke. Only the LI and the SCU really seem to have measured up to the Pope's vision.

The question that remains to be answered is why there was such a contrast between papal vision and actual achievement. It is perhaps too easy to answer that the Pope was surrounded by people who either did not comprehend his intentions or actively opposed them. That there were such people is not to be denied, of course, and one could make the case that the men who prepared most of the practically oriented texts fell into the first category and the leaders of the TC into the second. But there remain certain ambiguities in the activities of the Pope himself.

On the one hand, it was, after all, the Pope who was finally responsible for the structure and direction of the preparations of the Council, and he did make many important decisions to orient the conciliar preparation in the direction he wanted. He insisted that the antepreparatory consultation be as broad and as free as possible. He did not hesitate to make adjustments in the machinery of the preparatory period that Tardini had drawn up. He established the SCU to pursue his treasured ecumenical hopes and supported Bea's efforts to give it very broad responsibilities. He insisted on the distinction between the conciliar preparation and the Curia.

On the other hand, there are other decisions more difficult to comprehend. He approved the appointment of curial heads to chair the PrC, only moderating this fatal link with the structure of the Roman Curia by prohibiting secretaries and assessors from serving as secretaries of the PrC. The concrete supervision of the preparatory work he entrusted to Felici. He approved a set of *Quaestiones* that reflected little of his vision, broadening this narrow focus only by leaving the PrC free to add other issues they thought important.

All the evidence is not yet available on how closely the Pope followed the course of the preparations. He appears to have met with Felici at least once a week, meetings about which almost nothing is known. On several occasions he received written reports on the work of the PrC.[629] He paid an apparently largely ceremonial visit to each of the PrC during the course of their work, but no full record of his remarks on these occasions has been published.[630] It is not clear how closely the Pope followed the work of the individual PrC nor whether he examined their many schemata before they were presented for review by the CPC.[631] His speeches to the CPC are usually very general in content and hortatory in tone; and his remarks about the schemata it would be considering never give much indication of what he thought of them.

At the end of the process, the Pope's approval was required before any schemas could be inscribed on the conciliar agenda and sent out to the bishops. A few published fragments of the Pope's comments on the schemata brought to him for approval are generally favorable, but they are insufficient to permit a certain judgement about his views.[632] In any case his approval appears to have been sought only at the very end of the process of selection, when it would have been difficult for him to ask for major changes in the agenda without postponing the opening of the Council indefinitely.

But if it is unclear how closely the Pope followed the preparatory work while it was in course, there is no doubt that he was made aware fairly early about criticisms of the preparation of the Council. By the late spring and summer of 1961, many people, including important Cardinals, began to complain to him, both privately and publicly, about certain of its features: the lack of coordination in the work, the absence of a pastoral orientation, the exclusion of lay people, complaints of the press about the lack of information about the work, and the absence of an ecumenical orientation. But there is not much

[629] Carbone, "Il cardinale Domenico Tardini," 84; for examples of written communications to the Pope about the work of the TC, see Tromp Diary, 31 Jan 1961, 11 April 1961, 29 April 1961, 6 May 1961.

[630] See *ADP*, I, 60, 62-65, 78, 80-82, 84-85, 88-89, 100, 115, 186-87; only these last two pages reproduce the Latin text pronounced by the Pope for the SCU; for all of the other encounters only the vague reports *in oratione obliqua* printed in *OssRom* are given.

[631] In his lengthy discussion of the role of the General Secretariat, Caprile, I/2, 413, does not mention that Felici sent the texts to the Pope before transmitting them to the CPC; but in vol. II, 3, he claims, without supporting authority, that "with no exceptions," the Pope had seen all the texts before they were printed and sent to the CPC.

[632] See V. Carbone, "Genesi e criteri," 587-88; Fagiolo, "Il cardinale A. Cicognani," 234. It would be more useful to know what the Pope's judgements were on the texts while they were being elaborated, and whether any criticisms he might have had of them were communicated and exercised any effective influence on the history of the texts. At least one text, the TC's schema *De ordine morali*, Pope John found too harsh and negative; see Caprile, I/2 279n.

evidence that Pope John was willing or, if willing, able to respond to these criticisms effectively.

On the first two complaints, his only known response was the establishment, announced in November 1961, of a subcommission on mixed matters, which would attempt, after the several PrC had completed their independent work, to give it a coherent and pastoral character. As for the laity, for whom a greater role had been requested by Frings and Döpfner, the Pope's response seems to have been the one stated at the conclusion of the first session of the CPC: he considered that the wishes of the laity had been sufficiently indicated in the *vota* received from their bishops in the antepreparatory consultation. Pope John was no more yielding on the question of public information. While grateful for the interest on the part of non-Catholics and journalists, he recalled that the Council was exclusively concerned with the internal life and organization of the Catholic Church.[633]

Finally, on the ecumenical dimension of the Council, the Pope continued to make his passionate interest more than clear not only in multiple references in his speeches and in his establishment of the SCU, but also in his authorization of the Secretariat to go beyond the explicit language of *Superno Dei nutu* and to prepare texts on ecumenically sensitive topics. But he does not seem to have responded effectively when criticisms of the preparatory work's lack of ecumenical sensitivity were registered.[634] Certainly nothing changed in relations between the SCU and the TC.

Even more puzzling is the Pope's tolerance of the OR's inactivity with regard to the Orthodox. Patriarch Athenagoras in particular had multiplied expressions of affection for Pope John and of his willingness to come to Rome to meet the Pope. The latter was considered at Rome to be impossible, at least if it required as a condition a reciprocal action on the part of the Pope. But what is astounding is that there were no serious efforts even to begin a conversation with the Orthodox.[635] It would not be until June 1961, long after far more serious conversations had

---

[633] *ADP* I 37; *DMC* III 21.

[634] A private letter from Congar in July 1961 warning the Pope about the potential betrayal of his ecumenical aspirations appears to have gone unanswered. Sometime later, when Congar told Bea that he had written to the Pope, Bea replied that the Pope "was very astonished to learn that there had never been a mixed commission between the Secretariat and the Theological Commission;" Y. Congar, *Mon journal du Concile*, 6 March 1962.

[635] Dumont details the story, including his appeals to Cicognani and Tardini, in February 1961, in a chapter of his still unpublished memoirs. See also A. Wenger, *Les trois Rome*, 53-101.

been initiated between the SCU and Anglicans and Protestants, that an official delegation visited Athenagoras. This visit remained without effect, however, and the Orthodox eventually asked that their relations with the Vatican be channelled through the SCU and not the Congregation for the Oriental Church or the OR. It was not until the end of 1961 that the Pope entrusted all ecumenical contacts to the SCU; and at this point relations improved. The Pope's slowness to act on a matter so close to his heart remains to be explained.

A few other more particular interventions of the Pope during the preparatory period may usefully be mentioned here. When Romeo's bitter attack on the Pontifical Biblical Institute (PBI) was published in early 1961, the Pope privately communicated his disgust at the article and gave public support to the PBI by appointing its rector to the TC. The Pope's actions appear to have been motivated more by the excesses of Romeo's argument and by its part in institutional conflicts between the Lateran and the PBI than by considerations of personal sympathy — in fact, Pope John appears to have been troubled by recent developments in Catholic biblical studies.

A year later another public controversy was provoked by the publication of R. Lombardi's book, *Concilio: Per una riforma nella carità*, accompanied by articles in the press maintaining that its proposals for reform, including that of the Roman Curia, were shared by Pope John. The Pope, who had never been an enthusiast of the Jesuit's "Movement for a Better World," seems to have seen the book and its interpretation as a threat to the delicate relations he had tried to establish between the Curia and the Council. After refusing Lombardi's request to write an article acknowledging mistakes and deploring press-interpretations of his work, the Pope authorized the publication in *OssRom* of an article which, after general remarks urging responsible commentary on the Council, explicitly mentioned Lombardi's book as a contrary example, declared it to be of purely private provenance, and criticized its comments on the clergy and the Roman Curia.[636] Lombardi's work was withdrawn from circulation and all translations forbidden. A few days later the Pope seemed to be referring to Lombardi when in his speech to

[636] The article in *OssRom*, 11 Jan. 1962, is summarized at some length in Caprile, I/II, 265-66. The following day, Fr. Janssens wrote a letter to Jesuit superiors, warning against Jesuit writers leading lay people "to nourish hopes that, given the basic dogmas of the Church and the mind of the Supreme Pontiff, are bound to be disappointed;" *ARSJ* 14 (1961-66) 163. For the whole incident, see G. Zizola, "Roncalli e padre R. Lombardi," *CrSt* 8 (1987) 73-93; idem, *Il microfono di Dio*, 448-71.

the CPC he urged prudence and respect for truth on people who write about the Council, "especially if writers enjoy a certain authority, lest their methods generate disturbance and worry."[637] The whole incident attracted much attention, some of it fearful that the actions taken against the Jesuit would inhibit the free speech in the Church thought to be desired by the Pope.[638]

Finally, there is the Pope's attitude towards the many-sided question of Latin. With regard to its use at the Council, his first statement, when the topic came up at the CPC, was to say that Latin would be the official language but that room would be provided, when necessary, for other languages to be used.[639] But the *Ordo celebrandi* he approved left room for the vernacular only in meetings of the conciliar commissions. In February 1962, his apostolic constitution *Veterum sapientia* settled the question of the use of Latin in clerical education by adopting a much stricter discipline than was under consideration in two PrC. This document also appeared to take a stand on the question of the use of Latin in the liturgy, when it forbade revolutionary criticisms of the Church's discipline. This paragraph, especially when coupled with the Pope's earlier exaltation of Latin in solemn liturgies, appeared to be foreclosing the question before the Council could address it. It was only, it seems, through private communications that bishops were assured that the Council would have an opportunity to address the issue.

The least that one can say about a number of these papal actions is that they remain mysterious. Why did the Pope regularly make decisions or remarks that seemed to discount the criticisms that the direction and results of the preparatory process were threatening to betray his vision of the Council? Why did the Pope wait nearly a year before taking seriously the criticisms of the preparatory work by such important figures as Frings, Döpfner, König, Alfrink, Léger and Suenens? It appears that it was only in the spring of 1962 that he began to give a sympathetic ear to the complaints and fears, when he privately commissioned Suenens to draw up a coherent plan for an integration of the preparatory material. But even this sympathy did not have any concrete effect on the determination of the agenda of the first session of the Council.

[637] *ADP* I 157.

[638] B. Häring says he openly criticized the action, supported in his view by Montini; see *Fede storia morale*, 51. See also J. Ratzinger, "Freimut und Gehorsam," *WuW* 17 (1962) 409-21.

[639] *ADP* I 95.

For whatever reasons, Pope John seems to have preferred to intervene by way of his formal statements, which throughout the preparatory period continued to call for a profound and broad conciliar program, rather than to act decisively to ensure that such a program would guide the preparations. This preference gave great freedom, of course, to all the bodies involved in the work: the General Secretariat, the individual PrC, and the CPC. But although the CPC was supposed to have some authority over the preparation of the Council, it was never able to assume that task effectively. Its meetings were marked by great freedom and frankness, but the more important methodological and substantive concerns articulated there had little effect. The Pope seems to have preferred to leave it to the Council Fathers themselves to decide what they wished the Council to be and to do. The drama of the first session of the Council — and the final judgement on the preparatory work — would lie in the fact that to prove equal to the Pope's vision the bishops of Vatican II felt it necessary to repudiate so much of the work done to prepare for it.

CHAPTER IV

THE EXTERNAL CLIMATE

J. OSCAR BEOZZO

I. PUBLIC INFORMATION ABOUT THE WORK OF PREPARATION

The interest and expectations aroused by the announcement of January, 1959, led the press and other mass media to undertake to keep public opinion informed. But it became clear after the first weeks that it was very difficult to advance beyond the level of general information or more or less hasty conjectures. When the antepreparatory phase began, it seemed natural to expect a constant and organized flow of information. Such was the hope aroused by the official communiqué in the second half of July, 1959, which told of the establishment of a special commission, the invitation sent to the Catholic bishops asking them what they expected of the Council, the establishment of a secretariat, and the request that the Catholic universities and Roman Congregations prepare studies and proposals.[1] In addition, at the end of the following October Secretary of State Tardini actually held a press conference, the first in the history of the Holy See, at the end of which he announced that a press office would soon be set up to supply information "on the various phases of the Council."[2]

1. *Expectations Regarding News*

Despite all this, throughout the entire first six months of 1960 no information on the antepreparatory activity was given out, even though thousands of expressions of opinion had been reaching Rome from the bishops and were being sifted and summarized by the secretariat team. Only at the end of May and the beginning of June did John XXIII announce the formation of preparatory commissions and give a brief summary of the work done during the preceding twelve months. On this occasion the pope noted that the antepreparatory commission had performed "a task carried out with respectful discretion," and said that

[1] Complete text in Caprile I/1, 175-76.

[2] *ADA* I, 153-58. The announcement was repeated by Tardini on January 26, 1960, in an interview with *La Croix* on French television: *DC* 57 (1960) 393-98. During these years this Paris Catholic daily did valuable work in supplying information; this was due especially to the zeal of its editor-in-chief, A. Wenger.

the activity of the preparatory commissions would be marked by "a prudent confidentiality."[3] In addition, as has already been noted, the members of the commission were bound to a rather strict secrecy concerning the work in which they were engaged.

The desire to be informed about the work of a Council is a recurrent theme in the history of these assemblies; this was especially the case, although in very different modalities, with Trent and Vatican I. At the beginning of the 1960's the desire for news was no longer limited to an elite but, due to the spread of television in Europe as elsewhere, had become part of the cultural scene generally. In this area as in others the pontificate of John marked a turning point.[4] No past Council had reached the masses or been affected by the masses: the experience of Vatican II would be different. The tremendous importance of public opinion during the war but especially after it whetted this desire; in fact there were even references to it in some episcopal vota, which suggested the establishment of a center "for public relations or information, in order to prevent the spread of inaccurate news and to report, instead, news of the Council, the Holy See, and the Church, that would be true and accurate (*secundum veritatem et fideliter*)."[5] In their turn, several groups of competent journalists expressed the wish that authoritative steps be taken to ensure accurate and continual information,[6] since at that time information depended on sporadic initiatives which, even when authoritative, were often limited in scope.[7]

---

[3] *DMC* 2, 390-402; citations on 393. The pope would return to the subject of "reticence" and *amor silentii* on November 14, when he addressed the members of the preparatory commissions (*DMC* III, 21-22).

[4] See M. Marazziti, *I Papi di carta. Nascita e svolta dell'informazione religiosa da Pio XII a Giovanni XXIII* (Genoa, 1990).

[5] Caprile I/1, 175, note 13. Because of the divisions of the Code of Canon Law that were used in it, none of this appeared in the *Analyticus Conspectus* of the vota. *OssRom* for June 20-21, 1960, announced the appointment of Msgr. M. J. O'Connor as president of the press secretariat (the secretary was A. M. Deskur; there were fifteen members and eighteen consultors), but in July O'Connor explained that the secretariat would make suggestions to the Central Preparatory Commission but would not concern itself with the participation of the press in the Council (Caprile I/1, 273).

[6] On July 9 the final statement of the International Catholic Press Union, meeting in Santander, had expressed the desire for information about the Council (*DC* 57 [1960] 1136-38). Caprile (I/2. 128, note 6 [1961/62]; 402-3 [1961/62]; 455-58 [1961/62]) and *DC* 58 (1961) 853-58 report statements in the press pointing out the problem created by secrecy on preparation for the Council.

[7] In mid-June, 1960, Cardinal Bea held a press conference in New York (*DC* 42 [1960] 1099-1102). On June 24 Bishop Felici took part in a discussion on Vatican Radio (Caprile I/1, 178-79). Taking advantage of John XXIII's mandate to the Secretariat for Unity to keep non-Roman Christians informed about the Council, Bea held frequent public lectures; see Stejpan Schmidt, *Augustin Bea: The Cardinal of Unity*, trans. Leslie Wearne (New Rochelle, NY, 1992) 382-411, and Caprile, I/2, 28-29, 72-73, 242-46, 288, 317-18, 512-14.

It is not yet possible to determine whether there were differences of opinion within the Holy See on the question of information about the Council. It may be recalled that the preconciliar steps taken by Pius XI and Pius XII had been surrounded by secrecy, partly as a result of the control exercised by the Holy Office in the matter. The spontaneous tendency of John XXIII to be communicative and the early press conference of Cardinal Tardini in October, 1959, had raised hopes of a new attitude. Had the pope meant to introduce a more flexible standard when he spoke of "reticence" and an *amor silentii*, but not of "secrecy"? If he did, not many were aware of it, and not a few preferred an atmosphere of radical distrust of the press. In any case, throughout the whole of 1960 and 1961 preparation for the Council was carried on in a completely "airtight" silence that was broken on only a very few occasions. Secretary Felici held a conference at the beginning of December, 1960, on the Council and the press; two weeks later Tardini granted an interview on English television; toward the end of February, 1961, Bea appeared on French and German television, and Cardinal König met with journalists in Vienna.[8]

These few driblets were completely unsatisfactory. The international press grew increasingly restless, while the lack of information killed the attention of mass public opinion and stirred fears in ecclesial circles of a Roman manipulation of the preparation. In this atmosphere initiatives took shape that were independent of the circles occupied with the preparation for the Council. Thus *La Civiltà Cattolica*, the journal of the Italian Jesuits, which enjoyed an exceptional reputation, took the initiative of proposing to the pope, via its editor, Fr. Robert Tucci, and at the suggestion of Fr. G. Caprile, that it write and publish a "Chronicle" of the preparation. John XXIII

> expresses a desire that this be done...in a special section of the journal; he adds that he knows that on that occasion [during Vatican I] we had been in a privileged position, and he thinks the same can be the case now; he is glad that we have been the first to offer our services and that we are the best fitted for the task because of the importance of the journal, because it is published every two weeks, and because we have men prepared for the task. But first he will have to speak to Cardinal Tardini about it.[9]

[8] Felici: *DC* 58 (1961) 669-71; Tardini: Caprile I/1, 38; Bea: Caprile I/2, 38; König: *DC* 58 (1961) 443-47. In addition, Cardinal Cento appeared on French television on February 12, 1961: Caprile I/2, 57-59.

[9] Caprile I/1, VII; Caprile here transcribes a note written by Father Tucci after a papal audience on June 7, 1960. The note goes on to say that the pope "has from the beginning made it his practice to do nothing without consulting the cardinal secretary of state and vice versa, so as to ensure unity and harmony in government." As a result, *Notiziario*, No. 1, was published in the issue for the second half of June, 1960.

Not long after, on occasion of the International Eucharistic Congress held in Munich in August, 1960, Fr. Tucci also sponsored a meeting of the editors of periodicals of religious information published by the Society of Jesus; similar meetings would be held weekly at the Roman offices of his periodical during the entire Council. At the end of April, 1961, two weeks after a press conference by Msgr. Felici, the latter met with the International Catholic Press Union; toward the end of June he would hold another press conference, followed by an interview in mid-September about the central commission.[10] Bea, for his part, granted interviews on the "ecumenical" preparation, first at the beginning of March, 1961, and again at the end of May.[11]

Almost a year after the meeting of the Jesuit editors, a small number of journalists engaged in reporting religious news met in Paris in mid-May, 1961, and agreed that it would be expedient to have periodic meetings for the exchange of ideas, especially in view of the Council. Thus was born the group of religious journalists.[12] On this occasion or, at the latest, at a subsequent meeting in Freiburg (Breisgau) toward the end of September, the group produced a document that emphasized the importance of news. The Council was to be a unique event and required that the expectations of people be met and that information systems be adapted to meet this need. Concrete suggestions were offered for organizing and financing a press office and for producing a bulletin. In order to inform those who would pass the information on, it was absolutely necessary to make use of the various methods of conveying news and to welcome and give guidance to journalists, especially if they were not Catholics. The document ended: "If journalists run into a wall of silence, concealment, and distrust, they will use every means to acquire information and will not hesitate to exaggerate what they do have and to invent. Openness and trust will be the best guarantees of truth and discretion with regard to the Council."

2. *The Press Office of the Central Commission*

Meanwhile, preparation for Vatican II entered its most important phase with the beginning, in mid-1962, of the working sessions of the Central Commission. At the end of the first cycle of work the pope

---

[10] Tucci: J. Grootaers, "L'information religieuse au début du Concile: instances officielles et réseaux informels," in *Vatican II commence*, 213; Felici: *DC* 58 (1961) 665-68 and Caprile I/2, 97, and then *DC* 58 (1961) 893-96 and Caprile I/2, 131-32 and 175.

[11] *DC* 58 (1961) 447-50 and 859-62.

[12] Grootaers, "L'information religieuse," 211-34.

summarized the preparatory activity already accomplished and made a reference to "journalists...their impatience and keen desire to be informed about activities concerning the Council." He assured the journalists that "there will not be lacking opportunities to provide the clergy and the faithful and all those around the world who are sincerely interested in this great event with news and ideas that will satisfy the impulses of generous hearts."[13] The promise was still a vague one and seemed to reflect an intention to be selective about the information to be released. Was it also influenced by the desire expressed by the group of religious journalists, who had shared their worries with, among others, high-ranking prelates?

What is certain is that in the autumn (October 12) the appointment was finally announced of an Italian prelate, Msgr. F. Vaillanc (already involved in the publication side of Italian Catholic Action) as director of the press office of the secretariat of the Central Preparatory Commission. John XXIII underscored the importance of this step by receiving the Foreign Press Association at an audience on October 24. November 6 brought the first issue of the *Notiziario* of the press office, the text of which appeared in *L'Osservatore Romano* for November 9.[14] This publication represented a qualitative leap by comparison with the complete lack of official information during the previous years, but it also resembled the mouse brought forth by the mountain. It consisted of a few mimeographed pages containing general information, without any precise description of the various positions at issue, much less any indication of the various persons who intervened in the preparatory discussions.

Expectations seemed disappointed rather than satisfied. The impression was given that the preparatory work consisted essentially of a trite, unvarying repetition of subjects dealt with in the abundant papal teaching issued during Pacelli's long pontificate. The creation of a press

---

[13] *DMC* III, 329-30.

[14] *DMC* III, 473-81. The full title of the *Notiziario* was: *Pontificia Commissione Centrale preparatoria del Concilio ecumenico Vaticano II — Segreteria Generale — Servizio Stampa — NOTIZIARIO*. The *Notiziario* appeared in ninety-seven issues, the last one dated June 23, 1962. The vast majority were devoted to the sessions of the Central Commission; there were also terse items about the meetings of the subcommissions of the Central Commission (amendments, regulations, mixed subjects). The *Notiziario* for March 23, 1962, reported the beginning of a course for the stenographers who would work at the Council; there was also some news about meetings of the commission for ceremonial, the commission for the technical organization of the Council, and the administrative secretariat. On September 5, 1962, the first issue of the bulletin from the press office of the Council was published.

office was a step forward, but news was still a desideratum.[15] Outside of
Rome and even outside of circles directly involved in the preparation
people continued to know nothing or almost nothing. This was so much
the case that at a new meeting in Brussels in late March and early April,
1962, the religious journalists insisted again on the importance of information, adding that if journalists were forced to invent, the non-Catholics
would be in a better position because they would have no scruples. "Up
to now, the information given does not meet the needs of the press, for
it has consisted solely in summaries and statements couched in language
that is too close to that of the Scholastic manuals." The journalists suggested that a group of experts be included in the press office.[16]

The uneasiness, which grew as the opening of the Council approached,
was echoed even in two addresses of John XXIII during the following
May. The pope assured his listeners that he had "thought of expanding
the press office so that public opinion might be kept suitably informed."
Some weeks later, addressing the congress of the International Federation
of Newspaper Editors, he spoke more specifically of his "intention to
reorganize and enlarge the press office... It is very much Our desire that
a lack of adequate information not compel journalists to think up more or
less likely conjectures and to spread among the public ideas, opinions,
and hopes that will then prove ill-founded or erroneous." There was thus
an unconditional acceptance of criticisms, although later in the address
the pope insisted once again on an ambiguous "need for discretion."[17]

Once again, the effect was felt primarily at the material level: on
October 5, 1962, Felici officially opened the new quarters of the press
office. At the same time, six rules were announced that would regulate
the activity of journalists accredited to the press office.[18]

---

[15] See F. Vaillanc, *Imagini del Concilio* (Rome, 1966), and R. Laurentin, "L'information au concile," in *Deuxième*, 359-78.

[16] *Nota sulla informazione concernente il concilio* (sent on August 8, 1962, to those who
had attended the meeting; complete text in Caprile I/2, 650-51; see Grootaers, 216-17). On
the preceding February 3-4 Vaillanc had spoken at the meeting of the Italian Catholic Press
Union (Caprile I/2, 318-19). It is an odd fact that some information about the work of the theological commission had been published in *La voix diocésaine de Besançon* (no. 33, 1961,
403-6) on the initiative of Archbishop Dubois, who was a member of that commission.

[17] *DMC* IV, 267 and 303. Grootaers (217) reasonably maintains that the pope's admission was the result of the Brussels document. On January 23 in Paris and on April 12 in
Berlin Bea had spoken of the ecumenical importance of the Council (*ICI* 162, 57-59).

[18] Complete text in Caprile I/2, 651-52. On September 28, Felici had given a lecture
to the Circle of Rome with the title "Alla vigilia del Concilio ecumenico" (*OssRom*, September 30, 1962), and on September 30 he had spoken on the same subject on Italian television. During the meeting of the coordinating commission on March 29, 1963, Bishop
Felici would give a "Relatio de nuntiis dandis" in which he painted a rosy picture of the
press office experiment (*AS* V/I, 508-11).

3. *Spontaneous Initiatives*

The Catholic world saw a growing number of spontaneous initiatives intended to stress the importance of the Council. Despite their variety and unevenness these undertakings also intended to provide news about the preparation for the Council and reflected widely different expectations. A typical example was the Spanish periodical *Concilio. Revista de orientación e información sobre el Concilio Vaticano II*, which began publication in June, 1962, but had no information to pass on about the preparation. The periodical was in fact devoted solely to providing information of a historical kind and to expressing wishes concerning problems it wanted the Council to take up. The same fate would befall the countless other press, radio, and television enterprises that multiplied everywhere in some measure as the opening of the Council drew near.[19]

In these circumstances a certain apprehension began to spread that was caused both by the lack of reliable and persuasive news and by the circulation of more or less fanciful hypotheses and inferences. On the eve of the Council's opening, public opinion lacked reliable points of reference, but so, for that matter, did even the participants in the Council, for, as we know, they received a small set of preparatory texts only a very few weeks before they left for Rome. The Council seemed to be not only an event internal to Catholicism but one that had been reserved to the "official personnel" in Rome. Was there not a danger that the calls and exhortations addressed to the faithful by almost all the bishops, asking them to pray for the success of the Council, would fall into a void? Was not the conciliar maturation of the bishops themselves being delayed, since they were not used to working together and were often prisoners of the limited problems of their own dioceses?

A reading of the section of Fr. Congar's *Journal* that covers the period of preparation provides a significant proof of the scarcity of information even for those who, like the French Dominican theologian, took part in the work of the doctrinal commission and had the advantage of many personal contacts. In these notes there is almost never any information about other commissions; much less does Congar know anything about what will happen at the point when the Council begins its work.

---

[19] Thus Italian television planned a series of broadcasts in the autumn of 1962 on the history of the Councils; the project was assigned to G. Alberigo. Reports on the initiatives of other television and radio networks may be found in the principal journals of religious news and in Caprile. An important regional example has been studied by D. Beloeil and M. Lagrée, "Le catholicisme breton devant le concile (1959-1962)," in *Vatican II commence*, 262-74.

One has an odd feeling when one comes across the note dated March 6, 1962, according to which Congar has learned that "commissions of experts will be at work during the Council" and that someone "is working to have me on these commissions, because they will need theologians to provide replacement texts, as Kleutgen did for the first Vatican Council."[20]

II. INFORMATION AND SPONTANEOUS DISCUSSIONS

Public opinion, ordinary Christians, and even not a few bishops and churchmen shared in the preparation for the Council solely through periodicals and reviews and such information as these supplied.[21] These publications had to grapple with the unwelcome but unavoidable fact that the work of the preparatory bodies was buried in secrecy and in the cryptic reticence of the Vatican's vehicles of communication, both official (*L'Osservatore Romano*) and semi-official (*Civiltà Cattolica*). They succeeded nevertheless in getting organized and benefitted from the spontaneous enthusiasm that inspired editorial staffs, associations, and even episcopates.

They sought to shed light on a scene that was far too vast: the vota of the bishops remained anonymous; no one, even among the major leaders, had an overall picture either of episcopal trends or of the preparatory commissions. Consequently, between 1959 and mid-1962 there was almost nothing to which the media and the theological journals could *react*. If and when they decided to express their own views and their own expectations of the coming Council, they did so as they pleased, for they could not systematically discuss the progress of the debate that was going on in the "dark room" of the Vatican agencies. On the contrary, they had to think things out on their own or else, as the months went by, concern themselves with what other reviews, newspapers, conferences, and books were saying about the Council.

[20] Y. Congar, *Mon journal du Concile*, March 6, 1962. Congar himself notes that in the late spring of 1960 there was talk of a Herder plan to set up a central secretariat for information on the Council.

[21] On this subject see H. J. Sieben, *Katholische Konzilsidee im 19. und 20. Jahrhundert* (Paderborn, 1993) 244-77. For a contemporary survey see H. Küng, "Veröffentlichungen zum Konzil," *Theologische Quartalschrift* 143 (1963) 56-82. Also: A. Melloni, *Lo spettatore influente: riviste e informazione nella preparazione del Vaticano II*, in *Attese*, 119-91; this work is based on the bibliography of Vatican II prepared by G. Turbanti and on a catalogue, drawn up by a team at the Istituto per le scienze religiose (Bologna), of literature published during the period of preparation.

Information in the outside world on the preparation was therefore not distinguishable according to source but was rather divided into levels. At one level there were scholars carrying on their discussions (not without effects on bishops and ecumenical leaders) in specialized periodicals that transcended geolinguistic boundaries. At an intermediate level there were the journals of religious information that were committed, with varying degrees of authoritativeness, to hunting out what sparse news there was, news which, paradoxically, the operation of the rule of secrecy concentrated on what the pope had to say.[22] Finally, general public opinion, both Catholic and noncatholic, brought to bear on the preparation the weight of its own expectations, its own illusions, its own hopes. Then the circle was closed and began again. What the media managed to figure out was brought into the many lecture series on the Council that bishops in little towns and seminaries permitted or even desired;[23] but this spread a consensus rather than information and fed a circulatory activity that crossed diocesan and linguistic boundaries.

Even amid the complexity of this phenomenon it is possible to identify two general trends: the quantitative spread and the hardening of ecumenical "doubt."

1. "Religion" Reporters

Except for a slight reduction in the middle six months of 1959, due to the disappointed realization that the curia was controlling the process of preparation, the four years of preparation saw a constant growth of interest in the Council, with a predictable upswing during 1962.

---

[22] See A. Melloni, "Parallelismi, nodi comuni e ipotesi conflittuali nelle strutture della preparazione del Vaticano II," in *Verso il concilio*, 445-82.

[23] A quite unique project was that of the Roman Theological Academy: a study-week, the results of which would appear in a special issue of *Divinitas* under the title: *Acta Hebdomadae de Conciliis Oecumenicis celebratae a Pontificia Academia Theologica Romana diebus 13-18 mensis novembris A. D. 1960*. More typical, especially of the Italian cultural climate, were the conferences sponsored by Giuseppe Cardinal Siri of Genoa in 1962 at the Colombianum. Only ranking cardinals were invited, as though in an effort to organize a network of contacts that would be centered in the archbishop, at one time a probable successor to Pius XII and a valiant opponent of reforms. Even joint undertakings such as the week of updating held by the Catholic University of Milan at Mendola or the course sponsored by the Pro Civitate association in Assisi in August, 1960, had to make room for these considerations. The atmosphere outside Italy was quite different; there the dominant concern was with inquiry; see, e.g., the XIIIth Missionary Week, held at Burgos, August 5-12, 1960, its theme being "Toward Unity through Charity."

The press agencies became more specialized.[24] It was through these agencies, the influence of which has been little studied but cannot be overestimated, that the first "press conferences" of the curial cardinals and prelates became widely known. The correspondents of the agencies also were successful in providing interesting material not only to the dailies but even to the journals of religious news,[25] which gradually made their presence more fully felt, without any important variations from one linguistic area to another.

The Tablet stood out as both authoritative and accurate. Its two analogues, *America* and *Commonweal*, differed among themselves: the former provided abundant details but was, on the whole, passive; the latter was rather cautious about committing itself in its rare editorials and paid little heed, on the whole, to the broad range of European discussion.[26] *The Tablet*, on the other hand, was more careful in observing the movement of the preparation and more attentive to the ecumenical problems raised by the pope and Bea. The voices of noncatholics, of the laity, and of troubled journalists found a place in its pages; at times there were even articles that got to the heart of what was being discussed in the commissions and other bodies, even if this eluded the readers. The bishops to whom *The Tablet* gave a platform were few but prominent: Alfrink and the episcopal conference to which he belonged, Frings, König, the Polish episcopate, and, unexpectedly, Bishop Bakole, who in his address to the Paris meeting of the Society for African Culture described the problem raised by participation of the Churches of that continent in the Council.

A highly professional journal, *Informations catholiques internationales*, made its presence increasingly felt after September, 1961. After having for a long time reported on the Council "from Rome," it inaugurated a special page "on the Council" that was edited by Fesquet (beginning in January, 1962, it was entitled *Informations Concile*). *La Croix*, the daily newspaper already mentioned, did the same. The French made

---

[24] The attitude of the Soviet press, whose correspondents in Rome always had a semi-diplomatic role, is a case apart. On Kolosov, for example, see A. Riccardi, *Il Vaticano e Mosca 1940-1990* (Rome-Bari, 1992) 255.

[25] It is worth noting that R. Graham, in his "Progress Toward the Council," *America* no. 110, October 22, 1960, reports the agenda of the coming Council on the basis of information about the draft decrees that was provided in a dispatch from the Katholische Nachrichten-Agentur. On the importance of the press see W. Kampe, *Das Konzil im Spiegel der Presse* (Würzburg, 1963) and Grootaers in *Vatican II commence*.

[26] The positions taken by Cardinal Cushing and Gregory Baum were approved in a few articles in 1961, but only in June of 1962 was note taken of König's insistence that the role of the laity be a subject of discussion.

the best use they could of the *Notiziario* published by the Central Commission, but they also devoted a study day to the difficulties created by secrecy.[27] By choice and for lack of alternatives, *Informations* made Bea its leading figure: he was interviewed, answered letters, was the subject of an editorial and a dossier, and so on. For this reason, attention to ecumenical matters grew and soon the Anglican, Orthodox, and Protestant worlds were speaking out and expressing their views on the Council, on John XXIII's invitations to observers, and on ecumenism at the periphery. Earlier than any other journal, *Informations* also endeavored to report on the positions taken by the future fathers: interviews with Alfrink, Léger, and Frings, as well as with members of the French episcopate, were published. Some interviews in Italy, France, and Poland and surveys of Denmark, Spain, and Germany completed the picture of an activity that gave a glimpse of what was at stake in the future conciliar assembly.

Herder Korrespondenz combined two functions usually carried out by different journals.[28] On the one hand, it provided accurate and analytical reports on the stages of the journey leading up to the Council (after the manner of *Documentation catholique* in France), with translations of the more important papal documents and updates on noncatholic reactions. On the other, it reviewed and gave a platform to important theological positions that had little place in the official discussion, the regulations of which clothed it in a secrecy that press conferences only made all the more irritating. The panoramic picture of the worldwide episcopate and the book review section were remarkable: on the one hand, the journal focused attention on what was being said by Jaeger and the Dutch episcopate, but also by Döpfner, Dubois, the Spanish bishops, the Polish bishops, König, Liénart, Suenens, and Montini; on the other, it continually stressed the themes of ecumenism and the laity.

Once the fervor evoked by the announcement of 1959 had passed, the review *Il Regno*, published by the Dehonian Fathers of Bologna, paid little attention to the two conventions on the Council that were held in Assisi and Mendola. Only with the editorial in the issue of November, 1960, did it return to the subject and claim that the issue at Vatican II

---

[27] *Un concile pour notre temps. Journées d'études des Informations Catholiques Internationales*, by J.-P. Dubois-Dumée, J. de Broucker, R. Voillaume,, M.-D. Chenu, Msgr. Marty, F. Houtart, L.-C. Baas, J. D'Souza, O. Rousseau, Y. Congar (Paris: Cerf, October, 1961). The book brings together opinions on what might be expected of the Council; in a conclusion, Congar speaks of the Council as a dawn needing help in order to break.

[28] For a list of the fuller surveys see Sieben, *Katholische Konzilsidee*, 244.

would be a choice between traditionalism and modernity. Beginning in 1961 almost every issue carried articles on what it continued to see as the main theme of the conciliar activity (unity) and on the participation of the laity, which was urgently called for, at least in the preparatory phase, by the Dutch episcopate. *Il Regno* also deplored the difficulties facing reporters and the secrecy of the preparatory groups, but it did not have much to say about areas outside Rome. Thus the only news about Italian preparation during 1962 was a review of Fr. Lombardi's book and an account of a meeting of the laity of the diocese of Florence that was sponsored by Cardinal Florit. As for what was happening outside of Italy in 1962, Italian readers were told of the results of a poll taken in two Paris parishes; the journal pointed out, as was to be expected, that public opinion about the conciliar agenda gave first place to the subject of unity. Then in the ninth issue of that year, an issue devoted entirely to the Council, there was a survey of the progress being made in preparation in Europe, Canada, and Latin America, and the various "views" of what the Council would do were described.

2. *Theological Discussion and the Periodicals*

In summary, as far as news was concerned, there was a growing accuracy, an ever greater professionalism of the correspondents, a presentation of the views of theologians, and some firsthand impressions and judgments, especially about the meetings of the Central Commission. In the theological journals, the increase in attention was slower, due to the very pace of publication. The ecumenical journals (*Irénikon* and *Istina*), of course, were attentive to the development of thinking on the unity of the Churches, a subject on which a good many statements were coming down from the pope and from Bea.[29] The same might have been expected to be true of the reviews that were the "organs" of other movements (the biblical, the liturgical), but it was not. These journals maintained a prudent reticence and did not discuss any "strong" demands with regard to the preparation. Only one special issue of *La Maison-Dieu* took up the subject of expectations of the Council and expressed desires similar to those under discussion in the liturgical commission, a body of which some editors of the journal were members.[30]

---

[29] At the time when the Council was announced the most discussed question was the ecumenical character of the Council; see, e.g., H. Bacht, "Sind die Lehrentscheidungen der ökumenischen Konzilien göttlich inspiriert?" *Catholica* 13 (1959) 128-39.

[30] *La Maison-Dieu*, no. 66 (1961). *Fêtes et Saisons* did better in a popular style.

Amid the countless theological journals, the most original idea at the beginning of the preparatory process was that of *Esprit*, which sponsored a poll aimed at allowing the Catholic laity to express their own vota,[31] after the model of those sent by the bishops, the universities, and the curial congregations. *Wort und Wahrheit* took over this idea in 1961.

Then, as the Council drew nearer, the identification of issues vital for the future of the Church became the predominant theme in essays and issues devoted to a single subject.[32] The most widely discussed questions had to do with the nature and ecumenical character of the Council, the ecclesiological problem and especially the episcopate, and the problem of the unity and the reform of the Church.

In the French-speaking world the *Nouvelle revue théologique* brought together Thils' studies of the episcopate, those of Dejaive on Council and catholicity, and those of Häring on mixed marriages. *Ephemerides Theologicae Lovanienses* published an up-to-date chronicle and kept carefully abreast of publications. Under the heading of current religious events *Études* reported papal statements and studied them carefully. *Signes du temps* reported on the preparation with little enthusiasm, but it did publish essays and a translation of part of a book of Küng of which I shall speak further on.

In the Dutch- and Flemish-speaking area there was extensive discussion; the journals showed some traces of it, but the receptivity of the bishops turned theological pleas into a subject of public debate.[33]

The English review *Blackfriars* emphasized the atmosphere of ecumenical dialogue as the decisive and enduring fact, while at the end of the period of preparation it published an article of Baum on the laity. It also offered its readers a survey of attitudes in the German and Austrian world, and with good reason, since although the amount of information that appeared in the German-language journals was modest, they published a series of rather important and worthwhile contributions.

---

[31] This esteemed journal published the results of the poll on different occasions; later, it would give M.-D. Chenu, one of the great men excluded from the preparation, a chance to speak: "Vie conciliaire de l'Église et sociologie de la foi," *Esprit* 12 (1961) 678-89.

[32] Sieben surveys the appearance of these themes as early as 1955-58; see *Katholische Konzilsidee*, 244-77.

[33] In Brussels *De Maand* published essays surveying the ecumenical scene with an eye on the coming Council and, as early as February, 1962, began a special issue with an essay on the theology of Councils (H. Küng). On the Netherlands see J. Y. H. A. Jacobs, *Met het oog op een andere kerk. Katholiek Nederland en de voorbereiding van het Tweede Vaticaans Concilie* (Baarn, 1986) and J. A. Brouwers, *Vreugde en hoopvolle verwachting. Vaticanum II. Terugblik van een ooggetuige* (Baarn, 1989) for the part played by Fr. Schillebeeckx.

The questions which the *Theologisch-praktische Quartalschrift* raised for the Council covered a rather broad spectrum (episcopate, laity, language of the liturgy, diaconate, communion under both kinds, marriage, censorship, fasting, celibacy), although it gave priority to canonical and theological questions. *Theologie und Glaube*, published in Paderborn, outlined possible doctrinal understandings with the other Churches, giving a great deal of space, as we would expect, to the theses of Jaeger and Bea. During the period of preparation *Stimmen der Zeit* published only an essay of Bea, but in an article of 1959 it had analyzed the preparation for Vatican I, the influence of which on the preparation for Vatican II is rather clear today.

In the Spanish-speaking world *Razón y Fe* distinguished itself, beginning in 1960, by thorough theological studies that were dedicated to the point of view of a Council conceived in strictly confessional terms. *Estudios Eclesiásticos* and *Salmanticensis* spoke out on the Council for the first time only in 1962: the one to emphasize the orientation of the Council: toward a new code; the other to provide a survey of studies of the episcopate that had appeared during the preparation. In the Portuguese-speaking world the announcement of the Council and the preparation for it were largely ignored by the reviews.[34] The ones that published the largest number of articles were the Portuguese reviews *Lumen* (which listed freedom, ecumenism, celibacy, and liturgy as the most urgent of the problems to be tackled by the future Council) and *Brotéria* (with a panoramic view of the subjects most widely spread). In Brazil the *Revista eclesiástica brasileira*, despite restrictions, did important work in supplying information, especially with the help of its editor-in-chief, Bonaventura Kloppenburg, a consultor of the preparatory theological commission.[35]

The Italian journals were not exceptionally active. The editors of *Vita e pensiero* (Milan) dealt with the Council in the form of various essays and an issue devoted to the subject in 1960, with a preface by Cardinal Montini; after that, it reduced its coverage to some slipshod reports and a reappraisal of ecumenical expectations. *Humanitas*, too, after publishing a series of lectures delivered in Brescia, abstained from making a

[34] Knowledge of the world of journals of a scientific kind published in Portuguese is derived from the "Sumário de revistas" published in the *Revista da Universidade Católica de São Paulo*.

[35] In July, 1962, Kloppenburg himself published *Concilio Vaticano II. Documentario preconciliar* (Petrópolis; Vozes), with extensive documentation on the preparation for Vatican II.

contribution of its own. After having shared the initial enthusiasm of the first six months, *Testimonianze* likewise limited its attention to the point where it became negligible: it reported to its readers on the congress of the laity of the archdiocese which Cardinal Florit wanted to hold in Florence, and then focused all its attention on an issue planned to cover the opening of the Council, but these plans were overtaken by the events of the first week of the Council. *La Scuola Cattolica* published an article of Carlo Colombo, as well as other contributions that were focused on the ecclesiological problems which the Milanese theologians had already raised in the votum of their faculty. *Studi Cattolici* spoke out at set intervals, but only on relations with the Orthodox. *Questitalia* collected what was said in other reviews (*La missione, Le messager du coeur de Jésus*, etc.) and by theologians in various countries; when the opening approached and this journal descended into the arena on its own, it issued a harsh and clear critique of the preparatory work and — for a purpose rather different from that of *Esprit* and *Wort und Wahrheit* — published the results of a questionnaire sent to sixty-four intellectuals and laypersons.[36]

Did this piling up of themes and expectations represent perhaps an unconscious protest against the lack of proportion between the expectations of the Church and the content of the schemata? No, because between 1959 and 1962 there was, in quantitative terms, only a small increase in available information! What happened was that this information was repeated and reechoed in all the editorial offices, producing an ever greater volume of crossreferences and an extraordinary amplification: a mountain of hopes rose upon a very tiny base. While, then, the first effect of secrecy was a dearth of news and a demand that the "rights" of journalists be respected, the further result was to encourage groups and theologians to listen to one another: this was the more far-reaching effect and one that truly "prepared" the way for the atmosphere that would prevail at the Council.[37]

Only a few journals (but, significantly, they were the ones that had their centers in the theological faculties that were playing a dominant role in the preparatory groups) kept an eloquent silence which the atmosphere of expectation could not breach. *Angelicum, Augustinianum,*

[36] "Attese del laicato cattolico italiano davanti al concilio ecumenico. Questionario di quattro domande," *Questitalia* 5 (July-September, 1962) 346-508.

[37] Recall the interplay of crisscrossing citations and the drawing up of shared bibliographies; the pastoral letters of bishops and episcopates became part of this exchange of information, but the same was not true, it seems, of particulars about material to be found in the bulletins of dioceses assigned to bishops who were members of commissions.

Laurentianum, and *Studia patavina* remained completely silent. *Apolli-naris*, *Euntes docete*, *Gregorianum*, *Antonianum*, as well as *Orienta-menti sociali*, *Divus Thomas*, and *Rivista di Ascetica e Mistica*, paid occasional attention to the Council in the form of one or two interventions that were authoritative but not repeated.[38] This silence was not peculiar to Italian journals, but in the rest of the world the editors who decided to remain spectators were few and were offset by the activism of their colleagues. In the French-speaking world *Laval théologique et philosophique* remained silent, while *Nova et Vetera* and *Lumière et vie* gave a little space to their own views. Although the *Revue des sciences philosophiques et théologiques* did accept articles on questions that were important for the coming Council, only in 1961 did it note the publication of articles on Vatican II in the periodicals that it mined for its bibliography. In the Anglo-Saxon world *The Harvard Theological Review*, *The Heythrop Journal*, *The Catholic Historical Review*, and *The International Review of Missions* remained silent.

3. *The Circulation of Books: Unity, Reform, Episcopate*

Books played a decisive role in this interest that fed on itself and grew; even more extensively than the journals, books bore witness to a hope to which no reference was made in the discussions in the commissions,[39] but which was changing the Church itself.

The lack of information about the discussions going on in the preparatory commissions was confirmed by the number of works that came pouring out on the entire history of the ecumenical Councils,[40] following, with more or less gratifying results, the path opened by H. Jedin in 1959.[41] The historian of the Council of Trent had shown, concisely but effectively, how in the course of history Councils had responded to the

[38] Recall the articles of S. Tromp, "De futuro concilio oecumenico," *Gregorianum* 43 (1962) 5-11, and U. Betti, "De membris concilii oecumenici," *Antonianum* 37 (1962) 3-16.

[39] The Central Commission published, in two editions, the list of the members of the preparatory commissions, and in 1961 it published statistics of the responses to Tardini's circular letter: *Consultazione per la preparazione del Concilio Vaticano II. Dati statistici* (Vatican Polyglot Press, 1961).

[40] J. L. Murphy, *The General Councils of the Church* (Milwaukee: Bruce, 1960); X. Andro (A. Rey Stolle, S.J.), *Los Concilios Ecuménicos. Veinte siglos de historia* (Barcelona: Borras, 1959). In Spain there also appeared A. Fabrega y Grau, *Historia de los Concilios Ecuménicos* (Barcelona, 1960). F. Dvornik's little book, *The General Councils of the Church* (London: Burns & Oates, 1961), was completed in 1960.

[41] H. Jedin, *Kleine Konziliengeschichte* (Freiburg im. B.: Herder, 1959). The same publisher issued translations into English, Italian, Spanish, and Portuguese (Sao Paulo) in 1960.

needs of an age; he had thus attested to and prepared the way for a state of mind.[42] Jedin had also taken part in other undertakings.[43]

That expectation of the Council had produced perceptible changes was shown by the sad fate of Father Lombardi's book, *Concilio. Per una riforma nella carità*.[44] This very powerful Jesuit, who had enjoyed almost unlimited esteem in the last part of Pacelli's pontificate, maintained the need for decisive action to renew Church structures and in particular the Roman Curia along the lines of a top-down simplification. The book annoyed various circles and even the pope himself and on January 11, 1961, was torn to pieces on the first page of *L'Osservatore Romano*, which harshly criticized its style, its theses, and its intentions.[45]

On the other hand, writings by and about bishops[46] were given great prominence, as were the opinions of theologians who had not been allowed to speak in previous years or to take part in the preparatory commissions.[47]

[42] R. Spiazzi, *Il Concilio Ecumenico nella vita della Chiesa* (Rome: Mame, March, 1962), had a different purpose in his reading of history: a review of conciliar history and the ecumenical character of the Councils of the Roman Church; questions on the guidance of the Spirit and the goal of charity in the Church as salient aspects of the coming Council, which would have to take its place in a well-established tradition.

[43] On *Conciliorum Oecumenicorum Decreta*, edited and published in Bologna, see above. E. Iserloh also wrote about conciliar history: "Gestalt und Funktion der Konzilien in der Geschichte der Kirche," *Ekklesia — Festschrift für A. Wehr* (Trier, 1962) 149-69.

[44] Rome: Aspes, 1961.

[45] The General Curia of the Society of Jesus saw to it that the book was withdrawn from bookstores; see G. Zizola, "Roncalli e padre R. Lombardi," *CrSt* 8 (1987) 73*-93*. On the other hand, an editorial, "Theory and Practice," *Commonweal* 72 (1962) 480, agreed with Lombardi's book.

[46] Congress of Recoaro, 1961, published in *Sacra Doctrina*, N.S. 6 (1961), with addresses by Lercaro, Bortignon, Ciappi, Cicognani, Urbani, and others. C. A. Rijk, *Het Concilie in de Beleving van het Geloof* (German translation: *Das Zweite Vatikanische Konzil und die Wiedervereinigung im Glauben* [Essen: Ludgerus-Verlag, 1961]), is an extensive commentary on the 1961 letter of the Dutch bishops, the example of which Rijk follows in emphasizing the ecumenical aspects.

[47] *Qu'attendons-nous du Concile?* (Brussels-Paris: La pensée catholique & Office général du livre, November, 1960): a collection of articles that had appeared in *Revue nouvelle* and *Évangéliser* in 1959-60; R. Aubert, P. Bourghy, T. Dhanis, C. J. Dumont, J. Grootaers, J. Hamer, F. Houtart, P. Kovalevsky, P. Leemans, R. Snoeks, and J. N. Walty offered possible directions the Council might take (with an ecumenical emphasis) and presented the results achieved by a Belgian working group. O. B. Roegele, *Was erwarten wir vom Konzil? Gedanken eines Laien* (Osnabrück: Fromm, 1961), called attention to the shift from the phase of enthusiasm to that of preparatory reflection and emphasized the German contribution — through the biblical, liturgical, and ecumenical movements — to the preparation of the soil out of which the work of the Council would emerge; he also predicted an anticentralist reform and a new style for the Church of the Council. *Erwartungen zum kommenden Konzil* (Würzburg: Echter, September, 1961) contained essays by P. Brunner, H. Tüchle, A. Brandenburg, M. Schmaus, and O. B. Roegele; this little book from the Bavarian Catholic Academy touched on themes on which they expected progress would be made at the Council, namely, ecumenical encounter, the laity, the key problems of ecclesiology.

Another large shelf is filled with books that, beginning in the preparatory phase of the Council, debated the problem of the unity of Christians. These do not represent a homogeneous viewpoint but include works that translated the pope's statements back into the language of uniatism,[48] texts giving voice to the variations within the group making up the secretariat,[49] statements from circles involved in "historical ecumenism,"[50] and reactions from noncatholic communities.[51] All these works, however, took as their starting point the supposition that the only positions "visible" during the preparatory period — that of the Pope and that of Cardinal Bea — really showed the direction that would be taken

---

[48] C. Algermissen, *La Chiesa cattolica e le altre Chiese cristiane* (Rome, 1960[3]); B. Leeming, *The Churches and the Church. A Guide to the Problem of Christian Disunity and the Attempts to Solve Them* (London: Darton, 1960).

[49] A. Bellini, *Il movimento ecumenico* (Rome, 1960; see the review by R. Tucci in Caprile I/2, 325), as well as the volume by various writers, *Il problema ecumenico oggi*, ed. C. Boyer (Brescia, 1960).

[50] See, e.g, the acts of the Chevetogne conference, *La concile et les conciles. Contribution à l'histoire de la vie conciliaire de l'Église* (Paris, 1960), in which the ecumenical center gave expression to the hope of unity through a historical rereading, by the best experts, of the major conciliar events. On this subject see also O. Kèramé, *Le prochain Concile Oecuménique. Catholiques et Orthodoxes bientôt réunis?* (Bulletin d'orientations oecuméniques; Beirut, 1960), with a preface by Msgr. P. K. Medawar, auxiliary of the Melkite Patriarch of Antioch; and L. Jaeger, *Das ökumenische Konzil, die Kirche und die Christenheit. Erbe und Auftrag* (Paderborn, 1960) (ET: *The Ecumenical Council, the Church and Christendom*, trans. A. V. Littledale (New York, 1962).

[51] A. Spindeler, *Das 2. Vatikanische Konzil. Wende oder Enttäuschung?* (Cologne: Wert und Werk, 1959), on the varying understandings of the Council in the Christian confessions and in the perspective of the impulse the Council was giving to Catholic ecumenism. *The Papal Council and the Gospel. Protestant Theologians Evaluate the Coming Council* (Minneapolis: Augsburg, 1961); German translation, *Konzil und Evangelium. Lutherische Stimmen zom kommenden römisch-katholischen Konzil*, ed. K. E. Skydsgaard (Göttingen: Vandenhoeck und Ruprecht, 1962; pp. 215): essays by Lutheran theologians and historians and a bibliography of writings that appeared during the preparation and bore witness to an as yet incomplete change in the Catholic outlook. The book was the official response of the commission for interconfessional study of the Lutheran World Federation, of which Skydsgaard was director. P. Meinhold, *Der evangelische Christ und das Konzil* (Freiburg im B.: Herder, 1961): on expectations in the Evangelical world. There was a response to this: A. Brandenburg, *Evangelische Christenheit in Deutschland am Vorabend des 2. Vatikanischen Konzils in katholischer Sicht* (Osnabrück: Fromm, January, 1961). Meinhold's book was published at almost the same time as E. Schlink, *Der kommende Christus und die kirchlichen Traditionen* (Göttingen: Vandenhoeck und Ruprecht, 1961). R. Pfister, *Das Zweite Vatikanische Konzil und wir Protestanten* (Zürich-Stuttgart: Zwingli Verlag, 1962, around October): a summary of information on Germany and an explanation of the ecumenical possibilities provided by the Council. In 1961 and 1962 there also appeared *Die ökumenische Konzile der Christenheit*, ed. H. J. Margull (Stuttgart, 1961), and K. Stürmer, *Konzilien und ökumenische Kirchenversammlungen* (Göttingen, 1962).

in the coming Council.[52] In addition, more farsighted theological thought about what the results of the Council would be, especially in the area of ecclesiology,[53] was rendered fertile, as it were, by the concern for ecumenism and by the rethinking of the dimension of tradition.[54]

These last two points were the key to the extraordinary success of Hans Küng's book, *Konzil und Wiedervereinigung. Erneuerung als Ruf in die Einheit*, which appeared in German in 1960 and was quickly translated into several languages.[55] The point which the German theologian emphasized was that the Catholic Church *could* advance along the road to unity by renewing its own tradition, by an adequate reception of what the biblico-liturgical movement had rediscovered, and by the increased emphasis on the common priesthood of the Christian people. These steps would be taken if the Church would welcome the hope offered by the Council and avoid new theological (and especially Marian) definitions that would only add to the reasons of conflict with noncatholics. Conversely, noncatholics would be reassured by the

[52] On the reaction which this supposition elicited from the journals of the patriarchates of Moscow and Constantinople see Caprile I/1. The multiplier effect of the western ecumenical periodicals closes the circle; on this see Ph. Chenaux, "Le Conseil oecuménique des Églises et la convocation du Concile," in *Veille*, 200-14. On *Irénikon, Istina, The Ecumenical Review, Oekumenische Rundschau, Unitas*, and *Catholica* see Sieben and Küng, cited above. Especially attentive to the ecumenical scene, and optimistic in tone, was the survey "Présence au Concile," edited by O. Rousseau, in *Irénikon* 34 (1961) 500-14.

[53] In January, 1961, the volume *Episkopat und Primat* by K. Rahner and J. Ratzinger appeared in the Quaestiones Disputatae series (Freiburg-Basel-Vienna: Herder); ET: *The Episcopate and the Primacy*, trans. K. Baker and others (New York: Herder & Herder, 1952). The historical background of this question was also the subject of G. Thils, *Primauté pontificale et prérogatives épiscopales. "Potestas ordinaria" au Concile du Vatican* (Louvain, February, 1961) and of J.-P. Torrell, *La théologie de l'épiscopat au premier concile du Vatican* (Paris: Cerf, July, 1961). Another book in the same Unam Sanctam series that had published Torrell's book, but one that was on a different level by reason of its wide readership and its impact, was *L'épiscopat et l'église universelle*, ed. Y. Congar and B.-D. Dupuy (Paris, June, 1962); here twenty-three authors (among them a good many of those whom we have already seen taking positions in the journals) analyzed the relationship of the episcopate to Christ, to the apostolic college, to the people of God, and to the pope.

[54] Y. Congar had taken a position on this problem in his *La tradition et les traditions* I. *Essai historique* (Paris, 1960), in the first part of the work, p. 8 (written in 1958). On the effects of this method of analysis see *Diakonia in Christo. Über die Erneuerung des Diakonates*, ed. K. Rahner and H. Vorgrimler (Quaestiones Disputatae; Freiburg-Basel-Vienna, June 1962).

[55] Freiburg im B.: Herder. J. M. T. Barton reviewed the book in *The Tablet* 215 (1961) 910; this had been preceded by extracts in translation (ibid., 848-51, 872-74). ET: *The Council, Reform, and Reunion*, trans. C. Hastings (New York: Sheed & Ward, 1962). On the genesis of the book see what Küng himself had to say at the Würzburg Colloquium of 1993 on "Der Beitrag der deutschsprachigen und osteuropäischen Länder zum Zweiten Vatikanischen Konzil."

incorporation into the praxis of the Church of a legitimate pluralism on which the bishops would have to keep a watchful eye.[56]

The explosive spread of Küng's idea of a necessary and sufficient connection between reform and unity shows how news about the preparation was now being turned into the preparation of news.[57] The commissions were working in airless secrecy, without comparing their work with anything else, and only a few periodicals connected with the ecclesiastical universities published articles and special issues about the Council, in which some spokesmen for the various commissions took positions that had to do mostly with the discussion going on within the preconciliar commissions themselves.[58]

But these were rare events and the messages were in code. Elsewhere, theologians and essayists attempted to bring themes and problems into focus for the Council on the basis of the very few certain things that John XXIII and Cardinal Bea had made known to public opinion and that strengthened the positions taken by bishops and theologians, positions often reprinted and translated in anthologies of statements.[59]

Books that departed from this pattern were few.[60] A pretty much isolated case was the book of M. Tedeschi, *I pericoli del concilio*, which

[56] Küng's book, which in German had a preface by Cardinal König, was quickly translated into French (with an imprimatur from Liénart) and into English (with no imprimatur!) and was reviewed in the more important journals. A significantly conciliatory note was struck in the review in *CC* that was signed by the editor, Fr. Tucci, and is reprinted in Caprile I/2, 42-43.

[57] See Küng, "Veröffentlichungen zum Konzil," 56-82.

[58] Such was the attitude of *Divinitas*.

[59] Daniel-Rops, *Vatican II. Le concile de Jean XXIII* (Paris: Fayard, April 1961). G. Huber, *Vers le concile. Dialogue sous la colonnade de Saint-Pierre* (Paris: Centurion, 1960) and *Vers l'union des chrétiens* (Paris: Centurion, 1961): in the form of a dialogue between a librarian and a journalist, this book discussed the hopes kindled by the Council of a reform of the Church and a movement toward unity; the second book carried a preface by Bea. *Prendre part au Concile. Choix de textes du Pape et des évêques*, ed. R. de Montvalon (Paris: Fleurus, September, 1962): an anthology of passages from John XXIII and other bishops (Bea, Frings, Jaeger, Veuillot, König, Guerry, Liénart, Felici, the Dutch episcopal conference), grouped around six key points for the Council: definition of the purposes of the Council, ecclesiology, relations with the nations, unity of Christians, convocation, prayer. M. Gozzini, *Concilio aperto* (Florence: Vallecchi, 1962), contained excerpts from eighteen sources on the risks associated with a Council, on the end of the Constantinian era, on the laity, the Church, ecumenism, and relations with the world; the authors anthologized were Montini, König, Feltin, Jaeger, Gerlier, Léger, Nabaa, Bea, Alfrink, Merella, and the bishops of Holland, Canada, Congo, Tanganyika, and Upper Volta.

[60] Worth mentioning is the little book of B. Pawley, *Looking at the Vatican Council* (London: SCM, April, 1962), a careful survey of the preparatory work; Pawley also gave a good deal of space to the books of Küng and Jaeger, Skydsgaard's collection, and Schlink's theses. See also F. Legrand, *Le concile oecuménique et l'évangélisation du monde* (Mulhouse: Salvator, and Paris-Tournai: Casterman, April, 1962), with a preface

was published in Rome, in October, 1962, by the Fascist publishing house, Il Borghese; it attacked the pope and published the press conferences of Tardini (1959) and Felici (1962) in order to show how to avoid the "dangers" of infiltration of the Roman Church by noncatholics through dialogue and ecumenical groups.

III. PREPARATION FOR THE COUNCIL BY THE EPISCOPATES

John XXIII intended the broad involvement of members of the episcopate in the preparatory commissions and in the Central Commission to be a way of giving a universal, that is, not simply "Roman" and curial, character to the preparation. It is of interest, therefore, to see to what extent this involvement went beyond personal participation by individual prelates in a commission and gave rise to joint enterprises, even if they were only informal. In a good many countries the episcopates were already organized into conferences, and this normally provided an institutional center for that kind of participation. We have already seen, however, that only in very few cases did the bishops work together in producing the votum requested by Cardinal Tardini.[61] The most common undertaking of the episcopal conferences was the publication, especially during the months preceding October, 1962, of one or more pastoral letters calling the attention of the faithful to the importance of the Council and urging them to pray for it. These provided very many occasions for a humble but heartfelt popular participation; as a result, millions of the faithful became aware of the Council. In this way many Catholics experienced for the first time that it was possible for them to share in a great ecclesial event. In many dioceses, in addition, occasions of prayer for the Council were successfully combined with collections of funds to cover the expenses of episcopal participation.

Some episcopates, however, took more incisive steps. As early as 1959, as we have seen, the German episcopate had devoted an extraordinary

by L.-J. Suenens: Legrand, editor of *Le Christ dans le monde*, a periodical dealing with the missions, and a consultor to the preparatory commission on the missions, expounded the necessity of increased missionary activity as a result of the Council, this as a means of meeting the challenges (communism and laicism) of the modern world.

[61] Thus the episcopates of Ivory Coast, Guinea, and the Province of Fianarantsoa in Madagascar; the Indonesian, Melkite, German, and English episcopates. The Belgian bishops also consulted with one another; see Cl. Soetens, "Les 'vota' des évêques belges en vue du concile," in *Veille*, 39 and 47. On the other hand, the nuncio's effort to have the Swiss episcopate produce a common votum was not successful; see Ph. Chenaux, "Les 'vota' des évêques suisses," in *Veille*, 111-12.

session to a fuller reflection on the significance of John XXIII's announcement; the Dutch episcopate did the same in August, 1959, and the Austrian in November of that year, while the Polish episcopate set up a commission within its ranks for the purpose.[62] Still in 1959, the Melkite Patriarch, Maximos IV, writing in the name of all the Melkite bishops, sent the pope a letter on the seating of the Oriental patriarchs at the Council. If they were placed behind the cardinals, this would symbolize a lack of respect for their Churches, since "the importance of the Churches is signified by precedence."[63]

In mid-1960, a few days after the establishment of the preparatory commissions, Cardinal Frings of Cologne sent the pope a letter that had been agreed upon by the German episcopate during a special meeting; in it he asked that a *Commissio de re pastorali* (Commission for Pastoral Matters) be set up.[64] The suggestion was not accepted but it showed the keen insight of the German bishops into the central problem of Vatican II and of the preparation for it. At the beginning of 1961, the Dutch episcopate in its turn published a joint letter on some important subjects it wanted the Council to take up: the distinction between the kingdom of God and the Church; the communion that precedes the differentiation between clergy and laity; the relationship of the *sensus fidei* to the magisterium; the Council and the *sensus fidelium*; the Council as a liturgical action; the distinction between the internal problems and the external problems of the Church; the importance and urgency of Christian unity.[65]

Toward the end of 1961 the Congolese conference drew up vota on liturgical reform. No less important was a document of the French

[62] The German episcopal conference set up three different working groups within its ranks to prepare it for the Council. See J. Jacobs, "Les 'vota' des évêques néerlandais pour le concile," in *Veille*, 101; J. Kloczowski, "Les évêques polonais et le concile Vatican II," in *Deuxième*, 167. See also J. Wnuk, *Vatikanum II. Episcopat polski na soborze watykanskin (Vaticanum II. L'épiscopat polonais au concile du Vatican)* (Warsaw, 1964).

[63] Caprile I/1, 673-76. In August, 1962, Maximos IV would write to the secretary general of the Council and repeat the same claim (ibid., 676-77).

[64] K. Wittstadt, "Der deutsche Episkopat und das Zweite Vatikanische Konzil bis zum Tode Papst Johannes' XXIII.," in *Papsttum und Kirchenreform. Festschrift G. Schwaiger*, ed. M. Weitlauff and K. Hausberger (St. Ottilien, 1990) 745-63, especially 755-56.

[65] *De Bisschopen van Nederland over het Concilie* (ET in *The Furrow* 12 [1961] 365-81); at the end the bishops thanked Fr. Schillebeeckx for his collaboration in the redaction of the text. See Jacobs, *Met een oog op een andere Kerk*, 83-92. See the reservations of Cardinal Montini (J. Grootaers, "L'attitude de l'archévêque Montini au cours de la première période du Concile [oct. 1962 — juin 1963]," in *G. B. Montini arcivescovo di Milano e il concilio ecumenico Vaticano II. Preparazione e primo periodo* [Brescia, 1985] 283) and of Fr. Tromp (shared by Msgr. Felici: Tromp Diary, February 16, 1961).

episcopal conference on the universality of the Council, its importance for contemporary society, and the need for an internal renewal of the Church.[66] During the spring of 1962 two conferences in the Americas — first the Brazilian, then the Canadian — published joint statements in anticipation of the Council. The Brazilian bishops emphasized almost exclusively the importance and fruitfulness of fraternal exchanges between the bishops. Vatican II was to confirm and give new impetus to this conviction. The Canadian bishops, for their part, stressed the point that the convocation of the Council bore witness to the youthfulness of the Church. They hoped that the Council would move in the direction of Christian unity and would commit itself to a dialogue with the contemporary world.[67]

The following August, the United States conference came out with a joint letter which said that Vatican II would be a new and unique kind of Council. The United States bishops asked: What contribution can the Church of the United States make to the Council? They answered by asserting their determination to play an active part and not simply to give passive approval.[68] At the end of August, the German bishops, for their part, published a letter that was intensely spiritual in tone and placed the emphasis on the conversion of Catholics and therefore on the need for a sincere *mea culpa* for the divisions in the Church. No less important was the zeal of the *Pro mundi vita* commission.[69] Heard from quite unexpectedly, it seems, was Msgr. Ghattas, Coptic Catholic Bishop of Thebes in Upper Egypt who harked back to his votum of two years earlier and on June 29, 1962, sent a substantial collection of thoughts that had been developed in collaboration with his clergy.[70]

This brings us to the weeks immediately preceding the opening of the conciliar assembly, weeks dominated on the one hand by the papal radio

---

[66] The text of the Congolese bishops is in *DC* 59 (1962) 1271-72; the "Note d'enseignement doctrinal en vue du prochain Concile," ibid., 1341-46. The very brief reference to the problem of unity is surprising.

[67] Complete texts in, respectively, *REB* 22 (1962) 485-90, and *DC* 59 (1962) 737-42. *OssRom* for April 24-25, 1962, published an Italian translation.

[68] Text of the "Statement on the Ecumenical Council" (August 19, 1962) in *Pastoral Letters of the United States Catholic Bishops* III. *1962-1974* (Washington, D.C.: USCC, 1983) 11-16. See J.A. Komonchak in *CrSt* 15 (1994) 324-25.

[69] *HK* 17 (1962-63) 49-51; *DC* 59 (1962) 1283-88.

[70] A printed booklet of 30 pages, divided into "theses" on the priesthood, the liturgy, mixed marriages, *communicatio in sacris*, and courts to deal with faith and morals. These were followed by a draft of a statement to the Orthodox Churches; four points regarding the responsibilities of Oriental Christians in dealing with Muslims; a draft of a statement on freedom of conscience.

address of September 11 and on the other by reactions to the first group
of preparatory drafts. It was in order to conduct a thorough examination
of these that a couple of Dutch bishops met with sixteen missionary
bishops who were natives of the Netherlands. From this meeting came
the plan for a memorandum containing a critical analysis of the drafts;
the text, written by Fr. Schillebeeckx, would be distributed to the bishops of the world who were already in Rome.[71]

Acknowledging the relative incompleteness of our information, we
may conclude that as the Catholic bishops prepared to set out for Rome,
their attitudes and perspectives were, on the whole, not very different
from those that had inspired the vota they had composed in 1959-1960.
At least, the paucity of information about the preparation going on in
Rome and the lack of practice in collective reflection caused the vast
majority of the bishops to set off for Rome in a state of relative passivity. However, the climate of John's pontificate, the very convocation of
a Council, and the publication of *Mater et Magistra* had at least made a
crack in this passivity by sowing the seeds of more responsible attitudes.
The initiatives already mentioned of some episcopal conferences made it
possible to foresee the emergence of episcopal personalities — from
Léger of Canada to Suenens of Belgium, Alfrink of the Netherlands,
Malula of the Congo, König of Austria, Helder Cámara of Brazil, Maximos IV, the Melkite patriarch, and Frings of Germany — who would be
the key figures during the course of the Council.

The coming together of African intellectuals that took place in Rome
brought an important confirmation of the interests and expectations that
had been stirred up by the prospect of a Council, even in areas "remote"
from the European center of things.[72]

IV. The Ordinary Life of the Church

During the preparation for the Council the life of the Church went on
at all levels. John XXIII's concern that the institutional structure of the
preparation be distinct from that of the Roman Curia evidently did not
mean erecting a screen between expectation of the Council and everyday
Christian life. On the contrary, it was not difficult to see in almost every
public utterance of the pope an anxiety that the atmosphere of the Council

---

[71] J. A. Brouwers, "Vatican II. Derniers préparatifs et première session. Activités con-
ciliaires en coulisses," in *Vatican II commence*, 354-55.

[72] *Personnalité africaine et Christianisme* (Paris, 1963).

should permeate the entire life of the Church. It is certainly not possible to recapitulate the endless aspects of this relationship in even a summary way. It is only right, however, to recall how a far-reaching and fruitful "osmosis" gradually took place between the expectation of Vatican II and the "ordinary" experience of the Church.

1. *The New Style of John XXIII*

Roncalli the Christian, whom obedience had brought even to the Chair of Peter, remained faithful to the method and style he had slowly developed in over seventy years of life, prayer, and service to the Church. What was most startling about his pontificate was the very fact that a pope avoided stereotyped and official models and allowed sparks to be struck from a lifegiving contact between, on the one hand, a lengthy and deep Christian experience that had developed within grooves established by tradition and had been nourished by an unceasing personal fervor, and, on the other, latent expectations of a prophetic service inspired by the gospel.[73] Roncalli was not reluctant to allow his own private virtues to become the public virtues of the pope, and this was even the very reason why he won unprecedented approval and exercised a historical influence inversely proportionate to the short duration of his pontificate. The "papal office" was given new life by the authentic and therefore bold holiness of a Christian, and the entire Church, and even every human being, was illumined and warmed by it.

It had been centuries since a pope so enhanced the Roman papacy as Roncalli did, not so much by the actions which he was able to complete (however important: Council, ecumenism, commitment to peace) — others were to bring them to completion — but because the elderly "Angelino" from Sotto il Monte once again gave the papacy an evangelical and therefore authentically human face. It was because he helped millions of women and men, often poor in possessions and hope and "at a distance," to feel close not to a powerful but benevolent and condescending man, but to a brother who pointed to Jesus and invited every human being to hope in him and feel close to him. For centuries, the style associated with service had been eclipsed by the exercise of a princely power; the possibility of playing a prophetic role, such as was included in the biblical understanding of infallibility and primacy, was compromised when popes identified themselves with a role of conservative

---

[73] See G. Alberigo, "Il pontificato di Giovanni XXIII," in *La Chiesa del Vaticano II (1958-1978)*, *Storia della Chiesa*, XXVII (Milan 1995) 15-51.

immobility that tended to face the future by looking into the mirror of the past and distrusting history. The result was the image of the pope as sovereign over a perfect society, as unaffected by history, and as the intransigent guardian of a revelation too often made inflexible by dogmatic formulas and juridical systems. Roncalli, on the other hand, had developed a style that shrank from intransigence and dogmatism out of a profound respect for all human beings, to the point where he was mistaken for a good-natured but unimportant fellow. He had a precise view of the nature of the Church, of the historical juncture through which it and the world were passing, and of the answer which the times were calling upon Christianity to give, an answer which he derived from the gospel and the most authentic tradition.

This tendency was translated into a climate and a style that provide the key for understanding the life of the Catholic Church during those years. In August of 1962 Cardinal Léger, Archbishop of Montreal, observed: "You [John XXIII] have created this climate in the Church since your announcement of the Council. Your words and your personal attitude have stimulated a fruitful quest within the Church, have encouraged a profitable dialogue among Catholics, and have altered relations between Catholics and our separated brethren in the direction of greater charity and better understanding."[74]

An important and solemn expression of this orientation was the publication, on the occasion of the seventieth anniversary of *Rerum novarum*, of the encyclical *Mater et Magistra* (May, 1961),[75] in which the pope, while faithfully repeating many formulations of Catholic social teaching, introduced important new ideas. First of all, the document dropped the usual deductive method that rigidified social doctrine by assimilating it to a code of abstract principles; instead it applied an inductive method, that is, it took current problems in their concreteness as its starting point. Aided by this method, the encyclical took as a major focus of interest the unqualified use of the term "socialization," analyzing its origin, its breadth, and its impact as a mass phenomenon. Even when the encyclical repeated traditional teaching on many points (property, labor, enterprise, and so on), it stripped it of its usual moralistic tone. Certain points evoked an especially strong echo in the "Third World": the social question was

---

[74] Petition of Léger to John XXIII, sent on September 11, 1962.

[75] The pope's first encyclical was *Ad Petri cathedram*, June 29, 1959; two others, *Sacerdotii nostri primordia* and *Grata recordatio*, were published on August 1 and September 25, 1959. Other encyclicals followed on November 28, 1959, May 15 and November 11, 1961, July 1, 1962, and the final one, *Pacem in terris*, on April 9, 1963.

no longer identified solely with the labor question, but problems having to do with the land, agriculture, and farmers were also taken up; colonialism and underdevelopment were denounced. This document of John had a direct effect on the work of preparation in the area of social questions.

2. Tensions in Ordinary Government

Some circles reacted harshly to these papal initiatives aimed at creating a new climate by promoting an active involvement of the various members of the Church and especially of the episcopate. A seemingly marginal but in fact crucial issue was the monopoly held by Latin. People were therefore disconcerted by the publication on February 22, 1962 of the Apostolic Letter *Veterum sapientia*, which was devoted to the uncompromising praise of Latin as the language of the Church and which the most unyielding circles in the curia had managed to obtain from the pope.[76] Representative of the same kind of thinking was the monitum against Jesuit palaeontologist Teilhard de Chardin, which the Holy Office published at the beginning of July. It was an expression of hostility toward many theologians beyond the Alps — H. de Lubac first of all — who had always maintained the complete orthodoxy of the French Jesuit. The Holy Office reasserted its own "supreme" authority, while the pope's proposals for renewal were correspondingly discredited to some degree in the eyes of the episcopate.

For his part, Pope John seems to have endured this constant trickle of actions that departed from the line he was taking, but he did not deviate from the convictions that were directing his pontificate. Thus on July 12, 1962, he arranged for the transfer to St. John Lateran of the entire structure of the vicariate of the diocese of Rome, an action that undid the symbiotic relationship between papal curia and diocesan curia and made visible, even at the bureaucratic level, the combination in the person of the pope of the role of bishop of Rome with central responsibility for the universal Church.

Disagreements over the pastoral value of the French worker-priest experiment, in which Roncalli had already been involved during his time as nuncio in Paris, re-echoed during these years.[77]

---

[76] A, Melloni, "Tensioni e timori nella preparazione del Vaticano II. La *Veterum sapientia* di Giovanni XXIII (22 febbraio 1962)," *CrSt* 11 (1990) 275-307.

[77] See F. Leprieur, *Quand Rome condamne. Dominicains et prêtres-ouvriers* (Paris, 1989).

3. *The College of Cardinals and Episcopal Appointments*

John XXIII did not fail to satisfy the expectations of those who elected him that things would return to normal, and in fact as early as October 30 he revived the practice of scheduled audiences with those in charge of the curial congregations, which Pius XII had let fall into disuse. On November 17, 1958, he assigned to D. Tardini the post of secretary of state which had been vacant for fourteen years. On December 15 he saw to a creation of cardinals, something awaited in vain since 1953; on this occasion he gave a red hat first of all to G. B. Montini, who had previously been punished by Pius XII. The pope created twenty-three cardinals, thereby going over the maximum of seventy that had been set by Sixtus V. On this occasion the pope asked those cardinals who held two offices in the curia to choose only one of them; the request, desired by many, elicited strong general approval, but also resentment in some of those affected. In any case, in the following October and November Cardinal Pizzardo left the Holy Office, Cardinal Tisserant the Congregation for the Oriental Church, and Cardinal G. Cicognani the Tribunal of the Apostolic Signatura. All the other creations of cardinals took place before the opening of the Council: December 14, 1959 (eight cardinals), March 28, 1960 (seven, including a Japanese, a Philippino, and an African), January 16, 1961 (four), and March 19, 1962 (ten).

The effect of the pontificate on the ordinary order of the Church was to be seen especially in the appointment of bishops: 1076 during the entire pontificate. The appointments were marked by growing attention to continents other than Europe, by a sharp increase in the choice of clerics from the dioceses to which they were appointed, and by a lowering of the average age of the new bishops, especially in dioceses of the Third World.[78] In all, the number of bishops changed from 2480 in 1958 to 2809 in 1963; residential sees also grew in number from 1638 to 1916 (all the new ones, except one, were outside of Europe).

On November 10, 1959, native hierarchies were established in Congo and Burundi; on May 8, 1960, the pope personally consecrated Third World bishops; on June 5, 1960, he sent a message to the Africans, which he repeated on November 5, 1961; at the beginning of 1961 he also established native hierarchies in Vietnam, Korea, and Indonesia.

---

[78] It is also significant that the average age of the appointees decreased notably as one moved from Europe (63) to North America (60), Asia (59), Latin America (57), and Africa (54).

Another important aspect of ordinary government had to do with interventions of the Holy Office, which were much less frequent, pointing to the change of climate since the pontificates of Pius XII and his predecessors.

4. The Roman Synod

The Roman Synod was celebrated from January 24 to January 31, 1960, a year after it had been announced.[79] On February 23, 1958 the pope installed the preparatory commission for the synod; this was then organized into eight subcommissions; the celebration took place in the cathedral of St. John, January 24-31, 1960; finally, the synodal decrees were approved on June 28 and then published.[80] Its positive importance consisted essentially in the fact that it brought out the pope's role as bishop of Rome and the authentically diocesan nature of the Church of Rome: two points that are obvious and yet seemed to have been forgotten by the Church. As Pope John repeatedly insisted, this was the first diocesan synod of Rome in the entire modern age.

John XXIII, who as a young man had been secretary of the synod of his diocese and who as patriarch had celebrated the synod in Venice in 1957, was in a hurry. On January 30 he summoned Cardinal Micara, his vicar for the diocese of Rome, in order to start preparations for the synod with him. The first difficulties arose precisely in understanding the respective responsibilities of each of these two men. The pope made clear the way in which he wanted to exercise his responsibilities as bishop of the diocese: he meant in fact to assume these responsibilities in full, as he would confirm in the address with which he promulgated the synodal decrees.

In both its contents and its effects the Roman synod turned out to be a failure. The synod lacked something resembling what the Secretariat for Christian Unity was to be for the Council, namely, a suitable instrument for grasping and channeling the deepest insights of John XXIII. This role might have been played by the "Office for Pastoral Activities"

[79] The announcement of the synod was not enthusiastically received. On the contrary, it caused puzzlement: no diocesan synods had been held in Rome since 1461; a single provincial synod had been held by Benedict XIV in 1725. The idea elicited astonishment and resistance. In the view of many, Rome, being the center of Christianity, was a sacred city and therefore could not be compared to any other city or diocese nor be bound by normal procedures and pastoral measures.

[80] *Primo Sinodo Romano A. D. MCMLX* (Vatican City, 1961). See M. Manzo, *Papa Giovanni vescovo a Roma* (Cinisello B., 1991), and S. Ferrari, "I sinodi diocesani di A. G. Roncalli," *CrSt* 9 (1988) 113-33.

that some parish priests had asked for and that might have been able to promote creative and innovative pastoral action for the entire city by securing the commitment of all apostolic energies, especially those of the laity. On the other hand, the way in which the synod was prepared for and celebrated, limited as it was by its heavily clerical character, never allowed an involvement and real participation of all the apostolic energies of the city.

Moreover, the diocese, too, was unprepared and was in a state of centuries-old disintegration; much of the vicariate structure was not attuned to the pope's intentions and the synod itself seemed to be an instrument in need of adaptation. On the other hand, it must be added that, if we look beyond the synod as such, the Roman Church felt the beneficial results, even if only a decade later, of the impulses to renewal to which John XXIII's initiative had given rise. The pope, for his part, did not hide his reservations, as in his address to the Roman clergy on November 24, 1960:

> From the very first meeting on January 24 in Our sacred Lateran basilica to the more solemn one of June 29th close by the Tomb of St. Peter, We were able, with the help of the Lord, to celebrate what was certainly an *opus bonum*, even if not, in some respects, an *opus perfectum*. We were all at the apostolic meeting. If a respectful comparison may be permitted Us, all of the twelve were there in full agreement. Even Thomas was there — that is, even those who had been timid and uncertain in the beginning. All were equally impressed by the Lord's goodness toward those who invoke him and serve him trustingly.[81]

Nor may we forget that the pope was concerned to prevent a critical assessment of the synod from reflecting negatively on the planned ecumenical Council, as some perhaps expected that it would. At least the organization of the preparation probably served as a kind of general test of the approach taken to the preparation for Vatican II.

---

[81] *DMC* 3, 38; *TPS* 7 (1961-62) 10. Manzo (214) remarks: "It is surprising to see the frankness with which John XXIII manages to review, at a public audience, the troubled *iter* of the synod's work. His confirmation of the tensions that accompanied the event in the ecclesiastical world is unusual. In addition, the distinction between *opus bonum* and *opus perfectum* shows John's awareness of the limitations of the Roman synod. The synod is more important in the history of pastoral action than canonically or in terms of its decrees. At least, the latter is the more fleeting result in the pope's view. Finally, it is not difficult to suppose that in the person of Thomas and the 'timid' and 'uncertain' John intended to describe all those who had resisted the plan for a synod."

5. *The International Eucharistic Congress in Munich*

In the years that intervened between the announcement and the opening of the Council, the International Eucharistic Congress that took place in Munich from July 31 to August 7, 1960,[82] provided a unique occasion for many of the future participants in Vatican II to meet one another. Although the coming Council did not appear among the topics set down in the congress program, the event, held about half-way between January 25, 1959, and October 11, 1962, was an opportunity for contact, inasmuch as many cardinals and several dozen bishops from throughout the world were present.[83] Even the universal horizon within which the congress was set anticipated, albeit remotely, the climate of Vatican II. The echo which the Munich meeting found in public opinion seemed to prefigure the great power of the conciliar assembly, two years later, to capture public attention. On the other hand, two of the basic themes of the coming Council were already central to the Eucharistic Congress: a sympathetic attention to contemporary society and a longing for the union of Christians.

6. *The New Delhi Assembly of the World Council of Churches*

Toward the end of 1961 (November 19 — December 5) the International Assembly of the World Council of Geneva took place in the capital of India. Although the meeting had been planned for years and although the Catholic Church still had no part in the Council, the preconciliar climate and the Assembly undeniably influenced each other. I need only recall that at New Delhi the World Council defined the Trinitarian dimension of its theological platform better than it ever had before. At the same time, this made it possible for the Churches of the eastern Orthodox tradition to become full members of the Genevan Council of Churches. From this, as well as from the membership of many Asiatic and African Churches, came a new impulse to ecumenism that found an echo also in Rome and then at Vatican II.

The Holy See, for its part, after a difficult maturation and despite the opposition of the Holy Office, which wanted Catholics to be present only as "reporters," had reached the decision to send a group of "observers" to the Assembly, thus reversing a deep-rooted attitude of distrust and utter aloofness. This new direction had also been demanded

---

[82] *Statio Orbis. Eucharistischer Weltkongress 1960 in München* (22 vols.; Munich, 1961).

[83] See *HK* 15 (1960) 7-34.

by the World Council of Geneva as a condition for its accepting the invitation to send observers from the Council itself to the coming ecumenical Council. On the other hand, even at New Delhi the imminence of the Catholic Council accelerated the development of the watchword that was to characterize the World Council in subsequent decades, beginning with the Uppsala Assembly of 1958: "The Conciliar Character of thhe Church."

V. Echoes in Other Religious and Ideological Spheres

1. *The Attitude of the Muslim World*[84]

Neither the preparatory phase nor the Council itself, being internal affairs of the Catholic Church, aroused either reactions or special expectations in the Muslim world, which was a broad and complex reality of about four hundred million believers. Islam, although oppressed in the communist countries of the east and the Balkans and in the Asiatic republics of the USSR, was experiencing a full-scale revival in Africa and Asia, where struggles for independence and national self-assertion were breaking out: from Mossadegh's Iraq to Nasser's Egypt, from Pakistan to Indonesia.

The authoritative Egyptian periodical *Magallat Al-Azhar*, for example, never spoke of anything having to do with Christian events from 1958 to 1978. It preserved "silence about such great events of contemporary history as the Second Vatican Council."[85]

On the other hand, its columnists did urge Catholic and Muslims to agree on certain points of common interest: "While from the dogmatic standpoint there is no great possibility of agreement, this does not rule out collaboration in other areas, the economic and the political, for example. The struggle against common enemies is a form of collaboration that is encouraged and desired."[86]

---

[84] This section is based chiefly on: *Proche-Orient Chrétien*, a periodical published by the White Fathers in Palestine, especially the issues of 1959 to 1962; on F. Dore, *Cristianesimo e Cristiani in Magallat Al-Azhar (1958-1978). Riflesso e percezione di una realtà religiosa presso una differente coscienza comunitaria* (excerpts from a doctoral dissertation for the Pontifical Institute of Arabic Studies and Islamology; Jounieh, 1991); and on M. Impagliazzo, "Mondo islamico e Vaticano II: prospettive di ricerca," a paper read at the Würzburg Colloquium (1993) on "Der Beitrag der deutschsprachigen und osteuropäischen Länder zum Zweiten Vatikanischen Konzil."

[85] Dore, *Cristianesimo*, 78: "This is something that has left us puzzled and is difficult to understand. Did the periodical wish perhaps to turn up its nose at this great religious event? Was it dissatisfied with the Declaration *Nostra Aetate*? One thing is certain: the periodical gave no response, either positive or negative."

[86] Ibid., 349.

The first of these enemies was atheism: "It would be possible indeed for the two worlds, the Muslim and the Christian, to unite against atheistic communism, which is an obstacle to stability and peace. But this union will only come about when Christianity recognizes Islam as a revealed religion, just as, after all, Islam has done for Christianity."[87]

The second enemy was Zionism. In reply to an article in the English Catholic periodical *Universe*, which urged Muslims to join Christians in the fight against atheism, Al-Sarqawi had this to say: "The answer is that we would like to take this outstretched hand on condition that Catholics recognize another common enemy: Zionism. We are waiting for the Holy See to take a stronger and clearer position against it and to condemn it publicly and persistently, so as to convince American Catholics to do battle against Zionism."[88]

A third field of mutual concern was the sacred places in Palestine and the tragedy of the Palestinian refugees, which affected both Christian and Muslim Arabs in the same way. "Christians and Muslims are closely linked by the fact that they share the same Palestinian holy places: Jerusalem and Bethlehem... The two groups have always lived here in full harmony and respect... Thus they are also united in trying to have the holy places returned to their rightful owners... rejecting the Jewish occupation and all plans for internationalization."[89]

2. *Catholics and the Muslim World*

For its part, the Catholic world did not show any greater interest in the Muslim world. This lack of interest can be seen in the infrequent references to Islam in the discussion of the Council that went on in the universities, the periodicals, the press, and public opinion inside and outside the Church,[90] as well as in the *consilia et vota* of the bishops, the

---

[87] Muhammad 'Abd Allàh AL-SAMMAN: "The preceding pope confessed Islam, but death prevented him from proclaiming this confession"; *Magallat Al-Azhar* (February 31, 1960), article 47, 856-59, in Dore, *Cristianesimo*, 351-52.

[88] Mahmud AL-SARQAWI, "Come, let us struggle together," *Magallat Al-Azhar*, January, 1962, 942-49, in Dore, *Cristianesimo*, 354-55.

[89] See articles 84/607; 199/15-16; 285/359-60; 203/482; 199/15 and 16; 284/133; 285/358-64; Dore, *Cristianesimo*, 364.

[90] For a survey of the infrequent references see Caprile's analytical index: I/1, 435; I/2, 768.

universities, and the Roman curia. A careful reading of the vota shows that "the nonchristian religions have a very low place in the concerns of the bishops and groups that were consulted."[91]

On this attitude of the bishops of the non-Latin rites, "it is to be observed, finally, that, whatever their orientation, the Oriental prelates show no interest in the Muslim world in which to a great extent they live, or at least they are not concerned to show this interest in their vota for the Council. References to the subject are in fact very rare... It is certain that one will search in vain through the vota of the Orientals for words indicating a benevolent attention to believers in Islam. The impression given is that they usually regard the Muslims as pagans to be converted or as a society so unlike their own that it leaves them indifferent."[92]

When we turn to the bishops of the Latin rite in Africa, the Near East, or Asia, we find a range of rather contradictory reactions. First of all, there were those who, like their brethren of the Oriental rites, were not even aware that their pastoral ministry was being exercised in the midst of peoples and states that were in the majority Muslim. In their vota they dealt only with matters internal to their Churches: liturgical and, above all, canonical and disciplinary issues.

Among those who did touch on the subject, three groups may be distinguished. The first spoke of Islam in aggressive language, complaining of the difficulties the Church and the faithful had in the exercise of the faith and in community life. Thus Msgr. Leclerc of Bimako in the Sudan: "Christians (16,000 in the entire Sudan, a country of animists but above all of Muslims) are scattered, drowned."[93] Or Msgr. Mercier of Laghout in Algeria: "Islam, located at the very doors of Holy Church and increasingly blending with its faithful, remains its most implacable adversary."[94]

---

[91] "There is complete silence on the part of the entire hierarchy of Europe and the Americas. Only the universities of the Propaganda (Rome) and of Nijmegen, and, above all, the Gregorian (Rome) and the Lovanium (Congo-Leopoldville) call for studying and teaching the nonchristian religions in a positive spirit but without relativism....The bishops of mission countries speak at length of missionary problems, little of the nonchristian religions as religions, and hardly at all of Islam. One is a bit surprised to see the total silence of the Oriental Churches on a subject they faced every day": R. Caspar, "La religion musulmane," in *Vatican II — Les relations de l'Église avec les religions nonchrétiennes* (Unam Sanctam 61; Paris, 1966) 201-2.

[92] R. Morozzo della Rocca, "I 'voti' degli orientali nella preparazione del Vaticano II, in *Veille*, 144-45. The same scholar notes that "the followers of the prophet are simply 'fanatics,' according to Zaya Dachtou, Archbishop of Urmya. On the other hand, he does not use this word in an exclusively contemptuous sense, since he wants his Iranian Christians to be able to be 'fanatics' in effectively opposing the Muslim."

[93] *ADA*, II/5, 41.

[94] *ADA*, II/5, 149.

A second group looked upon Islam as an object of missionary conquest, although a difficult one and one that was already the scene of wearying defeats. Msgr. Lacaste of Oran in Algeria even charged that behind the renaissance of Islam were the communists and the naive irenicism of Catholics:

> Shall I dare address the missionary problem in Muslim countries? Our missions, which have been cruelly ravaged by communism, risk losing sight of the threat posed by the Islamic expansion in Africa and elsewhere. While communism, proud of its gigantic conquests, uses all the resources of a matchless propaganda, Islam, which yesterday lay humbled, is today raising its head, encouraged, on the one hand, by communist diplomacy, despite official denials that the press has been won over to its cause, and on the other, oddly enough, by the naivete of too many Catholics who believe that they must never speak of Islam except to allow it publicly a spiritual value equal to that of Christianity, although nothing calls for such an admission. It is quite to be expected that they do not ask their Christian brothers and sisters to have as strong a faith and vigorous a hope as the Muslims themselves do.[95]

In the third group, which likewise looks upon Islam as mission territory, but in an atmosphere of dialogue and cooperation, were such bishops as Msgr. Moloney of Bathurst in India. In his view, since the apostolate to the Muslims was insufficient, it was desirable that Catholic and Muslim theologians come face to face at the Council.[96]

C. Quillard, Apostolic Prefect of Niamey, also had a clear position along the same lines.[97] Léon Duval, speaking of an Algeria destroyed by the war for independence, by torture, and by terrorism, asked the Council to give an impulse to cooperation between Catholics and noncatholics in behalf of peace and the dignity of the human person:

> ... and to noncatholics and even nonchristians. Since it is the foundations of society, the defense of the dignity of the human person, and universal peace that are at stake, it would be most appropriate for the Council to issue a summons not only to Catholics but to all men and women of good will. This would lead the Council to establish prudent norms for the collaboration of Catholics and noncatholics, not only in regard to the areas of this collaboration (the promotion of justice, the defense of belief in God, the defense of ethics, the exercise of works of charity...) but also in order to avoid the danger of syncretism or *communicatio in divinis*.[98]

[95] *ADA*, II/5, 114.
[96] *ADA*, II/5, 215.
[97] *ADA*, II/5, 92.
[98] *ADA*, II/5, 102.

In the chapter on the missions in the *Analyticus conspectus*,[99] there is
a summary and synthesis of remarks on the Muslims in the vota, but the
summary does not faithfully reflect everything the bishops had said.[100]
A more serious matter was that at the moment when the preparatory
commissions were being organized, the question of Islam completely
disappeared.[101] As a result, the question of Islam would not be present
either in the preparatory phase or in the first period of the Council, and
would return only in the debates of the second period in connection with
the draft document "On the Jews," which was suggested at that point as
the fourth chapter of the draft on ecumenism.

3. *The Attitude of the Jewish World: Judaism, an Unexpected Theme*[102]

Unlike the immediate effect which it had in Orthodoxy and in
the Protestant world, the announcement of the Council does not seem to
have provoked either reactions or interest on the part of Jews. This was

---

[99] *ADA*, II, App. 1-2.

[100] *ADA* II, App. 2, 641-42: "Missions among the Muslims. 1. The conversion of
Muslims should be encouraged. 2. Religious syncretism must be avoided, and a more
suitable way must be sought of making clear and refuting the wives and fables that have
been admitted into the Quran and Islamic traditions, but always in a charitable way. 3.
There is a frequently expressed desire for Catholic experts who are able to argue on
Islamic subjects. 4. If possible, let teachers of the Church, and especially those versed in
Muslim doctrines, debate at the Council with Muslim teachers, especially a) about the
spread of materialism, and b) the status of our Lord Jesus Christ and the Blessed Virgin
Mary in the Quran. 5. There should be greater charity shown in dealing even with the
followers of Muhammad, and similarities between the teaching of Christ and that of
Muhammad should be brought out. 6. Missionaries do not preach the gospel directly to
Muslims; they are content with works of charity, but what these lead to is simply the
grateful remembrance of benefits and not by any means conversion. 7. Let the similiari-
ties with the teaching of the Muslims not make us forget the profound differences
between Muslim and Christian Catholic teaching. 8. In the minds of Muslims Christianity is identified with western culture."

[101] Caspar, "La religion musulmane," 202: "According to the antepreparatory commissions the subject belonged in the draft on the missions; but, at the very first meeting
of the commission in question, it was decided to deal only with general problems, without getting into the study of particular religions."

[102] For a survey of Jewish-Christian relations during the last forty years: J. Kaplan,
"Le nouveau regard chrétien sur le judaïsme," *Revue des sciences morales et politiques*
(1987) no. 3; J. W. Delamire, "Vatican II et les juifs," in *Deuxième*, 577-606. The most
important texts on the Jewish-Christian dialogue: *Les Églises devant le judaïsme —
Documents officiels 1948-1978*, ed. M.-Th. Hoch and B. Dupuy (2 vols.; Paris, 1980);
*Stepping Stones to Further Jewish-Christian Relations. An Unabridged Collection of
Christian Documents*, ed. H. Croner (New York, 1977); *Le Chiese Cristiane e
l'Ebraismo, 1947-1982. Raccolta di documenti*, ed. G. Cereti and L. Sestieri (Casale
Monferrato, 1983); *Die Kirchen und die Juden — Dokumente von 1945 bis 1985*, ed. R.
Rendtorff and H. H. Henrix (Munich, 1988).

understandable, however, in view of the fact that John XXIII had only two main objectives in convoking the Council: the internal reform of the Church and dialogue with the other Christian Churches.

It must also be said that it is not possible to speak in a generic way of "the Jewish world," because of Judaism's great complexity, the diversity of its representatives, and its integration into a plurality of cultures and traditions. To this it may be added that in our century the history of the Jewish people has been radically altered by two important events: on the one hand, the Shoah with its six million dead and, on the other, the return to the promised land, which gave rise to the state of Israel and caused a succession of wars and conflicts both with the population of Palestine and with the neighboring Arab states.

At the beginning of the 1960s there were thirteen million Jews in the world, twenty-five percent of them in Europe. The two most dynamic centers of Judaism had shifted to the United States and Israel. At that same period the three million Jews in the USSR were living in silence and surrounded by suspicion. In Poland only three thousand remained of the original three and a half million; in the two Germanies, no more than fifteen thousand of the five hundred thousand before the war. These facts were a challenge to the Christian conscience, which asked itself how such a tragedy had been possible.

4. *John XXIII and the Jews*

In the broad consultation conducted by order of John XXIII as a way of beginning the preparation for the Council, the subject of Judaism came up in only two cases, and the contrast between the two was significant: the first was the text of the eighteen professors of the Pontifical Biblical Institute, which asserted the need to combat antisemitism; the second was the request of a bishop "to condemn international freemasonry, controlled by the Jews."[103]

Small gestures, however, awakened consciences and led to steps being taken almost simultaneously on both sides. John XXIII, with the sensitivity of one who had lived in the East for over twenty years and had become aware of the Jewish tragedy,[104] was one of the creators of

---

[103] T. Stransky, "The History of *Nostra Aetate*," in *Unanswered Questions — Theological Views of Jewish-Christian Relations*, ed. R. Brooks (Indiana, 1988) 55.

[104] On Roncalli's interventions with the secretariat of state and the other munciatures in an attempt to save Jews condemned to deportation and the death camps, see A. Melloni, *Fra Istanbul, Atene e la guerra. La missione di A. G. Roncalli (1935-1944)* (Genoa, 1992), especially 258-68 and 275-79.

this little miracle. Among others who contributed to it were French historian Jules Isaac and German Jesuit Augustin Bea.

John XXIII took the first step on the occasion of his election to the pontificate. News of this was communicated to the government of the state of Israel even though the Holy See did not recognize it and had no diplomatic relations with it. In reply Dr. Isaac Halevy Herzog, Grand Rabbi of Israel, telegraphed his "sincere blessings" to the pope. Another little step was taken in connection with Holy Week, 1959. Up to that point, Catholics used to say in the "Solemn Intercessions" of the Good Friday liturgy: "Let us pray also for the perfidious Jews" and, again, "Almighty, eternal God, who in your mercy do not reject even Jewish perfidy." These expressions obviously sounded hostile to Jewish ears and wounded more sensitive Christian consciences. John XXIII ordered their removal.[105] Among his papers there is a short note, written perhaps a few days before that Good Friday:

> For some time now We have been concerned about the *pro perfidis Judaeis* in the Good Friday liturgy. We know from reliable testimony that Our predecessor Pius XII of holy memory had already removed the adjective in his own praying of the text and had been satisfied to say "Let us pray...also for the Jews." Since We have the same thought, We decree that in the next Holy Week the two petitions [be shortened in this way].[106]

John XXIII subsequently saw to the omission from the liturgical books of expressions or references that might be offensive to Jews and Muslims, to Protestants and pagans.[107] This seemingly simple gesture was immediately appreciated and greeted with gratitude and joy in those sectors of Judaism and the Church that were sensitive to the question. Among Protestants too the novelty of the gesture was understood, as was the openness which it implied.[108]

At the same time, however, on the occasion of the opening of the new synagogue in Cologne, which should have symbolized a changed attitude to the Jews, the shadow of recent antisemitic persecutions was seen again. On the morning of that day the walls of the synagogue were

[105] Capovilla, *Lettere*, 484.

[106] Ibid., 484.

[107] See *AAS* 51 (1959) 595. Deleted from the formula for the baptism of adults were expressions concerning pagans: "Tremble at idols, reject unreal images"; the Jews: "Tremble at Jewish perfidy, reject Jewish superstition"; Muslims: "Tremble at Muslim perfidy, reject the wicked sect of unbelievers; heretics: "Tremble at the wickedness of heretics, reject the deadly sects of wicked N." See *Ephemerides Liturgicae* 74 (1960) 133-34, cited in Caprile I/1, 252-53, notes 8 and 9.

[108] *Service Oecuménique de presse et d'information* (= SOEPI) (Geneva), August 26, 1960; cited in Caprile I/1, 253.

daubed with swastikas, and a new wave of antisemitism struck even the United States and other countries of Europe. On January 18, 1960, a delegation of the international Jewish organization B'nai B'rith went to the pope in the Vatican to discuss the new outbreak of antisemitism and "to thank him for the help he gave persecuted Jews when he was delegate in Turkey (1935-44) and for having eliminated the epithet *perfidus* from the Good Friday liturgy."[109]

Two other actions of John XXIII were much appreciated by Jews. The first took place on October 17, 1960, when the pope received 130 representatives of the United Jewish Appeal: entering the audience hall with his characteristic graciousness, he opened his arm wide and exclaimed: "I am Joseph, your brother." Recalling as it did the moment in which Joseph revealed himself to his brothers in Egypt (Gen 45:3), the words stirred lively feelings.[110] The other, and perhaps the more important one for Jews, took place on March 17, 1962. Driving along the Lungotevere John XXIII found himself in front of the Roman synagogue. The pope had the roof of the car removed and blessed a group of Jews who were leaving the temple. Rabbi Toaff, an eyewitness of the event, recalled that "after a moment of understandable bewilderment, the Jews surrounded him and applauded him enthusiastically. It was in fact the first time in history that a pope had blessed Jews and it was perhaps the first real gesture of reconciliation."[111]

5. *The Initiatives of Jules Isaac*

It was, however, Jules Isaac (1877-1963) who realized all the concrete possibilities that this climate of dialogue and friendship opened up for relations between Jews and Christians. This historian, formerly inspector general of public education in France, was persecuted under the Vichy regime because of his Jewish descent. After having lost wife and children in the Nazi persecutions, he returned to the faith of his forebears and dedicated himself to dialogue between Jews and Christians. He sought to uncover the roots of antisemitism in order better to fight it.

As early as 1947, at the Seelisberg Conference sponsored by the National Council of Christians and Jews, he had suggested the ten points which the conference then proposed to the Churches in the form of a call

[109] A. Gilbert, *The Vatican Council and the Jews* (Cleveland-New York, 1969), Appendix G, 292; see *DC* 57 (1960) 318-19.

[110] *DC* 57 (1960) 1419-20. The words also appeared in the pope's address at his coronation and were used again once in 1959 and once in 1960, in speaking to Christians.

[111] E. Toaff, *Perfidi giudei — fratelli maggiori* (Milan, 1987) 219-20.

for the needed revision of Christian attitudes, catechesis, and teaching in relation to the Jews.[112]

On June 3, 1960, Isaac handed John XXIII a memorandum and a file on the question that constantly preoccupied him: a reformulation of Christian teaching, preaching, and catechesis for the purpose of eradicating the roots of antisemitism.[113] After Isaac's visit, the pope immediately entrusted the study and examination of the file to Cardinal Bea and the Secretariat for Christian Unity, within which a working group on this subject had been established at its first meeting. This group had set up a network of contacts and exchanges with the Jewish world and with its principal associations, especially in France, the United States, and Israel.

The discretion practiced by the Secretariat had made possible a gradual maturing of views on this complex question, as the Secretariat emphasized the exclusively religious character of its own approach and worked up a short draft of a conciliar statement *De Judaeis*. On the other hand, independently of the intentions of all concerned and especially of the secretariat, any document on the Jews already had an inherent political significance. This did not escape the Catholic bishops in Arab countries, especially those countries closer to or in direct conflict with Israel, just as it did not escape the Arab governments or international Jewish organizations or the state of Israel itself.

Rumors of a planned declaration *De Judaeis* had caused uneasiness and then debates and opposition in both Christian-Arab and Muslim-Arab circles. The statement was interpreted as a rapprochement with the state of Israel and a prelude to diplomatic recognition of it. Arab pressures, initially at the level of chanceries, were brought to bear both on the secretariat of state and on the governments of friendly countries, asking for their intervention in the matter. The controversy and the pressures became more spirited and public as the result of a gaffe by the World Jewish Congress, which on June 12, 1962, announced the appointment of Dr. Chaim Wardi as its own "unofficial observer and

---

[112] *Les Églises devant le judaïsme*, ed. Hoch and Dupuy (note 102, above) 20-21. Together with other prominent figures in the Jewish, Catholic, and Protestant worlds, Isaac formed the initial group of *Amitiés judéo-chrétiennes*, an organization that received a great deal of attention in France. In 1949 Isaac was received by Pius XII. Despite the emotions felt by the two men, the meeting had no practical consequences.

[113] J. Isaac, *Della necessità di una riforma dell'insegnamento cristiano nei riguardi di Israele*, a memorandum presented to John XXIII in 1960. See M. Vingiani, "Jules Isaac. Il promotore del dialogo ebraico-cristiano a venti anni dalla morte," in *Ecumenismo anni '80* (Verona, 1984) 323-38).

representative" at the Council.[114] Thinking about relations between the Church and the Jews had been carried on very discreetly until the point when it was decided to invite to the Council personalities from the Jewish religious world as guests of the secretariat, despite the fact that a poll taken on this proposal would have shown strong resistance among orthodox Jews.

6. *The Political Horizon of the Debate*

It was right at this sensitive moment that, without consulting the secretariat, the World Jewish Congress made known the appointment of Dr. Wardi. Moreover, Wardi was living in Israel and the Israeli ministries of foreign affairs and religious affairs approved his appointment, thereby giving it political overtones. "The Vatican was immediately besieged with protests from Arab countries and requests for similar representation at the Council. Jews protested too."[115] The false step taken by the World Jewish Congress and the negative reaction of the Arab countries[116] created an unfavorable climate that finally led to an unusual step by the secretariat of state: in agreement with Cardinal Bea, discussion of this draft in the Central Commission was stopped, thereby removing it from the conciliar agenda.[117] To justify these steps it was said at the commission that "since the disagreements between Jews and Arabs in our time are well known, the suspicion of political intent, or of favoring the one or other side, easily arises; false rumors to this effect are already being spread."[118]

[114] Gilbert, *The Vatican Council and the Jews*, 61. On the entire incident see the section "The Wardi Incident," 61-64. As a matter of fact, Dr. Chaim Herzog had played an active role at the New Delhi Assembly of the World Council of Churches, taking part in the drafting of a declaration condemning antisemitism.

[115] Ibid., 61.

[116] See J. Oesterreicher, *The New Encounter between Christians and Jews* (New York, 1985) 160-61: "The Arab governments saw their worst fears confirmed and let loose a storm of protest against the allegedly preferential treatment of the Jews. It seems that at a given moment Arab leaders assumed that the Jewish Congress' decision had Vatican approval. Yet, they certainly believed that the State of Israel stood behind the plan and was trying to force its way, under false pretenses, into the Council, or at least into its 'antechambers.'"

[117] See A. Bea, *The Church and the Jewish People*, trans. P. Loretz (New York: Harper & Row, 1966) 23: "The first of these difficulties arose in June 1962 when the first schema, dealing only with the Jews and hammered out by the Secretariat in the course of many long sessions, was included in the agenda of the Central Preparatory Commission of the Council. Unfortunately, at this precise moment, news came that certain Jewish organizations were to be represented at Rome in connection with the Ecumenical Council and this produced some vociferous protests on the part of the Arabs. It was therefore considered prudent to allay anxiety by removing the schema on the Jews from the agenda of the Council."

[118] *ADP*, II/4, 21.

After stating that discussion of the draft was inopportune, Cardinal
Cicognani went on to say in harsh and polemical language: "It would be a
waste of time to recall our connections with the Jewish people: Christ our
Lord himself was of that people, and we hold to the Old Testament as well
as the New. But we should stick to the purpose of this Council, at which the
Church desires solemnly to affirm its faith and to strengthen its apostolate.
And why this particular decree? If a decree on the Jews, why not one on the
Muslims? They certainly boast of their descent from father Abraham."[119]

7. *The Attitude of the Marxist Archipelago*

When John XXIII ascended the papal throne, he inherited a situation
that had by then reached a dead-end. Its character was determined by the
immobilism of the Holy See in its relations with the communist countries. The policy of religious persecution practiced by those countries
and Catholic intransigence had led to a complete impasse in many disputes. The Church in China, while not completely suppressed, finally
consecrated some new bishops that were chosen locally and not by
Rome. Pius XII had condemned this schism, even though the Holy See
was unable to offer any way out of the conflict.

The transition from Pius XII to John XXIII brought no immediate
change in this Vatican policy, whether in relation to the countries of eastern Europe or in relation to communist countries generally, from China in
Asia to Cuba in Latin America. Still in force was the Holy Office decree,
issued in 1949 and confirmed in 1959, that threatened excommunication
of Catholics who voted for communists or made any contributions to that
political party; reminders that this decree was in force were issued on the
occasion of all Italian political crises and at times of elections.

What had changed, however, was the climate, as the previous "intransigence" gave way to a less ideological and more practical, less political
and more pastoral attitude and one, therefore, that was open to dialogue.
The changed attitude was not immediately perceptible, as was shown by
the address of John XXIII to the secret consistory of December 15,
1958. In what it said of China the address still reflected the pessimistic
and almost apocalyptic perspective of the last years of Pius XII:

> For some time, as you know, the Catholics of China have been living in
> extremely painful and difficult conditions. Missionaries, peaceful heralds
> of the gospel, have been slandered, imprisoned, and finally expelled,
> among them a great many archbishops and bishops. Zealous Chinese bish-
> ops have been thrown into prison...interned, or in any case hindered in the

[119] Ibid.

free exercise of their pastoral office, while churchmen legitimately appointed to replace or succeed them have found themselves in the same position, and all this simply because they were not prepared to obey harsh demands which they could not in conscience accept... Unfortunately — We are forced to say it with sorrow — there have not been lacking some who, fearing the orders of men more than the holy judgment of God, have yielded to the demands of the persecutors and even gone so far as to accept a sacrilegious episcopal consecration that can give no jurisdiction over the faithful because it was bestowed without an "apostolic mandate."[120]

Furthermore, on January 12, 1959, the pope wrote to Cardinal Micara, asking that he request the people of Rome to join him in prayer for China during the Week of Unity that was to end on January 25 in the basilica of St. Paul's Outside the Walls. But in his homily for that day his pastoral style, which avoided condemning or offending, was shown when, after recalling the sufferings and dangers to which the Church was subject in so many places in Europe and Asia, he said:

Because duty requires great reserve and a sincere and considered respect and also because of Our confident hope that the storm will gradually dissipate, We avoid specifying ideologies, places, and persons. But We are not indifferent to the latest evidence that continually passes before Our eyes and reveals fears, acts of violence, and the obliteration of the human person.[121]

Such were the sentiments of John XXIII, even in the midst of his anxiety about the peoples and the Church in those countries, for as he would tell De Gaulle in 1959, "among all the peoples of Europe and Asia which had been subjected to Communism, the Catholic community was oppressed and cut off from Rome."[122]

After the death of Cardinal Aloizije Stepinac of Zagreb in Yugoslavia (February 10, 1960),[123] the pope asked Cardinal König to represent him at the funeral. While celebrating Mass for the deceased in Rome, he "recalled the sufferings of the archbishop and spoke of his constant exercise of forgiveness and peace; he also expressed his appreciation of the Yugoslavian authorities who allowed a public celebration of the

[120] *DMC* I, 80.

[121] *DMC* I, 126.

[122] Charles de Gaulle, *Memoirs of Hope: Renewal and Endeavor*, trans. T. Kilmartin (New York: Simon and Schuster, 1971) 193.

[123] Stepinac, Archbishop of Zagreb, the first bishop in eastern Europe to be arrested, was condemned to sixteen years of hard labor on October 31, 1946. In 1951 Tito vainly offered Rome his freedom in exchange for his leaving the country. The archbishop was finally set free but forced to continue living in his native land. When Pius XII created him a cardinal in 1952, the regime regarded the act as a provocation and broke off diplomatic relations with the Vatican. See H. Stehle, *Eastern Politics of the Vatican 1917-1979* (Ohio, 1981) 260.

funeral."[124] Such gestures of humanity and reconciliation paved the way for the new pope's personal style, in which pastoral mission took precedence over politics.

John XXIII took a cautious position in regard to Cuba, which, after the revolution of January 1, 1959, and an agrarian reform that had expropriated the large estates of North Americans, was experiencing increasing hostility from the United States and was therefore aligning itself with the USSR. At the time when J. F. Kennedy was establishing a total commercial blockade against the island, supporting an armed invasion, and demanding, at the meeting in Punta del Este, that all the other countries of the Americas break off diplomatic relations with Fidel Castro's regime, the pope did not yield to those who called for his excommunication and the end of diplomatic relations. As a result, all the bishops of Cuba would be able to take part in the Council.

Cardinal Agostino Casaroli, who as secretary of state under Paul VI would be the prime mover of the *Ostpolitik*, liked the image of a "thaw." He recalls the moment when "the personal warmth of John XXIII seemed to melt a thick barrier of ice, as this warmth was completely new and rejected positions consecrated by the sacrifice of so many."[125]

But the "thaw" was not due solely to John XXIII; it was an international movement that aimed at the peaceful coexistence of differing social and political systems. The need of activating such a thaw even within the Church was all the more urgent in view of the growing opposition between those who wanted the Church to be involved in the politico-ideological conflict between West and East and those who wanted the Church pastorally oriented to the salvation of all human beings. One of the key points in this opposition was the attitude taken towards communism. One example, among many, was the clashes in the Central Commission when *De cura animarum pro christianis communismo infectis* ("The care of souls in dealing with Christians infected by communism") was being discussed.[126]

A very clear norm for Roncalli, and one that was confirmed by the whole of his earlier life, was that pastoral zeal and service should be kept separate from politics. He had felt the need to reassert this conviction immediately after his election, perhaps also in order to distance himself from certain aspects of the preceding pontificate and from internal and external pressures aimed at making the pope fill specific

[124] *DMC* II, 204-5.

[125] A. Casaroli, *Nella chiesa per il mondo. Omelie e discorsi* (Milan, 1987) 274; see A. Santini, *Agostino Casaroli uomo del dialogo* (Milan, 1993).

[126] A. Indelicato, *Difendere la dottrina o annunciare l'evangelo. Il dibattito nella Commissione centrale preparatoria del Vaticano II* (Genoa, 1992) 224-29.

political roles.[127] Consequently, communism no longer had a predominant place in the Roman magisterium; John did not underestimate it but he did relativize it; in his view, the historical horizon of the Church's activity was much broader and more complex. At the beginning of Lent, 1959, he warned preachers "to enlighten consciences, not to confuse and coerce them...to heal the brethren, not to frighten them."[128] The pope gave expression to this attitude in a serene appraisal of the present time, unlike many who "are discouraged or give up, or are tempted to give up, the effort or at least to slacken it." In his view, the Church on its pilgrimage through the centuries has not always triumphed nor, because it overcame so many enemies in the past, may it consider itself victorious over present enemies; rather it must "trust entirely in the never-failing help of its founder."[129]

John's main interest was not in political interventions, which were often dictated by circumstances internal to Italy, but in the various aspects of the problem of peace, which was to enter a new phase during the coming years, due in part to his contribution. John XXIII's commitment to peace allowed him to find room for common action with the communist countries. Instead of interpreting Soviet proposals for peace and disarmament as simply a cunning way of persuading the West to lower its guard against communism, he believed that a nation that had lost twenty million people in the last war could really want nothing but peace.

Thus, at a moment of serious international tension, when the Soviets built the Berlin Wall and the Americans responded by renewing nuclear testing, which was immediately followed by a series of explosions of Soviet experimental bombs, John's addresses took on a stronger note. On September 10, 1961, he moved out of the framework of the cold war and supported the disarmament proposals of the non-aligned countries, which, for the first time since Bandung, had met in Belgrade under the leadership of Tito, Nehru, Nasser, and Bourguiba. His appeal was especially welcome in the USSR, where Khrushchev himself told *Pravda*: "John XXIII pays tribute to reason when he warns governments against a widespread catastrophe and exhorts them to realize the immense responsibility they have to history. His plea is a good sign. In our age,

[127] The most open sign that these pressures existed can be found in the article published, despite the pope's disagreement with its views, in *OssRom* for May 18, 1950, under the title "Punti fermi." It was evidently the result of the curia's dissatisfaction with the political reticence of John XXIII and, at the same time, an effort to force his hand. As a result of the publication Cardinal Ottaviani's scheduled audiences were frozen for a while.

[128] *DMC* I, 142.

[129] *DMC* I, 351.

given the existence of utterly destructive means of slaughtering people, it is inadmissible to play with the destiny of nations."[130]

John's ecumenical aim created a movement of dialogue and reconciliation and presupposed recognition of and respect for others, trust in their good faith, and the ability to accept their qualities and evaluate them positively. Heretics and schismatics thus became brothers and sisters who had to be found again.

As early as his address on the day of his coronation, November 4, 1958, John XXIII had outlined some basic points of his program. Among these was that he wanted to be, first of all, a pastor and the pastor of all: "We want to emphasize this point, that my very special concern is the task of being the pastor of the entire flock."[131] What might have seemed to be merely a figure of speech was in fact a decision that had controlled an entire life and was now becoming the program for a pontificate. The program was destined to find its practical application very soon, in the pope's surrender of himself to the guidance of providence and in his obedience to divine inspiration that came to him through persons and events, while at the same time not losing confidence and interior peace: *Obedientia et pax* ("Obedience and peace"). The program was soon challenged by the divisions, irreconcilable blocs, and hard realities of politics. Peace, along with truth and unity, was at the center of the programmatic encyclical *Ad Petri cathedram* of June 29, 1959.

8. *Bishops and Observers from the East*

In March of 1962 John XXIII, now increasingly involved in the preparation for the Council, summoned Msgr. Francesco Lardone, apostolic delegate in Istanbul, where his assignment was the one Roncalli had once had, and received him twice in the course of a few days.[132] According to Lardone, John XXIII went directly to the point: "You have connections with the Soviet ambassador in Ankara and can tell him of my desire to see the Russian Catholic bishops, too, at the Council."[133] But the Holy See and Moscow did not have diplomatic relations, and information was lacking about the Catholic hierarchy in Lithuania, Estonia, and Latvia. Lardone returned to Ankara and was able to tell Cardinal Cicognani as early as April 11 that he had met

---

[130] G. C. Zizola, *Giovanni XXIII. La fede e la politica* (Rome-Bari, 1988) 141-42.

[131] *DMC* I, 15.

[132] Cicognani, Secretary of State, was upset and had told Lardone: "The Holy Father wants to deal with the Reds...and he intends to give the job to you. I don't know..."; see A. Riccardi, *Il Potere del Papa. Da Pio XII a Paolo VI* (Rome-Bari, 1993²) 233.

[133] Ibid., 234.

with Rjov, Soviet ambassador to Ankara, and that the latter had told him that to satisfy the Holy Father's wish his government agreed that the Russian Catholic bishops should take part in the Council. On the basis of this reply Lardone approached all the other ambassadors from communist countries in order to win their good offices for the participation in the Council of the Catholic bishops of their respective countries. He was very cordially received and won a promise that they would pass the request on to their respective governments.[134] Attempts were also made through the Chinese embassy to the United Arab Republic in Cairo to gain the attendance of the Chinese bishops, but without success.

All in all, in view of what had gone before, the participation in the first period of the Council of a bishop from Bulgaria, two bishops and an apostolic administrator from Hungary, four bishops from Czechoslovakia, and three capitular vicars from the USSR was a considerable and unexpected success. The total number of bishops from the Soviet area who took part in 1962 was thirty-five, after the arrival of a large Polish delegation that was due to the initiative of the primate.

9. *The Russian Observers*[135]

From the very beginning of its work the Secretariat for Christian Unity had discussed the question of inviting observers from the other Christian Churches to the Council. As far as the Orthodox in the countries of eastern Europe were concerned, it had been planned to have the invitation reach the patriarchates of Moscow, Sofia, Bucharest, and Belgrade through the ecumenical patriarchate of Constantinople. But while Patriarch Athenagoras had rejoiced at the idea of a Council and was doing his best to effect a reconciliation with Rome, in July, 1961, the official journal of the Moscow patriarchate opposed the sending of its own observers with a solemn *Non possumus*.[136]

At New Delhi, in that same year, the Catholic observers, representing their Church for the first time at an Assembly of the World Council of

[134] Ibid., 183.

[135] See Schmidt, *Augustin Bea*, 357-63; A. Wenger, *Concile Vatican II. Première Session* (Paris, 1965) 222-56; idem, *Les Trois Romes — L'Église des années soixante* (Paris, 1991) 79-89; 95-99.

[136] Wenger, *Les Trois Romes*, 80: "The patriarchate of Moscow...has already made known its feeling about the Council, which it regards as exclusively the business of the Catholic Church. But the statements of Cardinal Bea testify to the claim of the See of Rome to absolute power in the Christian world, a claim that served as the basis for the forging of the new dogmas that have separated the Church of Rome from the universal Church.... This being the case, the familiar *Non possumus* of the Roman Church was met with the *Non possumus* of the Orthodox Church."

Churches, had been able to meet with the delegates from the patriarchate of Moscow and the Orthodox Churches of Rumania, Bulgaria, and Poland. Metropolitan Nicodemus explained to the Catholic observers the attitude of his own Church to Rome:

> Russian Orthodox Christians cultivate the finest fraternal sentiments toward the Roman Catholic Church and toward its hierarchy and faithful. But the Russian Church does not approve of the activity of the Vatican in the political sphere. In this area the Vatican often shows itself hostile to our country. We, the faithful of the Russian Orthodox Church, are loyal citizens of our country and we have an ardent love for our fatherland. That is why anything done against our country cannot improve our mutual relationship.[137]

The invitations to the Orthodox Churches had already been sent via the patriarchate of Constantinople, but the mediation of Constantinople was not acceptable to Moscow.[138] When Msgr. Willebrands' attention was called to this, he met Metropolitan Nikodim in Paris in August 1962. Nikodim then met with Cardinal Tisserant in Metz, and between September 27 and October 2 Willebrands made a sudden and secret journey to Moscow, in order to inform the Synod and the patriarchate's synodal commission for interchristian relations of several matters: the final preparations for the Council, the conciliar agenda, and the invitations to the Churches. On October 4 Cardinal Bea telegraphed Metropolitan Nikodim that an official invitation had been sent directly to the patriarch.[139] Moscow's acceptance came quickly and the observers reached Rome on the afternoon of the twelfth.[140]

In Constantinople, however, Patriarch Athenagoras, who had always been the one most in favor of sending a delegation, did not receive a reply from Moscow and believed in good faith that the Russian Church would not be sending observers. He therefore assembled his synod and in order not to harm the unity that was settled at Rhodes, declared it impossible to send Orthodox observers to Rome.

---

[137] Ibid., 88.
[138] In 1962 Patriarch Alexis stated: "The Russian Orthodox Church has not received an invitation to the Council of the Roman Catholic Church" (Wenger, *Concile Vatican II*, 213). On March 21 of that same year Metropolitan Nikodim presented a well-organized report on the coming Council to the Holy Synod of Moscow.
[139] *Revue du Patriarcat de Moscou* 11 (1962) 9-10.
[140] See also N. A. Kovalsky, "The Role of Vatican II for the Normalization of Relations between the Vatican and Russia," a paper read at the Würzburg Colloquium of 1993 on "Der Beitrag der deutschsprachigen und osteuropäischen Länder zum Zweiten Vatikanischen Konzil." On the reactions of western communists see A. Casanova, *Vatican II et l'évolution de l'Église* (Paris, 1969), and *Le concile vingt ans après. Essai d'approche marxiste* (Paris, 1985); R. Garaudy, *From Anathema to Dialogue: A Marxist Challenge to the Christian Churches*, trans. L. O'Neill (New York: Herder & Herder, 1966).

CHAPTER V

ON THE EVE OF THE SECOND VATICAN COUNCIL
(JULY 1 — OCTOBER 10, 1962)

KLAUS WITTSTADT

I. THE FIRST SEVEN SCHEMATA AND
THE REACTIONS OF THE EPISCOPATE

1. *The General Attitude of Expectation before the Council.*

During the final three months before the solemn opening of the Second Vatican Council the expectations raised by the announcement of this event became especially clear. Not only the Catholic world but all of Christendom and, beyond that, all people of good will were filled with hope. They all sensed that in the person of John XXIII something had begun that might answer some of the deepest longings of human beings, such as the yearning for peace, the desire of community, the dream of a better world. All this was becoming increasingly clear from the very diverse statements issued and from the reports carried in the world press. M.-D. Chenu, O.P., captured the mood accurately when, in a text prepared for the Council fathers on September 15, 1962, he spoke as follows: "All of us, Christians and non-Christians, have been very responsive to the announcement of a Council."

On July 1, 1962, the pope issued his encyclical *Paenitentiam agere*; it was published in *L'Osservatore Romano* for July 6.[1] In this document the pope urged clergy and people to a more intense preparation through prayer and penance. He stressed that "there is need especially of interior repentance." But he also emphasized exterior penance: "The faithful must be encouraged to subject their bodies to the control of reason and faith and to make reparation for their own sins and the sins of others." The pope wanted all to cooperate in the work of redemption. "All know that the ecumenical Council has for its aim the spread of the divine work of redemption." "Nothing is more desirable, nothing can honor us more, than to work together for the salvation of people." If each person "does everything in his or her power, Christians can contribute greatly to a

[1] *ADP*, I, 275-83.

happy and successful outcome of this Second Ecumenical Council of the Vatican, which has for its purpose to lend a new luster to Christian life."[2] The pope's intention in this encyclical was to focus the gaze of all on Christ the Lord and call them to follow him; he was conveying one of his own convictions. As in the other documents of John XXIII, so in this one it is clear that the pope's desire was both to lead people to faith and to deepen the faith of believers.

Many of the statements issued on expectations for the Council took this passage of the encyclical *Paenitentiam agere* as a point of reference. Thus Cardinal Paul Émile Léger, Archbishop of Montreal, had this to say: "The Council's purpose is to restore a Christian meaning to the contemporary world. This requires energy, an affirmation of what is positive, love for human beings, and an understanding of life here on earth... The Council, then, will promote the renewal of the Church and thereby — in a broader perspective — the rapprochement of Christians."[3]

Others formulated their expectations of the Council in these terms: "The Council calls for an immense effort on the part of the entire Church, an effort directed both within and without."[4] Cardinal Döpfner expected from the Council "a deepening and strengthening but also a differentiation and adaptation of the inner life of the Church." He repeatedly insisted that the Council would have a "pastoral character." As he understood the phrase, it meant two things. "First of all, the Church will not pay any heed to the fact that it is surrounded by enemies. Its aim is to rediscover itself in order then to gain a deeper understanding of its mission to the world." The cardinal continued: "On the other hand — and this is the second thing — the Church soberly recognizes, as it seeks its self-renewal, that it exists in an age that does not grasp its ultimate mystery."[5]

The entire world had its eyes on the Council, and the common dream was that it would contribute to the making of a better world. The various statements issued gave voice to longings and desires. In France people were hoping for "a faith purified of routine and outward conformism."[6] Dutch Catholics made the point that "it is clearly the Holy Spirit who is

    [2] Ibid., 283.

    [3] Cardinal Paul Émile Léger, "'Mit den Samenkörnern seines Wortes.' Verchristlichung aller irdischen Werte als Aufgabe," Katholische Nachrichtenagentur, *Sonderdienst Zweites Vatikanisches Konzil*, no. 9 (September 25, 1962) 2-3 [henceforth: KNA, *Sonderdienst*].

    [4] O. B. Roegele, "Vigil des Weltkonzils," ibid., 4-7 at 7.

    [5] Konzilsnachlass Döpfner, Archiv des Erzbischofshofes München (AEM).

    [6] "Frankreich blickt auf das Konzil. Eigene Probleme nicht anderen aufdrängen," KNA, *Sonderdienst*, no. 14 (October 8, 1962) 2-4 at 3.

guiding the Church, and not so much the bishops as human beings."[7] The hope of the Swiss was formulated in this way in the Catholic newspaper *Vaterland*: "The Church will always be Roman Catholic, but there may be a shift of emphasis away from the 'Roman.'"[8] Poland was concerned especially "with the relationship of Polish Catholics to people in other churches, nonbelievers, Judaism, and the Old Testament."[9]

Clarification of the place of the laity in the Church was central to the conciliar expectations of the approximately four million Catholics in England. In their view, the Council fathers should satisfy the express desires of many leading laypersons and clerics and state clearly that since the laity are "the Church" they may propose their suggestions and ideas (Pope Pius XII!) without fear of being viewed as heretics, malevolent critics, or eccentrics. Furthermore, said the English Catholics, the Council should go so far as to allow, in the near future, Anglicans and Catholics to pray together on special occasions such as marriages and funerals. All English Catholics would welcome the use of the vernacular in the celebration of Mass. Many clerics wanted a reform of the breviary, including the use of the vernacular. In the eyes of the English, the Index and the prohibition against cremation, among other things, were in need of radical revision.[10] Of the approximately twenty million inhabitants of the Scandinavian countries about 60,000 profess the Catholic faith. They were worried, to some extent, that the Council might further hinder their contacts with their Lutheran brethren in the faith.[11]

In the Italian Catholic world the statements of Cardinal Montini, Archbishop of Milan, about the coming Council were especially significant. He made known his ideas and expectations of the Council in an extensive Lenten pastoral letter. He hoped for internal reforms. Although he did not see in the Church "any deep-rooted and widespread malady" that was so conspicuous as to be a public scandal, he thought that the Church was in need of a spiritual renewal; it needed new vitality so as not simply to refrain from evil but to do what is good. He singled out ecclesiology as the most important topic for the Council. He assumed

[7] "Die Niederlande blicken auf das Konzil. Wer gibt den Ton in der Kirche an?" ibid., 4-7 at 6.

[8] "Die Schweiz blickt auf das Konzil. Hunger nach Information," ibid., 7-9 at 9.

[9] "Polen blickt auf das Konzil. Verhältnis der Katholiken zum Andersgläubigen," ibid., 10-11 at 11.

[10] "England blickt auf das Konzil. Was erwarten die englischen Katholiken vom Konzil," ibid., 11-13.

[11] "Skandinavien blickt auf das Konzil. Hl. Messe dem Volk zugänglich machen," ibid., 13-15 at 14.

"that the Second Vatican Council will include in its agenda the question
of the episcopal office, in order to show its origin in the gospel, its sacramental gifts of grace, and its power of teaching, ministry, and jurisdiction, and this in reference both to the individual bishop and to the episcopal college." "The royal priesthood of the laity" would also have
to be given closer consideration. In particular, Montini emphasized the
ecumenical task of the Council, although he did not fail to recognize the
difficulties on the road to reunification.[12]

In Spain the situation was rather confused. José Pont y Gol, Bishop of
Segorbe-Castellón, complained that the degree of general participation
in the Council still left something to be desired. He saw a tendency to
isolationism in Spanish Catholicism and called for an openness to the
worldwide Church.[13] In order to make the public more aware of the
Council, a new monthly periodical entitled *Concilio* began to appear in
Madrid in 1962.[14] The role of the lay apostolate seems to have been a
special problem for Spain. Archbishop Moreillo of Zaragoza in his pastoral letter "The Laity and the Council" expressed a desire for a
reassessment of the lay apostolate. At the same time, however, he considered it necessary to differentiate carefully between the task of the
priestly office and the service of the laity to the world.[15] By and large,
there were great tensions to be seen in the Spanish Church as the Council drew near; as a result, the openness to modern values which the
Council envisaged could not but radically challenge the situation of the
Church in Franco's Spain.[16]

The range of expectations in the Church of the United States of America can be seen in the joint pastoral letter which the bishops issued on
the occasion of their annual meeting in August of 1962. The American
bishops were convinced that they could make a special contribution to
the Council by bringing to it the experiences of a new kind of Church
such as could develop only under the conditions of pluralism that characterized North American society. Although the Church of the United
States was not so rich in tradition, it could represent the advantages
"which have come to the Church from living and growing in an atmosphere of religious and political freedom." It could serve the present-day

---

[12] *HK* 16 (1961-62) 392-94; complete text: Giovanni Battista Montini, *Discorsi
e scritti sul Concilio (1959-1963)*, ed. A. Rimoldi (Quaderni dell'Istituto Paolo VI, 3;
Brescia-Rome, 1983) 72-108.
[13] *HK* 16 (1961-62) 489f.
[14] Ibid.
[15] Ibid., 394f.
[16] Ibid., 560-69.

Church as a model for the future, inasmuch as it had achieved an intense vitality "unaided by political preference but unimpaired by political ties."[17] The bishops regarded as the most important thing of all the spiritual impulse that the Council could give.

In South America the hope was the Council would supply the solution for the desperate pastoral and social situation. The Council must bring the worldwide Church to acknowledge its responsibility for the human race. The Council "reveals and at the same time intensifies a new ecclesial self-awareness that will also find expression, to a greater degree than in the past, in collaborative action."[18] The expectation was that the renewal of the liturgy and, in particular, the introduction of the national vernaculars, would lead to a greater participation of the people in the Mass and to a deepening of religious life. Both of these would make it possible to eliminate pagan practices and habits of thought.[19]

If we may judge by what Christians and priests in Togo were saying, the people of Africa hoped for a new impulse for the ecumenical movement, since the division among Christians could only have a negative effect on the credibility of missionary work. "People feel that the division is a cause of distress for religion, since unity in love suffers due to doctrinal divergences; people here do not consider those with different beliefs as brothers and sisters, the way they do in Europe, but as rivals and enemies." In particular, it was hoped that the Council would lead to better contacts, at the level of the universal Church, between the young mission countries and the old European Churches. Difficulties both spiritual and material would thereby be alleviated.[20]

These few examples show how people everywhere felt that "the Church which John XXIII had summoned to a Council was now emerging from a lengthy period of mistrust of history and from a doctrinal rigidity that looked upon the truths of the gospel as a treasure to be safeguarded rather than a blessing to be shared."[21] In almost every country people felt that Roncalli had let the entire world know that today more than ever before Christians are called upon to bear witness to the Christ who is in our midst. The result was to arouse great expectations of the approaching Council. Bishops and theologians in particular anxiously

[17] "Statement on the Ecumenical Council" (August 19, 1962), no. 12, in *Pastoral Letters of the United States Catholic Bishops, III, 1962-1974* (Washington, D.C., 1983) 13.

[18] See *HK* 17 (1962-63) 72f.; 167-69 (these pages report the contents of a booklet by Fr. Houtart, *Die Kirche von Lateinamerika in der Stunde des Konzils*).

[19] See "Lateinamerika blickt auf das Konzil," KNA, *Sonderdienst*, no. 20 (1962) 3f.

[20] See "Togo blickt auf das Konzil," ibid., 2f.

[21] Giuseppe Alberigo, "Cristianesimo e storia," *CrSt* 5 (1984) 577-92 at 592.

awaited the texts that would be sent to them and then, beginning on
October 11, be discussed in the meeting-hall of the Council.

2. *The Sending of the Seven Schemata*

The preparatory commissions and secretariats were formed by Pope
John XXIII on the feast of Pentecost, June 5, 1960, and charged with the
development of schemata, or drafts, for Vatican Council II. In his
address after Vespers on Pentecost the pope divided the Council into
four periods. The first was to be one of general introduction, positioning,
and preliminary preparation (the antepreparatory period); an important
element in this period was the obtaining of vota from the Council fathers
throughout the world. The second period was that of direct preparation:
this was the business of the eleven preparatory commissions, the three
secretariats (for the press and communications media; for the unity of
Christians; and for administration), and the Central Preparatory Commission. The third period was to be the actual Council, and the fourth,
the solemn proclamation of the conciliar decrees: "of what the Council
has decided to decree, explain, and suggest in regard to the improvement
of thought and life, the progressive deepening of spirit and activity, and
the exaltation of the gospel of Christ as this is applied and lived by his
holy Church."[22]

The instructions and content for the actual work of the preparatory
commission were submitted to the pope on July 2, 1960, by Pericle
Felici, General Secretary, and were then sent out, with an accompanying
letter of July 9, to the presidents of each commission.

As a result of all the preparatory work, the secretary general was able,
during the summer of 1962, that is, just in time for the opening of the
Council, to send the Council fathers a volume containing the first seven
schemata that were to serve as the basis for discussion during the general
meetings (*congregationes generales*).[23] On July 3, 1962, John XXIII had
decreed that these first seven schemata, which bore the official title
*Schemata constitutionum et decretorum de quibus disceptabitur in
Concilii sessionibus. Series prima* (Drafts of Constitutions and Decrees,
to be Discussed during the Meetings of the Council. First Series), should
be sent to all the Council fathers throughout the world.

The volume thus dispatched contained the following drafts in the following order: I. Schema of a dogmatic constitution on the sources of

---

[22] *ADA*, I, 101.
[23] *Schemata*, I, 1.

revelation. II. Schema of a dogmatic constitution on the preservation of the purity of the faith. III. Schema of a dogmatic constitution on the Christian moral order. IV. Schema of a dogmatic constitution on chastity, marriage, the family, and virginity. V. Schema of a constitution on the sacred liturgy. VI. Schema of a constitution on the communications media. VII. Schema of a decree on the unity of the Church (including the Eastern Church).

"Despite all Pope John's urgings, only seven draft texts were ready to be sent to the bishops..."[24] The noteworthy thing in the present context is that the schema on what was regarded as a main theme of the Council, namely, the position of bishops in the Church, had not yet been handed in. This was interpreted as meaning that the Curia was trying to delay debate on this delicate subject.

On the other hand, the seven schemata were but a small part of the texts drafted by the various commissions. Seventy schemata in all were composed, amounting to over two thousand printed pages. Archbishop Lorenz Jaeger described the situation this way:

> The volume entitled *Conciliorum Oecumenicorum Decreta* that appeared in 1962 contains all the decrees of the previous twenty Councils in 792 pages. This simplistic comparison already shows that Vatican II cannot possibly discuss the prepared drafts in detail and pass resolutions on them. ... Without exception, the drafts that have been prepared suffer from the fact that the preparatory commissions worked quite independently of one another, with the result that overlapping was unavoidable... The central commission has not succeeded in eliminating the resultant repetitions and in turning the various texts on the same subject into a unified whole.[25]

John XXIII himself recognized the problem. He showed Cardinal Suenens the texts from the various commissions and asked him to give his opinion and to develop a plan for better coordinating the work and for achieving an intelligible order in the contents of the conciliar documents. Suenens privately developed a plan for the Council that was later made public during the first session when the work of the Council was not advancing.[26]

---

[24] Peter Hebblethwaite, *John XXIII. The Pope of the Council* (New York, 1984) 416.

[25] Wolfgang Seibel, *Zwischenbilanz zum Konzil. Berichte und Dokumente der deutschen Bischöfe* (Recklinghausen, 1963) 161f. The passage cited is from an article by Archbishop Jaeger, "Die erste Periode des Zweiten Vatikanischen Konzils."

[26] Klaus Wittstadt, *Erneuerung der Kirche aus dem Pfingstereignis. Leon-Joseph Kardinal Suenens zum 80. Geburtstag* (Würzburg, 1984) 113-16.

The first of the dogmatic constitutions was *De Fontibus Revelationis* (The Sources of Revelation). It was divided into five sections: I. The twofold source of revelation; II. Inspiration, infallibility, and the literary structure of the scriptures; III. The Old Testament; IV. The New Testament; and V. The sacred scriptures in the Church.

> The striking thing about this organization of the subject is that while "two sources" of revelation are mentioned (scripture and tradition), there is subsequently no proper discussion of the problem of tradition. The entire draft expresses an obvious positivism that is interested less in a coherent set of arguments than in a juridically unambiguous statement of facts that are to serve as a basis of legitimation. As a result, the question of revelation as such is excluded, as is the question of its historical origin. The Old and New Testaments are not seen primarily as the historically original witnesses that exert an influence in the present and indeed constitute this on the basis of the experience of the past, but rather (as in positive law) as an objectively given, timelessly valid ordinance of the divine legislative will that is untouched by the problem inherent in all historicity. Juridical thinking thus becomes the basic category for dealing with divine revelation.[27]

Central to the understanding of revelation in the schema is the idea that the hierarchical office alone guarantees the authenticity and legitimacy of revelation.

During the discussion of revelation at the Council it was around the question of the relationship of scripture to tradition that the debate erupted. The point most criticized was the rigid separation of scripture and tradition. The draft wanted to distinguish scripture and tradition as precisely as possible. It represented the view that the truths of revelation are to be found partly in the scriptures and partly in tradition. Too little attention was paid to the fact that the revealed word of God is the only source of revelation, and that "Christ himself not only spoke the saving word but is himself also the living and eternal Word of God that expresses itself in the good news that is handed on in the apostolic preaching."[28]

In this draft the conception of revelation and the conception of the Church conditioned each other to a high degree. Paragraph 6 of the first chapter dealt with a question that is basic for an understanding of the

---

[27] Hanjo Sauer, *Erfahrung und Glaube. Die Begründung des pastoralen Prinzips durch die Offenbarungskonstitution des II. Vatikanischen Konzils* (Frankfurt-Berlin-Bern-New York-Vienna, 1993) 23-24.

[28] Eduard Stakemeier, *Die Konzilskonstitution über die göttliche Offenbarung. Werden, Inhalt and theologische Bedeutung* (Konfessionskundliche und kontroverstheologische Studien 18; Paderborn, 1966) 62.

Church, namely, the relationship of each of the two sources of revelation (scripture and tradition) to the teaching office or magisterium of the Church. According to what was said here the magisterium is bound neither by the community of believers nor by the scriptures. The draft said: "In order that both sources of revelation may act in harmony and more effectively for the salvation of humanity than when taken separately, the Lord in his providence has entrusted them as a single deposit of faith, not to the individual faithful, however learned they may be, but solely to the living magisterium of the Church, in order that it may preserve and protect them and give an authentic interpretation of them."[29]

In this draft the viewpoint of a single school, that of the Curia with its center in the Holy Office, had prevailed in a very one-sided way. A particular objection to the draft was that its tone was very negative.

> Text and notes were filled with anxiety and suspicion; everywhere the authors scented dangers to the faith and errors against which the faithful must be on guard. In fact, it was not very difficult to see in the first chapter of *De fontibus* a condemnation of the view of Geiselmann, the Catholic historian of dogma, whose new interpretation of the Tridentine decree on scripture and tradition had won widespread agreement, or to perceive, in the following chapters, warnings to Catholic biblical scholars who were zealously following the open-minded encyclical *Divino afflante Spiritu* of Pius XII.[30]

It was perhaps Yves Congar who best put his finger on the problem when he said: "There is not a single dogma which the Church holds by scripture *alone*, not a single dogma which it holds by tradition *alone*."[31]

The schema had been composed by a subcommission of the preparatory theological commission and approved both by the full Theological Commission and the Central Commission, but later on it was withdrawn after being discussed and voted on in the Council hall. It was recognized even in the stage of preparation that the idea of two sources of revelation, as formulated here, would make ecumenical dialogue more difficult and would reinforce differences in the understanding of

[29] *Schemata*, I, 11.

[30] Pieter Smulders, S.J., "Zum Werdegang des Konzilskapitels 'Die Offenbarung selbst,'" in Klinger and Wittstadt, *Glaube im Prozess*, 99-120 at 104.

[31] *Informations catholiques internationales*, December 1, 1962, p. 2, cited in Xavier Rynne, *Letters from Vatican City. Vatican Council II (First Session): Background and Debates* (New York: Farrar, Straus, 1963) 141.

revelation, especially with the Protestant Churches.[32] For this reason the Secretariat for Christian Unity composed an entirely new draft.[33]

The schema on revelation was followed by the *Schema Constitutionis Dogmaticae de Deposito Fidei Pure Custodiendo* (Schema of a Dogmatic Constitution on Preserving the Deposit of Faith in its Purity).[34] The preface spoke of the right and duty of preserving the patrimony of faith (the "deposit of faith"). The first chapter dealt with "the knowledge of the truth"; the second had the title "God"; this was followed by a section on "the creation and evolution of the world" and then by one on "revelation and faith." The fifth chapter dealt with "the development of doctrine" and the sixth with "private revelations," while the seventh bore the title "On the natural and supernatural orders." The eighth chapter was devoted to "Original sin in the children of Adam." The ninth was entitled: "On the last things," and the tenth, "On justification through Christ."

The next document, *Schema Constitutionis Dogmaticae de Ordine Morali Christiano* ("Schema of a Dogmatic Constitution on the Christian Moral Order"), had a similarly didactic and restrictive character. In the first chapter an attempt was made to explain the basis of the moral order; the second chapter dealt with "The Christian conscience"; the third had the title "On ethical sujectivism and relativism," the fourth, "On sin," and the fifth, "On the natural and supernatural dignity of the human person."

The fourth draft, the *Schema Constitutionis Dogmaticae de Castitate, Matrimonio, Familia, Virginitate* ("Schema of a Dogmatic Constitution on Chastity, Marriage, the Family, and Virginity"), was in the same style. The first chapter of the first part dealt with sexuality and the second with "the chastity of the unmarried"; these two made up the first part. The second part had the general title "On Marriage and the Family." The first chapter developed "the order of Christian marriage, which was established by God," the second chapter dealt with "the rights, duties, and virtues proper to Christian marriage," and, finally, the third chapter was on "the Christian family, which was established by God." The second part ended with an explanation of "the rights, duties, and virtues proper to the Christian family." The third part took up "holy virginity." The

---

[32] See Heribert Schauf, "Auf dem Wege zu der Aussage der dogmatischen Konstitution über die göttliche Offenbarung 'Dei Verbum' N. 9a: 'Quo fit ut Ecclesia certitudinem suam de omnibus revelatis non per solam Sacram Scripturam hauriat,'" in Klinger and Wittstadt, *Glaube im Prozess*, 66-98 at 66.

[33] See Stakemeier, *Die Konzilskonstitution über die göttliche Offenbarung*, 62-67.

[34] *Schemata*, I, 23-69.

draft ended with an epilogue, intended as an *Admonitio brevis*, a "brief exhortation."[35]

The drafts which I have outlined originated with the theological commission over which Cardinal Alfredo Ottaviani presided and of which Father Sebastian Tromp, S.J., was the secretary. The drafts of the dogmatic constitutions could not but show his hand; they reflect the spirit of Roman Neoscholastic theology and of the Holy Office.

> Of course, the people close to Cardinal Ottaviani were pushing in the same direction. All the concerns of the "supreme" congregation to maintain the purity of the faith found systematic expression here. All dangers were carefully noted. The predominantly negative tone was already perceptible in the titles: "Maintaining the purity," "Moral order," "Chastity," and these were then followed by lists of condemnations.[36]

The theological commission assumed that their drafts would pass the Council's scrutiny without difficulty. "Father Tromp... remarked with great confidence that the theological drafts were so painstakingly prepared that the Council would adopt them in a couple of weeks."[37] But these were the very drafts that made many bishops uneasy. The texts were controlled by "the rules of a strict and shallow scholasticism, concerned almost exclusively with defense and lacking in discernment, tending to condemn all that did not fit perfectly with its own perspective."[38]

"Pope John also read the texts and he was not happy with them."[39] He did not, indeed, say anything directly against the content of the drafts, "but he did not like their tone. In conversations he constantly complained of the length of the texts devoted to condemnations."[40] But it went against the grain of John XXIII to intervene directly. He preferred an open and honest debate.

The Curia undoubtedly set most store by the dogmatic constitutions. Only in fifth place came the *Schema Constitutionis de Sacra Liturgia* ("Schema of a Constitution on the Sacred Liturgy").[41] The original plan indeed was to begin with dogmatic subjects. The idea was to move, in a deductive process, from the contents of the faith as defined in abstract formulas to moral questions and finally to ecclesiastical practice.

[35] *Schemata*, I, 71-96.
[36] Mario von Galli and Bernhard Moosbrugger, *Das Konzil und seine Folgen* (Lucerne-Frankfurt a. M., 1966) 116.
[37] Smulders, "Zum Werdegang," 100.
[38] Henri de Lubac, *A Theologian Speaks* (Los Angeles, 1985) 7.
[39] Galli and Moosbrugger, *Das Konzil und seine Folgen*, 116.
[40] Henri de Lubac, *Entretien autour de Vatican II* (Paris 1985) 20.
[41] *Schemata*, I, 157-201.

The draft of a liturgy constitution that was presented by the preparatory commission was discussed in the Central Commission on April 3, 1962, but the discussion produced no definitive result. The draft was then referred to the third subcommission, which was under the direction of Carlo Confalonieri, a curial cardinal. This subcommission completed the draft in the form in which it was sent out on July 13, 1962. "When the members and consultors of the preparatory commission again saw the draft on the liturgy, but now in the official edition, they saw that violence had been done to it at important points. But to a reader who did not know the situation the draft seemed even now to be still a good piece of work."[42]

In particular, those passages were changed that provided for a decentralization of decision-making on liturgical questions.

> The power of the competent ecclesiastical authority of a region now no longer consisted in making decisions with the force of law, but was reduced to offering suggestions to the Holy See. Consequently it was no longer possible to speak of "power." This change was a decisive one, since the granting of permission for the vernacular, the decision on certain adaptations, and the settling of local cases, to take but some examples, were no longer in the hands of the bishops, as the new juridical norms had provided within certain limits.[43]

The chalice for the laity and the breviary in the vernacular were subjects no longer discussed, and concelebration was permitted only in exceptional cases. The members of the preparatory commission did, however, let the Council fathers know of these changes. In the discussion during the first session of the Council the fathers went back to the original text.[44]

In summary it can be said that the liturgy commission did their work well, and although their draft angered the loyal supporters of Latin, "their strategy was to claim that they were merely continuing the liturgical reforms that had started with St. Pius X and been further extended under Pius XII."[45]

It was evident that there were circles in the Curia that wanted to block any effective renewal of the liturgy. They were dissatisfied with the draft from the liturgical commission. Bugnini, the secretary of the liturgical commission, was relieved not only of his post as secretary but also of his professorship in the Lateran University, and was banished from Rome.

---

[42] Hermann Schmidt, *Die Konstitution über die heilige Liturgie. Text -Vorgeschichte-Kommentar* (Freiburg i. Br., 1965) 75.

[43] Ibid.

[44] See Annibale Bugnini, *The Reform of the Liturgy: 1948-1975*, trans. M. J. O'Connell (Collegeville, 1990) 29-38.

[45] Hebblethwaite, *John XXIII*, 449.

Caprile does not regard the changes in the text as so serious. He says that the text remained unchanged in its essential lines and was simplified by the removal of the *declarationes*.[46]

While, then, certain circles in the Curia looked with suspicion on the draft on the liturgy, it met with widespread approval among the bishops, even in its "censored version." In its basic plan they found the tone to be pastoral and positive.

The schema had eight chapters: 1. General principles for the renewal of the liturgy; 2. The sacrament of the Holy Eucharist; 3. The sacraments and sacramentals; 4. The divine Office; 5. The Church year; 6. Liturgical furnishings; 7. Sacred music; 8. Sacred art.

The first chapter called for special attention, for in it general principles on the nature of the sacred liturgy and on its importance for the life of the Church were expounded. Here, more than in purely external questions regarding liturgical actions, could be seen the heart of a new vision of worship, one that also affected the image of the Church. The chapter was concerned with God's relationship with human beings, the effects of this relationship in daily life, the people of God and the long neglected universal priesthood that was presupposed by the ministry of the ordained priest; in short, with "that entire conception of God that is essential and proper to Christianity and in accord with our times, but hard to discern in the past form of the liturgy."[47]

Conditions were especially favorable for the liturgy constitution, which could reap what had already been begun in the liturgical movement. Mention must be made especially of Pius X and Pius XII. Cardinal Lercaro and Professor Jungmann, to name but two, were outstanding representatives of the liturgical movement. Their central idea was: the closer to the source, the clearer the water. Mario von Galli wrote:

> It is not surprising, then, that the preparatory liturgical commission could present a text that suited the bishops right from the outset. It was the only text to do so. It alone retained, in essentials, its original form. It was opposed only by isolated groups of bishops in whose countries the liturgical movement had not gained a secure foothold, such as the United States. Cardinal Spellman described the ideas emanating from the liturgical centers as "romantic reveries of scholars with their heads in the clouds," while another bishop even called them "half-mad." But the real center of opposition was the Roman Curia, or, more accurately, a section of the Roman Curia: the people for whom liturgy was identical with rubrics. They had a premonition of the disaster that threatened them.[48]

[46] See Caprile I/2, 511-12; but in footnote 2 Caprile mentions Schmidt's criticism.
[47] Döpfner papers, Council Archives (AEM).
[48] Galli and Moosbrugger, *Das Konzil und seine Folgen*, 118.

The sixth draft of a constitution dealt with a quite topical question, that of the communications media; at the same time, it showed the problems the Church had in dealing adequately with the media.[49] After an introduction on the importance of the communications media, the first part contained principles drawn from Church teaching on the importance of these media and on their proper use. The right and duty of the Church to pronounce doctrinally and pastorally on the subject followed from its commission, which is to help human beings to cope with their task in this world. A decisive element in this coping is the primacy of general moral principles. This first section ended with considerations on the duties of specific groups of people and of the civil authorities.

The second part had to do with the Church's utilization of the media. The third made suggestions for ensuring the carrying out of responsibilities in this area and dealt with the juridical position and duties of priests and religious working in this field, as well as with the rights and duties of laypersons. The fourth part turned to the several media and discussed each separately. A first section dealt with the press, with the news services (it suggested that an international Catholic news agency be set up), with magazines and periodicals, and with the Catholic press. A second section dealt with the cinema, a third with radio and television, with the attention to be paid to juridical and administrative forms, and with religious broadcasts for mission areas. Even comics, records and tapes, posters, and leaflets, and similar forms of journalism were addressed. The draft closed with a plea for the drawing up, by order of the Council, of a pastoral guide for the entire Church. This draft, too, ended with an exhortation.

The entire structure of this draft was quite unconvincing; it contained many platitudes and hardly did justice to the role of the media in a modern, open society.

The last of the seven drafts dealt with ecumenism. Under the title, *De Ecclesiae Unitate "Ut omnes unum sint"* (The Unity of the Church: "That all may be one") the following questions were dealt with in 52 sections: the work of redemption; the earthly and the heavenly Church; the hierarchic Church; the unity of the visible Church under Peter; the unity of the invisible Church; unity in diversity; losses through division; the vestiges of unity; the work of the Church for the attainment of unity; supernatural means; theological means; liturgical means; juridical and disciplinary means; psychological means; practical means; conditions for and ways to unity.[50]

[49] *Schemata*, I, 240-50.
[50] *Schemata*, I, 251-68.

The draft on the unity of the Churches took into account only the eastern Churches. It stressed the unity of the Church that rests on the oneness of its leader, that is, Peter and his successors, but it also took into account the difficulties of the separated eastern brethren, while also emphasizing the principle that unity cannot be achieved at the cost of truth. The draft then explained the manner and conditions of reconciliation, in which everything that was part of the religious, historical, and psychological heritage of the eastern Churches had to be preserved. The draft nonetheless lacked a genuinely ecumenical spirit, as can be seen in the fact that nothing was said of the guilt and transgressions of Catholics in connection with the various divisions.[51]

But the greatest defect of the draft was that it looked only to the eastern Churches and did not mention the Protestant Churches of the West. There was no genuinely ecumenical perspective. But Bea and his newly established Secretariat for Christian Unity were only beginning their work. Cardinal Bea was very much concerned to ease any tensions in relations between the Roman Catholic Church and the other Christian confessions. For this reason he visited Archbishop Michael Ramsey of Canterbury in August, 1962. He wanted to emphasize in a public way the ecumenical goal of the Council, as this was repeatedly voiced by John XXIII.

3. The Reactions of the Bishops

The bishops received the seven drafts only in August and had to submit the changes they desired by September 15; many of them thought this impossible.[52] They complained that the drafts had been sent to the bishops only a very short time before the opening of the Council and that this made any thorough study and analysis impossible.[53]

Despite the shortness of the time allowed, 176 future Council fathers submitted their *Animadversiones* (comments) on the drafts. This meant indeed that less than 10% of the Council fathers gave their opinion of the drafts; on the other hand, the input came from 38 countries and all parts of the world, so that they represented an interesting cross section. The largest number of responses came from Italy (38), but these limited themselves for the most part to polite phrases and a few remarks on

[51] See Heinrich Reuter, *Das II. Vatikanische Konzil. Vorgeschichte -Verlauf- Ergebnisse dargestellt nach Dokumenten und Berichten* (Cologne, 1966²) 32.

[52] See Döpfner papers to Father Bernhard Häring, 7 September 1962; Döpfner Council Archives.

[53] See ibid.: Cardinal Paul Émile Léger to Döpfner.

stylistic and conceptual points. Substantial critiques came chiefly from France (28) and regions influenced by France (former French colonies; French-speaking Canada), from Germany (11) and the Netherlands, but also in the submissions of bishops from the developing countries and mission lands.[54]

Cardinal Pierre Gerlier of Lyons pointed out a clear contradiction between the expositions in the dogmatic schemata and the expectations which both Church and society had of the Council. John XXIII had spoken of a renewal of the Church and an ecumenical orientation of the Council. The texts were on a high philosophical and theological level, but the question of the pastoral task of the Church in the present age was not raised at all. No heed was paid to the Holy Father's intention of having a pastoral Council. Gerlier therefore maintained that prior to any discussion of the individual drafts, there should be a declaration of principle as to the goal and task of the Council. Such a statement of goals should make it clear that the Church was taking a new direction, namely, that its concern had to be to bear witness to the Father's love. The Church had to say that it wanted to contribute in every way to the promotion of the fraternal and peaceful coexistence of human beings in solidarity. The Cardinal of Lyons emphasized that the theologians, who often lack the feel for pastoral matters, should not become judges of faith. The Council should not become a Council of theologians but must be a Council of bishops who, in union with the Holy Father, desired to bring the message of salvation to all human beings.[55]

Similar concerns and desires were expressed by Alfred Ancel, Gerlier's auxiliary bishop. He wrote: "I am very much afraid that the way in which sacred teaching is presented here is not adapted to the goal which John XXIII had in mind when he convoked the Council." Especially lacking in the texts was the positive direction given by a straightforward proclamation of the message of salvation: "People are looking neither for a list of various errors against the faith nor for a scholastic explanation of the truths of faith, but for a clear and vivid communication of the truth which God revealed to humankind." The dogmatic texts, however, would remind a reader of theological and philosophical courses that students take. "As I read the texts I was reminded once more of the lectures of the professors at the Gregorianum, those lectures that I once heard with great profit; but I must honestly admit that it does not seem possible for me to approve a text of this kind, which is to be

---

[54] See *AS* App., 67-350.
[55] See *AS* App., 77-79.

presented to the world by the bishops gathered in Council together with the pope."[56] André M. Charue, Bishop of Namur, had a similar criticism: "The Council cannot play the part of the Holy Office." That is, what was needed was not a theological explanation of individual questions nor condemnations, but the simple proclamation of the good news.[57]

Almost all the French replies contained the criticism that the perspective in the drafts was *ad intra*, focused on internal affairs, and then only in a very restricted form, whereas questions *ad extra*, dealing with matters outside the Church, were given no attention. Yet it was this that people expected, namely, that the Church would work out a healthy and fruitful relationship with the modern world, with science, and with nonbelievers and those of a different faith. These bishops were opting for a perspective that was hardly acknowledged in the preparatory period but that after lengthy discussion at the Council would lead to the Pastoral Constitution *Gaudium et spes*. It must be recognized that the French bishops in particular were highly sensitive to this approach; this was certainly a fruit of the renewal of theology in France during the second third of the twentieth century.

This view is confirmed by the especially voluminous petitions from Charles de Provenchères, Archbishop of Aix,[58] and from Léon Artur Elchinger, Coadjutor Bishop of Strasbourg.[59] Elchinger took up the question of the tasks of the Church in an increasingly nonchristian and secularized world. He asked: "Why must the Church involve itself with the peoples?" He then emphasized that "the Church must seek out people who are searching and lay hold of them where they are, so that it can be a friend to them in the name of God. For this reason the Church must transform the present world. It may not wait for people to come to it, but must go out to them. The Church may not simply reject and refute contemporary atheism as an error, but must bend all its powers to see to it that atheism cannot even arise either among its own children or among other human beings." Elchinger then spoke of the difficulties that Christians face in a world not yet Christian. He raised the question of "spiritual tolerance"; he brought up the connection between the Church and bourgeois society. In an epilogue to his votum he said: "The Church is prepared to purify its behavior and its action as it seeks to find its way

[56] See *AS* App., 90-93.
[57] See *AS* App., 135-43.
[58] See *AS* App., 160-67.
[59] See *AS* App., 173-80.

into the world. It is not trying to dominate but to serve (see Mt 20:25-
28). It intends to instill in people a salutary restlessness and then to pen-
etrate the world like yeast, in order finally to be radiant light and sure
truth in the midst of humanity."[60]

The episcopal conference of Chad sent the pope and the Curia a very
courageous document. The four bishops of the country, Frenchmen by
birth, called for a comprehensive reform of the Church's structures.
They referred to a paper of the bishop of Congo, dated July 4, 1962, in
which catholicity was taken to mean unity in diversity ("Catholicité -
Unité dans la Diversité"), with a series of consequences for the life of
the Church. In particular, on the basis of this principle, Roman central-
ism must be opened to discussion; in light of a theology of the episcopate, the apostolic responsibility of bishops must be more strongly
emphasized and the scope of the local bishop's activity must be
expanded. The variety of the challenges facing the worldwide Church
requires that bishops be able to make independent decisions at the
national and regional levels, especially in regard to the liturgy and the
administration of the sacraments. The bishops of Chad also demanded
that the reform of the Roman Curia be put on the Council's agenda.
Along with a decentralization of what were presently the Curia's competencies, an internationalization of the Curia was also desirable. In
addition, the external image of the Vatican also had to change:

> It is, then, extremely important that Rome inspire respect and an evangeli-
> cal love in the Christian world, not only through the words and acts of the
> Supreme Pontiff but also through the very setting, ceremonials, and other
> external signs that surround the venerable person of the pope and the mem-
> bers of his household. It is desirable that the outward trappings of the
> Roman papacy be more conformed to the simplicity of the gospel and to
> the spirit of poverty and love that ought to shine forth in the Church.[61]

The understanding of the Holy Office must also change; in particular, the
various schools of thought in theology should also be represented there.

Maurice Baudoux, Archbishop of Saint Boniface in Canada, discussed
the seven schemata in great detail. He too found fault especially with the
negative and apologetic tone that prevailed in lengthy sections of the
texts. Their style and manner of expression would not promote the real
goal of the Council.[62] A great many bishops agreed with this judgment.
Cardinal Raul Silva Henriquez, Archbishop of Santiago in Chile,

[60] See AS App., 170f.
[61] AS App., 340-49 at 341f.
[62] AS App., 99-110.

described the first schemata very concisely but aptly as "excessively apologetic," "excessively juridical and scholastic."[63] Abbot Christopher Butler, President of the English Benedictine Congregation, justifiably asked, with regard to the first four schemata: "The words 'we anathematize' are indeed absent, but does not 'we condemn' say practically the same thing?"[64]

The German bishops likewise were not restrained in their criticism of the schemata. Cardinal Frings of Cologne stressed the point that on no account could the schema "on preserving the deposit of faith in its purity" be presented to the Council ("completely unsuitable," "so inadequate..."). The other schemata of the theological commission needed to be radically revised. It was very regrettable that too little heed had been paid to the suggestions of the Central Commission. It was therefore necessary that the schemata be publicly discussed at a general meeting of the Council.[65] The objections of Bishop Hengsbach of Essen were almost identical: "The language of the first four schemata is overly negative, apologetical, and polemical, nor is it in many respects consonant with the present state of theological studies."[66] The German bishops were especially critical of the basic trend of the texts as being insufficiently ecumenical.

Many bishops were greatly disappointed with the first four schemata of the theological commission. "The view of the German bishops was that the dogmatic schemata should be flatly rejected."[67] The German bishops expressed this view during their meeting in Fulda in August, 1962. Cardinal Döpfner made the following remark in his notes: "Theological commission: mostly trouble, very negative." Döpfner characterized the work of this commission as "especially important because basic, but also especially problematic."[68]

In the many letters that reached Cardinal Döpfner the bishops repeatedly stressed the point that "the pastoral requirement does not find satisfactory expression in the texts"; thus Cardinals Suenens, Alfrink, and Liénart.[69] Bishop Elchinger wrote very frequently to Cardinal Döpfner. He wished that there might be closer contact between the German and

[63] *AS* App., 82-85 at 82.
[64] *AS* App., 122-23 at 122.
[65] *AS* App., 74-77.
[66] *AS* App., 211f.
[67] Yves Congar, O.P., "Erinnerungen an einer Episode auf dem II. Vatikanischen Konzil," in Klinger and Wittstadt, *Glaube im Prozess*, 22-32 at 22.
[68] Döpfner papers, Council Archives.
[69] Ibid.

French episcopates and that they might develop a close collaboration at the Council. Elchinger, an Alsatian, offered to mediate between the two. He wrote to Döpfner: "We must not accept the schemata for dogmatic constitutions. Cardinal Tisserant, with whom I spoke recently and who sets great hope on you [Döpfner], feels the same way."[70]

The schemata that had been sent out awakened a holy disquiet in many bishops and hastened the development of an informed opinion. As the Council approached, a group of bishops formed who were concerned by the way things were moving. They intensified contacts with one another; they were in agreement that a Council taking the direction predetermined by the schemata would end in a great disappointment and be a great setback for the Church. In collaboration with open-minded theologians they began to compose new documents that also included the intentions repeatedly expressed by Pope John XXIII. Commentaries on the schemata were prepared and counterproposals drawn up, and these were circulated among the bishops.[71] In this work the collaboration of important cardinals who could speak for the episcopate of an entire country probably played a role that was decisive for the Council. For example, Léger sent Frings a communication addressed to Pope John XXIII, with the request that he, Frings, also sign it.[72] In addition to Döpfner, Cardinals König of Vienna, Alfrink of Utrecht, Montini of Milan, Liénart of Lille, and Suenens of Malines were persuaded to sign this joint statement.[73]

On September 21, 1962, Cardinal Döpfner received a paper written by Yves Congar. This "Draft of an Opening Declaration" contained the points which many French bishops had already brought up in their petitions to Rome; for this reason it is highly likely that this paper had already made the rounds of the French bishops.[74] The idea of an opening proclamation went back to Father Chenu.[75] Congar, who received Chenu's text in mid-September, was in general agreement with the plan

---

[70] Ibid.

[71] See Karl Rahner's letter of September 19, 1962, to Cardinal König, in which he reports conversations with Cardinal Döpfner and a meeting of German theologians with Bishop Volk of Mainz; in *Karl Rahner, Sehnsucht nach dem geheimnisvollen Gott. Profil, Bilder, Texte*, ed. Herbert Vorgrimler (Freiburg i. Br., 1990) 150-65.

[72] See Gilles Routhier, "Les réactions du Cardinal Léger à la préparation de Vatican II," *Revue d'Histoire de l'Eglise de France* 80 (1994) 281-302.

[73] On this matter see Döpfner's Council Archive, August 27, 1962 (Léger to Döpfner) and September 24, 1962 (Döpfner to Alfrink).

[74] See André Duval, "Le message au monde," in Étienne Fouilloux (ed.), *Vatican II commence... Approches francophones* (Leuven, 1993) 105-18.

[75] The information that follows is from Father Y. Congar, *Mon journal du Concile*.

and offered his assistance, but he thought that Chenu's remarks needed improvement from the religious and theological points of view. He passed on word of the plan to Liénart, Alfrink, König, Döpfner, Montini, Frings, and Suenens, to Archbishops Marty of Rheims and Hurley of Durban, and to Bishops Charue, Weber, Ghattas, and Volk. He received approving answers from Liénart, Alfrink, and Döpfner. Liénart thought it would be good to draft a text like that which Chenu had written in French and which Congar had revised but which would be expanded by a paragraph on ecumenism. Congar sent the revised text to Hans Küng, who was to translate it into German; to this end Küng and Congar met in Strasbourg on September 27.

Küng agreed with Congar's criticism of the schemata. He thought that in their present form the four theological schemata were not capable of improvement and that their complete rejection should be urged. In addition, an effort should be made to have the practical schemata discussed first at the Council and only then the theological. To this end Küng and Congar agreed to approach the bishops. They drafted a statement which Küng translated into Latin and Congar sent back. Küng wanted the text to be signed by well-known theologians; Congar urged caution here, lest the impression be given of a second Council of theologians who were influencing the real Council of bishops. Congar also told Küng that he was skeptical of the idea of an assembly of theologians in Rome during the Council. Such an assembly would be acceptable only if theologians of an integralist mind were also represented. No suggestion of a conspiracy of theologians must be given, for it would be a provocation to the scholastic party, who were still a numerical majority.

On October 1 the Latin text of Chenu's document was sent to Liénart, Suenens, Döpfner, and Alfrink who had pronounced themselves in favor of the project. On October 2 Congar gave Weber the French and the Latin versions. Weber told Congar that Bishop Elchinger and he had sent Cardinal Cicognani a request that a step along Chenu's lines be taken.

The German and French bishops appointed Karl Rahner to compose a statement "rejecting the schemata drawn up by the theological commission."[76] The Dutch bishops discussed the schemata at s'- Hertogenbusch. A suggestion was made to compose and distribute to the Council fathers a commentary that would point out the weaknesses of the dogmatic constitutions. A plea was made to give the schema on the liturgy

[76] Marie-Dominique Chenu, O.P., "Ein prophetisches Konzil," in Klinger-Wittstadt, *Glaube im Prozess*, 16-21 at 16.

first place on the agenda. An anonymous commentary was made public that was in fact written by Edward Schillebeeckx. It urged "that the first four schemata be completely rewritten." It suggested that the Council avoid dealing with questions on which the theologians were still in disagreement. In both language and treatment a scholastic style should be avoided, and "the good news should be proclaimed with good will and in a positive way."[77] Latin, English, and French translations of this commentary were prepared.[78]

With regard to the reception of the first seven schemata Suenens reported that together with Döpfner and other cardinals he had written a letter to the pope to make it clear to him that a large part of the schemata should not be distributed to the Council, for he would have to count on their being rejected.

The election of members of the conciliar commissions that was due to take place right at the beginning of the Council was likewise prepared for even before the fathers arrived in Rome. The explanations of Cardinal Liénart and Frings to the general meeting of October 13, in which they rejected the electoral procedure proposed by the Curia, were the result of careful planning. This is made clear by the mention in Father Congar's journal of the fact that Bishop Elchinger had visited him on October 2 and asked him for a list of such bishops as he thought to be the right kind, that is, who would be open-minded.

To a greater extent than researchers have hitherto brought out, important bishops, especially members of the central commission, had been in close contact even before the Council opened, so that the often quite heated clashes of the first session were not the product solely of group dynamics in the course of the Council but were already emerging in the months before the Council, although the fact was still largely concealed from the public. Bishops were showing themselves disillusioned and provoked especially by the highhanded action of the theological commission, which had not allowed the ideas and criticisms even of the Central Commission to influence the schemata except in a limited degree. In this context Döpfner complained "that open-minded theologians, even when consultors, were very much repressed."[79]

Cardinal Bea's Secretariat for Christian Unity played a special role among the institutions of the Curia, for it shared the views of the open-minded

---

[77] J. Jacobs, *Met het oog op een andere Kerk. Katholiek Nederland en de voorbereiding van het Tweede Vaticaans Oecumen. Concilie, 1959-1962* (Baarn, 1986).

[78] See *HK*, September, 1962.

[79] Döpfner papers, Council Archive.

bishops. It was aware of the limitations of the texts provided by the theological commission. For this reason the Secretariat composed a second schema on the sources of revelation, and this was to play as important role in the discussion during the first session.[80] The Secretariat also worked up a schema on the very controversial question of tolerance and religious freedom.[81]

As petitions to the Curia proved and as the discussions in the background attested,[82] there was a growing and widespread desire that the dogmatic schemata be put last and that the Council begin its work with the schema on the liturgy.

Not all the bishops by any means reacted negatively to the first seven schemata that had been sent to them; there were also many positive responses. Here, in the preparatory period, the groups were already emerging that would be more or less in opposition during the Council. Broadly speaking, two trends were to be seen in the thinking of the bishops: one that was based on the Bible and the Fathers and one that was governed more by juridical or, as the case might be, organizational considerations. The radical differences were clearest in the different evaluations of the schema on the sources of revelation. Thus Cardinals Ruffini and Siri, as well as the great majority of the Spanish bishops were supporters of De fontibus. While I do not want to pass any judgment, I must say that in this group problems were seen in an entirely different way; a different view of pastoral activity prevailed; the didactic element was more to the fore. In the view of the Spaniards, the schema was sufficiently pastoral in its style. The Patriarch of Lisbon, Cardinal Manuel Goncalves Cerejeira, likewise regarded the schema an acceptable basis for discussion. So too did Cardinal Jaime de Barros Camara of Rio de Janeiro. These bishops saw in the schema a clear attestation of Catholic teaching; so said, for example, Cardinal James Francis L. McIntyre, Archbishop of Los Angeles. Cardinal Antonio Caggiano of Buenos Aires took the same line. Cardinal Giovanni Urbani, Patriarch of Venice, was another supporter of the schema. In many cases the only argument given was that the text had been prepared by many "learned men."

To sum up: the critics of the schema came chiefly from Germany, France, Belgium, and the Netherlands, while its supporters were

---

[80] See Stakemeier, *Die Konzilskonstitution über die göttliche Offenbarung*, 62-70.

[81] See Bea to Döpfner, July 24, 1962, Döpfner papers, Council Archive.

[82] See, e.g., a letter of Bishop Josef Stangl to Cardinal Döpfner, in which he reports that on October 10 and therefore at the beginning of the Council a proposal was to be submitted by leading personages that the schema on the liturgy be taken first; Döpfner papers, Council Archive.

residents of Spain, Portugal, and Italy. North and South America did not offer a clear picture. Especially in North America, Irish influence probably led to a positive judgment on *De fontibus*.

A difference of views comparable to that seen in the question of the sources of revelation was also to be seen in the question of the use of the vernacular in the liturgy. But many bishops regarded as overly cautious the attitude taken to the use of the vernacular in the liturgy. The schema read: "The use of the Latin language is to be maintained in the western liturgy. But since use of the vernacular has been accepted as very useful in not a few rites, more room is to be made for it in the liturgy, especially in readings and instructions and in a good many prayers and songs."[83] Therefore, Benedikt Reetz, President of the Beuron Congregation of the Benedictines, wanted an addition made to the first sentence of the article: "but a carefully regulated use of the vernacular is to be allowed."[84]

But there were also those who spoke out against too extensive a reform of the liturgy. Geraldo de Proença Sigand, Archbishop of Diamantina in Brazil, wrote:

> 1. A great deal of novelty should not be introduced into the liturgy, lest the Catholic people think that the Church has been in error for a long time. 2. The diversity allowed in various regions should be so structured that the characteristics which the rite possesses everywhere are not destroyed or weakened. The oneness of the Roman liturgy is the source and expression, throughout the world, of a consciousness that allows Catholics from various regions to recognize one other almost instinctively as brothers and sisters and that gives rise to a lively sense of their oneness under the leadership of the pope. Even noncatholics detect and marvel at this profound sentiment.[85]

In the preparatory period the two groups had already made their appearance that would also be in opposition at the Council. Schillebeeckx saw in them two radically different approaches: "The thinking of the one group is essentialist, that is, they think in concepts (we are dealing here with more than simply a way of thinking); the thinking of the other is existential." Because the first group was so strongly anchored in the Curia and in the theology of the Roman schools, it was able, during the period of preparation, to determine the spirit of the systematic schemata. "The chief concern of the preparatory commissions was to formulate the faith as exactly as possible. 'As exactly as possible'

---

[83] *Schemata*, I, 167.
[84] *AS* App., 286-87 at 286.
[85] *AS* App., 158-60 at 159.

meant: to pay no heed to historicity, to define the content of faith as an abstract essence."[86]

Thus it was already clear in the preparatory period that two different ways of thinking, both of which were surely sincere, would clash at the Council: one that was shaped more by the administrative life of the Church, and one that was shaped by pastoral concerns and therefore by the experience and real life of human beings in the present age.[87]

The bishops repeatedly recommended that the liturgy schema be the first to be discussed at the Council, because they thought it to be the one that was most completely worked out and because in their opinion its language, too, struck just the tone they thought needed. The only other schema that won a similar agreement was the one on ecumenism, although here the bishops said plainly that it needed to be completed in important respects. What the bishops suggested in their responses turned out to be the case at the Council: except for *De fontibus* the schemata of the theological commission no longer appeared at all on the agenda. As for *De fontibus*, it gave rise to heated debate in the first session, was removed from the agenda, and had to be completely redone. Apart from the innocuous schema on the communications media, only the main parts of the liturgy schema found a place later on in a conciliar document.

II. POPE JOHN XXIII DURING THE FINAL PERIOD
BEFORE THE OPENING OF THE COUNCIL

1. *Various Statements and Audiences*

The Second Vatican Council was John XXIII's Council. He initiated it; he determined the emphases that would be decisive for the course taken by the Council. In so doing, he was not the victim of a superficial activism; his desire was for a spiritual atmosphere of love and readiness for reconciliation. He communicated a sense of great openness about the coming Council, as well as a special trust in the working of the Holy Spirit.

This outlook found expression especially in the entries he made in his spiritual journal. During the months before the Council John XXIII

---

[86] E. Schillebeeckx, *Die Signatur des Zweiten Vatikanums. Rückblick nach drei Sitzungsperioden* (Vienna-Freiburg-Basel, 1965) 41f.

[87] See Döpfner papers, Council Archives.

endeavored in two ways to find the right path for the Council. In prayer and inner contemplation he looked for spiritual guidance; at the same time, however, he did not cut himself off from others, but tried, through living contact with them, to gain a sense of their cares and needs but also of their hopes. Interior listening and exterior listening gave Roncalli's spiritual life an indivisible unity; he heard God's call in the words of sacred scripture and in his contacts with his fellow human beings.

Roncalli himself described this twofold orientation:

> This retirement to Castel Gandolfo for my usual, and rather better orga-nized, work, still concerned with the daily occurrences in the life of Holy Church, has enabled me to follow the preparatory work for the Council. The large Audiences were very useful for this purpose. They were perhaps too crowded, as they included representatives from every country of the world, but full of spiritual and religious fervor, and a sincere and pious enthusiasm which is edifying and encourages optimism.[88]

On June 20, 1962, the activity of the Central Preparatory Commission came to an end. John XXIII praised its work and also expressed his hap-piness with it. But in his words to the members of the Central Commis-sion the pope said hardly anything about their work nor did he discuss questions about the doctrine and content of the texts prepared for the Council. He did express respect for what they had accomplished: "What more could have been looked for, considering the capabilities of human nature, augmented as they are by God's abundant, inestimable grace?"[89] He did not criticize anyone and thereby exclude ideas and traditions, for then he would have himself betrayed his own conception of the unity of all Catholics and would have given rise to new confrontations. He wanted to tear down walls; he was obliged therefore not to work "within a system" and not to place himself on the level of one or other theolog-ical trend, but to remain aloof from these trends.

The address just cited showed once again that the pope's main emphases were different and that he did not regard as centrally important the prepared schemata with their unquestionable erudition. He was turn-ing people's eyes to other dimensions, not to say the real dimensions of faith. Christian truth does not bear witness to itself through dogmas and theoretical statements. John saw the next three months before the opening of the Council as the time, first and foremost, for the bishops "to collect

---

[88] Pope John XXIII, *Journal of a Soul*, trans. D. White (Image Books; Garden City, NY: Doubleday, 1980) 344.

[89] *AAS* 54 (1962) 461-66 at 462; *ADP*, I, 261-65 at 262; translation in *TPS* 8 (1962-63) 182-87 at 183.

your thoughts" (*apti ad animos colligendos*).[90] This period was to be a time for seeking in the sacred scriptures the center of faith and the sustaining roots of a Christian life. He was here saying, indirectly, that this center cannot be found by intellectual discussion in the form of theological treatises. He said, therefore:

> We wish you, during this time of preparation for the Council — clearly an event of the highest order and a singular privilege of divine providence — to read each day a few pages of St. John's Gospel and to meditate on them for a while. Consider the first chapter. There it is as though the heavens are opened for us and we are allowed to contemplate the mystery of God's Word. It is as though the whole earth reverberated to the sound of John the Baptist's preaching, heralding the Lord's coming. Indeed, the entire Gospel narrative is charged with his witness, the austerities that went with it, his words and his blood. Consider the tenth chapter, containing the parable of the Good Shepherd...
> Consider, too, those last words of our Lord recorded in chapters 14, 15, 16 and 17, and especially His final prayer in chapter 17: *ut unum sint*, — that they may be one.[91]

Almost all of the pope's activities during the last three months before the Council — audiences, addresses, prayers — offered similar inducements: he wanted the Council to make a significant contribution to the renewal of Christian life and to facilitate a deepening of the Christian spirit. To this end he regarded the personal sanctification of each individual, beginning with the pope himself and including all the faithful, as the primary prerequisite.

An expression of his fundamental attitude was to be found in the Encyclical *Paenitentiam agere* of July 1, 1962. In this encyclical he earnestly summoned Catholics to the Council, for which he said that prayer and penance were the best preparation. Only if hearts were changed could the Council become a new and fruitful breakthrough in the service of God's kingdom: "If each person does everything in his or her power, Christians can contribute greatly to a happy and successful outcome of this Second Ecumenical Council of the Vatican, which has for its purpose to lend a new luster to Christian life."[92]

On July 2, the pope wrote to religious sisters, urging them to offer their prayers and ascetical practices for the successful outcome of the coming Council. He saw in the spirit of the evangelical counsels the most important basis for a following of Christ. At the end he spoke again

---

[90] *AAS* 54 (1962) 463; *ADP*, I, 262; *TPS* 8 (1962-63) 183.
[91] *AAS* 54 (1962) 465; *ADP*, I, 264; *TPS* 8 (1963-63) 185-86.
[92] *ADP*, I, 282.

of the Council, saying: "On the eve of the Second Vatican Council the Church has called all the faithful, urging each of them to an act of participation, witness, and courageous activity."[93]

This call to a religious renewal was insufficient for many of the faithful, and a certain dissatisfaction spread abroad, once it seemed that original expectations were not to be fulfilled. Skepticism grew, since not only "had the general public not been suitably informed about the preparation," but in addition "too little had been done to come to grips with the wealth of suggestions, ideas, and recommendations from the members of the Church and to take account of them in composing the drafts."[94]

The behavior of the Curia and especially of the Holy Office seemed to betray the great hopes for an opening up of the Church. We may think here, for example, of the attempts not only to exclude the representatives of a forward-looking theology from the work of preparation but even to subject them to increased censure. This was a sign of a fearful, defensive attitude toward something new that was emerging and "that seemed to be heralded in the increasingly lively discussion going on within the Church, in the desires expressed by quite a few bishops and part of the clergy before the Council, and especially in the many comments, written and oral, of Catholic laypersons, especially in the countries of Central Europe."[95] Shortly before the Council Cardinal König felt "a great embarrassment at the mountain of documents and at the practical impossibility for the Council to study them seriously."[96]

The steps taken by the Curia did not originate with Pope John XXIII, but he did patiently accept them. "Pope John embraced the whole world in his thoughts and prayers. From time to time he was made aware of underhand maneuvers taking place before his eyes. He followed St. Bernard's basic principle: 'See everything, turn a blind eye to much, and correct a little.'"[97]

John XXIII's "leadership style" was subtler and gentler than people had been accustomed to from popes; as result they repeatedly got the impression that he allowed himself to be carried along by opinions and influences or that he would lose sight of the broad picture. Roncalli knew how to speak between the lines and to develop his ideas while

---

[93] *ADP*, I, 284-93 at 292.

[94] David Andreas Seeber, *Das Zweite Vaticanum. Konzil des Übergangs* (Freiburg i. Br., 1966) 62.

[95] Ibid., 67.

[96] Cardinal Franz König, *Where is the Church Heading?*, trans. T. Kala (Middlegreen, 1986) 24.

[97] See Hebblethwaite, *Pope John XXIII*, 339.

trusting that in the long haul they would prove convincing. Giuseppe
Alberigo has repeatedly emphasized this characteristic of John XXIII:

> He avoided polemics and harsh expressions, but he certainly did not refrain
> from communicating his own viewpoints and making responsible and care-
> ful judgments. This prefatory remark must be kept in mind when speaking
> of "the essentially pastoral goals of the Council," since these were often,
> then as now, regarded as lacking any specifically theological character. On
> the contrary, one must realize that for Pope Roncalli the description was a
> way both of distancing himself from the doctrinal goals (definitions) or
> condemnations or ideological purposes that came spontaneously to mind
> for many people, and of underscoring the urgent need of a commitment to
> a renewal of the spirit and ways in which the Church bears witness and
> exercises her evangelical presence in history.[98]

Roncalli tried always to emphasize what unites and binds and so to
find a new basis for coexistence that would be valid both within the
Church and in relation to all people. Just a day before he went to Castel
Gandolofo (July 30, 1962) he received Shizuka Matsubara, head of a
Shinto temple in Kyoto, Japan. He wrote of this visit in his journal: "It
gave me great satisfaction to receive a visit marked by such kindness
and courtesy... It pleased me greatly to speak of the sympathy I felt for
Japan from my earliest years... The pope likes to feel united with all the
upright and honorable souls on earth, to whatever nation they belong, in
a spirit of respect, understanding, and peace."[99]

On July 3, 1962 John XXIII received President Antonio Segni. During this audience he made a statement about relations between Church
and state: "The pope in the Vatican is one thing, the President in the
Quirinale is another."[100] The pope emphasized his own worldwide
vision of the Christian task as compared with the more limited perspective of the president: "All the nations of the earth, all decent and receptive souls are invited to cooperate in this great undertaking of global
restoration in the gleaming light not of material weapons of destruction
but of the eternal principles of the Christian order as this is understood,
reconstructed, and applied to the varying conditions of peoples and families." He made clear the point at which the Council was to enter the
scene and what message it must proclaim:

> You know that a year ago, by way of approach to the work of the Council,
> We published an important document on social matters, one that continues

---

[98] Giuseppe Alberigo, "Giovanni XXIII e il Vaticano II," in G. Alberigo (ed.), *Papa
Giovanni* (Rome-Bari, 1987) 215-16.

[99] Loris Capovilla, *Ite Missa Est* (Padua-Bergamo, 1983) 188.

[100] Cited in Hebblethwaite, *Pope John XXIII*, 355, 366.

very successfully to elicit in all the countries of the world fervent agreement and applause. *Mater et Magistra* calls attention to problems of justice
and social charity, and it proposes agreements and solutions that are a
preparation and foretaste of very important principles that deserve to be
proclaimed by a Council.[101]

No statement of the pope failed to refer to the Council. Everyone was
asked to pray for the Council, that is, in the final analysis, to view the
Council existentially and even to identify with it. The world-transform-
ing power of the Spirit was to be rediscovered and made fruitful through
prayer and personal sanctification.[102] The intention of the pope during
the months before the Council was summed up in his radio message to
the Deutscher Katholikentag in Hannover: "To the extent that you
follow Christ and are united among yourselves, the ways of divine providence will be made level and the breath of the Holy Spirit will prepare
'a new heaven and a new earth' everywhere in the world."[103] Here are
the key words and phrases that were the focus of the pope's thoughts and
desires: The following of Christ and internal unity; Holy Spirit and
Church; Church and vocation.

At the end of July the pope went to Castel Gandolfo, where he studied the texts drafted for the Council. He wanted to set an example for the
bishops, since he was requiring the same of them. John XXIII undoubtedly distanced himself from the schemata that had been composed. Like
many bishops he felt that they were not in keeping with the pastoral aim
of the Council. Thus he wrote with regard to the schema "That all may
be one": "And, in general, this way of taking a draft made up of elementary concepts and principles and decorating it with sentences from

---

[101] *AAS* 54 (1962) 522; *ADP*, I, 293f.

[102] The pope wrote to Cardinal Cento, his representative at a jubilee celebration of the
Carmelites: "In addition, this fervent charity will lead the entire Teresian family to be
concerned for the good and advancement of the Church and therefore, through special
prayers and voluntary sacrifices, to win for it the divine forbearance, thanks to which
there may arise from the coming Second Ecumenical Vatican Council a new spring, the
harbinger of a greater spiritual beauty" (July 16, 1962; *AAS* 54 [1962] 569-70; *ADP*, I,
300). See especially *Prayers to be Offered for the Council* (July 18, 1962; *ADP*, I, 300)
and *Prayer for the Success of the Council* (July 24, 1962; *ADP*, I, 301). On August 1,
1962, the pope spoke to acolytes: Make your contribution "to a good outcome for the
Council"; what he had in mind was "fervent religious piety, holiness of life" (*ADP*, I,
304). On the anniversary of his priestly ordination, August 10, 1962, the pope spoke at
Castel Gandolfo to the students of various seminaries and the Brothers of various orders
and congregations and said the following, among other things: "The first step toward the
plan for an ecumenical Council arose from the desire that the grace of the Lord should be
more effectively operative within the Catholic Church and in the broad, universal horizons which Providence has marked out for it and made known to it" (*ADP*, I, 330).

[103] *ADP*, I, 335; *AAS* 54 (1962) 591-94 at 594.

the Bible, with ready citations from scripture that could also be applied to other themes than those being discussed, causes confusion in simple minds of average intellectual ability, such as the majority of good Christians are."[104]

Cardinal Suenens likewise reported the pope's concerns. He had an audience at Castel Gandolfo and wrote as follows: "That same morning he also said to me: 'I know what my part in the Council will be... it will be to suffer.' I did not know what kind of suffering he had in mind; I think he was referring to the struggle he would have to engage in to keep those around him from reining in the Council or blocking it."[105]

Such meetings and his own analysis of the schemata strengthened the pope's conviction that the Council had to find a new form of proclamation that would not be content to issue lengthy explanations which would not really make contact with the modern world. All the more, then, did the pope emphasize his goals. On September 2, 1962, he spoke to 350 young architects from fifteen European countries. He took that rather unimportant occasion to abandon a defensive posture and to make clear his own theological and pastoral guidelines, even, to some degree, in opposition to the thinking of the Roman and curial tradition:

> The purpose of the Council is to raise a new edifice on the foundations laid in the course of history, using the divine and human means that the Church has at its disposal... Making its own the words of John the Baptist, which Jesus repeated: "Repent, for the kingdom of heaven is at hand" (Mt 3:2; 4:17), the Council will expand the scope of charity to meet the varied needs of peoples and will present the message of Christ to them in a clearer way. This will require of people a conversion of heart, a new spiritual strength, and an enlightened and active faith.[106]

Charity as the expression of a lived faith was more important to Roncalli than a theoretical system of doctrines. These ideas were, as it were, a prelude to the pope's radio message of September 11, 1962, in which he expressed these convictions.

2. The Radio Message of September 11, 1962

The pope began by saying: "The great anticipation of the ecumenical Council, just a month away from its official opening, is shining in the eyes and the hearts of all the children of the holy and blessed Catholic

---

[104] *Lettere 1958-1963*, 546; Alberigo, "Giovanni XXIII e il Vaticano II," 238.
[105] Léon Joseph Cardinal Suenens, *Souvenirs et Espérances* (1991) 89.
[106] *AAS* 54 (1962) 667-69; *ADP*, I, 338-39.

Church."[107] The pope let it be known, once again, that he was satisfied with the preparation for the Council, but he also pointed out that the "wealth of doctrinal and pastoral material" that had been gathered together only provided "themes" for the Council fathers and had not by any means decided anything.

John XXIII attached great hopes to the beginning of the Council. "Considered in its spiritual preparation, the Ecumenical Council, a few weeks before it meets, seems to deserve that invitation of our Lord: '... When their buds [those of the fig tree and other trees] burst open... know that the kingdom of God is near.'"[108] It is the kingdom of God that orients the Church and gives it its meaning. It also sets the standard for the Council: "This phrase, 'Kingdom of God' expresses fully and precisely the work of the Council. 'Kingdom of God' means and is in reality the Church of Christ, one, holy, catholic, and apostolic, the one which Jesus, the Word of God made man, founded and which for twenty centuries he has preserved, just as still today he gives her life by his presence and his grace."[109]

Further on, the pope speaks of the perennial interior vitality of the Church. He does not view the Church as an abstraction or an institution, for it lives "in every chosen soul."[110] Referring to the symbolism of the Easter candle, he says: "At one point in the liturgy, see how his name resounds: '*Lumen Christi* [Light of Christ].'" He follows this remark with characteristic exclamations that would later on become to some extent guidelines for the Council: "*Lumen Christi, lumen Ecclesiae, lumen gentium* [Light of Christ, light of the Church, light of the nations]."[111] In his message the pope adopts a strong Christological emphasis: "What in fact has an Ecumenical Council ever been but the renewing of this encounter with the face of the risen Jesus, glorious and immortal King, shining upon the whole Church, for the salvation, joy, and splendor of the human race?"[112] It is this religious conviction that gives rise to the pope's prevailing mood, one that was to bear fruit in the

---

[107] Italian original: *AAS* 54 (1962) 678-85; *ADP*, I, 348-55. English translation in *Council Daybook Vatican II. Session 1, Oct. 11 to Dec. 8, 1962; Session 2, Sept. 29 to Dec. 4, 1963*, ed. F. Anderson (Washington, D.C.: National Catholic Welfare Conference, 1964) 18 [this translation has been emended at several points. — Tr.].

[108] *Council Daybook*, 18.

[109] Ibid. John XXIII here identifies the Church to a remarkable degree with the kingdom of God; he avoids this in his later utterances (see Giuseppe Ruggieri, "Appunti per una teologia di papa Roncalli," in *Papa Giovanni*, 245-271.

[110] Ibid.

[111] Ibid.

[112] Ibid.

Council: "The new Ecumenical Council wishes to be true joy for the universal Church of Christ."

He then moves on the several reasons for the calling of the Council. For the division of the Council's work the pope here uses the distinction between *ad intra* and *ad extra*, which probably goes back to the plan of Cardinal Suenens for the Council. In connection with the *ad intra* he says: "The Council's reason for existence... is the continuation, or better the most energetic revival, of the response of the whole world to the testament of the Lord... The Church wishes to be sought again as she is, in her internal structure — vitality *ad intra*." The remarkable thing about these statements is that Roncalli thinks of the Church not in static or juridical, but dynamic and historico-processual categories.

But the pope avoids, quite deliberately in all likelihood, the question of how the essence of the Church is to be further described theologically. He is not interested in a bloodless theory or a concept of the Church. He quickly shifts from the interior aspect of the Church to its external activity, since only here does the reign of God become visible and alive, and the message of the gospel concrete.

> Considered in the relations of her vitality *ad extra*, that is, the Church facing the needs and demands of peoples — those human situations which turn them instead to appreciate and enjoy the things of earth — the Church considers it her duty to do justice to her responsibilities by her teaching... It is from this sense of responsibility before the duties of the Christian called to live as a man among men, as a Christian among Christians, that all the others, although not Christians in fact, ought to feel themselves drawn by good example to become Christians.[113]

Here, once again, formulations and ideas are brought to bear that were nourished by the experiences of Roncalli's life; deeply impressed convictions here find utterance. Thus he had already written, as Vatican representative in Bulgaria: "Let us let go of the old disputes and see to it that we make people good by our example."[114]

In the desire for "love" and "peace" the pope sees at work the yearning of mankind, but also a common mission, a spirit that binds all humanity together. Thus he says in the message of September 11: "Man seeks... love... He aspires and feels the duty to live in peace... He is sensitive to the attractions of the spirit... "[115] Given this starting point, it

---

[113] Ibid., 19.

[114] Cited in Francesca Della Salda, "Oboedientia et Pax: Roncalli in Bulgaria," Die Erfahrungen Roncallis in Bulgarien (1925-1934)," *CrSt* 8 (1987) 23.

[115] *Council Daybook*, 19.

follows that one goal of the Council is to offer, "in clear language, solutions demanded by the dignity of man and of his Christian vocation."[116] The pope then lists the main guiding ideas: "The fundamental equality of all peoples in the exercise of rights and duties within the entire family of nations; the strenuous defence of the sacred character of matrimony, which imposes on spouses a conscious and generous love."

The pope sees at work everywhere in the modern world concepts that contradict the Church — indifferentism, denial of God and a supernatural order, exaggerated individualism that does not acknowledge the person's responsibility for the neighbor. He does not condemn them, however, but says only that the voice of the Church must make itself heard once again; in this context he refers to his encyclical *Mater et Magistra*. But the voice of the Church is heard only when the Church cares about people and takes up their defense and not the defense of its own institutional interests. In this connection, the pope makes these impressive points: "Confronted with the undeveloped countries, the Church presents itself as it is and wishes to be, as the Church of all, and particularly as the Church of the poor (*la chiesa dei poveri*)"; "The miseries of social life which cry for vengeance in the sight of God: all this must be recalled and deplored." All people, but especially Christians, are exhorted to solidarity with one another. The social and communitarian sense "which is intrinsic to authentic Christianity... must be vigorously affirmed."

The discourse also addresses the relationship between Church and state. Here the Church claims the right to religious freedom, "which is not simply freedom of worship." The Church must demand this freedom in order to "place man upon the path of truth. Truth and freedom are the building-stones upon which human civilization is raised." John XXIII here calls freedom a positive value; this was a view that still met with resentment in curial circles and also gave rise to intense controversy at the Council.

The pope turns again to the subject of "peace." He speaks with a great intensity that is the result of his experiences; his image of the human person and the Church emerge clearly: "Mothers and fathers of families detest war. The Church, mother of all without distinction, will again raise that cry which rises from the depths of the ages and from Bethlehem, and from there on Calvary, that it may spread abroad in a prayerful precept of peace, a peace that prevents armed conflicts, a peace

---

[116] Ibid.

that must have its roots and its guarantee in the heart of every man."[117] It must be the aim of the Council "to cooperate in the triumph of peace, thus to make earthly existence more noble, more just and more deserving for all." The Council must develop "the concept of peace, not only in its negative expression... but much more in its positive demands, which require of every man a knowledge and constant practice of his own duties."[118]

In these remarks the pope gives expression to the questions that were very much on his own mind. He was aware that the Church had to review its tasks and to set different emphases in its preaching in the future. But in his case the task of renewing and improving the world had theological and religious motives. This can be seen when he takes up this theme again at the end of the radio message. He alludes to the seventeenth chapter of St. John's gospel: "'That all may be one.' 'One': one in thought, word, and work."[119] The Council must give expression to this vision; everything else is secondary and unimportant by comparison. The desire for the union of brothers and sisters is decisive for the pope. He ends his message by repeating his earlier exclamation: "*Lumen Christi, Deo gratias*. This light shines and will shine on for centuries: '*Lumen Christi, Ecclesia Christi, lumen gentium.*'"[120]

After the tensions of the preparatory period the radio message gave a clear direction for the Council: "Of fundamental importance is what is said about the very reason for the Council's being held: at issue is 'the response of the whole world to the testament of the Lord' which he left us when he said: 'Go, teach all nations...' The purpose of the Council is, therefore, evangelization."[121]

The importance of the radio message was underscored by, for example, the reaction of Father M.-D. Chenu, O.P., who wanted to draft a conciliar message to the world that would be modelled on the pope's address ("Plan for an Opening Statement in the form of a 'Message' inspired by the Message of His Holiness John XXIII on September 11, 1962").

Regarding the origin of the text of the radio message Henri de Riedmatten, O.P., claimed in 1967 that it "was to a great extent inspired by Cardinal Suenens' memorandum," so much so that the next day the pope gave Cardinal Suenens a gift of his books as a sign of his approval

---

[117] Ibid., 19-20.

[118] Ibid., 20.

[119] Ibid.

[120] Ibid., 20-21.

[121] Ludwig Kaufmann and Nikolaus Klein, *Johannes XXIII. Prophetie im Vermächtnis* (Fribourg-Brig, 1990) 68.

and gratitude.[122] This influence did not mean, however, that the message did not bear the special stamp of the pope. Hebblethwaite rightly insists: "But 'to a very large extent inspired' does not mean that Pope John XXIII simply copied down a Suenens text; as was his practice with a draft that he liked, he thought it through, made it his own, and added personal touches. One effect of this collaboration was that from now on Cardinal Suenens became still closer to Pope John."[123] Suenens himself had this to say about the episode: In the radio message the pope described the Council as "a continuation of our Lord's commandment: 'Go, teach all nations, baptize them in the name of the Father, of the Son, of the Holy Spirit; teach them to observe all that I have commanded you" (Mt 28:19-20).' These words formed the subject matter of the plan."[124]

In language and content the radio message was very much Roncalli's own work. He devoted himself for weeks to the manuscript of the address and consciously and deliberately set out emphases that were completely different from those in the schemata of the preparatory commissions. The radio message was in contrast to the theological and dogmatic rigidity of texts composed in traditional Roman and curial language. Without directly opposing the schemata, John XXIII did respond to them by opening up a different perspective for the Council. Thus the Church of the poor did not appear as a topic in any of the drafts, which were composed almost exclusively by first-world theologians. Furthermore, the pope wanted this Council, which was meeting seventeen years after the end of the Second World War, to be more "universal" than all the preceding Councils and therefore truly catholic.[125] His understanding of catholicity emerged with special clarity in the way in which he combined the *ad intra* and *ad extra* points of view and identified them with Peter, the guarantor of order and institutional continuity, and Paul, who devoted himself to all "who had not yet received the gospel." The pope saw catholicity ensured by the union of the Petrine and the Pauline heritages; both points of view had to be brought out at the Council. John XXIII also made it clear where the Roman Church had to catch up when he dealt only briefly with the

---

[122] Riedmatten is cited in Hebblethwaite, *Pope John XXIII*, 424; Suenens, *Souvenirs et Espérances*, 70f.

[123] Hebblethwaite, *Pope John XXIII*, 424.

[124] Léon-Josef Cardinal Suenens, "A Plan for the Whole Council," in *Vatican II Revisited* (Minneapolis, 1986) 90.

[125] Angelina Alberigo and Giuseppe Alberigo, *Giovanni XXIII. Profezia nella fideltà* (Brescia, 1978) 357.

internal manifestations of the Church's life and more extensively with its external manifestations: the need of a solution to the social question, the relationship between Church and state, the right to religious freedom, justice and peace.

In his memorable address of October 11, 1962, John XXIII again picked up the themes of the radio address of September 11. The assembled Council fathers responded to the pope's appeal in their first conciliar message to the world, in which they expressed their readiness to promote peace and justice through a love that serves. Lines can undoubtedly be traced leading from passages in the September 11 radio message to *Gaudium et spes*.

That the pope's message was perceived as a special sign of hope is shown by the special echo it found in the world press. The Roman daily, *Il Tempo*, gave a detailed report of the radio message, in which it emphasized especially the references to the human race as a whole. The pope was addressing the problems of humanity and its longing for freedom, peace, and justice. As a result, the Council would have a broader scope. It was not only Catholics who would be involved, but all human beings of good will. The Christian Democratic paper, *Il Popolo*, stressed the admirable combination of the two areas of activity of the Church as proclaimer of truth and helper in gaining mastery of earthly life.

Another newspaper, *L'Italia*, published the complete text of the pope's address. In a commentary, Giancarlo Zizola appraised the speech as a "straightforward introduction to the Council." It was also clear that the pope's words raised new expectations that out of a sense of pastoral responsibility, the Council would take seriously the problems of humanity.

Left-leaning and socialist Italian newspapers also dealt with the radio message. Although in these cases the interior distance from the Catholic world remained very perceptible, the concerns listed by the pope were recognized as being, in the social and cultural spheres, a basis for joint action by means of which ancient prejudices might be overcome.[126]

It was not only Christians but all people of good will who were inspired to hope by the message. It showed that in the pope's eyes peace was more than a moral imperative or a heavenly utopia, it was the very essence of Christianity. The message also showed that Roncalli's optimism sprang from his faith. He realized that since Vatican I Rome had come disturbingly close to self-isolation, and in the message he broke free of this restricted vision because he knew that Christianity is meant

[126] See the lead-article in *Avanti*, September 13, 1962; *Paese-Sera*, September 12-13, 1962.

for all. Here one cannot help but think of Teilhard de Chardin, in whose view the coming age will be marked by a universal human conscious-ness. The Christian anticipates that there will be a single human race, the people of God, as part of the plan of salvation in which the incarnate divine Son is the center of salvation history.

John XXIII confirmed his conception of the Council in various addresses during the period remaining before its opening. On September 16, 1962, the pope told young people that his radio message of a few days earlier had had for its motto "The Church of Christ, light of the nations," "as if to open the doors of the Council."[127] The main theme of the general audience of September 19 was again "Looking forward to the celebration of the Council."[128] "Only a few weeks separate us from the great event that will begin on October 11 and will perhaps be con-tinued, after a short interval, in the coming year."[129] The pope ended his address with the remark that at this historic moment forces were being mobilized to intensify prayer and sacrifice. On September 23 the pope visited the church of Christ the King where he stressed the point that the Council would concern itself with truth, goodness, and peace, values which everyone desires. The Council was to be "a glorification, a tri-umph, of truth, goodness, and peace. That is the pope's desire."[130]

3. *Spiritual Preparation*

In the final period before the beginning of the Council John XXIII never wearied of asking for prayer and holiness. He himself regarded the prepa-ration for the Council as primarily a spiritual exercise for acquiring the capacity for hearing the call of the Spirit. He wanted to keep up a dialogue with himself and with the history and tradition of the Church, to which he wished to remain faithful. It is this purpose that explains his visit to the tomb of Cardinal Tardini, his Secretary of State, on the first anniversary of his death, July 30, 1962,[131] and to the tombs of his immediate predecessors in the crypt of St. Peter's on September 23, 1962[132]; he wanted to pray and meditate there in order to see clearly the way he should follow.

On September 9, 1962, the pope addressed the rectors of seminaries, telling them that this meeting came just before the week of his retreat, in

---

[127] *ADP*, I, 357-58 at 357.
[128] Ibid., 359-61.
[129] Ibid., 359.
[130] Ibid., 363.
[131] Ibid., 303.
[132] Ibid., 363.

which he intended to prepare for the opening of the ecumenical Council.[133] On September 10 he wrote in his journal:

> At an early hour and in silence I accompanied Msgr. Loris Capovilla as he carried the Blessed Sacrament from the Vatican chapel to the chapel of the Torre San Giovanni, where I joyfully began my private pre-conciliar retreat. This retreat began with great fervor last night during the almost unexpected visit I agreed to make to the church of Santa Maria degli Angeli. This was to have been a private visit, but the great concourse of people turned it into a most impressive occasion.
>
> Although my soul is well disposed for this retreat I am making in preparation for the Council, present circumstances compel me to make inevitable alterations to the usual meditations on these Exercises. This time everything is with the intention of preparing the Pope's soul for the Council: everything, including the preparation of the opening speech which the whole world gathered in Rome awaits, just as it listened most attentively to the speech which was broadcast this very evening to the whole world.[134]

On September 15 John XXIII finished his retreat in Torre San Giovanni. In his journal he wrote: "My retreat, with only Father Ciappi and Msgr. Cavagna to see me, in immediate and personal preparation for the Council, today comes to an end, although I have not been able to use it, as I wished, solely and entirely for the purpose I had set myself."[135]

The following entry also speaks of the pope's spiritual state:

> But it [the retreat] set a good example; it prevented me from being distracted by any exterior matters, business, literature or anything else. It was a more intense effort to find union with the Lord, in prayers, thoughts, and a calm and determined will. It leaves me with an increased fervor in my heart for all that concerns the substance of my ministry and my apostolic mandate. Lord Jesus, supply what I lack. "Lord, you know all; you know that I love you."[136]

These words show that he was prepared, in the highest possible measure, for the Council. He "was not going to panic if it took an unforeseen turn."[137]

After his retreat in Torre San Giovanni the pope submitted to a thorough medical checkup. The results were ready on September 23, but were never made public. In his chronology, which appeared in 1970, Capovilla had this brief notation for September 23, 1962: "First manifestation of the serious illness that threatened his health."[138]

---

[133] Ibid., 342.

[134] Pope John XXIII, *Journal of a Soul*, 345-46.

[135] Ibid., 348.

[136] Ibid.

[137] Hebblethwaite, *Pope John XXIII*, 424.

[138] Loris Capovilla, *Quindici Letture* (Rome, 1970) 760.

The pope's life was thus in danger, but he chose to act "as if" nothing were wrong. "Pope John's remark that his contribution to the Council would be suffering took on a deeper and more poignant meaning... It also gave him the freedom that came from knowing that, humanly speaking, he had nothing more to lose."[139]

In September, 1962, the pope wrote in his journal: "After three years of preparation, certainly laborious but also joyful and serene, we are now on the slopes of the sacred mountain."[140] Later on, this entry took on a double meaning: it could refer to the preparations for the Council and signify that these were successful to the point that the Council could now begin. On the other hand, it could also refer to the pope's health. In speaking of suffering to Cardinal Suenens he had a premonition of his fatal illness. Thus the final sentence in the journal read: "May the Lord give us strength to bring everything to a successful conclusion!"[141]

It was probably as a result of some such premonition that on August 2, 1962, the pope composed a *Motu proprio* dealing with the *sede vacante* period. He decided that no photographs should be taken of him on his deathbed; that only those persons should be admitted to the crypt who had an indispensable part to play in the burial; and that during this period no one should live in the papal apartments.[142] The text, *Summi Pontificis electio*, was published on September 5, 1962.[143]

Despite the first signs of his illness and coming death, the pope continued his rigorous work for the Council. He drafted his radio message and reflected on his opening address at the Council, which would be the most important speech of his life; in other words, he completed his program without heed for his health.

Another element in the pope's spiritual preparation was his pilgrimage to Loreto and Assisi on October 4, 1962. This was the first time since 1870 that a pope officially left Rome. At 6.30 the pope boarded the presidential train. At the station in Trastevere Premier Amintore Fanfani joined him on board. President Antonio Segni was waiting for him in Loreto. Thus the event also had a political significance in Italy. The pope was enthusiastically greeted by large crowds at every station.

The first goal of the journey, the Marian pilgrimage site in Loreto, drew some criticism, because this act of special devotion to Mary might

---

[139] Hebblethwaite, *Pope John XXIII*, 425.
[140] *Journal of a Soul*, 349.
[141] Ibid.
[142] Loris Capovilla (ed.), *Giovanni XXIII. Lettere 1958-1963* (Rome, 1978) 549.
[143] *AAS* 54 (1962) 632ff.

be interpreted as hindering ecumenical dialogue. Both Loreto and Assisi played an important part in the story of his life, for he had visited these places in 1900 before travelling to Rome on the occasion of the Holy Year. Then came a switch that was important for his future life: he received a scholarship for studying theology in Rome, with the result that he was snatched from the intimacy and security of Bergamo and began a new phase of his development. Loreto thus meant that Roncalli was confronted with the story of his own life. The pilgrimage offered a chance to reflect on the stages of his life and the convictions that had grown out of them. Here he would find the strength to continue perseveringly on the way that he knew was right.

In his homily at Loreto he took the incarnation of the Word as one of his themes and connected it with one of his theological and therefore pastoral goals when he spoke of the union of heaven and earth, thus transcending not only traditional distinctions between the sacred and the secular but also materialistic philosophies of life and purely immanent views of the world. In this homily he enhanced the value of human work in particular by seeing it as a collaboration with God the Creator. He linked in a convincing way three points: incarnation, family, and work.[144]

The special significance of the visit to Assisi was appreciated throughout the world. If the Council was to give prominence to the "Church of the poor," as the pope had indicated in his radio address of September 11, then Francis of Assisi was its appropriate patron. In his sermon at Assisi the pope linked poverty and peace: Only if the good and beautiful things that providence has put in this world are justly distributed can there be true peace. He uttered this moving apostrophe: "O holy city of Assisi, you are renowned throughout the whole world simply for having given birth to the Poverello, your Saint of wholly seraphic fervor! May you understand the privilege that is yours and offer the nations the spectacle of a fidelity to the Christian tradition that will be for you a further reason for authentic and undying honor."[145]

If we compare Francis of Assisi, the great reformer of the medieval Church, with John XXIII, reformer of the contemporary Church, it is certainly possible to see a spiritual affinity between the two men. Both reached an almost frightening closeness to Jesus. They did not engage in a scornful flight from the world; their program was one of giving and affirmation. The piety of each man sprang from an encounter with the crucified Jesus and a decision for him. It is not hard to understand that

[144] See *ADP*, I, 373-78.
[145] Ibid., 378-81 at 381.

in Assisi John XXIII found direction for the Council through which he desired to bring Christianity to the world.

The pope's spiritual preparation concluded with a procession from the Liberian Basilica to the Lateran Basilica that was devoted to prayer for reconciliation and for the Holy Spirit. The pope invoked "the perennial giver of life, the supreme organizer of Holy Church: the Holy Spirit."[146] Here it was made clear once again what the pope hoped for from the Council: his determining desire was that the Council should become a "new Pentecost."

4. *The Pope and Organizational Preparations*

During a general audience in St. Peter's on July 4, 1962, the pope mentioned that the work, begun in May, 1962, of turning the basilica into a Council hall was progressing well.[147] On September 23, he himself visited St. Peter's and inspected the almost completed technical preparations.[148] The *Motu proprio, Appropinquante Concilio*, issued on August 6 and published in *L'Osservatore Romano* on September 6, set out the regulations for the constitution and procedures of the Council.[149]

With the publication of the regulations in *L'Osservatore Romano* the distribution of offices in the Council was also made known. An Apostolic Letter of September 4 appointed individuals to their charges.[150] It is not difficult to establish that the distribution of offices bore Roncalli's signature. The choice showed great balance in regard both to international membership and to theological and ecclesio-political trends.[151] As

---

[146] Ibid., 383f. at 383.

[147] Ibid., 294f.

[148] KNA, *Sonderdienst*, no. 9 (1962) 22.

[149] *AAS* 54 (1962) 609-31; *ADP*, I, 306-25. The *Motu proprio* is translated in *TPS* 8 (1962-63) 282-84, followed by a resumé of the regulations (284-88).

[150] *AAS* 54 (1962) 687f.

[151] The distribution of offices in detail:
Council of Presidents: Cardinals Tisserant (Dean of the College of Cardinals), Liénart (Lille), Tappouni (Beirut/Rome) Gilroy (Sidney), Spellman (New York), Pla y Daniel (Toledo), Frings (Cologne), Ruffini (Palermo), Caggiano (Buenos Aires), Alfrink (Utrecht). Presidents of the conciliar commissions: Commission for Doctrine of Faith and Morals: Ottaviani; Commission for Bishops and the Government of dioceses: Marella; Commission for the Oriental Churches: Cicognani; Commission for Discipline of the Sacraments: Aloisi Masella; Commission for the Discipline of the Clergy and the Christian People: Ciriaci; Commission for Religious: Valeri; Commission for the Missions: Agagianian; Commission for the Liturgy: Larraona; Commission for Seminaries, Studies, and Catholic Schools: Pizzardo; Commission for the Lay Apostolate and for the Press: Cento. Secretariat for Extraordinary Questions of the Council: President, Secretary of State Amleto Giovanni Cicognani; Members: Cardinals Siri (Genoa), Montini (Milan),

compared with its role in the preparatory period, the curia no longer had such a decisive influence. Some of the cardinals working on the presidential commission were relatively open-minded, e.g., Liénart of France, Frings of Germany, and Alfrink of the Netherlands. On the Secretariat for Extraordinary Questions were to be found individuals of open mind and readiness for reform, such as Montini (Milan), Suenens (Mechlin-Brussels) and Döpfner (Munich-Freising).

Provision had been made in the regulations for observers at the Council, and on September 5 the Secretariat for Christian Unity, under Cardinal Bea, published a list of those appointed by the other Christian communities that Rome had invited to do so. Unfortunately there was no representative of the Patriarchate of Constantinople.[152] Also published in September, 1962, was the list of periti or official theologians of the Council; here again a certain shift in the center of gravity is discernible as compared with the preparatory period.[153]

The organizational requirements for the Council were thus met. As for the content of what would be discussed, the pope had tried to keep all

---

Confalonieri (Rome), Döpfner (Munich-Freising), Meyer (Chicago), Suenens (Mechlin-Brussels). President of the Tribunal of the Council: Roberti. General Secretary of the Council (and of the Secretariat for Extraordinary Questions): Felici. President of the Court of Arbitration (in case conflicts arose during the Council and complaints were lodged): Roberti.

[152] See KNA, *Sonderdienst*, no. 10 (1962) 8f., and *HK* 17 (1962-63) 57.
Anglican Church: Dr. John Moorman, Bishop of Ripon (Great Britain); Dr. Frederick Grant (USA); Dr. Charles de Soysa, Archdeacon of Colombo (India). Lutheran World Federation: Dr. Kristen E. Skydsgaard, professor of theology (Denmark); Dr. George Lindbeck, professor of theology (USA). Evangelical Church in Germany (EKD): Dr. D. Edmund Schlink, professor of systematic theology at the University of Heidelberg. World Federation of the Churches of Christ (= Disciples of Christ): H. Jesse Bader, Secretary General of the Federation (USA). World Committee of the Society of Friends (= Quakers): Dr. Richard Ullmann. World Council of the Congregationalists: Dr. Douglas Horton (USA); a second observer would also be appointed. World Methodist Council: Bishop Fred P. Corson, President of the World Council (USA); Dr. Harold Roberts, Principal of the Theological College in Richmond (Great Britain); Dr. Albert C. Outler, professor of theology in Dallas (USA). World Council of Churches in Geneva: Pastor Dr. Lukas Vischer of the Reformed Church of Switzerland, member of the Faith and Order Commission of the World Council of Churches; a second observer would also be appointed. Old Catholic Church (Union of Utrecht): Kanonikus Dr. Peter Jan Maan, professor of New Testament exegesis and homiletics in the seminary of Amersfoort, Pastor of the Old Catholic Cathedral in Utrecht. Coptic Church of Egypt: Father Youanna Girgis, Inspector in the Egyptian Ministry of Public Education; Dr. Mikhail Tadros, Adviser to the Court of Appeals. Syrian-Jacobite Church: Father Ramban Zakka B. Iwas; Father Paul Verghese. World Alliance of Reformed Churches: Pastor Herbert Roux of the Reformed Church of France; Dr. Douglas W. D. Shaw of the Presbyterian Church of Scotland; Professor James H. Nichols of the Theological College in Princeton (USA).

[153] See the next section, on the experts.

questions open, but at the same time had exerted pressure to counteract the heavily dogmatic and doctrinal orientation that seemed to be set in the period of preparation, so as to prepare the way for a Council that would be sensitive to the call of the Holy Spirit and to the questions and needs of humankind.

III. THE APPOINTMENT OF THE EXPERTS

1. *Task and Importance of the Experts*

Mario von Galli remarked that "in complete contrast to earlier Councils, in which theologians often addressed the assembled fathers at plenary meetings, this honor was given to almost no theologian at the Second Vatican Council." Galli then asked: "Was this in order to emphasize the pastoral character of the Council? Or would people have been embarrassed if the old practice were followed, since the minority could offer hardly any great theologians?" In any case, theologians were immensely important during the Second Vatican Council. "At times their influence became so great that a good many bishops vehemently opposed them… In fact, then, the theologians were 'the cooks of the Council.'"[154]

The experts worked according to the instructions given to them. They did not have the final say as to the topics chosen, but they did play a role of decisive importance when it came to the views of the bishops; the actual work of the commissions was largely in their hands.

The place and function of the experts were carefully described in *Appropinquante Concilio*, the *Motu proprio* of August 6, 1962, in which the pope gave the Council a set of regulations for the conduct of its business (*Ordo concilii oecumenici Vaticani II celebrandi*). In its 70 articles it defined the functions of the participants and established norms for the conduct of the Council's business.[155]

The fifth chapter of these regulations dealt with the duties of the theologians, canonists, and other experts. Article nine was entitled "Professional Advisers to the Council." It said that the theologians, canonists, and other experts at the Council, to be known as "professional advisers" (*periti*), were to be appointed by the pope. Article ten described their

---

[154] Von Galli and Moosbrugger, *Das Konzil und seine Folgen*, 130.

[155] See the resume of the regulations in *TPS* 8 (1962-63) 284-88. See H. Jedin, *Ecumenical Councils of the Catholic Church: An Historical Outline*, trans. E. Graf (New York, 1959, 1962⁴).

tasks: "The experts of the Council are to take part in the general congregations, but are to speak only when asked to do so." A subsequent paragraph said: "The presidents of the individual commissions can, as they see fit, call upon the conciliar experts who work with the members of the commissions in composing and revising the schemas and in drafting reports."

Article 11 said that the individual Council fathers could look for advice and help not only to the experts of the Council but also to a private theologian, canonist, or other specialist. But these personal advisers had no right to take part in the general congregations and the meetings of the commissions. They were, however, bound by oath to secrecy about the dealings and discussions of the Council.

The measures thus required in *Appropinquante Concilio* went back to canon 223 of the Code of Canon Law, which provided that theologians and experts in Church law could also take part in a Council, but according to the law then in force they were to have a purely advisory function.

2. *The Appointment of the Experts on September 28, 1962*

The first list of experts published in *L'Osservatore Romano* (September 28, 1962) contained 224 names.[156] The great majority on the list were members of the curia and members and consultors of the various preparatory commissions, as well as professors of the Roman universities. This way of proceeding was understandable, since the Roman experts were well-known, they had proved themselves in various ways, and they enjoyed the trust of the pope and his advisers. In addition, their collaboration did not entail any special financial outlay.

The experts came from all areas of the theological sciences, the auxiliary sciences, and other relevant areas of special expertise: dogmatics, moral, biblical sciences, canon law and jurisprudence generally, sociology, history, history of the Church and of the Councils, pastoral theology and liturgy, Latin, Eastern Churches activity and ecumenical activity, and the theory and practical use of the modern communications media.

The 224 conciliar experts came from over thirty different countries. Obviously the most evenhanded distribution that might have been

---

[156] *AAS* 54 (1962) 782-84. Also appointed were the two doorkeepers of the Council: Prince Asperno Colonna, Assistant at the Papal Throne, and Prince Alessandro Torlonia, to whom the pope gave the personal title of Assistant at the Papal Throne for the duration of the Council. In November, 1962, another 100 names were added to the list of periti. In the interim, individual appointments were frequently announced. See *Concilio Ecumenico Vaticano II. Commissioni Conciliari*, published by the General Secretariat of the Council (Vatican Polyglot Press, November 30, 1962); see *HK* 17 (1962-63) 435ff.

achieved was neither attained nor sought (even with regard to countries with a relatively high percentage of Catholics). The almost complete lack of theological advisers and canonists from the mission countries was probably due, among other things, to the financial difficulties created by the great distance of these countries from Rome. It was probably thought that further appointments might redress the balance somewhat.

According to their origin the experts were divided as follows: 53 from curial service (almost all of them canonists) and 84 from the Roman universities, institutes, colleges, and religious houses: thus over 60% were from the center of the Church. 59 came from various European countries (Austria 3, Belgium 7, England 4, France 11, Germany 7, Hungary 3, Italy outside Rome 12, Lithuania 1, Luxembourg 1, The Netherlands 2, Spain 6, Switzerland 2); 14 were from North America and Latin America (Brazil 1; Canada 1; United States 12); 1 was from Africa (Egypt) and 4 were from Asia (India, Jordan, Lebanon, Turkey).

If we divide all 224 experts, including the members of the curia and of the Roman institutes, colleges, and religious houses, according to national origin, the following picture emerges: Italy 85 (44 of them from the curia and 29 from the Roman universities, institutes, colleges, and religious houses); France 19; Spain 19; United States 16; Germany 15; Belgium 10, The Netherlands 7, England 4, Austria 4, Hungary 4, Canada 3, Switzerland 3, Ireland 2, Brazil 2, Lebanon 2, Yugoslavia 2, Luxembourg 2, Poland 2, and one each from the Ukraine, Greece, Egypt, Argentina, China, India, Jordan, Lithuania, Rumania, Syria, Czechoslovakia, and Turkey.

A large number of the conciliar experts were from the area of ecclesiastical administration (curial staff members, officials, vicars general, spiritual aides to Catholic associations, etc.) or from the area of the government of religious orders. Among the theologians, members of the various papal universities and of the institutes and theological faculties of the orders and congregations predominated. It can be said in general that experts from the area of pastoral care, for example, full time pastors, were almost completely lacking.

In purely quantitative terms, the Italian, curial, and Roman element supplied the majority of the experts. The universal Church was not reflected here. On the other hand, despite the predominance of persons from the world of traditional theology there was lacking a dynamic openness to the questions and problems raised by Pope John XXIII; into this vacuum individual theologians who were looking for new answers and had even formulated such answers could push their way. In this fashion they could introduce ideas that had developed in the twentieth century outside of Roman theology.

3. *Experts in a Renewal of Theology*

When we look back today it is not difficult to detect in the conciliar documents the influence of the great movements of renewal that had emerged at the end of the last century and the beginning of the present century: those that called for a renewed reflection on the Bible, the liturgy, early Christian literature, and the apostolate of the laity.

In this process, "the prevailing influence was that of the theological faculties and schools of Jerusalem, Louvain, Innsbruck, Saulchoir, Lyon-Fourvière, and the German faculties."[157] It is certainly correct that the Council hastened the process whereby Catholic theology as a whole aligned itself with the theological schools of Central Europe and France. "In southern Europe, eastern Europe, and outside our continent, the old apologetics still determined theological instruction in large measure. All these countries stood outside the development."[158] It seems justified, therefore, to look more closely at the trend-setting theological schools and experts of the German-speaking and French worlds.

In connection with the Second Vatican Council people often speak, rather simplistically, of "German theology." But among the German-speaking theologians who appeared on the list of experts in September 1962, very different approaches were to be found. Thus individuals such as Jesuit theologian Franz Hürth or Heribert Schauf, professor of theology at Aachen, represented the strict Roman and Scholastic approach. A large number of the German-speaking theologians from the Roman institutes of the religious orders hardly presented any strikingly different theological image from these two men.

Michael Schmaus, dogmatic theologian at Munich, had difficulty in connecting with theological discussion in the period before Vatican II, even though in his manual, *Katholische Dogmatik*, he had done pioneering work in the late thirties in giving a new methodological direction to systematic theology. "Here was a dogmatics that consciously took its direction from the scriptures and the theology of the Fathers and at the same time kept an eye on the questions of the present time."[159] From his

---

[157] Joseph Comblin, "Die katholische Theologie seit dem Ende des Pontifikats Pius' XII," in Herbert Vorgrimler and Robert Vander Gucht (eds.), *Bilanz der Theologie im 20. Jahrhundert. Perspektiven, Strömungen, Motive in der christlichen und nachchristlichen Welt* II (Freiburg-Basel-Vienna, 1969) 870-88 at 872.

[158] Ibid.

[159] Karl Forster, "Michael Schmaus," in Hans Jürgen Schultz (ed.), *Tendenzen der Theologie im 20. Jahrhundert. Eine Geschichte in Portraits* (Stuttgart etc., 1966) 422-27 at 422.

teacher, Martin Grabmann, who had a strong interest in the history of theology, Schmaus gained "an insight into the genesis and process of development of philosophical and theological problems. The simple passing on of important passages was replaced by a deeper understanding of the historicity of theology itself."[160]

It was already possible to see here basic orientations that would be characteristic of "German theology": strong ties to the work of historico-positive research and critical exegesis that was refined by coming to grips with the model provided by the Protestants and that made it intellectually irresponsible to allow certain ecclesiastical prejudices to go unchallenged. In Germany, with its independent theological faculties, traditions were still at work that had been nourished by the Catholic Enlightenment of the eighteenth and early nineteenth centuries and that had found new sustenance since the beginning of the twentieth.

In addition, a clear dissatisfaction with Scholastic theology had been growing. The person and the subjective encounter with God were rediscovered as necessary categories in the life of faith.

> It was this atmosphere and the reaction against the conceptualism and "reification" to which people objected in classical Scholasticism, that gave rise to the works of an Erich Przywara, S.J. (born 1889), who introduced Newman into Germany, of a Peter Lippert, S.J. (1879-1936), of a Romano Guardini, whose aim in all his writings is to bring into focus the situation of the human being before God, not from a static but an existential and even dramatic point of view, and who never tires of reminding his readers that God is not simply an omnipotent He but a living Thou, and, finally of a Karl Adam (1876-1966), who since the thirties exerted an influence far beyond the borders of Germany... The most prominent characteristic of his theological work is its rootedness in Christian life: his aim is not simply to enrich the reader's knowledge but to let the lifegiving power of Christianity pervade the entire person.[161]

As a result of such experiences the task of theology also changed. It acquired a mediating, dialogical function. No longer could there be a question simply of preserving the deposit of faith as a set of rigidified concepts. Theology had to find ways of communicating the content of the faith and the Church's message in a manner universally understandable and of enabling it to become an experiential reality in the life of the Church. "The desire for a less technical theology that could be fruitfully preached to the Christian people led to the call for a 'theology of proclamation' or

[160] Ibid., 423.
[161] Roger Aubert, "Die Theologie während der ersten Hälfte der 20. Jahrhunderts," in Vorgrimler and Vander Gucht, *Bilanz der Theologie* II, 7-70 at 24f.

kerygmatic theology."[162] Joseph Andreas Jungmann, S.J. (1889-1975) issued this call in 1936. The liturgy, the worship of the Church, was seen as the primary and original locus of proclamation. It was Jungmann, professor of pastoral theology at Innsbruck, who provided scientific liturgical foundations for the development begun in the liturgical movement and made this movement fruitful for theology. He was also a direct personal bridge to Vatican II. He was already at work during the preparatory period and left his firm imprint on the liturgical schema. As a peritus at the Council he was able to introduce his ideas on liturgical reform. At his side was another peritus from the German-speaking world: Johannes Wagner, director of the German Liturgical Institute.[163]

In addition to liturgical renewal, a further merit of theologians from the German-speaking world was to have emphasized ecumenism as a matter of concern to the Church. In this area Eduard Stakemeier, fundamental theologian from Paderborn, was able to make his influence felt as a peritus. "In the setting of the tasks undertaken for the Council by the Secretariat for Unity Stakemeier collaborated above all on a major topic and problem: the hierarchical structure of the Church."[164]

Another peritus who was heavily influenced by efforts in the ecumenical area was German Redemptorist Bernhard Häring, precursor of a renewed moral theology that abandoned a narrow casuistry for a personalistic and holistic approach. Father Häring submitted an alternative draft for the schema on "Chastity, Virginity, Marriage, and Family." In it he approached marriage entirely from the viewpoint of "the call to true love."[165]

German scientific Church history, which aimed at on objectivity free of prejudices, also bore fruit in the ecumenical dialogue. This discriminating viewpoint was introduced by Hubert Jedin (1900-1980; professor of Church history at the University of Bonn, 1948-1965), who was probably the best known German Church historian at that time. Jedin's speciality was the history of the Reformation and of the Councils, especially the study of the Council of Trent. In 1960 he became a member of the preparatory commission for studies and schools. His main contribution

---

[162] Ibid., 26.

[163] See Johannes Wagner, *Mein Weg zur Liturgiereform 1936-1986. Erinnerungen* (Freiburg-Basel-Vienna, 1993).

[164] Johannes Kardinal Willebrands, "Die Mitarbeit Prof. Eduard Stakemeiers im Einheitssekretariat," in *Eduard Stakemeier zum Gedenken*, ed. by the Johann-Adam-Möhler-Institut (Paderborn, 1971) 41-45 at 21.

[165] Bernhard Häring, *Meine Erfahrung mit der Kirche. Einleitung und Fragen von Gianni Licheri* (Freiburg-Basel-Vienna, 1989) 58.

here was the preliminary work on the regulations for the Council, into which he was able to integrate the various models and approaches of earlier Councils.[166]

Among the German-speaking theologians Jesuit Karl Rahner (1904-1984) deserves special attention. Although he played almost no part in the preparatory work, he was to become undoubtedly the most influential theologian at the Council. Trained in and shaped by the tradition of Roman scholasticism, Rahner became aware that a theology thus rigidified and regulated in its formal concepts, imposed on human beings from outside, and in the final analysis alien to them, was no longer capable of disclosing to them the contents of faith, the message of the gospel, and that the claim of that theology to be an integral, unsurpassable, and definitive explanation of the world was an obstacle to hearing and understanding the questions, criticisms, concerns, and problems of contemporary humanity.

One stimulus to this view came to the young Karl Rahner from the "kerygmatic theology" mentioned earlier. His insight was deepened during the period of his research-studies at Freiburg from 1934 to 1936, where his encounter with existentialist philosopher Martin Heidegger was a source of particular inspiration. Through an analysis of Thomas Aquinas' metaphysics of knowledge he came to realize that the Church had to revise its understanding of revelation and that a reflection on the foundations of theology was indispensable.

> In modern conditions [theology] could no longer say in the classical terms of fundamental theology: "If God speaks, man has to obey; now we prove that God has spoken, naturally and supernaturally, so all who do not hear are either intellectually inept or morally perverse." Modern thought raises the question: "How can a human being hear God at all? How does such a reception of a revelation of God take place, and in such a way that the hearer can stand surety for it, can share it with us in a credible way? This is where Rahner's theological programme began, in the steps of Thomas, in conversation with Kant, German Idealism, Heidegger, but also guided by Ignatius and the significance which human senses have for him in relationship with God. This course led to the elements of a Christian anthropology, a theological doctrine of man. And precisely by reflecting on *conversio*, the necessary self-surrender of man in the world, Rahner found further important additional elements for his theology: what has "always" been given only becomes concrete and capable of being experienced by us when we go out of ourselves and turn to face other individuals.[167]

---

[166] See Hubert Jedin, *Lebensbericht. Mit einem Dokumentenanhang* (Veröffentlichungen der Kommission für Zeitgeschichte, Reihe A: Quellen, 35; Mainz, 1984) 197-219.

[167] Herbert Vorgrimler, *Understanding Karl Rahner: An Introduction to his Life and Thought*, trans. John Bowden (New York, 1986) 61.

In *Hearers of the Word* (1941) Rahner developed further his approach of using philosophical anthropology to conceive anew the relations between God, revelation, and the human person within the coordinates of space and time, which are elements of the world, and thus in relation to historicity. Rahner wrote: "Man is the existent thing, possessing a spirituality that is receptive and open to history, who stands in freedom and as freedom before the God of a possible revelation which, if it occurs, appears in his history... in the world."[168]

It was characteristic of Rahner that he did not remain at the level of a theoretical philosophy of religion. He was much too aware that every philosophical approach is limited and open to revision. It was precisely here that his pioneering contribution to theology was to be located. He was skeptical

> of any self-enclosed system of thought that is prior to and independent of theology. The Scholastic system of thought — which he himself developed and used brilliantly — could no longer claim to be so indispensable as in the past... The later Rahner was "skeptical" in principle about any philosophy... There was a native missionary impulse at work here in Rahner the theologian, who was able to keep a firm hold on the ultimate, radical universality of the faith, above and beyond the supposed universality of any philosophical system. The cause of the faith was not to be made dependent on particular philosophical views; otherwise this identification would result in the faith's losing some of its proper explosive force, which can be illustrated by means of many philosophies but transcends all of these taken together.[169]

The pastoral aspect comes to the fore in his publications in the area of spiritual theology. Theology needs the personal search into the mystery of God and a conversion to the human beings of each age. Rahner struggled to grasp the ever new relationship between transcendence and concrete, personal human existence in which faith historically arises. Such a conception as this had far-reaching consequences for the history of dogma and especially for the open-endedness of dogmatic development. Historicity and with it the questions of each age acquired a new value. It seemed almost inevitable that this changed understanding of the place of theology should be accompanied by criticism of the Church itself.

Like not a few other theologians of the time, Rahner came into conflict with the magisterium during the fifties. The Order refused its

---

[168] *Hörer des Wortes* (Munich, 1941) 209; ET: *Hearers of the Word*, trans. M. Richards (New York: Herder & Herder, 1969) 162.

[169] Karl Lehmann, "Karl Rahner," in Vorgrimler and Vander Gucht, *Bilanz der Theologie* II, 143-81 at 164.

imprimatur for his *Mariology* (1951). His support for concelebration in
his little book *Die vielen Messen und das eine Opfer* (ET: *The Many
Masses and the One Sacrifice*) was criticized by Pius XII, and the Holy
Office forbade him to say anything further on this subject. His interpretation of the "virgin birth," in which he conceived of virginity not as a
biological phenomenon but as a religious and theological way of
expressing a complete submission to the divine will,

> caused serious disturbances in Roman circles. Rumours were circulated
> that now steps would really be taken against Rahner. They caused Cardinal
> Julius Döpfner, who had always shown Rahner signs of appreciation and
> sympathy, to intercede for him with John XXIII in an audience of 24 Jan-
> uary 1961. The consequence of this intervention was that not only were no
> proceedings set in motion, but on 22 March 1961 he was nominated by
> John XXIII as the consultor to the Council's preparatory commission on
> the discipline of the sacraments. This was a high-level official "settlement"
> of the matter.[170]

But Rahner's enemies did not rest. On June 7, 1962, his superiors in
the Order told him that henceforth all his writings were under Roman
censorship, a measure that was thoroughly in keeping with the mood in
the summer of 1962, when the Roman curia wanted to give the impression that it was capable of retaining the initiative in regard to the coming Council. Various German bishops fought for the cancellation of this
measure, but this came only in May of 1963. In the interim Rahner had
also been appointed an official theologian of the Council by John XXIII.
    Rahner had only a small part in the actual preparation for the Council.
He had been called to the commission for the discipline of the sacraments primarily because he was the only dogmatic theologian who had
spoken on the question of the permanent diaconate. He was, however,
never invited to a meeting of the commission, but was only asked for a
report on the renewal of the diaconate.
    From the fall of 1961 on, however, Cardinal König kept Rahner
informed about the details of preparation for the Council, and the texts of
the preparatory schemata were also made known to him. He shared the
general dissatisfaction. The schemata were the expression of a self-
understanding of the Church and of theology beyond which Rahner was
trying to move. Like König and Döpfner, Rahner was convinced that
every step had to be taken to keep the Council from proceeding along the
path planned by the curia. Rahner was eventually to become one of the
formative and path-breaking theologians of Vatican II. His effectiveness

---

[170] Vorgrimler, *Understanding Karl Rahner*, 91-92.

was due not only to the way in which he took part in the Council but also to the worldwide reception which his theological thought enjoyed before the Council and which helped prepare the way for the spirit of this Church assembly. As a result of this "authority" he succeeded at many points, along with Y. Congar, E. Schillebeeckx, J. Ratzinger, and H. Küng, among others, in breaking through the schemata that had been prepared as finished products into an open country of greater theological freedom.[171]

French theologians also had an especially formative influence in the work of the Council. The chief names to be mentioned are Fathers Yves Congar, O.P., Jean Daniélou, S.J., and Henri de Lubac, S.J. All three theologians were representatives of the "new theology," the designation used of writers who strove for a renewal of theology in both method and content and who were therefore accused of contributing to a resurgence of modernism. The Jesuits of Lyon-Fourvière and the Dominicans of Le Saulchoir were especially suspect.

Father Marie-Dominique Chenu, O.P., a theologian who never became an official peritus, said, for example, that theology is not first and foremost a science made up of logical conclusions, that is, speculative theology, but owes its life to the scriptures, piety, and faith. The theologians of the new theology made the study of the sources of faith the starting point for their theological work. They knew that Christianity had its origin in history and not in metaphysics. Consequently, the first need was to get to know history.

These theologians thus tried to make it very clear that a profound theology must take spiritual and historical experience into account. In his work *Surnaturel*, for example, de Lubac used arguments from the tradition to move beyond a formal metaphysics of two self-enclosed orders of nature and supernature. So, too, what Congar had to say "about reform, history, and freedom does not arise out of speculation cut off from reality, but is the reflection of a man who is affected and involved and who suffers from the inflexibility of Church government, the static thinking of Neoscholasticism, and ecclesiastical obedience."[172]

The following words of Congar are especially indicative of his intellectual and spiritual position: "What Teilhard de Chardin perceived in regard to the cosmos as a whole and the totality of its history, Father Chenu perceived in regard to the historical and social dimension of human life."[173]

---

[171] Lehmann, "Karl Rahner," 148.

[172] Johannes Bunnenberg, *Lebendige Treue zum Ursprung. Das Traditionsverständnis Yves Congars* (Walberberger Studien 14; Mainz, 1989) 375.

[173] Yves Congar, "Marie-Dominique Chenu," in Vorgrimler and Vander Gucht, *Bilanz der Theologie* II, 99-122 at 121.

In Congar's view the cross was a condition of every holy work. He wrote: "God himself is at work in what seems to us a cross. Only by its means do our lives acquire a certain genuineness and depth. Nothing is meant wholly seriously unless we are prepared to pay the price it demands."[174] "Congar repeatedly paid this price. His unremitting determination to serve truth in the Church, a patient determination that reached the point of sacrifice, won him an exceptionally respectful hearing among the fathers of the Council."[175]

Congar knew that modern unbelief can be overcome only if the Catholic world, priests and faithful, achieve a more comprehensive, more vital, more human vision of the Church. "We must clarify the whole temporal dimension of the Church by showing and stressing its inner connection with Christ, the decisive and ever present role of the Holy Spirit, and the primacy of grace, and clarify also the whole human dimension by showing to advantage the activity of the entire community of believers, its liturgical and apostolic role, its reality as fully ecclesial."[176] It is certainly not an exaggeration to say that Congar's at once traditional and prophetic statements show a certain similarity to utterances that can be found in John XXIII.

We can gain some realization of Congar's importance in the conciliar discussion of the Church if we recall something he wrote in 1937: "Everywhere we get a sense that it would be of great profit in our pastoral ministry and would allow Christianity to spread to a far greater extent throughout the world, if the concept of the Church were to recover the broad, rich, vital meaning it once had, a meaning deriving wholly from the Bible and tradition."[177]

Credit must go to Congar, among others, for one of the Council's essential achievements: "the shift from a predominantly juridical conception of the Church to an eschatological vision of the Church as the people of God, the body of Christ, the temple of the Holy Spirit; the rediscovery of the sacramental and communional nature of the Church, which helps us better understand that the episcopal and presbyteral priesthood is by its nature pastoral, apostolic, and therefore essentially 'a service of the gospel' (see Rom 15:16 and 12:1)."[178] Congar took to

---

[174] Y. Congar, *Dialogue between Christians. Catholic Contributions to Ecumenism*, trans. P. Loretz (Westminster, MD: Newman, 1966) 45.

[175] M.-J. Le Guillou, O.P., "P. Yves M. J. Congar, O.P.," in Vorgrimler and Vander Gucht, *Bilanz der Theologie* II, 181-91 at 187.

[176] Y. Congar, *Sainte Église* (Paris, 1963) 545.

[177] Y. Congar, *Pour une théologie de l'Église* (Paris, 1937) 97-99 at 99.

[178] Le Guillou, "P. Yves M. J. Congar, O.P.," 191

heart the new orientation of the Church to the paschal mystery. Many of the Council Fathers owed to Congar a broadening of their conception of the Church.

On the problem of modern man and the faith, which was central theme of the Council, Congar observed:

> The greatest obstacle that people of today encounter on the way of faith is their impression that there is no connection between, on the one hand, faith in God and the orientation to his kingdom and, on the other, the human person and work here on earth. The inner connection between these realities must be seen and shown. This is the most effective positive answer to the reasons for modern unbelief.[179]

Congar was increasingly impressed by the historical character of revelation, which in his view was essentially the history of what God has done in the life of human beings for the benefit of the entire race, so as thereby to carry out a specific plan of grace.[180] In order to overcome the difficulties which hold many people back on the way of faith, it was necessary, according to Congar, to make it ever clearer "how the world of God is connected with the world of human beings."[181] His own vocation was "to be the main motivating force in an extraordinary theological, ecclesial, and missionary renewal, the fruits of which, to his joy, he saw ripen at the Council."[182] In addition, Congar made a decisive contribution to the realization "that, although the Church remains always the same in its evangelical substance, it cannot be a Church of yesterday in a world of today and tomorrow. Its own future demands that it be present to the future of the world, in order to direct this toward the future of God."[183]

Alongside Congar stood Jesuits Jean Daniélou and Henri de Lubac. In an article of 1946, Daniélou had already touched on themes that had been in need of reappraisal ever since the condemnation of modernism: the historical study of the Bible; the bridging of the division between theology and spirituality, Church and world, dogmatics and exegesis; the need of integrating subjectivity and historicity into theology.[184]

A distinctive characteristic of de Lubac was his friendship with Teilhard de Chardin, S.J., whom he met for the first time in Paris in 1921 or

---

[179] Cited ibid., 192.

[180] Ibid., 194.

[181] Y. Congar, *The Wide World My Parish: Salvation and its Problems*, trans. D. Attwater (Baltimore, 1961), passim.

[182] Le Guillou, "P. Yves M. J. Congar, O.P.," 199.

[183] Y. Congar, *Église catholique et France moderne* (Paris, 1978) 53.

[184] Jean Daniélou, S.J., "Les orientations présentes de la pensée religieuse," *Études* 79 (1946) 6-21; see 6f.

1922. De Lubac's work, *Catholicisme. Les aspects sociaux du dogme*,[185] became the perfect example of a renewal of theology. De Lubac's student and friend, Hans Urs von Balthasar, called it a "programmatic book."[186] The description was justified because in it de Lubac had rediscovered the fraternal Church and "in this respect had outlined in advance the ecclesiology of Vatican II."[187] Given their basic outlook, it is not surprising that in 1941 Daniélou and de Lubac should have inaugurated the great series, *Sources chrétiennes*.

A certain spiritual affinity led John XXIII, immediately after his election, to make known his esteem for de Lubac; in 1960 he appointed him a consultor.[188] In the years after the Council de Lubac continued to concern himself primarily with the Church's self-understanding. He remained true to the principle that he had developed in his book *Surnaturel*: return to a simpler, more traditional, and more profound teaching. It was in the light of this principle that he criticized the productions of the preparatory commissions, saying of them:

> All the schemas of our commission stuck to the rules of a rigid and shallow scholasticism, concerned almost exclusively with defense and lacking in discernment, tending to condemn all that did not fit in perfectly with its own perspective... A choice had to be made between a theological style that was completely defensive — sometimes extremely limited in outlook, too dependent on the manuals of the day — and the desire to find new inspiration by means of a more thorough-going return to the great Tradition of the Church.[189]

According to de Lubac, some theologians explained as follows John XXIII's liking for him and other, chiefly French, experts: "Because the Church wanted to avoid the erroneous developments that took place after the first Vatican Council (which excluded theologians of opposing views), she had theologians such as Congar, Daniélou, Rahner, and de Lubac come to Rome in order that she might hold them by every means to her maternal bosom."[190]

---

[185] A fifth edition appeared in 1952; ET: *Catholicism. A Study of Dogma in Relation to the Corporate Destiny of Mankind*, trans. L. C. Sheppard (New York: Sheed & Ward, 1950).

[186] Herbert Vorgrimler, "Henri de Lubac," in Vorgrimler and Vander Gucht, *Bilanz der Theologie* II, 199-214 at 205.

[187] Ibid., 210.

[188] See Karl Heinz Neufeld, "Bishops and Theologians in the Service of Vatican Council II," in *Vatican II. Assessment and Perspectives Twenty-Five Years After (1962-1987)*, ed. R. Latourelle (New York/Mahwah: Paulist Press, 1988) 74-105.

[189] Henri de Lubac, *A Theologian Speaks* (Los Angeles, 1985) 7.

[190] Henri de Lubac, *Entretien autour de Vatican II* (Paris, 1985) 16.

Mention must be made of one French theologian who helped shape the Council even though he was not an official peritus: Marie-Dominique Chenu. Congar wrote of him: "At the Council, too, he was effective through his personal influence and not because of any official position. So much of what blossomed and bore fruit there was due to the seed he had sown,"[191] Chenu was available as consultor to a number of French bishops; for example, Léon-Arthur Elchinger, at that time coadjutor bishop of Strasbourg, kept in close touch with him.[192]

Chenu aptly described the specific character of Vatican II as follows: "As compared with all other Councils its distinctive trait is this: a renewal of the efficacy of God's word through the power that is native to it, while remaining in touch with the transformations going on in contemporary history. This is precisely the definition of prophecy."[193]

The following remarks of Congar about Chenu express his enthusiasm for the man: "With Father Chenu and those around him we believed in theology and thought it had something to say to the people of today, to the extent that it was not satisfied to warm up formulas discovered in the past but sought answers to questions of the age."[194] Chenu repeatedly attacked a certain kind of textbook Scholasticism as "primitive objectivism," "rationalism," and "baroque theology."[195]

Congar compared the intention and orientation of Chenu's work with those of Teilhard de Chardin. Chenu found especially attractive Teilhard's claim "that many are unable to believe because the evidence of the world is stronger than the light of Christ. Only if we take with complete seriousness the evidence of the world, its proportions, its unity, and its history, only if we believe fully in it, will we be able, working from within it, to restore God and Christ to their place in it and enable them to show themselves there once again."[196] It was fortunate for the Church that John XXIII appointed for conciliar work theologians who had fallen into disfavor prior to his pontificate.

A series of Belgian and Dutch theologians whom the pope appointed as experts should also be mentioned. The first to be cited is canonist Gommar Michiels, O.F.M.Cap., who was honorary professor at the

---

[191] Congar, "Marie-Dominique Chenu," in Vorgrimler and Vander Gucht, *Bilanz der Theologie* II, 101.

[192] See the Elchinger conciliar archive (Strasbourg): correspondence with Chenu.

[193] Marie-Dominique Chenu, O.P., "Ein prophetisches Konzil," in Klinger and Wittstadt, *Glaube im Prozess*, 16-21 at 21.

[194] Congar, "Marie-Dominique Chenu," 102.

[195] Ibid., 105.

[196] Ibid., 121.

Lateran University and active as consultor to the commission for bishops
and the government of dioceses. The experts also included Louvain
canonists Guillaume Onclin and Henri Wagnon. Mention must also be
made of Louvain exegete Lucien Cerfaux, who was a consultor to the
Pontifical Biblical Commission and a member of the theological commission.

Theologians Gérard Philips and Gustave Thils did outstanding theological work.[197] As early as 1954, in his book *Le rôle du laïcat dans
l'Église*, Philips, a professor at Louvain, had brought up viewpoints
that played an important role at the Council in the discussion of the
place of the laity in the Church. He exerted an influence particularly
on three Council documents: *Dei Verbum, Gaudium et spes*, and
Lumen gentium.[198]

Gustave Thils, dogmatic theologian at Louvain, was a member of the
Secretariat for Promoting Christian Unity and a driving force in the
creation of an ecumenical theology. In addition, he had already
attempted in 1947 an assessment of a theology of progress.[199]

An important theologian from the Netherlands was Johannes G. M.
Willebrands, secretary of the Secretariat for Promoting Christian
Unity. Willebrands was a man of great openness and, as such, was
really predestined to be a collaborator of Cardinal Augustin Bea.
Among the early experts were also Alfons J. M. Mulders of
Nijmegen, a missiologist. and Anton Ramselaar, director of the semi-
nary in Apeldoom. Edward Schillebeeckx, probably the most impor-
tant theologian from the Netherlands, was never an official peritus but
he exerted a decisive influence, especially on the Dutch fathers of the
Council.

IV. COMMUNICATIONS AND ORGANIZATIONAL PREPARATIONS

1. *Vatican Press Policy: Between Openness and Secrecy*

The importance to the Council of the work of the press is underscored
by the following remark of Jan Grootaers in a lecture entitled "Religious
News at the Beginning of Vatican II": "A sociologist has been able to

---

[197] *HK* 17 (1962-63) 440, 442.
[198] See C.-H. Baudry, "Philips (Gérard)," in *Catholicisme. Hier aujourd'hui demain*
(Paris, 1987) col. 193f.
[199] See his *Théologie des réalités terrestres*, 2 vols. (Paris/Bruges 1947).

say that Vatican II unfolded on three different levels: those of the bishops, the theologians, and the religion reporters."[200]

One reason in particular why news became a problem during the period before the Council was that the press was keeping a watchful eye on everything leading up to the Council. Journalists generally, but Catholic journalists especially, were tackling the problems raised by the Council. In numerous longer or shorter writings, whether in newspapers, periodicals, or booklets, they gave thorough, comprehensive explanations, intelligible to people generally, of all questions that were of interest and importance in connection with the Council; in the process they also gave expression to wishes and expectations.

In contrast to the situation at the time of Vatican Council I, there was hardly a press anywhere in the world that was hostile to the Council. Public opinion was on the side of the Council. This positive attitude was certainly due in great part to the fact that Pope John XXIII had succeeded in filling the world with new hope, and this hope was reflected even in the journalists. It was obvious that in their reporting the individual periodicals and newspapers had to keep "their" readers in mind, but almost all of them had a positive and expectant attitude toward the planned Council. This was true of Christians and nonchristians alike. It was clear what could be accomplished by someone like John XXIII, whose primary goal was to be there for "others."

On May 28, 1962, on the occasion of an international congress of journalists, the pope stated his views on the duties of the press.[201] He assured the journalists that they could "always count on a warm reception from Us." How serious the pope was in this matter was clear from his next words: "In fact, gentlemen, We rely on you, very specially now during the approach of the Second Ecumenical Vatican Council, that important event which it is hoped will have a positive influence, beyond the borders of the Church, on all people of good will. In the achievement of this goal the press is nowadays not only useful but an indispensable means."

Further on in his address the pope expressed the wish that "journalists not be forced by lack of information to engage in more or less probable conjectures and publish ideas, opinions, and hopes that later prove to be

---

[200] Lecture given at Louvain in 1989. See Jan Grootaers, "L'information religieuse au début du Conciile: Instances officielles et réseaux informels," in *Vatican II commence*, 211-34.

[201] *ADP*, I, 248f. I am indebted to Prelate Professor Gerhard Fittkau, at that time the head of the German-speaking group, for many references. — Translation of the address in *TPS* 8 (1962-63)

ill-founded or false." These words show that the pope was very well aware of the importance of a liberal policy on news.

But according to the Regulations for the Council (article 26) the principle of secrecy was still to be maintained. All the participants were "obliged to keep secret the discussions in the Council and the views expressed there." Against this background, it is understandable why until there should be proof to the contrary, journalists remained mistrustful and were very skeptical about the Vatican's policy on news. Swedish journalist Gunnel Vallquist, for example, wrote: "We do not expect much from the Vatican's news service. Its director, Msgr. Vallainc, is reported to have said in advance: 'We do not need the press.' In any case, the Vatican does not have a very modern conception of news."[202]

In 1961 the magazine of the Reformed Swiss Church published a critical article on "The Catholic Press and the Vatican Council." It began with the remark that "the lack of information is deplored by people everywhere." The author made clear the tensions affecting news about the Council.

> On the one hand, at a reception for the International Catholic Press Union the pope said that the climate is important if the Second Vatican Council is to be able to be really effective, and that the press can make an important contribution in this respect. On the other hand, Msgr. Felici, secretary of the Central Commission, recommended that the press maintain a 'reverent silence,' and he pointed out that the press office was set up to meet the needs not of the press but of the Council.[203]

Felici's words showed that there was "fear of interference by incompetent persons in the preparation for the Council." He advised journalists to prepare the public for the Council mainly by means of historical essays on the history of Councils.

The closer the Council came, the more strongly felt was the lack of an office that would provide continuous and reliable information to the press and the other media of journalism. As I have already said, the providing of news about the Council was something new for Rome and created problems. Initially the decision was to give "controlled" information.[204] Such an attitude caused discontent, and it was understandable that even before the Council the journalists were demanding entry into the Council hall.

[202] Gunnel Vallquist, *Das Zweite Vatikanische Konzil* (Nuremberg, 1966) 3.

[203] "Die katholische Presse und das Vatikanische Konzil," *Kirchenblatt für die reformierte Schweiz* 117 (1961) 281f.

[204] Philippe Levillain, *La mécanique politique de Vatican II. La majorité et l'unanimité dans un Concile* (Paris, 1975) 146.

Now and then news of resignations got out. For example, the *Washington Post* for September 1, 1962, said: "Msgr. Kelly resigns as church news chief." In Catholic circles in the United States Kelly's action caused astonishment. Kelly's view was that during the Council news should be managed according to the standards of the public press. He called for the greatest possible openness, but in his view prospects for this were unfavorable, and so he stepped down after seven years as news chief for the American bishops. He referred to Pope John XXIII, who wanted the greatest possible openness in dealing with the representatives of the press from around the world. Kelly believed that his action was fully in line with the pope's views. He said: "There is no doubt that Pope John XXIII wants to inform all people..."

Lorenz Jaeger, Archbishop of Paderborn, called keeping the press informed "the most difficult matter connected with the Council, because people in Rome were not accustomed to working with the press."[205] In the period before the Council very severe criticisms were voiced regarding Vatican public relations: "People were still living in the tradition of privy Council politics and as a favor allowed an occasional trivial communiqué to reach the journalists."[206]

As a matter of fact, even during the preparation for the Council secrecy about the discussions was regarded as essential. The members of the commissions had to swear on the gospel not to say anything about what they might learn during the work of preparation. The experts of the various commissions were even forbidden to talk about the questions on which they had to work.

In this situation people recalled that it was the secrecy which had earlier surrounded Vatican I that had done the harm. An observer wrote: "In reality the conciliar discussion were neither secret nor published. There was only an atmosphere of whispered news, of mistrust, of anecdotes; there were reports and rumors that could be neither proved nor rebutted."[207]

Despite all these difficulties, the representatives of the press, regardless of denomination and philosophy of life, trusted in John XXIII; they felt that he would not leave them in the lurch. On October 13, 1962, the pope addressed the journalists. He began by saying: "The purpose of today's audience is to express the esteem We have for the representatives of the press and the importance We attribute to your profession."

[205] Jaeger, Council papers (Archives of the Archdiocese of Paderbon).
[206] Vallquist, *Das Zweite Vatikanische Konzil*, 3.
[207] KNA, *Sonderdienst*, no. 8 (September 10, 1962) 13f.

This address once again clearly emphasized John XXIII's relationship with journalists and the press. The pope remarked:

> Your [responsibilities], gentlemen, are great. You are at the service of truth, and insofar as you serve it faithfully you meet men's expectations... As a result of the conscientious fulfillment of your mission as reporters on the Council, We look forward... to very happy effects on the orientation of world opinion regarding the Catholic Church in general, her institutions, and her teachings... The mere announcement of the Council has aroused in the whole world a remarkable interest to which you have abundantly contributed... It is Our earnest desire that your accounts should arouse the friendly interest of the public in the Council and help eventually to correct mistaken or incomplete views of it... In serving the truth you will have assisted at the same time that "interior disarmament" which is the absolutely necessary condition for the establishment of true peace on this earth.[208]

The pope's special appreciation of the work of journalists raised a justifiable hope that he would not be opposed to improving the access of journalists to the sources of information. His openness to the press was certainly known and acknowledged throughout the world. There was, however, considerable doubt about whether John XXIII would get his way against currents in the curia.

2. *Organization of the Work of the Press*

The announcement of the Council and the work of preparation for it had already met with great interest in the press. Evidence of this were the many meetings of journalists that dealt with the theme of "We and the Council." An example: a meeting in South Styria in May of 1961, attended by ninety participants from the German-speaking world. Their purpose was to locate the Council in the broad context of Church renewal and to make clear its aims. Another purpose of the conference was to counteract a certain sense of resignation that had resulted from the decline of initially very high expectations and from the impression that a "Chinese wall" had been erected against the public. The point was emphatically made that "it would be a great gain if journalists were put in a position in which they could keep the Catholic public throughout the world currently informed about the problems of the Council and the state of the preparations for it, and in this way place public opinion at the service of the Council."[209]

In order that they might keep the public better informed, the editors of the twenty Catholic newspapers in the Netherlands had already

---

[208] KNA, *Sonderdienst*, no. 23 (October 15, 1962) 7-9; *TPS* 8 (1962-63) 221-23.
[209] *HK* 16 (1961-62) 438f.

approached the Vatican in May, 1961, with a request that it facilitate the work of journalists at the approaching Council. The request stressed the point that if this suggestion were disregarded, the unavoidable result would be false news about the Council.

The German bishops appointed Walther Kampe, Auxiliary Bishop of Limburg, to set up a "Working Group for News" that would have as its function to prepare and be in charge of all news about the Council. In addition, the Katholische Nachrichtenagentur (Catholic News Agency) was to produce a *Konzils-Sonderdienst* (Special News Service for the Council) for the daily and weekly press, the radio, the clergy in pastoral ministry, and Catholic associations and organizations.

On July 4, 1962, through the good offices of Cardinal Bea, Auxiliary Bishop Kampe had an audience with John XXIII. The bishop told the pope what the German publishers wanted; their wishes were undoubtedly typical of the wishes of all journalists. Kampe himself reported: "The primary concern was that in addition to the official press office of the Council it be possible to set up press centers for the individual language groups."[210] This would also provide the structure for carrying out the commission which the German bishops had given for the promotion of publicity about the Council in the German-speaking world and to which the Austrian episcopate and the bishops of German-speaking Switzerland had given their agreement. The pope, who had repeatedly emphasized his understanding of the role of the press agreed with this plan.[211]

Despite the many well-founded fears there were also many positive signs. Just in time for the beginning of the Council, the new large hall for meetings of the entire press was officially opened at Via Conciliazione 52 and Via Rusticucci 5. Cardinal Secretary of State Cicognani dedicated the building. The technical arrangements in the conciliar press room that had been set up for this specific purpose were satisfactory. About a hundred typewriters were provided, and about thirty international telephone connections and teleprinters were installed.

Any comprehensive reporting depended entirely on Roman press policy. It was not easy to obtain admission as a press observer to the Council since the selection of observers was tightly controlled. How strict the press regulations for the Council were was clear also from the fact that journalists were forbidden to approach and interview visitors and persons residing in the Vatican.

[210] Walther Kampe (ed.), *Das Konzil im Spiegel der Presse* I (Würzburg, 1963) V (2); *ADP*, I. 248f.
[211] Ibid.

At the opening of the conciliar press office on October 2, 1962, 400 tickets for the opening celebration were to be distributed to journalists. But the press office had by this time already distributed over 600 press cards to journalists. It was calculated that the number of reporters would reach around 1000.[212]

The great interest of the world press in the conciliar event could be seen, for example, in the fact that over a hundred journalists came for a tour of the Council hall on October 8, 1962. The tour was set up by the conciliar press office for all journalists thus far accredited.[213]

The conciliar press office had seven sections for the most important modern languages: English, French, Italian, Polish, Spanish, German, and Portuguese. The director-in-chief of the office was Msgr. Fausto Vallainc. Msgr. James Tucek headed the English section; he was director of the Roman office of the North American news agency *News Service*. Head of the French section was Father Frank Bernard, from *La Croix* in Paris. The Spanish-language group was headed by Don Cipriano Calderon; the Portuguese by Father Bonaventura Kloppenburg from Brazil; Father Francesco Farusi, head of the news section, was responsible for the Italian group, and Stefan Wesoly looked after the Polish-speaking journalists. Prelate Professor Gerhard Fittkau was responsible for the German-language group.

But even the section chiefs for the individual language groups had first of all to see to it that adequate information reached them. It was said that Fittkau profited by his closeness to the German episcopal conference; Calderon had a special relationship with Msgr. Gonzales Casimoro Morcillo, Archbishop of Zaragoza, and Farusi had connections with Vatican Radio.

It was due to the heads of these language groups that the opportunities for acquiring informations improved steadily during the course of the Council. Just recently, in April, 1993, Fittkau insisted that this improvement had been very much a concern of his; he had repeatedly called the German bishops' attention to the need. On October 1, 1962, for example, Fittkau wrote to Cardinal Döpfner, saying the following, among other things:

> It looks as if Archbishop Felici will retain absolute control over our office and, with Msgr. Vallainc as go-between, be the only one to supply news for our communiqués. If we may judge by the talk Felici gave last Friday at the Circle of Rome, that news will be very scanty. He used elegant language to

[212] KNA, *Sonderdienst*, no. 12 (October 4, 1962) 11.
[213] Ibid., no. 16 (October 9, 1962) 3.

say nothing beyond what everyone already knew. Yesterday Felici even returned Vallainc's completely innocuous pamphlet on "Some Subjects Discussed in the Central Preparatory Commission" as being still "secret material." Yet it contains nothing more than has already appeared in *Osservatore* and much less than can be found in *Herderkorrespondenz*. Our work will not be easy. We hope that the Council fathers will influence the press policy of the Council, and in particular will win a clarification of our position in relation to Felici, who was supposed to have a board of Council fathers who would have a part in determining the press policy of the Council. I am afraid that the bad experiences of Vatican I may be repeated.[214]

The examples given above show that many journalists had their own channels. It is also clear that for the time being the Church and the Vatican, on the one hand, and journalists used to reporting on parliaments, on the other, held opposed views on news.

In order to be able to work efficiently, the Catholic news agencies of Central Europe combined to form a team for reporting on the Council, and they set up a joint editorial office at Via Domenico Silveri 30 in Rome. Members of the group were Kathpress (Austria), KNP (Netherlands), KNA (Germany), KIPA (Switzerland), and CIP (Belgium). The group took the name RICI (*Romanae informationes catholicae internationales*) and was in close touch with all Catholic news agencies. Associations of journalists were also formed to improve the communication of news; one such was *Recontres Internationales d'Informateurs Religieux* (RIIR)

A Catholic news office was established in Copenhagen. It set itself the task of keeping the Scandinavian press — about 1200 dailies in Denmark, Swede, Norway, Finland, and Iceland — informed about the Council. The initiative in setting up the office came from Johannes Suhr, Bishop of Copenhagen, and Archbishop Bruno Heim, Apostolic Delegate for Scandinavia. In addition, a center to assist Scandinavian journalists was opened in Bonn in association with the Catholic news office there.[215]

For reportage on the Council many newspapers increased the number of their representatives in Rome or set up offices there for the first time. On September 25, the KNA noted "that all the conditions are now in place for keeping the public thoroughly informed about the work of the Council, because the sources of news and information in Rome are now flowing in sufficient measure."[216]

---

[214] Döpfner, Council papers (AEM).
[215] KNA, *Sonderdienst*, no. 9 (September 25, 1962) 22.
[216] Ibid., 9.

This same flow of information, however, still left something to be desired. The press had first to clear a way for itself. But the pressure exerted by the journalists on the news system set up by those in charge of the Council did not fail to have its effect. A good month after the start of the Council an improvement in press policy was to be seen. Now two heads of the seven language groups in the conciliar press office were allowed in turn to attend the general congregations of the Council, whereas previously only the director of the press office, the Italian Vallainc, had access to the Council hall. On November 23, 1962, Fittkau, head of the German-speaking section, was present for the first time at a general congregation. The initiative for this new step came from an international group of Catholic journalists in Rome. This group, which had formed independently of the conciliar press office and to which no member of the conciliar press office belonged, had sent to the presidential commission, via the general secretariat of the Council, a five-page memorandum on the news policy of the Council.

The breakthrough to a comprehensive news policy did not come easily for the Catholic Church. Nor may we forget that dealing with the world press was something new and strange for the Church.

With the beginning of the Council as a world event the importance of the other media — film, radio, and television — also increased. It had been planned from the outset to film all the important events at the Council and to prepare a documentary in color. At the beginning of October, 1962, the Istituto Nazionale Luce, located in Rome, was commissioned to make filmed reports on the Council. Radio Televisione Italiana (RAI) had the exclusive right to make recordings for the radio.

3. *International Press Reportage*

The importance of the press becomes clear when we reflect that, for people who did not themselves take any part in the work of the Council, the Council meant what they learned about it from the press. From this fact also followed the great responsibility of the press in relation to the Council; it may be said that in very large measure it met this responsibility in an outstanding fashion.

It was of great importance not only to journalists but to the Church itself that the Council be suitably echoed in public opinion. In fact, never had so many religious events and theological problems been discussed in the modern press as in the period immediately before the Council and during the weeks of the first session.[217]

[217] Kampe (ed.), *Das Konzil im Spiegel der Presse* I, V.

An inspection of newspapers and periodicals shows that even a broad sector of noncatholic public opinion was informed about the Council to an exemplary degree. "Reportage even in the Evangelical press was on a very remarkable level."[218] Individual articles repeatedly showed "how astutely and sensitively a good many journalists acclimated themselves to the often quite tangled paths of theological science and how gratifying it was that the press also opened its columns eagerly to noteworthy views of professional theologians."[219] The Auxiliary Bishop of Limburg accurately evaluated the echo which the Council found in the press "as a first and promising sign of the reconciliation between Church and world that the Council had set as its goal."[220]

My aim in what follows is to show how the world press was reporting the news just before the opening of the Council. To this end I have taken some important newspapers in important countries as examples.[221]

The main points of interest in international reporting of the Council were these: the person of John XXIII; hopes for comprehensive reform; description of important events prior to the Council, for example, papal audiences; questions of Church policy, for example, the participation of bishops from the eastern bloc in the Council; reports on theological problems, for example, the structure of the Church; ecumenical desires.

Anyone comparing the major international newspapers will quickly observe that Pope John XXIII was a focus of reportage. In the *Frankfurter Allegemeine Zeitung* Schmitz van Vorst introduced into an article entitled "From Diaconate to Mixed Marriages" the following incident which he regarded as an important sign of a capacity for correction and of new directions: "It is reported that during these weeks the pope has very attentively read the book of an opponent of Vatican I and that at several points he exclaimed: 'He is right!' It is undoubtedly John XXIII's endeavor to avoid earlier mistakes at the coming Council."[222]

---

[218] Ibid., VI.

[219] Ibid.

[220] Ibid., VII.

[221] The newspapers studied were: German-speaking world: *Frankfurter Allgemeine Zeitung (FAZ)*; *Deutsche Tagespost*; *Neue Zürcher Zeitung*; *Der Spiegel*; Belgium: *Gazet van Antwerpen*; *Le Soir* (Brussels); France: *La Croix* (Paris); *Le Monde* (international edition); Italy: *Corriere della Sera*; Spain: *Diario de la Noche* (Madrid); England: *Daily Telegraph*; Sweden: *Stockholms-Tidningen*; Greece: *Athens Courier*; USA: *Washington Post*; *New York Times*; Argentina: *Diario Argentino*. Most of the newspapers used here are in the newspaper library of the Federal Press Agency in Bonn. Further references in Kampe (ed.), *Das Konzil im Spiegel der Presse* I (1963); II (1964), and Antoine Wenger, *Vatican II. Première Session* (Paris, 1963). Periodical articles dealing with the preparation for the Council are collected in Caprile, I/2.

[222] *Das Konzil* (Sonderdruck der Frankfurter Allgemeinen Zeitung), 12.

In an article entitled: "Church and State: A Theme of the Council. Advance of Integralism during the Preparations for the Great Church Assembly," which appeared in the same newspaper at the end of July, 1962, the same writer showed profound insight in his discussion of the central problem, namely, the Church's assessment of its role in the world. Schmitz van Vorst here expressed the hope that the subject would not be handled in the traditional manner. It is significant that he linked this hope to the person of John XXIII. He referred to the two addresses of the pope at the conclusion of the Central Commission and on the feast of Peter and Paul: "He brought up Innocent III, the pope of a universal monarchy. But he described only the priestly side of the man. In another place the pope spoke of the city of God as *inter turres*, 'among the towers.' The towers are the states. These are necessary. There in the midst of them the Church performs its humble service as helper and nothing more."[223]

In all the newspapers the pope was repeatedly seen as the man on whom hopes were pinned. The *Salzburger Nachrichten* said: "It thus seems to be increasingly clear that with Pope John a new epoch in the history of Christianity has dawned, an epoch of love, forgiveness, and understanding."[224] It was because of this that the pope's radio message of September 11, 1962, received very close attention from the press. The German news magazine, *Der Spiegel*, known to be highly critical of the Church, wrote appreciatively of the Church's changed outlook in social questions and questions of world politics, as this was sketched in the radio message[225]; so too did the *Neue Zürcher Zeitung*.[226] The *Gazet van Antwerpen* reported the content of the address in great detail and emphasized the new vision of the Church.[227] In an article "The Council and Politics" *La Croix* made extensive reference to the radio message. Antoine Wenger, author of the article, brought out the central concern: truth and freedom as the basis of human civilization, and in this connection also called attention to the change of direction in the Church.[228] *Le Monde* emphasized especially the point made in the radio message about the "Church of the poor."[229] The *New York Times* carried a report of the pope's radio message that was dated the very next day; the article had the characteristic title, "Pope Sees Peace Aided by Council."[230]

[223] Ibid., 10.
[224] Kampe, *Das Konzil im Spiegel der Presse* I, 14.
[225] *Der Spiegel* 43 (1962) 75.
[226] *Neue Zürcher Zeitung*, no. 252, p. 4.
[227] *Gazet van Antwerpen*, September 12, 1962, 1.
[228] *La Croix. Quotidien Catholique d'Information*.
[229] *Le Monde*, September 13, 1962, 10.
[230] *New York Times*, September 13, 1962, 6.

In all these instances the pope himself was seen as the cause of the new tone heard from the Vatican.

This strong focus on John XXIII emerged even in the *Daily Telegraph*, despite the fact that it hardly had to take a Catholic readership into account. The *Athens Courier*, among others, was proof that newspapers which usually kept their distance from the Catholic world were especially fascinated by the pope himself.

The figure on whom the journalists focused was John XXIII. The entire press showed great sympathy for him; he had shown himself credible and convincing. He determined the atmosphere that was reflected in reportage. A further point is that North American reporting, in particular, took a very positive attitude to John XXIII. The North American newsmagazine *Time* even made Pope John XXIII its "Man of the Year" for 1962. The staff of *Time* felt that the pope "wanted to communicate a sense of our oneness as a human family" and that he had set in motion ideas and forces which were releasing hopes throughout the world.

A characterization of John XXIII by Katharina Herkenrath in *Echo der Zeit* very aptly captured the phenomenon of Roncalli, a man not fully understandable in intellectual terms but one who touched so many people:

> The fine words of Theodor Haecker can be applied to our Holy Father: that in the oneness of the spirit "beatitude as a fullness of feeling" is "at the same time the fullness of thought in the intellectual vision of absolute truth... " This makes him outstanding and causes him to say and do things that are not of an everyday kind but new and surprising, that are in line with tradition but not inflexible, that add an element of liberation to the conventional, that are official and yet constantly transcend the bureaucratic, that are intuitive but nevertheless fit easily into real situations, that, in summary, are original, deriving from a creative marriage of the natural and the supernatural.[231]

It was in light of this changed atmosphere that expectations of the Council were formulated. Thus *Welt am Sonntag* for October 7, 1962, carried an article by Luise Rinser on the question "What does the world expect of the Council?" Summing up, she wrote:

> This Council is not at all about increasing the prestige of the Church nor is it about politics. It is about the spirit and about awakening sleeping spiritual and religious forces, especially those of the laity. It is, I might say, about the official recognition of the pluralism of modern life; that is, it is

---

[231] *Echo der Zeit*, October 7, 1962; cited from Kampe (ed.), *Das Konzil im Spiegel der Presse* I, 100.

about the resolute surrender of a centralized Roman administrative authority that has become overly powerful, in favor of a vitally flowing Christian
life in its many forms, without in the process losing even the slightest part
of essential Christian teaching and ethics.[232]

The desire was repeatedly expressed that the Catholic Church break
out of its institutional rigidification and that a new spirituality and religious spirit develop from the laity. A few days before the Council began,
Herbert Leicher wrote in the *Rhein-Zeitung*: "The reform which people
hope for from the Council might begin even now. The faithful, for
example, might devote themselves more intently to questions of faith;
communities might attend worship more fervently; pastors might scruti-
nize their efforts in ministry and religious might on their own initiative
already undertake in their communities a good many reforms that the
Church expects of them."[233] The spirit of reform, indeed almost a
euphoria about reform, echoed repeatedly in many articles.

But the same mood was not to found in equal measure in all countries.
To the extent that expectations of reform grew, so too, usually, did the
amount of reportage in the newspapers. Consequently, the preparation
for the Council received more attention in the press of German-speaking
countries and in Belgium, The Netherlands, Italy, France, and North
America as well, than it did in Spain or South America. In the *Diario de
la Noche* (Madrid), for example, there were only very meager reports on
the Council, and they did not raise theological questions; the same was
true of *Diario Argentino*. The level of public intellectual and theological
discussion within a region or country was reflected in the level of attention in the press.

In Catholic countries or in countries with quite large groups of
Catholic inhabitants the desire for news was, of course, significantly
greater and the editorial staffs of the newspapers responded accordingly.
Corriere della Sera gave continuous coverage to events having to do with
the Council; it is noteworthy that it went into great detail, while also
publishing in-depth discussions. On September 11 it carried an article by
Ernesto Pisoni, "The Assembly of the Church: A Model of Democracy
— Not even the pope can say how long the Council will last."[234]

This Italian newspaper did not, however, achieve the depth of reflection to be found in newspapers of Western and Central Europe. The
important Belgian paper *Le Soir* (Brussels) ran a five-part series of

[232] Cited from Kampe (ed.), *Das Konzil im Spiegel der Presse* I, 32.
[233] *Rhein-Zeitung*, October 5, 1962.
[234] *Corriere della Sera*, September 11, 1962, 5.

detailed and illustrated articles on the Council from August 21 to August 25, 1962. The author, Henri Poumerol, gave his series the overall title "Vatican II, Universal Council. A Historic Event." The first article was a survey of Church history; the second, "A New Face," went into the question of how 500 million Christians would determine the face of tomorrow's Church. The third article emphasized the contrasts to be expected at the Council:"Traditional pomp and liturgy, but shorthand Latin, electronic voting, and simultaneous translation." The fourth turned to the central question: "Collective self-criticism or concerted renewal and deeper reflection on doctrine?", while the final article dealt with the ecumenical hopes that had emerged with the Council: "You shall all be one."[235]

Le Monde, too, concerned itself very intensively with the entire range of problems connected with the Council. Like *Le Soir*, *Le Monde* was interested not only in superficial news but also in discussions of central problems that stressed content and difficulties. Thus it published a theological article by Fr. Congar entitled "The Theological Meaning of the Council,"[236] as well as a historical article dealing with general principles, "The Historical Meaning of the Council," by André Latreille.[237] In a front-page article on September 26 Fr. R. Rouquette examined the subject of the pope and collegiality,[238] and on September 28 Jacques Madaule took up the question of "The Council and the Jews."[239]

The press repeatedly tackled such fundamental problems as these. In an article on "Rome and the Bishops: Reform of the Constitution of the Church?" the *Frankfurter Allgemeine Zeitung* examined a difficult subject, namely, the extent to which Roman centralization can make way for a more collegial Church structure. With great sensitivity to the internal procedures by which decisions are reached in the Church, the article drew this balanced conclusion: "The Church will not incline toward reforms that turn everything upside down. But cautious and experimental steps toward a greater independence of the bishops do seem to be on the agenda."[240]

As in the major newspapers of Western and Central Europe, so too in the national newspapers of the United States there were accurate reports

[235] *Le Soir* (Brussels), August 21-25, 1962, p. 5 in each issue.
[236] *Le Monde*, September 6, 1962, 7.
[237] Ibid., September 20, 1962, 8.
[238] Ibid., September 26, 1962, 1.
[239] Ibid., September 28, 1962, 8.
[240] *Frankfurter Allgemeine Zeitung*, September 17, 1962; *Das Konzil* (Sonderdruck der FAZ), 12-14

on the preparation for the Council. The *Washington Post* informed its readers about the regulations for the Council, the history of previous Councils, the sending of observers to the Council, and the pope's journey to Loreto and Assisi. On October 6 this newspaper published an almost full-page article under the title, "Vatican Council to Weigh Church's Modern Role." In this article Harry Gabbett took up central questions with which the Council would deal, for example, the role of the laity.[241] Reportage in the *New York Times* was of a similar kind, with the objectivity and detail of the presentation being especially outstanding. The information conveyed in the *New York Times* often went beyond that provided by the news agencies. The central themes of the Church and the Council were made clear; subjects such as the unity of Christians, spiritual renewal, and commitment to peace were examined. Like the other newspapers cited, the *New York Times* made a very positive contribution to preparing its readers and attuning them to the Council.

Suspicion marked the press's reporting of events that seemed to bypass the process of renewal; this was especially the case with the monitum against Teilhard de Chardin.[242]

Consciously Catholic newspapers and periodicals reportage on the Council, of course, appears to have been abundant and detailed. A clear German example of this was the *Deutsche Tagespost*, which made extensive use of such Roman sources as *L'Osservatore Romano* and *Civiltà Cattolica*. The same was true of *La Croix* (Paris), to name another Catholic organ.

It is evident that reporting on the Council in noncatholic countries was less extensive than in Catholic countries. In Great Britain, Sweden, or Greece, there were only a few articles, and these were often very brief. It seems no less evident that in these countries ecumenical expectations played a special role. On October 3, 1962, the *Daily Telegraph* carried a picture of John XXIII; the hope which the accompanying article associated with the pope was the hope of Christian unity; this was clearly the area in which other confessions had a sympathetic interest in the Council.[243] The *Athens Courier* took up the long unresolved question of participation by observers from the Orthodox Churches.[244]

In confessionally divided countries such as Germany and Switzerland the ecumenical problem was discussed both at a high theological level

---

[241] *Washington Post*, October 6, 1962.
[242] See *Le Monde*, July 3, 1962, and July 7, 1962, 8.
[243] *Daily Telegraph*, October 3, 1962, 6.
[244] *Athens Courier*, October 11, 1962, 1.

and in a critical and sophisticated way. The *Neue Zürcher Zeitung* published an article entitled "Luther and the Council."[245] The issue of October 10 carried an article, "A Protestant Preview of the Council," by Pastor Paul Wieser, Director of the Swiss Evangelical Press Service. In it he noted that the fact that even "in noncatholic Christendom people are eagerly and attentively waiting for the Council to take place can be regarded as a sign of an ecumenical awakening that would have been unthinkable only a few decades ago." He went on to say: "If non-catholic ecclesiastical leaders are inviting their faithful to pray for the Council, they are doing so in the realization of the common responsibility of Christians, as part of their confession of the common Lord, and in the hope that the Council will be guided by the word of God, the gospel of the love of the God who alone redeems and brings humanity home."[246]

In the period immediately before Vatican II the press kept a sharp eye on relations between the eastern bloc and the Catholic Church; the central question here was whether the bishops from the East would be allowed to take part in the Council. Communist policy on the Churches was an important indicator for the development of East-West relations in the setting of the "Cold War." On September 26, 1962, the *Frankfurter Allgemeine Zeitung* discussed problems with the communist countries under the heading, "Warsaw Puts Pressure on the Bishops. Cardinal Wyszynski Protests Conditions Placed by the State on Participants in the Council." A summary, with commentary, was given of a sermon which the cardinal had delivered in Warsaw.[247] Observations on "The Polish Route — Toward Rome" brought out the problems with which the bishops of the communist world had to struggle.[248] Just before the Council, on October 7, the same newspaper reported the enthusiastic reception which the Polish delegation to the Council had received in Rome; it noted, in particular, that for tactical reasons four theologians sympathetic to the Marxists had been invited to the Council.[249]

In the communist controlled press of eastern Europe news of the Council was scanty.[250] Most newspapers were not permitted to write anything at all about the Council. The press or the political authorities,

[245] *Neue Zürcher Zeitung*, no. 250 (September 12, 1962), 6.
[246] Ibid., no. 277 (October 10, 1962), 7.
[247] *Das Konzil* (Sonderdruck der FAZ), 14.
[248] *Frankfurter Allgemeine Zeitung*, October 8, 1962; *Das Konzil* (Sonderdruck der FAZ), 20.
[249] *Das Konzil*, 21.
[250] For the following remarks see Wenger, *Vatican II. Première Session*, 312f.

as the case may have been, were not interested in informing the masses about an event that would give a look at the life of the Catholic Church. Articles dealing with the Council appeared therefore only in newspapers meant for the intellectual or political elite; for example, *La Literatour-naia Gazeta*, the periodical *Neue Zeit*, and the journal of esthetics, *Naouka i Religia* (Science and Religion).

The first articles in this last-named periodical cast discredit on the Council and the Catholic Church. In the issue of March, 1962, for example, an ironic judgment was passed on the program for the Council: The subjects of the Council would be sacred scripture, prayer, ecclesiastical discipline, communion, the missions, and so on, while subjects affecting the whole of humanity would not be addressed, for example, the struggle for peace, disarmament, the liquidation of the colonial system. The first real treatment of the Council appeared in the issue of July, 1962, in which the Council was represented as being an alliance of religious forces against communism. The September, 1962, issue of the same periodical published an article "The Vatican on the Eve of the Council," by Scheinmann, author of numerous works against the Vatican. Here the pope's concern for "The unity of the Christian Churches and for a rapprochement with nonchristians" was interpreted as an attempt to form an international alliance of Churches against communism.

Volume 6 (1962) of the *Jahrbuch des Museums der Geschichte der Religion und des Atheismus* (Journal of the Museum of the History of Religion and Atheism), published by the USSR Academy of Sciences, contained two articles on the Council. The author of the first, "The Papal Policy of Church Unity," was Eduard Winter, member of the East German Academy of Sciences, who had published a book on Russia and the papacy. Winter, too, accused the Church of taking a stand against communist and the socialist countries. A further article on the ecumenical Council of 1962 and on Catholic teaching about the oneness of the Church was largely historical. The idea of unity was seen as a declaration of religious war on atheistic communism. But such a policy, the author concluded, did not do justice to the longing of all peoples for peace. In this context Wenger remarked that in fact the Council was of greater concern to the communist authorities than they were willing to admit.[251]

Mr. Krassikov, the TASS representative in Rome, gave a benevolent description of the opening ceremony and the pope's address; he must have gotten a positive impression of John XXIII. *Isvestia* carried a

[251] Ibid., 314.

similar account on October 12, 1962. The point was made here that while the Church would concern itself primarily with matters of faith, it would also take up questions having to do with the international situation.

In summary it can be said that a comparison of the international newspapers of the so-called western world confirms that there was, by and large, a positive attitude to the Council. At the same time, there were definitely differences of focus. In more Catholic countries a predominant theme was the renewal of the Church; in noncatholic countries the question of the reunification of Christians was to the fore. In all, however, the problem of peace on earth and fraternal coexistence was dominant. At this point the hopes of humanity converged with John XXIII's expressed intentions for the Council.

V. THE COUNCIL HALL AND ITS SERVICES[252]

1. *Planning Phase and Tasks*

In order to ensure an adequate place in St. Peter's for all the Council fathers, theologians, observers, and journalists, the basilica had to be rearranged. Plans for the rearrangement were drawn up by the Technical and Organizational Commission, which had been established by the Central Preparatory Commission. The importance assigned to this commission, which had been appointed on November 7, 1961, with Cardinal Döpfner as one of its members, became clear from the fact that Archbishop Felici, General Secretary of the Central Preparatory Commission, was appointed its secretary. According to a description supplied by Felici in the name of the pope, the function of this commission was to anticipate and prepare everything that might be useful to the work of the Council.

The first meeting of the Technical and Organizational Commission took place in the Sala delle Congregazioni in the Apostolic Palace on Wednesday, November 8, 1961 at 5.00 p.m. Present were Cardinals Gustavo Testa (curia) as president, Paul Marie Richard (Bordeaux), Julius Döpfner (Munich). Paolo Marella (curia), Luigi Traglia (curia), and Alberto di Jorio (curia), as well as Felici and undersecretaries Sergio Guerri, Agostino Casaroli, and Iginio Cardinale. Unable to attend were

---

[252] My guides in this exposition have been Pericle Felici, *Sancta Aula Concilii* (1967), and Silvano Stracca, "L'aula delle Congregazioni," *L'Osservatore della Domenica. Il Concilio Ecumenico Vaticano II*, No. 10 (March 6, 1966) 186ff.

Cardinals Francis Spellman (New York),[253] Fernando Quiroga y Palacios (Santiago de Compostela), and Giovanni Battista Montini (MIlan).

Cardinal Testa began by explaining the directives governing the commission's work. The first item on the agenda was the reception and housing of the participants in the Council; a second subject was "the length of time for the celebration of the Council"; a third was the question of the Council hall; and a fourth had to do with "initiatives and external manifestations."

The fathers were to be given comfortable and appropriate lodging and assistance so that they would feel themselves to be welcome guests. Felici explained that the pope wished the Council to begin in October, 1962, and to end in December, 1962. The cardinals presents thought this plan rather optimistic.

The Cortile della Pigna and the Pius XII Auditorium were suggested as the venue for the meetings of the Council; St. Peter's Basilica would be used for solemn gatherings. The Ospizio S. Maria in the Vatican was suggested as the location for the general secretariat and for the technical and organizational commission. News offices were to be housed outside the Vatican.

Once John XXIII had decided on St. Peter's Basilica as venue for the Council, detailed planning could begin. The chief engineer for the work was Dr. F. Vacchini, Director of the Technical Office of the Fabbrica di S. Pietro. He was in charge not only of organizational and technical matters but of the no less difficult artistic problems. According to Vacchini, on the one hand, the Council fathers needed to be provided comfortable arrangements suitable for their labors and discussions, while, on the other, the interior architecture of the basilica had to be preserved. The purpose of any rearrangement was to ensure both practicality and comfort.

The following topics were on the commission's agenda for their meeting of June 7, 1962: 1. Arrangement of the Council hall in St. Peter's; 2. Clothing to be worn during the sessions; 3. Timetable of the sessions; 4. Liturgico-religious arrangements; 5. Languages to be used at the sessions; 6. Voting procedures; 7. Various Matters.

The organizational and technical commission presented a detailed sketch of the arrangement of St. Peter's. The set-up of the Council hall in the central nave (96m × 22m) had to satisfy the following basic requirements:

[253] On February 6, 1962, Cardinal Spellman wrote to Cardinal Testa, thanking him for his appointment to the Technical and Organizational Commission. He apologized for not having been able to attend the first meeting of the Commission (conciliar archive of the Istituto per le scienze religiose, Bologna).

1. At least 2000 seats and work stations, with good lines of vision, were needed. 2. The papal throne was to be placed at the very front and had to be visible from all seats. 3. The seats for the cardinals had to be specially marked. 4. Sufficient space had to be left free in the middle of the hall for the services provided by the secretariat. 5. Unobtrusive places had to be found for the catering and health services and for sanitation arrangements. 6. It should still be possible during the Council to have solemn ceremonies in which the public might also take part.

Since only the central nave and the Confessio were reserved for the Council, all the altars, except for those of St. Michael and St. Petronilla, were still available for liturgical ceremonies, and all works of art remained visible. During the construction work only the central nave would be inaccessible to the public. If necessary, the work could be done at night, so that the basilica could be kept open.

The furnishings were to be simple in style but made of fine material and in keeping with the dignity of the place and the importance of the solemn event.[254]

The actual work of turning St. Peter's into a Council hall began after the planning was complete, on May 15, 1962, and continued until October 10. the day before the opening of the Council. John XXIII followed the work in St. Peter's very attentively and repeatedly made suggestions of his own.

2. The Council Hall[255]

The 2500 square-meter surface of the Council hall provided room for 2905 places: 102 for the cardinals, 7 for the patriarchs, 26 for the general secretariat and its employees, 2440 for the Council fathers, 200 for the experts, and 130 for observers.

The original overall plan had the papal throne in front of Bernini's baldachin that arches over the Confessio, the papal altar; the chamber with the stairs leading down to the tomb of Peter would thus have been covered over. In keeping, however, with his understanding of the vital unity and continuity of the Church, the pope himself ordered that the entrance to the tomb of Peter be left completely free, open, and visible and be made an integral part of the Council hall. For this reason, the papal throne was moved back to a place at the center of the four twisting columns of Bernini's baldachin.

---

[254] Council archive of the Istituto per le scienze religiose, Bologna.
[255] See Caprile, I/2, 680-81.

The pope also rejected the planned movable altar that could be moved to the center when needed for the celebration of the conciliar liturgies and, in its usual place somewhat to the side, was to display the book of the gospels that would be solemnly placed there as at every Council. The pope did not like this arrangement at all. He wanted a "fixed altar" for the community Mass with which every working day of Council debates was to be begin. He regarded it as very important to place "the book of the gospels, the word of God, always at the center." The book in this case was a richly decorated manuscript codex from the year 1472. As a result, a fixed altar was placed directly in front of the papal throne, at the point where the stands began and thus in the center of the hall, so that the book of the gospels might always be right in the middle as the soul and inspiration of all the conciliar labors of the fathers.

In front of the Confessio and the papal throne was the table for the board of presidents. To the left of this and at an angle to the hall the general secretariat had its place and behind were four tables for employees of the secretariat, members of the conciliar press office, and stenographers. To the right of the papal throne, opposite the statue of Peter, at the head of the central nave, a row of places were reserved for the cardinals. The seats in this section were covered with a red material.

The fathers' seats were arranged symmetrically in ten or more rows down the sides of the central nave, each row being about 30cm higher than the one in front of it, so that a good view in all directions was guaranteed. A lengthwise passage running along the top of these rows, with numerous side passages leading up to it, ensured that every seat was accessible even during the meetings. These side passages divided the rows of seats into sections containing from 60 to 80 places.

The central passageway of the hall was about 5,60m wide. Two underpasses, located at about the middle of the rows of seats, made it possible to enter and leave the hall without having to walk the length of it.

Almost 2500 seats were set up for the Council fathers. Each place consisted of an upholstered chair with a folding seat, a long board that swung up into place and was wide enough to be used as a writing desk, and, finally, a kneeler that likewise folded up.

The eight archways to the side naves were blocked off by high walls, in order to close in the hall and to permit the erection of six elevated tribunes reached by steps from behind. Each of the first two tribunes on both side had sixty places for the fathers, and each of the last two had 100 places for the experts.

The observers had their eighty places in the tribune of the basilica itself, in front of the pillar of St. Longinus; fifty places were provided for auditors in the tribune in front of the pillar of St. Andrew. Both groups sat close to the papal throne and the altar and were therefore able to follow the proceedings with great ease.

The framework of the tribunes was made of 25300 meters of steel tubing that was covered with 5cm thick wooden boards. The vertical surfaces of the structure were covered with over 150 cubic meters of fir boards, these in turn being covered with fabric.

The horizontal surfaces of the rows of seats and the tribunes were covered with a layer of rubber, and red runners were laid on the passageways; in all, 2300 square meters of rubber and 800 of carpet were put down. For decorations using cloth preference was given to the combination, traditional in St. Peter's Basilica, of damask and velvet with gold trimming.

Large tapestries over the tribunes completed the decoration of the hall. These tapestries, belonging to the Vatican Museum, were by the "New School of Raphael," woven in the 16th century in Brussels by disciples of Raphael and from designs of the master. At the express wish of the pope, who wanted an image of the Mother of God in the Council hall, a tapestry depicting the coronation of Mary was hung behind the papal throne, above Bernini's baldachin. The center of the basilica was adorned by a mosaic of Giacomo Manzù that contained the papal coat of arms, the name of John XXIII, and the date of the opening of the Council.

In the setting up of the hall an effort was made to have it harmonize with the cathedral of St. Peter. The form which the hall took was meant to make it clearly visible to the fathers that the Council was an extraordinary event.

3. *Technical Equipment*

Costly technical equipment had to be installed for the work of the Council. In addition to lighting, this included means of communication such as telephones, sound equipment, devices for television transmissions, and a punchcard machine for electronic data processing.

3.1 *Electric Lighting*

The main source of illumination was 42 floodlights that were suspended from the cornice of the church. This installation, together with the normal illumination from the vault, ensured that each Council father would have enough light for reading and writing. The tapestries received special lighting so as to show them at their best.

The illumination of the tapestries, together with that from the flood-lights, provided sufficient light in the tribunes. All the underpasses and the neighboring spaces were adequately lit. The tables of the presidential Council and the secretariat had metal table lamps.

A special installation working on lower current (for safety's sake) took care of the spaces beneath the tiers of seats. A installation that pro-vided stronger lighting was also set up in the hall for the televising of open sessions and solemn ceremonies of the Council.

A special need was to isolate lighting appliances that were close to wooden structures and to decorations using cloth; for this purpose about 12 square meters of asbestos were used.

3.2 *Microphones*

At earlier Councils people had often complained about poor acoustics; at Vatican Council I, for example, the Council fathers criti-cized the "deafness" of the hall, and in the end a sail had to be stretched across the vault to improve the acoustics.

The goal of the sound technicians was to achieve an even distribution of sound and thus complete audibility. This was all the more necessary since the proceedings were to be in Latin. The problem was not an easy one to solve, but the equipment that was finally installed proved its worth. It con-sisted in all of 68 loudspeakers that were located at key points in the hall and a further 24 loudspeakers distributed on the tables of the presidential Council, the general secretariat, and the secretarial services.

The 37 microphones in use were regulated from a control room located to the left of the first tribune and from which there was an excel-lent view of the hall. The microphones of the presidential Council and the general secretariat could be turned on from there. 24 microphones were set up among the Council fathers. They were placed, one for each section, at the lowest row of seats, so that a speaker would not have to walk more than 20m and would always remain fully in view. Each of these places for speakers also had a lectern and a telephone.

The remaining 13 microphones were at the papal throne, on the tables of the presidential Council and the general secretariat, on the altar of the Council, on the lectern from which the general secretary spoke, in the choir, and at the organ.

3.3 *Tape Recording*

The recording center had four tape recorders that were controlled directly by the center; the result was a high tonal quality. Two of the four machines were always running in order to provide two continuous recordings, one that went directly to the archive, the other for the 15 stenographers who kept the minutes each day. The stenographers were priests of various nationalities who had attended a course in Latin shorthand that Prof. Aloys Kennerknecht (Mainz) gave before the Council. But the shorthand soon proved quite inadequate when the results were compared with the tape recordings, and in the end the stenographers were mainly transcribing the minutes from the tapes.

Throughout the Council the sound equipment functioned extremely well, and, despite initial worries, the technical and organizational commission, in combination with the punchcard system, provided a very accurate documentary record of the Council.

3.4 *Television Equipment*

Immediate video recordings of the most important conciliar events in St. Peter's and their transmission, in the Eurovision area and throughout the world, were made possible by a number of television cameras, and this without disturbing the assembly. Radio Televisione Italiana was responsible for all transmissions. A small closed-circuit television installation allowed the pope to follow the meetings in the Council hall even from his private office.

3.5 *Telephones*

Inside the hall a special telephone line connected the tables of the board of presidents and the general secretariat with the various sectors and with all the speakers' posts. The installation consisted of a central telephone switchboard with which were connected the presidential board and the general secretariat, all the microphones, the tribunes, the microphone control room, the recording center, the punchcard center, the Vatican Radio post in the loggia of St. Longinus, and the three first-aid stations. There were 34 pieces of telephone equipment in all. In order to avoid disturbing noise, the telephones emitted only visual signals.

In the various sections of the tiers of seats an *assignator loci* was charged with taking calls and informing the father in question. The *assignatores loci*, 50 in all, were young priests of all nationalities, between 25 and 30 years of age, whose task it was to assist the bishops in the hall.

The telephone system already in place in the basilica was also upgraded in order to permit communication with the outside from certain places in the hall. For this purpose, telephones were placed, for example, on the tables of the presidential board and the general secretariat and in the first-aid stations.

3.6 *Data Processing*

One of the factors that played a decisive part in determining the course and duration of the Council was the management of the flood of information. Personal data on the Council fathers had to be worked up; it was also necessary to keep quick track of presences and absences and to tabulate votes. For this purpose. a punchcard system of the Olivetti-Bull type was used.

From June, 1962, on, a section within the general secretariat of the Central Commission was given responsibility for this area. The most important information about each Council father was entered into a main card file that was continually updated.

A second punchcard office was set up in the hall for immediate analysis of the data that became available each day. This office functioned only during the working sessions of the Council; it was located in a place specially set up for the purpose, near the altar of the Madonna Gregoriana.

These two centers were primarily responsible for the collection of personal data and the assignment of places to the Council fathers. They kept tab on absences and votes.

a) *Particulars about the Council Fathers*

A punchcard was started for each father that contained the following information: alphabetical code, last name and first name, diocese, nationality, date of election or appointment, and office held. A special card contained the man's complete present address. The cards were arranged both alphabetically and according to the various offices.

When the date of appointment was replaced by a number representing the office and the length of service (seniority number = *codice de decananza*), the result was a further card (in a seniority list) that was used for assigning seats in the hall.

b) *Assignment of Places*

The Council fathers were assigned their places in the hall strictly according to office or rank and then according to their age. Those who held higher offices and were older thus sat closer to the papal throne.

Since the hall was divided into two halves, it became necessary, in order to preserve this arrangement, to assign places to the right and left alternately according to age. The number of places in the hall was less than the number of those fathers who had a right to take part in the Council, since allowance was made for the fact that inevitably and for valid reasons a number of Council fathers could not be present. In order to assign places, therefore, it was necessary to wait for the opening meeting and first determine the number present. In addition, some places were kept open in the various sections for latecomers. Finally, special places were reserved, in the lowest tier of seats, among others, for fathers who needed them for specific reasons.

It was not easy to satisfy all these requirements. Only the punchcard system made it possible to solve the problem quickly and accurately. After ascertaining who was present on the first day of the gathering, a list of attendees was compiled. With the help of the system each attendee's card could easily be given the number of the place to be assigned to the particular father. For this purpose a list of the numbers of the seats had already been prepared. This list was then arranged alphabetically, making it possible to draw up lists of the places assigned to the fathers.

c) *Attendance Records and Vote Counting*

Checking for attendance and the counting of votes were done with the help of data processing. The cards on which the fathers confirmed their presence or cast their vote by marking it with a lead pencil were read, sorted, and counted by nine modern Olivetti-Bull machines.

An "identity card," or master card, was started for each Council father, giving his place number, family name and first name, hierarchical rank, episcopal see, nationality, year of birth, day of appointment, and whether he belonged to the secular or the religious clergy.

Each country received a code number: for example, 111 for Germany, 118 for Yugoslavia, 121 for Luxembourg, 125 for the Netherlands, 127 for Poland, 130 for Russia, and so on.

At the upper edge of the identity card an explanation of the various perforations was given in ordinary language. An example of this (without the seat number): "Se Frings Joseph CpKöln 111 887 18024601s." This was the identity card of "His Eminence Joseph Frings, cardinal priest, Archbishop of Cologne, of German nationality, born in 1887, created cardinal on February 18, 1946, belonging to the secular clergy."

The data from this identity card were copied onto the white attendance cards and the green voting cards on each occasion. Each Council father received a white attendance card from the *assignatores locorum* as he entered the Council hall before every public meeting and every general congregation. In addition to the data copied from the identity card, the date of the particular meeting was recorded on the attendance card. On the right-hand side (at the point where the three rectangles for the three possible votes were printed on the voting cards) the attendance card had a rectangular, lightly hatched area with *Adsum* printed on it. In this rectangle the father signed his name with a special machine-readable, magnetographic pencil. The cards were collected and brought to the punchcard department.

From these cards the department in a very short time compiled a list of those present, with the rank and therefore the place of each person. There, too, forms were printed containing the names of the present or absent fathers. These lists supplemented the minutes of the meeting. Each day saw an accumulation of approximately 2500 cards; the analysis of these took about a half-hour.

The voting cards were likewise distributed to the fathers by the *assignatores locorum*, collected after they made their decisions, and sent on to the punchcard department. Each father had places for three possible votes on his card: *placet, non placet,* and *placet iuxta modum.* The machine checked whether the voting card had been filled out and signed, and was therefore valid. It scanned the card to see which of three possible voting areas had been marked with a cross, and then punched out a small hole at the lower left-hand edge of that voting area. Any voting card that had not been properly filled out (for example, two areas were crossed out, or the intention of the Council father was not clear beyond any doubt) was rejected by the machine. The voting cards that had been properly filled out and punched were counted by machine. On a wide sheet of continuous paper the machines first recorded the names and data for all the Council fathers who had voted *placet iuxta modum.* This list was immediately handed to the president of the general congregation, who could use it to look over the reservations of all the Council fathers who had voted in this way. According to the regulations for the Council every *placet iuxta modum* vote had to be accompanied by an explanation. In the same way the machines then also listed by name all those voting Yes or No.

The counting and analysis of the votes was checked several times from various points of view, in order to discover any "erroneous decisions" of the machine.

The machines took approximately an hour to analyze the voting cards. In addition, of course, the entire voting process included the actual voting as well as the distribution and collection of the voting cards. It is not surprising, then, that for the first major votes, that is, for the analysis of the voting cards for the election of the members of the commissions six whole days were allotted: In four general congregations during the first week of the Council members were elected of two commissions at a time; thus 32 persons in all each time. The machines thus took a day and a half for the analysis of about 100,000 voting cards. In all, 538 votes were taken and more than a million cards were distributed.

d) *Other Arrangements*

After careful examination the organizational and technical commission rejected installations for simultaneous translation and for voting "by push-button."

All the work done for the Council in St. Peter's supposedly cost more than 600 million lire.[256]

4. *Services*

During the session the Council hall needed some indispensable facilities: medical care, catering, sanitary facilities, and a security service that would also keep order. These facilities had to be immediately available at the hall but at the same time kept separate and have no access from outside. It was not easy to find space in St. Peter's that could be converted for these services.

If, along with the fathers, the *assignatores locorum* and the other service personnel are included in the count, over 3000 people streamed into St. Peter's Basilica every day during the periods when meetings were held. It is obvious that this required major organizational feats.

4.1 *Health Services*

Three first-aid stations were set up in the basilica, one each on the right and left at the front end of the hall, the third on the right at the back. The largest of these was on the left in a large area under the funeral monument of Pope Lambertini and accessible through this monument. The space was ventilated from the outside and at the back had running water, two washbasins, and two lavatories. This station was fully outfitted medically and had two beds separated by curtains.

The stations began their work an hour before the meeting started and ended it a half-hour after the meeting closed. Each station had a physician, two religious orderlies from the Fatebenefratelli, and two stretcher-bearers in constant attendance.

---

[256] KNA, *Sonderdienst*, no. 8a (September 10, 1962) 15.

The medical installation was intended for first aid; for more extended medical care immediate transfer was provided to specific hospitals in which rooms were kept in readiness at all times. Two ambulances were always at the ready during the meetings of the Council.

Rarely did the doctors go into action. The fathers turned to them, for the most part, only for prescriptions. In addition, the health service provided medical care inside and outside the hall; drugs were provided to the Council fathers by the Vatican Pharmacy.

4.2 *Catering*

Two catering stations were set up: one on the left in the sacristy of the Chapel of the Sacraments, the other on the right, near the passageway between the choir chapel and the sacristy. These locations were thus connected with the hall but at the same time separated from it. The spaces used had to be completely remodeled.

The personnel began their work every morning at 11.00 and finished their service at the end of each Council meeting. The Council fathers would obtain warm and cold drinks here, as well as pastries. No alcoholic drinks were served. About 3000 people had to be served in an hour and a half.

Many objections were initially raised against having this service, but it received the approval of the fathers, as the crowds proved. "At this 'secondary Council' the universality of the Church... found such spontaneous expression that it became clear to all that in the future even a non-Italian cardinal had a chance at the papal throne."[257]

4.3 *Sanitary Facilities*

The Basilica of St. Peter's was poorly equipped from the viewpoint of sanitation, and what it did have was not always in an acceptable hygienic condition. New installations were therefore needed. They had to be isolated from the hall but easily accessible. The best solution seemed to be to equip each catering post with sanitary facilities.

In a space near the first catering station, the one on the left side, there were ten lavatories. near the second, six more. In addition, six lavatories outside the church were rebuilt and expanded. Each lavatory was surrounded by a 2,20m high wall that was clad in majolica tiles; each had a stone floor and hot and cold running water. These installations remained permanent equipment of the church.

---

[257] Henri Picher, *Johannes XXIII. Der Papst der christlichen Einheit und des II. Vatikanischen Konzils* (Kettwig-Velbert, 1963) 163.

There was, however, no place in St. Peter's Basilica for changing one's clothes. The fathers thus had no choice but to board one of the waiting buses wearing their full regalia or else to change out in the open in the car park under the colonnade.

4.4 Security and Order

This service seemed needed in order to facilitate the orderly progress of the Council's work and to protect the technical installations in the hall, especially since two attacks had occurred during the construction work on the hall. On July 13, 1962, a rather small device exploded at the right side of the altar, close to the organ. The marble base of the statue of Clement X was slightly damaged. Twenty days before the Council, on September 21, 1962, another bomb attack on the basilica was attempted. About 150 men, almost the entire papal guard, was called up to keep a close watch on the basilica.

During the Council the ordinary liturgical life of the basilica had to continue and the church had to remain open to the public; this aggravated the security problem. Primary responsibility for security belonged to the papal guard, which worked day and night in collaboration with the Italian police, both inside and outside the basilica.

As a first security measure, taken as early as the beginning of the work on the hall, teams of two papal guards, firemen, carabinieri, and Italian policemen took turns patrolling the church during the night. During the periods when the church was open to the public, barriers were erected around the areas belonging to the Council hall, and guards kept anyone from entering the hall. This service was performed by six papal guards, two firemen, six carabinieri, and six Italian policemen. Surveillance at the entrances and outside the church was beefed up by members of the papal guard and the Italian police.

Immediately after the end of the first session of the Council, a tour of inspection was instituted; this was performed twice a day for three years by a policeman and a fireman.

Special steps were also taken to prevent fires; these were all the more important since before the construction of the hall there was practically no fire protection equipment available.

During meetings of the Council (from 9.00 a.m. to 12.30 p.m.) the church was closed to the public. 18 sampietrini, 20 papal guards under the command of three officers, and 8 firemen formed a special security service. The main function of the sampietrini was to control the various entrances to the hall and the church. Seven policemen in mufti checked all parts of the hall every morning and then took up their stations in the tribunes. Their task was to keep unauthorized persons from slipping in and remaining in the church during the meeting. After the liturgy and a further check of the hall the policemen took up positions at particular points, for example, near the general secretary, at the punchcard unit, and at the catering locations. The police assigned to this task were bound to secrecy by their service oath, but care was taken to assign only officers who knew no Latin. At the end of each meeting of the Council, a further check of the hall was made in order to collect forgotten belongings which were then returned to their owners the next day. This service proved to be especially efficient.

In addition, seven papal guards were on duty at the main entrances to the church, and, finally, a group of six police were at the St. Martha entrance. The firemen also took up their positions in the hall early in the morning. From 2.00 p.m. on, when the basilica was opened to the public, the usual security service took over.

It is evident that just the maintenance of security and order required the commitment of extensive resources.

VI. THE ARRIVAL OF THE FATHERS IN ROME

1. *The Arrival of the Fathers*

A few days before October 11, 1962, the great flood began: of Council fathers, secretaries, advisers, and experts, and of journalist, pilgrims, tourists, and curious folk.

On January 2, 1962, the Central Commission had sent an invitation to all bishops and ecclesiastics who were entitled to take part in the Council, and had urged them to send quick confirmation of their participation. But since some responses were a long time in coming and since more precise personal information on individual Council fathers was also lacking, as were details of their arrival and lodging, the secretariat of state wrote to all the nunciatures on June 19, 1962. The latter were commissioned to acquire this information with the assistance of the president of each episcopal conference. In addition, a more detailed questionnaire was sent to the nunciatures, to be filled in by the participants in the Council. It asked each to give his own or, as the case might be, his authorized representative's surname, first name, title, and address, then their Roman address, the means of transportation on their journey, and the date and hour of their arrival. The participants also had to say whether they could pay for their own lodging or wanted to be guests of the Holy See. They were asked, further, to say whether they would be accompanied and by whom (surname, first name, title, and Roman address). A short curriculum vitae was also to be supplied as well as six signed passport photographs. The secretariat of state wanted the answers back by July 15.[258] 2856 invitations were sent, to 85 cardinals, 8 patriarchs, 533 archbishops, 2131 bishops, 26 abbots, and 68 religious superiors.

The Council fathers came from 79 countries. They were divided into the following geographical groups: 38% from Europe, 31% from the Americas, 20% from Asia and Oceania, and 10% from Africa. The bishops departed from their sees without knowing when they would return.

About 500 bishops were unable to accept the invitation. Almost 200 of these were bishops from the eastern bloc. About 200 told the pope that their health would not permit a journey to Rome.[259]

According to the pope's intention and the statement of Cardinal Testa to the technical commission (see the minutes), all the guests for the Council were to be made comfortable in Rome. To this end, informational signs were posted at the Roman airports; delegations were sent to the train station to give individual groups a friendly and dignified reception.

With feelings of expectation and hope the fathers and their entourages made their way to Rome by airplane and then by train or auto.

One of the first bishops who wanted to come to Rome for the Council died on his arrival in Naples: John Forest Hogan, Bishop of Bellary in India. Antonio Barbieri, Archbishop of Montevideo, arrived in Rome as early as the end of the September. On Saturday, October 6, 1962, the Hungarian bishops reached Rome by train and went immediately to the Hungarian College.

Cardinal Stefan Wyszynski, Archbishop of Gnesen and Warsaw, reached Termini, the main train station of Rome, at 8:55 a.m., on October 7, 1962; he was accompanied by fourteen Polish bishops, among them Karol Wojtyla of Krakow. The pope had sent a special sleeping car of the Italian railroad to Warsaw. The Primate of Poland was greeted at the station by Cardinal Raul Silva Henriques, Archbishop of Santiago de Chile, and by the substitute secretary of state, Archbishop dell'Acqua. A large crowd had gathered on the platform. Archbishop Boleslaw Kominek, one of the most prominent representatives of the Polish episcopate, had received his exit visa too late to make the journey to Rome in the company of Cardinal Wyszynski and the other Polish bishops.

[258] See Caprile, I/2 (1961-62) 536f.
[259] *Gazet van Antwerpen*, September 23, 1962, 3.

Kominek, whose pastoral charge was the department of Wroclaw, accompanied by his auxiliary, Bishop Wronka, reached Vienna by the Chopin Express on October 9, 1962; on that same day, at 11.30 a.m., they continued their journey to Rome. On October 9, three Hungarian and two Yugoslavian bishops arrived; on October 10, three Czech bishops and Petras Mazelis, Apostolic Administrator of Telshiai in Lithuania, one of the republics of the Soviet Union. The pope was especially gladdened by the arrival of the bishops from the eastern bloc; he received them in a private audience on the days immediately following.[260]

For the first time in the history of Councils, the fathers came from all parts of the world, and yet most of them reached Rome in a few hours, since the majority travelled by plane. A reception pavillion, draped in red, was erected at Leonardo da Vinci Airport in Fiumicino; trained personnel handled all matters of protocol. The Council fathers were then brought by automobile from the airport to the city.[261] The Fiumicino airport looked like a clerical institution during the days before the Council.

239 Council fathers came from the United States of America; of these, 5 cardinals, 23 archbishops, and 116 bishops came by air. A special Air France plane flew the French archbishops and bishops from Paris to Rome on October 9, 1962. 71 spiritual leaders from almost all the dioceses of France were accompanied by bishops from Laos, Tahiti, Iran, and India. The French bishops brought four tons of baggage, vestments, and documents to Rome. On October 9, Cardinals Suenens and Alfrink also reached Rome.

Many Council fathers started from the Frankfurt airport. Most flew with Alitalia, the only airline that had set up a reception committee at the airport of Rome in order to process Council fathers quickly and without any hitch. Among the twelve bishops who either flew to Rome from Frankfurt on October 7, or else changed planes at Frankfurt, were Bishops Volk of Mainz, Lommel of Luxembourg, and Schmitt of Bulawayo in Africa. Cardinal Frings flew from the Cologne-Wahn airport to Rome on October 8. On Thursday afternoon (October 8), the largest group thus far, 18 Council fathers and advisors, left Frankfurt; among them were Bishops Hengsbach of Essen, Kempf of Limburg, and Bolte of Fulda, as well as auxiliaries Rudloff of Hamburg and Schick of Fulda, Bishop Wember from Scandinavia, and Drs. Hirschmann and Semmelroth, professors at the Jesuit school of higher studies in Frankfurt. On September 30, 1962, Cardinal Döpfner had told the nunciature in Bonn that he

---

[260] Wenger, *Vatican II*, 44.
[261] Caprile, I/2, 682.

would go to Rome by auto and that his secretary, Dr. Gerhard Gruber, would accompany him. He arrived in Rome on Monday, October 8. Cardinal Godfrey, Archbishop of Westminster, flew to Rome from London on October 8, 1962.

Many prelates preferred to travel by sea. The Australian bishops had decided to go to Rome by sea and not by air. Their journey lasted over two weeks, and they used the available time on board to make a detailed study of the schemata which the preparatory commissions had drafted for the Council.

On October 11, 1962, the two official extraordinary observers from the Holy Synod of the Russian Church also arrived at the Council: Vitali Borowski, professor of theology, and Archimandrite Kotlarov.

There was a reception office for all arrivals, in the same building that housed the press center; here the arriving bishops received documents containing instructions, the arrangement of places, and the opening prayers for the Council.

The bishops from the various parts of the world formed a colorful picture, reminding onlookers that the Catholic Church is a worldwide Church. Participants in the Council reported, later on, that from the very start of the Council the prevailing atmosphere was one of friendliness. Alfons Dalma captured the mood of the arriving fathers when he wrote: "A further picture takes shape in my mind:... old and young, tall and short, figures powerful and frail, faces of fighters and of thinkers, of administrators and of pioneers, of scholars and of men of action, of ascetics and of esthetes."[262]

2. The Housing of the Fathers

When all the secretaries and theological experts were included, about 7500 persons were expected in Rome as direct or indirect participants in the work of the Council. All of them needed accommodations. If the observers and representatives of the press were counted in, there were about 10,000 people in Rome for the Council.

Rome was prepared to receive the Council fathers and their companions. The housing in Rome of the Council participants, the observers, and the press caused no great difficulties, since in addition to the numerous hotels many religious houses and colleges were available.[263]

---

[262] Alfons Dalma, in *Die Presse*, October 20, 1862, 5.
[263] Emil Schmitz, S.J., "Rom ist gerüstet. Konzilsstadt wird nicht aus den Nähten platzen, " KNA, *Sonderdienst*, no. 3 (July 30, 1962) 5f.

Problems of logistics had been tackled long before the Council; for example, months before the Council each father had to fill out a form giving his Roman address during the Council; in other words, the housing question was resolved before October 11, 1962. This activity was handled by way of the nunciatures (so it was in Germany, for example). It is to be assumed, therefore, that the curial authorities were not overly burdened by logistical problems.

To anyone in Rome it was obvious that the Church was a worldwide Church, for seminaries, houses of study, and religious houses of almost all nationalities were to be found there. Almost all the religious Orders received Council fathers. This made it possible for national groups to remain together, with the result that international contacts were not made until during the Council itself.

15 of the French bishops stayed at St. Louis des Français, 45 at the French Seminary, 15 at the headquarters of the Sulpicians, 20 at St. Martha's in Vatican City, 12 in religious houses belonging to Sacré-Coeur d'Angers and in various other communities.

When we examine the Roman addresses of the German participants in the Council, we find that four bishops lived at the German College of S. Maria dell'Anima in the Via della Pace, two at the German College of S. Maria in Camposanto, three at the Pontifical Germano-Hungarian College. The other German Council fathers found lodging in various houses, for example, the generalate of the Congregation of the Sisters of Our Blessed Lady; the Casa Palotti at Via dei Pettinari 54; the Villa Mater Dei at Viale delle Mure Aurelie 10; the Istituto S. Elisabetha at Via del Olmata 9; the house of the Carmelite Sisters of the Divine Heart of Jesus at Via Trionfale 227; the Villa San Francesco; San Anselmo College; the Villa Salvator Mundi; the generalate of the Holy Family Missionaries; the Villa Stuart; and elsewhere. Almost all of the German bishops stayed at religious institutes.[264]

Cardinal Alfrink moved into the Dutch College. The Poles were housed in the Pontifical Polish College and the Pontifical Polish Institute; Cardinal Wyszynski, for example, stayed here with five other bishops. One bishop found lodging with the Polish Sisters of Nazareth and another with the Polish Resurrectionist Fathers.

Six bishops — Bishop Danilo Catarzi from Uvira, Zaire, and bishops from Sierra Leone, Indonesia, and Brazil — lived with the Xaverians. Thirteen bishops, among them Bishop Aristide Pirovano of Macapà, Brazil, spent their nights at the Pontificio Istituto Missioni Estere. Thirty

---

[264] Döpfner Council papers (AEM).

bishops, among them Cardinal Rufino Santos, Archbishop of Manila, were housed at the Pontifical Philippine College in the Via Aurelia.

The majority of the fathers were lodged in religious houses. The bishops from the United States — about 140 in number — rented three hotels for themselves and their companions (about 400 persons in all); one of these was the Grand Hotel, where Cardinal Spellman, among others, had his headquarters.

The addresses which all the fathers had at the beginning of the Council were given in a register entitled *Peregrinatio Romana ad Petri Sedem*, which was available in the reception office at Via della Conciliazione 10; it was intended as a ready reference for participants in the Council. The curial authorities and the hospitals were also listed there. The main section of this vade mecum had the heading: *Domicilium in Urbe Patrum Concilii Oecumenici Vaticani Secundi*. An appendix listed 90 houses in which the individual fathers found lodging: "Alberghi ed istituti che ospitano i padri conciliari."[265]

3. Finances

People in the Vatican observed silence in the matter of the Council budget. No information was given out regarding financial matters. *Superno Dei nutu* (Pentecost, 1960) established an administrative secretariat to handle these questions. In the regulations for the Council that were issued in the *Motu proprio Appropinquante Concilio* (August 6, 1962) this secretariat became one of the five sections of the general secretariat of the Council. Responsibility rested on the shoulders of Cardinal de Jorio, President of the Commission for the Administration of the Patrimony of the Holy See; he could be described as the banker for the Council.

On the assumption that the Council would last a year (three sessions of two months each, with the bishops returning to their dioceses in the intervals) it was calculated that the cost of the Council would be between 15 and 20 billion lire (25 and 33 million dollars).[266] This esti-

---

[265] See Douglas Horton, *Vatican Diary 1962. A Protestant Observes the First Session of Vatican Council II* (Philadelphia-Boston, 1963) 11-17.

[266] *Römische Warte*, Series 38, October 9, 1962, 299. Auxiliary Bishop Walter Kampe (Limburg) calculated that the average daily expense for each bishop during the period of the Council would be $5.00. For 2700 bishops and 5000 accompanying persons the daily cost would thus be $38,500.00; for a session, then, about $2,500,000.00 would be needed. Bishop Kampe figured $190,000.00 for travelling expenses (one round trip). For the technical preparations in Rome Kampe gave a figure of $1,250,000. According to these calculations, a single session of the Council would cost over $3,900,000.

CHAPTER V

mate seemed realistic. Shortly before the Council began, the Italian press calculated that the total cost of the Council would be 74 million dollars; this figure, however, was regarded as exaggerated.

Just the work done in St. Peter's Basilica — the alterations in the basilica, the buying and installing of a public address and communications system, and a series of other installations — cost over $950,000. The setting up of various offices, for example, the press office with its sections, required rather large sums, as did the aids for the Council's work, for example, the printing of documents for the Council.

John XXIII's view was that self-respect required the father of a family to provide his guests with only the best; any bishop who wished might be the guest of the Holy Father, with all expenses defrayed. The pope certainly had not thought through the financial consequences of such an invitation.

People in the Vatican supposed that the bishops themselves would pay for the travel and stay of the participants in the Council. In July, 1961, Pericle Felici observed, with regard to the financing of the Council, that many bishops and religious communities would be proud to pay for the journey to Rome and the costs of residence there. If this were not possible, the Central Commission would guarantee financial help; in no case should participation in the Council be frustrated by financial difficulties.

In fact, many bishops were not in a position to pay the costs, so that the Holy See had to help out. In the end, about 1000 Council fathers accepted the pope's invitation, and the Holy See had to pay their expenses. Since each Council father brought one or two companions with him (a secretary and a theologian), the pope had to defray the costs for about 3000 participants from the poor regions.

The financial problems with which many Council fathers had to deal were underscored by the following incident: A missionary bishop from Cameroon was almost out of money for his journey by the time he reached Paris; he had to continue on to Rome by second-class train, and this while fasting, until finally some French soldiers gave him some of their provisions. The Vatican had to pay for his stay in Rome and his journey home.

The Vatican already had to bear the brunt of the expenses during the four-year period of preparation. But in this period, too, the question of expenses was not allowed to influence in any decisive way the choice of the almost 880 persons involved in the preparation for the Council. About half of those working on the preparatory commissions had to be supported by the Vatican.

These financial obligations definitely caused trouble for the Holy See. For a time, the idea was even entertained of alienating some of the properties owned by the Vatican in order to meet the costs of the Council, but this idea was dropped.[267] Funds were supplied through collections from the faithful throughout the world.[268] At the beginning of the Council the German episcopal conference contributed a million DM to the Vatican. The North Americans also showed themselves generous. Council fathers still alive in very diverse parts of the world have repeatedly attested that no one was left in need and that a balance based on sharing was achieved. Thus the Council was not, strictly speaking, affected by economic problems.

The American, German, French, Spanish, Belgian, Austrian, and Swiss bishops, in particular, took care of their own lodging and maintenance in Rome.

4. *Contacts among the Fathers in Rome*

There is not very much to be said about contacts among the Council fathers, since, as individual fathers confirmed, it was only during the Council that groups and friendships, as well as theological circles, were formed. To a certain extent, the first stimulus to these contacts came after the meeting of the Council at which it was decided that the members of the commission should be freely elected.

If we consider how national groups were living together, we may assume that international contacts were not yet especially developed before the beginning of the Council, except among religious, although even these met only other Franciscans, Dominicans, etc. Most of the fathers reached Rome immediately before the Council, and in many cases only on October 10, 1962, so that there was hardly any opportunity for introductory contacts and conversations.

It is obvious that contacts between the bishops and their theologians in the various countries were very intensive during the final months before the Council, since despite the fact that the first seven schemata reached them only at a late date, they were nonetheless asked for their views.

In any case, both before and after the arrival of the bishops in Rome most meetings occurred between members of the same national groups. The German bishops met for a conference at the Anima on October 10.

---

[267] Ibid.

[268] P. Lambert, in KNA, *Sonderdienst*, no. 8a (September 10, 1962) 15-16 at 16.

At 7:15 in the evening all of them were invited to a reception given at
the German ambassador's to the Vatican in honor of German Foreign
Minister Gerhard Schröder. Cardinal Frings noted: "During the week
before the opening of the Council we were already able to hold a meeting of the German bishops in the hall of the Anima... The German missionary bishops joined us. Other German-speaking bishops, for example,
those of Luxembourg and Austria, likewise took part in their weekly
preparatory sessions."[269] At the first gathering of the German bishops
Professor J. Ratzinger gave a talk on the schema "on divine revelation."

The first contacts of the fathers in Rome took place in the large
houses that gave lodging to bishops from various countries, for example,
the Domus Mariae and the houses of Orders and congregations where
bishops and experts from various geographical regions were staying.
Participants in the Council who had known one another as fellow students in Rome also met. Meetings of journalist and press agencies were
also arranged.

All were certainly looking forward with great eagerness to the Council. It is also certain that the prevailing expectation among members of
the Curia was that the Council would be over in a few weeks, for they
figured that the prepared schemata would simply be adopted.

A clear sign of an "interior contact" was the fact that without any
prior arrangement an overwhelming majority opted for free elections to
the commissions. Of this event Cardinal Suenens remarked: "This was
the salvation of the Council." By this he meant that the Council had now
become a Council of the Council fathers.

If a general appraisal of the situation be wanted, one must say that the
"preliminary contacts" that took place in Rome after the arrival of the
fathers were rather cautious and reserved. Bishop Elchinger pointed out:
"When we came together in Rome, we did not know one another."

---

[269] Frings, *Für die Menschen bestellt*, 252.

CONCLUSION: PREPARING FOR WHAT KIND OF COUNCIL?

GIUSEPPE ALBERIGO

The preparation for Vatican II was rich and full. Not only did it take longer than the Council itself, it had very pertinent institutional characteristics. The pope was its supreme moderator, the Roman curia was its protagonist, and bishops and theologians, especially from Europe, were deeply involved in it.

Over and against these data is the drastic refusal of the great majority of conciliar fathers and their collaborators to recognize themselves in the proposals that came from this preparation. On October 11, 1962, it would seem that the Council would begin its work from scratch; more than 90% of the preparatory schemata would not even be considered by the conciliar assembly.

On the basis of very rich documentation, published and unpublished, this volume has reconstructed the journey first of the antepreparatory and then of the preparatory phases. It has revealed the complexity of this work and the considerable energies it required, beginning with the enormous mass of data and proposals sent to Rome during the general consultation of 1959-1960.

Before any other consideration, we have to recognize that despite the deep research which prepared and accompanied the writing of this volume, it has not been possible completely to dissolve the uncertainty about how heavily concern for the restoration of unity among Christians weighed upon Pope John's original intentions. This is a question which, it may be, will never recieve a univocal answer not so much because of the lack of sources as because of the very fluidity of this concern. If it is clear enough that the pope "dreamed" that the Council could promote the *causa unionis*, how he might have imagined that the one church could be recomposed remains unclear. The pope does not seem to have verified his own intuition with others, and even less was he in contact with spokesmen from other Christian churches, to the point that the impression could be had that the casual invitation sent out by Pius IX on the eve of Vatican I was being repeated.

In retrospect, one has the impression that the rapid decline in importance of the goal of Christian unity weakened the preparation of the Council by depriving it of an inspiration and a center. Even if it was, at least in immediate terms, a utopia, a drive toward union would have given the path to Vatican II a lofty soul and goal. No one now can know whether the risk of setting an unattainable goal, and therefore of disappointment, might nevertheless have been run with profit.

John XXIII, for his part, desiring to open the road to the actual celebration of the Council, gave the preparation an autonomous institutional space; repeatedly he stated that the preparation represented a sphere of the Catholic church's life distinct from its ordinary government. It is true that research conducted so far has not allowed us to clarify who was the source of the idea to have the Council preceded by a preparation that was so long that it had to be articulated in two distinct phases (ante-preparatory and preparatory). We do know that the announcement of January 25, 1959, in substance Roncalli's own mature judgement, was conditioned by suggestions which led him to add to his own project of a Council the two other projects of a Roman Synod and the revision of the Code of Canon Law. But it is not clear how the idea of a preparation was born that, after the vast consultation desired by the pope, would pass to a classification of the proposals and, finally, to the redaction of base-texts for the Council's work.

Could one have expected that from the consultation there would come proposals able to give content to John XXIII's surprising project? Or, instead, was the surprise provoked by the announcement such that it dissuaded people from expecting significant reponses? On the other hand, we have to recognize that it would not have been possible to open an assembly of more than two thousand members without a coherent preparation. Well then, independently of the origin of the preparatory mechanism, was it not perhaps fated that its function, objectively, would be to put the brakes on and to delay the beginning of the Council? Or could one really expect anything more than what it did produce, a plethora of texts, almost all mediocre, defensive in attitude and preoccupied to set in stone the condition of Roman Catholicism in the 1950s?

Paradoxically, the control which the Roman curia obtained over the antepreparatory phase and the hegemony it exercised in the preparation were compromised to the degree that they were exercised at a bureaucratic level and within an historical horizon limited to the last century, rather than by means of an ample and universal vision of faith and of the church. Even the impulse which Pius XII sometimes showed in addressing the pressing rhythms of history and its profound changes seems to have been obfuscated by defensive preoccupations and by the detailed efforts to have the Council sanction the orientations pursued by the individual congregations. We do not find indications that people were perceiving the epochal evolutions that were beginning to show themselves at the beginning of the 1960s: from détente between west and east to the end of the colonial era; from the neo-industrial explosion on both sides of the Atlantic to the impoverishment of the "Third World." Euro-centrism, often interpreted as Romano-centrism, was still the dominant optic. The experiences of renewal that had matured in Europe since the 1930s continued to be seen with distrust when they were not simply rejected.

From so many points of view, it seems that the criteria that guided the preparation of a Council between 1948 and 1952 had been taken up again, with an implicit: "As we were saying yesterday." If it is true that only a decade had passed since then, it is also undeniable that the orientation of John's pontificate and the firm decision to celebrate a Council, together with the move out of the post-war climate, were signalling a dramatic epochal shift, something which Pope John had seen in all its density.

On the other hand, the very idea that governed the Pope's project — of a "new" Council and not just of a conclusion to the interrupted First Vatican Council — was still too unripe in that January of 1959. Did it not have still to mature just about everywhere, confirmed even in the pope himself by the immense echo his announcement had received?

In addition, the simultaneous announcement of the revision of the Code of Canon law clearly and considerably had the effect of "diverting" the attention of almost all the bishops, comforting them with the hope that the Council's chief work would be a myriad of administrative adjustments. That is why the "pastoral" character which the pope wished to prevail in the new Council was for a long time banalized and understood to locate the Council at a non-theological level. It was only on the very eve of the Council that a stronger meaning of the term "pastoral" began to gain ground: the subordination of every other aspect of the church's life to the image of Christ as "Good Shepherd."

Considerations such as these are not intended to hide the fact that it would have been possible to avoid at least some of the disadvantages from which the preparation suffered. Perhaps, only as an example, one could think that an effective involvement of different energies, alongside those of the Roman circles, might have broadened and enriched the dialectic by including in it urgings and proposals already developed elsewhere. Similarly, assigning the Central Preparatory Commission the responsibility to directing and coordinating the activities of the commissions, which were numerous because parallel to the curial congregations, might have reduced the often repetitive plethora of preparatory schemata. But it is also true that the infrequent examples of involvement — as, for example, of Y. Congar in the Theological Commission and of H. Jedin in the Commission for

Studies — appear to have been vitiated by a prejudiced distrust; they themselves minimize their own contribution to the work. And even in the Central Commission some personalities who only twelve months later would play dominant roles in the development of the Council — Alfrink, Suenens, Léger, König, and Liénart, not to mention Montini — for a long time acted timidly and awkwardly; perhaps Bea is the only exception here. An explicit clash of different positions only began in the spring of 1962.

More than anyone's testimony, it is the years of the preparation themselves that provide the clearest documentation not only of the church's unreadiness to take up the tasks of participation and co-responsibility demanded by the celebration of a Council but also of the static and passive condition of Catholicism. Almost unconciously it had entered upon a road that led all things to Rome and, even more, concentrated them in the person of the pope; Catholicism was becoming monolithic. For Catholicism to live like a besieged fortress of truth was a condition of apparent strength and substantial weakness. From this point of view, one can understand why some people denounced the "delay" in the convocation of the Council and why others instead were convinced that it had come "too soon."

Synthetically, then, what was the contribution of the years 1959-1962? An historical perspective, however brief it is, allows us to go beyond manichean assessments which would like to demonize the perversity of the preparation for Vatican II or, on the other hand, to exalt it as the one "sane" moment in the whole conciliar experience.

A first observation concerns Catholicism as a whole and, to a considerable degree, all of contemporary Christianity. Although studies of the different geo-spiritual areas are still not exhaustive, there are enough of them to see how the announcement of the Council gave rise to a myriad of intense, if latent, expectations of a profound shift in the life of the church. This surprised everyone, giving hope to many, provoking fear in others. Then, while the institutional gestation was quite quickly concentrated in Rome and wrapped in nearly impenetrable secrecy, a parallel gestation began to take place. The latter had a myriad of anonymous protagonists almost everywhere, sustained and inspired by the succession of John XXII's public acts and interventions in which he continued to mould an image of the Council as a call, differentiated it is true, to all Christians to come together in union and to embrace an "*aggiornamento*". It was chiefly this informal, diffuse, and spontaneous preparation that created the conditions that made the Council an effectively innovative event.

A second aspect concerns the slow, still confused, emergence of specific requests by which many people sought to give concreteness to the "*aggiornamento*." The liturgical movement urged the active participation of the faithful in worship and the related use of the vernacular. The movement for the promotion of the laity insisted on an ecclesiological assessment of the non-clerical condition. The biblical movement was restoring the centrality of the Word of God and, in parallel, the renewal of theology was promoting "*ressourcement*." The ecumenical movement wished to move out of the stage of Roman intransigence. Finally, there was a widespread conviction that Catholicism had a duty to complete the definitions of 1870 on the pope's prerogatives by a theological and sacramental delineation of the episcopate. It is true that these expectations found little room in the vota sent in by the bishops; requests for condemnations and for Marian definitions were much more frequent, and there was a very broad range of proposals for modifications of canon law. But many Catholic circles were increasingly aware that they were lagging behind as "modernity" continued to spread, at least in western culture. If the need was felt finally to emerge from the psychosis of a siege-mentality, it was still not clear how to do that. It is not without significance that the Pastoral Constitution on the church in the Modern World is the only one of the major conciliar texts that does not have an ancestor among the numerous schemata of the preparatory period.

We have seen how the preparation was selectively filtered by the preparatory structure and how it was presented to the Council in jumbled forms alien to Pope John's spirit of search for "*aggiornamento*." The structure of the "Synthentic Report" at the beginning of 1960 and the consistent formulation, some months later, of the "Questions" for the work of the preparatory commissions crucially determine what would characterize the work of the next two years, down to the threshhold of the Council.

But it is also true that as they faced the conciliar opportunity, people gradually became aware that those who were hoping for renewal still had only immature notions of what it involved; this is something which Bea repeatedly noted during the work of the Secretariat for Christian Unity. This is not the least cause of the difficulty and ineffectiveness with which these circles, with the sole exception of the liturgists, made their vain attempt to check the hegemony which the Roman and curial theology was exercising over the whole preparation. This hegemony, although qualified by the jealousies of the various Roman universities, had first in Tardini a shrewd moderator, who knew how to be supple; then in Ottaviani it had an authoritative leader, but one who was often too intransigent and ill-equipped to deal with the tough flexibility of Bea, who was supported by the unshaken trust of the pope.

Some people have been tempted to ask whether John XXIII did not entrust the effective preparation of the Council to Bea and to the Secretariat the latter had "invented" and directed. It is certain that the collaboration between Roncalli and Bea can be abundantly documented, to the point that the historian cannot but wonder whether this fruitful convergence did not also project upon the pope the limits of the personality, the preparation, and the experience of Bea.

But this relationship does not mean that the pope did not show trust in the preparatory structure the curia was directing. It seems rather that he gave the same opportunities to this structure that he gave to Bea's Secretariat. Later, during the open confrontation of the Council, it would be decided which approach reflected the church's *sensus fidei*.

From 1960 on these two perspectives developed, but instead of their trajectories converging, they grew ever farther apart. The differences between them led people to emphasize their own perspective, and this resulted in a scissors-movement. In addition, the preparation guided by the curia was burdened rather than helped by its parallelism with the congregations, since each of these trusted that the Council would sanction its own line of government and even particular aspects of it. The shadow of concerns for everyday governance falls over a large part of the preparatory schemata. Perhaps Msgr. Felici did not see the need for the preparation not to remain a prisoner of these concerns, even if he did not have a personal culture really different from that of the representatives of the congregations. In any case, between 1960 and 1962 Felici's unceasing dedication gained him a knowledge and a control of the preparation that made him a candidate for the direction of the Council.

To what degree the dialectic generated by the preparation was filtered to the Catholic bishops in their different sees and milieux becomes clear in the interventions that first sporadically and in isolated fashion then more frequently and in concert began to express dissatisfaction with a large number of the texts produced by the preparation itself. From the letter of Frings in 1960 to the collective pastoral letter of the Dutch bishops in 1961 to the alarm expressed, with surprising but spontaneous convergence, by Léger, Rahner, Schillebeeckx, and Dossetti in the summer of 1962, down to the many responses on the eve of the Council that criticized almost all the schemata finally sent to the bishops, a slow but unequivocal evolution was underway in many milieux.

They began to become aware that their own involvement in the upcoming conciliar event must be as protagonists and not just passive attendants. At the same there was a growing awareness of the centrality of *"aggiornamento"* and of "the pastoral" as inalienable characteristics of the Council and of the church as a whole. The conviction was spreading that an effort at research is necessary, and it then became easy to distance oneself from the received texts, even if perhaps only a few were aware how hard it would be to construct effective alternatives.

In this climate, Suenens submitted to John XXIII an organic image of a program for the Council. The bishops, as they began to arrive in Rome and to meet one another, discovered how widespread the dissatisfaction was; some theologians began the hard work of preparing more or less completely new texts.

Less than forty years later, it is quite obvious how impervious the ecclesiastical machinery was to the historical conjuncture of humanity and even to the urgency of renewal that, following the announcement of the Council, was pervading the whole Christian world. There was a hiatus, not only of sensibility but of awareness and of perception of the meaning of the faith, between the groups that had central ecclesiastical responsibility and the great majority of the faithful. For their part, the bishops, almost all of them slow to perceive the new climate of expectation and of hope, still found themselves in a condition in which, precisely because of the appeals of Pope John and then by their participation in the conciliar event, they could rapidly develop a new awareness.

We can thus understand how many of the difficulties that the Council would encounter during its work had their roots precisely in the limits and deficiencies of its preparation. Today it is clear that this also conditioned the results of the Council themselves much more than might have been suspected as the products of the preparation were being rejected by the great majority of the assembly. Perhaps it was the empiricism that dominated the perspective of the preparatory works that allowed it to happen that much of what had been elaborated during that period filtered into the conclusions of Vatican II, despite the often ingenious barriers erected by the majority. It was a majority which, because it was endowed with a fragile and immature doctrinal background, was easily contented by the euphoria generated by its unexpected success when it confronted the mythical power of the curia.

The profile begins to appear, almost insensibly, of one of the dominant characteristics of Vatican II, namely, the tension between the conciliar assembly and the Roman curia. The curia, now dominated by the Secretariat of State, at first under Tardini and then under Cicognani, and now dominated by the Holy Office, seems jealous of the preferential relationship established between pope and Council besides being hostile to conciliar conclusions not determined by itself. The phenomenon of a conflict between Council and curia had been displayed during the Council of Trent, where it was tamped down by Morone and Borromeo; it remained tacit during Pius IX's Council; but it was to explode spectacularly at Vatican II. The historical dialectic between pope and Council was being transformed into a complex and inextricable three-part dialectic.

The risk that such a dialectic would have paralyzing effects was balanced by the pressure exercised by public opinion. After the explosion of expectations in the spring of 1959, the impossibility of a miraculous unity among Christians and the secrecy of the preparatory labors had reduced interest. But the nearing of the opening of the assembly, the convergence of the thousands of participants on Rome from all over the globe — in clear contradiction to the suffocating atmosphere of the Cold War — and the resounding echo of John XXIII's radio message of September 11 reignited trust and hope in unforeseen degrees. A great deal was being expected of the Council, even if everyone was free to fill his expectations with whatever content was dearest to his heart.

As for the substance of the problems that Vatican II would address, a deepened knowledge of the preparatory years leads to considerations that are only apparently contradictory. On the one hand, the schemata then formulated would in fact condition the conciliar decisions in unexpected ways, despite their rejection by the assembly. Many of the preparatory positions, so ignominiously abbandoned, would surreptitiously find their way back into the various constitutions and decrees. On the other hand, however, it seems that perhaps without the shock produced by the noisy lack of harmony between the schemata and the conciliar assembly, it would have been difficult for the Council to gain a sufficient level of awareness and of creativity.

Finally, from a sociological point of view, the preparation appears to have been concentrated in the hands of a proportionately restricted group, composed exclusively of males who were celibate, of rather high median age, and of European culture. This composition, although it had its dialectical tensions, promoted a strong impermeability to the general social situation. One has the impression during the years between 1959 and 1962 that the major world events did not find much echo within this group. Even the most important acts of John XXIII, for example, the encyclical *Mater et magistra*, do not seem to have even scratched the universe of the preparation, as is clear from the texts prepared on pastoral responses to communism.

Was it a Council of epochal transition that was about to begin?

INDEX OF NAMES

INDEX OF SUBJECTS